THE MODERN BRITISH NOVEL OF THE LEFT

THE MODERN BRITISH NOVEL OF THE LEFT

A Research Guide

M. KEITH BOOKER

GREENWOOD PRESS
Westport, Connecticut • London

Library of Congress Cataloging-in-Publication Data

Booker, M. Keith.
    The modern British novel of the left : a research guide / M. Keith Booker.
        p.   cm.
    Includes bibliographical references and index.
    ISBN 0–313–30343–6 (alk. paper)
    1. English fiction—20th century—History and criticism.
    2. Politics and literature—Great Britain—History—20th century.
    3. English fiction—20th century—Stories, plots, etc.   4. Right and left (Political science) in literature.   5. Political fiction, English—History and criticism.   6. Political fiction, English—Stories, plots, etc.   I. Title.
    PR888.P6B66   1998
    823'.9109358—dc21   97–43861

British Library Cataloguing in Publication Data is available.

Copyright © 1998 by M. Keith Booker

All rights reserved. No portion of this book may be reproduced, by any process or technique, without the express written consent of the publisher.

Library of Congress Catalog Card Number: 97–43861
ISBN: 0–313–30343–6

First published in 1998

Greenwood Press, 88 Post Road West, Westport, CT 06881
An imprint of Greenwood Publishing Group, Inc.

Printed in the United States of America

The paper used in this book complies with the Permanent Paper Standard issued by the National Information Standards Organization (Z39.48–1984).

10 9 8 7 6 5 4 3 2 1

For Eric Hobsbawm

and dedicated to the memory of
Christopher Caudwell, Ralph Fox, Lewis Jones,
and all of those who have carried on the fight

CONTENTS

Preface	ix
1. Introduction to the Literature of the British Left	1
2. Selected Critical and Historical Studies Relevant to the British Novel of the Left	21
3. Selected British Novels of the Left	41
4. Selected Postcolonial Novels of the Left	317
Appendix: Novels of the Left Listed by Subject	377
Works Cited	383
Index	405

PREFACE

The following is a reference work intended to provide a useful starting point for students and scholars interested in the cultural production of the British Left, a phenomenon that has been largely ignored in mainstream accounts of British cultural history but that is coming more and more to be recognized as a crucial element of British culture in the twentieth century. The book begins with a general introduction that includes both a historical survey of the development of the British novel of the Left and an introductory discussion of Marxist literary theory. This chapter thus provides both historical and theoretical background for the rest of the book. Chapter 2 of this research guide seeks to provide additional supplemental information through a presentation of brief summaries of some of the most important critical, historical, and theoretical works by British leftists from Christopher Caudwell, Ralph Fox, and Alick West to Eric Hobsbawm, Terry Eagleton, and Perry Anderson. Chapter 3, the bulk of this guide, then presents discussions of a number of British novels of the Left, seeking not to encompass all British novels of the Left (which would be impossible for such a large literary phenomenon), but to cover the most important works and to suggest the magnitude and scope of British Left cultural production in the past century. These summaries are followed in chapter 4 by summaries of a small number of postcolonial novels of the Left, both because the issues raised by these novels are relevant to British history and British culture and because it is important to recognize the genuine vitality of Left cultural production in the Third World in the last quarter of the twentieth century. The guide ends with an appendix arranging individual novels by category (most novels are listed in more than one category) in order to provide a convenient organizational tool for users particularly interested in specific issues.

1

INTRODUCTION TO THE LITERATURE OF THE BRITISH LEFT

The use of the spatial metaphor of a Left vs. Right opposition (originating in the tendency of nineteenth-century European legislatures to seat the more radical members to the left of the presiding official) has long been a standard part of the vocabulary of politics, even though it is clearly the case that most issues at the end of the twentieth century are too complex to be reduced to simple polar oppositions between a forward-looking Left and a backward-leaning Right. This confusion is particularly apparent in American politics, where the gap between the nominally Right and the nominally Left is miniscule. At century's end, Democrats (traditionally seen as the left wing of American politics) are scrambling frantically to identify themselves as moderates whose main goal is to restore traditional American values. Conservative Republicans, meanwhile, draw upon an imaginary past to derive the formula for what they claim to be a "revolutionary" thrust into the future.

This particular confusion derives from the narrow range of political opinions—all of which are basically liberal despite the unfashionable status of that term within the mainstream of American politics. And British politics are not much better, as the gradual convergence over the past few decades of Conservative and Labour Party positions on various issues clearly indicates. But the terminology of Left vs. Right is inherently vague on a larger scale as well—each orientation potentially suggesting up to half of all available positions on any given issue.

The situation has been complicated still further in both Britain and America by nearly five decades of consistent and intentional distortion in which leftism was identified as a form of extremism roughly analogous to any number of other shibboleths of Cold War rhetoric, including totalitarianism, ideology, and (ultimately) even ostensibly neutral terms such as government and politics. The central referent of all of this rhetoric is, of course, communism, the most successful "leftist" program of the twentieth century and the one that has most seriously threatened to work fundamental social, political, and economic change that was not in the interest of capital. Meanwhile, in a sort of modern version of "might makes right," the ultimate victory of global capitalism in the recent Cold War has often been taken as a vindication of the capitalist rhetoric in that war and as proof that capitalism is the only logical basis upon which to build an advanced modern society.

Among other things, the end of the Cold War has led to a situation in post–Soviet Russia in which the Communist Party is typically regarded in the Western media as "right wing," further complicating notions of political Left and Right at the end of the twentieth century. And, if the political Left is now hard to define, defining the literary Left is even harder. The works of literature described in this research guide encompass a range of political positions. To a large extent, however, this study follows the tendency of Western Cold War rhetoric to identify the Left essentially with a rough constellation of ideas revolving around the central concepts of Marxism, communism, and socialism, especially insofar as these concepts suggest a fundamental critique of the social and economic injustices of capitalist class society and propose, instead, a more equitable distribution of wealth and power.

This focus on class means that William Empson's definition in *Some Versions of Pastoral* of proletarian art as "the propaganda of a factory-working class which feels its interests opposed to the factory owners" (6) has been useful, but in Britain any definition of leftist literature is complicated by a rich tradition of working-class culture and socialist politics that are not necessarily aligned with Marxism or communism. Meanwhile, even a quick look at the range of literary works that can be included within this understanding of "Left" immediately calls into question the widely promulgated Cold War notion that a leftist political orientation is somehow inimical to the production of a rich and varied literature. As part of a general effort to demonstrate the cultural superiority of the West, Western Cold War rhetoric tended to characterize leftist literature as dogmatic and doctrinaire, crippled by the requirements of ideological orthodoxy and by the demands that leftist writers adhere to the party line. The supposedly sterile, monological, and impoverished products of leftist literature were then opposed to a capitalist literature that was portrayed as complex, sophisticated, and inherently multiple in meaning and ideology—thus the apotheosis in these years of modernism as the official high culture of the West.

This narrative came to be accepted almost universally by Western cultural historians, especially in America, where the pitch of Cold War rhetoric was always especially strident, even hysterical. But such Manichean visions that present leftist politics as the antithesis of genuine culture were prominent in Cold War Britain as well, where they were promulgated by former quasi-leftists such as George Orwell, just as the same model was promoted in America largely by the supposedly left-leaning critics who came to be known as the New York Intellectuals. The works summarized in this research clearly challenge that vision. They indicate, first of all, that the sheer volume of Left cultural production in Britain in the twentieth century has been far greater than most accounts of modern literary history would acknowledge. Perhaps more importantly, they indicate that the range and diversity of this production, in terms of genre, style, subject matter, political orientation, and other criteria, have been extremely broad. In short, Left cultural production in Britain in the twentieth century has been rich, varied, and extensive, constituting a tradition the suppression and denial of which has been one of the major cultural/political phenomena of the century.

This research guide is intended as a contribution to the recovery of that tradition. The sheer volume of Left cultural production, especially in the genre of the novel, has been so extensive that this guide cannot hope to be literally comprehensive. This guide does seek, however, to indicate the range of British leftist novels produced in the twentieth century, balancing a desire to provide fairly detailed descriptions of individual novels with a desire to describe as many individual novels as possible. It is hoped that the result will provide a valuable introduction to the modern novel of the Left as well as a reference resource that will be of use to both beginning students and professional scholars of Left culture.

BASIC CONCEPTS IN MARXIST LITERARY THEORY

A number of theoretical issues complicate the very notion of leftist literature, including the fact, as Terry Eagleton repeatedly reminds us in *The Ideology of the Aesthetic*, a recent historical survey of aesthetic theory, that the very notion of the aesthetic as we know it arose in conjunction with the rise of capitalism and bourgeois society. And the complicity between bourgeois ideology and the whole notion of the aesthetic is particularly powerful in the case of the novel, which any number of observers (Ian Watt's landmark study of the rise of the novel in the eighteenth century is still paradigmatic) have identified as a fundamentally bourgeois genre. Leftist novelists who seek to overcome the hegemony of bourgeois ideology must therefore face the challenge of doing so within a genre that developed historically as a way to express, rather than oppose, the worldview of capitalism.

Mikhail Bakhtin's vision of the novel as a genre that is inherently both plural and continually evolving might be seen as a quintessential expression of the bourgeois nature of the novel, a situation that leads Franco Moretti to conclude that "Bakhtin in fact reproposes in the domain of literary criticism some of the basic tenets of liberal-democratic thought" (*Way* 151). On the other hand, the broad sweep of Bakhtin's historical vision tends to suggest that the cultural impulses underlying the novel have fundamental roots in folk cultural energies that are both older and broader than European bourgeois culture. Thus, while Bakhtin grants that the novel emerges as a genre "with special force and clarity in the second half of the eighteenth century," he also wants to insist that this emergence, which clearly occurs in conjunction with the rise of the European bourgeoisie is only one episode in a long history that begins in ancient Greece and presumably will extend well beyond the bourgeois era (*Dialogic* 5). In short, despite the essentially bourgeois vision that seems to underlie Bakhtin's characterization of the novel, his project could also be interpreted to imply that the novel as a genre transcends its recent bourgeois orientation and should thereby still be a valuable resource for socialist or other writers who would seek to go beyond the tradition of bourgeois aesthetics. Many observers, in fact, have even considered Bakhtin a Marxist, even if a rather unusual one, and it is certainly the case that numerous Marxist critics have found Bakhtin's theoretical insights useful.

Bakhtin's vision of the novel as an ever-evolving genre that constantly presents radical challenges to the literary status quo calls attention to the fact that the novel emerged as the favorite genre of the European bourgeoisie in the early days when the bourgeoisie themselves constituted a revolutionary class. One might argue, then, that bourgeois novels in the eighteenth century (and perhaps even up to the middle of the nineteenth century) are, in fact, leftist novels. From this point of view, the novel is not an inherently bourgeois genre but an inherently leftist genre, an insight that supports the extensive attempts of Georg Lukács to identify ways in which modern antibourgeois writers can learn from their bourgeois predecessors. Lukács's energetic promotion of early nineteenth-century bourgeois realism as a model for twentieth-century socialist writers is based on the fundamental insight that the bourgeoisie were at one time a revolutionary class and that bourgeois literature played a major role in the historical victory of the emergent bourgeoisie over their aristocratic predecessors. Here Lukács directly follows Marx, who himself regarded the revolutionary victory of the bourgeoisie in the then-recent past as the prototype of class-based revolution and as the best historical evidence that a proletarian revolution could be successful in the relatively near future. Lukács reminds us that the European bourgeoisie, however decadent and conservative they would become once their power had been consolidated, were in their younger days the most successful revolutionary class in history, making early bourgeois literature arguably the most effective revolutionary literature of all time.

Lukács began his studies of literature with the early *The Theory of the Novel* (1916), which is an essentially Hegelian account that was written before Lukács became a Marxist. But, through his later studies of great early nineteenth-century realist writers such as Balzac and Scott, Lukács went on to develop what is still the most thoroughly elaborated system of Marxist aesthetics to have been produced. Firmly rooted in the work of Marx and Engels and centrally based on a materialist vision of history as moving (at least potentially) toward the eventual achievement of socialism, Lukács consistently privileges literary realism as the mode best suited to capture the sweep of history toward socialism and to indicate the functioning of society as a totality all of the aspects of which are interrelated in a coherent, if complex, fashion. For Lukács, this ability of the great realist novels to comprehend society as a totality directly counters the tendency of decadent capitalism to fragment human experience into separate realms, thus impoverishing and unsettling the human subject.

Lukács, especially in his important work *History and Class Consciousness* (first published in 1923), describes this fragmentation in terms of the phenomenon that he calls reification, or the conversion of all aspects of human life (including abstract concepts, social relations, and even humans themselves) into "things." Reification is clearly related to the Marxist concept of commodification. However, whereas the notion of commodification emphasizes the participation of commodities in a single overarching economic system, Lukács's discussion of reification focuses on the dialectical flip side of this process, in which the separation into discrete things implies that human life is radically fragmented, individuals losing all sense that the different aspects of life fit into a coherent whole. Thus, reification is also closely related to the process of alienation and, in particular, to the effacement in capitalist society of all traces of the actual production of commodities, leading to a further separation between production and consumption of goods. This aspect of reification has become particularly important to Marxist critics in recent years, as consumers in "First World" countries like the United States so often buy and use goods that were manufactured in the distant "Third World." Reification thus becomes a sort of repression through which citizens of rich countries can enjoy their luxury products without thinking about the lives of the workers who produced those products under the most oppressive of conditions.

Meanwhile, Lukács further argues that individual perception in a capitalist society is limited by class consciousness, which enables members of a certain class to understand the world only in ways allowed by their class position. He argues that the bourgeoisie are by definition incapable of seeing through the process of reification; concerned only with the manipulation of commodities, the bourgeois owner acts essentially as a consumer of commodities with no real access to an understanding of the details of their production. The proletariat, on the other hand, is intimately involved in production. As a result, despite the alienated condition of workers, they can potentially develop a revolutionary class consciousness that will allow them to see through the mystifications of the commodity and gain access to the idea of society as a totality. For Lukács, literature can play an important role in the development of this new proletarian consciousness of totality, because the greatest writers are those who can effectively represent the totality of human life. Indeed, in a capitalist society, perhaps the most important single function of such literature is to promote the development of a proletarian class consciousness that can potentially contribute to the demise of the capitalist system.

In works such as *The Historical Novel* (first published in 1937), Lukács sees realism as the only literary mode capable of representing the totality of society by revealing through its narrative form the underlying movement of history. Great realists such as Scott and Balzac, regardless of their personal ideologies, thus provide potentially valuable models for socialist writers. Indeed, Lukács believes that the greatest realist literature, by embodying the forces in an epoch that enable historical change, is always progressive, regardless of the political leanings of the authors themselves. Thus, in *The Meaning of Contemporary Realism*, he argues that "for the Marxist, the road to socialism is identical with the movement of history itself.... Thus, *any* accurate account of reality is a contribution—whatever the author's subjective intention—to the Marxist critique of capitalism, and is a blow in the cause of socialism" (*Meaning* 101). But this accuracy need not imply the inclusion of exhaustive accurate details (which would be naturalism): Lukács notes that in the historical novel "it matters little whether individual details, individual facts are historically correct or not.... Detail ... is only a means for achieving ... historical faithfulness ... , for making concretely clear the historical necessity of a concrete situation" (*Historical Novel* 59).

Moreover, Lukács's insistence that the most effective literary works must strive to represent society as a totality does not imply that texts must seek, in an encyclopedic way (per Bakhtin), literally to represent all aspects of society. Rather, successful works of literature must seek to represent their characters and events in ways that show their participation in the totality of society. Crucial here for Lukács, especially in the case of characterization, is the technique of typification, or the ability of writers such as Scott to create characters who "in their psychology and destiny always represent social trends and historical forces" (*Historical*

Novel 34). Such writers are thus able to "give living embodiment to historical-social types" (*Historical Novel* 35). For Lukács, "the *typical* is not to be confused with the *average* (though there are cases where this holds true), nor with the *eccentric* (though the typical does as a rule go beyond the normal). A character is typical, in this technical sense, when his innermost being is determined by objective forces at work in society" (*Meaning* 122). Thus, typification involves the representation of characters who are distinctly and vividly portrayed as individuals, but in whom "certain, purely individual traits of character, quite peculiar to them, are brought into a very complex, very live relationship with the age in which they live, with the movement which they represent and endeavour to lead to victory" (*Historical Novel* 47).

Lukács's work also involves a firm sense of literary history. If the great age of realism corresponds to the rise to power of the bourgeoisie in the eighteenth and early nineteenth centuries, then the bourgeois turn to conservatism after this power is achieved leads to a decline in realist literature that eventually leads to the appearance of naturalism, which for Lukács is a sort of degraded form of realism that focuses on description instead of narration and that concentrates on local details at the expense of a loss of an ability to represent society as a totality. Meanwhile, in his important essay "The Ideology of Modernism" (included in *The Meaning of Contemporary Realism*), Lukács extends this narrative to modernism, which he sees as even more decadent and less able to represent reality accurately than is naturalism.

Lukács believes that the formal fragmentation of modernist texts participates in the process of reification that is itself central to the fragmentation of social life under capitalism. Moreover, he sees in the dazzling verbal constructions of modernist writers a reflection of the kind of reification and fragmentation that he finds rampant in modern capitalist society. He argues that modernist writers like Joyce and Kafka make technique an end in itself, without regard to the human realities that this technique is supposed to convey. For Lukács this "negation of outward reality" is a central project of modernist writing, which represents a turning away from the world and a retreat into an aesthetic realm divorced from social reality. And this disengagement is in direct complicity with the main cultural thrust of bourgeois society, which seeks to isolate art in a separate realm and thus deprive it of any potentially subversive political force. Modernist texts thus are for Lukács not progressive documents, interacting with history in a positive and productive way. Instead, they are sterile artifacts, divorced from history and totally caught up in the inexorable drive of capitalist society to convert all it touches into mere commodities.

A number of important twentieth-century Marxist theorists have been strongly influenced by Lukács's work. For example, Lukács's concern with issues of wholeness and fragmentation, along with a focus on the material aspects of cultural media, identifies an important area of contact between the work of Lukács and that of the German Marxist theorist and cultural critic Walter Benjamin. In his important essay "The Storyteller" (included in *Illuminations*), Benjamin argues in a mode reminiscent of Lukács's narrative of gradual historical fragmentation that in the modern world the ability to tell meaningful stories is rapidly becoming a lost art. Storytelling for Benjamin is first and foremost a means of conveying advice for dealing with "real" life, but he suggests, writing in the tumultuous days of post–World War I Germany, that the modern world no longer makes sense. "Reality" itself is thus increasingly problematic, and there is no longer any meaningful advice to give. Benjamin, like Marx and Lukács, sees the devaluation of experience in the modern world as the consequence of a long historical process. Meanwhile, always concerned with the relationship between works of art and the physical technology available to produce and distribute those works, Benjamin suggests that the demise of storytelling begins with the invention of the printing press and occurs as part of the shift from oral to print culture (and from stories to novels) that has characterized Western society for the past four centuries. Benjamin particularly emphasizes the contribution that the rise of the novel makes to the decline in the ability of individuals to relate to others, much in the way that the early Lukács (in *The Theory of the Novel*) sees the novel as the genre of a modern world that has lost the sense of wholeness characteristic of the earlier world of the epic. In contrast to the communal activity of telling (and listening to) stories, both the reading and the writing of novels are for Benjamin solitary activities, thus rendering particularly problematic the project of leftist writers to further a sense of solidarity among their working-class readers.

For Benjamin, the earliest forms of art were endowed with an "aura" that caused them to be viewed with a sense of quasi-religious awe. However, Benjamin believes that the mechanical reproduction of modern forms such as printed texts and (especially) film leads to the shattering of this aura and to the growth of a changed mode of aesthetic reception that produces a new kind of emancipated reader, free of the quasi-religious enthrallment associated with art in earlier eras and thus able to resist the authority of received ideas and to read in challenging and critical ways. For Benjamin, the formal fragmentation of modernist art can play a positive role in this process as well, and in this sense Benjamin differs substantially from Lukács. On the other hand, he resembles Lukács in his critique of the deterioration of the knowledge conveyed by traditional narrative into the ephemeral and fragmented kind of information conveyed by the modern newspaper.

Moreover, in making this distinction between genuine knowledge and mere information, Benjamin anticipates the critique of Enlightenment science carried out by the "Frankfurt School" theorists Max Horkheimer and Theodor Adorno in *The Dialectic of Enlightenment*. Noting the Enlightenment "motto" that "knowledge is power," Horkheimer and Adorno suggest that the scientific impetus of the Enlightenment is informed by a quest not for a liberating truth, but for a power that ultimately enslaves. In particular, they suggest that the emphasis on the power of the individual in Enlightenment thought is related to a drive to dominate nature, a drive that inevitably turns back upon itself and leads to the formation of individuals who are internally repressed and of societies consisting of individual subjects who strive for domination of one another. Importantly, Horkheimer and Adorno do not oppose science itself, but merely the mechanical application of science. Enlightenment science, they argue, seeks not knowledge but information, not understanding but practical application. Such science thus does not yield genuine enlightenment, but reinscription within the new myth of the power of technology: "With the abandonment of thought, which in its reified form of mathematics, machine, and organization avenges itself on the men who have forgotten it, enlightenment has relinquished its own realization" (*Dialectic* 41).

This emphasis on reification again identifies a Lukácsian strain in the work of Horkheimer and Adorno, though the powerful influence of Friedrich Nietzsche on their work leads to a number of differences from Lukács. Adorno in particular, though far more pessimistic than Marx about the possibilities of a coming socialist utopia, finds in modernist art a potentially powerful and progressive counter to the oppressive overemphasis on reason and rationality that he sees as central to the Enlightenment. In particular, he tends to place modernist art in opposition to popular culture, which he views as a debased form intended essentially to stupefy the general population and thus render them more susceptible to capitalist exploitation. Indeed, Horkheimer and Adorno, in their essay "The Culture Industry" (also included in *The Dialectic of Enlightenment*), provide the basis for one of the major strains of criticism of popular culture in the second half of the twentieth century.

In some ways, the opposition between modernism and popular culture in Horkheimer and Adorno is dangerously similar to the Cold War vision of modernism as the polar opposite of mass politics. But the analysis of Horkheimer and Adorno can also be seen as an important precedent to Fredric Jameson's later, and very different, attempt to distinguish between a modernism that still contains powerful elements critical of capitalism and a postmodernism that is thoroughly saturated with the "logic" of capitalism in its late, global/consumerist phase. For Jameson, the most important Lukácsian critic still working at the end of the twentieth century, postmodernist art arises from a sense of reality that is radically fragmented, discontinuous, and multiple, a direct reflection of the nature of late capitalism. Indeed, he views postmodernism as an "apotheosis of capitalism" (*Postmodernism* 77).

Jameson sees more critical potential in modernism, which he views not simply as a reflection of commodification and consumer capitalism but as a reaction against these phenomena that was at least in some ways effective. He indicates a strong link between the technical brilliance of modernist art and its supposed subjectivism with his suggestion that the distinctive personal "styles" of the various modernist artists themselves function as evidence that within the modernist cultural milieu the concept of a distinctive self still had meaning. Jameson's attention to fragmentation often integrates a consideration of art and literature with traditional mainstream Marxist social critique. For example, in *The Political Unconscious* he relates the bourgeois attitude toward art as separate from social reality directly to the ideology of bourgeois individualism. This ideology, according to Jameson, leads to the perception that private life is sharply distinguished from the public world of politics in a way that parallels the bourgeois tendency to treat art as a self-enclosed realm separate from the social and political world. But this perception of art does not elevate it as somehow superior to everyday reality; instead, it merely renders art irrelevant, diminishing its function in life. Similarly, Jameson insists that the ostensible privileging of the private over the public that is central to bourgeois individualism actually impoverishes private life by obscuring the domination of the individual by capitalism and creating a false illusion of individual autonomy. Far from creating the strong, independent individuals mythologized by bourgeois ideology, capitalism "maims our existence as individual subjects and paralyzes our thinking" (*Political* 20).

To oppose this tendency, Jameson elaborates a Marxist interpretive practice (related, at least metaphorically, to Freud's methods for reading the contents of the unconscious mind) that allows critics to detect the presence of a "political unconscious," or underlying ideological content, in literary texts. At the same time, Jameson insists on the need for critical self-consciousness and for critics (in the process he calls "metacommentary") to meditate on the ideological conditioning of their own work. He thus proposes a model for a Marxist critical practice, which (along with his own large and impressive body of criticism) has been of special importance to the re-emergence of Marxist critique in the United States after several decades in which Marxist literary criticism was virtually absent due largely to the political climate of the Cold War.

Jameson's 1971 book *Marxism and Form* can in many ways be taken as the founding text of contemporary American Marxist criticism. In this work, a critical introduction to the thought of a number of important Marxist thinkers (including Adorno, Benjamin, and Lukács), Jameson introduces a number of the key concepts that have since remained central to his career, including a Lukácsian concern with cultural and psychic fragmentation in the modern world, an emphasis on the importance of historical vision in cultural criticism, a firm belief that literature and culture cannot be separated from their social and political context, careful attention to both form and content in elaborating the political significance of cultural artifacts, and a strong commitment to the necessity for a utopian element (in the Marxist, scientific sense, rather than in the idealistic sense) in critical thought. Jameson's work is marked by a sophisticated use of concepts from poststructuralist, psychoanalytic, and other forms of critical thought, but it remains firmly rooted in the Marxist tradition. It also provides an important methodological model in its insistence on the importance of a metacritical approach, that is, on criticism that not only discusses its object but also performs self-conscious critical examinations of the grounds of its own inquiry. Jameson's work has been tremendously influential for American Marxist critics and for other American critics interested in exploring the social and political dimensions of literature and culture.

Jameson's most important debt to Lukács may reside in the central emphasis of both critics on history as the basic fabric of human existence. In particular, Jameson follows Lukács in placing great emphasis on the way literature reflects the Marxist notion of history as class conflict. Thus, in a recent essay, Jameson declares that history, in the modern sense, is an invention of the European bourgeoisie, designed to tell the story of the cultural revolution through which they rose to hegemony in Europe. The story of "the transition from feudalism to capitalism," suggests Jameson, "is what is secretly (or more deeply) being told in most contemporary historiography, whatever its ostensible content." Further, he argues, this view of history makes the bourgeois cultural revolution "the only true Event of history" (*Signatures* 226–27). Thus, the now famous injunction "Always historicize!" with which Jameson begins *The Political Unconscious* implies not only an insistence that critics be aware of the embeddedness of literary texts in their historical contexts but also an awareness of the way the discourses of both history and literature have been used to support and legitimate bourgeois hegemony in Europe.

Given the central role of literature in the establishment and maintenance of bourgeois hegemony in Europe, it is not surprising that so many

Marxist literary critics, like Eagleton, have focused particularly on the realm of ideology. The most influential figure in this vein of Marxist criticism has been the Italian Marxist Antonio Gramsci, whose work is principally represented in a series of notebooks he wrote while in an Italian fascist prison (for his left-wing political activities) from 1927 until his death in 1937. Gramsci focused on the way the European bourgeoisie gained and maintained their power through a complex of political and cultural practices that convinced the more numerous lower classes willingly to accede to bourgeois authority. Thus, bourgeois power resides principally in what Gramsci calls "hegemony," in the ability of the bourgeoisie to obtain the "'spontaneous' consent given by the great masses of the population to the general direction imposed on social life by the dominant fundamental group; this consent is 'historically' caused by the prestige (and consequent confidence) which the dominant group enjoys because of its position and function in the world of production" (*Notebooks* 12).

Literature, of course, can play a central role in the development of this "spontaneous" consent. Meanwhile, if absolutely necessary, this consensual obedience can be supplemented by "the apparatus of state coercive power," that is, by institutions like the police and the army, which use physical force to enforce "discipline on those groups who do not "consent" either actively or passively. This apparatus is, however, constituted for the whole of society in anticipation of moments of crisis of command and direction when spontaneous consent has failed" (12).

Gramsci's work has proved extremely influential for a number of subsequent Marxist critics. The most important of these Gramscian Marxist critics is probably Louis Althusser, whose extensive body of work is particularly distinguished by his attempt to integrate Marxist thought with the structuralist methods of analysis that were dominant in France during the 1950s and 1960s. This project centrally involves art and culture, and Althusser is especially concerned with delineating the complex relationship between art and ideology. From this point of view, Althusser's most important concept is probably the notion of "interpellation," or the "hailing of the subject"—the process through which individuals are formed as subjects by powerful forces working in the interest of the prevailing ideology of a given society. For Althusser, we do not form our attitudes so much as they form us, and "the category of the subject is only constitutive of all ideology insofar as all ideology has the function (which defines it) of 'constituting' concrete individuals as subjects" (*Lenin* 171).

Echoing Gramsci, Althusser emphasizes that the process of interpellation allows the existing power structure of capitalist society to maintain its domination over the general population without resorting to violence or force. Interpellation occurs in subtle ways through the workings of what Althusser calls "Ideological State Apparatuses" (ISAs), including official culture and specific institutions like churches and schools, though it is constantly backed up by the physical force represented by the "Repressive State Apparatus" of the police and the military. Althusser's discussion of interpellation has much in common with the frequent arguments of Marxist critics that ideological manipulation of individual psyches lies at the heart of the bourgeois conception of the free autonomous individual, a conception that turns out to be nothing more than a ruse to hide the fact that individuals are largely determined not by their own choices but by the needs of the economic and political systems in which they live. Indeed, Althusser directly contrasts ideology (as knowledge thoroughly conditioned by politics) with science (as direct objective knowledge). This opposition leads to a special emphasis on culture and literature, which for Althusser is situated somewhere between the poles of science and ideology. Moreover, for Althusser art plays a privileged role in ideological critique because the workings of ideology can potentially be detected in art in ways that they cannot in society at large.

The Gramscian vein of Marxist ideological critique has also been central to the tradition of British cultural materialism. A key founding figure in this tradition is Raymond Williams, whose work grows directly out of the strong British tradition of socialist class and working-class culture. However, especially later in his career, Williams also draws extensively upon the continental Marxist tradition of thinkers like Althusser. Emphasizing the important role played by literature and culture in the development of society as a whole, Williams employs analysis of cultural artifacts as part of a project to develop a general vision of British socialism. In *The Country and the City*, he presents nothing less than a Marxist revision of the entire history of British literature from the Renaissance forward. But Williams's work, perhaps influenced by his own working-class background, is marked by a distinctive emphasis on the creative potential of ordinary people. He pays serious attention not only to traditional "high" culture, but also to popular culture, and his work on popular media like television has been extremely influential for cultural critics in recent years. Williams's view of culture as the embodiment of the mutually lived experience of ordinary people and therefore as a source of organic unity has struck many contemporary Marxist critics as somewhat nostalgic and idealized. Nevertheless, his insistence on attention to the needs and experiences of common people as a necessary element of cultural criticism has provided a positive example for many subsequent critics.

Such attention, of course, has been precisely the project of much leftist literature in the past century. This project, however, is not an easy one, as indicated by Barbara Foley's compelling argument in *Radical Representations* that the inability to this point of modern leftist literature to contribute in a substantial way to the ultimate demise of capitalism can be attributed largely to the fact that leftist writers have all too frequently succumbed to the lure of bourgeois aesthetics (which the universalist tendencies of bourgeois ideology have identified simply as aesthetics) and have attempted to produce works that can meet the standards of bourgeois aesthetic judgment. To an extent, Cold War rhetoric to the contrary notwithstanding, it is the aesthetics of the bourgeois tradition (and not the dictates of the Communist Party) that in the twentieth century has proved a powerful, hegemonic force holding the imaginations of an entire generation of artists in its grip and placing strict limitations on the kinds of art they can produce. But hegemony (in its technical, Gramscian sense, at least) is never totally successful, and the specific nature of capitalist hegemony is such that there are always cracks and fissures in which resistance might begin to take root.

Thus, there has been an impressive volume and scope of Left cultural production in spite of all the ideological forces that have been aligned against Left culture in Britain and the United States in this century. For one thing, numerous middle-class writers have attempted to convince their own class to end its participation in the most extreme forms of exploitation of workers, either through satires of the fundamental dishonesty and inefficiency of capitalism or through graphic description of the suffering of the poor under the capitalist system. Meanwhile, working-class writers have attempted to promote a sense of solidarity among workers, sometimes calling directly for proletarian revolution. And they have done so through a variety of genres, including realistic descriptions of working-class experience, utopian projections of a better world under socialism, and dystopian projections of the evils to which capitalism might eventually lead. This research guide attempts to present a cross section of British novels of the Left that captures something of the breadth and scope of Left cultural production in the past century.

THE BRITISH NOVEL OF THE LEFT: A BRIEF HISTORICAL SURVEY

Although the notion of a literature of the Left as defined in this study ultimately has meaning only after the work of Marx, it is also the case that literature has often been regarded as a troubling and potentially subversive force throughout history. Thus, despite his insistence that the aesthetic is a thoroughly bourgeois concept whose very purpose is the perpetuation of bourgeois ideology, Eagleton argues that there is something inherently uncontrollable in the aesthetic that still gives it a considerable subversive potential: "The aesthetic as custom, sentiment, spontaneous impulse may consort well enough with political domination; but these phenomena border embarrassingly on passion, imagination, sensuality, which are not always so easily incorporable" (*Ideology* 28). Meanwhile, much of Bakhtin's work involves the delineation of the historical background of the novel in a long countertradition of "low," folk-based literature that is oriented in direct opposition to the dominant tradition of "high" culture. In British literature, not only are all early novels in some sense leftist, but there are novels explicitly radical in their orientation that go back at least as far as William Godwin's essentially anarchist *Caleb Williams* (1794). Meanwhile, the rudiments of a critique of capitalism can be found in the novels of Elizabeth Gaskell or even certain novels (*Hard Times*, *Dombey and Sons*) of the thoroughly bourgeois Charles Dickens. On the other hand, Dickens remained highly antagonistic to the idea of working-class political action. In texts such as *Barnaby Rudge* (1841) and *A Tale of Two Cities* (1859), workers who attempt to take action to improve their lot are depicted as debased savages devoid of human feeling, setting the tone for a series of such depictions that would resonate in bourgeois literature for the next century and then find new life in the rhetoric of the Cold War.

By the early nineteenth century, the political climate (in response to events in France) was specifically antirevolutionary, while the economic climate (in response to the Industrial Revolution) was more and more capitalist. This situation, combined with the low literacy rate and lack of access of the working class to the publishing industry, made the production of leftist novels in the modern sense virtually impossible. Nevertheless, as E. P. Thompson points out in his monumental work *The Making of the English Working Class*, English working-class culture developed in vibrant and dynamic ways during the nineteenth century as workers sought, within the confusion of sweeping social transformations such as the Industrial Revolution, to establish a viable cultural identity for themselves as individuals and as a class. Writers such as William Cobbett established a tradition of journalistic writing informed by "detailed social observation, from the point of view of the condition of the majority of men" (Williams, *Country* 108).

Mostly, however, working-class culture remained an essentially marginal phenomenon, promulgated through informal channels and generally set in stark opposition to an official English culture that tended to represent workers in negative and stereotypical ways. Indeed, the more workers sought to seize control of their lives, the more they became the objects of fear and loathing in the official English press—and in English literature. The Chartist movement of 1837–1848 marks a particular watershed in the history of this phenomena. This movement, which derived its name from the "People's Charter," drafted by the London Working Men's Association, called for reforms such as universal male suffrage, most of which would not be instituted until the crisis in capitalism at the end of the nineteenth century. Meanwhile, as the most significant attempt of English workers in the nineteenth century to gain both political and cultural power, this movement spurred the expansion of working-class culture into realms hitherto dominated by the middle and upper classes, including the production of working-class novels by writers such as Ernest Jones and Thomas Merton Wheeler. Not surprisingly, this movement triggered a reaction in middle-class literature as well, providing some of the inspiration for Dickens and Gaskell and even leading a decidedly right-wing writer like Benjamin Disraeli to warn, in novels like *Sybil* (1845), that economic inequality was making England into two nations that might eventually end up at war with one another. In Disraeli's case, the concern was less for the plight of English workers than for the possibility that these workers, given their brutelike tendencies toward savagery and mob violence, might wreak havoc on the upper classes. Nevertheless, "condition of England" novels by writers such as Disraeli and Gaskell helped to establish precedents for the literary treatment of issues that would be crucial to the literature of the Left in future decades.

The middle part of the nineteenth century, especially after the end of the Chartist movement, saw a relative dearth in the production of working-class literature in Britain, though works such as John W. Overton's *Harry Hartley, or, Social Science for the Workers* (1859) and W. Lynn Linton's *The True History of Joshua Davidson* (1872) continued to agitate for greater justice and equality in Britain. Working-class literature then underwent a resurgence late in the nineteenth century as the work of Marx and Engels stirred an international effort toward the radicalization of organized labor, while the Great Depression of the late nineteenth century worsened the plight of the working class and brought new urgency to the treatment of issues of social and economic equality. Specific events such as the Trafalgar Square Massacre in 1887 and London Dock Workers strike of 1889, along with broader developments such as the founding of the Second International in 1889 marked a renewed concern not only with the problems of capitalism but with the potential of socialism as a solution to those problems.

Meanwhile, literature played an important role in developments that led to a number of political and social reforms designed to alleviate the plight of the poor, a plight so extreme that many felt it might lead to revolution. Novels such as George Gissing's *The Nether World* (1889) and Arthur Morrison's *A Child of the Jago* (1896) attempted to make a middle-class audience aware of the miserable living conditions of the underclasses, especially in London. More important, writers such as William Edwards Tirebuck, Allen Clarke, and Margaret Harkness (publishing as John Law) produced novels designed to express a genuinely working-class perspective on contemporary social and political issues. Moreover, many of these writers were importantly influenced by socialism, as were writers such as William Morris, H. G. Wells, and George Bernard Shaw. The last years of the nineteenth century also saw an increase in the production of historical novels from a working-class perspective by writers such as William Hale White (*The Revolution in Tanner's Lane*, 1887), James Haslam (*The Handloom Weaver's Daughter*, 1904), and E. L. Voynich (*The Gadfly*, 1897).

Thus, by the end of the nineteenth century, there was already an impressive body of novels of the Left in Britain, ranging from naturalistic descriptions of working-class poverty, to rousing calls for working-class political action, to utopian visions of a better socialist future, to historical novels intended to help provide a usable past for working-class action in the present. It should be noted, however, that these novels tended to be leftist primarily in terms of content and did not pose fundamental challenges to bourgeois aesthetic conventions. Meanwhile, partially because of the success of democratizing reforms introduced around the turn of the century, the impetus for leftist literature seemed to wane in the first decade of the twentieth century; World War I contributed to a further decline in British Left literary production in the second decade of this century. Left novels did continue to be produced, however, including works such as *The Sorcery Shop* (1907) by the important socialist propagandist Robert Blatchford. Moreover, 1914 saw the publication (albeit in expurgated form) of Robert Tressell's *The Ragged Trousered Philanthropists*, probably the most vivid literary evocation of working-class experience to that date and a book that would become the single most influential text in the literature of the British Left in the twentieth century. Tressell's novel also broke new aesthetic ground and posed a fundamental challenge to the traditional bourgeois conventions of the novel, thus making it an important model for subsequent leftist novels in terms of style and technique as well as content.

The 1920s then saw another surge in the production of leftist literature in Britain, spurred by British social and economic problems in the wake of World War I and inspired partly by the success of the Russian Revolution and the project to build socialism in the Soviet Union. Works such as James Welsh's *The Underworld* (1920), Ethel Carnie Holdsworth's *This Slavery* (1925), Henry Green's *Living* (1929), and Ellen Wilkinson's *Clash* (1929) once again turned literary attention to class-related social and economic issues. With the coming of the Great Depression of the 1930s (and with the threat of fascism looming over British society—both internally and externally—during most of that decade), British literature of the Left underwent a veritable explosion of productivity. This decade saw the publication of hundreds of novels of the Left, in a wide variety of modes and from a significant range of political perspectives. Some of these works, such as Lewis Grassic Gibbon's trilogy *A Scots Quair* (1932–34) employed sophisticated modernist literary strategies that helped them to become accepted as classics of British literature.

Meanwhile, works such as Olaf Stapledon's socialist utopian fantasies (*Last and First Men*, 1931; *Star Maker*, 1937) eventually gained recognition as classics of science fiction. Writers such as Rex Warner (*The Wild Goose Chase*, 1937) and Edward Upward (*Journey to the Border*, 1938) produced experimental avant-garde works that attempted to convey the need for radical social and political change in Britain, while writers such as Walter Greenwood (*Love on the Dole*, 1933) and Walter Brierley (*Means-Test Man*, 1935) used realist and naturalist strategies to convey working-class experience to a primarily middle-class audience in ways that helped them to become best-selling popular successes. Writers such as Harold Heslop (*Last Cage Down*, 1935) and Lewis Jones (*Cwmardy*, 1937; *We Live*, 1939) began to make genuine progress toward the development of a legitimately proletarian literature that would break free of the limitations of the bourgeois aesthetic tradition. Other leading leftist writers of the decade included James Barke, Ralph Bates, Simon Blumenfeld, James Hanley, John Sommerfield, Storm Jameson, Naomi Mitchison, Sylvia Townsend Warner, and Mulk Raj Anand. Finally, critics such as Christopher Caudwell, Alick West, and Ralph Fox made important contributions in the 1930s to the development of British literary criticism from a genuinely Marxist perspective. Fox, incidentally, also wrote proletarian novels, while Caudwell (writing as Christopher St. John Sprigg) joined C. Day Lewis (writing as Nicholas Blake), historians G. D. H. Cole and Margaret Cole, and numerous others in writing detective novels sympathetic to the proletarian cause.

World War II interrupted this tremendously rich cultural production, and the subsequent climate of the Cold War made it impossible for that production to regain its former momentum in the years after 1945. It should be emphasized, however, that some of this lack of momentum was due to the fact that many reforms supported by leftist writers of the 1930s were actually implemented in the years after World War II. Nevertheless, social problems and class inequality remained, and leftist writers continued to respond to those phenomena. Jack Common wrote effective autobiographical novels of working-class experience, including *Kiddar's Luck* (1951) and *The Ampersand* (1954). Jack Lindsay, whose career began in the 1930s, remained a tremendously prolific writer of leftist texts, specializing in historical novels. "Angry young men" such as Stan

Barstow, John Braine, Alan Sillitoe, and Keith Waterhouse also continued to document working-class experience sympathetically, even if without a specifically socialist demand for change.

Doris Lessing, responding especially to issues related to gender and colonialism, produced works such as *Martha Quest* (1952) and *The Golden Notebook* (1962) that broke genuinely new ground in the literature of the Left, even if the latter book also documented the dispirited condition of the British Left at that time. Likewise, John Berger, who in novels such as *G.* (1972) brought the British novel of the Left fully into the realm of postmodernism. In the meantime, writers such as David Caute kept alive the Left tradition of historical novels, while writers such as Sillitoe, Barry Hines, David Storey, Pat Barker, James Kelman, and the Marxist critic and theorist Raymond Williams continued to produce novels centering on working-class life within the new context of post–1960s Britain. Of these, Storey, Kelman, and Barker would all become winners of the prestigious Booker Prize, suggesting the continuing vitality of working-class literature in Britain.

It is probably true, as is widely perceived, that the last twenty years have not been a particularly rich period of British Left cultural production, though on this score one might consult Andy Croft's spirited argument that the quality and diversity of texts associated in one way or another with leftist ideas is so impressive as to suggest that leftist culture is actually hegemonic in Britain even to this day (*Red Letter Days* 336–45). In any case, production in leftist history and cultural and literary criticism has certainly been particularly impressive in the period from the 1960s to the 1990s. Historians such as E. P. Thompson, Eric Hobsbawm, and Gareth Stedman Jones have helped to keep alive the strong British tradition of working-class culture, while Hobsbawm's magisterial four-volume history of the nineteenth and twentieth centuries has done a great deal to clarify, from a decidedly leftist perspective, the broad movement of world history in the last two hundred years. Critics such as Croft, H. Gustav Klaus, and Jeremy Hawthorn, meanwhile, have worked to bring renewed attention to the long tradition of British socialist and working-class literature. And theorists such as Williams, Terry Eagleton, and Perry Anderson have drawn upon the heritage of British cultural materialism to make important new contributions to the development of Marxist theory. Some of the most important work in this area is summarized in the next chapter of this guide.

2

SELECTED CRITICAL AND HISTORICAL STUDIES RELEVANT TO THE BRITISH NOVEL OF THE LEFT

PERRY ANDERSON: *CONSIDERATIONS ON WESTERN MARXISM* **(1976).** A general survey of the phenomenon of Western Marxism. Anderson argues that Gramsci was the last major Western Marxist thinker to focus on issues of class struggle and that subsequent Western Marxist thinkers have tended to focus primarily on analyses of the superstructure. In particular, Anderson points out the crucial importance of literature and culture in the work of Western Marxists, even ones so otherwise as different as Georg Lukács and Theodor Adorno. In Anderson's view, Western Marxism was born in the failed proletarian revolutions against capitalism in Europe immediately after World War I and has been marked by its participation in a growing gulf between socialist theory and working-class practice. This gulf, meanwhile, has led to an increasingly parochial focus that has sometimes resulted in analyses of Western society to the exclusion of a properly Marxist global vision and a retreat into cultural theory to the exclusion of broader working-class social concerns.

F. C. BALL: *ONE OF THE DAMNED: THE LIFE AND TIMES OF ROBERT TRESSELL, AUTHOR OF THE RAGGED TROUSERED PHILANTHROPISTS* **(1979).** An informative supplement to Tressell's classic work of proletarian fiction by the editor who was responsible for the restoration of Tressell's full text in the 1955 Lawrence and Wishart edition. Important aspects of Ball's book are its description of the complex publication history of Tressell's text and a discussion of popular and critical reactions to it. However, *One of the Damned* is probably most valuable for its substantial biographical information on the mysterious Tressell as well as a good description of the historical context of *The Ragged Trousered Philanthropists*.

DAVID BELL: *ARDENT PROPAGANDA: MINERS' NOVELS AND CLASS CONFLICT, 1929–1939* **(1995).** A broad and useful study that focuses on the work of Harold Heslop and Lewis Jones in an attempt to ascertain and describe the aesthetic principles that underlie their fiction. Bell argues that these two writers attempt to appropriate certain bourgeois literary forms for use as antibourgeois socialist propaganda.

CHRISTOPHER CAUDWELL: *STUDIES IN A DYING CULTURE* **(1938).** In the 1930s, Christopher Caudwell was a leading figure in the attempt to develop a sophisticated form of Marxist literary criticism in Britain. Though his career was cut short when he was killed in 1937 while fighting in the British Battalion of the International Brigade in the Spanish Civil War, Caudwell produced an extensive body of Marxist literary criticism, most of which is available in volumes published posthumously. Under the name Christopher St. John Sprigg, he also published several detective novels during the 1930s. Book-length works of literary criticism include *Illusion and Reality* (1937), *Studies in a Dying Culture* (1938), and *Further Studies in a Dying Culture* (1949). Of these, the second is probably the most important, though all of Caudwell's critical work is similar in that it focuses primarily on readings of bourgeois literature (the "dying culture" of the title), attempting to develop a materialist approach designed to demystify the aesthetic concepts that have historically equated bourgeois literature with literature itself.

Studies in a Dying Culture also includes essays arguing that the works of writers such as George Bernard Shaw and H. G. Wells, traditionally associated with socialism, are in fact pervaded with bourgeois ideology. Although Caudwell's application of Marxist concepts to literary and cultural criticism is sometimes a bit mechanical, he provides a number of valuable insights into the nature and power of bourgeois ideology. It is also worth remembering that he was only twenty-nine years old when he died in the fight against fascism. A longer career no doubt would have produced increasingly sophisticated critical analyses, though Caudwell's willingness to die in the cause of freedom stands as a valuable lesson in itself.

JON CLARK, MARGOT HEINEMANN, DAVID MARGOLIES, AND CAROLE SNEE, EDS.: *CULTURE AND CRISIS IN BRITAIN IN THE THIRTIES* **(1979).** A useful collection of essays on a variety of aspects of British culture in the 1930s. James Klugmann's introductory essay provides valuable historical information about the political context of 1930s culture. Also useful is Peter Widdowson's general survey of English fiction in the 1930s (which includes discussions of Virginia Woolf, Aldous Huxley, Edward Upward, Rex Warner, George Orwell, Graham Greene, and Christopher Isherwood). Of most relevance to the novel of the Left is Carol Snee's essay "Working-Class Literature or Proletarian Writing?," which looks at the work of Walter Greenwood, Walter Brierley, and Lewis Jones within the context of a general discussion of the relationship between proletarian fiction and the bourgeois aesthetic tradition.

ANDY CROFT: *RED LETTER DAYS: BRITISH FICTION IN THE 1930s* **(1990).** An excellent and informative survey of British leftist culture in the 1930s. Croft includes relatively little in the way of detailed readings of specific texts, but he provides near-encyclopedic historical coverage of leftist novels published during the decade and of the cultural context in which those novels were produced. Croft is quite open about his own Gramscian perspective and about his desire to broaden traditional definitions of leftist fiction. His definition may, in fact, be a bit too broad and his estimate of the power of leftist culture in Britain a bit too optimistic. For example, he is probably too sanguine about accepting the Popular Front period as an era of leftist hegemony in British culture. Nevertheless, his arguments are always thought provoking and his extensive documentation is extremely valuable.

JAMES CRONIN: *LABOUR AND SOCIETY IN BRITAIN, 1918-1979* **(1984).** A sophisticated historical study that employs Foucauldian methods of analysis to trace the relationship between working-class culture and British politics during the period covered. Drawing upon contemporary accounts, Cronin begins by emphasizing the growth of working-class solidarity in specific opposition to bourgeois domination in the years after World War I. He also suggests that unemployment and other hardships associated with the Depression years of the 1930s often furthered this sense of class consciousness, especially in the realm of cultural production.

VALENTINE CUNNINGHAM: *BRITISH WRITERS OF THE THIRTIES* **(1988).** The most extensive published compilation of information on British literature of the 1930s. Written from a perspective sympathetic to the Left, the book gives extensive coverage to leftist culture, though Cunningham is a bit too dismissive of the accomplishments of leftist fiction in the decade.

C. DAY LEWIS, ED.: *THE MIND IN CHAINS: SOCIALISM AND THE CULTURAL REVOLUTION* **(1937).** A collection of essays describing the ways in which capitalism has inhibited development in a number of important disciplines and suggesting that socialism could lead to the liberation of the human mind in ways that would produce important new advances in these disciplines. Particularly relevant to a study of the novel of the Left are Rex Warner's essay on education and Edward Upward's essay on Marxist interpretation of literature. Other essays in the cultural realm focus on the film industry, the theater, art, music, and the media, while essays on psychology, science, and religion are included as well.

TERRY EAGLETON: *CRITICISM AND IDEOLOGY: A STUDY IN MARXIST LITERARY THEORY* **(1976).** A general study of Marxist literary theory, marked by Eagleton's typical intelligence and wit. As does much of Eagleton's work, it focuses especially on the role of ideology in Marxist criticism. In particular, it insists on the impossibility of an "innocent" criticism that neither addresses the ideology of the text nor employs an ideology of its own.

TERRY EAGLETON: *THE IDEOLOGY OF THE AESTHETIC* **(1990).** An impressive survey of the philosophy of aesthetics from its origins in eighteenth-century bourgeois thought, through the work of great bourgeois philosophers such as Kant and Hegel, and on to the oppositional Marxist philosophies of thinkers such as Marx, Benjamin, and Adorno. Eagleton also discusses the implications of the work of Nietzsche, Freud, and Foucault in terms of our understanding of the philosophy of aesthetics. The work is particularly valuable for its demonstration that the very category of the aesthetic is an invention of bourgeois thought and for its attempt to historicize the resolutely ahistorical inclinations of bourgeois aesthetics. Eagleton also maintains that, despite its bourgeois origins, the realm of the aesthetic still contains a number of potential energies that might be used to oppose bourgeois hegemony. The long chapter on Foucault and postmodernism contains numerous provocative challenges to postmodernist thought and is of particular relevance to contemporary cultural issues.

TERRY EAGLETON: *LITERARY THEORY: AN INTRODUCTION* **(1983).** Because of its wide use as a textbook in university-level introductions to literary theory, Eagleton's book may be the most widely read work of Marxist theory in America. The title, however, is a bit misleading, because Eagleton's book is not so much an introduction to literary theory as a historical study of the background of certain schools of bourgeois literary theory, including the New Criticism, phenomenology, hermeneutics, structuralism, and poststructuralism. Eagleton impressively reveals the politics that lie behind these supposedly apolitical approaches to literary study and ends with a call for an overtly political criticism that does not seek to hide its ideological agenda.

TERRY EAGLETON: *MARXISM AND LITERARY CRITICISM* **(1976).** A brief, accessible, and extremely useful introduction to the use of Marxist theory as the basis for literary criticism. The study begins with the work of Marx and Engels and moves through the work of twentieth-century theorists such as Georg Lukács, Lucien Goldmann, Pierre Macherey, and Walter Benjamin. Louis Althusser is discussed only in passing, though Althusserian ideas clearly lie very much behind Eagleton's own point of view. Eagleton also includes a useful discussion of the so-called Lukács-Brecht debate concerning the relative merits of modernism and realism as a mode for antibourgeois literature. The book ends with a reminder that Marxist theory is not merely an alternative method for interpreting literary texts but "a part of our liberation from oppression."

WILLIAM EMPSON: *SOME VERSIONS OF PASTORAL* **(1935).** A general survey of the pastoral mode in British literature, Empson's book begins with a chapter on proletarian literature, indicating the prominence of that literature in the British culture of the 1930s. The chapter is also notable for its very positive treatment of the postrevolutionary culture of the Soviet Union.

PAMELA FOX: *CLASS FICTIONS: SHAME AND RESISTANCE IN THE BRITISH WORKING-CLASS NOVEL, 1890–1945* **(1994).** A theoretically sophisticated study that includes illuminating readings of a number of works of British working-class fiction from the 1890s to the 1940s. Fox's perspective is more feminist than Marxist, which often leads her to call attention to issues of gender that are sometimes overlooked in studies of working-class culture. On the other hand, this perspective sometimes obscures class-related issues, and Fox's emphasis on the importance of "shame" as a constitutive aspect of working-class subjectivity could do more to locate the sources of this shame in the social and economic structures of capitalism. Similarly, Fox's notion of resistance, far more pluralistic and localized than the Marxist notion of class struggle, sometimes fails to apprehend the real nature of oppression and resistance under capitalism. Nevertheless, *Class Fictions* is an important addition to scholarship on British working-class literature and a valuable contribution to the important task of establishing a genuine dialogue between Marxism and feminism.

RALPH FOX: *THE NOVEL AND THE PEOPLE* **(1937).** A member of the Central Committee of the British Communist Party and one of the founders of the British section of the Writers' International, Ralph Fox was one of the leading British Marxist activist intellectuals of the 1930s. During the first half of this decade he published numerous articles in leftist organs such as the *Daily Worker*. His book-length works of social and political criticism include *A Defence of Communism* (1927), *The Colonial Policy of British Imperialism* (1933), and *The Class Struggle in the Epoch of Imperialism* (1933). Powerfully influenced by developments in the Soviet Union, Fox published an account of his first-hand observations of events in the early years of the Soviet Union (*People of the Steppes*, 1925) and a biography of Vladimir Lenin (1933). Fox translated works by such important early Soviet figures as Georgy Plekhanov and Nikolai Bukharin. He also wrote the novels *Storming Heaven* (1928) and *This Was Their Youth* (1937). In 1936 he joined the International Brigade and went to Spain, fighting in a unit that was primarily French but included a British company. He was killed in action soon afterward.

The Novel and the People, Fox's most important work of literary criticism, was published posthumously in 1937. The book is simultaneously an ambitious collection of essays on the political implications of the novel as a genre and a polemical contribution to a number of political debates in the 1930s. Drawing directly upon the work of Marx and Engels and influenced extensively by Russian thinkers such as Plekhanov and Bukharin, Fox develops in *The Novel and the People* a Marxist aesthetic that is in many ways highly reminiscent of that of Georg Lukács, though Fox did not have access to Lukács's work. In particular, he argues that, while the novel originates as a bourgeois form, its unique ability to represent society as a totality makes it a potentially powerful weapon in the socialist battle to overcome capitalism. His sophisticated work stands as a rejoinder to those who would claim Marxist thought on culture in the 1930s to be rigid and doctrinaire. His life, marked by an active fight for justice that eventually led to the loss of that life, should put to rest the invidious Cold War stereotype of Marxists as cold, uncaring ideologues.

JAMES GINDIN: *BRITISH FICTION IN THE 1930S: THE DISPIRITING DECADE* **(1992).** A useful survey of certain aspects of British fiction in the 1930s that discusses a number of leftist works but is marred by a reliance on bourgeois aesthetic criteria. Though somewhat eccentric in its choice of works on which to focus, it includes a number of texts that seldom get central attention in period studies, including works by Nicholas Blake, Patrick Hamilton, Winifred Holtby, and Rosamund Lehmann. It also affords significant attention to more prominent figures such as Lewis Grassic Gibbon, J. B. Priestley, Henry Green, and L. P. Hartley.

FRANK GLOVERSMITH, ED.: *CLASS, CULTURE, AND SOCIAL CHANGE: A NEW VIEW OF THE 1930S* **(1980).** An eclectic collection of essays that reevaluates a number of aspects of British politics and culture in the 1930s from varied points of view. Several of the entries deal specifically with literature, including Valentine Cunningham's essay on 1930s writers and political commitment, Gloversmith's essay on Orwell and Auden, and Stuart Laing's essay on John Sommerfield's *May Day*. Other essays deal with topics such as gender issues in the interwar period, the cultural position of the Communist Party of Great Britain in the first half of the 1930s, and the relationship between British intellectuals and the Popular Front in the mid-1930s. Although this volume is useful, it might have profited from a more extensive treatment of leftist literature and a more substantive discussion of the politics of literary criticism in the 1930s.

JEREMY HAWTHORN, ED.: *THE BRITISH WORKING-CLASS NOVEL IN THE TWENTIETH CENTURY* **(1984).** An extremely useful compilation of essays edited by a leading British literary scholar. Included are essays on such individual writers as Robert Tressell, Lewis Grassic Gibbon, Walter Greenwood, D. H. Lawrence, Jack Common, and Alan Sillitoe, as well as more general discussions of novels about miners, novels about the Irish working class, and the use of realism in the working-class novel. Together, the essays explore the various ways in which the novel, though a quintessentially bourgeois form, can be put to productive use for the expression of working-class experience. They also seek to call attention to the tradition of British working-class literature in ways that might lead to a reformulation of British literary history, which has so often ignored the works of working-class writers.

GRANVILLE HICKS: *FIGURES OF TRANSITION: A STUDY OF BRITISH LITERATURE AT THE END OF THE NINETEENTH CENTURY* **(1939).** In this volume Hicks, one of the major American Marxist critics of the 1930s, outlines aspects of British literature at the end of the nineteenth century that identify links between the Victorian tradition and modern British literature. In particular, Hicks seeks to identify transitional elements in the works of such figures as William Morris, Thomas Hardy, Samuel Butler, George Gissing, Oscar Wilde, and Rudyard Kipling, then to relate these transitions to historical changes in the economic and social context in which these writers worked. Hicks's major premise is that the industrial expansionism of the high Victorian age led to a severe economic crisis for which imperialism provided a temporary cure. He then elaborates the relationships of this historical development to the works of his transitional writers, arguing that their works signal the end of Victorian industrial capitalism and mark the rise of an imperial finance capitalism the inherent instabilities of which anticipate the coming collapse of capitalism as a whole.

PETER HITCHCOCK: *WORKING-CLASS FICTION IN THEORY AND PRACTICE: A READING OF ALAN SILLITOE* (1989). A useful study of Sillitoe's fiction as working-class literature, focusing especially on the novel *Saturday Night and Sunday Morning* and its later film adaptation. Hitchcock also places the work of Sillitoe in a broader context by beginning with a general historical survey of British working-class fiction that also includes helpful discussions of a number of critical studies of the subject. The work concludes with a meditation on the theory and practice of working-class fiction that provides a useful discussion of a number of Marxist critical concepts in relation to the novel as a potential mode for the expression of working-class consciousness.

ERIC HOBSBAWM: *THE AGE OF CAPITAL, 1848–1875* (1975). The middle volume in Hobsbawm's three-volume study of nineteenth-century history, *The Age of Capital* follows *The Age of Revolution* in describing the historical development of industrial capitalism during the classical period from 1848, when bourgeois hegemony had been firmly established in Europe, to 1875, when the decline of most capitalist economies into depression forced sweeping reforms in the workings of capitalist economies and the associated social and political structures. Like the other volumes in the trilogy, *The Age of Capital* is sweeping in scope, tracing the (often highly negative) impact of unfettered capitalist expansion on virtually every aspect of life in Western Europe and North America. Hobsbawm demonstrates with his typical insight and lucidity that the classic age of capitalism led to a growing gap between rich and poor that heightened tensions between the classes and made inevitable the near collapse of capitalism in the last decades of the nineteenth century.

ERIC HOBSBAWM: *THE AGE OF EMPIRE, 1875–1914* (1987). The final (and in many ways most impressive) volume in Hobsbawm's three-volume study of the history of the "long" nineteenth century. Like its predecessors, *The Age of Revolution* and *The Age of Capital*, *The Age of Empire* is a comprehensive study that considers virtually every aspect of life in Western Europe and North America during the period covered. For the Marxist Hobsbawm, of course, the economic is the principal driving force of history, and he relates in convincing fashion the way in which the sweeping reform and democratization of Western societies at the end of the nineteenth century came about in an attempt to save capitalism from a crisis that nearly brought about its end. Hobsbawm also explores the ways in which imperialist expansion helped to avert economic collapse in the West, while at the same time it fostered competition among nations, thereby heightening the tensions that would eventually lead to the outbreak of World War I. This work brilliantly captures the excitement, anxiety, innovation, and skepticism of one of the most eventful and tumultuous periods in history.

ERIC HOBSBAWM: *THE AGE OF EXTREMES: A HISTORY OF THE WORLD, 1914-1991* **(1994).** An extension of Hobsbawm's earlier studies of nineteenth-century history that, in its global rather than Western scope, is in some ways even more impressive than its predecessors. Hobsbawm brilliantly captures the flow of events from World War I, through the interwar period, through World War II, and through the postwar period of capitalist economic boom, Cold War, and decolonization. Maintaining a special focus on the realm of the economic, Hobsbawm traces the development of the wide variety of social, political, and cultural transformations that have marked our century. While regarding the Russian Revolution as clearly the most important event of the twentieth century, Hobsbawm argues that, in retrospect, the opposition between capitalism and communism (both, after all, products of the Western Enlightenment) may seem to historians less central to this century than the confrontation between Western and non-Western societies. Published soon after the fall of Eastern European socialism, *The Age of Extremes* contains a number of valuable insights into the historical causes of that fall and ends with a suggestion that the apparent global victory of capitalism at the end of the century may be a temporary one and that better times may lie ahead if we will only heed the lessons of history.

ERIC HOBSBAWM: *THE AGE OF REVOLUTION, 1789-1848* **(1962).** The first volume of Hobsbawm's magisterial three-volume history of the "long" nineteenth century—that is, the period from the French Revolution in 1789 to the beginning of World War I in 1914. This volume presents a lucid and compelling description of the sweeping transformation brought about in European life by the political impact of the French Revolution and the social and economic impact of the Industrial Revolution that followed soon afterward. Hobsbawm's Marxist historiographic approach is particularly good at placing this transformation within the context of the rise of capitalism and the establishment of bourgeois hegemony in Europe. For Hobsbawm the "age of revolution" ends with the general failure of the revolutions of 1848, which marked the point in history when bourgeois hegemony had been established and when the bourgeoisie ceased to be a force for revolutionary change.

RICHARD HOGGART: *THE USES OF LITERACY* **(1957).** A major work of British cultural criticism, focusing on the impact of modern developments such as the growth of popular culture and the mass media on the British working class. Hoggart envisions working-class culture as a source of community and stability that is stubbornly resilient and resistant to the pressures of modernity. Indeed, the individuals who suffer most according to his account are those, like the "scholarship boys" of one of his best known chapters, who become separated from their roots in the working class by attempting to rise beyond it and experiencing not the joy of upward mobility but the alienation of *déclassement*. As a result, Hoggart's account of working-class culture is sometimes rather sentimental and nostalgic, while at the same time it makes that culture appear oddly conservative and stodgy, with values such as family, home, and all-around decency lying at its heart. Nevertheless, partially based on Hoggart's own personal experiences, *The Uses of Literacy* is a rich and valuable account of British working-class culture that serves as a useful supplement to British working-class literature.

KATHARINE BAIL HOSKINS: *TODAY THE STRUGGLE: LITERATURE AND POLITICS IN ENGLAND DURING THE SPANISH CIVIL WAR* (1969). A general study of the impact of the Spanish Civil War on British culture in the late 1930s. Though not itself avowedly leftist in its orientation, the book emphasizes leftist culture, with separate chapters on leftist "argument," fiction, drama, and poetry. These chapters are useful, though not particularly comprehensive. Also included is a chapter on responses to the Civil War from the British Right.

PETER KEATING: *THE HAUNTED STUDY: A SOCIAL HISTORY OF THE ENGLISH NOVEL 1875–1914* (1989). An extremely useful study of the English novel at the end of the nineteenth and beginning of the twentieth century, focusing on the response of writers during this period to the rapidly changing social conditions around them. Keating particularly focuses on changing attitudes toward gender and class, and in so doing he provides valuable commentary on the works of writers from late-Victorian popular novelists such as Robert Louis Stevenson and Rider Haggard, to early modernist writers such as Joseph Conrad and E. M. Forster. Keating provides some especially valuable readings of late figures in the realist tradition, including George Gissing, Henry James, Arnold Bennett, and H. G. Wells. Though focusing on these mainstream figures, Keating also acknowledges the work of working-class writers such as Tirebuck and Tressell. Explicitly couched as an attempt to overcome the ahistorical tendencies of much literary criticism, Keating's book does an excellent job of identifying the social and political issues that lie behind the fiction he discusses, as well as relating literary innovations to larger historical developments. A comprehensive bibliography of British fiction published from 1875 to 1915 completes the work.

PETER J. KEATING: *THE WORKING CLASSES IN VICTORIAN FICTION* **(1971).** An impressive survey of the representation of the British working class in Victorian fiction, focusing on works published in the last two decades of the nineteenth century, though with constant reference to earlier works, particularly those of Charles Dickens. Keating concentrates on such writers as Walter Besant, George Gissing, Rudyard Kipling, and Arthur Morrison, all of whom at least attempted to provide realistic depictions of working-class life. In addition to these major figures, Keating also discusses the work of lesser known writers such as the Chartist novelists of the 1840s and the "Cockney School" novelists of the late nineteenth century. While Keating himself tends to accept bourgeois aesthetic criteria, he provides extremely useful background material for any study of the modern novel of the Left, which both builds upon and contests the nineteenth-century representations he analyzes. Keating also discusses, though not in great detail, the works of novelists such as Margaret Harkness, Constance Howell, and W. E. Tirebuck, who can be seen as the immediate predecessors of modern leftist novelists such as Robert Tressell and as founding figures in the entire tradition of the modern British novel of the Left.

PETER KEATING, ED.: *INTO UNKNOWN ENGLAND, 1866–1913: SELECTIONS FROM THE SOCIAL EXPLORERS* **(1976).** An anthology of selections from the works of upper- and middle-class "social explorers" who have attempted to describe the lives of the lower classes in an effort to further the cause of social justice. This work provides useful background for any understanding of class-related issues within the context of late nineteenth- and early twentieth-century British history.

ARNOLD KETTLE: *AN INTRODUCTION TO THE ENGLISH NOVEL: VOL. II: HENRY JAMES TO THE PRESENT DAY* **(1953).** The second volume of a sweeping history of the English novel from its beginnings in the eighteenth century to the early years after World War II. In this volume Kettle concentrates on a relatively small number of works by such canonical writers as Henry James, Thomas Hardy, Joseph Conrad, D. H. Lawrence, and James Joyce, but he does so within the context of a genuinely historical analysis and from a Marxist point of view, both of which set his work apart from most Western literary criticism in the 1950s and maintain its value even today.

H. GUSTAV KLAUS: *THE LITERATURE OF LABOUR: TWO HUNDRED YEARS OF WORKING-CLASS WRITING* **(1985).** An important historical survey that attempts to delineate an alternative literary tradition including both working-class writers and middle-class writers who sympathize with the agenda of the working class. Klaus traces the contributions of literature to the development of working-class subjectivity, discussing writers ranging from the plebeian poets of the eighteenth century, to socialist utopian writings of the early nineteenth century, to Chartist fiction, to the proletarian novelists of the twentieth century. A special focus is placed on socialist literature of the 1930s, including a full chapter on the work of Harold Heslop and another on a series of novels published in 1936.

H. GUSTAV KLAUS, ED.: *THE RISE OF SOCIALIST FICTION, 1880–1914* **(1987)**. A collection of essays on a variety of writers and movements during the period indicated by the title. Provides extremely useful background information that helps to place the rise of the socialist novel at the end of the nineteenth century within its historical context and that identifies the works of writers such as W. E. Tirebuck, Margaret Harkness, and Robert Tressell as the foundation of later developments in the British socialist novel. Entries such as Ingrid von Rosenberg's essay on Harkness, Tirebuck, and French naturalism and Ronald Paul's study of Tressell and international leftist writers such as Maxim Gorky and Martin Anderson Nexö also help to place the development of British socialist fiction within the context of the rise of an internationalist leftist literary tradition.

H. GUSTAV KLAUS, ED.: *THE SOCIALIST NOVEL IN BRITAIN: TOWARDS THE RECOVERY OF A TRADITION* **(1982).** An extremely useful and informative collection of essays covering the works of a wide variety of British leftist and socialist writers, ranging from the Chartist fiction of the 1840s to the contemporary works of writers such as Raymond Williams and John Berger. Entries such as Ramón López Ortega's essay on the language of the working-class novel in the 1930s and Raymond Williams's meditation on the general problems facing Welsh proletarian novelists address important theoretical issues, while other essays provide insightful readings of the works of specific socialist novelists, including Williams, Berger, Margaret Harkness, Robert Tressell, Lewis Grassic Gibbon, Ethel Carnie Holdsworth, Lewis Jones, and several others.

GEORG LUKÁCS: *THE HISTORICAL NOVEL* **(1937).** One of the most important work of Marxist literary criticism ever written, Lukács's impressive survey traces the development of the historical novel from its beginnings in the eighteenth century to its embattled status in the 1930s. Lukács focuses, however, on the nineteenth century, and this book is probably most valuable for its delineation of the characteristics that make the early nineteenth-century historical novels of writers such as Walter Scott examples of bourgeois realism at its best. In particular, Lukács's comments on such novels help to clarify his belief in realism as the literary mode that best represents the forward movement of history (eventually toward socialism). His comments on Scott, Tolstoy, and other great historical novelists also exemplify his insistence on the importance of representing society as a totality, though for Lukács such representations involve less an attempt at encyclopedic completeness than capturing the forces that drive history,

For Lukács, following such predecessors as Friedrich Engels, the most important technique in the representation of such historical forces is "typification." Meanwhile, for Lukács the power of early nineteenth-century bourgeois literature derives from its ability to capture the historical energies involved in the rise to power of the European bourgeoisie. *The Historical Novel* also includes valuable discussions of writers such as Flaubert, whom Lukács regards as symptomatic of the decline of bourgeois literature into decadence as the bourgeoisie themselves became a conservative class after solidifying their power in Europe. For Lukács, the crucial marker of this change from revolutionary class to reactionary class is the decision of the bourgeoisie all over Europe to oppose rather than support the revolutions of 1848. In his view, this decline in bourgeois realism eventually leads to the development of naturalism and then modernism as increasingly decadent offshoots of the realist tradition. Although Lukács's readings of literary history have been widely challenged, they have nevertheless been highly influential and still stand as exemplary attempts to place literary history within the broader context of social and political history.

JANET MONTEFIORE: *MEN AND WOMEN WRITERS OF THE 1930S* (1996). A useful study of British fiction of the 1930s, concentrating on politically engaged fiction and particularly concerned with women leftist writers who have been largely ignored in mainstream accounts of British literary history. Writers such as Storm Jameson, Naomi Mitchison, and Sylvia Townsend Warner thus emerge as major figures in this study, though Montefiore contextualizes the work of these writers with a discussion of numerous other writers and of the social and political context of the decade. The focus is primarily on fiction, though the book includes discussions of autobiographies and a chapter on women poets of the 1930s as well. An entire chapter is also devoted to Rebecca West's *Black Lamb and Grey Falcon*, which Montefiore reads as a veiled critique of fascism.

GEORGE ORWELL: *HOMAGE TO CATALONIA* **(1952).** Orwell's account of his experiences in Spain during the Spanish Civil War is generally considered one of the most important documents of that conflict. The book includes graphic accounts of actual combat as well as meditations on the background and implications of the conflict. Orwell's sympathy with the Spanish Republicans, for whose cause he himself fought, is never in doubt in the book. However, his argument that the failure of the Republican cause was largely due to the self-interest and internal bickering of the communists who supported them is typical of Orwell's problematic relation to the British Left. Of course, this argument does not do justice to the genuine dedication of the many communists who fought and died for the Republican cause while remaining entirely loyal to the Communist Party, nor does it adequately address the fact that the liberal democracies of the West failed to come to the aid of the Republicans in their fight against fascism.

GEORGE ORWELL: *THE ROAD TO WIGAN PIER* **(1937).** Orwell's account of his firsthand observations of life among coal miners and the unemployed in England's industrial north, written on commission for the Left Book Club, a prominent force in British leftist culture of the 1930s. Part I contains vivid accounts of the difficult conditions under which miners must work and the squalid conditions in which all of the poor must live. These images stand as a powerful indictment of the capitalist system and as a strong argument for socialism. Part II, though also theoretically written in support of socialism, contains many criticisms of the socialist movement as it actually existed in Britain in the mid-1930s. Orwell's conclusion that British socialists should drop all talk of economics and class struggle and concentrate on calls for liberty and justice show the superficial nature of his commitment to socialism and the fundamentally bourgeois workings of his strongly individualist consciousness. A foreword by Victor Gollancz disputes many of Orwell's comments about British socialism.

RONALD PAUL: *"FIRE IN OUR HEARTS": A STUDY OF THE PORTRAYAL OF YOUTH IN A SELECTION OF POST-WAR BRITISH WORKING-CLASS FICTION* **(1982).** A study of the theme of youth in the fiction of a number of post–World War II working-class writers, including Jack Common, Brendan Behan, Alan Sillitoe, and Barry Hines. Paul notes that this theme has been prominent in working-class fiction since the Chartist period, so that its study can help to uncover continuities in the tradition of working-class culture.

BRUCE ROBBINS: *THE SERVANT'S HAND: ENGLISH FICTION FROM BELOW* (1986). An excellent survey of the representation of servants in British bourgeois fiction of the nineteenth century. This work is particularly useful for its suggestion that, despite the marginal position of servants in canonical British fiction, the representation of servants had a destabilizing influence that caused bourgeois writers to modify their techniques in order to attempt to deal with characters who were a foreign class presence in the bourgeois novel. In so doing, Robbins argues both for a revaluation of the British literary canon and for a careful consideration of servant figures in British fiction as the agents of a stubborn moral resistance to oppression that can serve as a valuable source of utopian images in our own day.

ALAN SINFIELD: *LITERATURE, POLITICS, AND CULTURE IN POSTWAR BRITAIN* (1989). Reviews the utopian hopes and dreams that led to the establishment of the post–World War II welfare state, then traces that attempt to reorganize British society through to its demise in the Thatcher years. The author notes that postwar welfare capitalism was really a form of corporatism rather than socialism and that it was ultimately designed more to preserve capitalism than to promote social and economic equality. Looking at wide-ranging issues involving class, race, and gender, Sinfield analyzes the role of culture in a process of social construction of values that was central to the historical development of postwar Britain. He pays particular attention to the impact on this development of the Cold War and interactions between British and American culture. This work also pays significant attention to the role of Left cultural production during this period, including a useful account of the rise of the New Left. It concludes with a hope that the tribulations of global capitalist dominance at the end of the twentieth-century may ultimately lead to a new period of fertile development in the thought and culture of the Left.

DAVID SMITH: *SOCIALIST PROPAGANDA IN THE TWENTIETH-CENTURY BRITISH NOVEL* (1979). Probably the most comprehensive historical survey of the modern British novel of the Left, focusing on the period from 1906 to 1956. While the title sounds disturbingly reminiscent of pejorative Cold War stereotypes about the literature of the Left, Smith does not in fact consider propaganda as a necessarily negative category of expression. However, he does seem to accept the bourgeois premise that propaganda and art are two separate categories which for him are often at odds in the socialist novel; this leads him to conclude that the best socialist novels (such as Tressell's *The Ragged Trousered Philanthropists* and Grassic Gibbon's *A Scots Quair*) are those that succeed in effecting a conciliation between the two modes. Although Smith does occasionally produce judgments of socialist novels that are clearly derived from the application of bourgeois aesthetic criteria, all in all his book is relatively evenhanded and extremely useful as a source of information about the tradition of the novel of the Left in Britain.

GARETH STEDMAN JONES: *LANGUAGES OF CLASS: STUDIES IN WORKING-CLASS HISTORY* **(1983).** An interesting analysis of nineteenth-century political discourse that attempts to track the historical development of working-class consciousness as a discursive formation. The author argues that the working class does not necessarily constitute itself through its own discourse (as E. P. Thompson tends to imply) but is sometimes the product of radical discourses that are not specific to the working class.

GARETH STEDMAN JONES: *OUTCAST LONDON: A STUDY IN THE RELATIONSHIP BETWEEN CLASSES IN VICTORIAN SOCIETY* **(1976).** An encyclopedic compilation of information documenting class differences in London in the latter part of the nineteenth century, including detailed statistical charts and tables in an extensive appendix. Jones focuses particularly on the conditions of working-class life and on the way London's lower classes were treated as a marginal element of British society. He provides extremely valuable contextual background to phenomena such as the late nineteenth-century concern with degeneration and the rise of socialism and working-class political activism at the end of that century.

E. P. THOMPSON: *THE MAKING OF THE ENGLISH WORKING CLASS* **(1963).** Thompson's careful description of the rise of English working-class culture within the difficult early nineteenth-century context of the industrial revolution and the English reaction against Jacobinism stands as perhaps the single most important historical work to have been produced by the rich British tradition of historical materialism. It is a fascinating account that includes massive amounts of information and documentation and also makes a number of useful points about the ultimate unreliability and incompleteness of much historical information about this period. Thompson begins by noting the element of radicalism that informed English culture in the eighteenth century. He then notes that the French Revolution led to an outburst of Jacobin agitation in England in the 1790s, but that anti-Jacobin reaction (strengthened by anti-French sentiment in the Napoleonic Wars) led to a quick end to this version of English radicalism. Thompson then proceeds to discuss the development of a specifically English version of working-class culture — and thus working-class consciousness — in the early nineteenth century.

In Part II, Thompson focuses on the oppressive conditions faced by the English working classes in the early years of the nineteenth-century Industrial Revolution. Here Thompson is especially concerned to counter numerous revisionary Cold War-inspired accounts from the 1950s that sought to demonstrate that conditions in the Industrial Revolution were not as bad as they had been depicted and that industrialization and the rise of capitalism were actually boons to the English working classes. Much of Thompson's argument in this chapter thus deals with technical matters like the analysis of statistics indicating the standard of living of English workers during this period. Thompson, however, emphasizes that the oppression suffered by the working classes resulted from phenomena far more complex than the rise of factories and mechanization. In particular, he notes the important element of political oppression spurred by anti-French fears. He also pays considerable attention to the negative impact of religion. During the early 1800s, the working classes grew increasingly alienated from the Anglican Church, leading to a dramatic rise in "working class" religions, especially Methodism. However, Thompson shows that Methodism, with its ethos of obedience and its horror of human physical life, worked strongly to the detriment of workers.

Part III of *The Making of the English Working Class* details the powerful tradition of resistance that continued to thrive among the English working classes even amid the repressive climate of the early nineteenth century. Thompson delineates this climate by demonstrating the widespread infiltration of virtually every working-class movement by government spies and pointing out the high frequency with which radical leaders were executed during this period. He pays particular attention to the Luddites (1811–16) and argues that they were far more sophisticated and politically motivated than has been traditionally depicted. Calling the postwar period 1815–19 the "heroic age of popular radicalism," he notes the proliferation of radical rhetoric during the period, culminating in the crucial Peterloo Massacre of 1819. Thompson then shows how a thriving working-class culture arose in the quieter days of the 1820s, including extensive efforts at self-education and the development of working class newspapers, periodicals, theater, and so on, despite extensive attempts at government censorship. He notes that the great increase in working class consciousness during this decade culminated in the crisis period of 1831–32 when England hovered on the brink of revolution. He then shows how the alliance of the aristocracy and the new bourgeoisie (together with reforms that shifted the upper echelons among the workers into the bourgeoisie) managed to defuse these revolutionary energies. After 1832, the working-class movement put most of its energy into political solutions, especially into seeking the vote.

MARTHA VICINUS: *THE INDUSTRIAL MUSE: A STUDY OF NINETEENTH-CENTURY BRITISH WORKING-CLASS LITERATURE* **(1974).** A survey of working-class literature in the nineteenth century that provides a useful background for studies of such literature in the twentieth century, especially in its delineation of the contestation of representations of the working class in literature. Vicinus includes a particularly detailed discussion of the literature of the Chartist movement and of the attempts of writers such as Thomas Martin Wheeler and Ernest Jones to adapt the bourgeois form of the novel to the expression of working-class consciousness. Other chapters on such phenomena as literature associated with coal miners' unions in the early nineteenth century and the dialect literature of the industrial north not only document the beginnings of a working-class literary tradition but provide important social and historical background to that tradition.

ALICK WEST: *CRISIS AND CRITICISM* **(1937).** A collection of essays on literature and culture by one of the leading British Marxist cultural theorists of the 1930s. West, incidentally, was one of the few such theorists to survive the 1930s both literally and professionally, continuing to write works of cultural criticism into the 1950s, including *A Good Man Fallen Among Fabians* (1950, a study of George Bernard Shaw) and *The Mountain in the Sunlight* (1958). His autobiography, *One Man in His Time*, was published in 1969. *Crisis and Criticism* begins with essays on bourgeois literature and criticism, centering on the work of such figures as T. S. Eliot and I. A. Richards and arguing that this work indicates a crisis in bourgeois individualism. It continues with essays on Marxist aesthetics that take Marx's notion of society as an organic totality as a starting point. The work concludes with discussions of two specific texts, James Joyce's *Ulysses* and Harold Heslop's *The Gate of a Strange Field*. While ultimately finding Joyce's attitude rather nihilistic, West sees much of value in *Ulysses*, including an argument that individual motifs in Joyce's book are presented "within the totality of relations existing at the moment," providing "an expression of those forces to which Marx gave formulation when he said that society is the totality of relations" (118). Much of the discussion of Heslop's book is in direct comparison to *Ulysses*—mostly to the advantage of the former.

RAYMOND WILLIAMS: *THE COUNTRY AND THE CITY* **(1973).** An impressive survey of the history of British literature, focusing primarily on the developing theme of the opposition between urban and rural settings and associated values. Among other things, Williams usefully points out that capitalism in England was both an urban and a rural phenomenon and that the traditional tendency to attribute social problems created by capitalism simply to urbanization tends to obscure the real causes of those problems. The work includes insightful commentary on canonical bourgeois authors such as Dickens and Hardy, while also usefully indicating the importance of working-class writers such as Alexander Somerville and Lewis Grassic Gibbon. There is also a discussion of the relevance of postcolonial literature to the issues discussed in the book.

RAYMOND WILLIAMS: *CULTURE AND SOCIETY, 1780–1950* **(1958).** In this important early work, Williams describes the historical development of the notion of culture, arguing that the concept of culture is actually a rather recent one that came into wide use in England only during the period of the Industrial Revolution. In short, Williams demonstrates that the very notion of culture as we have come to understand it is an inherently bourgeois concept. In so doing, he focuses primarily on literature, with readings of nineteenth-century Romantic poets and industrial novelists serving to delineate the development of a literary tradition that came to be seen as central to English culture, while readings of twentieth-century figures such as T. S. Eliot, D. H. Lawrence, and George Orwell trace the further development of culture in the twentieth century. Williams also discusses the development of Marxist theories of culture and ends with a discussion of modern mass media within a context of an attempt to redefine culture in a broader sense and in a way that might contribute to the growth of culture beyond its bourgeois origins.

RAYMOND WILLIAMS: *WRITING IN SOCIETY* **(1983).** A collection on essays on a variety of authors ranging from Racine, to Shakespeare, to David Hume, to Dickens, to Robert Tressell. The volume is extremely instructive for its insistence on reading all of these authors in historical context, and the particular combination of authors selected is typical of Williams's style of expanding the canon to include traditionally marginal cultural figures. Also included are some useful comments on the politics of literary criticism.

3

SELECTED BRITISH NOVELS OF THE LEFT

JAMES BARKE: *LAND OF THE LEAL* **(1939).** *Land of the Leal* is a sweeping historical saga that narrates the process of modernization in Scotland from the 1860s to the 1930s. The book focuses on the lives of David and Jean Ramsay, effectively placing their personal histories within the context of larger developments in the world around them. Beginning with their childhoods in rural Galloway, the book vividly describes the peasant culture within which David and Jean grow to maturity and marry. David grows up in a household dominated by his mother, especially after his father, a farmer with vaguely radical tendencies, is drowned when David is still a child. Jean, on the other hand, is the daughter of Tom Gibson, a sort of Old Testament patriarch who tyrannizes the entire family, imposing his own religious fanaticism on them with an iron hand. David, who has trained in cheese-making, and Jean, who has a natural gift for working with cows and dairy products, meet and marry and soon leave Galloway seeking better opportunities in dairy farming.

Eventually, the couple moves to Caddomlea to work on the large estate of Sir Charles Laidlaw-Scott. Here, Jean's hard work and skill make her one of the estate's most valued workers, while David's intellectual leanings help him become a favorite of Sir Charles. On the way, one daughter has been lost to diphtheria, but the other daughter, Barbara, proves to be a gifted student in the local school and grows to be a beautiful young woman. Because of her exceptional personal qualities she is taken into the manor house as a lady's maid, but is then cast out in disgrace when the son of Sir Charles, having unsuccessfully attempted to seduce her, is diagnosed with a venereal disease and then claims to have contracted it from Barbara. David believes Barbara's protestations of innocence, which are verified when the local doctor confirms her virginity.

Outraged at the unfair treatment of their daughter and saddened by this lesson in class and gender inequality, David and Jean move with Barbara and their son, Andrew, to a new position at the estate of Captain Carsewell of Blackadder, in Fifeshire. The new estate, built on nineteenth-century coal money, is large and luxurious. The dairy is a marvel of modern technology, and the family moves into a house that amazes them with its modern appointments. There, the practical Jean rapidly impresses Mrs. Carsewell and again becomes a valued employee. David, on the other hand, occupies a strictly subordinate position; at one point he is nearly dismissed when he leads a revolt of field workers who are asked to work overtime without extra pay. In general, the family does well, and a second son, Tom, is born. Barbara, however, still troubled by the scandal at Caddomlea, moves to Glasgow, then London, and finally to India.

World War I brings special economic hardships to the family, but they still get by, aided especially by Jean's success in raising hens and selling eggs, which are now in great demand. Immediately after the war, however, Captain Carsewell dies of a heart attack. The estate is sold off, and most of the employees, including the Ramsays, are dismissed, providing still another lesson in class society. As David's friend and fellow employee Jock Simpson puts it, "It's no' good enough that we should all have to depend on one man and his money. He goes and drops down dead—and we've to be hounded off the place like a pack o' beggars" (423). Following the book's inexorable historical logic, the family next moves to urban Glasgow, where David finds work in a shipyard until the postwar depression in shipbuilding leads to his unemployment. Indeed, unemployment is only one of the many hardships faced by David and Jean, whose rural roots make adjustment to the city especially difficult. David is especially unhappy in this urban world, his fundamental incompatibility with which is eventually symbolized by his death as the result of having been hit by an automobile.

In the meantime, Andrew and Tom grow to adulthood, the former training as a machinist and the later for the ministry, signifying their contrasting personalities. Andrew inherits the vaguely radical sympathies of both his grandfather and father, but he goes beyond his forebears when he discovers socialism and is thus able to give his political beliefs a coherence that theirs lacked. Not surprisingly, Andrew's growing class consciousness often sets him at odds with his brother. The book makes clear the historical complicity between religion and class exploitation, and Tom is alienated from his working-class roots not only by his work in the church but by his marriage to a haughty upper-class woman. However, when Andrew joins the International Brigade and goes to Spain to fight fascism, the growing fascist threat begins to awaken Tom as well. He compliments Andrew on having recognized the "dormant" evils of the capitalist system, which fascism has awakened—though Andrew responds that these evils were not all that dormant even in Glasgow had Tom not been too blinded by his religion to see them (582). After Andrew is killed in hand-to-hand fighting, Tom is further radicalized and begins to call for action against fascism from his pulpit.

The book ends as the aging Jean, nearing death, dreams of being reunited with David and Andrew in the "land of the leal." "Leal" is a Scottish word connoting justice and genuineness, and the book's title refers to a utopian realm free of the injustice and the falsity of the modern world. For Jean this utopia is envisioned through nostalgic memories of her childhood Galloway, but the book is driven by a forward historical movement that makes clear the impossibility of a return to the past. Indeed, when David and Jean pay a visit to Galloway late in the book, they find it much changed and much decayed, and David, musing on his childhood in the area, realizes that the past is irrecoverable: "But there was no way back to that life: there was no way forward. He had come back to find that the past was dead and dying and that the future was more uncertain than ever it had been" (493). Jean's aging ruminations on the land of the leal thus clearly offer no real solution to the social problems faced by the family in urban Glasgow. However, through the socialism of Andrew (and the budding socialism of Tom), the book does offer a viable utopian alternative. The book ends with Jean's dreams of a past that cannot be retrieved, but its overall movement clearly keeps open the hope for a better future.

Barke's narrative is coherent and well motivated. The behavior of each character is scrupulously developed as a result not only of that character's personal experiences in the past but in relation to events in the changing world around him or her. Vivid descriptions of private experience are carefully integrated with descriptions of historical events, such as the Boer War, World War I, the General Strike, and the Spanish Civil War. As John Burns puts it in his introduction to the book, the development of the Ramsays is carefully sketched, so that "each move, in a progression from backbreaking work on the land to working in the great Glasgow shipyards, brings them right up to date as participants in one of the greatest social changes of our time—the move towards an increasingly technological society" (xi). In this sense, the book has much in common with Lewis Grassic Gibbon's *A Scots Quair*, a book to which it is in fact often compared. Burns makes precisely this comparison, citing Francis Russell Hart, who also invokes Gibbon in praising Barke's book not only for its ambitious scope but for the "moving and believable" presentation of its characters (241). This individualist language suggests Hart's own bourgeois perspective, of course, and it is not surprising that he goes out of his way to downplay Barke's politics, arguing that the book is "misremembered for a doctrinaire socialism" (241). David Smith, on the other hand, calls the similarities between *Land of the Leal* and *A Scots Quair* "superficial" and suggests, contrary to Hart, that Barke's book suffers from a "harsh and naively expressed dogmatism" that marks it as a product of an age of "repetitive harangues" (70–71).

In point of fact, however, *Land of the Leal* is far clearer in its espousal of socialist politics than Hart wants to claim, yet far more subtle in its development of this message than Smith believes. One might say that Hart concentrates on the private dimension of the book, while Smith concentrates on the public dimension, neither fully appreciating the effect of the combination of the two—somewhat in the vein praised by Georg Lukács in relation to the novels of Walter Scott. Even Smith grants that the book "has partially solved the propagandist's problem: the natural and artistic development of the political message" (70). Indeed, while some of Barke's episodes may be a bit too transparent in their allegorical significance, all in all, the long, patient development of the hardships faced by the Ramsays in the midst of the modernization of Scotland makes clear the difficulties of both the backbreaking labor of a bygone peasant life and the shameless exploitation of workers under modern capitalism. And the book makes clear the desirability of socialism as an alternative to either of these. If the inexorable forward movement of the book's historical narrative makes clear the inevitability of the triumph of capitalism over feudalism, it also suggests the historical logic of the ultimate triumph of socialism over capitalism. ***Selected bibliography:*** Burns; Hart; David Smith (*Socialist Propaganda*).

PAT BARKER: *THE CENTURY'S DAUGHTER* (1986). The title character of *The Century's Daughter* is Liza Wright, née Jarrett, born precisely at the stroke of midnight at the beginning of the twentieth century, which would make her birthdate January 1, 1901. The events of the narrative present in the book occur when Liza is eighty-four years old, which would place them in 1985. These events revolve around the attempts of the state (particularly through the efforts of Stephen, a twenty-nine-year-old social worker) to convince Liza to move out of her crumbling row house so that it, along with all of the other houses on the street, can be demolished in the interest of urban renewal. The narration of these events is interwoven with Liza's memories of the past, which together represent a sort of history of Britain in the twentieth century from her particular working-class woman's perspective. These memories are symbolized in the text by an ornate metal box, painted with the figures of dancing women, which Liza has inherited from her mother. This box contains numerous written documents from Liza's family history (including a newspaper clipping proclaiming her the "Century's Daughter" because of the timing of her birth), but it also serves, as Lyn Pykett points out, as a sort of image of oral matrilineal history, passed from mother to daughter.

Stephen is unable to convince the stubborn Liza to move from her longtime home to one of the nearby high-rise public housing projects, which she views as sterile and dehumanizing and which function as one of the text's most effective representations of the creeping homogenization and reification of British society under late capitalist modernization. Many of these projects are already in decay, thus symbolizing the decadence of Thatcherite England. This decadence is also shown in the fact that the neighborhoods in which these decaying projects exist are terrorized by bands of roving delinquents who, devoid of hope or of the communal supports formerly offered by British working-class culture, take out their frustrations in vandalism and other forms of violence. Indeed, one gang of such delinquents eventually breaks into Liza's home, having heard rumors of her treasured box, which they (being unable to imagine that anything else might have value) assume is full of cash. Liza is injured in the ensuing scuffle and dies in the night, alone except for her parrot, Nelson.

Liza's death is not entirely tragic, however poignant. She has lived a long and productive life and has exercised a powerful positive influence on many of the people whom she has met in the course of the troubled century. A strong and selfless woman who has spent much of her life caring for her mother, her daughter, and her granddaughter, Liza functions as an image of the continuity of certain positive (generally feminine and working-class) cultural energies that have survived the tribulations of two world wars and of rampant modernization. As her neighbor, Mrs. Jubb, says to Stephen after Liza's death, "There's a lot'll miss her. It's surprising how much she meant" (288). And Stephen understands this point very well. The formerly cynical Stephen has, himself, has been powerfully affected by his relationship with Liza, which, among other things, has helped him to begin to resolve some of his alienation from his working-class family, particularly from his recently deceased father, who had never quite been able to come to grips with the fact that Stephen is gay. Liza's influence will thus live on in Stephen, as it will in her daughter and granddaughter, a continuity symbolized by the fact that Stephen agrees to assume the care of Liza's parrot, which has already passed through a succession of owners and is in itself a symbol of continuity. Liza's daughter takes the memory box, and presumably will pass it to her own daughter in turn.

As a result of this sense of continuity, *The Century's Daughter* is essentially an optimistic work, despite the long litany of abuses and hardships that Liza has suffered and despite the sordid manner of her death. She, as an individual, may die, but the community she represents lives on. Indeed, the greatest strength of *The Century's Daughter* is its ability to get beyond the individualism of the typical bourgeois novel and to present vivid individual characters with powerful subjective emotions who are nevertheless first and foremost members of a community. In particular, Barker, partially through endowing Liza with a quasi-allegorical status, is able to focus on private experiences and personal relationships without lapsing into sentimentality and without losing sight of the fact that private individuals are the products of historical phenomena and participants in a public community. In the same way, Barker is able to trace the decline of British working-class culture and the demise of certain communal energies during the course of the twentieth century without sliding into nostalgia for the past. Liza herself is the book's strongest antidote to nostalgia, and whenever her friends begin to wax poetic about the golden past, she insists, while granting that much has been lost, that much has also been gained. In particular, she argues that women have made great strides in the course of the century and now have far more rights and opportunities than they had at the beginning. Barker is thus able to detail the negative consequences of growing capitalist modernization in Britain in a mode that still leaves room to hope for a better future.

The major historical events related in the book are the two world wars, which have a crucial impact on Liza's life, both because of the direct changes they bring in her existence during the wars and because she loses a cherished loved one in each war (her brother, Edward, in World War I, her son, Tom, in World War II). And Barker does a good job of detailing the impact of these wars on British society as well, perhaps anticipating her convincing treatment of the milieu of World War I in her later trilogy of novels about that war. If *The Century's Daughter* has a weakness, however, it is in the treatment of British history between the wars, and especially in the 1930s. While Barker effectively indicates the economic hardships of the Depression years, she does little to capture the richness of leftist political and cultural activity during that period. She shows Liza joining the Labour Party (and even has one of Liza's friends become an important party leader), but there is little representation of real political action, and the Communist Party is missing altogether. Thus, while Barker suggests through the figure of Liza that there is a fundamental strength in British working-class culture that endures through all tribulations, she does little to suggest ways in which this strength might lead to genuine social and political change. *Selected bibliography:* Hitchcock (*Dialogics*); Pykett.

PAT BARKER: *UNION STREET* (1982). Pat Barker, winner of the prestigious Booker Prize for her 1995 novel, *The Ghost Road* (the third volume in a trilogy of novels about World War I that also included the 1991 *Regeneration* and the 1993 *The Eye in the Door*), is one of the most respected novelists in contemporary Britain. Her work is consistently informed by strong political statement. In addition to this powerful antiwar trilogy, she is the author of works such as *Union Street* and *The Century's Daughter* (1986) that are strongly rooted in working-class experience. These works are also strongly rooted in feminine experience, and Barker's most important contribution to British working-class literature is probably her demonstration that feminist resistance to patriarchal oppression need not be at odds with resistance to capitalist oppression on the basis of class. Indeed, the difficulties of Barker's women clearly arise at least as much from their class positions as from their genders, while her work suggests in subtle ways that oppression suffered by these women at the hands of working-class men is actually produced as part of a divide-and-rule strategy through which the capitalist system seeks to interfere with the development of a sense of solidarity among workers of all genders and races. Novels such as *Union Street* are thus extremely important and deserve more attention than they have received.

Union Street is an excellent example of the intelligent and sophisticated exploration of the interrelationship between gender and class that has made Barker perhaps the most important contemporary novelist of British women's working-class experience. The book actually consists of seven stories, each centering on a different working-class woman. Nevertheless, it is rightly considered a novel, partially because the events of the stories often literally overlap but more importantly because Barker carefully weaves the stories together by presenting her seven protagonists not as isolated individuals but as members of a community. For one thing, all of the protagonists reside on the same street (Union Street) in an English industrial town. Most of them are thus directly acquainted with one another, and all of their stories occur within the context of a single neighborhood. They also share the broader background of an economic and political crisis represented most centrally by a looming miners' strike—presumably the 1973 strike that would lead to the fall of the Conservative Heath government the following year. Moreover, the women in these stories are tied together in subtle ways by common experiences of gender and class. Indeed, each protagonist is slightly older than the one before, and there is a clear suggestion in the book that these stories sequentially represent a kind of exemplary working-class woman's life story.

The first segment of *Union Street* focuses on Kelly Brown, a preadolescent girl who lives with her mother, her older sister, and a succession of "uncles" with whom her mother seeks solace from loneliness. Kelly's already difficult life is disrupted when she is lured into a dark factory yard and raped, an event that becomes not only the center of the story but the center of Kelly's life. Much of the story deals with her attempts to deal with the trauma of this experience and with her rejection of most of the efforts of her neighbors to provide support. Kelly even turns to vandalism, striking out to try to rid herself of her bitterness. But she begins to find true healing only when she encounters an old woman sitting on a park bench on a freezing winter night. Kelly is concerned that the woman (unnamed here, but later identified as Alice Bell, protagonist of the seventh segment of the book) will freeze, but then realizes that the woman actually wants to die. The woman falls asleep, and Kelly leaves her on the bench to die. It is clear as the story ends that Kelly has experienced a moment of genuine human contact that promises to set her on the road to recovery.

In the next segment, eighteen-year-old Joanne Wilson copes with the discovery that she is pregnant and contemplates her future life with the child's father, who promises to marry her but is clearly less than enthusiastic about either marriage or parenthood. In the meantime, Joanne receives solace from the friendship of Joss, a midget who lives in the neighborhood and whose small size places him in a subaltern position similar to that occupied by the women. The story also focuses on Joanne's work in the local cake factory, where working conditions are made considerably worse by dissention among the women triggered by one woman's racist persecution of a black West Indian worker. Yet Joanne, knowing that her future husband will refuse to allow her to work, sadly contemplates leaving her job, where she can at least feel a certain sense of community with the other workers, however disrupted this community may be by race and other divisions. The next story essentially presents a picture of the future that faces Joanne by focusing on Lisa Goddard, a young mother whose abusive, unemployed husband hardly provides the companionship she requires. Her principal contact, in fact, is provided by her children, whom she loves despite her occasional impatience and frustration with them. This segment then culminates when Lisa gives birth to her third child, a girl, and then eventually bonds with the girl despite an initial inability to feel any sense of connection to her.

Muriel Scaife, the protagonist of the fourth segment, is a somewhat older married woman whose two children, Sharon and Richard, are now approaching adolescence and whose husband, John, is ill with a fatal lung disease. Richard is a studious boy whose successes in school identify him as a common figure in working-class literature, though he is particularly set apart from his father by the fact that John is entirely illiterate. This illiteracy, however, serves as a source of connection between John and Muriel, who helps him to conceal his inability to read or write from all but herself. After John's death, the community comes together in mourning and in support of Muriel as the neighbors come by the Scaife home one by one to view the body.

Iris King, the protagonist of the book's fifth segment, is particularly supportive, though Muriel's most important support comes from her children, the devotion to whom keeps her going. Iris is a tower of strength, who in fact provides support for many of the inhabitants of Union Street, though she herself, receives very little support from her abusive husband, Ted. Iris experiences a personal crisis when her teenage daughter, Brenda, becomes pregnant. When a doctor declares that Brenda is too far along to have an abortion, Iris arranges for the girl to visit an illegal abortionist, who triggers a miscarriage. The baby, a boy, is so far developed that it is born alive, though it soon dies. Iris buries the body beneath a pile of rubble behind the house and does not let Brenda know that it had ever been alive. Meanwhile Iris copes with the care of an elderly schizophrenic aunt who eventually has to be taken away and institutionalized. In the end, Iris goes on with life and continues to provide help and support for her neighbors, despite her own personal difficulties.

The sixth segment actually centers on a male character, George Harrison, who has recently retired after forty years in the local steel mill and who now finds that he has great difficulty finding things to do with his time. George realizes that it is a nuisance to his wife to have him around the house all day. He eventually finds a part-time job and spends more and more time out of the house. One night, he runs into Blonde Dinah, a legendary local prostitute, now in her sixties and near George's own age. Much to his own surprise, George finds himself going back with Dinah to her place to avail himself of her services. The two actually have a rather tender encounter, and he ends up spending the night. The next morning, he carefully examines her nude body, including her genitals, as she sleeps. He realizes that, even after decades of marriage, this is the first time he has seen an entire nude female body. George leaves, invigorated and ready to go on with his life, which still has years remaining. The final segment then tells the story of the aging Alice Bell, a devoted socialist whose long memory provides a sort of personalized history of twentieth-century working-class culture in Britain. Alice's health finally deteriorates to the point that her family concludes that she should be placed in a nursing home. But she is a proud and independent woman who does not wish to go on living in such an institution. Alice thus goes out into the freezing night, where she will encounter Kelly Brown and then die with her dignity intact.

As Peter Hitchcock notes, *Union Street* is an extremely interesting piece of radical writing that draws significantly upon the traditions of oral history and storytelling to produce narratives that demonstrate important dialogic relationships between women's and working-class issues (*Dialogics* 54-55). Hitchcock also emphasizes the positive and even utopian aspects of this seemingly bleak text, the ultimate effect of which is "not one of hopelessness, but a lesson in the discourse of resistance" (66). Barker manages to show her women protagonists facing life with dignity and determination, despite the tremendous difficulties they face. Yet she does not romanticize or heroicize their lives. These women simply do what has to be done, helping each other as best they can along the way. Indeed, it is not as individual heroines but as members of a community of women with common problems and common goals that they function most effectively. *Selected bibliography:* Dodd and Dodd; Hitchcock (*Dialogics*).

STAN BARSTOW: *A KIND OF LOVING* **(1960).** As Mary Eagleton and David Pierce note, "one of the most important cultural movements in Great Britain this century was the explosion of interest in working-class life in the decade from the late 'fifties to the late 'sixties" (130). Stan Barstow, the son of a Yorkshire miner, was a principal figure in this movement, and *A Kind of Loving*, his first and best known novel, draws substantially upon his own experience of working-class life. With this book, the young Barstow gained immediate critical and popular recognition as a writer and joined figures such as Alan Sillitoe, John Braine, and Keith Waterhouse, all of whom were writing novels of working-class experience in the late 1950s and 1960s, and all of whom met with a substantial amount of commercial success. Like Sillitoe's *Saturday Night and Sunday Morning* and *The Loneliness of the Long-Distance Runner*, Braine's *Room at the Top*, and Waterhouse's *Billy Liar*, *A Kind of Loving* was made into a successful film (released in 1962, scripted by Waterhouse and Willis Hall and directed by John Schlesinger).

Also like these other books, *A Kind of Loving* centers on the portrayal of working-class life under capitalism rather than on the exploration of specific alternatives to capitalism. Indeed, while Barstow's book does imply certain criticisms of class inequality under capitalism, it also acknowledges that the social reforms instituted by the Labor government that was swept into power in 1945 led to substantial improvement in the lives of Britain's working-class citizens, so much so that the characters of *A Kind of Loving* tend to suspect that current conditions are too good to last and that harder times lie ahead. Barstow's book thus provides both an important reminder that the British tradition of working-class culture has not been confined to literature but has at times achieved real reform and an anticipation of the way many of those reforms would begin to be dismantled by the Conservative Thatcher government in the 1980s.

Vic Brown, the twenty-year-old protagonist and first-person narrator of *A Kind of Loving*, is the son of a miner who has risen to lower-middle-class status by becoming a draftsman—as did Barstow himself. Vic is an extremely complex character, a mixture of swagger and insecurity, of rogue and hero. The book, often extremely humorous despite a consistently tragic undertone, centers around Vic's infatuation with Ingrid Rothwell, a young woman from a middle-class background who works in the typing pool at the same engineering firm where Vic is employed as a draftsman. Uncomfortable with Ingrid's seemingly vacuous talk of love, Vic soon realizes that his attraction for her consists mainly of physical lust, contrasting strongly with his own romantic fantasies of what a relationship should be. In particular, Ingrid, who shares none of Vic's budding interest in matters cultural and intellectual, begins to strike him as a sort of superficial philistine. Nevertheless, he finds his sexual attraction for her irresistible—with the ultimate result that she becomes pregnant and the couple marry, despite Vic's misgivings.

Not surprisingly, this marriage quickly leads to misery for both partners. With insufficient funds to set up housekeeping on their own, Vic and Ingrid move in with Ingrid's parents. The snobbish mother becomes Vic's constant tormentor, putting an additional strain on the already shaky marriage. Eventually, Ingrid suffers a miscarriage as a result of falling down the stairs, after which Vic feels more and more an outsider in the household. Frustrated with Ingrid's unwillingness to support him in his conflict with her mother, he dreams of escape from the relationship and eventually moves out. The book ends on a somewhat hopeful note, however, as Vic and Ingrid (partly through the intervention of Ingrid's father) reconcile and get a flat of their own where they can hopefully achieve "a kind of loving" away from the interfering mother-in-law. Indeed, Ronald Paul argues that this solution is so neat as to be "facile" and "manipulated" (69). On the other hand, it is not at all clear that anything has really been solved. In fact, Vic's final statement of determination to make the best of things reads more like a statement of resignation to defeat than a determination to strive for better times in the future. And his understanding that millions of others around the world are in much the same predicament does not go very far toward establishing a basis upon which those millions might work together to improve their lot—especially as Vic seems to imply that those millions are all male and that their collective enemies are not the bourgeoisie but women. *Selected bibliography:* Eagleton and Pierce; Paul (*Fire*).

RALPH BATES: *THE FIELDS OF PARADISE* (1940). Set in Mexico during the presidency of Lázaro Cárdenas (1934-40), *The Fields of Paradise* describes the attempts of the peasants of the agrarian village of San Lorenzo to overcome the oppressive domination of Judge Braulio Acosta, a local political boss, and Don Epigmenio Rosas, the illegitimate landlord of the village. The peasants of the book bear many similarities to the Spanish peasants described in earlier Bates novels such as *Lean Men* and *The Olive Field*, while Acosta's regime has many of the characteristics of the fascism that by 1940 had Spain in its grip. There the similarities end, however, because Mexico is a postrevolutionary country where the federal authorities, led by the leftist Cárdenas, are sympathetic to the cause of the peasants. It is therefore possible to envision a credible scenario in which a peasant revolt such as that which occurs in San Lorenzo might succeed, as it in fact does, though considerable difficulties still lie ahead for the peasants at the end of the book. One might, in fact, interpret Bates's shift from Spain to Mexico as the setting for his fiction as the result of his frustration over the victory of the Spanish fascists and as an attempt to find a way to build a more viable utopian element into his work.

To that extent, *The Fields of Paradise* is successful, but the success is bought at a high cost. In particular, the book is a sort of pastoral fantasy and is almost entirely lacking in any coherent political vision. The conflicts in the book are presented not as class struggles but simply as clashes between good and evil, justice and tyranny. Acosta is not an ideologue but a criminal; he has no political goals other than his own personal gain. To an extent the same can be said for the peasants, though they are at least willing to work to produce wealth and to share the wealth of San Lorenzo among themselves. But the element of community in *The Fields of Paradise* is greatly diminished relative to that in Bates's Spanish fictions. As opposed to the Spanish fictions, which present Spanish peasants, with their strong sense of community, as a collective protagonist, *The Fields of Paradise* is highly individualistic. The peasant uprising in San Lorenzo thus succeeds only because the outsider, Felipe Mantanzas (an almost Byronic hero), arrives in town to lead the revolt. And Felipe—who himself continually expressed his disinterest in, and even distaste for, politics—remains the central figure throughout the narrative. The moderation of *The Fields of Paradise* can be seen in its treatment of Catholicism, which is much more positive than in the Spanish novels. The parish priest of San Lorenzo, Father Ignacio, is rather sympathetic to the peasants all along. And even the Church theoretician, Canon Mendoza (who is initially appalled by the breakdown in order that the revolt represents), eventually comes to realize that the cause of the peasants is just. At the end of the book, the peasants seem well on their way to reestablishing their golden past, in which the people and the Church had worked harmoniously together to earn their lands the utopian title of "the Fields of Paradise."

The Fields of Paradise is also less vivid and powerful than Bates's earlier novels in its description of the lives and cultures of its peasant villagers, no doubt largely because Bates had spent little time in Mexico (he was there for two brief visits in 1938) as opposed to Spain. But the presentation of the book's conflicts in a virtually apolitical manner also clearly shows Bates's retreat from serious engagement in leftist politics, a retreat influenced by the Hitler-Stalin pact of 1939 and by the Soviet invasion of Finland (which Bates denounced in an article in *New Republic*) in that same year. As Katharine Hoskins puts it, *The Fields of Paradise* "lays its chief stress on caution, moderation, limited expectations, and the avoidance of fanaticism" (128). Granted, Bates does not specifically repudiate communism in the book, and he remains sympathetic to the communist goal of social justice. But Hoskins is probably right that the very moderation with which the book moves away from the political agenda of Bates's earlier fiction suggests that Bates (who was never a member of the Communist Party) was never specifically devoted to communist ideals but was instead merely "a practical Englishman [who] seems to have looked upon communism as the best and most practical means for achieving the free and just society he wanted" (129). **Selected bibliography:** Hoskins; Munton and Young.

RALPH BATES: *LEAN MEN* **(1934).** Ralph Bates, listed by Ralph Fox in *The Novel and the People* (1937) along with Mikhail Sholokhov and André Malraux as among the world's "very best" revolutionary writers, was one of the more successful of the British leftist writers of the 1930s. Indeed, Bates gained recognition not only from the Left but from the mainstream, as can be seen by the fact that *Lean Men* was reissued in 1938 in a Penguin edition, thus giving it a sort of momentary and unofficial canonical status. *Lean Men* was Bates's first novel, though he published a volume of short stories (*Sierra*) in 1933. Like most of Bates's work, *Lean Men* is set in Spain and shows a close firsthand knowledge of and sympathy for the Spanish people and their culture. In particular, it centers on events surrounding the abdication of King Alfonso XIII in 1931 and the subsequent founding of the Spanish Republic.

The central character of *Lean Men* is Francis Charing, an English leftist whose love of Spain and participation in the Spanish Revolution clearly align him with Bates. The book opens with Charing preparing to leave London for Barcelona, where he is being sent by the Comintern to help in the organization of the Communist Party there. Once in Barcelona, Charing establishes a "Centre for Free Studies," in which open discussions of politics, art, literature, and music can be conducted in a rather utopian environment that encourages each individual to live up to his or her creative and intellectual potential; in that sense it clearly anticipates the nature of society under socialism. The center is a success, but Charing's work is complicated by his own chaotic personal life and by the tendency of many of the radical opponents of the Spanish regime toward anarchism rather than socialism. Meanwhile, after the sweeping Republican victories in the municipal elections of 1931 and the subsequent abdication of Alfonso, the new government pursues only moderate reforms, leading to substantial discontent on the Left and to the eventual outbreak of violence. Charing's supporters suffer substantial casualties in the ensuing disorder, and Charing himself narrowly escapes, vowing someday to return to resume the fight for justice in Spain.

Bates's extensive knowledge of Spain (where, at the time of the writing of *Lean Men*, he had lived off and on since 1923) is put to good use in the book, which contains a number of vivid and insightful descriptions of Spanish life and culture. Although Bates's presentations of Spanish workers are sometimes rather idealized, his treatment of Spanish culture is even-handed, showing both the contribution of that culture to the strength and endurance of the Spanish people and the oppressive role of that culture in the economic and ideological enslavement of most of the people of Spain. Bates's treatment of Catholicism is an especially important part of the latter project, and the book captures well the centrality of Catholicism to Spanish life, a centrality that makes Charing's work particularly difficult. Not only is the Church itself a powerful opponent of communism, but even the communists who support Charing often seem merely to have shifted their surface vocabularies without having overcome the fundamentally Catholic nature of their view of the world.

Bates also does a good job of capturing the chaotic texture of political life in Spain in the 1930s, though sometimes at the expense of making *Lean Men* itself appear a bit muddled. David Smith thus argues that the narrative is disjointed and sometimes awkward, while he sees the presentation of Charing's motivations as confusing and contradictory (73–75). Indeed, Charing's loyalties to the workers of Spain sometimes seem to come into conflict with the program of the Communist Party, while Charing himself, while devoted to collective action, is often presented as an individual hero in a mode that comes dangerously close to the individualism of bourgeois literature. Such contradictions occur from the book's very first scene, which includes a brief biography of Charing that clearly strives to identify him as a typical "Bolshevik," but in which one of his communist associates in London identifies Charing as "the only man the Comintern could have chosen" for the upcoming mission (12).

Much of this tendency toward individualism in the presentation of Charing may have to do with the fact that he is an outsider in Spain and is never fully integrated into the community of Spanish workers. But much of it also comes from the fact that Charing's basic idealism sometimes comes into conflict with the exigencies of revolutionary action, which may require deceit and ruthlessness. But Bates can hardly be criticized for the latter point. Revolutions tend to be led by idealists, but revolution is by definition a dirty business that leads precisely to the kinds of conflicts for revolutionary leaders that Bates describes. While Bates could have done more in *Lean Men* to make precisely clear the historical and theoretical framework of the Spanish Revolution, his portrait of a revolution in action is generally effective and moving, while avoiding romanticization of the ease with which revolutionary change can be achieved. ***Selected bibliography:*** Ralph Fox (*The Novel*); David Smith (*Socialist Propaganda*); Munton and Young.

RALPH BATES: *THE OLIVE FIELD* **(1936).** *The Olive Field* continues the fictional chronicle of the Spanish Revolution begun in Bates's earlier *Lean Men*, though it dispenses with the English protagonist of the first book to concentrate on a purely Spanish setting and cast of characters. *The Olive Field* is epic in scope, showing the involvement of a wide range of characters in the dramatic historical events that swept across Spain in 1932–34. The first part of the book centers on Los Olivares, an olive-growing community in Andalusia in southern Spain. It begins in early 1932 as the town attempts to adapt to the political changes initiated in 1931, when King Alfonso XIII was removed from the throne to be replaced by a Republican government. The second part of the book, though featuring some of the same characters as the first, takes place in the Asturias, where a miners' uprising in 1934, though put down with much bloodshed, sets the stage for the Popular Front electoral victories of 1936, leading to the Civil War of 1936–39, in which Bates was one of the many British participants on the Republican side.

The Los Olivares section of the book, marked by a vivid evocation of the landscape and culture of the area, is probably the more effective of the two in a traditional (bourgeois) literary sense. This section is populated by a number of striking characters who together represent a cross-section of agrarian Spanish society in a time of historical turmoil. These include now-besieged representatives of the old regime, such as the local priests, Father Martínez and Father Soriano, and the local aristocrat, Don Fadrique Guevara y Muñaroz, the Marquis of Peral. Also important is Don Fadrique's domineering estate manager, Argote. But the central figures of this section are the olive workers and their families, particularly those who are involved in local efforts to further the demise of the old order and to institute revolutionary change. The majority of these are aligned with the anarchist cause, which is clearly characterized by Bates as a sort of substitute religion that cannot offer an effective alternative basis upon which to build a new Spanish society. The anarchists derive much of their leadership from the "Anarchist doctor," Aguiló, who has recently returned from prison. The most important anarchist characters are the olive workers Diego Mudarra and Joaquin Caro, though the latter will eventually convert to Communism under the guidance of Justo Robledo, the major communist spokesman in the community.

The Los Olivares section includes a number of important motifs. For one thing, Don Fadrique's continuing domination of the community demonstrates the persistence of the old regime under the Republican government in the early 1930s, even as the aristocrat makes preparations to flee with much of his wealth in the event of an all-out uprising. Bates also emphasizes the continuing influence of Catholicism in the young Republic, both in the way the priests continue to cling to power and in the way the olive workers continue to be influenced by their Catholic backgrounds. On the other hand, there is also a growing resentment of Catholicism, leading to a violent confrontation early in the text when Father Martínez insists on holding a traditional Holy Week procession. The procession is attacked by anarchists, who are then fired upon by the Civil Guard, showing the continuing loyalty of the latter to older structures of power.

Another important motif in the first part of the book is the failure of anarchism, which Bates depicts as sincere in its quest for liberty but flawed both because it offers no coherent alternative social system and because its fundamentally individualist basis undermines the kind of collective action needed to mount a successful revolution. This individualism is represented in a vivid way when Mudarra seduces (actually, rapes, would be closer) Lucía Robledo, sister of Justo and the longtime object of the romantic attentions of Caro. This episode leads to a violent confrontation between Mudarra and Caro, in which the former is nearly killed. It also leads to Lucía's pregnancy, which, in turn, makes her the object of Argote's insults. This ignites the already tense situation created by an economic crisis resulting from a hailstorm that destroys much of the olive crop. The resultant anarchist uprising is rather easily put down, and the shortcomings of anarchism become clear in both the wanton destruction that accompanies the rebellion and the ultimate failure of the rebellion, which ends in bloody failure when its leaders (including Mudarra) are arrested and a delegation protesting the arrests is massacred by the Civil Guard.

After the failure of the peasants' rebellion in Los Olivares, Caro and Mudarra move on to the Asturias, where they will take part in the 1934 miners' revolt. Though better organized and more politically sophisticated than the one in Los Olivares, this revolt also fails, partially because of anarchist lack of discipline. Mudarra is captured, tortured, and finally killed while trying to escape. Government troops wreak havoc in the region, massacring defenseless villagers suspected of complicity with the rebellion. Caro and Lucía, now married, manage to escape and return to Los Olivares, presumably to gather strength for further action, though this seemingly backward step is certainly problematic from the point of view of Caro's evolution as a communist. Nevertheless, Bates does leave open the hope of future revolutionary success, despite the failure of the rebellions in Los Olivares and the Asturias.

Thus, while Smith finds the narrative connection between the two rebellions forced and artificial, he concludes that *Lean Men* and *The Olive*

Field, Bates's two novels of the Spanish revolution, are both "interesting and intelligent books [that] contributed something of more than minor distinction to the revolutionary novel" (78). Moreover, as Gustav Klaus notes, Bates's depiction of the rebellions (especially the latter one) includes images of collective action that suggest the ultimate possibility of revolutionary success in Spain (113). In particular, there is a clear suggestion in the book that the rural revolution in Los Olivares and the more urban one in the Asturias might have succeeded had they only occurred simultaneously rather than sequentially. Indeed, Bates had planned to write a second volume pursuing the possibility of further revolution, but his involvement in the Spanish Civil War made that project impossible. (Indeed, Bates's involvement in the Civil War made it impossible for him to participate in the publication process of *The Olive Field*, the original edition of which contained numerous errors that Bates corrected in the revised edition issued in 1966 — and reprinted again as late as 1986.) The ultimate defeat of the Spanish Left by Franco and his fascist-backed rightest forces does not, in retrospect, negate this utopian aspect of Bates's work but instead serves as a poignant reminder of the difficulty of positive revolutionary change and of the collective moral failure of Western "democracy" to oppose the spread of fascism in Europe in the dark years leading to World War II. *Selected bibliography:* Klaus (*Literature*); David Smith (*Socialist Propaganda*); Munton and Young.

JOHN BERGER: G. (1972). Winner of the 1972 Booker Prize, *G.* remains John Berger's best-known novel. It is an impressive work, aptly described by Fred Pfeil as "a giant gorgeous fugue of history and desire, a Marxist mobile built to dance in a revolutionary wind to come" (231). A complex metafictional meditation on historical events in Europe at the end of the nineteenth century and beginning of the twentieth, the book conducts a profound investigation of the political implications of those events as well as an extensive interrogation of the means by which we remember and interpret history in general. *G.* has thus been appropriately identified by Linda Hutcheon as a central example of what she calls "historiographic metafiction" — of a postmodernist text that interrogates and challenges official modes for the narrative reconstruction of the historical past. As Ryan puts it, *G.* is "an experimentally transfigured historical novel of extreme intellectual and imaginative virtuosity" that "seeks to project . . . the first great liberating surge of energy towards social and sexual renewal galvanizing Europe at the dawn of this century" ("Socialist Fiction" 182).

G. is a sort of bildungsroman that outlines the growth and maturation of its eponymous protagonist. "G.," the book's title character, is the illegitimate son of Umberto, a wealthy Livorno candied fruit manufacturer and his liberated Anglo-American mistress, Laura. Much of the action centers on his personal development, especially on his growing awareness of and eventual extensive experience (in some ways he is a figure of the Don Juan legend) with sexuality. But even such private experiences have a public dimension, as G.'s sexual life parallels a growth in sexual awareness in the world around him. The events of G.'s life are always presented in historical context, as occurrences such as the Boer War and (especially) the events leading to World War I play a central role in the text. The growth of technology in the early twentieth century is important as well, as in the story of the attempts of the aviator Geo Chavez to become the first man to fly over the Alps. Echoes of revolution enter the text early on in the form of Umberto's memories of the 1848 revolutions, which he considers (along with anything else that threatens the social order) a form of madness. The birth of G. is related immediately after a section identifying Garibaldi as the national genius of Italy. Indeed, though G. is born in the late 1880s, after Garibaldi's death, the Italian revolutionary leader is clearly one of many cultural and historical personages (also including Don Giovanni, the Italian political leader Giolitti, Gabriele d'Annunzio, and Gavrilo Princip) who are clearly meant to be recalled by the protagonist's initial-name.

G. thereby has a sort of allegorical quality as the embodiment of the forces of modernity. For Ryan, he "acquires increasingly profound resonance as the mobile internal index of all the tumescent propensities and as yet unstructured aspirations—social, political, sexual, and technological—forcing their way out through the old, superseded formations" (182). The exact nature of this allegory is, however, unclear. Indeed, G. is an inherently enigmatic figure. Sent to Trieste as a British agent in the early days of World War I, he is suspected by the Italians there of being an Austrian agent and by the Austrians of being an Italian agent. In any case, G.'s participation in the confusing events leading to World War I is narrated within the context of the birth of nations such as Italy and Yugoslavia, both markers of the triumph of the European bourgeoisie over their feudal-aristocratic predecessors (as imaged specifically in the fall of the Austro-Hungarian Empire). G.'s apparent death at the end of the book can be taken, as a sign of the way World War I itself led to the death not only of Austro-Hungary but of a number of mass political liberation movements in Europe. G. thus may reflect Berger's own disappointment at the failure of the oppositional political movements of the 1960s to effect lasting systemic change. On the other hand, World War I also enabled the Russian Revolution, and the book's extensive attention to revolutionary energies provides a powerful reminder that the historical triumph of the bourgeoisie also created the conditions necessary for the development of a proletariat that could in turn eventually defeat the bourgeoisie. The text thus shows, as Joseph H.

McMahon puts it, that "the forces needed to change history are already present in, though not yet at work on history" (216).

Thus, *G.* is essentially a narration of the culmination in the early twentieth century of the sweeping historical transformation that took Europe from a feudal to a capitalist mode of production. It succeeds in capturing the sense of crisis and confusion that informed the early decades of this century, a phenomenon that was central to the growth of modernist art in ways that Berger himself has nicely described in some of his influential art criticism. If *G.* has a weakness, it is that it reflects this confusion all too directly and thus has difficulty anticipating a better future. Its fragmentary and reflexive method of composition may be inadequate to convey the powerful forces sweeping history forward during the transformation that it describes. At the same time, one could take Berger's postmodernist form as a potentially critical indication of the fragmentation and loss of historical sense that Marxist critics such as Fredric Jameson have identified as the ultimate consequence of this historical transformation. *Selected bibliography:* Dyer; Hutcheon; Jameson (*Postmodernism*); McCallum; McMahon; Pfeil; Ryan ("Socialist Fiction"); Weibel.

JOHN BERGER: *INTO THEIR LABOURS* **(1979-90).** *Into Their Labours* is the collective title for a trilogy of works comprising *Pig Earth* (1979), *Once in Europa* (1987), and *Lilac and Flag* (1990). Together, these volumes present a series of stories that detail the passing away of the peasant mode of life under the insistent pressures of modernity. The first volume is a sequence of stories that together present a picture of peasant life in a French mountain village in the twentieth century. The second is essentially a series of love stories set against the background of the dissolution of peasant traditions. The third is a novel detailing the experiences of peasants who have left the village and moved permanently to the city to pursue a new way of life. In essence, then, the trilogy narrates the final consolidation of the bourgeois cultural revolution in Europe; it provides a fresh perspective on this process by describing it from the point of view of a peasant class that is often nearly forgotten in Marxist historical narratives of the triumph of the bourgeoisie over the aristocracy and the rise of the proletariat as the ultimate historical nemesis of the bourgeoisie.

The stories (and poems) that make up *Pig Earth* deal with labor, food, marriage, birth, and death — the back-to-basics essentials that constitute peasant life yet somehow fail to encompass its richness. The gist of the book is best represented by its longest section, a sequence of three stories narrating the life of the peasant woman Lucie Cabrol. Lucie is marked as an outsider from birth, and her small size and tendency periodically to disappear confirm in her childhood the suspicion of those around her that she is someone apart, as indicated in her nickname, the "Cocadrille." Except for a brief affair with the narrator and a momentary encounter with a resistance fighter fleeing the Nazis, Lucie is essentially alone throughout her life. She never marries and eventually becomes a literal outcast whose troubling behavior leads to her expulsion from the village to an isolated house in the forest, where she survives by foraging for mushrooms, berries, and other products of nature. Eventually, she begins to learn the ways of modern commerce, selling these products across the Swiss border and smuggling back cigarettes and other contraband that she can sell for higher prices in France. Now an old woman rumored to have accumulated great wealth, she again proposes marriage to the narrator, who has returned, a widower, after decades in South America and Canada. However, she is suddenly murdered before he can give his answer. The third story in the sequence, narrated in a mode of magic realism, then relates the narrator's communications with Lucie's ghost and with the ghosts of others who have recently died in the village.

Viewed as a whole, Lucie's personal story, despite her unusual status, becomes representative of the historical experience of the peasant class as a whole. By endowing her with a vivid individuality that is nevertheless shaped by larger social and historical forces, Berger thus makes her a typical character of the kind praised by Georg Lukács in relation to the best works of nineteenth-century realism. A similar combination of personal and public perspectives informs the stories of *Once in Europa*. For example, the long title story of this volume consists of the musings of a peasant woman as she hang glides in the mountains high above her village, which is now dominated by a manganese factory. Yet, despite this highly unusual narrative situation, this story captures, in a representative way, the impact of modernization and industrialization on life in France's former peasant villages; the soaring narrator nevertheless suggests the uplifting nature of the dogged spiritual stamina of the peasantry in the face of this impact. All in all, the story leaves us, as Bruce Robbins puts it, "with an image of Europe already penetrated by difference, where peasant traditions coexist with unprecedented mixtures and marvels—an image that injects some buoyancy into the bathos of the 'disappearing peasantry' narrative" ("John Berger's Disappearing Peasants" 67).

Lilac and Flag is the only volume of the trilogy that consists of a single continuous narrative, the story of the lovers Zsuzsa (a.k.a. Lilac) and Sucus (a.k.a. Flag) as they struggle to make a life for themselves in the city of Troy, a sort of amalgam of modern cities everywhere. The fast-paced, problem-beset lifestyle of Troy is contrasted throughout with the simpler, purer lifestyle of the peasantry, both through the musings of the intrusive narrator (herself an old peasant woman) and through the fact that Trojans such as Sucus and Zsuzsa are often only one generation away from their own peasant backgrounds. But these characters are entirely cut off from their peasant roots, which seem to them to provide little in the way of guidance in the modern city. In fact, there are few sources of guidance in this decadent urban environment, though the depiction of the leftist activist, Murat, does provide a potential utopian dimension. But the city is not kind to former peasants. In one of the more transparently symbolic motifs in the book, Sucus's father, Clement, is killed by an exploding television set, suggesting the damaging impact of modern technological society on peasant life. The next generation, though born in the city, fares little better. Poverty is rampant, jobs are hard to come by, and workers who have jobs are ruthlessly exploited by their bosses. Crime is rampant as well, and Zsuzsa's brother, Naisi, is heavily involved in the trafficking of drugs, stolen passports, and other illegal items. Both Sucus and Zsuzsa become involved in Naisi's activities. Sucus, meanwhile, discovers Zsuzsa, now his wife, performing in a sex show in Troy's red-light district. He assaults her and some customers, leaving her for dead. Soon afterward, Naisi is killed in a gunfight during a police raid, and Sucus is captured. Sucus then dies from a gunshot wound, apparently self-inflicted, while he is being interrogated by the aging police superintendent, Hector (who turns out to be from the same village as Clement). As the book ends, Hector (also shot and killed during the interrogation), Naisi, and Sucus are aboard a ship of the dead, sailing into the afterlife. Zsuzsa lives on in Troy.

Given Marx's characterization of the peasantry as a hopelessly reactionary class, it is not surprising that Berger's turn to the peasantry as the subject of his fiction has drawn criticism from Marxist commentators such as Fred Pfeil, who finds *Into Their Labours* devoid of any productive vision for the future. And it is clearly the case that Berger wants to contrast a certain authenticity and solidity in peasant experience with the facticity and impermanence of experience under late capitalism. Thus, the rootedness of peasant life in tradition provides for Berger a stark contrast to the ruthless drive for constant innovation that is particularly central to capitalism in its consumerist phase but that as early as *The Communist Manifesto* could already lead Marx and Engels to describe capitalism as a system under which "all that is solid melts into air."

In its 1992 single-volume edition, the trilogy is preceded by a long introduction in which Berger clarifies the background and goals of the work as a whole. In particular, he attempts to explain what some might see as the trilogy's nostalgic romanticization of a peasant way of life, which many (including Marx) would see as backward and benighted. Granting that the peasant's tradition-oriented view of time contrasts radically with the future-oriented Enlightenment narrative of progress, Berger nevertheless argues that the notorious conservatism of the peasantry is due to the fact that peasant life is fundamentally uncertain and insecure. Exposed to life-threatening flux and instability on a daily basis, the peasant must seek some source of continuity in order to survive at all. Moreover, Berger points out that modernization (marked ultimately by the triumph of consumer capitalism) has hardly been an unequivocal boon to humanity in this century, so that "the peasant suspicion of 'progress,' as it has finally been imposed by the global history of corporate capitalism and by the power of history even over those seeking an alternative to it, it is not altogether misplaced or groundless" (xxviii). Expressing solidarity with the peasants themselves, Berger nevertheless maintains a future-oriented vision by making clear his understanding that to restore the peasant way of life would be neither possible nor desirable, peasants constituting an exploited class whose hardships are hardly to be longed for. Instead, Berger seems to hope (somewhat in the mode of the recent cultural criticism of John Gray) that we can learn some valuable lessons from the peasant past that will help us to envision a new future that escapes the constricting and dehumanizing domination of capital. Thus, Michael W. Messmer concludes that Berger's project in *Into Their Labours* goes well beyond the representation of rural peasants to suggest alternative ways of representing the experience of the "techno/peasants of the late twentieth century" (222). **Selected bibliography:** Gray; Harvey J. Kaye; Messmer; Pfeil; Quillian; Robbins ("Feeling Global"); Robbins ("John Berger's Disappearing Peasants").

JOHN BERGER: *A PAINTER OF OUR TIME* **(1958).** *A Painter of Our Time* shows many of the same concerns and sophisticated insights into the relationship between art and society that marked Berger's important early essays and art criticism written at about the same time for the *New Statesmen* (many of which were collected and published in *Permanent Red*, in 1960). Formally, *A Painter of Our Time* consists of a journal kept from 1952 to 1956 by painter Janos Lavin, a Hungarian communist who has lived in England since 1938, when he sought refuge there from the Nazis. Interspersed with the journal entries is a running commentary by the narrator, John, an art critic who clearly has much in common with Berger. This main section of the book is then framed by brief beginning and ending segments in which John explains how he found the journal in Lavin's deserted studio after the painter suddenly disappeared on October 16, 1956, leaving his life in England (including an English wife) to return to Hungary to participate in the building unrest in his home country, though the text leaves the exact nature of that participation open to speculation.

The time covered by Lavin's diary, in fact, corresponds roughly to the period of unrest in Hungary that eventually led to a large scale rebellion against the ruling communist regime, beginning on October 23, 1996—at just about the time Lavin would have arrived in the country.

The rebellion, suppressed with Russian military assistance, became a key locus of Western anticommunist propaganda. Berger, however, treats the rebellion in a sophisticated and evenhanded way, acknowledging that the issues involved were so complex that it is impossible even for Lavin's closest friends and associates to predict whether he will be on the side of the anticommunist rebels or the pro-Soviet government. Indeed, Berger's narrator (and to some extent spokesman) expresses the hope that Lavin is working in support of the government of János Kádár, who came to power with Soviet support in the midst of the 1956 rebellion — and who would remain a powerful figure in Hungary until 1988, during that time instituting numerous reforms and promoting substantial economic development while remaining a consistent supporter of the Soviet Union.

It is clear that Lavin returns to Hungary to work for the communist cause; it is not clear whether this work will involve support for the ruling regime or for the rebels against that regime. Such complexities contribute to an important range of images through which *A Painter of Our Time* seeks to challenge simplistic Cold War stereotypes, arguing for a greater complexity and sophistication in our understanding of global politics in the 1950s. And Berger's success in challenging the Cold War rhetoric of the West can be seen from the fact that the book was virulently attacked in most early reviews, so much so that the originally publisher, Secker and Warburg, withdrew the book from distribution within a few months after its publication (Dyer 36-7). For example, a central motif in the book involves Lavin's relationship with his lifelong friend, the poet Laszlo, who, unlike Lavin, returned to Hungary to work to build socialism there. Laszlo, however, runs afoul of the Rákosi regime and is executed in July 1952, initiating a period of severe psychic trauma for Lavin, who must come to grips not only with his friend's death but with his own feelings of guilt for being away in comfortable England while Hungary attempts to struggle toward socialism. In light of Cold War stereotypes, it is important that Lavin never waivers in his commitment to communism, understanding that Laszlo's arrest, trial, and execution are part of an extremely complex political process that cannot be reduced to the Manichean terms of Cold War rhetoric. Lavin thus finds himself unable to talk to anyone in England about the death of his friend because of their tendency to reduce such events to simplistic terms. In particular, he realizes that the English regard a political execution as "first and foremost a *primitive* act," though the English themselves carry out such executions quite commonly, in a colonial context, "on primitive people — the Irish, the Africans, the Malays, people who have been misled into provoking them with unnecessary barbaric violence" (87).

Among other things, Berger here shows a sophisticated understanding of the complex discursive complicity between the Cold War rhetoric of anticommunism and the long tradition of colonialist stereotyping of non-Europeans, a complicity described in greater detail by Booker in *Colonial Power, Colonial Texts*. Berger also undermines such stereotypes in relation to the execution of Laszlo by having Lavin describe the execution not as an act of oppression but of war. Lavin understands, as his English friends (and wife) cannot, that the situation in Hungary is akin to civil war and that war always has casualties and consequences that cannot be reduced to the polar opposition of good versus evil. Lavin is thus perfectly willing to admit that Laszlo may indeed have been guilty of the crimes with which he was charged; he also knows that, even if Laszlo had not been guilty, his execution might conceivably have served a positive political purpose. There is thus no suggestion that Lavin returns to Hungary in order somehow to attempt to avenge his friend. Rather, he returns to work partially for better conditions in his native country but primarily to work in the cause of communism.

Berger's most important challenge to Cold War stereotypes in *A Painter of Our Time* is embedded in Lavin's extensive meditations on the social responsibilities of the artist, meditations that radically undermine the Western notion that art and politics are separate spheres and that the failure to separate these spheres was somehow evidence of communist oppression and cultural primitivity. While Lavin (and perhaps Berger as well) occasionally seems to lapse into the terms of bourgeois aesthetics, he radically rejects the romantic notion of the alienated artist, insisting that artists must "never make a virtue of our lonely burrowing" (94). Further, he suggests in his diary that those who accept the bourgeois notion that art is "transportable, timeless, universal, understand it least of all" (77). Lavin argues that art in a class society always has a class basis and always participates in class struggle. Meanwhile, he concludes that the contemporary decadence of bourgeois society in the West has led to the production of art that is informed by a "sickening futility" and involves a separation between the work of the artist and life in the social world (182). Rather than accept the bourgeois notion that art and politics are fundamentally incommensurable, Lavin believes that all art is in the last instance political and that all genuine art must recognize its political role. "All good art is for Man," Lavin concludes, "and therefore for us," that is, for communism (181). While Lavin seeks to make a distinction between art and propaganda, he believes that both can play positive and valuable roles and that the relationship between the two is so important that propaganda is "*the* problem of art in our time." As a modern painter, then, the principal issue with which he must deal is "the problem of propaganda — the problem of facing other men as a man" (176).

Much of Lavin's personal difficulty in England is that, as an exile, he does not quite fit in; he experiences an alienation that separates him from the social world around him, rendering his art ineffectual. For most of his stay in England he gains very little recognition as an artist. Even when he sells a number of paintings at an exhibition of his work, finally achieving financial success, the triumph is an empty one. It is, in fact, only a week after this exhibition that Lavin leaves for Hungary, realizing that he has no real role to play in English life, where he is an outsider and where artists in general have been safely contained within an aesthetic realm that has little contact with political reality. Thus, Lavin's alienation as an exile in England is closely associated in the text with the bourgeois belief in a separation between politics and art, anticipating Fredric Jameson's later argument that "the convenient working distinction between cultural texts that are social and political and those that are not becomes ... a symptom and a reinforcement of the reification and privatization of contemporary life ... which—the tendential law of social life under capitalism—maims our existence as individual subjects and paralyzes our thinking about time and change just as surely as it alienates us from our speech itself" (*Political Unconscious* 20). Lavin's musings on art, history, and politics seek to heal this crippling rift, as does Berger's book itself, simultaneously an aesthetic tour-de-force and a powerfully argued political statement. **Selected bibliography:** Berger (*Permanent Red*); Booker (*Colonial Power*); Dyer; Jameson (*Political Unconscious*); H. Kaye; McMahon.

NICHOLAS BLAKE: *A QUESTION OF PROOF* **(1935).** Nicholas Blake was a pseudonym of Cecil Day Lewis, one of the leading figures of British leftist culture in the 1930s. Known primarily as a poet, Day Lewis wrote vigorously leftist political verse in that decade, though he later turned to a more traditional lyric vein, a change that no doubt helped him to be named England's Poet Laureate in 1968. As Blake, he also wrote numerous detective novels, beginning in the 1930s with such books as *A Question of Proof* and *The Beast Must Die* (1938) and continuing throughout his career, becoming one of the century's best known and most successful writers of British detective fiction. Blake's detective novels are consistently clever but, even in the 1930s, are relatively conventional, even formulaic, in structure. However, the early ones, at least, also contain considerable social commentary and carry a leftist political message, though the political statement is more subtle and subdued in the detective novels than in Day Lewis's poetry or polemical writings of the 1930s. Valentine Cunningham thus somewhat sardonically describes Day Lewis, in his guise as Blake, as a Communist Party "mole toiling for it under the lawn of popular writing" (261).

A Question of Proof, Blake's first detective novel, is representative of his early work. The book begins with the revelation that a murder has been committed in the seemingly pastoral setting of Sudely Hall Preparatory School for Boys, the victim being one of the young students. The police who investigate the murder are baffled by the lack of clues. Super-sleuth Nigel Strangeways (who will continue to be the central detective of Blake's detective novels throughout his career) is then called in. Strangeways proceeds, in a Holmes-like manner (the book is replete with allusions to Conan Doyle's character), to piece together the seemingly insignificant details of the case, concluding fairly quickly that he knows who committed the murder. Unfortunately, Strangeways has no evidence that will stand up in court, so he refuses to divulge his conclusion. In the meantime, the situation is further complicated when a second murder, that of the school's headmaster, is committed. Strangeways, convinced that the cases are related, sets about acquiring proof (thus the title of the book) of the murderer's identity, primarily by the careful orchestration of events that will lead the murderer (who turns out to be one of the schoolmasters) openly to confess his crime. This stratagem succeeds, and the book ends with a final chapter in which Strangeways explains his process of deduction and reveals the plan that led to the confession.

Though perhaps a bit more erudite and literary than most works of the genre, *A Question of Proof* ostensibly participates directly in the British tradition of "well-heeled" detective fiction, following in the footsteps of predecessors such as Conan Doyle and Agatha Christie. This tradition relies upon a perception of the world as an orderly place in which events can be explained and in which those responsible for disruptions in the social order (i.e. crimes) can (and should) be identified and punished. Blake, however, undermines this sanguine social vision in a number of ways. The very idea that such shocking murders can occur at an elite boys' preparatory school calls attention to the perception of such schools as a bastion of British society and as the central training ground for the leaders of the British Empire. After all, if there is a dark underside to life in such schools, perhaps there is a similar dark side to the British imperial ideal itself. Blake enhances this suggestion with numerous references to class inequalities in British society and with reminders that, in the British justice system, murderers sometimes go free, and innocent men sometimes hang. The investigation of the murder uncovers other details as well, such as the fact that Wrench, one of the masters, is carrying on a sexual liaison with Rosa, one of the maids, while Michael Evans, another master, is having an affair with Hero Vale, the wife of the headmaster. Indeed, the latter detail contributes to the fact that Michael (an old schoolmate of Strangeways) and Hero are the prime suspects throughout most of the book. They are even at one point arrested for the crimes. Strangeways, however, is able to ascertain that Sims, another master, is a puritanical religious fanatic who violently resents the carnal activities of Michael and Hero. Indeed, it turns out that Sims committed the murders with the specific intention of implicating the two lovers. The seemingly genteel Strangeways himself shows a dark side when, knowing that Sims will be declared insane and thus escape execution for murder, he intentionally arranges to have the criminal commit suicide to avoid capture. Strangeways may thus have the flair of a Holmes or Poirot, but his ethics are, in fact, a bit suspect, as his name perhaps indicates.

In its suggestion that society is not really so orderly as some would like to believe and in its presentation of a well-heeled detective who is willing to break the rules to achieve a rough form of justice, *A Question of Proof*, despite its genteel tone, has much in common with the American tradition of hard-boiled detective stories, pioneered in the 1930s by Raymond Chandler and Dashiell Hammett. Indeed, the gun-toting Strangeways has more in common with Sam Spade or Philip Marlowe than one might at first expect, despite his smooth manners and Oxford education. On the other hand, Blake avoids the traditional individualism of American detective fiction by constructing his book such that it is Evans, not Strangeways, who is the central character. Nevertheless, *A Question of Proof* directly addresses (and implicitly rejects) the notion that such crimes of violence occur in America but not in the more civilized Britain. For instance, Police Superintendent Armstrong complains of the pernicious influence of American gangster films on Britain's youth, but notes with relief that "boys of the class we are dealing with now" are surely beyond that influence. It is, however, in its attention to class that *A Question of Proof* is distinctively British (and leftist), and Blake's point is clearly that such crimes occur not just in America (where both capitalism and puritanical religion reach their zenith) but wherever the capitalist emphasis on competition and the Christian rejection of the body combine to create pathological forms of human relations. ***Selected bibliography:*** Bargainnier; Cunningham; Sean Day Lewis; Gindin.

ROBERT BLATCHFORD: *THE SORCERY SHOP* **(1909).** Robert Blatchford, a founder of the Independent Labour Party, was one of the leading British socialist thinkers and political activists of the last years of the nineteenth century and the first years of the twentieth. As the author of political tracts such as *Merrie England* (1894) and *Britain for the British* (1902) and the editor of the socialist newspaper *The Clarion*, Blatchford was an influential proponent of a certain vein of (non-Marxist) socialism, based largely on rather conventional bourgeois notions of family and morality. He was also the author of several novels and short stories, though only one of his works of fiction, *The Sorcery Shop*, is directly constructed as an argument for the socialist cause. Clearly influenced by William Morris's *News from Nowhere*, Blatchford's relatively simple novel focuses on two bourgeois paragons (and members of parliament), the magnate Samuel Jorkle and the retired Major-General Sir Frederick Manningtree Storm, who are whisked away from their London businessman's club and taken for a tour of the socialist future by the magician Nathaniel Fry. In particular, Fry takes them to Manchester, now transformed from an industrial eyesore into an idyllic paradise, rich in natural beauty and populated by gentle, intelligent, and hard-working exemplars of socialism.

Blatchford's central structural device is favorably to contrast his socialist utopia with the England of his own day, at the same time providing answers to the kinds of charges that were typically leveled against socialism by its opponents at that time. He thus places a great deal of emphasis on the efficiency of his socialist system, which leads to material abundance for all citizens—as opposed to the capitalist system where waste, duplication, and greed lead to great wealth for a few but material deprivation for the many. In this idealized socialist Manchester, there is no crime and no government; all citizens play their proper roles and fulfill their duties strictly out of the pleasure they derive from a job well done and from the approval of their fellow citizens for doing so.

One reason they do so is their high level of education and enlightenment, and Blatchford pays a significant amount of attention to a description of the educational system, which is largely based on the concept of allowing students to pursue study in the subjects that interest them most. The effectiveness of this educational system is demonstrated by the fact that even common laborers show a high degree of learning and culture, a situation facilitated by the fact that the material wealth of this society leaves all citizens much free time for reading and travel. Most education is conducted not in schools but on an informal basis, with mothers being the principal educators of children. There is, in fact, a certain amount of idealization of mothers—and of women in general—in Blatchford's vision of the future, perhaps in part as a response to contemporary charges that socialism would lead to immorality and to the degradation of women through free love. Thus, while there is no organized religion in Blatchford's Utopia, he puts a great deal of stress on the high moral standards of this socialist community and, in particular, on the central role of the family in all aspects of community life.

The latter part of *The Sorcery Shop* virtually dispenses with the fictional framework and consists mostly of Fry's arguments to Storm and Jorkle for the achievability and viability of socialism—very much along the lines of Blatchford's own polemical writings. Indeed, the fictional framework is rather weak throughout, which perhaps partially accounts for the lack of popularity of the book when it was first published. Moreover, aside from any shortcomings in Blatchford's literary imagination, the book also suffers from excessive idealization and from the fact that this future socialist Utopia must be conjured up by a magician, something that combines with the subtitle, *An Impossible Romance*, to make the book less than entirely effective as a argument for the practical desirability of socialist. All in all, however, the book stands as a representative statement of a certain kind of moderate early twentieth-century British socialism. It is also a good specimen of the turn to works of utopian fantasy that informed much fiction at the turn of the century, when conventional realist fiction seemed to be struggling more and more to maintain an ability effectively to envision a better future. *Selected bibliography:* Blatchford (*Merrie England*); Blatchford (*Britain*); David Smith (*Socialist Propaganda*).

SIMON BLUMENFELD: *JEW BOY* (1935). *Jew Boy*, as its defiant title perhaps indicates, is the product of a Jewish culture that thrived on the East End of London in the 1930s but that was at the same time marginal to British culture as a whole. Indeed, Ken Worpole, in his introduction to the 1986 re-publication of the novel, identifies *Jew Boy* as the "founding work in what developed into a unique school of fiction, autobiography and drama: the literature of the Jewish East End" (4). Worpole goes on to compare this phenomenon to the Harlem Renaissance in America, and it is certainly worth noting that Blumenfeld's text specifically alludes at one point to Harlem Renaissance writers such as Langston Hughes and Claude McKay, suggesting that Blumenfeld consciously thought of them as predecessors—both in terms of their focus on a marginalized ethnic group and in the fundamentally leftist orientation of their politics (327). On the other hand, despite its focus on Jewish characters and their East End culture, *Jew Boy* resembles any number of British leftist novels of the 1930s, dealing with many of the same themes as those novels. Blumenfeld, himself a committed communist, was an active participant in the British leftist culture of the 1930s, serving as a member of the editorial board of *Left Review* and helping to found (and write plays for) the Rebel Players, who were prominent in the Workers Theatre Movement of the time. Central to *Jew Boy* is the exploitation of workers, including the experience of poverty and unemployment. The text also offers a depiction of working-class collective action as a potential means to improve the conditions under which workers live and work. The book also pays special attention to the exploitation of women and to their frequent reduction to sexual commodities within the capitalist economic system.

As the book opens, the protagonist, twenty-three-year-old Alec Benjamin, is awakened by his mother so that he can rush to his job as a tailor in a garment factory. Alec is the son of Russian Jewish immigrants, and most of the other workers in this East End factory (including the owner and management) are Jewish as well. Indeed, within the virtually self-contained world of the Jewish East End, most of the people with whom Alec comes into contact are Jews. Beyond the specific story of Alec, *Jew Boy* presents a vivid picture of various aspects of the culture of the Jewish East End. Alec spends much of his time at the Workers' Circle, where he and others can meet to discuss various issues, attend concerts, and participate in other cultural activities. The book introduces other figures of Jewish culture as well, such as the poet and intellectual Leopold Hartman, whose modernist verse Alec finds pointless and pretentious.

Alec and the other workers in his factory are ruthlessly exploited, while seasonal slowdowns leave many of them (especially those who, like Alec, are given to complaining about their treatment) unemployed during substantial portions of the year. Alec is, in fact, something of a leader among the workers, though he is politically unsophisticated and remains focused primarily on his personal concerns. For example, he spends considerably more time worrying about his late-adolescent sexual frustrations than about politics or fair treatment of workers. In the course of the book, we also meet some of Alec's friends, including Sam, recently returned from a disappointing attempt to make his fortune in America, and Dave, a sexual predator who shamelessly exploits women. Sam's experience makes it clear that America is not a capitalist utopia that provides magical solutions to the poverty experienced by Jews and others in Europe. Dave is central to Blumenfeld's treatment of gender. He treats his various girlfriends as sexual objects and at one point nearly murders one of them. He also rapes Olive, a Catholic girl working as a housekeeper for his family. Later, he marries an unattractive rich woman for her money but continues to consort with a variety of other women, including Olive, who has now been driven to prostitution.

Olive eventually becomes important in Alec's life as the two establish a relationship that eventually leads her to give up prostitution and live with him. She works as a waitress in a café, supporting the two of them after Alec enters an extended period of unemployment. Alec, who has read widely despite his lack of formal education, begins to grow bored with Olive, whom he regards as his intellectual inferior. At one point, he has a sexual encounter with Elspeth, a rich, beautiful blonde, but leaves feeling disgusted, realizing that the sophisticated woman has regarded him as a sort of exotic plaything because of his class and ethnicity. In the meantime, Olive suffers from her grueling work and feels so estranged from Alec that she does not tell him when she becomes pregnant and then has an abortion. He eventually finds out about the abortion and begins to realize how little he has appreciated Olive and her suffering. In the meantime, he becomes more politically aware, especially after he hears John Thomas ("Jo-Jo") King, a black communist, speaking in Hyde Park.

The depiction of such political activity is quite central to *Jew Boy*. Particularly important is the book's depiction of Jewish political activism in the London of the 1930s, either to demand improvement in conditions in England or to protest the increasingly outrageous treatment of Jews in Nazi Germany. Among other things, this aspect of the book calls attention to the failure of the British government to take action against the oppression of Jews in Germany — while at the same time suggesting that one reason for this failure might have been the antisemitism of British society itself. The black communist King allows Blumenfeld to extend his critique of oppression beyond the treatment of Jews to encompass the treatment of all of those who suffer oppression and exploitation under capitalism. Indeed, the book is internationalist in its orientation and shows little sympathy with Zionism, which Alec rejects out of hand. Alec, in fact, eventually finds the Communist Party a far more effective source of community than his religion. He is so impressed by King's description of conditions in the Soviet Union that he decides to return to Russia, the home of his ancestors. However, he is denied entry into the Soviet Union, which has a surfeit of manual workers like Alec and is currently giving preference in its immigration policies to engineers and other technical experts. Alec is dejected, but King explains to him that such policies are necessary; otherwise all of the world's workers would want to move to the Soviet Union. The point is clear: rather than flee to the workers' haven of the Soviet Union, the workers of the world need to work for revolution in their own societies. Alec resolves to do so and remains convinced that a better world must be possible even after an antifascist demonstration in which he participates at the end of the book is violently broken up by the police.

Blumenfeld went on to write three additional novels. *Phineas Kahn: Portrait of an Immigrant* (1937) presents Jewish culture as a source of strength for a young Jewish musician who travels about Europe fleeing antisemitism, eventually finding a home in the Soviet Union in the 1930s. *Doctor of the Lost* (1938) focuses on the Victorian slums and on the attempts of a doctor (based on the historical figure of Dr. Barnardo) to help the poor. *They Won't Let You Live* (1939) is the only Blumenfeld novel in which the protagonists are not Jewish. It features a Christian family in the East End and explores the conditions that might make such people susceptible to fascism and antisemitism. After the 1930s, Blumenfeld produced no more novels, but he continued to write journalism and drama into the 1980s. *Jew Boy*, however, remains Blumenfeld's best-known and most successful work. It stands not only as an important product of the culture of the 1930s but as an important predecessor to the identity politics of the end of the twentieth century. **Selected bibliography:** Croft (*Red Letter Days*); Worpole.

JOHN BRAINE: *ROOM AT THE TOP* **(1957).** *Room at the Top* was a highly successful book (later the basis for a successful and groundbreaking film of the same title) that helped its author to join other members of the "angry young men" of the 1950s (such as Kingsley Amis and John Osborne) as leading figures of contemporary British culture.

Though lacking any specific agenda for bringing change to contemporary British society, the book is nevertheless a biting critique of that society. This critique centers on the attempts of the working-class protagonist, Joe Lampton, to achieve a higher social standing through the opportunistic manipulation of personal relationships. Lampton does, in fact, succeed in rising to wealth and power, but only at the expense of dehumanizing both himself and those around him. The book thus emphasizes the role of rigid class distinctions in the overall reification of human relationships under the British capitalist system.

Room at the Top is narrated by Lampton, now a wealthy businessman in the mid-1950s, as he looks back on his younger self in the years just following World War II, in which he had served in the British forces and spent several years in a German prisoner-of-war camp. A native of the dingy Yorkshire mining town of Dufton, Lampton is the son of working-class parents who are killed by a German bomb during the war. After the war, having received training in accounting, Lampton gets a position as a clerk in the office of the town treasurer in Warley, a light industrial town that is near Dufton by road but, as a clean, bright, and relatively affluent community, light years away in terms of atmosphere. Soon after arriving in Warley, Lampton, sipping tea in a café, sees a rich young man getting into an expensive automobile accompanied by an elegant blonde. This experience changes Lampton's life. Describing both the Aston-Martin and the woman as possessions marking the man's class superiority, Lampton vows to do whatever it takes to acquire such possessions of his own (29–30). He then sets about making social contacts among the higher classes in Warley, a project that soon brings him into contact with Susan Brown, the beautiful eighteen-year-old daughter of a rich local industrialist. Lampton is smitten at once, presumably by her beauty, but as the book proceeds it becomes clear that Susan's main attractions are her wealth and social standing and that even her beauty is a sort of commodity. Meanwhile, Lampton, twenty-five, begins an affair with thirty-four-year-old Alice Aisgill, whose working-class origins are similar to his own, though she is now the wife of a rich mill owner.

Through most of the book, Lampton continues his affair with Alice, which he regards as pure physical release necessitated by the fact that his sexual relationship with the virginal Susan is less than fully satisfying. Meanwhile, he sets about his courtship of Susan via strategies reminiscent of a military campaign, aware that he must overcome not only the social and economic gulf that lies between Susan and himself but also the fact that she is simultaneously being courted by the dashing Jack Wales, a Cambridge student and a member of Warley's richest family. In the course of the book, Joe and Alice seem to develop a genuine love for one another, while Joe finds Susan increasingly trite and boring. He opts to continue his pursuit of her nevertheless, eventually making her pregnant—a move he had envisioned as a potential strategy from the very beginning. Susan's father reluctantly agrees to a wedding and offers Joe a position in his firm on the condition that he end the relationship with Alice immediately. Lampton does so, and the distraught Alice goes on a drinking binge and is afterward horribly killed in a car crash. Lampton himself is nearly overcome with guilt when he learns the details of her death but is determined to marry Susan (and her family fortune) nevertheless.

As the book closes, Lampton is being consoled that no one will blame him for the behavior that led to Alice's death, to which he responds, "That's the trouble" (301). Indeed, much of Braine's point is that Joe's manipulative and exploitative behavior is merely standard fare in a modern British capitalist society in which those who strive ruthlessly for success are not condemned but admired and in which a reduction of all kinds of social interaction to purely economic terms leaves little room for meaningful human contact. As Lampton says of Susan in the midst of his courtship of her, "I was taking Susan not as Susan, but as a Grade A lovely, as the daughter of a factory owner, as the means of obtaining the key to the Aladdin's cave of my ambitions" (173–74). And, while Joe's relationship with Alice seems more genuine, he also treats her as a representative of her class, in this case of the working class that he hopes to escape. Indeed, overcome by feelings of class inferiority in relation to his affluent acquaintances in Warley, Joe rejects anything associated with working-class values or experience. At the same time, however, he has no particular respect for the rich individuals to whose class he hopes to ascend. It is not rich people he admires but their possessions and power.

While Lampton does not feel entirely comfortable with his own unscrupulous quest for success, the values instilled in him by the society around him make it impossible for him to resist the opportunity to realize his dreams of an advance in class by marrying Susan. His society places great emphasis on class differences (and the inferiority of the working class amid these differences), driving him to seek to advance in class not only in order to have a bigger house and nicer car but to have a higher evaluation of his own personal worth. But it is also clear in the text that the realization of his dreams to advance can bring Lampton no true happiness. His tendency to treat other human beings (especially women) as objects to be used for the pursuit of his own ends only furthers his already strong sense of alienation, as does the experience of *déclassement* associated with his abandonment of his working-class origins without necessarily being able to feel at home in the class to which he rises. *Room at the Top* thus stands as powerful dramatization of the inability of capitalist society to fulfill the basic human needs of its citizens, even as the book's lack of commitment to specific social change anticipates Braine's own later drift into conservatism. *Selected bibliography:* Gråboek; Laing (*"Room"*); Lee; Marwick.

WALTER BRIERLEY: *MEANS-TEST MAN* **(1935).** *Means-Test Man* explores the material and psychological impact of unemployment on a single working-class family in Britain in 1934. Jack Cook, a miner by trade, has been unemployed for three years, during which he, his wife, Jane, and son, John, have struggled to maintain a decent existence while living off the dole. By the time of the action of the book, the family's savings—once a source of great pride to both Jack and Jane—have dwindled essentially to nothing. As a result, their economic condition is growing steadily worse, despite the fact that the National Government of the time was boasting that economic recovery was well underway. Meanwhile, the humiliation of unemployment is beginning to work powerful strains on the marriage. The book focuses on a single week in the life of the Cook family, leading to a Friday on which the means-test inspector will make his monthly visit to survey the family's financial situation and to verify that they still qualify for the dole. This visit, experienced by the Cooks (especially Jane) as a personal violation, is the focus of the book's depiction of the powerful psychological impact of unemployment on individuals who have been taught to regard work as a central source of their identities. This depiction, in fact, is extremely powerful and affecting, and it is not surprising that the book was an immediate commercial success upon publication in 1935. However, much like Walter Greenwood's *Love on the Dole* (a sort of companion text), *Means-Test Man* achieved much of its popularity by focusing on individual concerns and by avoiding any explicit political statement, thus remaining palatable to a middle-class audience.

The strength of Brierley's book is clearly in its depiction, in naturalistic detail, of both the physical and the psychological conditions under which the Cooks struggle to survive. Moreover, as Carole Snee notes, Brierley manages to present these details "as synthesised and artistically wrought experience which comments meaningfully upon the external world" (180). This process of synthesis gives the book a recognizably literary quality and may account for much of its initial success with middle-class readers. On the other hand, as Andy Croft notes in his introduction to the 1983 edition of the book, *Means-Test Man* has generally received an unfavorable response from leftist critics, the major reason for which is summed up in Ernie Wooley's conclusion in a *Daily Worker* review in 1935 that the book's chief weakness is that "the unemployed worker who sits timidly at home waiting for the investigator is not the rule, but the exception. . . . A book which brought out this fighting spirit of the unemployed would have been a much greater use to the working-class" (qtd. in Croft xiii). It is certainly the case that Jack Cook seems to be accepting his predicament rather passively and that the book seems to offer little in the way of a suggestion that collective action by the working class might be able to prevent the kind of humiliating experience that the Cooks are currently undergoing. On the other hand, Croft concludes that "the great strength and importance of the novel is in dramatising the utter helplessness of Jack and Jane Cook in the face of circumstances they simply do not understand" (xv).

Croft, in fact, labels ongoing leftist criticisms of *Means-Test Man* as "absurd," arguing that they fundamentally fail to appreciate Brierley's development as a writer attempting to assimilate the techniques of the British literary tradition. But this assimilation is, of course, the primarily weakness in Brierley's writing because it makes it impossible for him to write from a position that poses any real challenge to bourgeois ideology. For example, *Means-Test Man* does effectively make the case that Jack is a victim and not simply a shiftless parasite who prefers living off of public support to working. To this extent, the book is valuable as a refutation of middle-class stereotypes of the unemployed, both in the 1930s and still in the 1990s. Indeed, this project becomes quite clear when Jack, after the visit of the means-test man, tells Jane, "If all the women in England could feel for a minute what you've gone through this morning, there'd be no more of it, no more homes upset" (267). On the other hand, this project is part of a larger phenomenon in which it is clear that the book's primarily audience is not the working class, but the middle class, who are given a sympathetic, but nonthreatening view of workers throughout. As Roy Johnson puts it, "Brierley's is a typical case of the working-class writer who accepts middle-class values rather uncritically, incorporates them into his world-vision, and at the same time chooses . . . a form of expression which meshes perfectly with the imported world-vision but clashes with the actual facts of his working life and inhibits the development of a genuinely working-class form of literary expression" (8).

There are significant problems with Brierley's book that go beyond the lack of any depiction of collective resistance. For example, the differing reactions of Jack and Jane to their situation tend consistently to privilege his position. According to Pamela Fox, Jane's concern with appearances seems excessive, and her "preoccupation with reputation is finally deemed less dignified and tolerable because it is assimilationist in the worst sense" (141). There is, in fact, in Jane's attitude a sort of contempt for working-class culture, as when she continually insists that Jack and John speak "proper" English rather than the working-class dialect into which they frequently shift. In addition, Jane seems concerned mainly with the direct material consequences of their poverty, while Jack is depicted as capable of more thoughtful consideration of deeper consequences. Jack thus envies the employed for their "security and content," while Jane is occupied with "concrete repinings, clothes for her and her child and her husband at the same time, a nice home to which you could ask your friends, a steady wage which covered necessities and then left a bit over" (Brierley 209-10). In short, the dichotomy between Jack and Jane repeats a standard stereotype of Western culture, in which, as Simone de Beauvoir points out, the male opposes himself as "spirit" to the woman as flesh, as "the Other, who limits and denies him" (129).

In a similar vein, Jack's humiliation is clearly linked to his reduction to a sort of feminine predicament as he is forced to hang around the house and help Jane with various cooking and cleaning chores. In short, unemployment violates the separation of experience into the masculine realm of productive work outside the house and the feminine realm of domestic work inside the house. Yet this separation, part of a larger drive toward separation of public and private experience, is one of the mainstays of bourgeois ideology. Indeed, the most important way *Means-Test Man* fails to escape the confines of bourgeois ideology is in its thoroughgoing endorsement of this separation of public and private spheres. To an extent, Graham Holderness is correct that the experience of unemployment for Jack is one of "extreme alienation" as he is separated from his former employment (26). But it is his work, not his fellow workers, from which Jack feels alienated; he has, in fact, always felt himself somewhat apart from his fellow workers. Jack is a fervent individualist who loves to spend time alone and who finds it humiliating not to be able to support himself and his family without help from others. He also wishes to be able to "put a ring around" his private life, "showing definitely how far the world could come" (155). Jane, meanwhile, is fiercely protective of her domestic sphere. For her, the visit of the means-test inspector is clearly a "violation of the home," an intrusion of the public world into her private one with which she simply cannot cope (229). For the Cooks, the most traumatic effect of unemployment is clearly the way in which they are forced to rely on public support to meet their private needs—and to allow the public world (personified by the means-test inspector) into their private lives.

Given this individualist ideology, it comes as no surprise that the Cooks (and, apparently, Brierley) are unable to envision themselves as participants in a collective resistance to the system that has thrust them into their current situation. One might, of course, view the acceptance of bourgeois ideology by the Cooks (despite the fact that the capitalist system is clearly not working to their advantage) as a commentary on the insidious pervasiveness of this ideology. But it is the failure to present any alternative to this ideology that most seriously limits *Means-Test Man* in its function as a work of proletarian literature. ***Selected bibliography:*** Croft; De Beauvoir; Pamela Fox; Holderness; Johnson ("Walter Brierley"); Neubert; Snee.

WALTER BRIERLEY: *SANDWICHMAN* **(1937).** *Sandwichman* relates the story of Arthur Gardner, a young English coal miner in the 1930s who is struggling to achieve a better life through education. While working at the coal pit near his home village of Wingrove, he also attends classes at nearby Trentingham University College, pursuing a course of studies that he hopes one day will allow him to become a teacher. The task, however, is difficult. Although Arthur has a relatively easy job at the pit, the work still takes a great deal of time and energy away from his studies. He also finds that his attempts to educate himself alienate him from the other mine workers, who believe that he thinks himself better than they. Arthur's ambitions also lead to trouble with his bosses, who sometimes find him studying during slack moments on the job. Arthur's home life is difficult as well. His mother is supportive of his studies, but she is in ill health. His stepfather, Mr. Shirley, also a coal miner, resents Arthur's attempts at education (partially because his own sons are not motivated to put forth such effort); this leads to considerable tensions between Arthur and Mr. Shirley.

As Arthur nears his crucial Intermediate Arts Examination, his mounting troubles make it harder and harder for him to study. First, he is fired from his job at the mine after a moment of inattentiveness on his part (caused by an argument with another worker) causes an expensive accident. Meanwhile, Arthur's longtime girlfriend, Nancy, becomes increasingly impatient at having to wait for marriage until Arthur can complete his seemingly interminable education. She finally becomes involved with another man, gets pregnant, and breaks off her relationship with Arthur so that she can marry the father of her baby. Arthur continues to pay for his room and board through his unemployment benefits and by drawing upon his meager savings. Nevertheless tensions in the home increase; the night before his logic examination, he and his stepfather literally come to blows, and his mother is knocked unconscious trying to break up the fight. Arthur spends a sleepless night, then fails his logic examination the next day, derailing his plans eventually to take a university degree.

Much of the rest of the book concerns Arthur's experiences with unemployment, including a futile search for work amid the depressed economic climate of the 1930s. He does succeed in landing a temporary teaching assignment giving a series of lectures on literature in a nearby village, but the lectures do not go especially well. The only other job he manages to get involves an afternoon of work in the town of Pirley carrying a sandwichboard (hence, the title of the book) outside a furniture store that is having a sale. He finds this job demeaning, and is embarrassed when his stepbrothers, his mother, and Nancy all see him in his role as sandwichman. He and his stepfather again have words when the latter expresses his shame at having a son in such a demeaning position. Eventually, Arthur's initial unemployment benefits run out, and he is forced to undergo the means test before he can qualify for further benefits. The means-test inspector arrives and is nearly assaulted by Mr. Shirley as he pries into the family's financial affairs. It seems clear that no further benefits will be forthcoming because Arthur is a single man living with his parents. Meanwhile, however, Mrs. Shirley's condition worsens rapidly, and she dies. Arthur now has nothing to keep him in Wingrove (though Nancy has meanwhile admitted that she still loves him). At the end of the book, he leaves home to begin a new life tramping about the countryside.

Sandwichman participates in a long tradition of British novels about working-class protagonists who find that their class background greatly inhibits their attempts to pursue a life of the intellect. As Philip Gorski puts it in his introduction to the 1990 edition, the book is "perhaps best seen as a study in the effects that a desire for education, or 'culture,' may have upon a working-class individual" (xv). Characters such as Godwin Peake in George Gissing's *Born in Exile* (1892), Jude Fawley in Thomas Hardy's *Jude the Obscure* (1895), and Leonard Bast in E. M. Forster's *Howards End* (1910) might all thus be identified as Arthur Gardner's literary forebears, though the most direct literary precedent would be Paul Morel in D. H. Lawrence's *Sons and Lovers* (1913). Brierley shows his awareness of this heritage through direct allusions to Hardy and Lawrence. Carole Snee, in fact, argues that the book depends so much upon *Sons and Lovers* as background that it might be unintelligible to readers not familiar with Lawrence's book (181).

However, *Sandwichman* is also very much a work of the 1930s and takes much of its specific character from the context of that decade. Moreover, the book differs greatly from its predecessors in numerous respects. Philip Gorski notes, for example, that Brierley's book can be seen as a sort of realistic rejoinder to the idealistic *Sons and Lovers*, the differences between Lawrence and Brierley perhaps arising from the fact that Brierley had himself been a coal miner and experienced that life first hand (xix). Gorski finds Brierley's book extremely effective at presenting its material, and he particularly takes issue with Snee's criticism of Brierley's style as "lifeless and static" (180). On the other hand, Snee's criticisms of *Sandwichman* are supported by the even more negative assessment of Roy Johnson, who believes the book "suffers from all the inflation, the use of cliché, the unrealistic dialogue, and the generally sloppy use of language" that characterized the earlier *Means-Test Man* ("Walter Brierley" 7).

It is important to note that both Snee and Johnson couch their stylistic assessments within a criticism of the book's failure to critique the fundamental structure of the system that causes Arthur's difficulties or to suggest ways in which the system might be changed. In particular,

Brierley fails to interrogate Arthur's rejection of his class origins or to suggest that collective action to improve the lives of all workers might be preferable to Arthur's project of individual betterment. In the final analysis, *Sandwichman* is at least less maudlin than *Means-Test Man* in its sentimentality, but both books lack any effective utopian dimension that might suggest possible alternatives to the dismal realities of life in Britain in the 1930s. **Selected bibliography:** Gorski; Johnson ("Walter Brierley"); Snee ("Working-Class Literature").

ROBERT BRIFFAULT: *EUROPA* **(1935) and** *EUROPA IN LIMBO* **(1937).** *Europa* is a sweeping historical novel whose numerous characters move throughout late nineteenth- and early twentieth-century Europe amid an atmosphere of decadence and decay that moves the continent inexorably toward the outbreak of World War I. *Europa in Limbo* then continues this narrative through World War I and the Russian Revolution. The true protagonist of both novels is Europe itself, as the titles perhaps imply. However, the two books also constitute a bildungsroman that centers on the growth and maturation of their central character, Julian Bern, whose own personal development is closely related to larger historical trends. Indeed, by combining the genres of the historical novel and the bildungsroman, Briffault is able to establish an organic connection between public and personal experience and to portray even the most private experiences of Julian and the other characters as integrally related to the historical context that surrounds them.

In the beginning of *Europa*, Julian is a boy growing up in Italy, where his father is a British diplomat at the end of the nineteenth century. As a result of the father's position, the family comes into contact with numerous important personages, including various representatives of European royalty. The book then follows Julian as he comes to England to complete his education, first at Winton, a prestigious public school, then at Cambridge, where he works hard at his studies, especially in science. In the course of his education, Julian is exposed to numerous new ideas and gradually becomes aware of a number of controversial issues of the time, including socialism and women's suffrage. Meanwhile, during vacations and other trips to the continent, he continues to come into contact with a variety of European aristocrats, the decadence of whom is one of the central motifs of the book.

Julian becomes romantically involved with the Russian girl Zena, the niece of Prince Nevidof and the daughter of Daria Nevidof, the Duchess of Friedland. The duchess is herself a central character of the novel. Among other things, she is a famous beauty; she once posed for a sculpture of Europa and the bull, a myth that provides one of the referents of the title. The adolescent relationship between Julian and Zena goes nowhere, but it is renewed near the end of the book, even though Zena is at this time married to the Russian Prince Hruzof, a homosexual who is interested in her only for her money. The book ends as Julian and Zena are in Berlin preparing to flee Germany in the wake of the assassination of the Archduke Franz Ferdinand in Sarajevo and amid rumors that a large-scale war is about to erupt in Europe.

By the end of the first volume, Julian has had little involvement in politics, putting most of his energies into his studies in biology and into private concerns like his courtship of Zena. He has, however, already come to the conclusion that capitalism is a rotten, hypocritical system that needs to be swept away before genuine justice can be achieved in Europe. This conclusion is solidified in *Europa in Limbo*, which depicts World War I as the inevitable consequence of the capitalist system, but also as the beginnings of the death throes of that system. Amid the chaos of the war, Julian continues his political development. Reported lost in combat, he makes his way to Russia, where he completes his transition to ardent support for socialism and joins the Red Army to fight against the Whites in the Civil War that followed the 1917 Revolution. In this struggle, his life finds true meaning at last. Zena, meanwhile, also undergoes considerable development in this volume, evolving from a spoiled and idle woman of leisure to a woman who begins to realize the corruption of Europe's ruling classes and to see that any hope for a better future lies with the workers. Indeed, the attraction of both Julian and Zena to the working class is a major motif of the narrative, though Briffault is careful neither to romanticize nor to oversimplify that attraction.

As Stephan Lieske puts it, a major strength of these volumes is Briffault's ability to create "fictional characters that are convincing in themselves as characters acting in a specific time and place in history" (84). Indeed, characters such as Julian and Zena are good examples of the "typification" recommended by Georg Lukács in connection with the historical novel. Meanwhile, these novels, like those of Walter Scott and other historical novelists praised by Lukács, include marginal appearances by "world historical individuals," who are centrally involved in major historical events. In the course of the two volumes, for example, Julian encounters a wide range of important historical personages, including such cultural figures as Henry James and G. B. Shaw and such political figures as Rosa Luxemburg, Karl Liebknecht, and V. I. Lenin. If the books have a weakness as historical novels, it is that they pay much more attention to the decadence (especially sexual) of the European ruling classes than to the vitality of the working classes. As a result, the books sometimes seem dangerously close to showing a lurid fascination with the very decadence they condemn. But this project is an extremely difficult one, and David Smith is probably a bit too strong in his critique of the books as "revelling" in "immorality" (103).

Much of Smith's problem with the books has to do with the unapologetic way in which both attempt to address themselves to a mass audience. Indeed, Smith reveals his prejudice against popular forms when he describes both *Europa* and *Europa in Limbo* as "hastily written books for mass consumption" (103). Yet both are extremely interesting novels, and their attempts to attract a popular audience (which they did, in fact, do) constitute a leading example of the attempts of the British Left in the 1930s to contest for cultural dominance in popular, as well as literary, genres. Meanwhile, despite their sometimes lurid content, the books never lose sight of their political mission, and they are clearly informed by a fundamentally Marxist sense of history, however decadent some of their imagery. This historical vision is also spelled out in some of Briffault's nonfiction writings, particularly the historical study *Breakdown: The Collapse of Traditional Civilization*, which makes clear his view that the crisis in capitalism extending from World War I to the Depression of the 1930s was the culmination of a long period of decadence and decay. *Breakdown* also demonstrates Briffault's belief that the death of capitalist civilization, whatever the negative short-term consequences, is ultimately a good thing because it clears the way for the birth of socialism. Together, Briffault's two historical novels vividly dramatize this historical vision in a style that is attractive to a mass audience and in a tone that is neither strident nor sanctimonious. **Selected bibliography:** Briffault (*Breakdown*); Lieske; David Smith (*Socialist Propaganda*).

ALEC BROWN: *BREAKFAST IN BED* **(1937).** While lacking the magnitude of Brown's earlier *Daughters of Albion*, *Breakfast in Bed* is still ambitious in its attempt to capture the essence of middle-class life in Britain in the mid-1930s. In particular, it seeks to portray the impact on the consciousnesses of its middle-class characters of the growing sense of economic and political crisis that informed British life during that period. In that sense, the book is something of a fictional accompaniment to Brown's sociological treatise *The Fate of the Middle Classes*, published one year earlier. In that book, Brown discusses the nature of capitalism and attempts to argue that the middle class does not necessarily profit from the capitalist system and therefore need not feel threatened by challenges to the capitalist order. In particular, he argues that communism can represent a step forward for everyone and need not be feared by the middle class as the ultimate evil, even though the communist revolution must by historical necessity be led by the proletariat. *The Fate of the Middle Classes* ends with a warning that tyranny typically succeeds through divide-and-conquer strategies and that opposition between the middle class and the proletariat therefore works in the interest of tyranny, in this case fascism. The book is thus essentially a contribution to the Popular Front effort to rally both liberal and radical groups to make common cause against the threat of fascism. In *The Daughters of Albion*, Brown enacts this same thesis, though with a stronger sense of crisis and a more specific emphasis on the Civil War that had meanwhile erupted in Spain. He shows his protagonist, Michael Frobisher, in the process of overcoming his antagonism to communism (while remaining essentially an English liberal) to the point that he decides to go to Spain to fight side-by-side with communists against Franco and his fascist forces.

Other important characters in the book include Michael's wife, Jean, who is unsympathetic to his interest in Spain—and who indeed begins to see fascism as a positive defense against the breakdown in traditional morals that she believes informs the society around her. Jean is treated rather unsympathetically by Brown, though she is, herself, something of a victim, a woman who is unable to provide any emotional support to her husband because the cultural forces to which she has been exposed have rendered her cold, repressed, and inhibited. The fascists indeed emerge in the book as staunch defenders of precisely the forces that have made Jean this way, in particular as defenders of traditional bourgeois family values, but those values themselves are treated as highly suspect. For example, the marriage between Michael and Jean is empty and hollow, a purely economic and contractual arrangement.

The depiction of their relationship thus continues the critique of bourgeois marriage that Brown had begun in *Daughters of Albion*, and it therefore comes as no surprise that both Jean and Michael become involved in adulterous affairs in the course of the book. On the other hand, Brown treats the relationship between Michael's brother, John, and his lover and eventual wife, Molly Battys, in a very positive light. Both John and Molly are Party members who devote much of their energy to the communist cause. As a result, John, a research chemist, finds himself harassed by surveillance and fired from his job. Meanwhile, Molly's father, a wealthy surgeon, is appalled by their relationship and does everything possible to impede it. The two stay together nevertheless, joined by a love that survives despite societal pressures, as opposed to the marriage of Michael and Jean, who are together simply because it is what society expects.

John and Molly are the most positive characters in the book; the other communist characters (and all of the proletarian characters) are minor figures, though they help to flesh out Brown's portrayal of the political climate of the era. That climate consists of a growing fear of socialism on the part of the bourgeois characters, most of whom devote their attention to abstract art and to a rhetoric of spirituality, whiling away their time in frivolous dalliances—fiddling while Spain burns. *Breakfast in Bed* insists that these characters to not represent the real essence of British democracy. It also insists that the real threat to the British way of life resides not in socialism but in the increasing power of fascism. Especially in the second half of the book, this threat is represented primarily by events in Spain, where Franco and his forces seem gradually to be gaining the upper hand in their battle against the country's legally elected leftist government. And the book is clear in its warning that, if the fascists are not stopped in Spain they will have to be confronted somewhere else, perhaps on the shores of Britain itself. Brown's insights regarding this point are sometimes extremely keen, as when the communist worker Simon Wall warns Michael that attempts to avoid war with the fascists may eventually require the British to look the other way while the Germans invade Czechoslovakia (220). Michael, who at this point still desires peace at any cost, merely responds that Wall, like all "Reds," is a scaremonger. Michael will eventually come to realize, however, that Wall is right and that the fascists can never be appeased by appeals to "reasonableness."

In opposition to the fascist threat, the communist leader Rupert Wolf joins the International Brigade and goes to Spain to fight for the loyalist cause. John Frobisher wants to go as well, but Molly convinces him that, at least for the time being, he is needed to work for the cause in England. Thus, in keeping with the Popular Front ideology of *Breakfast in Bed*, it is not the communist John but the liberal Michael who goes to Spain to fight. Importantly, however, Brown makes it clear that Michael has not become a communist. Indeed, he retains his faith in the glories of British democracy and Western bourgeois culture. He believes, however, that democracy is in danger of extermination at the hands of the fascists. When Michael arrives in Spain and is asked whether he is there as a representative of the Communist Party, he responds that he is there simply to defend "civilization" (386).

Michael, who has experience as a gunnery officer from World War I, is a welcome addition to the loyalist cause. Initially, he uses that expertise in training Spanish gunners. However, he becomes directly involved in battle as the fascist forces approach Madrid and threaten to take the city. He is killed while valiantly fighting to hold off the vastly superior forces of the fascists, and the book ends as Rupert Wolf contemplates his fallen comrade. Asked by a Spanish soldier whether Michael had been a communist, Wolf replies, "No, just an Englishman" (402). The implication is clear: one need not be a communist to see that the fascists must be stopped, and any Englishman who really believes in the democratic principles officially espoused by the British nation has a duty to join the fight against fascism. Michael himself makes this position clear in the thoughts that run through his head as he fires his gun during his final, fatal fight: "As he held his finger to the little lever thought came to him of the bloodstained path of England, Tudor and Cromwellian, to that degree of democracy she had attained, and thus, smiling, through blood he saw a wider world democracy of peace, with fascist lawlessness finally crushed" (400). *Selected bibliography:* Brown (*Fate of the Middle Classes*); David Smith (*Socialist Propaganda*).

ALEC BROWN: *DAUGHTERS OF ALBION* (1935). Spanning the period from Christmas 1930, to Christmas 1932, *Daughters of Albion* is a massive work that details the lives of the Etchams, a rich English bourgeois family, as a means of conducting a biting satirical critique of what Marx and Engels called the "bourgeois clap-trap about the family" (487). In particular, Brown builds upon the observation of Marx and Engels that "the bourgeoisie has torn away from the family its sentimental veil, and has reduced the family relation to a mere money relation" (476). Indeed, all human relationships in the England portrayed by Brown have been reduced to money relations, but the focus of *Daughters of Albion* is on the family, identified in the book as the most revered (and hypocritical) of all bourgeois institutions. In so doing, Brown deconstructs the entire complex of sentimental bourgeois rhetoric about the family and conducts a searing examination of the ways in which bourgeois attitudes toward marriage contribute to the reification of human relationships under capitalism and especially to the objectification of women.

Roger Etcham, the patriarch of the family, serves in the text as a representation of the typical bourgeois husband and father. A wealthy lawyer in his fifties, he provides his family with a luxurious lifestyle but is entirely estranged from them emotionally, except for an annual Christmas gathering during which he attempts to compensate for the rest of the year with a sudden outburst of family sentiment. Meanwhile, he ignores his lonely and sexually frustrated wife, Violet, in favor of a string of young mistresses, each of whom he uses, then discards. The book begins during the family Christmas gathering of 1930, the last year in which Roger will be able to assemble the entire family for the event. Here we learn of Etcham's devotion to Christmas as a British national institution and of his belief that British culture "is built on the family. Our family life is sacred" (3). We also meet Etcham's five daughters: Cynthia, age 27; Muriel, 25; Charlotte, 23; Irene, 20; and Mary, 18. It soon becomes clear that, despite his supposed devotion to family, Etcham regards his five daughters essentially as commodities; most of his thoughts concerning them have to do with the necessity of marketing them to appropriate husbands, though he also harbors only slightly repressed sexual desires for Irene, the most attractive of the daughters.

The rest of the text focuses primarily on these daughters and on the various difficulties they encounter in their lives as a result of their upbringing and of the fundamental nature of the British bourgeois society in which they live. Cynthia, the oldest, is a rather mannish young woman who has attempted throughout her life to compensate her father for his lack of a son. She attempts to find fulfillment by owning and operating a poultry farm, thus making her father proud of her and meanwhile sublimating her repressed sexual feelings into the management of the farm. There is also a powerful element of sublimation in her relationship with her hired man, Roger Kidnup, for whom she clearly harbors vague (unconscious) sexual feelings, which she expresses in a project to "improve" him by introducing him to British culture, especially literature. Not surprisingly, Kidnup shows little interest in this endeavor, finding the stories in the bourgeois literature she gives him to read irrelevant to his life. Cynthia ends up frustrated and alone, tired of the farm and of her life, feeling old at twenty-nine.

Muriel is similar to Cynthia in her refusal to acknowledge her own sexual nature. Enthralled by the handsome parson, Percy Longbatten, Muriel convinces herself that she is interested not in his physical charms but in the charity work he does in London's slums. She becomes involved in this work as well and eventually joins Percy as his wife. The two set up housekeeping in a flat in the slum area where he does his work, though Muriel gradually decorates the flat in a more and more luxurious style that clearly separates them from Percy's poor parishioners. In the meantime, Percy becomes frustrated at the inability of Christianity substantively to improve the lives of the poor, while Muriel's primary contribution to his mission seems to be a campaign to discourage the poor from marrying, practicing birth control, or experiencing sexual love of any kind. By the end of the book the couple has moved to a pleasant house in a nice neighborhood far away from the depressing slums. Percy and the sexually repressed Muriel have grown estranged, and she has become a bitter and humorless harpy.

Charlotte, the voluptuous third sister, follows through on her sexual instincts at least to the point that, as the book begins, she is married and has a child. She attends the Christmas gathering with her infant son, though her husband (who turns out to be an inveterate womanizer, much like her father) is vacationing on his own in the south of France. Charlotte has married her husband, a schoolmaster, out of a romantic notion of his devotion to education. She discovers, however, that his concern is purely with financial gain, which leads him to abandon teaching in the interest of a business career. Meanwhile, his philandering causes an outraged Charlotte to seek a separation. However, her mother, who has long had to endure similar infidelities on the part of her own husband, advises Charlotte to stay in the marriage for the sake of appearances and financial security. Charlotte thus ends up following very much in the footsteps of her mother, remaining a wife out of economic and social necessity but being emotionally abandoned by her husband. Indeed, she is physically alone as well; she lives with their son in their home in England, largely withdrawn from the world, while her husband takes a job in Paris and spends most of his time there, living his own separate life.

The marriages of Violet and Charlotte, and to some extent of Muriel, are clearly presented by Brown as forms of legalized prostitution. Here again, Brown builds directly on the comments of Marx and Engels on bourgeois marriage. Indeed, in an explanatory note appended to the end of the book, Brown quotes from *The Communist Manifesto* to the effect that the bourgeois family is founded "on capital, on private gain. In its completely developed form this family exists only among the bourgeoisie. But this state of things finds its complement . . . in public prostitution" (694, Brown's ellipsis). Also particularly relevant to Brown's purposes is Engels's argument that bourgeois marriages are inevitably matters of mere economic convenience, and that "this marriage of convenience often turns into the crassest prostitution—sometimes on both sides, but much more generally on the part of the wife, who differs from the ordinary courtesan only in that she does not hire out her body, like a wage-worker, on piecework, but sells it into slavery once for all" (Marx and Engels 742).

Many leftist writers, of course, have employed prostitution as a metaphor for the reification of all social relations under capitalism. This metaphor is reinforced in *Daughters of Albion* in the treatment of Irene, who becomes involved with Doushan Matitch, a Serbian student studying in Paris, and goes there to be near him. For a time, the couple experiences a fulfilling sexual relationship, but family pressures eventually lead Irene to seek to formalize the relationship in marriage. Knowing that Doushan will want to live in Yugoslavia, Irene travels there (chaperoned, for appearances, by her sister Mary) to get the flavor of life there. Irene arrives with Orientalist notions of Yugoslavia as a picturesque land of romantic antiquities but finds, instead, an emerging modern nation in a frantic state of modernization and capitalist development. Brown's vivid and compelling description of conditions in the new nation of Yugoslavia (which draws upon his own experience there while serving as a lecturer at the University of Belgrade) provides the basis for a sort of allegory of the history of capitalism. The new Yugoslavia, in fact, is much like England but with the workings of capitalism stripped bare of the complex English ideological superstructure. Appalled, Irene concludes that she can never live in such an environment and breaks off the relationship with Doushan. Soon, however, she learns that she is pregnant, to which her mother responds by frantically arranging for an abortion by a top surgeon, followed by a quick marriage of convenience to a homosexual diplomat who needs a presentable wife for professional appearances. Shocked by these arrangements, the proud Irene refuses to cooperate and breaks off relations with her family.

Now alone and nearly destitute, Irene realizes that her only practical course is to go through with the abortion, which she does by going to a squalid illegal abortion clinic that caters primarily to prostitutes. While recuperating in the clinic, she meets the prostitute Maud Gayner, whom she does not realize is a former mistress of her father. After the abortion, Irene lives in squalor and semi-starvation while unsuccessfully seeking office work. Eventually, this life takes its toll, and she falls seriously ill, after which Maud comes to her rescue and takes her in. Living with Maud, Irene concludes that prostitution is her only recourse as well, though Maud, now stricken with an advanced stage of syphilis, attempts to discourage her. After discovering Maud's former relationship with Roger Etcham, Irene again falls ill. Maud goes to both Muriel and Charlotte to try to convince them to come to Irene's aid, but both refuse. Mary does come, but Irene declines her help. Irene remains on her own, facing a life of prostitution and inevitable disease and degradation.

Among other things, Irene's story dramatizes the lack of choices available to women in bourgeois England. If Violet, Charlotte, and Muriel become virtual prostitutes because they are willing to carry on marriages under false premises, Irene is forced into literal prostitution because she refuses to enter a marriage with Doushan when she cannot share his view of the world. Mary, a devoted student of Marxism, does share the worldview of Jimmy Wingfield, a wealthy young man who is striving to become a good communist despite his class position. Jimmy, however, is married, though estranged from his wife. England's divorce laws eventually lead Jimmy and Mary to live together out of wedlock in order to enable Jimmy's wife to sue for divorce on the grounds of adultery. The book ends just as this arrangement is beginning, and Jimmy and Mary face tremendous social pressures, including the strong disapproval of her father. Nevertheless, their relationship, based on intellectual honesty and a shared devotion to socialist ideals, does at least have a clear potential for success.

The communists Mary and Jimmy are clearly the most positive characters in the book, though Jimmy, in particular, still has a great deal to learn. He has not yet actually read Marx, and his tendency toward romantic idealism strains against the requirements of dialectical materialism. Indeed, if the book has an ideological weakness, it may be the failure fully to interrogate the shortcomings of Jimmy's excessive concern with integrity and moral "purity," which among other things prevents him from taking the expedient of committing adultery (or even pretending to do so) with a prostitute in order to get his divorce. Mary, meanwhile, has a more sophisticated understanding of Marxism, but she is probably the least vividly presented of all of the daughters. Finally, Jimmy and Mary clearly plan to be married as soon as legally possible, so that the book, despite its powerful critique of the institution of marriage, fails to reject that institution altogether.

Despite such flaws (to which one might add that it is longer than necessary and yet still lacks a satisfying conclusion), *Daughters of Albion* is an impressive and effective satire of the hypocrisy of bourgeois morals and "family values," which makes quite clear Brown's belief in Marxism as the key to building a better society based upon more honest and equitable premises. The book is entertaining, clever, and ironic in its merciless exposure of bourgeois mendacity and venality, making one wonder if critics who see *Daughters of Albion* as an example of Brown's supposedly heavy-handed propagandizing are reacting to the novel or just to Brown's reputation and polemical writings. Ramón López Ortega, for example, objects to Brown's stated goal of escaping the inherited traditions of British literature, then identifies *Daughters of Albion* (though misquoting the title) as perhaps the saddest example from the 1930s of "literature overrun by political doctrine" in ways that reveal "the sterility of the author's theorising" (126). In point of fact, the book presents an engaging narrative that is peopled by believable characters, however symbolic their function. The book convincingly dramatizes Marxist critiques of the bourgeois family, but it contains very little in the way of overt "theorizing." When such overt passages do occur (as in Jimmy Wingfield's explanation to Cynthia that Kidnup's lack of interest in British literature arises from the alignment of that literature with the bourgeoisie), they are neither sterile nor excessively intrusive. Indeed, Wingfield may not understand Marxism all that well, but his understanding of the class orientation of the British literary tradition is quite astute, and he makes Brown's argument for the need of a departure from this tradition quite well.

Similarly, David Smith accuses Brown of a "pompous and often long-winded didacticism" and complains that it is almost impossible to find anything positive to say about *Daughters of Albion* despite its vast length (82). Smith's complaint, however, seems based upon strictly bourgeois aesthetic conventions, which Brown is openly attempting to break. In any case, the book has numerous virtues and is considerably shorter than the typical classic of nineteenth-century British realism to which Smith seems to want to compare it. If anything, the problem with Brown's book is that it is too well executed by the very bourgeois standards that he, himself, seeks to overcome. Indeed, part of Smith's objection to the book is that it is not nearly as linguistically radical as might be indicated by Brown's goal, stated in his author's note, of achieving a new mode of literary expression that escapes the artificiality of the bourgeois past in order to establish a new literary language that is "the mass language of the people" (693). On the other hand, Smith's characterization of Brown's innovations as trivial is not fair. Many of Brown's sentence constructions are at least as inventive as those of modernists such as James Joyce or Virginia Woolf, while his unusual metaphors and images are, if not always effective in themselves, often recuperable as effective parodies of conventional literary language. Part of the problem may be Brown's own suggestion that he is developing a proletarian mode of expression when, in fact, *Daughters of Albion* is not a proletarian novel and contains no major proletarian characters. Taken for what it is, however, the book is an effective satire of bourgeois society that deserves more attention and respect than it has received. **Selected bibliography:** López Ortega; Marx and Engels (*Reader*); David Smith (*Socialist Propaganda*).

JOHN BRUNNER: *STAND ON ZANZIBAR* **(1968).** *Stand on Zanzibar* is a massive and highly ambitious science-fiction novel that employs a number of complex literary strategies to project an early twenty-first-century world in which many of the social and political tendencies of the late 1960s have been extended to near-disastrous lengths. In this sense, it has much in common with Brunner's other dystopian looks at the future. Indeed, one could see *Stand on Zanzibar* as combining with *The Jagged Orbit* (1969, which focuses on racism and the criminalistic tendencies of the military-industrial complex), *The Sheep Look Up* (1972, which focuses on future environmental degradation), and *The Shockwave Rider* (1975, which focuses on the impact of a worldwide communications explosion) to constitute a sort of dystopian tetralogy. The title of *Stand on Zanzibar* refers to its central emphasis on overpopulation, in particular to the fact that the world population has reached the level where, for the first time, it would no longer be theoretically possible for all of the world's people to stand shoulder-to-shoulder on the island of Zanzibar. In the book, international strife is a fact of life, with the United States and China engaged in an interminable war of attrition that bears obvious similarities to the war in Vietnam, ongoing when the book was written.

Though Brunner is a British writer, he focuses particularly on America, still the world's richest—but also most violent—nation, replete with commodities, but also with economic inequities that keep most urban areas on the verge of riots. Gender relations in an overpopulated America ruled by strict eugenic legislation are also rather strained, though Brunner does little to explore the implications of the fact that so many young women, unable to have children under the current circumstances, are reduced to the status of roving sexual objects, or "shiggies," drifting from one man to another, providing sexual favors in return for food and lodging. The American social fabric is further disrupted by the terrorist activities of pro-Chinese partisans and by the ever-present threat of "muckers"—individuals who snap under the pressure of modern life and run amuck, killing and maiming anyone in their path. Most of the populace cope with these pressures via an array of strategies that include mind-numbing drugs, casual sex, and popular culture. Indeed, the latter is a particularly powerful force as new technologies allow the media to extend their reach worldwide—symbolized by the fact that the chief figures in global advertising are the allegorical Mr. and Mrs. Everywhere (who can be made to resemble, via special high-tech televisions) whoever happens to be watching at the time.

Stand on Zanzibar presents this vision of the future via a complex literary form that is clearly reminiscent of John Dos Passos's *U.S.A.* trilogy—though Brunner himself has suggested that Dos Passos's later *Midcentury* may have been an even more direct inspiration ("Genesis" 36). Relatively brief narrative segments that advance the major plot sequences are interspersed with other segments that contribute primarily to the elaboration of the texture of life in this future world, through either additional narrative segments that relate the experiences of an array of minor characters or nonnarrative segments that involve collages of discourse from advertising, popular culture, and other sources. Many of the latter include quotations from the works of the antiauthoritarian pop sociologist Chad Mulligan, who also becomes an important character in the second half of the book.

Stand on Zanzibar is far less plot-driven than most science fiction, concentrating instead on creating a complete fictional world, thus recalling Lukács's emphasis on representation of the social totality. The mixture of discourses involved in this sort of construction also recalls Bakhtin's concepts of dialogism and polyphony, which Patrick Murphy has used to describe the effect of all four of the novels in the "tetralogy." There are, however, two major plot sequences, respectively centering on the experiences of Norman House and Donald Hogan, who begin the text as roommates in New York but then go their separate ways. The African-American House, an executive with the gigantic General Technics Corporation (GT), becomes involved in a massive project to develop the "backward" African nation of Beninia (in the process creating new markets for GT products); Hogan, meanwhile, after ten years of employment in "research" for the U. S. government, is pressed into active service as an espionage agent and sent to the Asian island nation of Yatakang to investigate reports that a world-famous Yatakangi scientist, Dr. Sugaiguntung, has developed new genetic techniques that will allow the Yatakangis to produce genetically superior human beings. Hogan, having been "eptified" into an efficient killing machine, eventually goes insane after he kills a number of people in the course of his mission, finally including Sugaiguntung himself. Hogan, meanwhile, becomes the effective head of the Beninia project, employing Mulligan as a principal adviser.

Much of the suspense of the plot involves the attempts of Hogan and other Westerners to unravel the mystery of the fact that life in Beninia, which is economically impoverished to the point of squalor, seems unaccountably richer and more humane than life in the "advanced" countries of the West. The entire country of Beninia operates like one large family, under the benign leadership of its patriarch, President Zadkiel Obomi, whose impending death has triggered the GT project. Beninia is a land essentially free of violent crime, with a language that makes it almost impossible even to describe anger, except as a form of temporary insanity. As such, the book explores contrasts between the individualism of modern capitalist society and the communalism of traditional African society in potentially productive ways. Unfortunately, Brunner's depiction of the Beninians has a tendency to succumb to colonialist stereotyping, as when ancient Beninia is described as a timeless land without history, inhabited only by the peaceful Shinka tribe until slave trading brought an influx of foreigners into the region. Most important, the mystery of Beninian tranquility and cooperation is ultimately attributed not to social but to biological differences. Mulligan discovers that the Shinkas bear a mutant gene that causes them to secrete a substance that suppresses the normal human (masculine) tendency toward aggression—thus making not only them, but those they encounter, behave in peaceful and cooperative ways.

This appeal to biological difference comes dangerously close to stereotyping in terms of both race and gender. Indeed, the highly patriarchal nature of this ideal Beninia is highly problematic, as is Brunner's failure to interrogate, in any effective way, the role of gender relations in his twenty-first-century America. In the end, Mulligan assumes, somewhat to his own horror, that capitalism will appropriate the Shinka mutation, developing a way to synthesize and market the secreted substance, then distributing it to prevent the human race from destroying itself. But the text does not address the fundamental incompatibility between capitalism, built on competition and aggression, and the Shinka mutation, which may not only spell the doom of the GT project to develop Beninia along capitalist lines but could also, if widely distributed, spell the doom of capitalism itself.

Ultimately, then, Brunner misses a number of opportunities to make important political points, perhaps because of his own apparent assumption that human social problems arise primarily from the biological predilections of the human race and are therefore not amenable to solution by social and political means. Indeed, while the book's critique of capitalism is sometimes trenchant, it does not really offer socialism as an effective alternative. The book is, in fact, sometimes quite critical of the communist regime in its future China, though it does suggest that Western complaints about the lack of individual freedom in China reflect a lack of understanding of the Chinese situation, which has been substantially improved under communism (586). Though John J. Pierce describes *Stand on Zanzibar* as a Wellsian satire "committed to utopian socialism and a world state," the book ultimately has no clearly articulated political agenda (189). It is also, as science fiction goes, not particularly imaginative in its projection of the impact of technology on future human societies. For example, the computer technologies that are central to much of the book are rather clunky in comparison with what has actually occurred in the past thirty years. But Brunner's book is clearly more a satirical commentary on the present world of 1968 than a literal attempt to envision the future. As Robert Scholes and Eric Rabkin put it, Brunner's dystopian novels are not predictions of what will happen but warnings of what might happen if we continue the way we are going (82). Moreover, *Stand on Zanzibar* is extremely insightful in its projection of a media-dominated world system that clearly reflects the spread of what critics such as Ernest Mandel and Fredric Jameson have called late capitalism. It also presents, in a vivid and effective fashion, the dehumanizing consequences of this late capitalist system, under which the quiet desperation described by Thoreau has reached epidemic and spectacular proportions. **Selected bibliography:** Brunner ("Genesis"); Murphy; Pierce; Scholes and Rabkin.

KATHARINE BURDEKIN: *SWASTIKA NIGHT* (1937). Originally published under the pseudonym Murray Constantine, *Swastika Night* is a leading example of the genre of dystopian fiction that became prominent in Britain in the 1930s, largely as a reaction to the perceived threat of fascism. Among other things, this trend provides important background to George Orwell's *Nineteen Eighty-Four*, which would become the best-known work of the genre. In fact, *Swastika Night* and *Nineteen Eighty-Four* have frequently been compared, sometimes very much to the advantage of the former, especially in the way Burdekin's novel is able to maintain a genuinely utopian hope for the future even as it centers on the dark consequences of a potential Nazi victory throughout Europe. Burdekin's novel is also striking for its focus on gender issues and for its understanding of the way the patriarchal orientation of fascism makes the threat of a fascist takeover particularly horrifying for women.

Swastika Night is very much a novel of ideas. Its plot and characterization are extremely rudimentary and are used simply to give Burdekin an opportunity to explore the nature of the threat posed by fascism in the 1930s. The book is set in the far future, more than seven hundred years after the initial Nazi victory. The entire world is split between two vast empires, one ruled by Germany, the other by Japan. Burdekin's book focuses on the German Empire (which includes all of Europe and Africa), but implies that the two empires are rather similar in their ideologies, though competition over resources has frequently led to warfare between the two regimes. The dissemination of information in this future world is strictly controlled. Books, in fact, have been entirely banned (except for one sacred "Hitler book"), and virtually all citizens are illiterate. History has been almost entirely forgotten, the only records of the past being highly mythologized versions in which Hitler has been promoted to the status of a god and all memories of any civilizations before German Nazism forgotten.

In Burdekin's fascist dystopia, much of the social structure has a feudal quality, with medieval conceptions of "blood" crucial to one's social status. There is a strict hierarchy among Germans, with a small hereditary elite group of aristocratic "knights" holding most power and ordinary Germans (referred to simply as "Nazis") doing their bidding. But Germans, of course, are regarded as a master race, and even these ordinary Nazis occupy a position far superior to that of subaltern peoples such as the British. In this society, the very texture of life has highly mythical quality, and politics has merged into a religion based on a cult of Hitler worship. One of the most despised groups, in fact, are the Christians, who insist on maintaining a separate religion of their own, though they, too, have largely forgotten the past and base their current beliefs on only the vaguest (and sometimes highly distorted) memories of pre-Hitlerian Christianity. Meanwhile, women constitute the most despised group of all. Reduced to the status of animals tolerated largely because they are needed as breeding stock to perpetuate the race, women are treated with disgust and revulsion, allowed to live only in separate women's compounds because they are not judged civilized enough to live among men. Women and men sometimes have long-term relationships, but in these relationships women are viewed strictly as the property of men, somewhat in the mode of cattle. Meanwhile, rape is common and entirely legal, resistance on the part of women being forbidden.

The protagonist of *Swastika Night* is Alfred, a dissident Englishman who comes to German to tour some of the sacred sights of fascism. While there, he meets Hermann, a Nazi farm worker whom he had previously known in England. Though presumably convinced that he, as a German, is a member of the master race, Hermann finds that he idolizes Alfred, who is clearly the more intelligent and sophisticated of the two. Through Hermann, Alfred comes into contact with the German knight, Friedrich von Hess, who reveals to him that he is in possession of a book compiled by one of his ancestors that contains details of world history before the Nazi takeover. A great deal of the narrative of *Swastika Night* consists of von Hess's explanation of this book to Alfred, who is excited to learn, among other things, that the British themselves once had an empire. This book has been passed down through the von Hess family for generations. However, von Hess has no heirs, so he entrusts the book to Alfred, who manages to take it back to England. Hermann comes to England as well, after intentionally having himself exiled from Germany. Both Alfred and Hermann are subsequently killed by Nazis, but Alfred's eldest son manages to rescue the secret book, leaving it in the possession of a local Christian, Christians being so despised that Nazis would not stoop to searching their quarters. The book thus ends on a hopeful note, with the suggestion that the truth contained in the book can at least potentially serve as the seed of an eventual revolt against the rule of the German Empire.

Within the confines of this minimal plot, Burdekin is able to carry out a satirical assault on fascism, militarism, and, especially, patriarchy. Because of its treatment of gender and its understanding of the complicity between fascism and patriarchy, Burdekin's book is identified by Andy Croft as "the most original of all the many anti-fascist dystopias of the late 1930s" (238). Indeed, if Burdekin's novel resembles *Nineteen Eighty-Four* in a number of ways, it also strikingly anticipates recent feminist dystopias such as Margaret Atwood's *The Handmaid's Tale*, which projects a similar patriarchal dystopian future, though aiming its commentary at the American religious right of the 1980s rather than at German fascism. In retrospect, of course, the highly religious orientation of the fascist regime depicted by Burdekin suggests parallels between these two phenomena that should be carefully pondered. Indeed, Burdekin's book, while aimed very directly at German fascism of the 1930s, is careful to suggest that fascism has its roots in patriarchal attitudes that go well beyond that specific phenomenon. Among other things, the book suggests that the ideology that drives the British Empire is not as different from the ideology of Burdekin's fictional German Empire as some might like to believe. The book's clear support for pacifism seems, in retrospect, problematic, while some of the book's portrayal of gender verges on essentialism. Nevertheless, *Swastika Night* calls attention to a number of crucial issues from the 1930s that remain important for us today. **Selected bibliography:** Croft (*Red Letter Days*); McKay; Patai ("Imagining Reality"); Patai (Introduction); Patai (*The Orwell Mystique*).

ARTHUR CALDER-MARSHALL: *PIE IN THE SKY* (1937). *Pie in the Sky*, described by Andy Croft as "a panoramic view of social disorder in contemporary Britain," employs a number of complex modernist narrative strategies to present a cross-section of British life in the mid-1930s (118). The book pays particular attention to the impact of political issues and activities on the lives of its characters and, in so doing, usefully indicates the extent to which politics had become an integral part of everyday life in the Britain of that time. The title phrase of the book, indicated in the epigraph as originating in an "I. W. W. Song," is actually taken from the song "The Preacher and the Slave" by the American labor activist and poet Joe Hill, first published by the I. W. W. in its *Little Red Song Book* in 1909. Hill's song lampoons the false promises of a better future life offered by Christianity as a way of discouraging political action in the present, and Calder-Marshall's book contains similar parodic energies. On the other hand, the phrase is also frequently used in *Pie in the Sky* in reference to the utopian promises offered by communism. The political orientation of the book is actually quite ambiguous, though Calder-Marshall himself seemed committed to leftist ideas at the time, as can be seen from the evidence of his contribution (on the film industry) to C. Day Lewis's collection, *The Mind in Chains*.

The plot of *Pie in the Sky* is complex and includes a number of interlinked strands. One fairly independent subplot deals with the attempts of the ambitious Alexey Deuteropopoff to make his fortune in capitalism after losing his former faith in communism. However, most of the action of *Pie in the Sky* involves several plot strands that center on the wealthy Yorke family, led by patriarch Carder Yorke, who has risen from working-class origins to found a successful clothing manufacturing company in the town of Bursley, largely through his exploitation of opportunities opened up to him by World War I. Also prominent in the text are Carder's two sons, Bernard and Fenner. The priggish Bernard works with Carder in the clothing firm but actively disapproves of the tendency of his widower father to become involved in amorous adventures with his housekeepers. Fenner, on the other hand, has no interest in the firm but works instead as a journalist in London. He also has leftist tendencies and has become involved in the activities of the Communist Party, partially because of his romantic interest in Caroline Bolton, a young communist woman who also grew up in Bursley. If fact, their two families have had a long relationship dating back to the youthful friendship between Carder and Caroline's father, Henry Bolton. Henry, however, had gone off to fight in World War I, while Carder stayed home and became rich. After the war, Henry became an employee of Carder's firm, but by the time of the action in *Pie in the Sky* he has lost his job after a long layoff due to an injury. Unable to find other work, Henry runs away from home and goes on the tramp, seeking work as he goes and meanwhile spending time in jail after he is unfairly convicted of poaching on the grounds of a rich estate. Caroline works as a teacher in London, but she loses her job as well when forced to resign from her teaching post due to rumors about her involvement with Fenner. Fenner, however, is far too cynical to become a real communist, leading to tensions that soon end the relationship between himself and Caroline.

Caroline manages to find a secretarial job with the help of the communist leader Turlin, who has risen via talent and hard work from dire poverty to a position of prominence in the Party. Caroline also moves in with the Turlin family to serve as a companion and tutor to their young son. Fenner, meanwhile, becomes romantically involved with Wynne Morris, a young woman who had been Carder's housekeeper and mistress until she left him because of the interference of the sanctimonious Bernard. Carder is thus left alone and in poor health; he eventually goes away to the continent to recover. He is then nearly decimated when he returns to discover that Wynne has taken up with Fenner. The relationship between Wynne and Fenner is further complicated by the fact that she is still married, though her long-estranged husband, Charlie Morris, is ill and near death.

Eventually, many of these complications are ostensibly resolved. Caroline seems happily settled with the Turlins; Charlie dies, and Fenner and Wynne seem headed for marriage; Henry returns to Bursley and he and his wife are offered jobs as Carder's servants. Bernard seems fated to take over the family business, though his management of the firm in Carder's absence was considerably less than successful. Finally, Alexey becomes part owner of a cafe and tobacco shop and is engaged to marry one of his partners. At the same time, however, Alexey seems remarkably unenthusiastic over his coming marriage; there are indications that Caroline may eventually become a disruptive force in the Turlins' marriage; Henry Bolton is insulted by Carder's job offer and has yet to accept it; and Wynne does not, in fact, give an answer to Fenner's proposal of marriage.

There is thus a great deal that is left unresolved at the end of *Pie in the Sky*, which is perhaps in keeping with its overall tone of ambivalence. The book acts almost as a catalog of political concerns in the 1930s and of attitudes toward those concerns, treating unemployment, political activism, bourgeois decadence, ideological manipulation, and gender relationships from a variety of perspectives and in a variety of styles. Indeed, it is this virtuoso stylistic multiplicity that is probably the book's most striking feature, leading Croft to describe it as "a series of technical variations, pastiches and parodies of contemporary British fiction" (117). Croft goes on to note the way Calder-Marshall's novel experimentally explores a wide range of techniques for the presentation of its material, shifting along the way "from social realism through stream of consciousness, romantic journalism and provincial naturalism to Socialist Realism" (264). *Pie in the Sky* is thus, in a sense, not so much a novel about leftist politics in the 1930s as a novel about literary representations of leftist politics in that decade. If nothing else, it serves as an excellent illustration of the diversity of political literature in the 1930s and of the extent to which leftist political concerns impacted even mainstream British literature in the "political" decade. **Selected bibliography:** Croft (*Red Letter Days*); C. Day Lewis (*The Mind*).

ETHEL CARNIE HOLDSWORTH: *THIS SLAVERY* **(1925).** Though the production of British leftist novels in the 1920s was relatively slight in comparison with the 1930s, a number of such novels were written and published. Moreover, as H. Gustav Klaus notes, many of these 1920s novels have distinctive qualities that mark them as works of that decade; these novels therefore form an important chapter in the history of the British novel of the Left that should not be ignored (90). One of the novels discussed by Klaus in this regard is *This Slavery*, which joins earlier Carnie Holdsworth novels such as *Miss Nobody* (1913) and *Helen of Four Gates* (1917) to make her one of the leading British leftist novelists of the first quarter of the twentieth century. However, Klaus also notes that, while many leftist novels of the 1920s are strongly informed by a response to World War I, *This Slavery* shows concerns that are typical of the British leftist novel before World War I, when *This Slavery* may in fact have largely been written. For example, Carnie Holdsworth presents a vivid, naturalistic description of the poverty suffered by mill workers, while contrasting this poverty with the luxurious lifestyles of the rich. In this sense, her work recalls predecessors such as Margaret Harkness. But Carnie Holdsworth, who herself worked in a Lancashire cotton mill from the age of nine, moves significantly beyond Harkness in the elaboration of a legitimate socialist politics, a difference that can be seen most clearly in the consistently negative depiction of religion (including the Salvation Army with which Harkness was so fascinated) as a tool of capitalist ideological domination. On the other hand, Klaus points out that Carnie Holdsworth's particular brand of socialism seems reminiscent of early twentieth-century writers such as Bart Kennedy and Allen Clarke, while it is also clear that *This Slavery* builds directly upon the late-nineteenth-century British tradition of socialist utopianism associated with William Morris.

This Slavery focuses on the all-female Martin family in the mill town of Brayton. Mrs. Martin is the hard-working and long-suffering matriarch of the clan, who has survived the death of her consumptive husband to continue to provide a stable, if modest, home for her mother-in-law, Grandma Martin, and her two daughters, Rachel and Hester. As Part I of the book begins, Hester accepts a marriage proposal from Jack Baines, a local weaver and rising trade union leader. Mrs. Martin, however, intercedes on the grounds that Hester is too young for marriage, and the engagement is canceled. Meanwhile, Barstocks' Mill, where Rachel, Hester, and Mrs. Martin are all employed, is destroyed by a fire, putting them and four hundred others out of work and into dire poverty. The intellectual Rachel spends the free time created by unemployment in studying Marx and becoming more and more involved in politics. When she learns that the mill owner, Barstock, is actually her father, she refuses his offer of money but threatens to reveal his paternity unless he does something to help the unemployed mill workers as a whole. The beautiful and sensitive Hester, on the other hand, devotes her time to music and poetry. One day, she is playing her fiddle in the woods and gains the attention of Sandy Sanderson, a wealthy yarn merchant, who begins to pay court to her. In the meantime, Grandma Martin dies, leaving the remaining Martins to scramble to try to raise enough money to bury her. Sanderson, whose attentions initially receive no response from Hester, loans Mrs. Martin ten pounds to help the family through the crisis, and Hester, tired of poverty and beginning to show signs of the same consumption that killed her father, is no longer able to resist the opportunities afforded by his courtship. At the end of Part I, Hester is engaged to marry Sanderson, while Rachel is (wrongly) arrested and taken to jail for her part in a socialist rally that turned violent after being interrupted by the police.

Part II opens after an interval of six years, during which Hester has had two children, one of whom, Stephen, is crippled. Barstocks' Mill has been rebuilt and Barstock himself is now a member of parliament. Sanderson is running a mill of his own. Business is booming, but the weavers, tired of being worked to death for low wages, are growing increasingly discontent. Led by Baines, they soon go on strike. As the strike stretches from weeks into months, the union's strike fund runs out, and the strikers begin to starve. The mill owners, feeling the pinch as well, bring in scabs to work the mills and arrange to have the militia sent to Brayton to quell the rising threat of violence. Rachel, in the course of her work in support of the strike, becomes romantically involved with Baines. Meanwhile, Stephen contracts diphtheria because his father has been too concerned with business to attend to a sanitary problem in the drains of their mansion. The boy, a strange child who seems old beyond his years (somewhat in the vein of Father Time in Thomas Hardy's *Jude the Obscure*) dies, driving Hester, already torn because of the conflict between her loyalty to her husband and her fundamental class sympathy with the strikers, nearly to distraction. She secretly provides the strikers with inside information about the plans of the owners and eventually donates her jewelry to their strike fund. At one point, Sanderson, discovering these activities, bodily throws her out of the house, and she goes to Baines for shelter. Eventually, however, she decides to honor her marriage vows and returns to Sanderson. The book winds up in a flurry of action as an accidental fire ignites Sanderson's mill, while the owners appear ready to give in to the strikers' demands. Nevertheless, soldiers arrive to break up a rally of the strikers, leading to a violent confrontation in which Hester, attempting to intercede, is shot and killed and Baines is arrested. The book then ends with a final utopian vision of the socialist future, but many elements of the plot are left unresolved. The status of the relationship between Baines and Rachel is unclear; the final outcome of the strike is not revealed; and the impact of the fire in Sanderson's mill is never explored.

This ending has been criticized by observers such as Mary Ashraf, who finds it "abrupt and enigmatic" (190). On the other hand, Ashraf praises *This Slavery* for its portrayal of revolutionary political practice and for the way it makes "the problems of political education, of a mature leadership, of reformism, of mastering revolutionary theory and the lessons of a sharpening conflict in industry" an integral part of the narrative (195). Other critics, including contemporary leftist reviewers, have complained of Carnie Holdsworth's continuing focus on romantic relationships despite the ostensibly political focus of her novel. Still, Pamela Fox suggests that the book's interlacing of personal and political plots, while problematic in many ways, nevertheless contributes to an important investigation of the complex interrelationship of class and gender and to an elaboration of the ways in which women suffer special forms of exploitation that extend beyond capitalism to include patriarchal society as a whole. The book thus "becomes the constellation site for an alternate set of classed and gendered meanings that rewrite its classic story of resistance" (165). *Selected bibliography:* Ashraf; Pamela Fox; Klaus ("Silhouettes").

DAVID CAUTE: *COMRADE JACOB* **(1961).** *Comrade Jacob* is a historical novel based on the activities of the radical "Diggers" in England in 1649, just after the English Civil War had led to the execution of Charles I and to the establishment of a Commonwealth that would come to be dominated by Oliver Cromwell. In particular, the book describes the attempts of the Diggers, under the leadership of Gerrard Winstanley, to establish a utopian community, with complete social and economic equality, on St. George's Hill, near the town of Cobham. This community is based on the cultivation of land, officially owned by Sir Francis Drake, that has long been designated as common grazing land. The community thus poses a fundamental threat to the existing social and economic system, causing the local authorities to react strongly. Indeed, most of the book entails the efforts of the locals, led by Drake; Drake's bailiff, John Taylor; the local parson, John Platt; and Ned Sutton, a prominent local shopkeeper, to dislodge the Diggers from the hill.

When the locals are unable to disperse the Diggers, they call for assistance from Cromwell's army. In response to this call, General Lord Fairfax, a leader of the antiroyalist forces in the recent Civil War, comes into the region with his troops. However, Winstanley meets with Fairfax and makes a strong impression upon him, convincing him to leave the Diggers in peace. Fairfax withdraws, but, at the insistence of Platt and the other locals, he leaves a small detachment of soldiers in the area, under the leadership of Captain John Gladman. Gladman turns out to be an utterly unscrupulous figure, fiercely ambitious and willing to do anything to advance his own social and economic position. Gladman (who clearly serves in the text as a carrier of the new capitalist values that began to take hold in England in the wake of the Civil War) immediately sets about persecuting the Diggers, whose egalitarian philosophy is particularly galling to him as it would make impossible the kind of advancement to which he is ruthlessly devoted. At one point, Gladman horrifies even Platt and the other enemies of the Diggers when he leads a vicious assault in which a small group of Diggers are ambushed while cutting wood. The men among the woodcutters are brutally assaulted and tortured, and a small boy is killed.

Fairfax then intervenes, insisting that no further attacks be made on the Diggers by the soldiers, though Sutton and Taylor continue to lead periodic raids on the hill by groups of local civilians. In response to continuing harassment and to an economic boycott in which local tradesmen refuse to do business with the Diggers, the latter, despite Winstanley's objections, conduct a raid on Cobham in which supplies are taken from various shops (including Sutton's) under threat of violence. Gladman is nearly killed trying to break up the raid, the ultimate result of which is official retribution that leads to the final destruction of the community on St. George's Hill. By the end of the book, many Diggers have been killed or imprisoned, and the rest have been scattered. Winstanley is being taken away in fetters as the book closes, thus completing the defeat of the Diggers.

There is a strong religious element to the beliefs of the Diggers, whose community on St. George's Hill is founded on the basis of a vision experienced by Winstanley in which Jacob (representing the forces of good) defeats Esau (representing the forces of evil) on a hill. At the same time, Caute clearly wants to suggest parallels between the radically egalitarian and communitarian principles of the Diggers and the secular program of modern communism. As Winstanley muses on the demise of his community just before his arrest, the destruction of the Diggers is clearly presented as a marker of the beginning of the era of bourgeois domination in England, while the experiment on St. George's Hill is clearly presented as the forerunner of more modern—and potentially more successful—antibourgeois movements: "The centuries of private ownership are closing in. Some may look back on us as mere ignorant peasants, which is true enough, but we were more than that, we were the pioneers of a great movement, a great ideal, which will one day come to fruit, not when God wills it, but when man wills it. . . . Man's essence, after all, lies in man's existence, not in God's existence. Let the poor and the exploited find a way of coming together. Then, my masters, there will be rivers of blood" (219–20).

Bernard Bergonzi, in fact, criticizes *Comrade Jacob* for focusing too closely on the portrayal of the Diggers as forerunners of modern communism. According to Bergonzi, the book does a good job of describing the community and the principal characters but is ultimately "shackled by a rigid Marxist *schema*; it is a *roman à these* rather than a genuine novel of ideas, though there is no doubt about the author's intelligence and literary skills" (46). Of course, Bergonzi here displays a typical Cold War prejudice in which Marxist ideas are viewed as rigid and inauthentic by definition. In fact, Caute's attempt to locate early origins of the radical tradition in British culture is entirely legitimate and has much in common with the research of historians such as Robert Brenner, who has argued the class nature of the English Revolution, and, especially, Christopher Hill, whose book *The World Turned Upside Down* remains the seminal historical study of the radical groups, such as the Diggers and the Levellers, who played an important role in the social and political turmoil surrounding the English Revolution. Indeed, Hill is acknowledged as an important source of information at the beginning of Caute's book. The work of such historians clearly situates the transformations in seventeenth-century English society as an important beginning point in the overall process of modernity and in the development of both capitalism and opposition to capitalism. Caute's book does likewise, and, if nothing else, it, like Jack Lindsay's *1649*, helps to dramatize the length and richness of the tradition of radical politics in England, however marginal and suppressed that tradition may have become within the context of the capitalist domination of the last few centuries of Western European history. ***Selected bibliography:*** Bergonzi; Brenner; Hill.

DAVID CAUTE: *THE DECLINE OF THE WEST* (1966). *The Decline of the West* traces the history of the fictional African nation of Coppernica (a sort of amalgam of Algeria and the Congo) beginning in the French colonial period, continuing through a violent revolution that leads to independence, and focusing primarily on the postcolonial period when the postrevolutionary regime, led by new president, Raymond Tukhomada, finds itself threatened by enemies on all sides. British, American, and French capitalists (represented by Soames Tufton, Chester Silk, and Aristide Plon, respectively) seek to exploit the nation's rich copper reserves; holdover French military officers, led by the neo-Nazi Armand Keller and the sadistic André Laval, dream of retaking political power in the former colony; and indigenous opponents of the Tukhomada regime, led by the ambitious Fernand Ybele and his lieutenant, the religious fanatic Jean Liwele, work in complicity with these foreign forces in an attempt to overturn the existing order in Coppernica.

Despite his depiction of violence and depravity in Coppernica, Caute's book is surely one of the least Africanist European novels about

Africa, managing to avoid the use (in the tradition of Joseph Conrad's *Heart of Darkness* and carried on more recently in the African novels of Graham Greene and William Boyd) of Africa merely as a milieu for European adventures. For one thing, Caute's Coppernica represents the classic postcolonial situation (warned against by Frantz Fanon in *The Wretched of the Earth*) of ongoing neocolonial capitalist domination by foreign powers working in league with an unscrupulous and decadent indigenous bourgeoisie. Caute, the author of a generally laudatory book-length study of Fanon and his thought, may in fact have derived some of his insights from Fanon.

Caute's backdrop is not only the violence of life in Africa, but the realities of spectacular violence in Europe and America. Caute also manages to treat Africans as sympathetic characters without condescending to them in the manner of Joyce Cary's *Mister Johnson*. In Caute's book the most positive characters are Tukhomada and his supporters, the former guerrilla leader Kundula Maya and the European-educated poet Amah Odouma. Moreover, while Tukhomada's forces do sometimes resort to violence, especially during the revolution through which they come to power, they generally do so only in direct response to the more extreme violence of their enemies. Indeed, it is the very hesitation to employ strong measures against their opponents that leads to the fall of the regime in a counterrevolution engineered by Laval, backed by Plon and Tufton, and featuring Ybele and Liwele as figurehead leaders. Caute, in fact, is quite careful to identify Europe as the principal source of the most extreme violence that afflicts Africa, linking the machinations of Laval, Keller, and others directly to the legacy of Nazism, which hovers like a specter over the text and functions as a key symptom of what Caute diagnoses as a fundamental sickness in the European psyche.

Caute's book is narrated in an essentially realist style, and to some extent it resembles the realist historical novels praised by Georg Lukács in *The Historical Novel*. In his later work, however, Caute moves away from realism and begins to challenge the bourgeois tradition in formal as well as thematic ways. In his book-length essay *The Illusion*, for example, he argues that "realism is burnt-out, obsolete, a tired shadow of a once-living force. It has to go." Meanwhile, in *The Occupation* and *The Demonstration*, a play and novel, which, with *The Illusion*, constitute an unusual multigeneric trilogy, Caute carries out this insight, writing in an antirealistic mode often reminiscent of Bertolt Brecht. Bernard Bergonzi, in fact, suggests that the turn away from realism in the trilogy represents "a defiance of the literary ideals of the Old Left and the central Marxist tradition; notably represented by Lukács's attempt to draw into the cause of progress and historical inevitability not just the historical fiction of Sir Walter Scott, but the whole of nineteenth-century bourgeois realism" (47).

The Decline of the West, on the other hand, might be taken as Caute's attempt to carry out Lukács's advice to look to writers like Scott as models. For example, Caute's characters, though vividly individualized, are also clearly linked to social and historical forces in the mode of the "typical" characters praised by Lukács. In addition to Tukhomada, Silk, Tufton, Plon, Keller, Laval, and Ybele, the book features characters like Jason Bailey (a typical talented, but alienated African-American), Zoe Silk (a dazzlingly beautiful blonde who preys on African American men in search of a sexual energy that she lacks), James Caffrey (an idealistic young British man with no acceptable focus for his idealism), the former British colonial solider Malcolm Deedes, the former Coppernican guerrilla leader Kundula Maya, and the European-educated Coppernican poet/politician Amah Odouma. All of these figures represent identifiable types as much as distinct individuals, and to this extent recall Lukács's emphasis on the central role played in the historical novel by characters whose typicality makes them the embodiment of large social and historical forces rather than individual eccentricities.

For Lukács such characters are effective in the work of a novelist like Scott because of the links they establish between the private (personal) and public (political) dimensions of life, allowing such novels to capture a sense of social totality in their representation of the movement of history. As the bourgeoisie drift into decadence after 1848, European social life is fragmented by a rift between public and private experience that shows up in literature as well. This rift, in fact, is an explicit theme of much of Caute's work, and Caute himself has identified "the tension between man's private and public existences" as the "central 'problematic' of my thinking and writing" (qtd. in Bergonzi 49). In one scene in *The Decline of the West*, Caute presents a confrontation between James Caffrey's idealistic brother, Alec, and their antisemitic father, who is defending the exclusion of Jews from his golf club. The father, who agrees that public British policy should oppose the kind of antisemitism represented by Nazi Germany, nevertheless argues that the club is a separate, private matter: "Now, my home, my private home, the home I have bought with my own money, my own savings and my own sweat— surely I can invite in whom I like? Am I not a free man? Am I taking away someone else's freedom? The club is the same; it's private" (197). Later, Caute presents the story of Malcolm Deedes's impoverished childhood in Scotland, which largely consists of an education in class difference, translating to a growing perception of the separation between the public and private realms and of the dog-eat-dog realities of alienated life under capitalism: "All joys, it seemed, were private, all sorrows public. To be private was to have, to be public was to have taken away, expropriated, distributed. When a friend cast covetous eyes on your ball, bat or stolen bike, it was time to remind him, "It's preevit!" —then fight on the piss-stained concrete, in dank, fetid alleyways, high treble voices shrill as dying birds, blood and yellow-green snot" (501).

Most of Caute's characters, especially the American and European ones, are radically alienated from the social world around them. As a result, despite their ability to represent typical positions within society, they lack the kind of connection to the social totality that for Lukács is central to the characterization of novelists like Scott. But the alienation of Caute's characters from the social totality should not be taken as a limitation in his vision so much as an element of his commentary on bourgeois society. Thus, although Caute's book may show signs of bourgeois decadence, it also presents an extended critique of decadence. The major shortcoming of *The Decline of the West* is its failure to present any sort of utopian dimension or to counter its pessimistic narrative of decline with the presentation of a viable alternative. Indeed, the book reflects a basic pessimism that has often (perhaps for good historical reasons) plagued European leftist thought in recent decades. ***Selected bibliography:*** Bergonzi ("Fictions"); Caute (*Demonstration, Fanon, Illusion, Occupation*); Fanon; Lukács (*Historical Novel*).

SID CHAPLIN: *THE DAY OF THE SARDINE* **(1961).** Narrated by the protagonist from the perspective of several years later, *The Day of The Sardine* relates the transition of teenager Arthur Haggerston from schoolboy to worker in post–World War II Newcastle. The book effectively captures many of the aspects of daily life in Arthur's milieu. It also dramatizes the consequences of a capitalist system that, in its postwar incarnation, is bringing unprecedented affluence to working-class youth but simultaneously bringing about a dehumanizing reification and routinization of every aspect of their lives. Older communal traditions that had sustained the English working class through their economic hardships are no longer viable, and English culture itself is caught up in a globalization of American-dominated late capitalist culture. Thus, Arthur's entry into the world of work is depicted as a sort of surrender, or fall, from the relatively romantic world of youth into the dreary routine of a factory worker in a capitalist system devoid of all spiritual value.

The process of Arthur's entry into the world of work is described as one of submission to mind-numbing routine and of disavowal of the romantic dreams of youth. This point is made clear in the book's title, which is explained early on when Harry Parker, the family boarder (and lover of Arthur's mother, Peg) tells Arthur about his earlier experience fishing for sardines in Norway, noting that the sardines, on their way to spawn, blindly swim by the million into the fishing nets. They are then put in barrels and shipped to England for processing and tinning. "Don't be a sardine," Harry then advises Arthur. "Navigate yourself" (22).

When Arthur assures Harry that he indeed plans to be somebody special and "get filthy rich," Harry simply responds that the rich are simply "another kind of sardine—plush-lined tin, that's all" (22). In short, to get rich one must devote oneself to participation in the capitalist economic system, and there is no escape from the routinization of daily life for anyone who participates in that system.

Harry, who sees himself as something of a free spirit, is at this time employed in a sardine-packing factory, but he argues that he is not a sardine because he lives not to work but works in order to live. The distinction, however, is largely lost on Arthur, and, indeed, by the end of the book Harry, still working in the factory, is married to Peg and is as settled into the routine of daily life as anyone. Arthur does resist incorporation into the capitalist system, primarily through his participation in a youth gang led by his friend, Nosey Carron. The petty criminal activities of this gang allow Arthur a sense that he is not swimming like a sardine into the nets of capitalism, while the group character of the gang's activities allows him to seek a communal dimension that is lacking in his life. But, as Ingrid von Rosenberg points out, gang participation in postwar works such as *The Day of the Sardines* or Colin McInnes's *Absolute Beginnings* (1959) is an ineffective substitute for the traditional structures of family and community that had earlier formed the heart of British working-class culture (162). Indeed, the gang is not a true group but a collection of individuals, and it is no surprise that the gang disintegrates in the course of the book.

Arthur also seeks escape from routinization through sexual and romantic adventures. He becomes sexually involved with Stella, an older married woman whose husband is often away. This relationship is in many ways fulfilling (and at least introduces Arthur to the world of sex), but it is also doomed. Eventually, Stella moves away, and Arthur loses touch with her altogether. Meanwhile, Arthur pursues a more spiritual kind of love with Dorothy, the daughter of an evangelical preacher, whom he regards as too pure to be sullied by sexual advances. But that relationship ends as well after Arthur discovers that Dorothy, too, is human, and has in fact been involved in a sexual dalliance with the brutish Nosey. In short, Arthur's romantic fancies of crime and sex (clearly derived from images he encounters as an avid consumer of American popular culture) all come to nothing, crashing upon the rocks of the world of work. Indeed, as Ronald Paul points out, Chaplin wrote the book after a stint as journalist reporting on the mining industry in the United States, which may account for "the decidedly American Western flavour of both the characterization and style of *The Day of the Sardines*" (65).

Arthur drifts from job to job, hoping to find some form of nonalienated labor that will allow him to derive the necessary income without becoming a sardine. The most important of these jobs is as a laborer helping with the laying of new sewer lines, a job he gets through the influence of his Uncle George, a trade union official. George is initially presented as the book's image of a "success." Not only does he have some modicum of power and respect but he also has considerable wealth, though it is a wealth derived primarily from corruption. He is, in fact, another kind of sardine, and he will eventually end up jailed for life. In any case, Arthur finds little to attract him in George's way of life, and George fires him out of fear that Arthur will reveal George's corrupt dealings. Arthur then makes one last protest against incorporation into the system when he runs away from home after he and Nosey assault the leader of a rival gang and then soon afterward see Nosey's brother, Crab, leaving the scene of a violent murder in which he has killed a woman in a fit of passion. But Arthur's bicycle is soon stolen by a tramp, and Arthur himself grudgingly returns to Newcastle, realizing he cannot escape.

Fortunately, Arthur finds that he is not needed as a witness in the murder case and that he and Nosey are not being sought for assault by the police. Crab, however, is not so lucky. As the only character in the book who had staunchly remained outside respectable society, he is executed for murder. Nosey, meanwhile, turns to religion and is safely reinscribed within the system. Arthur is effectively coopted as well, joining Harry in the sardine-packing plant. His sardinization is thus complete, as is Chaplin's chilling account of the powerful nets and tins of the modern capitalist system. In this sense, *The Day of the Sardines* is an effective novel. On the other hand, the book's depiction of capitalism as a total and inescapable system leaves no room for any suggested alternative or for any significant utopian dimension other than the bogus images offered by American popular culture. The book is, in fact, almost entirely apolitical, and, while its indictment of the dehumanizing consequences of capitalism is compelling, it offers no indication that life might be otherwise. In this sense, *The Day of the Sardines* is not an effective political novel, though it is quite representative of British postwar working-class fiction. ***Selected bibliography:*** Paul (*Fire*); Pickering and Robins ("Making"); von Rosenberg ("Militancy").

SID CHAPLIN: *THE THIN SEAM* **(1950).** Narrated by Christopher Jack, a young Durham coal miner, *The Thin Seam* gives a fictionalized account of one day of work in a mine. As such, it provides some of the most detailed technical descriptions of the actual experience of working in a coal mine that are available in English (or any other) literature. Moreover, this account is provided firsthand by an author who is himself a former miner; it therefore lacks the sometimes stumbling and uncertain quality of the description of coal mining that appears in works by nonminers, such as George Orwell's *The Road to Wigan Pier*. Chaplin himself has expressed the concern that the book is so technical that only other coal miners would be able to understand it (Pickering and Robins 149). And it is certainly true that some the book's vocabulary is difficult for nonminers and some of the scenes in the book are difficult to visualize for anyone who has not had firsthand experience of the mines. Nevertheless, *The Thin Seam* convincingly captures the hardship and danger of mining. For example, one of its central events concerns a fatal accident in which one of the miners is caught in the mining machinery and horribly mangled. Yet, Chaplin does not sensationalize the suffering of the miners. In fact, his book treats coal mines as almost romantic places, though it is reasonably successful at avoiding sentimentality.

The Thin Seam is somewhat autobiographical. A chapter early in the book provides a sketch of Christopher Jack's background, which turns out to resemble Chaplin's in a number of ways. For example, though Chris is not a writer, he has, like his creator, studied economics in college. He therefore feels somewhat distanced from the other miners because of his greater education and more intellectual bent. He has returned to the coal pits with some vague notion of becoming a leader among the miners, but it has become obvious to him that he can provide no such leadership, partly because he feels so isolated from the other miners. Indeed, one of the book's most trenchant political insights is provided by Chris's recognition that the educational system to which he has been exposed is designed not to provide enlightened leaders for the working class but to ensure that the most intellectually talented children of the working class will be lured away from participation in that class. Looking at the educational system as a whole, Chris concludes that "it appeared that its sole function was to draw away the potential leaders" from the working class (35).

The Thin Seam demonstrates just how effective this system has been. Even Chris, who understands how the system works and who remains staunchly sympathetic to the working class, can no longer really feel at home among the miners. Indeed, he spends much of the day narrated in the book dreaming of escape from mining into a better and more intellectually stimulating life. In a sense, *The Thin Seam* is, itself, a dramatization of this phenomenon. The book shows Chaplin's extensive knowledge of mining and it is certainly sympathetic to the miners. But it has no real agenda for political action and can provide no leadership for such action, which is presented in the book as pointless. Thus, the miner Andrews, who is the book's most antiauthoritarian figure, is described as an "impotent rebel" (158). Chaplin himself describes his project as a writer as an attempt to provide "insight and perception" to the people "who give him all his material." But he also suggests that he does not believe in "agitprop" or in the ability of literature to effect genuine social and political change (Pickering and Robins 149). *The Thin Seam* thus illustrates a trend typical of British working-class literature after World War II in which numerous writers retreated from calls for political action and simply concentrated on description of working-class life, often focusing on the phenomenon of *déclassement* and on the psychic tribulations of individuals isolated from their class rather than on solidarity and collective activity. *Selected bibliography:* Peter Lewis; Pickering and Robins ("Making").

ALLEN CLARKE: *THE RED FLAG* (1908). Allen Clarke, who worked for a time in the 1870s in the cotton mills of his native Lancashire before moving on to become a teacher and writer, was one of the leading British working-class novelists of the late nineteenth and early twentieth centuries. As Paul Salveson outlines, Clarke was a central figure in the Lancashire school of novelists (which also included such writers as Arthur Laycock, John Tamlyn, and Fred Plant), who described in their fiction conditions of working-class life in Lancashire around the turn of the century. Though sometimes critical of specific trade unionist practices, Clarke's political position was essentially that represented by the Independent Labour Party (ILP), a relatively moderate socialist organization that largely aligned itself with trade unionism and that tended to envision socialism as a matter of fairness and morality rather than the ultimate result of proletarian class struggle. Clarke elaborates this position in a number of works that address a variety of socialist and working-class issues in ways that tend to lack theoretical sophistication but that show a close connection to working-class life in Lancashire. The same might be said for nonfiction works such as *The Effects of the Factory System* (1899), which rails against the evils of modern factories within the context of a call for a return to the less automated and more decentralized system of craft industries.

Though a writer of historical novels such as *The Lass at the Man and Scythe* (1889, about the English Civil War), Clarke concentrates on relatively contemporary Lancashire settings in most of his novels. *The Knobstick* (1893), a strike novel based on the Bolton Engineers' Lock-Out of 1887, represents both this particular event and the general regional culture of Lancashire in a highly effective way, though it does sometimes descend into melodrama and does not really investigate the ultimate origins of the conflict (Klaus 84). Novels such as *The Little Weaver* (1893) and *Driving* (1901) contain particularly detailed descriptions of working conditions in contemporary factories, while works such as *A Daughter of the Factory* (1898, which features Rose Hilton, a female revolutionary) pay special attention to the plight of women workers. *Lancashire Lasses and Lads* (1896) is typical of Clarke's ability to present the life of a working-class community with an effectiveness that has been described by Jack

Mitchell as informed by an "inexhaustible curiosity about the lives of ordinary working-class men *and* women that leads straight into Tressell" (64). However, of all of Clarke's novels, *The Red Flag* is probably the most politically coherent in its direct presentation of socialism as a solution to the ills described in all of his works.

The Red Flag opens as an older woman, Mrs. Wilkinson, travels about Lancashire as a tramp, accompanied by her younger companion, May. In the course of their travels and their stays at various workhouses and other facilities for the poor, Mrs. Wilkinson and May gain an appreciation of the extreme hardships suffered by the unemployed, however virtuous they may be. They also meet a variety of other characters, including the upright Jim Campbell, who has lost his job because of his participation in a trade union, and the bitter Ronald Fordham, the illegitimate son of a millionaire who refuses to acknowledge him. In the course of the book, Campbell eventually makes his may to Brunborough (based on Burnley, in northeast Lancashire), where he comes upon a gathering being addressed by the socialist leader Summerfield. Campbell, already aware through direct experience of the evils of capitalism, is attracted by Summerfield's speech, and then goes with Summerfield to the socialist club where he is given food and lodgings for the night. As he drifts off to sleep that night, Campbell experiences a vision in which the masses of the poor arise behind the Red Flag of socialism to demand justice and humane treatment, described in what Salveson calls "one of the most moving pieces of imaginative socialist writing" (183). Summerfield then helps Campbell to get a job and to become involved in the socialist movement. Campbell also locates his old mother, for whom he has been searching in the course of his travels, and they live happily together in a modest house in Brunborough, though she, worn out by a lifetime of labor and hardship, dies soon afterward. Campbell also discovers that Mrs. Wilkinson, the middle-class wife of a minister, and May, a weaver in a factory, are not actually tramps; they were merely attempting to learn about tramp life first hand. Jim realizes that he loves May, and they are eventually married. Fordham, meanwhile, shoots and kills his father, the pompous magnate, Langdon, then shoots himself. He survives, however, and is convicted of murder, though widespread protests lead to the commutation of his death sentence.

That the plot of *The Red Flag* is weak and rather melodramatic is beside the point. Clarke's fictional structure is merely an apparatus to allow him to describe in vivid and shocking detail the conditions of the lives of the poor and to suggest that these conditions can only be improved by the greater justice that a socialist society could bring about. The book is also interesting in its presentation of factional disagreements within socialism, though Clarke makes clear his preference for the more moderate positions described in the text. In the speeches of Summerfield and in various debates and conversations among the characters, Clarke presents many of the basic tenets of socialism in a way that is clearly designed to convince the skeptical that a socialist society would not be nearly as threatening as they might fear. Indeed, there is a tendency in the book to present socialism as a sort of modern version of Christianity, thus making it more ideologically palatable to the British populace.

The book also tends to support moderate moves toward socialism and to depict violent revolution (espoused in the text primarily by the bitter, cynical, and deranged Fordham) as an unnecessary form of extremism. *The Red Flag* ends as the workers of the area gather on a hilltop for a massive socialist demonstration in a show of community and solidarity that is clearly intended to convey the utopian potential that resides in socialist fellowship as opposed to capitalist competition. This demonstration (based on the international demonstrations for an eight-hour work day organized for May Day of 1890 by the Second International) suggests the power — and ultimate triumph — of the masses, though again in a mode devoid of suggestions of revolutionary violence. **Selected bibliography:** Klaus ("The Strike Novel"); Mitchell ("Tendencies"); Salveson.

G.D.H. COLE AND MARGARET COLE: *CORPSE IN CANONICALS* **(1930).** *Corpse in Canonicals* is one a number of detective novels authored by the husband-and-wife team of G.D.H. and Margaret Cole in the 1920s and 1930s. Other such novels include *The Death of a Millionaire* (1925), *Poison in the Garden Suburb* (1929), *Burglars in Bucks* (1930), and *Off with Her Head!* (1938). However, despite their success as authors of detective fiction, the Coles are probably best known as leftist historians and social commentators. For example, G.D.H. Cole's *A Short History of the British Working-Class Movement* (first published in, then reissued in an updated edition in 1948) is one of the leading histories of British working-class activism, while Margaret Cole's memoir, *Growing Up into Revolution* (1949), is a rich source of information about British leftist culture through most of the first half of the twentieth century. The Coles coauthored one of the best sources of information about social and economic conditions in Britain in the 1930s, *The Condition of Britain* (1937). It might also be noted that Margaret Cole was the sister of Raymond Postgate, himself both a leftist historian and a detective novelist. Indeed, one of G.D.H. Cole's most important works of history, *The Common People, 1746–1946* (1949, reissued in 1992), was coauthored with Postgate.

Corpse in Canonicals is a representative example of the detective fiction produced by the Coles. Relatively conventional in form, the book begins with a perplexing murder, proceeds as a central sleuth (in this case Superintendent Wilson of Scotland Yard) unravels a confusing array of clues, and ends as Wilson reveals the identity of the murderer and explains the process of deduction by which he reached his final conclusions. There are, however, a few key characteristics that set *Corpse in Canonicals* apart from the mainstream of British detective fiction and perhaps subtly reveal the leftist orientation of the authors. For one thing, the victim, as the title indicates, is a clergyman, the Rev. Leconfield Barrington. For another, the body is found in the garden of the local chief constable, Colonel Welsh. Both the identity of the victim and the location of the corpse suggest an intrusion of violence into realms of British life that one might expect to be relatively placid, thus suggesting that a certain violence lurks beneath the seemingly calm surface of British bourgeois society as a whole.

This suggestion is reinforced by the fact that, through most of the book, the prime suspect seems to be the Rev. Almeric Prothero, a local parson. Indeed, though Wilson eventually concludes that Prothero was not involved in the murder, we find that Prothero was involved with the victim, who was blackmailing him with information about of a sexual indiscretion committed by Prothero earlier in his career. Moreover, the true killer, according to Wilson's reasoning, is another local parson, the Rev. Septimus Shaw. The suggestion that the official version of British reality may be inaccurate is further supported by the fact that both Reverend Shaw and Reverend Barrington have secret alternative identities (as the metal craftsman Stephen Smith and the explorer Matthew Boulton, respectively) and have for some time been involved in a series of spectacular jewelry thefts.

Wilson seems to be the only exception to this series of indications that the bastions of British society may not be what they appear. Yet, *Corpse in Canonicals* ends with a final subtlety that potentially undermines Wilson and suggests that justice may not be served in the case after all. Shaw-Smith protests his innocence to the very end, but he is convicted of the murder on purely—and somewhat shaky—circumstantial evidence. Moreover, Wilson, as he announces his deduction, predicts that this conviction will occur even without real proof. After all, Wilson points out, it is clear that the accused has been involved in a series of criminal acts, and this past involvement alone should convince any jury to convict him. When local resident Algernon Prior (who also turns out to have a secret identity, that of the vastly successful detective novelist Arthur Bentwich) protests that a conviction for murder on the basis of evidence of past acts of theft would be unjust and prejudicial, Wilson simply dismisses the protest as a quibble, assuring Prior that Shaw-Smith must be guilty and that any jury that uses "common-sense" will no doubt agree once they are made aware of his process of reasoning. In short, the British legal system is such that a man can be convicted of murder without convincing evidence, if only an authoritative figure, such as Wilson, assures the jury that the man is guilty. *Corpse in Canonicals* thus employs a number of subtle strategies to indicate that appearance and reality are not necessarily the same in modern British society, while also suggesting that the dependability with which justice is typically administered in the British detective novel is more a literary convention than a social truth. The book is thus a good example of the oppositional potential of the detective novel as a genre, just as the fiction of the Coles as a whole indicates the breadth of Left cultural production in Britain in the twentieth century. *Selected bibliography:* G.D.H. Cole (*Short History*); G.D.H. Cole and Margeret Cole (*Condition*); G.D.H. Cole and Postgate (*Common People*); M. Cole (*Growing Up*).

JACK COMMON: *THE AMPERSAND* **(1954).** *The Ampersand* is the sequel to Common's earlier *Kiddar's Luck*. Both books are autobiographical and feature a protagonist who is very similar to Common himself, though for some reason the name of the protagonist has been changed from Will Kiddar to Will Clarts in the later book. Clarts, however, is clearly the same figure as Kiddar, with the same background in a working-class family from the Newcastle suburb of Heaton. Indeed, *The Ampersand* begins precisely where *Kiddar's Luck* leaves off, as the protagonist, having finished his schooling at age fourteen (in 1917), contemplates his next move in life, a decision complicated by the fact that he wishes neither to pursue higher education nor to enter the dreary existence of the manual worker. Fascinated by the power and mysteries of the world of capitalist commerce (symbolized by all impressive looking firms with "& Co." in their names—thus the "ampersand" of the book's title), Will decides to enroll in Skilbeck's Commercial College in order to prepare himself for this new world. Much of the first half of the book details Will's experiences in the college, the curriculum of which he finds rather tedious but relatively easy. This section also details Will's own initial subversive foray into capitalism, in which he sells stolen pencils and other supplies (pilfered by his neighborhood friend, Alf, who works in a factory uncrating incoming shipments of such supplies) to his fellow students.

The second half of the book details Will's early experiences in the world of work, which he enters after completing the one-year course at the college. After some initial difficulty, he lands a job in Newcastle as an office boy for Mealing and Dillop, a firm of solicitors. Having learned the latest office techniques in his college, Will is at first put off by the antiquated procedures employed by his new firm, but he finds the surroundings in the dusty old office relatively congenial. The work is easy, and he has abundant spare time to spend reading books or playing chess against himself while on the job. He soon becomes the trusted minion of Mr. Dillop, one of the partners, running a variety of errands related to Dillop's mysterious (but clearly less than reputable) financial dealings.

These dealings also afford Will with ample opportunities for skimming, and for a time he lives a life of luxury that allows him to impress his friends and to conduct a somewhat half-hearted courtship of Mabel, a girl from his own Heaton, though he has no interest in marriage. Eventually, however, Will's friends abandon him out of fear that association with his ill-gotten gains will get them into trouble. Will breaks up with Mabel as well, and for a time he cultivates his sense of himself as a sort of Byronic loner, an image he has derived from his own voracious reading of adventure novels and avid viewing of American films. Soon, however, his embezzling is discovered, and he is dismissed from his job. Faced with arrest if he does not return the stolen funds and terrified of the reaction of his father if he should learn of the thefts, Will, now seventeen, runs away from home. The book then ends as he is on his way to London, hoping to make his fortune there.

Because it limits itself to the point of view of the teenage protagonist, *The Ampersand* is not terribly sophisticated in its political analysis. Indeed, Common, himself, was never strongly aligned with any particular political perspective other than an undying loyalty to the working class. The book does, however, present a vivid picture of working-class life in Newcastle and the surrounding suburbs during the period 1917-20, perhaps because it is so closely based on Common's own experiences— though, as Michael Pickering and Kevin Robins point out, the book is less directly autobiographical than *Kiddar's Luck* (80). Moreover, Will Clarts is an intelligent, well-read, and imaginative teenager, and he is already beginning to understand a great deal about the society that surrounds him. The book is particularly good in its exploration of the various internal conflicts within Will as he struggles with a number of competing inclinations. On the one hand, his great love of books makes the life of the mind attractive to him. On the other hand, the power and wealth offered by success in the world of business have their own allure. And both of these impulses must compete with Will's fundamental sense of loyalty to his class, from which he already knows he will be estranged either by scholarly accomplishment or financial success.

The key conflict in the book, however, may be that between Will's sense of collective solidarity with his class and the individualist tendencies encouraged by the bourgeois popular culture of which he is such an enthusiastic consumer and the capitalist economic system in which he is a rather ambivalent new participant. As Ronald Paul puts it, beneath Will's essentially comic (and somewhat Dickensian) adventures lies a serious attempt to "show a case of the individualist disorientation of a working-class outlook and attitude" (91). Thus Will's petty thefts, which ostensibly begin as a demonstration of contempt for bourgeois values (justified by the socialist slogan "Property is theft"), end up as the activities of a lone outlaw, alienated not only from his middle-classes bosses but from his working-class pals. In this, the book joins a whole family of modern British novels dealing with the phenomenon of *déclassement*, though, as Paul points out, its specific focus on the transmutation of class struggle into petty crime is especially typical of working-class novels from the post–World War II era (92). The book leaves off with its various conflicts unresolved (and perhaps unresolvable), though Common's own difficult struggle to be both a writer and a loyal member of the working class (which led to a life of poverty and frustration) suggests the direction Will's subsequent life might take. ***Selected bibliography:*** Paul (*Fire*); Pickering and Robins ("Revolutionary Materialist").

JACK COMMON: *KIDDAR'S LUCK* **(1951).** *Kiddar's Luck* is an autobiographical novel based on Common's working-class childhood in Heaton, Newcastle. It traces the life of its protagonist, Will Kiddar, from his birth in 1903 to his completion of school at age fourteen, during World War I. The book shows Will at home with his family, at play with the neighborhood boys, and in class at his working-class school. In so doing, it indicates the hardships and limitations encountered by British working-class children without becoming maudlin; it also shows the joys available to children via working-class culture without romanticizing that culture. The book clearly suggests, in fact, that the experiences of a working-class childhood are in many ways far richer than those available to children from the upper classes. At the same time, the special freedoms allowed to working-class children are presented as an all-too-brief prelude to an adult life of unending labor and responsibility.

Kiddar's Luck is particularly good at tracing the evolution of Kiddar's consciousness of class and indicating how his class position dictates the opportunities available to him in British society. In that sense, the book's treatment of education is particularly crucial. Will is, from the beginning, an intelligent and sensitive child who is especially attracted to literature. He can already read by the time he starts school at age five, trained by reading the comics with his father, a large and powerful railwayman. Indeed, young Kiddar learns many valuable lessons from his working-class father, despite the fact that the latter is an imposing and distant figure who looms over the household like an occupying army. In particular, Kiddar's father is a loyal trade union member who well appreciates the realities of class struggle in Britain. For example, when World War I begins, Kiddar is surprised to find that his father has absolutely no enthusiasm for fighting Germans in the interest of his "freedom as a Briton." In fact, the elder Kiddar insists that "as a Briton, he didn't have any; he was a British wage-slave, and what freedom he had he'd fought for through the trades union movement; he'd continue to fight for it whether the railway company was owned by Englishmen, Jews, Germans or Scots" (98).

Not surprisingly, young Kiddar finds the fare offered by his school boring compared to his experiences with popular culture. School is thus the first step toward the end of childhood freedom and the beginning of adult drudgery and routine. In fact, Kiddar, narrating the events from the perspective of later experience, concludes that the educational system is largely designed to accommodate working-class youth to the boredom they will experience throughout their lives as workers. The young Kiddar is forced to struggle against his school in order to keep his active imagination alive. After an early period of cutting school with one of his friends, Kiddar eventually begins to attend classes regularly, but he continues to find that the banal and repetitive offerings of his school pale in comparison to his own outside reading. This reading, meanwhile, is extensive; it eventually includes English literature as well as a variety of adventure novels and popular boys' magazines. However, it is particularly desultory because the boy largely reads the bits and pieces of books and magazines left in the family outhouse in lieu of toilet paper. As Kiddar grows older, he becomes more and more aware of the fact that the educational system in his school is oriented primarily toward identifying exceptional boys who can win scholarships and thus move on to "Better Things," that is, to further education that will allow them to move out of the working class. Indeed, Will eventually realizes that the goal of his working-class school was to turn out "less recruits for the working-class than any other of its kind in the district" (84). Meanwhile, the boys (like Kiddar) who are unlikely to win such scholarships are largely marking time in the school until they reach age fourteen and can go to work. It is clear that Kiddar's most valuable lessons in working-class life are learned not in his school but from his own reading, his experiences with his friends, and his observations of his father and other working-class men.

Because of these influences, Kiddar, despite the fact that his love of literature and his facility with English composition sets him somewhat apart from his friends, maintains his sense of himself as a member of the working class—as opposed to the scholarship boys, who are specifically trained in ways that alienate them from their working-class origins. On the other hand, when Kiddar finishes school, he finds that there are no jobs that really interest him. He wiles away the summer, then finally begins to think seriously about finding a job after his father complains about his idleness. Embarrassed, Kiddar scans the job listings in the local newspaper and prepares to write a letter of application. But the book ends as he instead envisions an imaginary ideal letter in which he openly declares his loyalty to the working class and his view of his potential boss as a class enemy. Moreover, in a reference that explains the book's title, he also honestly admits that he is interested in the job only because luck has brought nothing better his way, while he continues to hope that eventually his luck will change.

Kiddar's Luck provides a striking and vivid evocation of the day-to-day texture of working-class life. Moreover, despite the fact that Common has received very little recognition as a writer, the book is extremely well written, informed by a sophisticated, literate, and ironic style that nevertheless manages to stay true to the colloquial realities of its subject matter. Pickering and Robins summarize Common's technique: "What Common does is to marry literary technique and style, in this process of retrospection, with certain qualities and features of popular oral cultural expression, ranging from the commonplace but localized traditions of repartee and kidding, through the idiomatic narratives of the raconteur and folk-tale teller, to the more formal characteristics of monologue recitation and stand-up comic turns" (79). Though necessarily limited in scope because of its focus on a single protagonist who never gets beyond age fourteen, *Kiddar's Luck* thus not only accurately documents the realities of working-class childhood experience in the early twentieth century but points the way toward a genuinely working-class mode of literary autobiography. **Selected bibliography:** Paul (*Fire*); Pickering and Robins ("Revolutionary Materialist").

A. J. CRONIN: *THE STARS LOOK DOWN* **(1935).** The Scottish novelist and physician A. J. Cronin was the author of numerous novels during the period from the 1930s to the 1960s. Many of these were highly successful, and several were made into commercial films, including *Hatter's Castle* (1931, film version 1941), *The Citadel* (1937, film version 1938), and *The Keys of the Kingdom* (1942, film 1944). The latter two, respectively, draw upon his experience as a physician and his strong Roman Catholic faith, as does much of his work. But he is best known worldwide as a novelist of working-class life. His central achievement in this regard is probably *The Stars Look Down* (1935, film version 1939). This novel centers on social injustices in the Northern England mining town of Sleescale, near Tynecastle. The book is broad in scope, following the fortunes of a number of characters from its beginning in the first decade of the twentieth century to its end in the depression years of the 1930s. Cronin is clearly critical of the inequalities of British class society, and its sympathies are always with the working-class characters, who have a humanity and even a nobility that contrast strongly with the depiction of upper-class characters as either cold and heartless or ruthless and dishonest. But Cronin's politics are more liberal than radical, while his aesthetics are strictly bourgeois, seemingly designed not to promote proletarian class consciousness but to provoke emotional reactions in a middle-class readership.

The Stars Look Down begins as the miners in the Neptune mine, led by Robert Fenwick, protest the unsafe working conditions in a new area, the Scupper Flats, that has recently been opened to mining by the greedy mine owner, Richard Barras. The miners are locked out as a result of their protest and are soon forced to go back to work on Barras's terms. Luckily, however, Barras has by this time lost the new contract that made mining the Scupper Flats profitable, so he ceases work in the area for the time being. In the early part of the book, Cronin gets considerable mileage from the contrast between the living conditions of the working-class Fenwicks and the wealthy Barrases, much in the way that Émile Zola, in *Germinal*, had contrasted his miners and mine owners. As the book proceeds, the focus on these families continues, though shifting to the next generation, with Richard's son, Arthur, and Robert's son, David, emerging as major characters.

Arthur is a sensitive young man who lacks his father's ruthless drive to secure profit by any means necessary. When the reopening of Scupper Flats leads to an accident that kills dozens of miners, including Robert Fenwick, Arthur is horrified, especially as he suspects that his father had knowingly sent the men into danger. He becomes obsessed with the accident, and spends years seeking evidence of his father's true involvement in the disaster. Meanwhile, when World War I begins, Arthur, regarding the conflict as senseless, refuses to serve in the army and is sent to prison by a tribunal headed by his own father. Soon after Arthur's release from prison, the body of Robert Fenwick is finally recovered—and with it evidence of Richard Barras's guilt in the mine accident. When Arthur confronts his father with this evidence, the elder Barras collapses with a stroke, leaving Arthur to manage the mine. Arthur institutes a number of reforms and invests heavily in making the Neptune the safest and most modern mine in the region.

David Fenwick is the most important character in *The Stars Look Down*. Slightly older than Arthur, David works in the mines as a teenager, but also studies hard and eventually manages to win a scholarship to attend college in Tynecastle. There he struggles with poverty, but remains devoted to his studies until he falls in love with Jenny Sunley, who insists that he interrupt his schooling to take a job so they can be married. With the help of Richard Barras, he manages to secure a teaching position back in Sleescale. David remains determined eventually to get his B.A., though he finds most of his time taken up either by his teaching duties or by his demanding and pretentious wife. Jenny's shallow dreams of social advancement come strongly into conflict with David's devotion to his studies and determination to help the miners of Sleescale improve their lives. Indeed, one of the major weaknesses of *The Stars Look Down* is its tendency to treat women stereotypically as shallow and selfish and as impediments to men who are seeking to do important work. Meanwhile, David also tutors Arthur Barras, though he runs afoul of Richard Barras when he warns the latter of the dangers of mining in Scupper Flats. When these warnings are ignored, David publicly accuses Barras of guilt in the ensuing accident. As a result, David is fired from his teaching job and struggles with unemployment, eventually going to France with an ambulance unit during World War I.

After the war, David finds his marriage is in ruins. Indeed, Jenny runs away and disappears after revealing that the unscrupulous Joe Gowlan, supposedly David's friend, was actually the father of the son David had thought to be his. The boy had died of illness during the war. Nevertheless, David experiences a great deal of professional success during this period, devoting himself to the cause of the miners and eventually becoming an important trade union figure. Indeed, he is eventually elected to parliament as a Labour Party candidate. In parliament, David vigorously defends the rights of workers, but he finds that his efforts are largely in vain, even when the Labour government of Ramsay MacDonald comes into power. David discovers that many of the Labour Party politicians (and even union leaders) with whom he comes into contact do not share his idealistic devotion to the cause of the miners but are instead more interested in personal gain. Eventually, David loses his parliamentary seat as well as his union position, and by the end of the book he is forced to resume work as a miner in the Neptune, having thus come full circle.

Gowlan is the other major character of *The Stars Look Down*. The son of a Sleescale miner, Joe runs away to Tynecastle to seek his fortune. There, he finds a job working in a foundry owned by Stanley Millington. He also becomes romantically and sexually involved with Jenny Sunley, but gradually begins to tire of her and is delighted when she shows an interest in David Fenwick. This gives Joe an opportunity to get out of the relationship, claiming Jenny has forsaken him for David. Joe then wanders about, becomes involved in various shady dealings, including a renewed affair with Jenny that results in the birth of their son. During the war, Joe returns to Tynecastle and to the Millington Foundry, where he is given a job after claiming (falsely) to have been rejected for military service because of a bad knee. He advances quickly in the foundry and, through a combination of hard work and ruthless maneuvering, rises to become the works manager. When Millington himself joins the army and goes to Europe to fight, Joe is left to run the plant—and to begin an affair with Laura Millington, Stanley's wife.

Joe opportunistically converts most of the foundry's production to munitions, and the foundry prospers greatly during the war. Stanley returns from the war with shell shock, leaving the road open for Joe to seize control of the foundry, eventually buying it with his partner, Jim Mawson. The firm of Mawson and Gowlan, having gained considerable capital from war profiteering, gradually grows into a huge conglomerate, acquiring numerous other companies on the way. One of them is the Neptune mine, which they purchase at the beginning of the 1930s from Arthur when postwar financial difficulties combine with extensive damage caused by an attack of disgruntled miners on the Neptune's engine to bring him to the brink of financial ruin. Arthur becomes an employee of Joe in the management of the mine, while Joe buys and moves into the estate in which the Barras family has long lived in Sleescale. From there, he goes into politics, eventually using his power and wealth to unseat David Fenwick as the representative of the Sleescale area in parliament. Thus, while the idealistic David ultimately fails to achieve his goals, the unprincipled Joe succeeds mightily, becoming a powerful magnate.

In the sweeping scope with which it narrates the important historical changes occurring in the first decades of the twentieth century, *The Stars Look Down* is in some ways a sort of British version of John Dos Passos's *U.S.A.* trilogy—without the modernist literary innovations and with a healthy added dose of melodrama and sentimentality. The book is to some extent successful in linking the biographies of its individual characters to larger historical events, but there is no real sense in the book of history as a coherent process driven by understandable causes. Rather, the book's appeals to sentiment and melodrama greatly inhibit its effectiveness as a political novel, no matter how telling its critique of modern capitalism. The misfortunes of characters such as David Fenwick and Arthur Barras are ultimately presented as personal defeats that seem inevitable rather than signs of public, class-based oppression that might be effectively overcome. The different trajectories taken by the careers of David and Arthur, as opposed to that of Joe Gowlan, imply a clear criticism of modern capitalist society as one in which ruthless ambition and unscrupulous destruction of one's enemies is the key to success. Unfortunately, however, *The Stars Look Down* suggests neither that radical action should be taken to change the system nor that socialism might provide a superior alternative. **Selected bibliography:** Salwak (*A. J. Cronin*); Salwak (*A. J. Cronin: A Reference Guide*).

C. DAY LEWIS: *STARTING POINT* (1937). C. Day Lewis, one of the leading British poets of the twentieth century and the poet laureate of England from 1968 to 1972, is best known as a novelist for the numerous detective novels he published under the name of Nicholas Blake. *Starting Point*, which has some of the graceful ironic style of the Blake detective novels, is probably the best-known novel published by Day Lewis under his own name, and it is one of the literary works that best expresses the political position of its author as a member of the Communist Party from 1935 to 1938. Despite its clear leftist perspective, *Starting Point* is not a proletarian novel. Indeed, it confines itself to the representation of middle- and upper-class characters from Day Lewis's own middle-class perspective, presenting a sort of cross-section of this sector of British society within the context of the troubled climate of the 1930s. As such, the book is largely successful, and its exploration of the political responsibilities of its middle-class protagonists represents an important contribution to British leftist literature despite the lack of working-class characters. Indeed, many leftist commentators have found Day Lewis's focus on characters from class positions similar to his own a major strength of the book as it prevented him from having to attempt to represent working-class characters about whose lives he had very little direct experience, whatever his sympathies with their plight under capitalism.

Starting Point focuses on a group of four friends, beginning with their days together as students at Oxford in the mid-1920s. These four protagonists include Henry Voyce and John Henderson, of relatively modest middle-class origins; Theodore Follett, son of the famous actress Harriet Blair; and Anthony Neale, son of an old family of English landowners. They are first characterized through their varying reactions to the General Strike of 1926: Follett remains haughtily aloof from the entire event; Voyce and Henderson support the strikers but actually do very little to help them; Neale, who is identified by David Smith as a composite of Day Lewis and his friend Rex Warner and who will eventually become the most important of the central characters, sympathizes with the strikers but is so troubled by this radical challenge to the social order that he ends up working as a volunteer to keep public services running in London during the strike. However, he ceases his volunteer work after a conversation with a striking worker and decides to return to Oxford for the remainder of the strike.

The four friends soon complete their studies and begin to pursue careers in the early 1930s. Henderson, the son of a parson of relatively slight means, pays a visit to the impressive Neale estate, where he meets Anthony's younger sister, Brenda (who seems quite taken with him) and Anthony's titled father, who subsequently uses his influence to secure a job for Henderson as a chemist for Chemical Combines, a large London firm. Neale himself, with the advantage of wealth, is able to devote himself to improving conditions for the workers on his family estate, though he also pursues a career as a teacher in a local school. Voyce turns to social work, serving as a volunteer worker in and then the manager of a Boys' Club in the East End of London. The cynical Follett, in contrast, remains aloof from the world while working as a novelist. Through the paths taken by these four characters, Day Lewis is able to address the variety of opportunities available to Oxford-educated young men in England in the 1930s, always paying special attention to the various ways his characters deal with their political responsibilities amid the turmoil of this difficult decade.

Voyce makes his contribution on an essentially personal, local level, doing little to try to change the system, but dedicating himself to improving the lives of the underprivileged boys who come to his club. Meanwhile, he enters into a love affair with the much older Harriet Blair. Follett, on the other hand, makes no contribution whatsoever, and his depiction clearly serves as Day Lewis's critique of disengaged artists and intellectuals who attempted to ignore the crisis situation around them in the 1930s while retreating into their own ivory-tower worlds. Not surprisingly, Follett grows more and more bitter and cynical (he has some of the nastiness of an Evelyn Waugh), despite his success as a novelist. He eventually commits suicide after he accidentally shoots and kills his mother during an altercation over the affair she is having with Voyce. Voyce is then left to deal with his grief, feeling so guilty over the two deaths that he eventually retreats from the world altogether and enters a monastery.

Neale and Henderson have more sophisticated understandings of the political and economic situation in Britain in the 1930s than their two friends. But they also find that their class positions make it difficult for them to act on their beliefs. Henderson, a declared socialist even in his Oxford days, is troubled by his growing understanding of the complicity between Chemical Combines and the capitalist system he so deplores, especially after market considerations lead the firm to cancel a project that would have led to the development of an inexpensive supply of healthy food for the poor. But, wanting to keep his middle-class position, especially after marrying Brenda and starting a family, Henderson does nothing to protest the policies of his firm and even humiliates himself by groveling before his boss when the latter warns him to avoid participation in leftist political activities. Henderson thus puts his work as a scientist before his political responsibilities, somewhat along the lines of Bertolt Brecht's Galileo. Neale, on the other hand, has a modest independent income, even after the Depression brings hard times to his family, leading to the sale of their estate. Nevertheless, he still hopes to pursue his work as a teacher, feeling that he can make an important contribution to the education of the next generation. However, he finds that his growing leftist political commitment conflicts sharply with his teaching career, and his hesitation over whether to join the Communist Party (knowing it will cost him his job) becomes the central conflict of the text. As a compromise, Neale decides to join the Party and to work for its cause in secret, even while giving his pledge to the head master of his school that he will eschew politics.

Starting Point ends with an epilogue set in the late 1930s, a few years after the earlier events related in the book. Neale has now abandoned his earlier compromise, giving up teaching to work openly for the Party, helping to organize volunteers to go to Spain to fight against the fascists there. As the book ends, he announces to his sister and Henderson that he has decided to join the International Brigade himself and will soon depart for Spain. The family man Henderson, who has put his own political commitment aside in the interest of his career as a scientist, at first scoffs at the idea and tries to discourage his brother-in-law. Then, however, he admits that he, himself, is tempted to go to Spain, though Neale urges him to stay home with his family and to work within the Labour Party to generate support for the Spanish Republicans. The point seems to be that different individuals can contribute to the cause of social justice in different ways, and Day Lewis avoids any simplistic suggestion that all right-thinking individuals must pursue the course taken by Neale. The book ends as Neale meditates on his decision to go to Spain, content that he has made the right choice and that the fight in Spain is a step toward the establishment of a better world. Musing on his work of and that of his fellow communists, he realizes that he has at last achieved the sense of fellowship and community that he has long sought and concludes that their contribution will "guide a new world struggling out of the womb. They would live and die and be forgotten: but their lives would be built into the deep foundations of the future of these he was one. With these he was one" (318).

The sense of community that Neale experiences within the Communist Party culminates a major motif in *Starting Point*, in which all of the major characters struggle in one way or another to overcome their alienation by establishing a feeling of belonging to something larger than themselves. For example, Neale experiences something of a sense of community through playing rugby with this teammates in college and through his interaction with his students; to some extent, Henderson hopes to find a certain sense of community through his devotion to science; and it is largely a sense of community that Voyce seeks in his retreat into the monastery. Conversely, it is the absolute lack of any sense of community that leads Follett into radical alienation and eventual suicide.

Ultimately, it is only socialism that offers a viable sense of community by enabling Neale to think of himself as a member of a community that encompasses all of humanity. Similarly, it is only work toward the building of socialism that is presented in *Starting Point* as ultimately fulfilling and worthwhile. Neither Neale's teaching, nor Henderson's science, nor Voyce's religion, nor Follett's literature can offer a similar sense of belonging and accomplishment. The book also suggests that, in a socialist society, all of the characters might have been able to have fulfilling lives by pursuing their own favored activities. Thus, while *Starting Point* does little to explore the lives of those who suffer most extensively under capitalism, it does demonstrate that, in modern capitalist society, even those relatively affluent individuals who profit from the system are denied the opportunity to live happy and fulfilling lives. **Selected bibliography:** Croft (*Red Letter Days*); David Smith (*Socialist Propaganda*).

LEN DOHERTY: ***A MINER'S SONS* (1955).** *A Miner's Sons* combines a clear communist political perspective with a vivid portrayal of the lives of coal miners, both in the mines and in the community at large, to produce one of the most successful British miners' novel since the rich days of the 1930s, when writers such as Harold Heslop and Lewis Jones made the mining novel almost a genre in itself. Like many of his predecessors in this genre, Doherty was himself a miner, which perhaps helps to explain the vividness with which he is able to evoke the lives of miners in *A Miner's Sons* and in his two subsequent miners' novels, *The Man Beneath* (1957) and *The Good Lion* (1958). Doherty's work is especially remarkable for its continuing insistence on communism as the best means by which the miners can achieve social and economic justice, even though Doherty was writing in the 1950s, within the context of the Cold War. *A Miner's Sons* is especially successful in this regard, though it does manage to convey something of the troubled situation of communism in the early 1950s when the novel is set.

The book begins as Robert Mellers returns to the village of Mainworth, where he had formerly been a miner and a leader of the local branch of the Communist Party. Robert has been in prison for three years after accidentally killing Mathews, a turncoat union man, in a fight initiated by Mathews. In the meantime, the local Party branch has largely fallen apart, though it has gained some members among the young miners who have moved into a new housing estate built at one end of the village. Robert renews his relationship with Irene, his longtime girlfriend, as well as his mother and his father and brother, Herbert, both of whom are also miners. Robert also immediately resumes his work for the Party, though he is determined not to go back into the pit, partly because he feels he let the men down by allowing himself to be drawn into the fight with Mathews, thus bringing discredit upon the Party. In his Party work, Robert is aided by the veteran organizer Frank Wells and the leftist intellectual Mainwaring, a teacher in the nearby town of Killerton. He finds, however, that most of his former supporters among the miners of Mainworth, including the union representative Bill Barratt, are reluctant to return to the Party.

As the title indicates, much of *A Miner's Sons* focuses on Robert and Herbert Mellers and on their relationship with their father, a veteran miner who has been warned by his doctors that he will soon die (of silicosis) if he does not cease working in the mines, which he refuses to do. Robert, despite his dedication to the Party and its goals, must struggle with his own tendency toward individualism and with his own feelings of alienation from all of those around him, including Irene and his family. Herbert is a sensitive and creative young man who loves reading and secretly writes poetry. A forerunner of the "angry young men," he is a prototype of the frustrated worker who feels that his life is somehow unfair but who lacks the sophistication to understand the sources of this unfairness or to articulate his feelings. In particular, Herbert is thwarted and frustrated by a system that does not encourage him, as a miner, to dream or to be creative. Robert manages to introduce Herbert to communism and to help him identify the capitalist economic system as the fundamental source of his alienation and frustration. This identification made, Herbert is able to overcome his undirected anger and to work in a productive way to alleviate the causes of his frustration.

A major theme of *A Miner's Sons* is that the nationalization of the mines has done little to help miners like Herbert. Doherty suggests that the nationalized mines are not all that different from the formerly privatized ones and that nationalization has, in fact, been something of a windfall for the former mine orders—to the detriment of the miners. When the miners of Mainworth find that their pay is being decreased by order of the Coal Board, they organize to protest this cut, even though they receive little official support from their trade union, which is depicted here as a weak shadow of its former self working largely in complicity with the Coal Board. In the absence of effective union leadership, the Communist Party assumes a leading role in the protest, which takes the form of a refusal to work overtime, thus slowing production in the mines while still allowing the miners to draw a certain amount of pay. A representative of the Coal Board promises to investigate the situation if the men will meanwhile resume overtime work. Barratt, now again working with the Party, advises against accepting the offer, but Robert urges the men to return to overtime. They follow Robert's advice, which turns out to be a mistake, as the Coal Board does not subsequently act in good faith.

Barratt is once again alienated from the Party after this development, but he seems destined to return to the fold. When the Coal Board offers him a lucrative job working for them, he rejects the offer as an insult to his integrity and vows to go on fighting until the day when the miners themselves will at last control the pits in which they work. Robert, meanwhile, once again feels that he has let down the men and considers moving full time to Killerton, where he is now doing most of his work. Wells, however, convinces him that he is needed in Mainworth, urging him to assume the role of secretary of the Party branch there after Mainwaring moves to a new area, fearing that the men of Mainworth are becoming too dependent upon his leadership. Robert decides to accept this offer, especially after Irene pledges to support him in his work for the Party, thus culminating an emphasis throughout the book on the importance of women in the struggle for justice, even if they do not themselves work in the mines. The book thus ends on a positive note. Old Mellers has at last agreed to seek work outside the mines, while Robert has returned to the pit, working side by side with Herbert and the young communist George Rodgers and thereby enabling himself to provide organic leadership for the miners.

Among other things, *A Miner's Sons* clearly seeks to recover some of the cultural energies of the 1930s Left and Doherty draws very directly upon the work of predecessors like Heslop and Jones, which itself already drew upon forerunners such as Émile Zola's *Germinal*. This is a laudable project, and it certainly behooves leftist writers to make connections to the tradition in which they write, especially given that the thrust of most official literary scholarship is to discount or efface that tradition. On the other hand, one could argue that *A Miner's Sons* resembles its predecessors in the 1930s a little too much. The book itself reads very much like one of the miners' novels of the 1930s, and in that sense it fails adequately to reflect the substantial changes in the position of the cultural Left and of organized labor from the 1930s and the 1950s. The book does engage contemporary issues, such as nationalization of the mines, and it does portray the Communist Party as somewhat embattled, but it probably should have done more to place this embattled position within the context of the Cold War and the extreme pressures that were being brought to bear against leftist positions of all kinds in that era. All in all, though, *A Miner's Sons* is an impressive effort to keep the rich tradition of leftist miners' novels alive, and it deserves considerable more attention than it has thus far received. **Selected bibliography:** David Smith (*Socialist Propaganda*); von Rosenberg ("Militancy").

TERRY EAGLETON: *SAINTS AND SCHOLARS* **(1987).** *Saints and Scholars*, written by a noted Marxist literary critic, is a highly comic and erudite novel of ideas that addresses a number of important political issues. Though Eagleton has sometimes been highly critical of postmodernism in works such as *The Ideology of the Aesthetic*, his novel is written very much in a postmodern mode that collapses ontological levels, disavows historical authenticity, and pays little attention to verisimilitude. It begins with a detailed description of preparations for the execution by firing squad of Irish socialist leader James Connolly in the aftermath of the 1916 Easter Rising. But this chapter ends, as bullets race toward Connolly's heart, with the announcement that, for the purposes of this book, Connolly will not be executed in such a way but will, in fact, escape from Dublin. Eagleton then introduces the Austrian philosopher Ludwig Wittgenstein and the Russian intellectual Nikolai Bakhtin (brother of the celebrated critic and theorist Mikhail Bakhtin) into the book. After a lengthy discussion of their backgrounds (which includes some lively descriptions of the turmoil of turn-of-the-century St. Petersburg and the decadence of turn-of-the-century Vienna), Eagleton constructs a scenario through which Wittgenstein and Bakhtin meet at Cambridge, become frustrated with the pointlessness of the intellectual life there, and decide to remove to a small cottage in a remote village on the west coast of Ireland.

The debates between the cynical Wittgenstein (with his view that history has been a barbaric series of atrocities but that any action to improve matters would probably only make things worse) and the Nietzschean Bakhtin (with his quasi-anarchistic view that any disruption in the existing order is good as long as it doesn't lead to the establishment of a new order) allow Eagleton to address a number of abstract philosophical questions that have important concrete political implications. Meanwhile, their debates become more overtly political when Connolly, wounded and fleeing the British army, joins them in the cottage and explains the strategic logic behind the seemingly quixotic Easter Rising. Eagleton certainly knows his Irish history (and his Irish literature), and Connolly's description of the ravaging of colonial Ireland by the British provides the most effective political content of the novel. And, while Wittgenstein in particular views Connolly's justification of the doomed Rising as nonsense, we know in retrospect that the martyrdom of the leaders of the Rising (most of whom were captured and summarily executed by the British) led to such intense anti-British feeling that all-out war soon erupted between the Irish and the British, leading to the establishment of the Irish Free State by 1922. From our later perspective, then, Connolly's arguments have history on their side, though Connolly's attempt to maintain a faith in Catholicism amid his socialism also prefigures the way in which the Free State would become a Catholic theocracy and one of the most repressive states in Europe.

These historical personages are joined in the cottage by none other than Leopold Bloom, who has fled Dublin (and the pages of James Joyce's *Ulysses*) in disgust after his wife, Molly, has run off to Paris with young Stephen Dedalus. Of course, Bloom's appearance seems a bit anachronistic (by 1916, Stephen would be thirty-four, Molly would be forty-six, and Leopold fifty, all considerably older than they seem to be in Eagleton's text). There are other anachronisms as well, as when Nikolai makes references to aspects of his brother Mikhail's career that would not occur until decades later. But these anachronisms pale in comparison to the lack of verisimilitude that occurs when Leopold, as a literary character, joins Wittgenstein, Bakhtin, and Connolly in the same cottage. Indeed, the book eventually transforms into a playful exercise in allusion to Irish literature. The characters, sitting in the cottage and waiting for something to happen, obviously parallel the situation of Samuel Beckett's Vladimir and Estragon in *Waiting for Godot*; the whole book, with its comic allusions, its lively debates, and its mixtures of ontological levels, begins to read more and more like something out of Flann O'Brien.

Such literary shenanigans may provide an effective rejoinder to those who believe Marxists have no sense of humor, but they add little to the political message of the book. It is also telling that Eagleton's version of Irish literature features Joyce, Beckett, and O'Brien, not Sean O'Casey and Brendan Behan. All in all, though, *Saints and Scholars* effectively portrays the political situation in colonial Ireland, while addressing vexing issues, such as the necessity and desirability of violent revolution, that have wider implications for leftist politics. On the other hand, these issues are treated in a way that is clearly intended for an intellectual rather than a working-class audience. Indeed, while there is considerable sympathy in the book for the poor of Ireland, the only working-class characters are comic caricatures marginal to the story. *Saints and Scholars* is very much a book for those already in the know and should be enjoyed by those familiar with Eagleton's critical and theoretical work. But it makes no attempt to make its message accessible to a wider audience. Most aspects of the book seem designed more to produce comedy than to further class consciousness—though the comedy is somewhat muted by the fact that Connolly is eventually captured and executed after all. Of course, intellectuals need entertainment and amusement, too, and in that sense the book is effective. But *Saints and Scholars* is not likely to be enjoyed by nonintellectuals, nor is it likely to move intellectuals to take political action. **Selected bibliography:** Eagleton (*Ideology of the Aesthetic*).

J. G. FARRELL: *THE SINGAPORE GRIP* (1978). *The Singapore Grip*, focusing on the fall of British Singapore to the Japanese in World War II, is the third volume of Farrell's "Empire Trilogy." The other two volumes are the *Troubles* (1970), which deals with the Anglo-Irish war of 1919–21, and *The Siege of Krishnapur* (1973), which is set in the Indian War of Independence (or "Mutiny") of 1857. Each volume thus treats a moment of crisis in the history of the British Empire; together the three volumes constitute a historical narrative, backed by extensive historical research, of the gradual demise of that empire. Ronald Binns suggests that the Empire Trilogy performs much the same work of historical recovery as leftist historical texts such as E. P. Thompson's *The Making of the English Working Class* and *Whigs and Hunters* and Eric Hobsbawm and George Rudé's *Captain Swing* (35). Frances Singh, meanwhile, sees *The Siege of Krishnapur* as a radical change of direction in British fictions about the 1857 Mutiny, viewing it particularly as a positive move toward a Marxist conception of the role of the Mutiny in the forward movement of history.

Focusing on the same novel, A. V. Krishna Rao bemoans Farrell's sudden premature death as the truncation of what might have been the career of "one of the greatest historical novelists that England has ever produced" (41). Finally, according to Ronald Binns, Farrell's novels are often compared with those of Walter Scott, while Farrell himself admired the work of both Scott and Scott's great Marxist champion, Georg Lukács (27).

Though written in a comic-ironic vein that displays many of the characteristics of postmodernism, *The Singapore Grip* is serious in its elaboration of the economic underpinnings of British imperialism and is, in that sense, clearly the most sophisticated of Farrell's works. Its central character is Matthew Webb, an idealistic young Englishman who comes to Singapore on the eve of World War II, prompted by the death there of his father, one of the principals in the British firm of Blackett and Webb, which derives its income primarily from exploitation of the Malayan rubber trade. As his father's heir, Matthew has inherited a considerable portion of the company's stock, causing Walter Blackett, his father's partner, to try to consolidate control of the company within the family by marrying his daughter, Joan, to Matthew. This strategy links up with the book's many images of prostitution to suggest the commodification of human beings under capitalism. Joan, a willing accomplice, proceeds to attempt to seduce Matthew in an outrageously overt manner. The innocent Matthew, however, comes to prefer the exotic and mysterious Vera Chiang, the daughter, so she claims, of a Chinese tea merchant and a Russian princess, to the more bourgeois Joan.

Matthew comes to Singapore with little knowledge of business, and he is horrified when he learns that Blackett and Webb has gained most of its wealth through the ruthless exploitation of Asian workers. Indeed, much of the critique of economic imperialism that is so central to Farrell's book is achieved through the defamiliarizing lens of Matthew's innocence. Imperialism as a whole, with its built-in Manichean hierarchies, is strongly antithetical to the egalitarian philosophy of Matthew, who believes that the shared humanity of different nations will eventually allow them to "live in harmony with each other, concerning themselves with each other's welfare" (372). Matthew's belief in justice and equality is admirable, but it is also the case that his comprehension of these concepts is processed through a variety of literary fantasies. In a debate with his American friend Jim Ehrendorf, for example, he rightly excoriates British colonialism for its destruction of indigenous cultures in Asia, especially Burma. Within the ruthlessly Darwinian exigencies of the capitalist economies that Britain has brought to its colonies, Matthew argues, less efficient (and less materialistic) indigenous traditions have little chance of survival (184). Indeed, he argues that the British intrusion into Asia is beginning to cause the same kind of routinization that the bourgeois cultural revolution has already brought to Europe.

When the more practical Ehrendorf defends imperialism, pointing out that capitalism has brought the same kind of cultural decay to Europe, he is only reinforcing Matthew's point. Meanwhile, when Ehrendorf produces the standard argument that imperialism has brought economic improvement to Asia, Matthew responds that the workings of capitalism are such that any such improvements accrue to the benefit not of the Burmese but of their colonial masters. For the Burmese, he argues, "the coming of Capitalism has really been like the spreading of a disease" (184). Again, however, the same can be said of Europe, where the benefits of capitalism go primarily to the bourgeoisie and not to the workers who actually produce the wealth on which capitalism thrives. Thus, it is clear that Matthew's criticisms go beyond imperialism to capitalism itself. Amid a context in which fears of communist agitation are rampant, his belief in the equality of all men thoroughly undermines laissez-faire capitalism and takes on a decidedly (though inadvertently) communistic tone. He begins to wonder, for example, whether he, as a rich man, can possibly live a just life when so many of the people around him are poor. After all, he recognizes, the only way to become wealthy in a capitalist economy is to acquire wealth at the expense of others, which results in severe ethical dilemmas. When he visits Vera in the tenement cubicle to which the Blacketts have banished her to keep her away from Matthew (and thus clear the way for Joan), he wonders whether he can ever be justified in his life of comfort and luxury "while at the same time people lived in this wretched tenement riddled with malnutrition and tuberculosis" (428).

Ehrendorf, in the debate with Matthew over Burma, senses that his friend's criticisms of capitalism echo those of Marx. Thus, when Matthew characterizes capitalism as a disease, Ehrendorf, somewhat oversimplifying Marx's argument, points out that Marx himself regarded capitalism as a necessary stage in the historical movement from feudalism to communism, so that he "even saw the British in India as a force for progress" (184). Matthew responds by asserting that the movement from capitalism to communism does not usually happen, so that colonial peoples end up trapped in the transitional stage. Moreover, he concludes, even if the communist revolution were somehow to succeed, "my bet is that in practice Communism would be scarcely any better than Capitalism, and perhaps even worse" (185). Of course, it comes as no surprise that the idealistic Matthew would have little taste for communism with its firm foundation in materialism. And his romanticization of poverty is a far cry from the kind of proletarian class consciousness upon which any hope for a communist revolution must rest. Matthew's resultant inability to propose a viable alternative to capitalism greatly limits the power of his criticism of the capitalist system.

This limitation should come as no surprise. *The Singapore Grip* continually asserts that an estrangement from material reality renders the British incapable of understanding (and thus of effectively dealing with) the colonial world. This estrangement can be seen not only in the dreamy Matthew but also in the hard-hearted capitalist Walter Blackett, who is so convinced of the rightness of his quest for power and wealth that he is oblivious to the negative consequences for the Asians whom he exploits. Founded on a trade in opium, coolies, and prostitutes, and now principally engaged in a rubber business that thrives only by cheating independent Asian planters, Blackett and Webb (an obvious stand-in for capitalism itself) has no moral foundation whatsoever. Yet, Blackett is proud of his company's accomplishments. When not trying to market his daughter Joan to the highest bidder, he spends most of his time and energy planning for an elaborate jubilee in celebration of the fiftieth anniversary of his company's founding. This jubilee forms another of the important comic subplots of Farrell's text, while at the same time providing an effective reminder of the theatricality of British colonial power.

Blackett's inability to see beyond the limitations of his capitalist convictions is evident in his blindness to the implications of many aspects of his planned festival and parade. One of the floats in the parade is to be an artificial rubber tree spewing out gold, but Walter is one of the few onlookers who is unable to see that the yellowish water used to represent this gold looks suspiciously like urine (394). The planned centerpiece of the parade is a giant rubber octopus, whose tentacles encircle the necks of allegorical figures representing Shanghai, Hong Kong, Batavia, Saigon, and other colonial sites (390). Walter, caught up in his own businessman's version of *bovarysme*, is unable to see either the aesthetic tackiness of this display or the rather obvious implication that capitalism is a sinister force devouring the colonial world.

When the Japanese finally attack Singapore, the octopus is essentially destroyed, left with only two of its original arms, which had "not proved very durable" (594). And the fragility of this spectacular, if preposterous, allegory of capitalist imperialism can be taken as a comment on the fragility of imperialism itself. However much theatrical techniques might have contributed to the British domination of their vast empire, a typically *bovarystic* reception of colonial reality rendered the British ultimately unable to deal with that reality with the efficiency and effectiveness they had shown in their domestic rule of Britain. The ultimate weakness of British colonial rule in Singapore is demonstrated by the ease with which the Japanese capture the city, an event that has been characterized by Colin Cross as "the worst single military defeat the British Empire ever suffered" (232). But Farrell's book suggests that this defeat came about from fundamental weakness in capitalism as much as from specific failures in British policy.

The Singapore Grip interrogates a number of models of history, ultimately endorsing none of them but nevertheless suggesting the ultimate centrality of the economic in the historical process. Moreover, this focus on economic factors is often couched in terms of an overt critique of capitalism, as in the narrator's early, allegorical, description of the ruthless wresting of colonial Singapore from tropical nature by the "civilizing" forces of capitalist imperialism: "Down there in the city, taking the place of the rats and the centipedes which had once made it their home, seething, devouring, copulating, businesses rose and fell, sank their teeth into each other, swallowed, broke away, gulped down other firms, or mounted each other to procreate smaller companies, just as they do elsewhere in the great capitalist cities" (6).

Also important in this regard is the title metaphor of *The Singapore Grip*. Early in the book, Walter Blackett drops a hint about the meaning of the book's title when he brags of his company's "grip" on the rice market in Malaya, seemingly unconcerned that it was accomplished by ruthless exploitation of Malayan peasants (43). When Matthew Webb arrives in Singapore, he is jokingly warned by sailors aboard his ship to watch out for the Singapore Grip, which he proceeds to do. A central motif in the rest of the book is Matthew's (and the reader's) quest to find the meaning of this phrase, often to the amusement and surprise of those whom he asks. At one point Matthew believes that the Singapore Grip might be a kind of tropical disease, which he may, in fact, have contracted (210). But his friend Ehrendorf finally explains to him that the phrase refers to "the ability acquired by certain ladies of Singapore to control their autonomous vaginal muscles, apparently with delightful results." The grip is, in fact a specialty of Singapore prostitutes. Matthew, however, prefers his own version of Blackett's definition, immediately responding that the real Singapore Grip is "the grip of our Western culture and economy on the Far East . . . It's the stranglehold of capital on the traditional cultures of Malaya, China, Burma, Java, Indo-China, and even India herself!" (549, Farrell's ellipsis). Matthew, in short, clearly links the motifs of prostitution and imperialism, clarifying the double sense of the title and insisting that, if the British domination of much of Asia can be described in sexual terms, they are terms in which the economic nevertheless remains fundamental. ***Selected bibliography:*** Binns; Booker; Cross; Rao; Rignall; Singh.

RALPH FOX: *STORMING HEAVEN* (1928). *Storming Heaven*, written by an author who would go on to become one of Britain's leading Marxist theorists and literary critics in the 1930s, grows directly out of the tremendous excitement and optimism generated by the success of the Russian Revolution of 1917 and by the beginnings of the project of building socialism in the Soviet Union in the 1920s. Its protagonist is

John Johnson, who, at the start of the book, is a teenage boy growing up in San Francisco. In some ways, John is a walking emblem of the internationalism that informed the attitudes of the Left in the 1920s. Though he lives in America, he is the orphaned son of a British sailor and an "island woman." And, after years of hardship growing up in orphanages, he has finally been adopted by the Shurins, a Russian anarchist couple who have come to America to escape the Bolsheviks and in the hope that the husband's engineering skills will make them rich there. However, America does not turn out to be the golden land of opportunity that Shurin had expected. Indeed, America is presented as a ruthless land of cutthroat competition and hostility to dissident ideas, a characteristic that is presented most directly when John's friend, Pete Mason, a labor organizer for the Industrial Workers of the World, is murdered by the Ku Klux Klan.

Having lost his job, Shurin concludes that the Bolsheviks, whom he formerly despised, may be right in their criticisms of capitalism after all. So he decides to return to his native Russia. The family sails for Vladivostok, which is still occupied by the Japanese and ruled by a puppet White Russian government. Mrs. Shurin dies on the way, and Mr. Shurin, not one to be burdened by responsibilities to others, decides to send John back to America to fend for himself. John, however, has other ideas. He takes the $250 that Shurin gives him for his return to America and sets out on his own for the Soviet Union. The bulk of the novel then concerns John's rather picaresque journeys around the vast new nation, including an extended tour of the Asian provinces, with their diverse peoples and traditions. But *Storming Heaven* is far from a typical example of the stereotyping of non-European peoples as critiqued in recent works such as Edward Said's *Orientalism*. While John himself begins his journeys with the expectation that the Asians he meets will be mysterious and exotic, he is assured early on by his Bolshevik friend Yasha Schumann that they are really no different from John or himself, though many of them, like many peasants in Russia, still cling to traditional beliefs in ways that sometimes impede the Bolshevik project of modernization. Meanwhile, John finds that these provinces are continually plagued by attacks from partisan guerrillas, who, armed and supported by England and the West, are still holding out against Bolshevik rule.

Fox does a good job of portraying the complex cultural and political climate in the Soviet Union in the early 1920s, a phenomenon he, himself, observed first hand when he traveled there. He also conveys well the extreme difficulties that faced the Bolsheviks in trying to integrate these regions into the new Soviet Union. The difficulty of this task is indicated in the title of the book, which is taken from a reference in Marx to the difficult odds facing the Paris Communards in 1871. After all, the Bolsheviks must overcome centuries of tradition and superstition in order to bring modernization and socialist prosperity to the long-suffering people of the regions that now constitute the Soviet Union, while at the same time withstanding the extensive attempts of the West to undermine the new regime. John seems sympathetic to the Bolshevik cause. He becomes romantically involved with Nadya, a committed communist working as a teacher in the town of Buzuluk, but he functions primarily as an observer of, rather than a participant in, the historic process of transformation that is going on around him. In particular, he clings to an individualism that limits his ability fully to devote himself to the collectivist ideals of the Bolsheviks.

Eventually, John and Nadya move on to Moscow, to the heart of the Bolshevik efforts to build a new world. There, Nadya works in a factory while John, who has gained some experience in performing while on his travels, joins a troupe of actors. John is an immediate success on the stage, but he unfortunately begins to lead a profligate life that includes a doomed sexual liaison with Neura, a beautiful, but volatile, peasant woman who is also a member of the troupe. This liaison leads to the end of John's relationship with Nadya. It also causes John considerable unhappiness because the staunchly independent Neura refuses to allow him to possess and control her as he wishes. He soon discovers her in a compromising situation with William Whitehead, a famous British millionaire socialist who is visiting the Soviet Union as an observer. John, still only seventeen at this time, then murders Neura in a fit of passion. He is arrested, given a fair and sympathetic trial, and sentenced (under the extremely lenient procedures of the new state) to five years in prison.

Storming Heaven is an interesting and entertaining novel that addresses a number of important issues. The portrayal of Kirghiz tribesmen and other Asiatic peoples in the book is sympathetic without being romantic, building upon the observations contained in Fox's autobiographical travel narrative, *People of the Steppes* (1925). Indeed, Urszula Tempska describes Fox's writing in both *People of the Steppes* and *Storming Heaven* as "para-ethnographic," noting both its ethnographic focus and its tendency to challenge the epistemological assumptions of traditional Western colonialist ethnography. As Tempska emphasizes, Fox's writing rejects the dualistic stereotyping typical of Western ethnography, letting the people he represents speak for themselves and present their cultural perspectives in their own voices. From this point of view, both *People of the Steppes* and *Storming Heaven* deserve more critical attention than they have received, especially given the widespread interest in ethnographic representations that has been an important part of recent multicultural and postcolonial criticism. Fox's presentation of gender issues, drawing upon postrevolutionary attempts to correct the traditional oppression of women in Russian society, is similarly rich and complex, posing similar challenges to the traditional stereotyping of women and to conventional bourgeois notions of the proper relationship between men and women. From this point of view, Fox's work probably deserves renewed attention from feminist critics, as does the entire phenomenon of the attempt to reformulate gender roles in the postrevolutionary Soviet Union.

Ultimately, in fact, it is probably in its presentation of this historical context that *Storming Heaven* is most important. Fox's extremely positive depiction of the new Soviet society might strike some as naive, especially in retrospect. But it is surely more accurate than (and serves as a useful counter to) Western accounts that have tended to depict the revolutionary changes underway in the new state as an unmitigated evil. Fox's description of both the possibilities and the pitfalls faced by the project of the new Soviet state provide vivid reminders of that unique moment in human history. Granted, the book sometimes seems a bit chaotic and unstructured, but this lack of organization to some extent helps to capture the tumultuous climate of the postrevolutionary Soviet Union. Fox centrally understands this climate as informed principally by a struggle between the old and the new. And, while he openly endorses the Bolshevik project of technological modernization as a means of bringing better lives to the traditionally impoverished and oppressed peoples of the areas now included within the Soviet Union, he also knows that this modernization cannot be achieved without cost.

While Fox envisions the process of modernization as inevitable and irresistible, he also poses two clear alternative paths that this modernization might take. On the one hand is the Bolshevik path, with its devotion to social justice amid the drive for technological process. On the other is the capitalist path, specifically associated with America in the text, though primarily presented through the perspective of the Englishman Whitehead. Fox suggests that the capitalist path might be equally effective as a means of modernization, but he also argues, through one of his Russian characters, that the capitalist drive for profit will lead to a "soulless" modernity in which people may have food and clothing, but will lack direction or purpose in their lives other than the acquisition of material wealth. Moreover, the social inequalities that lie at the heart of capitalism inevitably lead to the production of "millions of mechanical men and women producing to keep a few in luxury, the deadly barrier of class still firmly in being, a kind of highly organized Chicago, spread across the earth" (263). In retrospect, this description provides a striking anticipation of the recent globalization of capitalism that Ernest Mandel, Fredric Jameson, and others have described as "late capitalism." Whitehead thus turns out to have been right in his belief that the coming world revolution would "come from America, not Russia" (279). But this outcome in no way invalidates Fox's critique of Americanization. Nor does it suggest that his presentation of socialist modernization as an alternative should not continue to be given careful and serious consideration, despite the ultimate historical failure of the Bolsheviks to implement their program in the Soviet Union. *Selected bibliography:* Ralph Fox (*People of the Steppes*); Fredric Jameson (*Postmodernism*); Lehmann, Jackson, and Day Lewis; Mandel; Said; Tempska.

RALPH FOX: ***THIS WAS THEIR YOUTH*** **(1937).** *This Was Their Youth* is a historical novel that relates the experiences of a number of inhabitants of an industrial town in Yorkshire in the years leading up to World War I. Tensions between Germany and England are already in the air as the book begins a few years before the war, as are international tensions arising from competition among colonial powers for control of the non-European world, especially in Northern Africa. Meanwhile, life in the once placid town is, itself, growing increasingly volatile. Modern technological advances in transportation, communication, and elsewhere are just on the verge of transforming the fabric of everyday existence. At the same time, the town's increasing economic reliance on manufacturing contributes to a growing separation of and antagonism between the classes. The town's factories are spewing out pollutants and giving the town a dingy and depressing look that provides an appropriate outward sign of the more subtle ways in which advancing capitalism is reducing the lives of individuals in the town to the dreary sameness of a routine dominated by the factory whistles. Fox's technique is to place these important historical developments in the background and to focus on the personal experiences of individual characters, always, however, keeping in mind the ways in which these characters and their experiences are shaped by larger social and historical forces.

The novel, in a move that helps to avoid the individualism of the traditional bourgeois novel, features an ensemble cast rather than a single protagonist. It also has little in the way of an overall plot, except for the movement of history itself as the world moves inexorably toward war. One important character is a middle-class teenage boy, Dan "Reefer" Stott, whose experiences in school, with his friends, and with his own emerging sexuality are subtly colored for the reader by the knowledge that Reefer will be just the right age to go to war when 1914 finally rolls around. Reefer, a student at Queen Elizabeth's Grammar School, is also introduced to the realities of class difference as he finds himself torn between his own middle-class origins and his friendship with some of the town's working-class characters, students at the Raw Top Council School. A very bright student, Reefer is the favorite of Jimmy Stuart, a teacher at his school who becomes involved in a passionate relationship with Elsie Wainwright, a teacher at Raw Top. Unfortunately, however, Stuart has tuberculosis, and he insists that the two postpone their wedding until he feels that his he is out of danger from his illness. Again, however, this situation is clouded by the fact that everything is about to change and that looming events may threaten their plans regardless of his health.

The difficulty of finding personal happiness within the environment of this town is also represented in the book in the story of Frank Whittam, a Boer War veteran who now serves as the school sergeant and gymnastics teacher at Queen Elizabeth's. Frank is the father of Mat Whittam, a student at Raw Top. He is also the lover of a young woman, Minnie, whom he eventually marries despite the fact that he has another wife living, totally mad, in an asylum. Frank and Minnie are very happy together until Sergeant Smitham, a town policeman who is blindly devoted to the strict enforcement of law and order at any cost, discovers the existence of Whittam's first wife, leading to Whittam's arrest for bigamy. Smitham serves as an emblem of the increasing regimentation and regulation of life in a reified bourgeois world. But he is also a sort of proto-fascist, thus serving to link the pre–World War I setting of the book to the late-1930s context in which it was written. Indeed, it is clear throughout the book that the shadow cast over the characters by the threat of world war prior to 1914 is very similar to the shadow cast over England by the looming fascist threat in 1937. Whittam receives a light sentence and is even offered a job in London, where he and Minnie plan to move after his incarceration. Again, however, the coming war looms over their plans.

Finally, the international dimension to the text is provided largely by the presence of Alan Brown, son of Tom Brown, the headmaster at Raw Top. Alan, a journalist who has traveled the world, visits the town in the course of the book, relating stories of his colorful adventures to the enthralled local boys. At the end of the book, however, he departs for Northern Africa, where war has broken out between Italy and Turkey (but where he will fall ill and have to return to Europe to convalesce). Alan Brown's adventures not only help to provide a sense of building international tensions but also introduce the theme of colonialism into the text. In particular, Alan's sympathies tend to be with non-Europeans in their confrontations with European power, while he strives to challenge a number of Orientalist stereotypes of the kind described by Edward Said in *Orientalism*. On the other hand, he sometimes comes close to such stereotypes himself. Meanwhile, Tom Brown's diatribes against Western capitalism and its domination of the rest of the world through superior military technology provide an interesting supplement to his son's position.

As a novel, *This Was Their Youth* is a bit rough and disjointed, and the various elements of its multiple plot structure do not come together as smoothly as they might. Thus, while the book in some ways exemplifies Georg Lukács's call for historical novels that reflect the sweep of history in ways that show the connection between public events and private experiences, it is certainly far less accomplished than Fox's earlier *Storming Heaven*. Of course, *This Was Their Youth* was written at a time when Fox's political activities left him little time to write. Moreover, it was brought to press after the author's death fighting with the International Brigade in Spain, so that he had no opportunity to make final corrections or changes to the manuscript. Nevertheless, *This Was Their Youth* addresses a number of important issues in subtle and significant ways and therefore stands, even in its unpolished form, as a suggestive example of potential directions for a leftist writing practice. **Selected bibliography:** Lehmann, Jackson, and Lewis; Lukács (*Historical Novel*); Said.

LEWIS GRASSIC GIBBON: *A SCOTS QUAIR* **(1932–34).** *A Scots Quair* ("quair" is a Scottish word meaning "book" or "volume") is the overall title of a trilogy of novels that includes *Sunset Song*, *Cloud Howe*, and *Grey Granite*. Together, these volumes constitute one of the most important examples of British working-class culture in the 1930s. Indeed, D. M. Roskies calls the trilogy a "proletarian masterpiece" and notes the way it "affronts entrenched ideas of the novel, undermining its etiquette in a way as eccentric as it is subversive" (178). The trilogy tells the story of its protagonist, Chris Guthrie, as she grows from her childhood in rural Scotland, to adulthood in a Scottish town, to late middle age in the urban setting of the fictional city of Dundairn. As such, the trilogy clearly participates in the generic tradition of the bildungsroman, even though it traces the life of its protagonist to an older age than is typical of that genre. However, by focusing on a female protagonist and by representing a variety of leftist political perspectives, the trilogy deviates from the nineteenth-century bourgeois bildungsroman in its effective invocation of feminist and socialist ideas. Moreover, the trilogy also constitutes an important work of historical fiction, the movement from country to town to city serving as a clear allegory of the historical process of modernization. Finally, as the title indicates, *A Scots Quair* is avowedly Scottish in its language, its setting, and its point of view. In this sense, it obviously recalls the historical fiction of Walter Scott. But the Scottish orientation of the book also serves as an important commentary on English expansionism that can be extrapolated to a commentary on imperialism as a whole.

Sunset Song focuses on the early life of Chris Guthrie as she grows up on Blawearie Farm in the Kinraddie Lands of Scotland, struggling to receive an education and dreaming of attending a university. She is generally ambivalent toward the land around her and confused about life in general, a situation little aided by her cold, humorless, domineering father, whom she is left to care for after her mother, frustrated by a dreary life consisting of little but back-breaking labor punctuated by frequent pregnancy and childbirth, commits suicide. After her father's death, Chris meets Ewan Tavendale, with whom she begins a passionate relationship that leads to her first marriage and to the birth of her son, also named Ewan. After the elder Ewan is shot as a deserter in World War I, Chris eventually marries the new minister Robert Colquohoun, whose progressive ideas lead many of the locals to brand him a "Bolshevik." Chris matures significantly in the course of the volume and learns a great deal from her experiences, much in the mode of the conventional bildungsroman. However, *Sunset Song* differs from the conventional bourgeois bildungsroman in several important ways. Most obvious, perhaps, is the fact that Chris is a woman, and, indeed, Gibbon is careful throughout the trilogy to try to construct a credible feminine point of view from which to tell the story. Deirdre Burton thus finds the trilogy as a whole striking for the effective way in which it establishes this point of view. And, as Pamela Fox notes, *Sunset Song* is "a particularly self-conscious feminine epic, its narrative merging the parallel rhythms of Chris's body and of the harvesting season" (195). Much of Chris's education in this first volume is explicitly political. Thus, in addition to her eventual husband, Colquohoun, she derives much of her understanding of the world from observing local figures, such as the socialist activist Chae Strachan and the draft resister Long Rob Duncan, with whom Chris has a brief affair before he finally submits and goes to the war, soon to be killed.

In *Sunset Song* Gibbon is also careful to connect Chris's personal experiences to larger historical developments in the world around her. The most obvious of these is World War I, which radically disrupts the relatively placid life led by Chris and her neighbors in rural Scotland, pulling them violently into contact with the modern world. The war has other implications as well. For example, Chae Strachan is killed on Armistice Day, perhaps signifying the way in which many thinkers of the left have seen World War I and its eventual settlement as an attempt to thwart the working-class political energies that were building at the beginning of the twentieth century and thus to kill off socialism as a serious political threat in western Europe. But the most obvious historical focus of *Sunset Song*, as indicated by its title, is its description of the end of a traditional rural way of life beneath the inexorable onslaught of modernity. Raymond Williams thus describes the book as "a classic statement of what is seen as the dissolution of the peasantry" (268). As Williams proceeds to point out, this process has special significance in areas such as Scotland, Ireland, and Wales, where the "English capitalist rural order" was resisted far longer than in England itself; but this process also participates in the larger historical movement from country to city that characterizes British history as a whole (269).

In *Cloud Howe*, Chris and Robert Colquohoun move to the town of Seggett, where his unpopular and somewhat vague socialism (the "cloud" image of the title) gradually gives way to a Christian mysticism with which Chris, an unbeliever, is unable to sympathize. In the meantime, she herself must come to grips with her own ambivalent feelings toward the growing proletarianization of her former peasant class, a development that is symbolized in the text by the antagonism between the workers in a local textile mill and the traditional "ploughmen" who live in the area. Chris's feelings in this regard are complicated by the fact that, as the wife of a minister, she no longer fully belongs to either of these classes but is essentially a member of the gentry. Much of this volume involves Chris's attempts to find happiness through purely personal experience, attempts that are clearly doomed as politics continually creeps into the text. The growing socialism of the mill workers is an important motif in the text, though their failure to improve working conditions through collective action contributes greatly to the frustration that eventually drives Robert away from politics. Meanwhile, the growing threat of fascism continually lurks in the margins of the text, especially as economic conditions worsen in the area. By the end of the text, Seggett has fallen upon hard times. The area mills have mostly been shut down, and Robert drops dead while delivering a sermon in favor of an unidentified "stark, cure creed" that is clearly neither socialism or Christianity, but might conceivably be either of the polar opposites of communism and fascism (350).

In *Grey Granite*, Chris and her son move to urban Duncairn, thus completing the historical movement from country to city that underlies the entire trilogy. The widowed Chris, with her partner Ma Cleghorn, manages to support herself by running a rooming house. In this text, however, Chris is somewhat supplanted as the central character by her son, Ewan, who in the course of the book becomes a dedicated communist. Indeed, the firmness of his political beliefs, as opposed to those of his father, is indicated by the granite of the title—which also refers to the determination in Ewan's gray eyes. Ewan becomes an apprentice in a steel mill, and his efforts to participate in the organization of the workers there make this volume of the trilogy much more of an example of proletarian fiction than are the first two volumes. Indeed, Williams concludes that the narrative of *Grey Granite* "more clearly than any other novel embodies the active labour movement of the thirties" (270).

An important motif in *Grey Granite* involves the attempts of the local police to disrupt and suppress the collective efforts of the workers, including one episode in which Ewan is brutally tortured and beaten by the police. Gibbon, thus, indicates the complicity of state power with the bourgeois class, but he also indicates the dedication of many who oppose the existing system. Thus, Ewan's humiliating torture at the hands of the police only hardens his resolve to work to overturn a system that thrives on the unfair exploitation of workers. By the end of the text, this resolve has led to the breakup of a promising relationship with the schoolteacher Ellen Johns, who has been forced to disavow the Communist Party in order to keep her teaching job. At the end of the text, Ewan is still being harassed by the police, while Chris, having experienced a brief and unsatisfactory third marriage, returns to the country and lives in the house in which she was born.

Chris's turn to the past shows an ultimate lack of development of proletarian consciousness that might be interpreted as a commentary on the weakness of the socialist movement in Scotland as a whole, just as the sometimes negative depiction of communist organizers and officials suggests problems with that movement. Burton finds Chris's development indicative of a complex ideological structure that suggests, among other things, important points of contention between feminism and Marxism. On the other hand, Burton's argument has a tendency to degenerate into a sort of neo-New Critical privileging of ambiguity—a quality of dubious value in a political novel. Fox finds the book less successful in its feminism (because Chris is consistently constructed as a sexual object) and more consistent in its socialism (though she grants its potential critique of the Communist Party as stunting the individual growth of its members). In particular, Fox argues that Burton overemphasizes gender and pays too little attention to the role of class in the trilogy. She then concludes that Chris's return to the country at the end of the trilogy is a "problematic, rather than laudatory, act of defiance" (197). Indeed, the historical vision of *A Scots Quair* is problematic in a number of ways, not the least of which is its frequent invocation of a romanticized Golden Age in the distant past. Jenny Wolmark, in fact, argues that the book, while presenting "a radical and positive criticism of capitalism" is nevertheless informed by "a profoundly conservative idealization of the past and a fatalistic acceptance of history as something to be endured rather than understood" (23).

From a Marxist perspective, the form and style of *A Scots Quair* are problematic as well, though these are the elements of the trilogy that have drawn the most praise from critics. The combination in the trilogy of a number of sophisticated modernist narrative techniques with a language that reflects the rhythms of country speech in northeastern Scotland, according to Fox, has gained Gibbon "a flawless critical reputation" that has made him more than any other writer since Robert Tressell, a "favorite son" of the genre of socialist fiction (194). Ramón López Ortega is typical when he argues that Gibbon "ranks with major twentieth-century writers," especially in his effective invocation, through style, of the voices of his working-class characters (139). López Ortega concludes that Gibbon's technique is revolutionary in its "mastery of the spoken word and the endowment of old literary forms with the most modern devices of radical expression (138, 141). One could argue, however, that the careful attention to style and technique in *A Scots Quair* suggests an attempt to adhere to bourgeois conceptions of aesthetic quality, a movement that combines with the problematic historical model that underlies the trilogy to create serious limitations in Gibbon's ability to break free of the bounds of bourgeois ideology and to make a genuine contribution to the development of socialist consciousness. This limitation (which, as Barbara Foley argues in *Radical Representations*, occurs all too often in the works of leftist writers) also frequently occurs in the visions of leftist critics, perhaps partially accounting for Gibbon's positive critical reputation. Nevertheless, there is no doubt that *A Scots Quair* is an important work and one to which leftists thinkers and writers would do well to attend. **Selected bibliography:** Burton; Foley; Pamela Fox; López Ortega; Roskies; Williams (*Country*); Wolmark.

GEORGE GISSING: *THE NETHER WORLD* **(1889).** Though he does not generally adopt a leftist stance toward British class society, George Gissing's vivid depictions of the lives of the British working class in novels such as *Workers in the Dawn* (1880), *The Unclassed* (1884), *Demos* (1886), *Thyrza* (1887), and *The Nether World* (1889) give him a special place in the history of British literature of the Left. Gissing's attitude toward the working class was complex and highly ambivalent, and it is only in *Workers in the Dawn*, the first of his working-class novels, that he attempts to contribute directly to a radical project of social change. Indeed, by the time of the writing of *The Nether World*, Gissing, whose growing success seemed to alienate him more and more from the working class about which he wrote, had become an avowed antisocialist. Nevertheless, *The Nether World* is generally regarded as Gissing's best working-class novel, and John Goode even goes so far as to identify it as "probably the best novel about working-class London in the late nineteenth century" (107).

The Nether World well illustrates David Grylls's description of the "characteristic feel of Gissing's fiction" as "busy-ness overshadowed by despair" (1). The book, which involves numerous characters and multiple subplots, describes in vivid detail the debased living conditions of the denizens of London's poorer quarters. One of the book's grimmest aspects is an unrelenting suggestion that little can be done to improve these conditions. Plagued by sickness, alcohol, and unemployment, many of the characters of *The Nether World* slide into crime or decline into despair. Although there are vague echoes of politics in the book (as in John Hewett's ineffectual radicalism), there is no real hint that the poor might improve their lot through collective class action on their own part. Indeed, as Fredric Jameson has pointed out, the denizens of Gissing's nether world are not figured as a class at all, but merely as some vague notion of "the people" (189). The few attempts at improvement that are made occur strictly at an individual level and generally involve an effort to escape from the working class rather than to elevate the class as a whole. Thus, the clerk Scawthorne manages, after years of study and hard work, to become a full-fledged lawyer. But even these attempts generally fail. The beautiful Clara Hewett, who has some promise as an actress, must give up her budding career when a rival throws acid in her face, badly disfiguring her. Similarly, the demands of daily life eventually make it impossible for Sidney Kirkwood, the book's ostensible protagonist, to fulfill his dreams of being an artist. Meanwhile, his efforts toward intellectual improvement serve only to alienate him from his own class, while economics exclude him from the upper classes as well.

The book ends as Kirkwood and Jane Snowdon struggle on in their small ways to help a few fellow citizens of the nether world live better lives, and to this extent it closes on a positive note, however meager. But utopianism in general is dismissed, as figured in the sad state of the poor who visit the Crystal Palace, itself a central nineteenth-century utopian image, in chapter 12. The central utopian motif in *The Nether World* has to do with the dream of Michael Snowdon, who has inherited a fortune from his son in Australia, to leave that fortune to his granddaughter, Jane, who will then use it to do good works for the poor not from above, as in the usual case of charity, but from within, as a genuine daughter of the people. She will, in short, become a sort of organic philanthropist. This project, however, leads to nothing but misery, overwhelming Jane with anxiety and disrupting a planned marriage between Kirkwood and Jane when the former backs away for fear that the inheritance will prove a corrupting force. Meanwhile, through a sequence of mishaps, Snowdon dies intestate, so that his fortune actually goes to his rather shiftless son, Joseph, who then absconds to America, where he loses the money in speculation.

This deconstruction of the inheritance plot so central to much of nineteenth-century British literature is part of a larger movement through which *The Nether World* tests a variety of standard literary formulas for happiness and success but finds that none of them work in the world of the poor. In particular, the more general formula of upward mobility turns out to be unavailable to Gissing's lower-class characters. More spiritual forms of salvation are unavailable as well. Religion, represented in the text only by the street-corner fanatic, Mad Jack, is simply irrelevant in these conditions. And marriage, a typical literary resolution, leads generally to misery and at best to burdens and responsibilities, as when the kindhearted Kirkwood weds the disfigured Clara and then must support her entire family on his modest income while she grows more and more despondent.

At one point in the text, Clara's father brings her a novel to read in order to help her get her mind off her disfigurement. But the novel, which deals with the glamorous lives of the rich, fails to address her condition in any productive way. Gissing, by devoting so many of his novels to the lives of the poor, attempts to counter the long-standing British literary tradition of focusing on the rich and in that sense performs a positive service, even though his novels are clearly directed at a middle-class audience. In particular, he provides a reminder that the poor are just as human as the rich, with many of the same strengths, failings, and aspirations, but with far fewer opportunities. In so doing, Gissing wrestled with many of the same problems later faced by more legitimately leftist writers. Gissing's extended literary meditation on the oppressive conditions of working-class life represents a genuinely new departure in mainstream British literature, while his analyses of class inequality in British society are often quite consonant with those of Marxist or socialist commentators, even if his own ideology was never genuinely socialist and then drifted gradually to the right in the course of his career. *Selected bibliography:* Goode; Grylls; Fredric Jameson (*Political Unconscious*); Keating (*Working Classes*); Poole.

J. C. GRANT: *THE BACK-TO-BACKS* **(1930).** Though not informed by a specifically socialist political consciousness, *The Back-to-Backs* helped to set the stage for the explosion of British leftist literature in the 1930s by calling attention to the oppressive plight of Britain's poor workers at the beginning of that decade. Though flawed by a certain amount of sensationalism and sentimentality, *The Back-to-Backs* is a powerful and shocking novel that was somewhat successful in its attempt to stimulate public outrage at the brutal and dehumanizing conditions under which coal miners in the North of England must work and in which they and their families must live. As Liam O'Flaherty emphasizes in his introduction to the novel, it is a "terrifying" account with ominous implications for the future of British society: "For if this abject slavery exists among us, if we allow vast hordes of our people to live in such a manner, more corrupt, more filthy, more bestial than cave-dwellers in primeval times, then the crash of our civilization can only be avoided by an immediate revolution" (v).

The Back-to-Backs is set in the hellish mining village of Hagger, where occasional moments of pleasure (as during the annual feast day celebration) provide only momentary relief from lives that consist primarily of an unending mixture of back-breaking toil and mind-deadening hopelessness. The plot focuses on the lives of the various members of the Shieldyke family, which includes the miner Geordie Shieldyke, his long-suffering wife, Jane, and their two sons, Willie and Tom, both of whom are also miners. The young woman Ailie Burt also lives with the family, her father, a friend of Geordie, having been killed in a mining accident. By Hagger standards, Tom is unusually sensitive and introspective, as is Ailie, though it is understood in the family that she will eventually wed the brutish Willie. She finally does so, in an attempt to cope with the shame of having finally succumbed to his animalistic sexual advances. The reduction of the various inhabitants of Hagger to the status of animals is, in fact, a central trope of the book, which employs a number of images of dehumanization in its presentation of the consequences of work in the pit and life in the village. We learn, for example, that Geordie in his youth had been harnessed like a horse to pull carts of coal from the mine. The later shift to ponies for this job was then, as Grant puts it, merely a "transference of the harness from one sort of creature to another" (29).

Predictably, the marriage of Willie and Ailie is not a happy one, and Ailie finds Willie's behavior increasingly repugnant as he continues to drink heavily and consort with prostitutes. Eventually, he is horribly killed when he catches fire and burns to death, running through the streets and screaming in agony, ending up on the gruesome slag heap that hovers over the village. Geordie, crushed by the death of his favorite son, commits suicide soon afterward. Jane, meanwhile, has already died, largely from overwork. Ailie is thus left alone to care for Tom, who has by now been maimed and paralyzed in a cave-in at the mine. These dark events are then capped off by a positive ending of sorts, as Tom, though helpless without her, nobly convinces Ailie to leave him and go away to marry the schoolteacher Tentergarth, who had earlier been forced to leave Hagger because of his controversial political views.

The plot of *The Back-to-Backs* is, however, secondary to the dark environment in which the events occur. For example, the book takes its title from the cramped and squalid rows of adjoining back-to-back hovels in which the miners must live, forced into such close proximity that they, themselves, must literally live back-to-back as well. And, while this environment is to some extent characterized through naturalistic detail, Grant's primary device is a series of striking, essentially expressionistic images of poverty and dehumanization, as Andy Croft rightly observes (75). Croft is probably also right that protests (often by the miners themselves) against the novel's presentation of miners as subhuman brutes arose largely from a misunderstanding of this technique and from a misplaced expectation of documentary realism. On the other hand, it is also true that the book, in its attempt to shock its readers, not only focuses on negative aspects of mining life, but exaggerates those aspects without presenting positive alternatives. In particular, as the image of the paralyzed Tom indicates, the book presents miners as essentially helpless victims unable to improve their lot, suggesting, instead, that the general population of Britain, especially the middle class, needs to take action to end the brutalization of the miners. *Selected bibliography:* Croft (*Red Letter Days*); O'Flaherty.

HENRY GREEN: *LIVING* (1929). In his autobiography, *Pack My Bag*, Green referred to class differences as "those narrow, deep and echoing gulfs which must be bridged" (68). *Living*, like many of Green's novels, is an attempt to do just that. It is structured around a parallel presentation of the lives of the workers in the Dupret Engineering Works and of their rich bosses, particularly the Dupret family itself. Management personnel, such as the works manager Bridges and the chief designer Tarver, who reside midway between these extremes, figure prominently in the book as well. The book also parallels public and private life, its multiple plot lines dealing both with private experiences such as illness, friendship, and courtship and with the public world of work and business. *Living* is written in a highly experimental style that seeks (through various devices such as the dropping of articles) to convey the feel of everyday life in a more direct way than is possible in conventional fiction. The result is a rather rough prose that Stokes identifies as "essentially the industrial workers' style," though the same style is used to represent the experiences of all of the classes in the book (199).

The public plot of *Living* deals primarily with the operation of the Dupret plant in Birmingham and with the attempts of the company to turn a profit in increasingly difficult economic times. These efforts sometimes lead to corner-cutting that results in unsafe working conditions; this also leads to the institution of oppressive practices, such as the stationing of a guard on the door of the lavatory to ensure that the men do not spend too much time there. The rivals Bridges and Tarver continually seek to undermine each other through various intrigues, while the business is also upset by the illness and eventual death of its founder and head, Old Dupret. Dupret is then succeeded by his son, Richard, age twenty-six, who understands very little about the operation of the business but who proceeds to institute new "efficiency" measures, such as divesting the company of all of its older workers, including Bridges, regardless of their years of service to the company, on the premise that they are less productive than younger men.

The private plots of the book deal with Dupret's illness (including one scene in which Mrs. Dupret hires a prostitute to try to perk him up a bit) and death and with Richard Dupret's ill-fated courtship of the socialite Hannah Glossop. An unsuccessful courtship is central to working-class life as well. Lily Gates, courted by both Jim Dale and Bert Jones, eventually chooses the latter, despite the preferences of her father and her benefactor, Craigan, for the former. She elopes with Jones to Liverpool, only to be abandoned there when he gets cold feet. Humiliated, she returns to Birmingham, but manages to get her mind off her troubles when the neighbor, Mrs. Eames, has a charming new baby that provides Lily with an effective diversion.

In the course of the book, Green makes clear the differences in the economic situations of the wealthy Duprets and workers such as Craigan and Gates. He also makes clear the sometimes ruthless ways in which workers are treated as their bosses strive to increase profits. Yet, one of the most striking effects of *Living* is to convey a sense that, especially on a private level, the workers and their bosses have a great deal in common. The two groups have many of the same kinds of personal experiences and feel many of the same emotions, despite their economic differences, and Green's goal seems to be to remind his readers that class-based distinctions between owners and workers are largely artificial, developed to serve as supports for the class inequalities of the economic system. It is nevertheless clear that Green's sympathies are with the workers rather than the rich Duprets, despite (or perhaps because of) his own upper-class origins—Green's father, like Dupret, owned a factory in Birmingham. In his introduction to the 1993 edition of the novel, John Updike compares Green's subject matter to that of D. H. Lawrence, "whereas Lawrence escaped from the working class, Green escaped into it, finding there a purpose and a gaiety hitherto lacking from his life" (12). Green ultimately seems to want to claim that the lives of his working-class characters are somehow humanly richer and more authentic than those of his upper-class characters. This reminder that capitalism does not bring happiness even to the rich is potentially an important one, but Green's suggestion of the greater authenticity of working-class life comes dangerously close to romanticizing the lives of the poor and to embracing the status quo, while ignoring the economic hardships under which the workers must struggle to survive. Perhaps more important, there is no real indication that the workers might be able to take action to improve their working and living conditions or to narrow the social and economic gap between them and their bosses. Thus, Ramón López Ortega, who finds Green's style basically effective in presenting the feel of working-class experience, concludes that "a better appreciation of the possibilities behind the squalor and misery would have contributed to a fuller picture" of working-class life (126). *Selected bibliography:* Green (*Pack My Bag*); Holmesland; López Ortega; Mengham; North; Stokes (*Henry Green*); Updike.

GRAHAM GREENE: *IT'S A BATTLEFIELD* **(1934).** *It's a Battlefield* is one of several novels produced by Greene in the course of the 1930s that, together, provide one of the most important fictional evocations of the texture of British life during that decade. While Greene is not typically listed among leftist novelists (partially because of his Catholic religious beliefs), his work was heavily influenced by leftist ideas during the 1930s, and much of his writing during that decade is highly critical of capitalism. For example, *A Gun for Sale* (1936) details a plot of large munitions firm to try to trigger World War II in order to increase business, while *England Made Me* (1935) depicts capitalist business activities as a form of organized theft. *Brighton Rock* (1938) picks up on this same theme in a more oblique way, portraying a debased every-man-for-himself criminal society that is in many ways reminiscent of Bertolt Brecht's *Threepenny Opera* (1928) as an allegorization of capitalism. Finally, *The Confidential Agent* (1939) involves an international intrigue centering on the Spanish Civil War, showing a concern with many of the issues that were central to the thought of the British Left in the 1930s. Of Greene's novels in the 1930s, however, it is probably *It's a Battlefield* that most thoroughly captures the mood of England in the 1930s and most effectively relates this mood to a crisis in capitalism itself. Grahame Smith, referring to the British tradition of writers such as Elizabeth Gaskell and Benjamin Disraeli, thus notes that the book is "a condition-of-England novel for its own time" (117).

It's a Battlefield combines naturalistic detail with modernist narrative techniques such as stream-of-consciousness vividly to evoke the impoverished climate of London during the Depression, and a general atmosphere of poverty and seediness underlies all of the action of the book. At the center of this action (though he never actually appears in the novel) is Jim Drover, a communist bus driver who sits in prison awaiting possible execution for killing a policeman (who was apparently about to assault Drover's wife, Milly) in the midst of a riot surrounding a political rally in London's Hyde Park. Drover's prison serves as the anchor for a number of carceral images (especially involving schools and factories) that combine to characterize modern English society as a sort of prison, while the title of the book is the center of a metaphorical pattern that characterizes this antagonistic society as based on a battle of all against all. The rally at which the killing occurs helps to set the historical context of the early 1930s, in which numerous demonstrations (many of which were organized by the Communist Party) were conducted in England to protest worsening economic and social conditions. As Norman Sherry notes in his biography of Greene, the most spectacular of these demonstrations was the Hunger March of 1932, when 3,000 people set out from the provinces to walk to London and were then joined by others along the way, their numbers swelling to over 100,000 by the time they gathered in London (460). This gathering did, in fact, lead to violent confrontations with police, and so can probably be considered the basis of the demonstration in which Greene's Drover killed the policeman. The anxiety of the authorities in *It's A Battlefield* over Drover's fate—they fear that leniency might encourage the enemies of the state and that his execution might trigger a violent response on the part of his supporters—indicates the seriousness of the political crisis that informed British society in the 1930s.

This anxiety causes the authorities to delay Drover's execution and to debate whether his sentence should be commuted to eighteen years in prison. Much of the action of the book involves the ultimately successful efforts of various characters, including Milly and Conrad Drover, Jim's brother, to work for that commutation. Indeed, most of the characters of the book are involved in one way or another in these efforts, though Greene seriously problematizes this motif by suggesting, among other things, that a lengthy prison term would hardly be a godsend for Jim Drover and would might, in the long run, impact the lives of those close to him more negatively than would his execution. In the meantime, the real story of the book centers on the attempts of the various characters to find some meaning in their lives amid the economically depressed and spiritually barren atmosphere that surrounds them. For example, one of the central figures in the book is the newspaper reporter, Conder, whose life is so empty that he attempts to escape into a whole network of fantasy identities. More down-to-earth is the "Assistant Commissioner" of police, whose identification by job title rather than name indicates the way in which he relies entirely on his work as a source of meaning in his life. But this meaning turns also out to be empty, especially as the Assistant Commissioner, who consistently maintains that it is his job to provide order, not justice, does not really believe in the values of the society that he is sworn to defend. In particular, he is entirely aware that the system he defends is unfair and works through the exploitation of the poor by the rich: "When he thought of the heavy sentences passed on men who stole a little jewelry from a rich man's house, the Assistant Commissioner was more than ever thankful that justice was not his business. He knew quite well the cause of the discrepancy; the laws were made by property owners in defence of property; that was why a Fascist could talk treason without prosecution; that was why a man who defrauded the State in defence of his private wealth did not even lose the money he had gained; that was why the burglar went to gaol for five years; that was why Drover could not so easily be reprieved" (169).

Meanwhile, Conrad Drover is also to some extent defined by his job in that he suffers from a radical alienation, largely because his intelligence and education have allowed him to advance to a position as a chief clerk that separates him from his working-class origins. He thus illustrates Richard Hoggart's discussion of English scholarship boys in the early twentieth century, noting their sense of being "emotionally uprooted from their class" and yet unable to win the genuine respect of cultivated middle-class people: "at one boundary the group includes psychotics; at the other, people leading apparently normal lives but never without an underlying sense of some unease" (225). Conrad (whose name is one of many signs in the book of the influence of Joseph Conrad on Greene's work) seeks to overcome this alienation through a romantic conception of love that leads him to a growing obsession with his sister-in-law, Milly. The two do, in fact, finally initiate a sexual relationship, but Conrad finds that the experience does not live up to his exaggerated expectations. Milly's sister, Kay Rimmer, also seeks escape (from the drudgery of her work in a match factory) through sexual relationships, but she lacks Conrad's romanticism. This approach leads her to become involved with the bitter and cynical Jules Briton, a sort of proto-Nazi who seeks any possible source of order and stability, preferably in the form of strong authority: "He wanted someone to say to him: 'Do this. Do that. Go here. Go there'" (41). Similarly vague is the approach of Lady Caroline Bury, a wealthy socialite and philanthropist who seeks meaning through a reliance on "faith," though she is unable to identify a stable object for this faith. And, finally, there is the prosperous leftist intellectual, Mr. Surrogate, who dedicates himself to abstract studies of economic injustice but is appalled by actual working-class people as individuals.

By the time Greene was writing *It's a Battlefield*, the Depression (and Greene's own financial insecurity) had led him to a decided left-wing orientation, despite the fact that his Catholicism made it impossible for him fully to accept communism. As Sherry puts it, "Greene's experiences of extreme financial insecurity had finally put paid to any lingering conservatism" (469). Indeed, the leftist sympathies of *It's a Battlefield* are clear, though the tone of skepticism and pessimism that runs through the book obviously limits its potential as a political novel. However, as Smith points out, the expression of these sympathies is "complicated both by Greene's hostility to communism and by a degree of uncertainty in his artistic presentation of working-class characters" (119). The book is fundamentally an investigation of the emptiness of spiritual life under capitalism, set against a material background of extreme social and economic inequality. In that sense, it provides a valuable supplement to more overtly leftist political novels from the 1930s, demonstrating the extent to which the ideas expressed in those novels found currency even in the works of more "mainstream" authors such as Greene. **Selected bibliography:** Allott and Farris; Couto; Greene (*Ways*); Hoggart; Sherry; Graham Smith.

WALTER GREENWOOD: *LOVE ON THE DOLE* (1933). *Love on the Dole* presents a vivid account of the tribulations of the working-class inhabitants of the impoverished "Hanky Park" district of the town of "Pendleton," based on Greenwood's own Salford, near Manchester. The book focuses primarily on the Hardcastle family and the increasing hardships they suffer in the course of the book. It opens in 1923 as young Harry Hardcastle, sixteen, completes his schooling and manages to obtain a position as an apprentice machinist in Marlowe's Engineering Works, one of the largest local employers. Harry's beautiful eighteen-year-old sister, Sally, works in the local cotton mill, their father is employed at a colliery, and their mother struggles to keep their household running. Harry begins his new job with extremely romantic expectations, which are soon to be disappointed. Indeed, he eventually realizes that Marlowe's is pursuing a policy of employing as many apprentices as possible because of their low wages and then dismissing them when their seven-year apprenticeship is finished. By the time Harry himself is dismissed, the English economy has taken an overall downturn. Mr. Hardcastle soon loses his job as well, while Sally is employed only part time. Harry and Mr. Hardcastle go on the dole, but conditions for the family become still worse when the introduction of the means test results in Harry being removed from the dole because he still lives with his family, who have Mr. Hardcastle's dole and Sally's meager salary for support.

Much of the book details the efforts of the residents of Hanky Park to maintain their humanity amid the brutal poverty in which they are forced to live. These efforts include the maintenance of underground economies revolving around local pawnshops and bookmakers, but the *Love on the Dole*, as its title indicates, focuses on the attempts of the various characters to establish and maintain meaningful human relationships, especially romantic ones. In the course of the book, Harry becomes engaged to Helen Hawkins and is forced to marry her after she becomes pregnant. This pregnancy leads to a violent confrontation between Harry and Mr. Hardcastle, and Harry and Helen are forced to live on their own, taking a squalid room as boarders with Mrs. Dorbell, one of the several local women who are important presences in the book. Harry deteriorates both physically and emotionally; by age twenty-four he is a beaten man. The beautiful Sally has numerous suitors, including the brutish local bully, Ned Narkey, and the wealthy but disreputable bookmaker, Sam Grundy. Appalled by such suitors, Sally falls in love with Larry Meath, a local worker who provides the book's principal political consciousness. As Ramón López Ortega notes, Meath (who has a great deal on common with Robert Tressell's Frank Owen) is "a familiar figure in proletarian literature: the typical autodidact who puts his education at the service of his class" (128). However, Meath is clearly set apart from the other locals by his superior sensitivity and intelligence, and his efforts to educate his fellow workers in social ideas meet with very little success. Already frail, Meath dies of pneumonia after being beaten by police, and Sally, driven to desperation, eventually becomes the mistress of Sam Grundy. Consequently, she is thrown out of the Hardcastle home by her father, who is overcome by shame both at her relationship with Grundy and at his own inability adequately to provide for his family. Nevertheless, Sally convinces Grundy to use his illegal contacts to obtain jobs for both Harry and Mr. Hardcastle, reinforcing a suggestion running through the book that, in these conditions, only criminals prosper. The book then ends as the neighborhood awakens in the early morning to another day of hardship—the same scene, in fact, with which the book begins.

A major theme of *Love on the Dole* is the frustration of romantic (in both senses of the word) desires amid the impoverished conditions of Hanky Park. As Greenwood, himself, put it, his goal in the book was "to show what life means to a young man living under the shadow of the dole, the tragedy of a lost generation who are denied consummation, in decency, of the natural hopes and desires of youth" (qtd. in Constantine 235). And, in its elaboration of the living conditions of this "lost generation," the book must be judged a success. Thus, in one of the most important accounts of modern British history, A.J.P. Taylor identifies *Love on the Dole* as "one of the few genuinely 'proletarian' novels written in English (352). Taylor goes on to suggest (not entirely accurately) that Greenwood's novel is rivaled only by Tressell's *The Ragged Trousered Philanthropists* as a proletarian novel, and Taylor is only one of a number of modern British historians who have regarded Greenwood's book as an authentic document of working-class life in the Depression-ravaged industrial areas of England in the 1930s. Indeed, as Stephen Constantine points out, the novel was the most popular of the numerous examples of working-class fiction that were produced in the 1930s, becoming a popular play (first performed in 1934) and eventually becoming a successful commercial film (in 1941).

However, Constantine further indicates that much of the success of the book had to do with its ability to appeal to a middle-class audience. This appeal arises from sources that may seriously limit the effectiveness of the book as a proletarian political statement. For one thing, the book is rather restrained in its depiction of the hardships of the poor, opting not to describe in any detail some of the more abject material consequences of poverty. For another, the book focuses almost exclusively on working-class characters and does not depict any significant middle- or upper-class characters as villains and as exploiters of the poor. Indeed, the book pays very little attention to the class structure of English society, its fundamental tensions being not between the rich and the poor, but between the "respectable and non-respectable residents of Hanky Park" (Constantine 239). In addition, despite Meath's occasional lectures on economic theory, the book does little to identify the fundamental workings of capitalism as the ultimate cause of the poverty of Hanky Park.

Finally, the relative lack of emphasis on political action in *Love on the Dole* prevented the book from being alarming to a middle-class audience. This lack is a serious one, the only significant instance of working-class protest against exploitation being a demonstration late in the book against the means test, and even this demonstration (during which Meath is beaten by police, leading to his death) seems rather ineffectual. Indeed, the circular structure of the book suggests an unending repetition of the miseries of Hanky Park that shows no sense of possible historical change. Carole Snee summarizes this limitation of Greenwood's book: "He writes within the naturalistic mode, and that technique reflects and reproduces his deep-rooted pessimism about the working class, for it enables him to depict the surface of working-class life in all its sordid squalor, but does not allow the reader to penetrate beneath that surface to see either its potential richness, or the possibility of the working class changing its own conditions of existence" (171).

Snee believes that this limitation arises primarily from the author's inability to transcend his own bourgeois consciousness. For her, Greenwood's novel is "a cry of outrage, but the rage is impotent, for his own ideological position is essentially that of the liberal reformer" (171). Similarly, Roy Johnson concludes that the book ultimately upholds many of the most cherished values of "polite middle-class orthodoxy" (88).

For Snee, Greenwood's bourgeois position shows up not only in the content of the book, but in its individualist aesthetics, which are those of the conventional novel. On the other hand, López Ortega finds in the book's language an effective representation of working-class consciousness, while Roger Webster makes an extended argument that the book actually manages to subvert bourgeois literary conventions. He argues that *Love on the Dole* engages these conventions in such a way that it reveals their ideological foundations. Thus, rather than obscure the workings of ideology in the mode of the bourgeois novel, Greenwood's book links "the conspiracy or plot of fiction to that of capitalist society" and thus suggests an important new direction for the novel form (61). In short, Constantine is probably right that Greenwood's picture of working-class life in Britain in the late 1920s and early 1930s is enhanced by the author's "skills as a novelist" (239). But whether these skills themselves identify him as a fundamentally bourgeois writer is open to debate. ***Selected bibliography:*** Constantine; Johnson ("Proletarian Novel"); López Ortega; Snee; Taylor; Webster.

PATRICK HAMILTON: *HANGOVER SQUARE* **(1941).** Patrick Hamilton was a successful British novelist and playwright of the 1930s and 1940s. He produced a large variety and volume of work, though he is best known in America for the two plays that formed the respective bases of the 1948 Hitchcock film *Rope* and the 1944 George Cukor film

Gaslight (itself a remake of a 1939 film, also based on Hamilton's play, of the same title). Much of Hamilton's work arose from a distinctly leftist political perspective. For example, his trilogy of novels from the early 1930s, *The Midnight Bell*, *The Siege of Pleasure*, and *The Plains of Cement* (published in 1935 as a single volume under the collective title *Twenty Thousand Streets under the Sky*) is an important fictional exploration of working-class life that shows a tremendous respect and admiration for the common people of London while at the same time criticizing structures of oppression based on class and gender. Patrick Hamilton was the brother of Bruce Hamilton, a successful writer of detective novels and thrillers, who also became enthusiastically devoted to Marxism in the 1930s.

The novel *Hangover Square* is an excellent example of Patrick Hamilton's contribution to British leftist culture. Set during the months leading to the beginning of World War II in 1939, it explores certain aspects of modern capitalist culture that have made fascism a possibility. In particular, it uncovers certain weaknesses in modern British culture that led many citizens of Britain to become fascinated with fascism in the 1930s and that rendered the British too slow to resist fascism, making World War II unavoidable. *Hangover Square* is essentially a detective fiction, though it is a highly unusual one in that there is no detective and the murder around which the plot revolves occurs at the end of the book. Indeed, the central mystery of the book is whether the crime will occur at all.

The central character of the book is George Harvey Bone, an unemployed man in his mid-thirties who has become obsessed with Netta Longdon, a beautiful but untalented young actress. Netta takes full advantage of George's affections, repeatedly humiliating and manipulating him with the collusion of her circle of decadent friends, particularly Peter, a young man of humble origins, whose bitterness at his own inability to enter the upper classes has driven him to fascism. Netta is attracted to the spectacle of fascism as well, while George, who embodies decency and traditional English values, is horrified by the specter of what is going on in Germany and much of the rest of Europe. However, George (like British culture) is also mentally ill, afflicted with a multiple personality disorder that finds him switching repeatedly between his relatively innocuous "normal" self to another self that is determined to murder both Netta and Peter. Eventually, the murders do occur, after which George, realizing that the killings have solved nothing, commits suicide by gassing himself, just as news of the declaration of war between England and Germany comes over the radio. Thus, George's private disaster and the public disaster represented by the outbreak of the war converge in a single moment, completing the function of

George's personal failures as a metaphor for the failure of modern civilization. *Selected bibliography:* Croft (*Red Letter Days*); Gindin.

JAMES HANLEY: *BOY* **(1931).** First published in two different editions in 1931 (with asterisks replacing certain "obscene" passages in one version), *Boy* became one of the most notorious works of British literature from the 1930s when it was republished in an unexpurgated edition in 1934 only to be seized by the police and subsequently banned for obscenity. Many writers, including such famous figures as E. M. Forster, in his address to the 1935 Congress of Writers in Paris, defended the book on the basis of its artistic merits. Nevertheless, Hanley himself, disgusted by the controversy, forbade further publication of the book during his lifetime. This move probably enhanced the book's fame; it remained his best known work, though he produced numerous stories of the darker side of working-class life during the decade. Hanley showed a remarkable capacity for describing not only the details of working-class life but the violent emotional impact of those details on the workers. Thus, Valentine Cunningham, though concerned at the extreme violence that tends to inform Hanley's work, calls Hanley "by far ... the best proletarian realist" of the 1930s (56). Hanley's other fictional works included *The German Prisoner* (1930), *A Passion Before Death* (1930), *Men in Darkness* (1931), *The Last Voyage* (1931), and *The Furys* (1935). He also wrote important nonfiction works, such as *Broken Water: An Autobiographical Excursion* (1937) and *Grey Children: A Study of Humbug and Misery* (1937, an account of impoverished conditions in the industrial regions of South Wales). Hanley died in 1985, and *Boy* was finally republished in 1990. It is now regarded as something of a minor classic in modern British literature.

The Irish-born Hanley grew up in Liverpool but left his Liverpool home to go to sea at age thirteen, and *Boy* is to some extent based on that experience. Its title character (generally referred to in the text simply as "the boy" rather than by name) is Arthur Fearon, who is forced to leave school to go to work at age thirteen to help support his impoverished family. Sensitive, introspective, and small for his age, Arthur finds his hellish job at the local docks (which consists primarily of descaling the insides of hot, smelly ship's boilers) difficult and degrading. Meanwhile, he continues to suffer abuse at home at the hands of his violent father. In desperation, Arthur stows away on board a ship bound for Alexandria so that he can escape the squalid conditions in which he lives. This motif, of course, is a staple of British adventure stories, and Arthur, himself, harbors a number of romantic expectations concerning the journey. His story turns out to be anything but romantic, however. Having nearly suffocated in a boiler in his previous job, he again nearly suffocates beneath a pile of coal on the ship, thus emphasizing the confining and carceral nature of nearly every aspect of his life. Once he is dragged out, half-dead, from beneath the coal, he finds that things improve very little. In particular, he suffers constant abuse at the hands of the crew, who take advantage of his small size and youth to make him the object not only of derision but of crude sexual advances. The frank treatment of this abuse was, in fact, one of the principal reasons why the book was originally banned. Arthur's subsequent sexual experience in Egypt is treated frankly as well. Ashore in Cairo, he attempts to proves his manhood by visiting a local brothel, and this experience momentarily reawakens his dreams of romance. These dreams end abruptly, however, when the prostitute he visits throws him down the stairs of the brothel. Moreover, he contracts syphilis from the encounter and falls seriously ill on the return voyage to England. As the delirious boy, now fifteen, cries for his mother, he is silenced by the ship's captain, who (in one final reenactment of the book's central metaphor of suffocation) smothers the boy and then throws his body overboard. Arthur is then reported lost at sea, thus avoiding the scandal of having such a young boy on board with syphilis.

Hanley's frank and vivid description of Arthur's brief but tortured life is viscerally powerful. It is also politically effective in that Arthur's experiences are clearly presented as examples of the kinds of dehumanizing and brutalizing treatment to which workers are frequently subjected. Moreover, the fact that Arthur suffers so much abuse from his fellow workers enhances rather than weakens this message, suggesting that the domination of workers by bosses is enabled by the participation of the workers themselves and therefore could presumably be ended by collective resistance on the part of the workers. Indeed, while the violence and brutality depicted by Hanley in his work can be overpowering, they are clearly demonstrated to be the result of dehumanizing social conditions and not of human nature. Therefore, despite their dark tone, Hanley's works suggest that the gruesome conditions he describes are not inevitable but might be subject to change by human intervention. *Selected bibliography:* Cunningham; Hanley (*Broken Water*); Stokes (*James Hanley*).

MARGARET HARKNESS: *A CITY GIRL* **(1887).** *A City Girl* was the first novel of Margaret Harkness, who, publishing under the pseudonym John Law, was a pioneer in the representation of working-class experience in British literature. This novel also has a special historical importance for leftist aesthetics because of Friedrich Engels's critique of the novel, contained in a letter written to Harkness in 1888, which puts forth a number of fundamental ideas that have remained influential for Marxist critics and theorists ever since that time (Marx and Engels, *Literature and Art* 41–43). In the letter, Engels diplomatically praises Harkness for her focus on the working class, so long neglected in British literature. On the other hand, he concludes that Harkness needs to make her working-class characters less passive and that she must work to achieve greater realism and detailed accuracy in her representations, preferably through the "truthful reproduction of typical characters under typical circumstances" (41). He also puts forth his influential notion that Honoré de Balzac, despite his personal reactionary philosophy, is "a far greater master of realism" than the left-leaning Émile Zola; Engels thus urges Harkness, who was so obviously influenced by Zola, to turn to Balzac as a model instead (42–43).

A City Girl does lack realism and, in fact, reads like a sort of fable. It focuses on Nelly Ambrose, a young woman who lives in poverty in the West End tenement known as Charlotte's Buildings but who harbors a number of romantic dreams of a better life. She works hard sewing trousers for a local "sweater," but nevertheless carries herself with such airs that she is famed among the local inhabitants as one who "fancies herself." As the book begins, Nelly seems fated to wed George, a former serviceman who now works as the caretaker of Charlotte's Buildings. Through George, however, she meets Arthur Grant, a middle-class journalist and sometime radical. Nelly is smitten by Grant's education and culture, so superior to those of George, and the two begin a brief clandestine relationship, though Grant has a wife and family in his comfortable West-End home. The relationship soon breaks off, but Nelly finds herself pregnant and winds up fleeing Charlotte's Buildings in disgrace. George, who feels unable to marry her in her fallen condition, still helps her to find lodgings with an old woman who works for the Salvation Army. The woman treats Nelly kindly, and the Salvation Army is generally treated quite sympathetically in the book as a genuine friend of the working class, though Nelly's own Catholic Church is consistently shown, in contrast, as merely contributing to the further misery of the poor. Nelly's baby, a boy, is born in the new lodgings, and the Salvation Army's Captain Lobe (protagonist of one of Harkness's subsequent novels) helps Nelly to find work, again sewing trousers.

The undernourished child soon becomes ill, and Nelly is forced to take him to a local hospital, where she encounters a great deal of institutional indifference to working-class suffering. When Nelly returns the next morning to visit her son, she finds that he is already dead. In a scene of somewhat maudlin melodrama, she then emerges from the hospital with the dead child in her arms, runs into Grant, and shows him his dead baby, the existence of which he had hitherto been unaware. The book ends as George, who has been offered a position caring for the gardens at a rural writers' colony, asks Nelly to go there with him as his wife. This situation, however, is less than the ideal one of which Nelly had formerly dreamed. For one thing, it is clear that George feels that she is marriageble only because the illegitimate child is conveniently out of the way, and only then if they move to a new locale where her past will not be known. Nelly does not, in fact, give George an answer, and, in the closing lines, he mutters to himself that he should have never left the army.

Harkness shows a sympathy with the working class that was unusual in British literature of the 1880s, though the Dickensian sentimentality (and even condescension) with which this sympathy is tinged tends to reduce the effectiveness of the novel. And Harkness's clear fascination with the Salvation Army as a potential means for the improvement of working-class life is highly problematic, all the more so because of the lack of any sense of genuine political action on the part of the working class. Indeed, Harkness's working-class characters are rather wooden figures who tend to be passive victims of social forces over which they have no control. Thus, even Peter Keating (who finds much to admire in Harkness's portrayal of working-class life) concludes that Harkness was unsuccessful in reversing the class bias of mainstream Victorian fiction and that her fiction is, in fact, valuable primarily for the way it contrasts with that mainstream tradition and thus illuminates the bourgeois bias of most Victorian literature. *Selected bibliography:* Goode ("Margaret Harkness"); Keating (*The Working Classes*); Marx and Engels (*Literature and Art*); von Rosenberg.

MARGARET HARKNESS: *OUT OF WORK* **(1888).** *Out of Work* was the second novel published by Harkness (under the pseudonym John Law), and the book, as John Goode notes, "shows many signs of a sophisticated response" to the advice given her earlier by Friedrich Engels with regard to her first novel, *A City Girl*, published in 1887 ("Margaret Harkness" 57). *Out of Work* is much more firmly rooted in reality than its predecessor and is in fact structured around two real historical events that occurred in 1887, the Queen's Jubilee, celebrating the fiftieth anniversary of Victoria's reign as Queen of England, and the Trafalgar Square riots of November 1887, growing out of discontent over the depressed condition of the British economy. The contrast between these two events not only provides a framework upon which Harkness can build her fictional narrative, but provides important thematic material as well, demonstrating the radical inconsistency between the increasingly grand and theatrical presentation of the British monarchy during this period and the increasingly impoverished conditions under which the lower classes of Britain are forced to live.

Out of Work begins as Victoria and her procession visit the East End in an obvious attempt to impress the poor inhabitants there, much as various imperial spectacles during this period were designed to impress the inhabitants of India and other parts of the British Empire. As John L.

Kijinski points out, the parallels between these domestic and colonial spectacles demonstrate the extent to which impoverished areas such as London's East End were envisioned as foreign and exotic locales and described via many of the same colonialist stereotypes that were being applied to more distant regions of the Empire. Moreover, as David Cannadine notes, the growing splendor of late-Victorian royal ceremony was a marker not of the growth of Victoria's power but of her gradual loss of real political clout as parliament assumed more and more of the actual responsibility for ruling Britain and the Empire. The growing ritualization of the British monarchy, then, involved "not so much the re-opening of the theatre of power as the premiére of the cavalcade of impotence" (121).

Indeed, in *Out of Work*, the starving inhabitants of Whitechapel are far from being overwhelmingly awed by Victoria's visit, which draws as many grumbles and hisses as cheers. The hypocrisy of this visit sets the stage for the next scene, in which the complacent and relatively well-to-do congregation of a Methodist chapel attempts to ignore the social injustice that surrounds them. A ragged man who wanders into the service is clearly far from welcome, especially when he begins to ask embarrassing questions of the ministers, who respond by giving him a penny as a bribe to leave. Harkness uses Christian imagery throughout the text to suggest that the ragged poor are the true constituents of Christ and that those who abandon the poor are not true Christians no matter how self-righteous they may be. This chapel scene sets the stage for the introduction of Mrs. Elwin, a Methodist widow, who runs a boarding house in the area, and her daughter, Polly, a "pretty Methodist," who has recently become engaged, somewhat to her mother's chagrin, to Joseph Coney, a young carpenter who has come to London from the provinces to seek his fortune. For workers such as Jos, however, there are no fortunes to be made in London at this time. In fact, he is unemployed and fast running out of money. Meanwhile, Polly is increasingly attracting the attentions of William Ford, the leader of her Methodist study class, who warns her against marrying Jos, supposedly because the carpenter belongs to the Church of England, but actually because he hopes to have Polly for himself.

Jos gradually descends deeper and deeper into poverty, moving from the Elwins' boarding house to some cheaper rooms and finally to a squalid doss-house, gradually growing weak and ill from hunger. In the doss-house, he meets a young girl known as the Squirrel, who has grown up on the streets and helps Jos to make his way in the unfamiliar underworld of London's poor. Jos finds occasional work on London's docks but soon takes to alcohol to such an extent that he is often unable to work. Eventually, he and the Squirrel leave the doss-house and begin sleeping, along with large numbers of other poor Londoners, out of doors in Trafalgar Square. The police soon crack down on this practice, however, and begin to clear the square at night. Jos briefly goes into a workhouse where he is to earn his keep by breaking slabs of granite. He is soon released, however, when a flying chip of granite injures his eye. He and the Squirrel move back into the doss-house and live off of the money she makes selling flowers in Trafalgar Square.

Conditions go from bad to worse for Jos. He is inadvertently caught up in the Trafalgar Square riots, then beaten by a policeman and arrested. The Squirrel uses her last pennies to pay his fine, but soon after his release he is jilted by Polly, presumably because he is not a Methodist but more because of his degraded and impoverished condition. Jos, defeated by London, decides to return to his rural village, though he no longer has family or friends there. He leaves without a word to the Squirrel, whom he has never regarded as a woman—or even as entirely human—despite all she has done for him and despite the fact that she obviously loves him. Heartbroken, she throws herself in the Thames and drowns as the narrator quotes the last words of Christ in accompaniment. Jos staggers homeward, reaching the village in a state of near starvation, then crawling onto the grave of his mother, where he dies of hunger. He is buried in his mother's grave, and his sad story thus comes to an end.

The exaggerated sentimentality of this ending may be a bit overdone, but in general the characters of *Out of Work* are reasonably believable both as individuals and as representatives of their class. And the suffering of Jos and the Squirrel, however extreme, is no more extreme than that suffered by many of the inhabitants of the East End of London during this period. Moreover, while Jos and the Squirrel are both victims of a powerful and heartless system, the book contains at least the beginnings of a depiction of collective action in the way the poor characters of the book are often shown sharing their resources and helping one another. The disturbances in Trafalgar Square, however quickly they are squelched by official action, even suggest the possibility of mass action against official power, while specifically socialist ideas are promulgated in the text by George, Jos's dockworker friend, and by a speaker that Jos and George hear on the street near the end of chapter 4. *Out of Work* thus represents a significant advance beyond *A City Girl* and deserves to be regarded as an important founding text in the tradition of the modern British novel of the Left. *Selected bibliography:* Cannadine; Goode ("Margaret Harkness"); Kijinski; Kirwan; von Rosenberg.

MARGOT HEINEMANN: *THE ADVENTURERS* **(1961).** *The Adventurers*, although presumably written from a leftist perspective, is less an argument for socialism than a documentation of the doubts and disagreements that plagued the British Left in the late 1950s and early 1960s.

In particular, the book is informed by a strong sense of the disillusionment with communism that marked that period in the wake of Nikita Khrushchev's disavowal of Joseph Stalin and the Soviet intervention in Hungary in 1956. *The Adventurers*, which actually begins during World War II, shows domestic disillusionment as well, particularly with the Labour Government that was elected in 1945 and that, under the leadership of Prime Minister Clement Attlee, held power until 1951, instituting a number of reforms but failing to carry out a genuinely socialist agenda, partly because of pressures brought about by the polarizing climate of global Cold War politics.

The Adventurers focuses on labor activism in the coal industry, something Heinemann knew a great deal about, having done substantial research during and after World War II into the status of Britain's coal industry while producing such studies as *Britain's Coal: A Study of the Mining Crisis* (1944) and *Coal Must Come First* (prepared for the Labour Research Department in 1948). The central character of *The Adventurers* is Dan Owen, the bookish son of a Welsh miner, who is determined never to go into the mines. Indeed, this determination is so strong that, as the book begins, he is sentenced to three months in prison because he refuses to work in the mines under a wartime emergency order, preferring instead to fight in the war, which strikes him as a more romantic endeavor. In response, some of his fellow "Bevin boys" (named for Ernest Bevin, the trade union and Labour Party leader who served as Minister of Labour in Churchill's wartime government) threaten a sympathy strike. Union leader Lewis Connor, a longtime leader of the Welsh miners, intervenes in the dispute and manages to avert the strike and to get Dan released from prison and reassigned to the Royal Air Force, partially by arguing that the young man has claustrophobia. But Dan's horror of the mines suggests the beginnings of an alienation from his working-class background that becomes more and more extreme as he grows older. Dan does well in the RAF and eventually wins a postwar scholarship to Keir Hardie College, at Cambridge, depicted here as a workingman's college. In college, Dan begins to suspect that the ideas and oppositions he had learned in his socialist-oriented working-class upbringing were overly simplistic, and it is thus not surprising that, when he later becomes a journalist and broadcaster, he does little to further the cause of workers. In fact, he often promulgates information that works to the detriment of the miners and that sometimes amounts to little more than anticommunist propaganda. In essence, he becomes an enemy of his own class, without ever openly breaking with his roots or apparently even realizing the depth of his own betrayal.

Dan thus functions as an image of the desertion of the working class by its intellectual leaders in postwar Britain. Meanwhile, this leadership goes awry in other ways as well, as when reforms instituted by the

Labour government (such as the nationalization of the coal mines) often seem to work against the miners. Connor, though, with strong roots in prewar trade unionism, continues to toil for his constituents, suggesting an older and more reliable tradition of leadership that contrasts strongly with that of the new generation represented by Dan. Of course, Heinemann was very much involved in the leftist culture of the 1930s, both through her own work and through her personal relationship with John Cornford, a prominent leftist poet who was killed in the Spanish Civil War. It might also be noted that Heinemann coauthored, with Noreen Branson, an excellent social history of the 1930s. The third important figure of leftist leadership in Britain in *The Adventurers* is Richard Adams, a classmate of Dan's at Keir Hardie who remains a loyal communist throughout the tribulations of the late 1950s, despite his shock and outrage at developments in Eastern Europe during that time. Through Adams, Heinemann thus apparently suggests the ongoing value of communism, or at least socialism, as a road to social justice, though Adams's own tormented doubts tend to call this point into question. **Selected bibliography:** Branson and Heinemann; Heinemann (*Britain's Coal*); Heinemann (*Coal Must Come First*).

HAROLD HESLOP: *THE GATE OF A STRANGE FIELD* **(1929).** *The Gate of a Strange Field* was the first of Heslop's novels centering on life in the Durham coalfields to be published in English. The book shows considerable knowledge of and sympathy with the hardships encountered by coal miners, hardships which Heslop had himself experienced first hand. The book also deals extensively with the attempts of coal miners to improve their lives through trade union activism. However, these attempts are rather ineffectual, and indeed the title of the book, according to Heslop's autobiography, *Out of the Old Earth*, is taken from H. G. Wells's description of the General Council of the Trade Union Congress as being confused and disorganized "like sheep at the gate of a strange field" (*Out of the Old Earth* 192). Partially due to its skeptical treatment of trade unions, *Goaf* lacks the strong sense of commitment to political action that informs a later work, *Last Cage Down* (1935), Heslop's best known novel. Indeed, David Bell describes *The Gate of a Strange Field* as a sort of "negative apprenticeship" on the part of Heslop, in which the lessons he learned by his own prior political mistakes are reflected in the mistakes made by Joe Tarrant, the protagonist of the book (117). In particular, Bell concludes that the purpose of the book is to demonstrate the limitations of trade union activity, limitations that would become all too clear to Heslop in his later, more radical, phase.

The first and longest segment of *The Gate of a Strange Field*, entitled "Adolescence," describes the beginnings of Joe Tarrant's career as a coal miner in the Hunton Pit after finishing his schooling at age fourteen. He works hard, does well, and gradually advances up the hierarchy of coal-mining jobs. Meanwhile, he begins a courtship with Molly Grahame that ends in her pregnancy and their marriage, though Joe is far less than enthusiastic about beginning married life at the age of eighteen. The segment ends as the couple begins their married life together, their adolescence abruptly brought to an end. In the second segment of the book, entitled "The Awakening," Joe gradually becomes more and more aware of the exploitation of miners by the mine owners and consequently becomes involved in trade union activities. Already, however, the union seems ineffectual, and conditions for the miners gradually worsen. Meanwhile, Joe continues his married life with Molly and their baby girl, Marie. However, he meets Emily Rutter at this time and becomes smitten not only by the young woman's beauty but by her devotion to the moderate socialist ideals of the Independent Labour Party. Emily returns his affection and the two begin an affair that results in a scandal. Molly takes Marie and leaves Joe, while Joe sets up housekeeping with Emily.

In the third segment of the text, entitled "Strife," struggles between the miners' union and the mine owners intensify, with the results generally favoring the owners. The confrontation culminates in the General Strike of 1926 and ultimately in an ignominious defeat for the workers. Left to fight on alone after the quick end to the General Strike, the miners, after much hardship, are forced to return to work on the owners' terms. Indeed, it seems clear that much of the pessimism and negativity of *The Gate of a Strange Field* arises from Heslop's attempts to come to terms with the failure of the General Strike. Joe is actively involved in the General Strike, his work in relation to which takes him to London, where he again meets Molly. After a brief period as a prostitute, she is now the mistress of a rich married man. Joe finds her beautiful and clearly finds her newfound sexual sophistication intriguing. He longs to renew their marriage, which further alienates him from Emily, whom he is beginning to find boring. He is also losing patience with the moderation of Emily's political views, and this segment ends as she goes away to Scotland to lecture for the Independent Labour Party, while Joe returns to work in the mine and moves back in with his mother. In the fourth segment, mining finally begins in a new section of the mine where the miners had long refused to work because of the danger of flooding. A flood does occur, and many of the miners are killed. Joe manages to escape drowning, but he is trapped, along with another miner, inside the mine. They are rescued, nearly dead from starvation, seventeen days later, when pumps are finally able to clear the mine of water. The doctor pronounces that there is a good chance they will survive, though the book ends before they regain consciousness.

The pessimism that informs *The Gate of the Strange Field*, combined with the rather antiheroic nature of its protagonist, drew considerable criticism from the Left at the time the book was published, including a strongly negative assessment by Anna Elistratova in *International Literature* in 1932. And it is certainly true that the book, by failing to suggest the possibility of radical political change through the collective action of workers, has serious limitations as a leftist novel. Thus, even Alick West, who finds much to value in the novel (comparing it favorably to James Joyce's *Ulysses*), concludes that it tends to depict conditions as static rather than as evolving historically, so that the events of the novel are estranged from the process of history, and "class-war in the novel is consequently a word, rather than a reality" (196). Nevertheless, Heslop's personal experience of the mines and his ability vividly to convey that experience in his writing made positive contributions to the development of British literature, while Heslop would later work to overcome the limitations of his early novels by building stronger utopian and historical dimensions into his writing. *Selected bibliography:* Bell; Elistratova; Heslop (*Out of the Old Earth*); West (*Crisis*).

HAROLD HESLOP: *GOAF* (1934). Though not published in English until 1934, *Goaf* is a revision of an earlier novel (*Pod Vlastu Uglya*, or "In the Power of Coal") that was published in its Russian translation in the Soviet Union in 1925 after the initial version had been rejected for publication in England. The semiautobiographical novel was apparently successful in the Soviet Union and was eventually reprinted there in a second, mass edition of half a million copies (Heslop, *Out of the Old Earth* 172). Thus, *Goaf* is, in a sense, Heslop's first novel; drawing directly as it does from Heslop's own firsthand experience of the Durham coalfields, it begins to establish the vivid fictional evocation of the experience of miners that would come to be the hallmark of his fiction. *Goaf* is somewhat less bitterly pessimistic than Heslop's *The Gate of a Strange Field* (1929), probably because *Goaf* was written before the abortive General Strike of 1926, an event that soured Heslop on trade unionism once and for all. However, *Goaf* already resembles *Gate* in terms of its skepticism toward the potential of trade union activism to win social and economic justice for coal miners and other workers. *Goaf* lacks the clear communist political message that would inform the *Last Cage Down* (1935), though *Goaf* does feature a protagonist who leans toward socialism and greatly admires the Russian Bolsheviks.

This protagonist is Tom Drury, a young coal miner from the Durham town of Shielding who becomes married early in the book to Cynthia Nesbit, a close friend of Margaret Wilson, the niece of "Big Bill" Watson, a former miner who has risen to become a Labour Member of Parliament (M. P.) from nearby Yarra. Watson is also a major figure in the text, and many of the book's political statements are conveyed via the debates between the Marxist Drury and the more conservative socialist Watson.

Watson has good intentions and is treated positively, but his inability to work genuine change through parliamentary politics functions in the text as a warning against the ineffectuality of such strategies. Tom Drury seeks to improve conditions for the Durham miners through direct trade union activism, quickly rising to the post of secretary of the Darlstone Miners' Association. Unfortunately, he manages to win very little for the miners, partly because of the machinations of Jack Hartley, a rival union leader who undermines many of Tom's projects while colluding with the mine management for his own personal advancement. Battles between the miners and management eventually lead to violence as the miners take to the streets and battle police. Tom, though he attempts to prevent this violence, is arrested on a charge of riot, but he is acquitted in court through the effective efforts of his Jewish solicitor, Stein.

Tom eventually wins out over Hartley, who is officially declared a traitor by the Hunton Lodge of the Miners' Association. Conditions in the mines continue to worsen nevertheless, and Tom is eventually trapped (with Hartley, now an overman in the mine) after a cave-in caused by unsafe working conditions. Tom attempts to get out of the mine by going through the dangerous goaf, the abandoned, previously mined area of the mine, while the cowardly Hartley remains in the area where they had been trapped. Hartley goes mad from the solitude and darkness and commits suicide with a knife left by Tom. Unable to get through the goaf, Tom collapses from hunger and exhaustion, but Watson leads a heroic rescue effort that manages to save him. Somewhat predictably, however, Tom is suspected of murdering Hartley and is brought to trial. Again, however, he is acquitted, largely through the spirited defense presented by Ben Purley a friend and fellow M. P. of Watson. At the end of the book, Tom returns happily to Cynthia and their new baby girl, so that, at least at the personal level, the book closes on a positive note.

At the collective level of the miners as a group, however, the tone of the book is largely negative. Watson, himself, comes to suspect that his career in politics has been useless, while Tom never really manages to follow through on his Marxist convictions but instead continues to operate (to no avail) at the level of rather conventional trade union activity. Purley is also an interesting figure in this regard. Something of a thinker, he authors a book entitled *Is Capitalism to Survive?* which causes Watson to compare him to the socialist historian G.D.H. Cole. Purley's thesis in the book (with which Watson entirely agrees) is that capitalism cannot survive but will eventually yield to socialism. However, he argues that Marx's analysis of this process, though in some ways brilliant, was confused and is inappropriate to conditions in modern England. For Purley, justice in England can never be achieved through revolution, but only through patient political and social reforms instituted by a Labour government (182–83). The bulk of Heslop's novel, however, suggests that Purley's evolution-over-revolution argument is a farce and that the current system will never yield to the kind of moderate reform proposed in Purley's book. What *Goaf* lacks, however, is any real sense that revolution can work either, ultimately leaving its miners very much at the mercy of powerful forces over which they have little control. It is only with *Last Cage Down* that this kind of positive statement will emerge as an important element of Heslop's fiction. **Selected bibliography:** Bell; Heslop (*Out of the Old Earth*).

HAROLD HESLOP: *LAST CAGE DOWN* **(1935).** Heslop's background as a Durham coal miner combines with his extensive writing experience and his sophisticated studies of Marxist theory to make his various novels of mining life among the more accomplished of the numerous mining novels that together constitute an important strand in the modern British novel of the Left. Central to his career is the sequence of three mining novels that includes *The Gate of a Strange Field* (1929), *Goaf* (1934), and *Last Cage Down*. The last is the best known and perhaps the most accomplished of the three. As Andy Croft puts it in his introduction to the 1984 edition of the novel, *Last Cage Down* shows "one of our most important working-class novelists at his most rhetorical and readable, the product of a literary patronage that helped encourage the most successful period of British working-class writing" (xiii). In the book, Heslop manages to convey much of the texture of mining life in the difficult years of the 1930s, while at the same time conducting a withering critique of the failure of British trade union leadership to defend the rights of workers during this period and conveying his firm belief that British workers needed to turn to the Soviet Union as an example in their attempt to achieve such justice.

The principal protagonist of *Last Cage Down* is Jim Cameron, a respected leader of the miners in the Franton Colliery and secretary of the local union lodge. Cameron leads the miners out on strike when the pompous and tyrannical mine owner, Tate, insists upon beginning to mine, using automated techniques, a new seam that has hitherto been regarded as unworkable because of its weak roof. However, the strike collapses after four weeks, largely because the Franton miners receive little support from the union leaders in the Darlstone Miners' Association and have to fight the battle essentially on their own. The miners return to work on Tate's terms, and work begins on the new seam. Cameron, whose own father earlier died in a roof collapse in the area of the new seam, is infuriated and swears that he will personally kill Tate if any miners die while mining the new seam; these threats lead to a nine-month prison sentence for Cameron. Meanwhile, Tate maneuvers to gain control of the Franton union lodge, managing to have his own candidate, the sanctimonious Jack Tasker, elected to replace the imprisoned Cameron as secretary.

When Cameron finally returns from prison, he finds conditions greatly deteriorated. Work continues in the new seam, with Jim's own brother, Jack, as one of the miners there. Jim's mother, Elsa, has been evicted from the house (owned by the mining company) where she has lived for decades, ever since marrying Jim's and Jack's father. And the miners, under Tasker's leadership, are unable to mount any effective challenge to Tate's exploitative practices. Jim, meanwhile, is denied the opportunity to return to work in the mines and thus finds himself suddenly an outsider in his own community, no longer a leader of the lodge or even a fellow worker of the other miners. Jim's new alienation is, however, in a sense symbolically appropriate because, despite his devotion to working for fair treatment for his fellow miners, he is a fierce individualist. Though an admirable figure in many ways, Cameron has been thoroughly interpellated by the ideology of bourgeois liberalism, leading him to reject communism as an alternative and to envision the class struggle between miners and owners as a personal confrontation between himself and Tate.

David Smith argues that Cameron is such a compelling character that his depiction tends to undermine Heslop's anti-individualist message (64). But it is clear that Cameron's individualism has disastrous consequences and makes him unable to lead an effective opposition to Tate, who sees his relationship with the miners as one of class struggle. On the other hand, Tate, capitalist that he is, is unable to exercise restraint and eventually brings about the destruction of the mine, many of the miners, and even himself. Work proceeds surprisingly well in the new seam, but Tate extends the work there, expanding operations until the inevitable roof collapse occurs. Two miners are killed, one of whom is Jack Cameron. Tensions mount as the community awaits Jim Cameron's revenge for his brother's death. He takes no action, however, dissuaded by both his fears of the retribution he will receive for killing Tate and his concerns for Elsa, who now has only Jim to care for her. Meanwhile, it is announced that the losses incurred in the recent collapse, together with a general slump in the mining industry, have made the Franton Colliery unprofitable. The miners are given notice and preparations for the closing of the colliery proceed. Then, on the last day of work in the mine, dangerous gas buildups lead to a massive explosion and fire that destroy the mine and kill many of the miners, as well as Tate himself when he descends into the mine to check on the damage. As the book closes, Cameron prepares to marry his longtime sweetheart, Betty, but otherwise conditions appear grim for the miners, who face a future of unemployment. Cameron, meanwhile, has learned some valuable lessons and now realizes, too late, that he should have taken a more radical and collective approach in his fight for justice.

That approach, of course, is communism, represented in the text primarily by the efforts of the miner Joe Frost, who has recently returned from the Soviet Union inspired by the heroic efforts of the Soviet people to build a socialist society in which workers can at last live decent and genuinely human lives. Frost functions throughout the text as a spokesman for Heslop (who had observed the Soviet experiment first hand) and as a sort of counter to Cameron. Frost argues stridently for his cause throughout the text, winning the respect and admiration of the miners for his learning and his dedication to justice. However, faced with the juggernaut of a British cultural system designed to demonize and discredit communism, Frost is able to win relatively few of the miners over to his cause. Meanwhile, the decline of the British economy is leading to a gradual increase in support for fascism, which Heslop envisions as a logical extension of the fundamental brutalities of capitalism. The book thus closes on an ominous note, with the Franton Colliery destroyed, the surviving miners out of work, and fascism looming as a genuine political threat in Britain. On the other hand, there are bright notes. The marriage of Cameron and Betty suggests a fundamental strength to the culture of the miners that allows them to go on in the face of all adversity, particularly as the miners remain firm in their resolve to continue "fighting the boss" (361). And, Cameron's ultimate conversion to Frost's cause, although too late to help the miners of the Franton Colliery, indicates at least some hope that the ideological conditioning of bourgeois ideology can eventually be overcome.

The most important utopian dimension of *Last Cage Down* resides in Heslop's unequivocal endorsement of Soviet-style communism as a positive alternative to a capitalist system on the verge of collapse into fascism. In this sense, the political message goes beyond that of Heslop's earlier books, which tended to focus on a critique of the failures of British trade unionism in the 1920s and 1930s. As Croft notes, the negative and critical orientation of these earlier books brought consideration criticism from the Left, while the additional positive dimension of *Last Cage Down* can be seen as a response to this criticism (Introduction x–xi). The book is thus intimately embedded in the political climate of the 1930s and should be read in that light. Among other things, while Frost's (and Heslop's) faith in the Soviet Union—and in Joseph Stalin—as a source of leadership for the workers of the world may strike many in retrospect as misguided, it is worth remembering that, in the 1930s, as capitalist economies all over the world were mired in a deep depression, the Soviet economy was shifting into full gear, growing and expanding at a rate unprecedented in world history.

As Eric Hobsbawm notes in *The Age of Extremes*, the Soviet communists, having been thwarted in their initial plans to export revolution worldwide, had little choice but to set about the desperate project of building socialism in the huge, impoverished, and unruly political entity that was the Soviet Union. Recognizing that this could not be done in a poor, backward country, the Soviets set forth on an astonishingly ambitious (and sometimes frightfully ruthless) campaign of rapid modernization based on a combination of "an all-out offensive against the cultural backwardness of the notoriously 'dark,' ignorant, illiterate and superstitious masses with an all-out drive for technological modernization and industrial revolution" (376). This project was not without its successes. As Hobsbawm points out, Soviet economic policies "turned the USSR into a major industrial economy in just a few years and one capable, as Tsarist Russia had not been, of surviving and winning the war against Germany in spite of the temporary loss of areas containing a third of her population and, in many industries, half the industrial plant" (382).

Moreover, Soviet policies provided a social safety net unheard of in the centuries of tsarist rule, while in education the "transformation of a largely illiterate country into the modern USSR was, by any standards, a towering achievement" (382). Nevertheless, the intense emphasis on modernization under Stalin meant that the socialist project of social and political emancipation had to take a back seat. The ultimate result was the demise of the Soviet state, which should not necessarily, according to Hobsbawm, be interpreted as discrediting Marxism. Indeed, that demise proves Marx to have been right in his insistence that socialism could be established only after human beings have reached a certain stage of material development, a stage that postrevolutionary Russia had clearly not reached (496–97). ***Selected bibliography:*** Bell; Croft (Introduction to *Last Cage Down*); Hobsbawm (*Age of Extremes*); Klaus (*Literature*); David Smith (*Socialist Propaganda*).

BARRY HINES: *KES* (1968). First published as *A Kestrel for a Knave*, Hines's book was reissued in 1974 with the shortened title to match that of the 1969 film adaptation, directed by Ken Loach. The book narrates a period in the life of teenager Billy Casper, who lives in impoverished conditions with his mother and half-brother, Jud, in government estate housing in a town somewhere in England's industrial north. Although not informed by any clearly stated political agenda, *Kes* is typical of Hines's work in its frank presentation of working-class life and its clear, but unsentimental, sympathy with those who live that life. The book describes in vivid naturalistic detail the grim environment in which Billy lives and shows, in convincing fashion, the powerful social and economic obstacles that combine to make Billy's existence a bleak one and to limit his prospects for a better future.

Jud, who works in the local coal pit, deals with his own frustrations by constantly tormenting his younger and weaker sibling. Their mother spends her days at work and her nights drinking and consorting with such a variety of men that Billy's numerous "uncles" supply his schoolmates with some of their favorite joke material. School, in fact, is the site of many of Billy's worst torments. Most of his fellow students, recognizing Billy's intelligence and sensitivity, reject and bully him. Most of his teachers, failing to recognize his intelligence and sensitivity, see no point in making an effort to educate him; thus, school is little more than a carceral institution designed merely to keep Billy and his fellow students off of the streets for a few hours each day until they reach the age when they can be sent to work in the coal mines or to do other manual labor.

Billy's life does have its bright spots. For example, one of his teachers, Mr. Farthing, befriends and sympathizes with him. Most importantly, Billy finds a refuge from his grim life when he captures and begins to train a young kestrel hawk, the "Kes" of the title. Fascinated with the bird, Billy reads widely about falconry and becomes a self-made expert in the field. He also has considerable success with the training, thus giving him for once a sense of both accomplishment and control. Kes, in fact, plays a number of symbolic roles in the book, serving not only as a haven where Billy can be momentarily empowered but also as an image of power and independence in its own right. The hawk is also a symbol of natural beauty and purity that contrasts dramatically with the grimy and squalid surroundings in which Billy otherwise lives. Finally, by the end of the book, we learn that Billy's father left home because of the infidelities of Billy's mother when Billy was still quite young and that Billy still cherishes pleasant childhood memories of time spent with his father, especially at the local movie palace. Kes thus functions for Billy as a sort of reenactment of the feelings remembered from these early times with his father.

Near the end of the book, Jud leaves a half-crown for Billy to place for him as a bet on two horse races. Both of Jud's horses win, which would have returned more than ten pounds on the bet. Billy, however, assuming that the horses would lose, has appropriated the money for himself, causing the enraged Jud to kill Kes in revenge. The shattered Billy, getting little sympathy from his mother, rushes from the home, carrying the dead bird under his jacket. He makes his way to the old movie palace, now closed and abandoned. He slips inside and entertains fantasies of viewing films that feature himself and Kes as the major characters, thus clearly linking his relationship with Kes to childhood memories of times with his father, while at the same time suggesting that Billy's tendency toward escapist fantasy has been largely produced by signals received from popular culture. Then, with nowhere else to go, Billy returns home, buries the hawk, and quietly goes to bed.

Billy's story is heartbreaking. Roy Johnson is correct, however, to identify *Kes* as an example of the fact that "it is possible to give an account of proletarian existence without falling into sentimentality or an overreverence for middle-class values" (94). Hines avoids sentimentality in a number of ways. For one thing, attentive readers realize early on that it is only a matter of time until Kes becomes the victim of either Jud or the various school bullies who torment Billy throughout the book. And, while the inevitability of Kes's loss may in some ways make that loss even more poignant, it also indicates the hopelessness of Billy's absorption in the hawk as a way of dealing with his life. The symbolic function of Kes in the book is highly problematic. The bird, kept in a small cage and released from it only while being trained, is hardly an effective image of independence or of nature in contrast to culture. In fact, it is as much a symbol of human domination of nature as are the slag heaps created by the coal pit. And, though the experience with Kes gives Billy something to live for and provides a focus for his previously unutilized intellectual abilities, Billy's growing obsession with the bird makes it more, not less, difficult for him to deal effectively with the exigencies of his everyday life. In the final analysis, Billy's absorption in nostalgic memories, bovarystic fascination with film, and emotional attachment to Kes offer him little in the way of strategies for dealing with reality, while at the same time serving to alienate him further from his fellow human beings.

Hines, a native of South Yorkshire and himself a former miner and then a teacher in a mining community, is one of the leading contemporary chroniclers of British working-class life. In *Kes*, the difficulties of that life are presented in vivid fashion. However, Hines makes it clear that, while life can and should have multiple dimensions, escapism is not the answer to the tribulations of working-class life, whether that escape involves the kind of extrasocial ideal represented by Kes, the kinds of unrealistic images presented in popular culture, or the kinds of idealized images associated with memories of a lost past. Billy's life is grim, and the future offers him little in the way of opportunity, a situation that is made clear in his interview with a Youth Employment officer to whom he is invisible as an individual and who suggests that, unless Billy is willing to work in the coal mines, there seem to be no jobs in England to suit him (171). Moreover, even were Billy to be recognized as someone with special intellectual and imaginative potential, the best he might hope for would be an education that would help him to rise to the middle class, alienating him from his working-class origins and leaving most working-class youth still in the position once occupied by Billy. And, given that escape into fantasy obviously provides no viable alternative to this grim situation, the only real solution to the dilemmas of youth like Billy would then be, by implication, to make fundamental changes in the economic system and class structure of Britain. Hines does not spell out what these changes might be, but *Kes* makes clear the urgency with which they are needed. **Selected bibliography:** Craig ("Roots"); Holderness ("Miners and the Novel"); Johnson ("Proletarian Novel")

BARRY HINES: *UNFINISHED BUSINESS* (1983). *Unfinished Business*, marked by the engaging narrative and a highly accessible prose style that is typical of Hines's writing, also continues the focus on contemporary British working-class life that is the distinctive feature of all of his work. In addition, the book resembles numerous other works of post–World War II British working-class fiction in its concentration on education as a potential key to upward mobility but also as a potential road to alienation from one's roots in the working class. However, *Unfinished Business* stands apart from most of Hines's work and from the works of upward-mobility writers such as Stan Barstow, John Braine, and Keith Waterhouse in its use of a female protagonist and in the exploration of gender issues that this use enables. In particular, the book explores the impact on a British working-class family when the wife and mother of the family begins to pursue a university degree in literature, only to discover that the new world of ideas opened to her by this education makes it impossible for her to continue to be satisfied with the suburban working-class existence into which she had previously been so comfortably settled.

As the book begins, Phil and Lucy Downs are living with their two children in a suburban home that is vastly superior to the impoverished conditions under which they grew up. Phil makes a decent income as a welder at a local engineering firm, and Lucy is primarily a housewife, though she has recently been attending a night-school course that will qualify her to enter the local university. Phil, however, is contemptuous of the notion, which he rudely mocks. But Lucy is determined and manages to gain admission to the literature program and to begin classes. Phil remains hostile to the idea, partly because Lucy is now away from home so much of the time but primarily because he secretly fears that Lucy's new education will make her regard him as crude and inferior. This hostility continues for some time, though Phil does his best to adjust, learning to perform domestic chores such as cooking and ironing to help out. Indeed, he finds to his surprise that he almost enjoys such tasks and that he certainly enjoys the increased time he is spending with the children.

Lucy is at first overwhelmed by the new world of the university and by the seemingly superior education and acculturation of all of those around her. She does well in her classes, however, and gradually begins to get accustomed to this exciting and stimulating new environment. She also learns that there are some things that she understands better than her fellow students, as when the literature department produces a play about a working-class housewife that only she seems able really to understand. In the process, she begins a flirtation with Dave Prybus, her literature tutor and the director of the play. Enthralled by Dave's knowledge and cultural experience and excited by the fact that such a sophisticated man obviously finds her sexually attractive, Lucy soon yields to Dave's advances and begins a full-blown affair. She is forced to reassess virtually every aspect of her previous life, partly because of the ideas she encounters in her coursework, partly because of the affair with Dave, and partly because of her encounters with other young women at the university, especially Tanya, a militant feminist. Eventually, the affair with Dave begins to cool, especially after the unpleasant experience of a visit by Dave and Lucy to his wealthy, snobbish parents. But Lucy finds that she is still unable to feel satisfied with her former life, which she now realizes has closed off many avenues for the exploration of her personal potential. In the end, she leaves Phil and the children, whom he insists on keeping with him. It is not clear whether the affair with Dave will continue, but it is certain that Lucy's education will, having already set her on a course from which there is no turning back.

Unfinished Business treats Lucy's troubled meditations on gender roles and expectations sensitively and in a way that makes clear that Lucy's growing estrangement from her husband results neither from her unfaithfulness nor from his lack of attention to her needs. Indeed, the estrangement between Lucy and Phil is treated as more social than personal and within a context that never loses sight of the fact of class as a primary determinant of the character of the lives of individuals of either gender in Britain. The principal issue in the book is, in fact, class rather than gender, and it is significant that Lucy finds the rhetoric of feminists such as Tanya rather unappealing, though intriguing. Lucy's growing dissatisfaction with her former role as wife and mother is certainly a reaction to the confinement forced upon her by these roles, but this reaction occurs not just as the result of the raising of her individual consciousness but also in response to the potential advance in class enabled by her new education. It is made clear, for example, that Lucy was always extremely intelligent and promising as a student but that she did not pursue her education earlier because, within the context of her working-class family, such a course simply did not occur to her or to her parents. As the wife of a skilled worker like Phil, she has moved to a better social and economic position than she had occupied as the daughter of a common laborer in a steel mill, and it is this very advance in class that makes it possible for her to envision herself as a university student. Her new education makes available still other possibilities, while making her former role as a suburban housewife untenable, both because it limits her as an individual and because she is thoroughly alienated from her husband, who now occupies a lower class position than does she. Thus,

Unfinished Business not only effectively dramatizes the limitations placed on women by conventionally accepted gender roles, but also convincingly demonstrates the close interconnection between gender and class in the description of the roles available to individuals in modern Britain. *Selected bibliography:* Behrend ("Second Thoughts"); Paul (*Fire*).

CHRISTOPHER ISHERWOOD: *GOODBYE TO BERLIN* (1939). *Goodbye to Berlin* is probably Isherwood's most widely respected novel. It is also his best-known work, partly because of the popularity of its stage and film adaptations, including the 1951 play *I Am a Camera* (which became a 1955 film under the same title) and the 1966 stage musical *Cabaret* (which became an award-winning film in 1972). As Isherwood explains in a prefatory note, the material in *Goodbye to Berlin* was originally intended to form part of a larger historical novel (to be entitled "The Lost") that Isherwood had intended to produce as a sweeping fictional account of the demise of Weimar Germany and the rise to power of the German Nazis. Isherwood's 1935 novel *Mr. Norris Changes Trains* (published in America as *The Last of Mr. Norris*) was also originally part of this same plan, so that the two novels overlap considerably, sharing many characters and settings. Indeed, the two were later published together as a single volume in America (under the title *Berlin Stories*), but each novel stands alone as a self-contained work. Further, each of the individual segments of *Goodbye to Berlin* (which include two extracts from the narrator's "Berlin Diary" that serve as a frame for four other narrative segments) is a self-contained story, but the segments overlap to form a coherent whole.

Partly because of this structure, *Goodbye to Berlin* has an episodic character with no firm central plot line. The first diary segment, dated Autumn 1930, serves to introduce the narrator (also named Christopher Isherwood but clearly not entirely identical to the author) and his distinctive style of detached reportage, announced in the famous early self-characterization, "I am a camera with its shutter open, quite passive, recording, not thinking" (13). This initial section also introduces the milieu of late-Weimar Berlin, where "Isherwood" works as an English tutor and lives in the somewhat shabby boarding house operated by Fraulein Schroeder. This first segment is essentially a series of character sketches of Fraulein Schroeder and the other lodgers (whom she prefers to refer to as "guests") in her boarding house. These boarders (who include a bartender, a prostitute, and a music hall yodeler) help to establish the atmosphere of decadence and the building sense of crisis that are crucial to the book, the real protagonist of which is clearly Berlin itself rather than any of the individual characters.

The next section of the book, "Sally Bowles," is probably the best known and was, in fact, published separately as a short novel in 1937.

This section is again essentially a character sketch, focusing on the eponymous Sally, an aspiring young British actress who has come to Berlin seeking opportunities in the film business, meanwhile supporting herself through singing (rather badly) in a Berlin night club and through sexual adventures with wealthy older men, maintaining an odd sort of innocence through it all. She and the narrator meet and become friends, and Sally soon moves to Fraulein Schroeder's boarding house. Sally falls in love with Klaus, a fellow performer, and she is heartbroken when he takes a job back in England and becomes involved with a woman there, leaving Sally alone and pregnant in Berlin. Sally, however, is nothing if not resilient, and she soon enters into an affair with Clive, a drunken millionaire, who also becomes fast friends with Isherwood. The three of them plan an extended trip abroad together, but Clive suddenly departs without them, leaving Sally stranded once again. Isherwood helps Sally arrange an abortion, but the friendship between the two gradually unravels. By the end of the segment, Sally has moved away to Paris, still seeking opportunities in show business, and Isherwood never sees her again.

The next segment, "On Ruegen Island," is set in the summer of 1931 in a Baltic summer resort that presumably provides its visitors with some respite from the increasingly troubled political climate of Berlin. But politics are not so easy to escape, and it is worth noting that "Ruegen Island" was in fact a German code word for Spain (another would-be sunny resort), used in conjunction with Hitler's intervention in support of the fascists there (Cunningham 185). The story centers on the deteriorating covertly homosexual relationship between Peter Wilkinson, a decadent upper-class Englishman, and Otto Nowak, a working-class German teenager with leftist sympathies. Otto pursues a sequence of young women, eventually leading the frustrated and highly neurotic Wilkinson to return to England in search of a new psychoanalyst. Isherwood, himself taking a holiday on the island, becomes acquainted with both Wilkinson and Otto and continues as a "camera," reflecting events in which he, himself, does not centrally participate. In the next segment, "The Nowaks," Isherwood renews his acquaintance with Otto when, in an effort to save money, he becomes a lodger with the Nowak family in their seedy tenement dwelling. The consumptive Frau Nowak constantly abuses Otto, comparing him unfavorably with his solemn and hard working brother, Lothar, a Nazi. Frau Nowak has certain sympathies with the Nazis as well, and her attitudes help to define the context in which the Nazi rise to power became a possibility. Eventually, she is removed to a sanatorium (in an obvious metaphor for the sickness of a Berlin society that would welcome the Nazis), and the segment ends as Otto and Isherwood visit her in the somewhat surrealistic surroundings there.

The last narrative segment centers on the Jewish Landauer family and thus brings to a focus many of the hints of German antisemitism that have circulated throughout the text. The Landauers are the wealthy owners of a Berlin department store, but their wealth turns out to provide little protection as the Nazis sweep to power. The narrator, Isherwood, gradually makes clear in the course of the story his sense that the Landauers are doomed, and in one key passage Isherwood attends a Jewish party (held on the eve of a referendum leading to the fall of the Brüning government in June of 1932, a key step in the Nazi rise to power) and describes the gathering as "the dress-rehearsal for a disaster. It is like the last night of an epoch" (271). Later, Isherwood learns that Bernhard Landauer has died of a "heart attack," but there is a clear implication that he has been killed by the emergent Nazis. Indeed, there is a direct reference at this point (published and widely read in the West by 1939) to the extermination of Jews in concentration camps, even though the Western powers claimed not to know about that project until years later (282).

The concluding diary segment of *Goodbye to Berlin* is set in the winter of 1932–33. Now once again boarding with Fraulein Schroeder, Isherwood goes out into the bitter cold for one last tour of the local "dives," which are likely soon to be closed by the Nazis. On this tour he becomes acquainted with the denizens of a "communist" café and subsequently observes their growing persecution by the Nazis, while the police increasingly look the other way. Isherwood prepares to return to England, while the apolitical Fraulein Schroeder prepares to welcome the Nazis. Indeed, the portrayal of Fraulein Schroeder in this segment is part of a general depiction of the German populace as passive and gullible and thus willing to accept the Nazis even without really agreeing with their extreme ideas. Hitler becomes chancellor by the end of January 1933, as Isherwood looks on with a sense of disbelief while maintaining his detached attitude, smiling at himself in a mirror despite the Nazi takeover simply because the weather is unusually fine that day.

Of course, this passage contains a great deal of potential criticism of the narrator, and one might interpret "Isherwood's" continuing detachment as a suggestion that it is not only the Germans who bear the blame for allowing the Nazis to come to power in Europe. In any case, the author Isherwood, his later fascination with Eastern mysticism notwithstanding, is clearly more politically engaged than his namesake narrator. Andy Croft notes that *Mr. Norris Changes Trains* and *Goodbye to Berlin* are the "most famous today of all the realist anti-Nazi novels," and it is certainly the case that, despite the ostensible focus on private experience (especially in the latter novel), both books are intensely political and strongly anti-Nazi in their orientation (328). The German communists, as the principal antagonists and first large-scale victims of the Nazis, are presented in a consistently favorable, if somewhat detached and ironic, light in both books. Together, Isherwood's fictional accounts of the rise of the German Nazis stand as important reminders not only of the failure of Western democracies to oppose the Nazis early on but of the historical role of communism as the principal bulwark against fascism. The German communists were defeated and virtually exterminated by the Nazis, treated just as brutally as Jews and gypsies. And it was the Soviet Red Army, with more than eighty percent of the German military machine committed to the Eastern Front, that was primarily responsible for the defeat of the Germans in World War II, however much the Western capitalist countries would like to claim that role. *Selected bibliography:* Croft (*Red Letter Days*); Cunningham; Heilbrunn; Lehmann (*Christopher Isherwood*); Rosenthal; Schwerdt; Stephen Wade; Wilde.

CHRISTOPHER ISHERWOOD: *MR. NORRIS CHANGES TRAINS* (1935). *Mr. Norris Changes Trains*, published in America as *The Last of Mr. Norris*, is a highly representative example of the work of one of the most successful British writers of the 1930s. The book, like the later *Goodbye to Berlin* (1939), was originally intended to form part of a single larger work (to be entitled "The Lost") that Isherwood had intended to produce as a sweeping fictional account of the demise of Weimar Germany and the rise to power of the German Nazis. *Mr. Norris Changes Trains* and *Goodbye to Berlin* thus overlap considerably, sharing many characters and settings. Indeed, the two were later published together as a single volume in America under the title *Berlin Stories*, but each novel stands alone as a self-contained work. Isherwood, widely regarded as a one of the least overtly politicized writers of the so-called Auden Generation, is generally known as a writer who focuses on private experience, especially psychological and sexual, rather than public phenomena. Yet *Mr. Norris Changes Trains* is a highly political book that is very much engaged with the issues of its time, thus demonstrating the extent to which even the most "apolitical" writers of the 1930s were unable to avoid extensive reference to such issues.

In fact, Isherwood's novel not only vividly evokes the historical and political context of Germany in the early 1930s, but depends quite heavily on this evocation for its success. The plot of the book, essentially that of a spy novel, is relatively simple, leading Isherwood to describe the book as "a sort of glorified shocker; not unlike the productions of my cousin Graham Greene" (qtd. in Lehmann, *The Whispering Gallery* 225). But (also like the productions of Greene) *Mr. Norris Changes Trains* is most valuable not for the events of its plot but for the detailed description of the historical milieu in which these events take place. As Ralph Wright put it nicely in a review of Isherwood's work published in the *Daily Worker* in 1937, Isherwood's stories of Berlin in the 1930s "not only paint an epoch, but explain to some extent why it yielded so easily before the onslaught of the Nazis, the bullies it itself had helped to form" (qtd. in Croft 329).

The book, written in Isherwood's distinctive crisp, clear style, begins as William Bradshaw, a young English teacher and the narrator of the book, boards a train in Holland bound for Berlin. On the train, he meets Arthur Norris, a puzzling and enigmatic figure. Indeed, much of the interest of the plot has to do with Bradshaw's attempts to ascertain the true nature of his mysterious new acquaintance. Thus, Alan Wilde suggests that "for the 'who-done-it' of the detective novel, *Mr. Norris* substitutes the 'what-is-he' of the modern *roman d'aventure*" (56-57). After arriving in Berlin, Bradshaw calls on Norris, who operates a mysterious "import and export" business there. Bradshaw gradually realizes that Norris's activities, business and otherwise, are not always quite above board and that Norris is apparently in some serious financial difficulties. The more Bradshaw learns, the more bizarre Norris seems. Among Norris's many interests are pornography (which he both authors and collects), sadomasochism, and politics. Norris is actively involved with the German Communist Party, and, through Norris Bradshaw, becomes acquainted with the Party as well, including their admirable local leader, Ludwig Bayer. Bradshaw also meets some of Norris's less virtuous acquaintances, including Norris's sinister secretary, Herr Schmidt, and the Baron von Pregnitz, the decadent aristocrat of the piece.

In the course of the book, Norris appears to sink deeper and deeper into financial difficulty, in response to which he supposedly cooks up an elaborate business deal involving Pregnitz that will make a great deal of money for both of them. He enlists Bradshaw in the scheme as well, and both Bradshaw and Pregnitz then travel to Switzerland to meet with a mysterious man, known only as "Margot," presumably in order to negotiate the sale to him of a glass factory in which Pregnitz owns an interest. Bradshaw, however, is suddenly recalled to Berlin by Bayer, who reveals to him that the trip to Switzerland involved not the sale of a factory but of information regarding the activities of the German Communist Party. Indeed, Bradshaw learns that Norris has been collecting and marketing such information for quite some time as a means of escaping from his overwhelming debts. Bayer, however, is a step ahead of Norris and has for some time been feeding him with inaccurate information in order to mislead the Party's enemies. Bayer also warns Bradshaw that Norris's activities have now caught the attention of the German police, who have Norris under surveillance. Bradshaw is infuriated to learn that Norris has been using him for such purposes, but is unable to remain angry with his charming friend, whom he helps to escape to Mexico to avoid the German police. Pregnitz, who has been selling state secrets in order to make money to pay Schmidt, who is blackmailing him because of his illicit sexual activities, commits suicide to avoid arrest for treason. Meanwhile, the Nazis take power in Germany and begin a brutal project to exterminate the communists. Bayer is captured and tortured to death. Bradshaw returns to London, where he receives a series of letters and postcards from Norris detailing the latter's movement through Mexico, California, and much of South America with Schmidt in hot pursuit.

Far more interesting than this plot is Isherwood's depiction of the social and political climate of Germany on the verge of and just after the Nazi takeover. Of course, the plot and its background are inextricable, and the private affairs of the various characters inevitably become entangled in public politics. Indeed, despite Isherwood's reputation as a chronicler of private, subjective experience, *Mr. Norris Changes Trains* continually suggests that private and public experience cannot be separated—as is symbolized early in the book by the fact that Norris's abode in Berlin has two separate entry doors, one for private life and one for public business, both of which, in fact, open into the same room (24). Bradshaw, who provides the narration, is a rather bland and uninteresting figure, a sort of neutral observer who maintains an ironic detachment from the ominous events around him. And it is of interest to note that he is in many ways modeled on Isherwood, whose full name was Christopher William Bradshaw-Isherwood. But, while Bradshaw's thinly veiled fascination with the opportunities for nontraditional sexual experience offered by Weimar Berlin may perhaps be interpreted as a reflection of Isherwood's own inclinations, it would probably be a mistake to see Bradshaw's attitude of neutrality to and detachment from German politics as that of Isherwood, who later rejected his own character as "heartless."

Indeed, the book itself is far from neutral, and even Bradshaw clearly regards the emergent German Nazis as evil, while his narration of the rise of fascism is in some ways made even more horrifying by his tone of ironic detachment. Bradshaw expresses considerable admiration for the German communists, who stand as the only real obstacle to the Nazi rise to power. *Mr. Norris Changes Trains* thus very clearly participates in the important phenomenon of antifascist literature in Britain in the 1930s, while its positive portrayal of communists as the chief enemies of fascism provides an important reminder of the political context of the 1930s. After all, leftist attitudes grew in influence in Britain in that decade not only because of the near collapse of the capitalist economies worldwide but also because of the perception of fascism as a serious threat to all of Europe. **Selected bibliography:** Croft (*Red Letter Days*); Cunningham; Heilbrunn; Lehmann (*Christopher Isherwood*); Lehmann (*The Whispering Gallery*); Rosenthal; Schwerdt; Wade; Wilde.

STORM JAMESON: *IN THE SECOND YEAR* **(1936).** *In the Second Year* is an antifascist dystopian novel that takes its title from the fact that it is set (at the end of the 1930s) in the second year after social and economic unrest in Britain has led to the revolutionary takeover of a new "National State" government. Conditions in Britain are still quite bleak, and most of the citizens live in considerable hardship—and fear. As the name indicates, this new government, though it continues to pay lip service to English democratic traditions and though it still seems headed inexorably toward war with Germany, has a great deal in common with the German Nazi regime. Civil liberties have been brutally suppressed under the new government, and those who have been judged enemies of the state, especially communists, have either been exterminated or interred in "Training Camps" that are presumably designed to further their political reeducation but that are suspiciously similar to the concentration camps of Nazi Germany. The new government is also strongly antisemitic, if in a more covert way than its German counterpart. Moreover, the specific details concerning the rise of the new government and its subsequent consolidation of power are clearly taken directly from German history, though they are enhanced with specifically British details. In her autobiography, *Journey from the North*, Jameson acknowledges recent German history as a direct source, but also suggests that she was attempting to "imagine an English Fascism, the brutality half-masked and devious, with streaks of Methodist virtue" (335).

In the Second Year is narrated by Andrew Hillier, an Englishman who arrives in England for a visit from Norway, where he lives and works as a college professor. Hillier is a liberal, and the book is narrated from his liberal perspective. He observes and comments on the events around him, but takes no real part in them, suggesting the way in which liberal inaction can contribute to the rise of fascism. Indeed, Hillier's indirect complicity with the State Government is made clear by the fact that he is the cousin of Prime Minister Frank Hillier, the dictatorial leader of the National State, whose very name indicates his proximity to Hitler. Andrew is also the brother-in-law of Richard Sacker, the leader of the "National Volunteers," a powerful private army of storm troopers that facilitated Frank Hillier's rise to power by eradicating his opponents, especially communists. Meanwhile, the National State government is able to hold power largely because many prominent liberals, trade union leaders, and Labour Party leaders have joined the government, presumably seeing its rule as preferable to anarchy. But most of the members of the new government are interested primarily in power, and much of the plot of the book has to do with the internal maneuvering of various members of the new government to consolidate their own positions.

In particular, Sacker, a childhood friend and loyal supporter of Frank Hillier, instigates a plot to prevent the dissolution of the National Volunteers and to undo what Sacker sees as the sinister influence of Big Business (as represented by financier Sir Thomas Chamberlayn) on Hillier's government. In this plot, he enlists the aid of a former army general, Smith, and two members of Hillier's government, former trade-union official George Body and Alexander Denham, a former Labour Party leader. Economist R. B. Tower, a Nobel laureate, is consulted as well, but does not actually join the plot. But the opportunistic Denham reveals the plot to the prime minister, who acts swiftly, leading to the arrest and execution of the others involved. Tower, whose prominence had protected him in the earlier purges of the universities despite his socialist leanings, is killed as well, although he (in a motif with a clear message for intellectuals) has taken no real action to oppose the new rejection. Andrew Hillier is also questioned, but is released: as a liberal, he is no threat to the National State. The power of the Hillier government is thus solidified, with the implication that its policies will become increasingly repressive and that its growing similarity to the Nazi regime in Germany will eventually lead to war between the two expansionist states. Only a few underground communists, such as Lewis, clearly the book's most positive character, remain to present any opposition at all to Hillier's (and Chamberlayn's) rule.

In the Second Year was generally well received by leftist critics in the 1930s, despite its seemingly pessimistic tone. But the book is clearly a cautionary tale, and its emphasis on the complicity of liberal and moderate socialist inaction with the rise of the National State government clearly implies that action on the part of liberals and moderate socialists could effectively prevent the rise of a fascist government in Britain. In this sense, the book is a sort of forerunner of the Popular Front, acknowledging the staunch and courageous opposition to fascism that characterized 1930s communism, but suggesting that the communists can triumph only with the help of liberal and socialist allies. Ultimately, then, the book emphasizes the seriousness of the threat posed by certain latent fascist tendencies in British society without concluding that these tendencies would ultimately lead to a fascist takeover. **Selected bibliography:** Croft (*Red Letter Days*); Jameson (*Journey*); Montefiore.

STORM JAMESON: *THE MIRROR IN DARKNESS* (1934–36). As Storm Jameson notes in an author's foreword still included in the latest edition of the first volume of the work, *The Mirror in Darkness* was originally conceived of as a sequence of five or six novels designed to "depict the contemporary scene." As it turned out, only three volumes would be completed, so the work stands as a trilogy consisting of *Company Parade* (1934), *Love in Winter* (1935), and *None Turn Back* (1936). Together, these volumes present an interesting historical account of British society from the end of World War II in 1918 to the end of the General Strike in 1926. This account is presented from a perspective sympathetic to socialism, though Jameson herself came from middle-class origins and her characters tend to be middle-class or even upper-class. Indeed, she does little in the trilogy to heed her own advice to leftist writers (in the 1937 manifesto "Writing in Revolt") to experience and then write about working-class life first hand. Moreover, Jameson's brand of socialism is distinctively moderate, and *The Mirror in Darkness* shows a suspicion of genuinely radical politics that makes Jameson's post–World War II anticommunist stance rather predictable.

A great deal of the material in *The Mirror in Darkness* is autobiographical, and the protagonist of the trilogy, Hervey Russell, is quite clearly based on Jameson herself. As a result, Jameson's autobiography, *Journey from the North*, provides extremely useful background to much of the material in the trilogy, though the most important background is history itself. *Company Parade* begins as Hervey moves to London just after the armistice in an attempt to make her fortune and thus provide financial security for herself and her family. She leaves her three-year-old son, Richard, behind in Yorkshire with a nursemaid, while her rather feckless husband, Penn Vance, continues to serve as a supply officer at an air force base in Kent. Hervey takes a job as an advertising copywriter at which, after a slow start, she is reasonably adept. Meanwhile, she pursues her career as a novelist, her first novel appearing in print soon after her move to London. Hervey, who herself has fallen in love with an American serviceman during the war, grows more and more estranged from her womanizing husband as the volume proceeds. We are introduced to numerous other characters as well, including David Renn, the partially crippled communist-leaning copywriter for whom Hervey works as an assistant, the socialist activist Louis Earlham, the prominent editor and journalist Evelyn Lamb, the wealthy publisher Marcel Cohen, the novelist William Ridley (perhaps based on J. B. Priestley), and Hervey's longtime friends, the scientist T. S. Heywood (married to Evelyn Lamb) and the leftist journalist Philip Nicholson.

In *Love in Winter*, it is 1924, and Hervey is still in London, with Vance now living in Oxford. She falls in love with her cousin, Nicholas Roxby, and the two are eventually married after each finally ends an unfortunate first marriage. This new marriage, based on Jameson's own second marriage, to historian Guy Chapman, is happy though not without its difficulties. The complex development of this relationship is played out against the background of a British society informed by increasing economic hardship and correspondingly increasing class conflicts. Once again, numerous other characters play important roles in the text, broadening Jameson's focus well beyond the personal relationship between

Hervey and Nicholas. Many characters from the first volume, such as Lamb, Earlham, and Renn, remain prominent, while others become important as well, including the mine owner William Gary and the shipping magnate Thomas Harben. Gary, a close friend of Nicholas and the former lover of Nicholas's beautiful sister, Georgina, is a particularly interesting figure. For one thing, he has been made impotent from a war wound, destroying his relationship with Georgina and causing him to funnel his energies into making money in business. As a result, Gary is, among other things, an emblem of the spiritual poverty of post–World War I Britain, in which human relationships have been replaced by economic struggles, even for basically decent people. Gary is a complex figure who in many ways sympathizes with the concerns of the trade unionists and socialists who, because of his position as a mine owner, are his natural antagonists. Cohen, incidentally, is treated rather sympathetically in the trilogy as well, and one could argue that Jameson's depiction of figures such as Cohen and Gary is a sign of sophistication that eschews the Manichean oppositions between workers and bosses sometimes found in leftist literature. On the other hand, one could also argue that Jameson's sympathy with such figures is a sign of her own class origins and of her lack of genuine devotion to the cause of the working class.

It is also important to recognize that Jameson includes Harben, a more negative figure of the exploitative rich, in her trilogy and that her treatment of Cohen and Gary is conditioned by her desire to identify fascism, rather than capitalism per se, as the true enemy of justice in Britain. Indeed, though the trilogy only extends to 1926, its origin in the 1930s is clear in that the sequence is centrally concerned with an exploration of the kinds of attitudes and conditions that made the development of fascism possible in Germany and that might make it a threat in Britain as well. The most important character in this sense is the sinister Julian Swan, obviously based on Oswald Mosley, a sort of protegé of Harben who spends much of his time organizing gangs of fascist thugs to break up labor meetings. By the time of *None Turn Back*, which opens during the General Strike of 1926, Swan has gained significant power and influence and is employed as the secretary of the Economic Council, organized to combat the strike. The ultimate failure of the strike is the real story of the third volume of the trilogy, although Hervey's personal experiences remain central as well. Throughout the book, she awaits the surgical removal of her uterus, knowing there is a possibility she will not survive the operation. She thus spends much of the text musing on her past life in an attempt to put her thoughts in order before the surgery. The operation is a success, however, and the book ends as Hervey recuperates, having just gotten word that the strike has been called off while having gained essentially nothing for the striking workers or for the locked-out miners in support of whom the strike was originally called.

None Turn Back is clearly sympathetic to the basic goals of the strike, though it also tends to treat the event as confused, misguided, and largely pointless. Indeed, as depicted by Jameson, the only thing the strike seems to accomplish is to divert attention from the threat posed by the appearance of Swan and his fascists on the British political scene. As Janet Montefiore puts it, the story of Hervey Russell is merely a unifying thread in a narrative "whose principal theme is the slow defeat of the Left by the sinister forces of wealth and reaction" (59). In this sense, the trilogy resembles John Dos Passos's *U.S.A.* trilogy, which similarly narrates the defeat of the American Left during the first decades of the twentieth century. However, Jameson was highly skeptical of modernist experimentalism throughout her life, and her trilogy, written in a single elegantly traditional style, lacks the formal inventiveness of Dos Passos's work. Furthermore, the focus on Hervey and her circle prevents *The Mirror in Darkness* from achieving the expansive social and historical scope of *U.S.A.*

Jameson's trilogy is also more narrowly focused than that of Dos Passos in its concentration on fascism, while in *U.S.A.* consumer capitalism as a whole is portrayed as the principal antagonist (and vanquisher) of the American working class and the American Left. However, Jameson's trilogy goes well beyond Dos Passos's in its sensitive treatment of gender issues, as Hervey struggles to build a career amid the patriarchal context of British society in the 1920s. Indeed, the entire trilogy was reissued in the 1980s (with useful introductions to each volume by Elaine Feinstein), primarily because of interest in its treatment of gender rather than its narration of the General Strike or its warnings against fascism. All in all, *The Mirror in Darkness* stands as an important document that presents a rich picture of British society from 1918 to 1926, even if that picture is essentially limited to the point of view of its well-educated, middle-class protagonist. Jameson, herself, is an important figure in twentieth-century British culture, having been a prominent participant in the literary Left in the 1930s and having become, at the end of that decade the first woman president of the British section of PEN. **Selected bibliography:** Jameson (*Journey*); Jameson ("Writing"); Montefiore.

GWYN JONES: *TIMES LIKE THESE* (1936). Centering around the General Strike of 1926, *Times Like These* relates the experiences of the inhabitants of Jenkinstown, a South Welsh coal-mining community torn by strife between miners and mine owners and gradually impoverished by a level of unemployment that grows steadily higher from the early 1920s into the Depression years of the 1930s. Important characters include the trade unionist Edgar Evans and the communist Ike Jones, though in general the book focuses primarily on the experiences of the Biesty family, made up of the miner Oliver, his wife Polly, and their children Luke and Mary. The real protagonist, however, is the collective constituted by the miners and their families. As Ramón López Ortega points out, "a consciousness of class, an awareness of belonging to an important group, pervades the entire novel. In it, the rejection of individualism in the interest of the macrocosm, the class, is complete" (136). Moreover, the book treats class very much in the manner emphasized by Marx, as a collective defined by opposition to other groups, in this case the mine owners and management. Marx's definition of a class in *The Eighteenth Brumaire* is, in fact, highly relevant here: "In so far as millions of families live under economic conditions of existence that divide their mode of life, their interests and their culture from those of the other classes, and put them in hostile contrast to the latter, they form a class" (Marx and Engels 608).

The class conflicts depicted in *Times Like These* are based on historical events. The book opens in 1925, at a time when labor tensions had been growing in South Wales for some time as mine owners employed increasingly exploitative labor practices in their quest for profit. Tensions came to a head in the spring of 1926, when government efforts to avert a crisis failed, leading to a lock-out of the miners on May 1, 1926. This move led to the declaration of a General Strike on May 3, with almost all of the manual workers of Britain striking in support of the miners. Middle-class volunteers, showing their own class loyalties, kept most services operating, however, and by May 12 (under questionable circumstances that are still being debated) the General Strike was called off, leaving the miners to fight on alone. Much of the action of *Times Like These* centers on this fight and on the way in which these experiences further a sense of solidarity among the miners. The book is not ultimately optimistic, however. After more than six months, the miners return to work essentially on the owners' terms, and many of the strike leaders lose their jobs. By the end, most of the miners who figure in the plot have been unemployed for years, and more and more are beginning to leave the valley in search of work elsewhere. The hardships of poverty, meanwhile, have taken their toll. Ike Jones is growing increasingly bitter and frustrated, calling for radical action in ways that alienate him from the bulk of the workers. Even the more moderate Edgar Evans is beginning to lose hope, feeling betrayed by the failures of the recent Labour government to bring relief to the miners. Polly Biesty is in poor health and virtually unable to walk. Luke's wife, Olive, having earlier barely survived after delivering a stillborn baby, has died from complications arising from peritonitis. Oliver, whose life has taken its meaning from his work, is grimly resigned to the fact that he will never work again. And Luke is on the edge of despair, mumbling to himself as the book closes, "What are we in the world for? Everything do seem so useless, somehow" (319).

Of the Biesty family, only Mary has some success, and she does so only by abandoning her class. Originally engaged to marry Edgar, she becomes estranged from him and from the life of the valley in general when her work as a secretary for the bus company executive, Broddam, opens to her a new way of life that leads her to dress differently, speak differently, and think differently from her family and the other inhabitants of Jenkinstown. After unfounded rumors of a sexual liaison between Mary and Broddam spread through the town, Mary finds another job in London, and her move to the city completes the process of *déclassement* that separates her from her roots in Jenkinstown and aligns her with the bourgeoisie. Most of the other bourgeois characters of the text meet with success as well. Broddam, himself, eventually takes a lucrative post in London. The mining executive Shelton, a sympathetically drawn figure who seems genuinely to care for the miners, inherits an estate and moves away from the valley, frustrated by long years of struggle in the interest of an owners' cause in which he does not really believe. In his place, the unscrupulous Webber becomes the head of the local mines, driving the remaining workers like slaves in search of higher profits for the mining company.

Times Like These is not entirely negative, however. For one thing, the lives of the miners, especially the Biesty family, are drawn in a richly human detail that is sympathetic while refusing to descend into sentimentality. For another, the miners and their families, buoyed by their communal values, continue somehow to survive in the face of all hardships. Thus, Glyn Jones, in her foreword, describes the strength of the book as its depiction of "a family, and around them a society, of decent, hard-working, honourable people who care deeply about their homes and their families and their jobs" (6–7). As a result of this emphasis, the political dimension of the book is somewhat subdued. Nevertheless, the book's focus on class and on collective experience is strong. And, while Ike Jones's calls for revolution are presented largely as the result of a personal bitterness that is not shared by most of the other miners, there is a clear utopian dimension in his vision of a "new start" after a violent destruction of the existing order, in which "we'll be masters of ourselves in a fine new world, and not just slaves to others" (294). Finally, there is a strong positive intonation to the characterization of Edgar Evans, whose intelligence and reading allow him to become an intellectual leader of the miners, while still remaining one of them, analyzing their plight in sophisticated ways but describing it in a language they can all understand. As López Ortega puts it, "Evans' voice is that of his community. He embodies the workers' hopes and his conviction that their cause will prevail" (136). Ultimately, *Times Like These* is a somber book describing somber times, but there are hints, however faint, of possible better times ahead. *Selected bibliography:* Glyn Jones; López Ortega; Marx and Engels (*Reader*).

LEWIS JONES: *CWMARDY* (1937). *Cwmardy*, subtitled "The Story of a Welsh Mining Valley," is precisely that. Though ostensibly a bildungsroman centering on the growth and maturation of the protagonist, Len Roberts, the book is simultaneously (and more importantly) a historical novel that traces the history of the mining community of Cwmardy from the 1890s to the years following World War I. Despite the focus on the point of view of the sensitive and introspective Len, the two central events of *Cwmardy* – a pivotal miners' strike and World War I – are both public in nature. Both of these events contribute in crucial ways to Len's education and maturation, thus demonstrating the shaping role played by public events in the development of individual consciousness. Meanwhile, the book (based largely on Jones's own experiences as a miner in the Rhondda region of Wales) presents a vivid, sympathetic, but unromanticized evocation of the working-class culture in which Len grows to maturity. As David Smith puts it in his introduction, "Its crucial quality, apart from considerable documentary value, is the skilled and knowledgeable manner in which the evolution of a political consciousness, with many checks and balances on its understanding, is shown as intimately related to a particular place and a special work experience."

The strike that occupies the central portion of *Cwmardy* is based on a real historical event, the 1910-11 Cambrian Combine dispute in which Churchill sent troops into the Rhondda to oppose the strikers and restore "order." Jones notes the hardships suffered by the striking miners during this long, difficult, and violent confrontation with the forces of authority, but most of his emphasis is on the solidarity fostered among the miners by this trying experience. Indeed, despite the repeated attempts of the police and military to break the strike through official violence, the strikers eventually win their demands, achieving not only better wages and working conditions, but also (and perhaps more important) a sense of the genuine power they can wield when they work together. Len, now a young miner, emerges as one of the leaders of the strike, especially as his youthful enthusiasm and determination provide vital supplements to the occasional pessimism of Ezra Jones, the miners' leader. The strike thus serves as an important educational experience in labor activism and in the potential power of working-class solidarity for the young Len.

World War I, occurring only a few years after the strike, is also a major watershed in the history of the valley – and in the growth of Len's socialist consciousness. As the war begins, a patriotic fervor sweeps the valley, and many of the miners (including Len's father, the powerful "Big Jim" Roberts) join the military to fight the Germans. Len himself, though ambivalent about the war, attempts to enlist, but is turned down for reasons of poor health. In the meantime, he begins to suspect that much of the propaganda that has been used to stir up anti-German hysteria in support of the war has been exaggerated or invented altogether. After all, the same British troops that have now been sent to fight the supposedly evil Germans had only recently been sent to oppose the striking miners of Cwmardy. Indeed, despite warnings from the company and the police, Len helps to organize an antiwar meeting at which a speaker describes the war as a battle between competing capitalist nations in which the capitalists themselves are making huge profits—often by doing business with both sides.

Meanwhile, prices in Britain skyrocket as the capitalists scramble to increase their profits. The miners of *Cwmardy* receive substantial increases in their pay, but the increases are not nearly enough to keep up with inflation, and the miners eventually are forced to threaten another strike to demand a living wage. As was true during the strike, the press depicts the miners in a highly negative light, contributing to Len's growing awareness of the ways the government, the police, the military, the media, religion, and other official institutions tend to work hand-in-hand with the members of the ruling class to maintain the existing order. The war ends before a strike ensues, and the miners who have been in the army return to work. New techniques of automation significantly increase the output of the mines, but render the work of the miners all the more tedious and dangerous. The book thus concludes on a seemingly negative note, with "progress" working to the benefit of mine owners, such as Lord Cwmardy, and mine officials, such as Mr. Hicks, but to the detriment of the miners themselves. Len, however, remains optimistic about the possibility of change for the better, as does Mary, Ezra's daughter, especially given the recent example of the Russian Revolution. As Len puts it, "If our people have the power to win strikes even against bullets and batons they have the power to do away with their poverty, to put an end to the struggle and begin to live clean, healthy lives" (310).

Cwmardy is clearly a book designed to promote a sense of working-class power and solidarity and to contribute to the development of a viable proletarian class consciousness among workers. Jones explains in a foreword to *Cwmardy* the very specific political motivation behind the writing of the book. He notes that he was encouraged to write the book by Arthur Horner, then president of the South Wales Miners' Federation, who suggested to Jones that "the full meaning of life in the Welsh mining areas could be expressed for the general reader more truthfully and vividly if treated imaginatively, than by any amount of statistical and historical research." In this foreword, Jones also puts forth his vision of the book's collective authorship, arguing that he cannot take credit for the creation of the book because it grew out of the real experiences of his fellow workers. "All of the events described," he points out, "though not placed in chronological order, have occurred, and each of them marks a milestone in the lives and struggles of the South Wales miners."

Jones could, of course, be criticized on the basis of the book's scrambled chronology, which sometimes leads to contradictions. Len, for example, seems to have been born after the Boer War (which ended in 1902), but seems to be a teenager by 1910. Indeed, Jones grants in his foreword that the book displays a certain "jumpiness," largely because it had to be written in "odd moments stolen from mass meetings, committees, demonstrations, marches, and other activities." Snee thus notes that the book "contains scenes of great power and strength," but argues that these scenes are not finally pulled together into a unified whole. For Snee, *Cwmardy* "is finally a collection of cameo portraits and vignettes" that fails to create the totalizing picture of Welsh mining life promised in Jones's foreword (183). Snee (who praises *Cwmardy* for its emphasis on the collective and for its refusal to conform to the individualist ideology of the bourgeois novel) here makes an argument that is somewhat reminiscent of the emphasis on the totality in the work of Lukács. On the other hand, organic unity in the work of art is the bourgeois aesthetic criterion par excellence and one of the principal means by which bourgeois works of art conceal the contradictions in the ideology that lies behind them. One could argue, then, that the very lack of unity in *Cwmardy* (perhaps somewhat in the mode of Brecht's epic theater) is a positive virtue that allows the work to conduct a critique of the contradictions that capitalism imposes on the miners' lives.

A more valid criticism of *Cwmardy* would be that the book, despite its attempts to evoke the entirety of community life and history, continues to place too much emphasis on the private aspects of Len's life, as in the ongoing focus on his difficulties in coming to terms with his adolescent sexuality. Still, one can read these very difficulties as a consequence of prevailing bourgeois notions of the separation of masculine and feminine spheres, a separation that clearly interferes with the development of a proletarian class consciousness that envelops both men and women. However, if the emphasis on family life in the book seems to be an expression of bourgeois attitudes, it is also the case that bourgeois ideology tends to privilege *bourgeois* family life and to regard working-class family life as debased. Jones's depiction of the genuine affection that links all members of the Roberts family (an unconventional family in which the parents are not married) can thus be taken as a counter to these bourgeois stereotypes. Moreover, as Raymond Williams points out, for a proletarian writer the family is often "the most accessible fictional centre, grounded in the reality of this kind of class community" (116).

In any case, Snee concludes that Jones goes beyond contemporaries such as Walter Greenwood and Walter Brierley in the attempt to escape bourgeois aesthetics and to develop a genuinely proletarian literature. Graham Holderness agrees, pointing out that Jones's "representations of work and community engage with a fully developed socialist consciousness to alter radically the nature of the novel form" (27). However, Snee and Holderness believe that Jones's second novel, *We Live* (which extends the story of *Cwmardy* into the 1930s and the Spanish Civil War) is even more successful in this sense. **Selected bibliography:** Bell; Holderness ("Miners and the Novel"); David Smith (Introduction to *Cwmardy*); Snee; Williams ("Working-Class").

LEWIS JONES: *WE LIVE* (1939). *We Live* is the sequel to Jones's *Cwmardy* and extends his narrative of the life of leftist activist Len Roberts—and, more importantly, of the Welsh mining community of Cwmardy—from the early 1920s to the late 1930s and the Spanish Civil War. The book begins as Len decides to join the Communist Party as the best way to work for justice for his beloved miners. Mary née Jones, now Len's wife, remains skeptical, however, largely because of the influence of her father, Ezra Jones, the longtime leader of the local miners, whose politics are more moderate (and more cynical) than those of the communists. More than the story of Len and Mary as individuals, *We Live* is the story of the local community, placed within the context of national and global political developments, including the General Strike of 1926 and the ominous rise of fascism in Europe in the 1930s. The book is also the story of the local communist movement in the Cwmardy Valley, which gradually gains influence among the miners as the only viable alternative to complete domination by Lord Cwmardy and his mining company, which effectively destroys Ezra's liberal Federation and instead coerces most of the miners into joining a nonpolitical company-backed union. The bankruptcy of any liberal solution to oppression is marked by Ezra's increasing alienation from the miners, culminating in his resignation from the Federation to become a company official, followed soon after by his death. Meanwhile, communist leader Harry Morgan manages to gain the support of a number of the local miners, including Len, Will Evans, and eventually even Mary. This support allows the communists to become the major force behind the continuing heroic resistance of the miners to exploitation by the mining company and oppression by the official forces, which always back the company in any dispute against workers.

At the end of the book, the miners have just won a major victory against the company. But, with the fascist assault on Spain well under way and with the specter of Nazi Germany haunting all of Europe, the communists are hardly in a position to relax and enjoy their victory. Instead, they recruit many of their leading members, including Len, to go to Spain to fight in the republican cause. Len, understanding the importance of the fight against fascism, is glad to go, despite his life-long aversion to violence and his close attachment to Mary, who must remain at home. The title of *We Live* emphasizes the way in which the collective is privileged over the individual in this work: Len is killed in Spain, but the community of Cwmardy and the communist movement live on. (Ironically, Jones, himself, would die of exhaustion resulting from his superhuman efforts to rally British support for the Spanish republicans, but his book would live on, published posthumously.)

In addition to the title motif, *We Live* consistently goes beyond *Cwmardy* in escaping individualism in the interest of a focus on collective action. Thus, while Len might still be described as the most important character, he is only marginally more prominent in this second novel than several others, including his parents (Big Jim and Shân Roberts), Mary, Ezra, and Will Evans. Moreover, Len, while a successful local leader of the movement, is less prominent as a political figure than Mary, Will, or Harry Morgan. If *We Live* is, like its predecessor, to some extent a bildungsroman focusing on Len's growth and maturation, it is also the case that his principal development in the course of the book is to learn to put aside his personal feelings in the interest of the good of the collective, while the central villain of the book (even more than the mine owner, Lord Cwmardy, and his manager, Mr. Hicks) is Fred Lewis, who claims to be a communist, but who cannot get beyond his own egotism and personal interests.

While its collective message is strong, *We Live* does an excellent job of demonstrating that devoted communists, such as Len and Mary, continue to have richly rewarding personal lives and that their devotion to the collective enriches, rather than diminishes, their lives as individuals. Len and Mary are so thoroughly integrated into the community as a whole that there can be no ultimate conflict between their interests and those of the miners as a whole. They are, in fact, figures of what Antonio Gramsci calls the "organic intellectual," so that, although they may become more educated and to an extent more intellectually sophisticated than the average miner or miner's wife, this development does not set them apart from the community so much as allow them to participate in it more fully. One might, then, contrast Len to a figure such as Étienne Lantier in Émile Zola's *Germinal*, which is perhaps the prototypical novel about coal miners. Lantier also becomes the intellectual leader of the miners in the French community of Montsou, but he is ultimately an outsider and never really fits in with the other miners. Len, on the other hand, has grown within the collective of the miners of Cwmardy and cannot conceive of himself as separate from his community, even though his experience in Spain causes him to realize that this community ultimately includes all of the workers of the world: "His body and mind had been moulded in the pit by his fellow workmen, and without them he knew his world would be empty" (93). The same, of course, might be said for Jones, and Graham Holderness rightly points out that Jones's effectiveness in representing working-class consciousness arises not from his personal genius, but from the fact that "the specific historical situation of the Rhondda valley in the 1920s and 30s, where Jones lived, worked and wrote, was capable of producing an image of class-struggle in the mining industry unrivalled in its clarity and simplicity" (29).

However, Holderness points out that the strong communal roots of Jones's fiction sometimes strain against the limitations of the novel form, with its own roots in the individualist ideology of capitalism. For Holderness, Jones's depictions of work and community challenge novelistic conventions and "engage with a fully developed socialist consciousness to alter radically the nature of the novel form" (27). It may be this unconventionality that leads David Smith, in his introduction to the book, to claim that *We Live* moves frenetically from one major political event to another, at the expense of turning its characters into "automated abstractions whose fictional duty is only to spill the historical beans." But in point of fact there is a great deal of attention to the private experiences of Len and his family, and the major characters all have vividly detailed emotional lives. As Snee argues, Jones's strong understanding of the relationship between the personal and the political "enables him to capture the complexities of individual lives and of political life as they intertwine and inform each other" (188). Thus, characters such as Len and Mary are what Georg Lukács would call "typical," that is, they are vividly individualized characters who are nevertheless shown as being shaped by larger historical forces of the kind that are shaping their society as a whole. The typicality of such characters, the establishment of close connections between private and public experience, and the building of the narrative upon a process of historical change all combine to make *We Live* a highly successful historical novel of the kind Lukács admires in the work of writers such as Walter Scott.

In the course of the book, Jones details the hardships suffered by the miners as a result of their dogged resistance, as when Len is imprisoned for six months merely for participating in a demonstration and when he spends most of his life impoverished and unemployed because of his opposition to the company. Jones does not revel in this hardship, however; instead, he focuses on the energy and vitality that help the miners to survive such adversity. This survival is due primarily to their sense of collective identity and to their mutual support for one another, which is demonstrated not only in private family life and in public labor activism, but also in a rich working-class culture that helps the miners to define themselves apart from the images of them purveyed by the official culture of Britain. This working-class culture relies greatly on folk tradition and has specific roots that clearly go back into the eighteenth- and nineteenth-century working-class cultures described by E. P. Thompson in his monumental study *The Making of the English Working Class*. But it also has the vitality and flexibility to respond to historical change and to remain ever-contemporary. Amid the alienating confusion of modernization and the rapid growth of their community from a small village into an emerging city, the workers of Cwmardy have maintained their class identity, as Smith notes, through the mediation of "ballads, games, choirs, jokes and anecdotes which mirrored their own collective endeavours."

One of the book's strongest features is its treatment of gender — or, in a sense, its lack of treatment of gender. For the communist movement depicted by Jones embraces full equality between the sexes. Men and women alike are comrades, and it is really no issue, for example, that Mary occupies a more important position in the Party than does Len. Moreover, the women of Cwmardy play a central role in political activity throughout the book, often, in fact, functioning more effectively than men in opposition to official power. Snee sums up Jones's achievement in this impressive novel: "In his treatment of women, of the working class, and of personal relationships, Jones breaks with the liberal ideology which has for so long surrounded and helped define the realist novel form, and in *We Live* in particular he begins to explore ways of opening up the form to allow the introduction of a proletarian consciousness" (190). **Selected bibliography:** Bell; Gramsci; Holderness ("Miners and the Novel"); Lukács (*Historical Novel*); David Smith (Introduction to *We Live*); Snee; E. P. Thompson (*Making*).

MERVYN JONES: *TODAY THE STRUGGLE* **(1978).** Mervyn Jones is an extremely prolific and versatile writer who has produced a number of novels dealing with issues of concern to the British Left. Jones first gained wide recognition for his 1966 novel *John and Mary*, which was the basis of a successful 1969 film starring Dustin Hoffman and Mia Farrow. This novel is also representative of much of Jones's work in that it focuses on a private (in this case sexual) relationship, but does so in ways that allow it to explore the social background of that relationship. *Today the Struggle* is probably Jones's most ambitious novel in this regard. This novel traces the lives of a number of characters from a variety of social backgrounds, beginning in the 1930s and extending to the late 1970s. In so doing, the book devotes most of its pages to describing the personal lives of the characters, including numerous affairs, marriages, and divorces. But it also carefully details the social and historical contexts in which the characters live, presenting in the process a sweeping history of Britain (and especially of the British Left) over the four decades encompassed by the book.

Jones carefully constructs his cast of characters to present a cross-section of British class society. Thus, Part I of the book, set in the 1930s, features three separate families, each from a different class background. One plot line centers on the working-class family of Alf Saunders, a railway signalman and devoted communist whose son, Len, goes to Spain to fight with the International Brigade. When Len is killed, he leaves his fiancée, Terry Flannery, pregnant with their child and thus rejected by her Irish Catholic family. So Terry goes to live with the Saunders family, which provides a great deal of support for her and her subsequent son, Joe. Another strain in Part I focuses on the bourgeois Charteris family, headed by prominent historian G. H. Charteris. This strain also features G. H.'s son, Basil, who intends to go to Spain, but only makes it as far as Paris before his sister, Nina, convinces him to return to England. Nina, meanwhile, is married to Roland Walmsley, a pacifist schoolmaster. She and Ronald have no children, but adopt two Jewish refugee children, Sophie and Max Friedemann, who flee Germany to escape Nazi persecution there. The class structure of Part I is completed with the Malet family, the patriarch of which is the Earl of Frome. This segment of the text focuses especially on the Earl's daughter, Fiona, a dazzling beauty who becomes involved with the dashing Kenneth Price, a world-famous mountain climber and a Nazi sympathizer.

These same families and characters remain central to Part II (set in the late 1950s) and Part III (set in the 1970s), though numerous other characters, many of them the offspring of the original characters, become important as well. Meanwhile, the lines of class become blurred, partly because members of the different families become involved with one another. Alf Saunders remains resolutely working class and maintains his loyalty to communism throughout the four decades, but the firm working-class structure of the family gradually deteriorates. Alf's son, Vic, becomes a trade union official, but his politics are decidedly moderate and his involvement with the union is simply his profession, rather than a political quest. Terry marries middle-class communist leader John Haslett, who leaves the Party in the 1950s. Young Joe Saunders, meanwhile, becomes a civil servant and essentially ascends into the middle class.

By the end of the book, the family is rapidly disintegrating. Terry's and John's granddaughter, Babsy Booth, still only sixteen, runs away to France to live with British painter Paul Ridley, now in his sixties and the former lover of Terry and the second husband of Fiona Malet. Meanwhile, Alf's grandson, Fred Kite, becomes a petty hoodlum, and Fred's son, Garry, becomes a gang leader who eventually rapes Francesca

Charteris, the thirteen-year-old daughter of Basil and his wife, the American novelist and feminist Gemma Lambiase. Basil himself becomes a successful historian, but never quite achieves personal happiness. Roland Walmsley dies of a heart attack in the 1960s, but Nina subsequently does well, opening a successful restaurant in London. Sophie Friedemann (now calling herself Sophie Walmsley) becomes a successful journalist. Max becomes a famous comedian, but never overcomes the trauma of his childhood and eventually commits suicide during a depression triggered by the Cuban missile crisis. Kenneth Prince turns out to be a homosexual, leading to the breakup of his marriage with Fiona. He is eventually killed in a jeep accident while commanding a group of British mercenaries in Africa. Caroline Prince, the daughter of Kenneth and Fiona, is for a time in her youth the lover of Joe Saunders, but remains aloof from most personal relationships, devoting herself to a series of political causes.

It is, in fact, such political causes that occupy the center of *Today the Struggle*, despite the frantic and soap opera-like action that provides most of the events of the plot. Indeed, the real story of the book involves large social changes that characterize British society in the movement from the 1930s to the 1970s. Most of these changes are presented as part of a gradual decline—in the family, in working-class culture, and in the power and commitment of the political Left. The 1930s, for example, are depicted as a time of great hardship but also as a time when one could count on one's family for support and when individuals could commit themselves with absolute conviction to momentous political causes, of which the Communist Party is among the most important. By the late 1950s, on the other hand, the Party has lost most of its influence, especially after Nikita Khrushchev's denunciation of Joseph Stalin and the Soviet intervention in Hungary. Many individuals have become cynical about politics altogether, while those who are still idealistic support causes, such as the nuclear disarmament movement, that deal with specific localized issues but not with the fundamental transformation of society. By the late 1970s, the economy is in decline, the fabric of the entire society is torn, cynicism is rampant, and about the only character still involved in any sort of politics is Caroline Malet, who seeks meaning in her life by joining a Palestinian terrorist organization that turns out to be headed by an Israeli intelligence agent. Through it all, as is indicated from the fact that Jones takes his title from W. H. Auden's poem, "Spain, 1937," the Spanish Civil War remains very much the moral center of the book, with the clear implication that the failure of the British to intercede in that conflict was the beginning of the end of British idealism. Yet the book ends on a positive note that centers on Spain as well. Basil Charteris, traveling in the south of France with his family, muses on his failure to go to Spain and concludes that unequivocal commitment is the only right way to live one's life. He confesses to Gemma his lifelong regret at not having gone to Spain, thus establishing a new closeness in their somewhat distant relationship. Gemma herself, meanwhile, muses on the course of the century in a way that provides a sort of summary of the book as a whole: "There had been, first of all . . . the challenge inspired by the Russian Revolution, when optimists counted on seeing socialism sweep away Europe's frontiers within a few years. Then the battle against fascism, which ought to have made dictatorships impossible for ever after. In America, within Gemma's own memory, the still incomplete struggle for equality of black and white. In England at the same time, the campaign against the bomb. And then the women's movement. Always something was gained, if only the awareness of greater possibilities; but always the success was partial, the impetus melted away. What mattered was to remember. What was vital was not to lose hope" (490).

The personal experiences of the numerous characters in *Today the Struggle* are clearly illustrative of larger social and historical forces, and to that extent these characters conform to Georg Lukács's insistence on the importance of typical characters in the construction of historical novels. The book is populated by numerous world-historical figures as well, as when Basil meets Josip Broz (Tito) in Paris or when Sophie interviews (and has sex with) John F. Kennedy in America. On the other hand, the utopian dimension of *Today the Struggle* is certainly weak, and the book conveys no sense that history is sweeping toward a more positive phase. Furthermore, there are gaps in the book's coverage of history, despite its panoramic scope. Colonialism and the phenomenon of decolonization, for example, are treated only superficially. The book concentrates on events (especially sexual relationships) that Lukács would probably regard as decadent, though it should also be said that this is largely the point of the book, which narrates the growing decadence of British society from the 1930s to the 1970s. All in all, *Today the Struggle* is an ambitious effort that suggests some of the possibilities of the historical novel, even if it does not always fulfill all of those possibilities. **Selected bibliography**: Lukács (*Historical Novel*); Ryan ("Socialist Fiction").

JAMES KELMAN: *THE BUSCONDUCTOR HINES* (1984). *The Busconductor Hines*, Kelman's first novel, already begins to anticipate the striking combination of working-class Glaswegian language and sophisticated literary technique that would come to distinguish Kelman's subsequent career. In particular, the book is narrated in an odd amalgam of demotic slang and mock scholarly discourse that provides a significant contribution to Kelman's assault on the assumed superiority of formal written language to the spoken language of ordinary people. The depiction of the protagonist, Glasgow bus conductor Robert Hines, is also typical of Kelman's writing in that Hines is not only a member of the working class, but a not very successful member at that. He chafes at the regimentation associated with his job as a conductor for the public bus company and is constantly in trouble with his superiors. Yet, despite his lack of devotion to his work, Hines is nevertheless defined by his job, as the book's title indicates. Meanwhile, he is sensitive, intelligent, well-read, extremely introspective, and, above all, vividly human despite his marginal position in the economic system of modern Glasgow. He is also quite politically aware, as when he explains to his driver, Reilly, that the company pays drivers more than conductors in order to disrupt any sense of solidarity between the two groups of workers (33). On a larger scale, Hines is also intensely aware of the subaltern position of Scotland in Great Britain, the "land of the regal brits" (221). Nevertheless, he is anything but a political activist, and the lethargy that makes it difficult for him to get to his job on time extends to politics and to all other areas of his life, perhaps because of a cynicism that leaves him unable to believe that any action on his part will lead to a genuine improvement in his life.

As is usually the case with Kelman's fiction, *The Busconductor Hines* focuses not on situations of unusual drama but on the ordinary events that transpire during the course of a series of typical days in the life of its protagonist. There are times in the text when Hines seems on the verge of the kind of dramatic experience that is normally the stuff of fiction, but these dramas consistently recede into anticlimax. At one point, for example, it appears that his wife, Sandra, has left him, taking their young son, Paul, with her to live with her parents. But she has second thoughts and returns that same night, reuniting the family. At several points, there are hints that Hines may have acquired a gun and may be on the brink of suicide or even murder, but no such events transpire, and by the end of the text it appears that the gun was merely a construct of Hines's sometimes vivid imagination. Near the end of the book, the workers at the bus company are on the point of going out on strike to protest the unfair treatment of Hines by the management, but he simply resigns from his job and averts the crisis. And even this resignation is inconclusive: as the text comes to a close, he is back on the job, and neither he nor we are certain whether his resignation was taken as final by the bus company. Through most of the book, meanwhile, we simply see Hines going about his daily routine: getting up in the morning, making and eating breakfast or other meals, taking his young son to nursery school, arguing with or making love to his wife. We also see him at work on his job, dealing with uncooperative passengers, bantering with his bus driver, debating with his superiors.

The drab banality of Hines's experiences is, in fact, much of the point of the book, and he himself feels increasingly suffocated by the routine in which he seems to have fallen. Throughout the book, he dreams of changing his life by moving to a better house, getting a better job, or even emigrating to Australia, but none of these things ever occur, partly due to the routinizing tendencies of the society around him and partially due to Hines's own passivity. He, like most of Kelman's protagonists, is not an energetic figure of action who leads the working class into conflict with their capitalist exploiters. Instead, he is too radically alienated to feel any real solidarity with the other members of his class, too glumly cynical to believe that any action he takes can really make a difference. As Cairns Craig puts it, "Kelman's central characters are symbols of the collapse of working-class life into a dispirited and isolated endurance: there is no hope of transformation; there is no sustenance in the community" (102).

Yet the book makes it clear that Hines's inaction does not make him unworthy of our interest, just as the lack of drama in his life does not mean that his life has no meaning. Among other things, it is not quite the case that nothing ever changes for Hines. Hovering over his inaction is an almost entropic process of decay in which virtually all aspects of his life are getting worse. Hines's family is a great source of solace; he and Sandra are very much in love, while he has high hopes that Paul, an extremely bright child, will be able to accomplish more than he ever has. But tensions are growing in the family, and Sandra, whose family has always felt that she married beneath her, is increasingly unhappy with their situation. The cheap dwelling in which they live is decaying by the moment, each day seeing a little more peeling of the wallpaper and the incursion of a few more mice. The neighborhood around the house, once relatively pleasant, is growing more and more squalid and dangerous. This decay informs Hines's work as a busconductor as well, as the bus company has for some time been gradually shifting to conductorless buses that will eventually render him obsolete.

The Busconductor Hines is formally fragmented, and each of the five chapters is broken into numerous shorter segments. The narrative consists more of a series of vignettes than a continuous plot, and even the individual sentences are often broken off in midstream. The book is thus typical of postmodernist literature in its formal fragmentation. However, while many postmodernist texts seem to celebrate fragmentation, Kelman treats the fragmentation of postmodern life (thematized by Hines's lack of any real sense of solidarity with his fellow workers) as a negative phenomenon that contributes in a central way to Hines's difficult psychic predicament. Kelman's book can thus be read as a diagnosis and critique of the unstable and fragmented status of the individual subject in the postmodern world of late capitalism, recalling among other things the work of Marxist critics such as Fredric Jameson. Kelman counters this fragmentation by weaving together Hines's public and private experiences, presenting Hines's private life at home and his public life at work as part of an interconnected whole. Kelman thus counters not only the fragmentation of experience under late capitalism, but the general tendency of bourgeois literature to treat public and private experience as separate and incommensurable realms. *Selected bibliography:* Cairns Craig; Jameson (*Postmodernism*); Klaus ("New Bearings"); Milne.

JAMES KELMAN: *A DISAFFECTION* **(1989).** *A Disaffection* narrates several days in the life of Glasgow high school teacher Patrick Doyle as he attempts to come to grips with a growing sense of alienation and frustration that is represented by the "disaffection" of the title. Doyle's malady might also be described as *déclassement*. As in all of Kelman's fiction, class is central to the book, and much of Doyle's difficulty arises from the fact that his university education and subsequent middle-class employment have separated him from his working-class roots without allowing him ever fully to feel himself a member of the middle class. Doyle is horrified by the bourgeois society that he sees around him—and particularly by his realization that, as a teacher, he is helping to instill the values of that society in his students, who respect him and trust him to tell them the truth about the world. Through most of the book, Doyle is thus on the verge of resigning from his job, but he can never quite do it given the depressed state of the Glasgow economy and his recognition that, even as a lowly teacher, he occupies a privileged position in his society relative to his married brother, Gavin, who struggles to get by during a lengthy period of unemployment, and his father, whose long life of toil has led to three strokes and left him aged and worn by his mid-fifties.

A Disaffection is typical of Kelman's fiction in its focus on the everyday experiences of ordinary people. Most of the plot has to do with Pat's various attempts to surmount his angst and find some source of pleasure and solace. To an extent, in fact, the book reads almost like a catalog of the various strategies available within a bourgeois society to escape from the realities of the injustices of the political and economic realm. The one escapist alternative typical of bourgeois society that Pat does not explore is religion, which he has rejected out of hand years earlier. Given Pat's intelligence and education, ignorance is not available as an alternative, either. He does, however, frequently consider suicide, that ultimate escapist gesture. But sex is the central concern of this lonely twenty-nine-year-old bachelor who has had very little experience or success with women. Pat has developed a powerful crush on the beautiful Alison Houston, a fellow teacher at his school, and spends much of his time trying to work up the nerve to reveal his feelings for her, even though he realizes that she, a married woman, will probably not respond. Alison eventually deduces his feelings from his behavior and tries as gently as possible to explain to him that an extramarital relationship would simply pose too big a complication in her life at this point. So Pat is once again left alone, the only woman he even knows being his sister-in-law, Nicola, on whom he also has a sort of crush and whom he wishes he could have married.

Pat resorts to other potential remedies as well. He frequently turns to drink as an escape from his troubles, though he gets very little solace from it and is trying to cut down. The world of art also offers its escapist attractions. Having once aspired to be a painter (Goya is one of his heroes), Pat occasionally tries to find some release in creativity, though the only project he actually undertakes in the course of the book is a somewhat unsatisfactory attempt to convert a pair of discarded electrician's conduit pipes into a musical instrument. Sport is a possibility as well, but Pat is not a great sports fan, and on the one occasion in which he goes to a soccer match to try to entertain himself he becomes so lost in thought that he misses the only goal of the game. Finally, Pat occasionally considers that great diversion of the middle class, the purchase of commodities. The driver of a small, aged car with rusty door hinges, he dreams of buying a luxurious automobile with extensive "in-car entertainment." Unfortunately, Pat cannot really afford such a purchase, and he understands the economic system of global capitalism too well to take much pleasure in commodities anyway. At one point, he muses on the possibility of buying something to get his mind off his troubles, "preferably an item of luxury but, an article sweated over by all the weans of Thailand for the wage of a lollipop, some article whose function they would be only vaguely aware of" (208).

This sort of awareness, gained as a result of his thoughtful bent, extensive reading, and university education, does a great deal to make Pat all the more miserable. His sympathies remain entirely with the working class, yet he can no longer feel himself a member of that class. In fact, he is firmly situated within the middle class whose values he rejects. Not only is he aware that he is contributing to the interpellation of his students, but he is aware of his own interpellation, horrified to realize that he not only looks and dresses like a teacher, but acts and talks like one as well. Intensely conscious of the exploitative nature of the capitalist economic system, of the subaltern position of Scotland in Great Britain, and of the growing global power of American capitalism and popular culture, Pat is haunted by the fact that his entire life centers on his teaching job, which he sees as a crucial contribution to the very system he so abhors. He is well aware, for example, that his school is designed very much along the same ideological lines as the cartoon shows watched by Gavin's children, which typically feature "a Northamerican white hero who was defeating socialist forces of evil who were of alien extraction" (293). Indeed, for Pat, these cartoons very much sum up the global political situation. He is able to comprehend socialism as an alternative to capitalism, but he is not able to believe that such an alternative can be achieved given the dominance of capital in his contemporary world. Although he is a great admirer of Marx (whom he describes as "fucking great"), he feels that, in the current situation, there is little point to being a Marxist. When one of Gavin's unemployed friends declares himself a Marxist and then asks Pat if he is a Marxist as well, Pat merely responds: "Seriously; you're asking me seriously, if I'm a Marxist, in a school like this, in a society like this, at a moment in history like the present" (191).

As is usual in Kelman's work, *A Disaffection* is technically accomplished and achieves many of its effects through style. The book employs a complex combination of stream-of-consciousness and indirect-free-style narration to provide very direct access to the contents of Pat's thoughts. Moreover, the language of the text, which is Pat's own, enacts his psychic state through style. In particular, Pat's language indicates his class position by freely intermixing the demotic slang of his working-class Glasgow roots, replete with expletives and sarcasm, with the sophisticated scholarly language of his British-dominated education and profession, replete with allusions to Greek philosophy, Shakespeare, Swift, Hölderlin, Hegel, Goethe, Dostoevsky, Dickens, Balzac, Joyce, Flannery O'Connor, *The Arabian Nights*, and (especially) Kafka.

This mixture of styles might be identified as a postmodernist gesture, but it is one with clearly political implications, especially in the way it refuses to grant the sophisticated elements of Pat's language any superiority to the working-class elements of it. Pat's language not only suggests that his education has been unable entirely to efface his working-class origins but also suggests that this working-class language and culture are too powerful to be entirely eradicated even by a thoroughly hegemonic bourgeois culture. This style is thus very representative of Kelman's "refusal to tolerate the slightest patronising attitude toward" the working-class characters that populate his fiction and of Kelman's "uncompromising critique of the convention in English fiction of draping the narrative voice in a neutral guise" (Klaus 187–88). Pat's plight is not only a comment upon the phenomenon of *déclassement* and on the radical alienation of the subject in an era of global capitalism, but also a demonstration of the impotent state of the Left in a 1980s Britain dominated by "fucking rightwingers."

Still, the book has a number of positive elements. In addition to its refusal to conform to bourgeois stylistic conventions or to grant the superiority of bourgeois language, there are occasional utopian moments in its content. For example, when Nicola suggests that Pat should perhaps simply appreciate what he has and stop agonizing over things that are beyond his control, he responds with a statement of great potential political power, despite its air of individualism: "Because I have a job doesni mean I have to stick it because people dont have a job I mean that's exactly what the system wants off ye; the last thing it wants is folk making their own decisions about working or not working and taking matters into their own hands, cause then the next thing ye know they'll be acting as if they're masters of their own fate and the next step on from there's making social change, structural change. Revolutions dont come, you've got to make them happen yourself. And once people start making their own decisions, well, that's when things might start to happen" (319).

A Disaffection thus provides a vivid portrayal of the alienation of a middle-class intellectual divorced from his working-class roots. It also suggests the lack of a viable political outlet for the frustrations of such intellectuals under late capitalism. It does not, however, suggest that this situation is inevitable or permanent. **Selected bibliography:** Cairns Craig; Harvie; Klaus ("New Bearings"); Milne; Morgan.

JAMES KELMAN: *HOW LATE IT WAS, HOW LATE* (1994). James Kelman has established a reputation throughout his career for representation of the experience of working-class Scotsmen with energy, humor, and humanity. *How Late It Was, How Late*, winner of the 1994 Booker Prize, is a particularly impressive and highly innovative effort in this direction. The book is narrated through a mixture of internal monologue and indirect free style that presents all of the events from the perspective of the protagonist, thirty-eight-year-old Sammy Samuels. In that sense, it does not seem very different from any number of modern bourgeois novels, beginning with James Joyce's *A Portrait of the Artist as a Young Man*. However, Sammy is an extremely unusual protagonist who differs dramatically from the tormented artists and intellectuals typical of the modernist novel. Sammy is a working-class character who has had few opportunities in life. While he has some skill and experience in the construction trade, he spends most of his time unemployed within the context of the depressed economy of contemporary Glasgow. Moreover, he has spent eleven of the past eighteen years in prison for crimes committed in an attempt simply to get by.

Sammy thus lives very much on the margins of modern British society, yet he is also clearly a sort of Scottish working-class Everyman, suggesting the way in which Scotland itself is marginal to Britain. Though life has made him extremely antagonistic and distrustful toward official society, he shows little bitterness and accepts his fate with a sort of stoic good humor. And, though he is a thoroughly alienated individual with a sense that no one can really understand him, he shows none of the misanthropy and existential angst that often serve as markers of alienation in bourgeois literature. For one thing, Sammy's alienation is at least partially due to the fact that, as a Scotsman, he occupies a semicolonial position within British society, making clear that the source of his condition is political and not metaphysical. Sammy is, moreover, a good-natured individual who has a number of drinking buddies, even if no close friends. And he has experienced virtually every form of human relationship, even if none of them were entirely satisfying. For example, he often recalls his working-class father, a dedicated union man who taught him to regard "fucking capitalists" as his class enemies (152). He has also been a husband, though he is now divorced, and he is the father of a son, now fifteen, who lives with the ex-wife. Sammy himself collects unemployment benefits, works when he can, and tries to pursue happiness through his somewhat strained relationship with Helen McGilvaray, the woman with whom he lives.

Sammy is thus an extremely unusual protagonist in relation to the mainstream tradition of British literature, especially when one considers his distinctive Glaswegian working-class dialect, which is also the language in which the text is narrated. Not only is his language extremely regional, it is also extremely obscene when judged by bourgeois standards. As one character tells Sammy, cautioning him about his language and exaggerating very little, "every second word's fuck" (238). Indeed, the "obscenity" of the book's demotic language was the center of considerable controversy when *How Late It Was, How Late* was awarded the Booker Prize, though it is hard to see how the book could have represented Sammy's perspective so convincingly without employing the language he would be likely to use.

The most unusual and innovative aspect of Kelman's use of perspective in the novel, however, has to do with the fact that, as the book begins, Sammy awakes from a weekend binge (triggered by a row with Helen) immediately to become involved in an altercation with the police that leaves him not only badly beaten but entirely blind. From that point onward, the novel is narrated entirely from the perspective of a blind man and therefore has no visual element whatsoever. To some extent, Sammy's blindness is clearly symbolic, suggesting his alienation from his surroundings and his inability fully to trust anyone around him. Indeed, Sammy's various infirmities are strikingly reminiscent of the afflictions that plague the characters of Samuel Beckett, making them figures of human inadequacy in the face of modern life. Sammy is particularly reminiscent of Beckettian figures such as Molloy, Malone, and the Unnamable in the way he doggedly plods on in the face of all adversity and of seeming hopelessness. Sammy's blindness also increases the sense of absurdity that surrounds his dealings with various government bureaucracies in the wake of his disability, clearly recalling the fiction of Franz Kafka.

Yet Kelman's novel also presents Sammy's experiences with an uncompromising realism that gives his book a concrete political dimension lacking in the work of writers such as Kafka and Beckett. Sammy's problems occur in a specific time and place and under specific social and political circumstances. If Sammy's story is an allegory of anything, it is not the human condition but working-class culture, which somehow goes on, with a style and language of its own, in the face of all adversity. At the same time, the book is an entirely realistic portrayal of life in modern Glasgow. The police, doctors, and social workers whom Sammy encounters in the course of the book may to some extent serve as allegorical representations of an official system of power that has Sammy very much at its mercy. But these functionaries are far from supernatural. They behave very much in the way members of the official bureaucracy in Scotland might, in fact, be expected to behave, and their motivations are not only entirely fathomable, but primarily economic. For one thing, the social service system, presumably designed for the benefit of citizens like Sammy, seeks to minimize expense by providing him as few services as possible. For another, the very fact that Sammy's blindness is apparently caused by his beating at the hands of the police causes the system to mobilize against him and to refuse to recognize the extent of his injuries. The attitude of the police is complicated not only by the fact that Sammy has a criminal record and is thus marked as a delinquent, but also by the fact that Charlie Barr, a slight acquaintance whom Sammy encountered during his lost weekend, is suspected of politically motivated terrorist activities, thus raising the question of Sammy's potential involvement in such activities as well.

To make matters worse, Helen has disappeared after their row, and her whereabouts remain unknown throughout the book. But Sammy does the best he can to accommodate himself to his blindness and to learn to survive alone and without sight. Meanwhile, in the midst of the attempts of the various minions of official power to intimidate, confuse, or just ignore him, Sammy shows a surprising strength and maintains his dogged determination to go on with his life. As he sees it, he has little choice: "Ye blunder on but ye blunder on. That's what ye do. What else is there man know what I'm talking about what else is there? fuck the suicide rates and statistics" (319). Sammy also maintains his equanimity and feels no bitterness toward anyone, even the police who beat him. "It's the system," he reasons, "they just take their orders" (63). Sammy's blindness is, thus, only one more in the series of obstacles that this system has placed in his path throughout his life, and to this extent he functions as a powerful image of working-class perseverance in the face of adversity. On the other hand, Sammy's alienation is so thorough that he feels very little sense of class consciousness. Nor does he expect to receive a great deal of support from the fellow members of his class. As he sees it, he is on his own, and, as such, it is not his hope to beat the system or to somehow cash in on his injuries. He merely hopes to go on as best he can, and by the end of the book he decides to head south for England, where he will be friendless but where he at least hopes that the police will bear him no specific grudge, thereby giving him a better chance to survive.

How Late It Was, How Late is thus a book that suggests little in the way of political action that might change the system that has victimized Sammy all his life. Yet, the very fact that the police are so intensely concerned about political "criminals" such as Charlie Barr suggests that they, themselves, feel vulnerable. In addition, the same skepticism that prevents Sammy from envisioning collective action to change the system itself serves as an important comment on the status of the individual subject in modern capitalist society and, in particular, on the way in which resistance has been squelched through the successful promulgation of the notion that such resistance is useless. Moreover, this seeming acquiescence is obtained in a way that allows Sammy to continue to see the "system" as his enemy. As a result, Sammy's acceptance of the system is obtained by a subtle form of coercion rather than by the far more stable and powerful method of consent that is typical of bourgeois hegemony. Indeed, Sammy's status as a subaltern within British society has, to some extent, interfered with the process of interpellation and prevented him from identifying with the official ideology of bourgeois Britain.

Kelman presents Sammy's plight in a matter-of-fact manner that avoids romanticism or sentimentality, just as Kelman's uncompromising use of Sammy's own distinctive language to narrate the book announces a refusal to surrender to the demands of bourgeois notions of literariness. Among other things, this language helps to establish the authenticity of Kelman's depiction of Sammy as a genuinely human and sympathetic character despite his numerous flaws. That accomplishment alone gives the book a significant positive dimension. In addition, there are also strong utopian resonances in the way Sammy's neighbor, "Boab," formerly a stranger, generously comes to his aid and in the way Sammy's son, Peter, offers help to his injured father. The most overt utopian dimension in the text resides in the character of Ally, an attorney who offers to represent Sammy in his attempt to get compensation from the authorities for his injuries. Ally is himself a former prison inmate who can thus very much sympathize with Sammy's position. However, he has gained enough knowledge of and insight into the system to know that the powers-that-be are themselves human and can be opposed by human action. Ally clearly sees Sammy's struggle for compensation as a form of class conflict in which the downtrodden Sammy has a legitimate chance at victory. Granted, Ally warns Sammy that the cards are stacked in the favor of their opponents, who after all have constructed the legal system within they must proceed. Moreover, he knows that the authorities themselves are willing to "fling away the rule book," especially if politics get involved. As he tells Sammy, "Ye have to understand about the law, it isnay there to apply to them it's there to apply to us, it's them that makes it" (310). On the other hand, Ally argues that people like Sammy and himself have the advantage that they are fighting for their lives, while their bourgeois opponents are simply fighting for money. He also believes that he and Sammy have a significant advantage in that the representatives of official authority hold them in such contempt that they are not really able to understand them: "It's a problem they've got I mean it's very hard for them to find out about us. That's cause we're repugnant. They don't even like being in the same room as us!" (239).

Sammy treats Ally with considerable skepticism. After all, he has never seen the man, nor can he read the legal documents that Ally presents him for his signature. Gradually, however, Sammy begins to trust the lawyer's sincerity, even if he finds it impossible to believe that he and Ally can beat the system on its own terms. The book thus ends with Sammy apparently preparing to head for England in an attempt to escape pressure from the police, though Ally, with the requisite documents already signed, may be able to proceed with the Sammy's claim for compensation in his client's absence. Actually, it is quite possible that Sammy will not go the England at all. One of the points of the book seems to be that it matters very little whether he remains in Glasgow or moves to Birmingham. It is, in fact, highly appropriate that the book ends with Sammy's plans unfinalized, the legal battle unresolved, and the question of a possible eventual restoration of Sammy's eyesight unanswered. Under the conditions in which they must live in capitalist society, people like Sammy may be able to envision temporary victories, but they can never hope to be victorious in the long run. They can simply hope to survive the slings and arrows that fortune brings them, perhaps getting in a few blows of their own along the way. Yet Kelman also suggests in a number of subtle ways that Sammy's condition is ordained not by fate but by the specific characteristics of British society at this particular point in history. And those characteristics might someday be subject to change. *Selected bibliography:* Cairns Craig; Donoghue; Milne.

D. H. LAWRENCE: *SONS AND LOVERS* **(1913).** Though *Sons and Lovers* is not particularly leftist in its political stance, the book stands out as one of the most important literary influences on subsequent British working-class writers. Not only does the novel center on working-class characters (something extremely unusual in British literature of its time), but Lawrence, himself, came from a working-class background. Thus, his ultimate success (and eventual canonization as one of the major figures of British modernism) provided important inspiration to other writers of similar backgrounds. As the son of a coal miner, Lawrence was an especially important figure in the development of the strong British tradition of coal-mining novels, setting the stage for later writers such as Walter Brierley, Harold Heslop, Lewis Jones, Len Doherty, and Barry Hines. Lawrence also demonstrated that writers who offend conventional bourgeois literary sensibilities can still become successful writers, though he (especially in the notorious censorship of texts such as *Lady Chatterley's Lover*) certainly had his troubles with the bourgeois authorities. On the other hand, the specific nature of Lawrence's transgressions against middle-class taste, which center on his open treatment of sexuality rather than on any suggestion of the possibility of collective working-class political action, suggests that writers who want to succeed in the West need to confine themselves to topics that can easily be absorbed within the existing structure of capitalist society.

One could argue, however, that the bourgeois reaction to Lawrence's "obscenity" was subtly reinforced by a discomfort over his treatment of class issues, however lacking in overt proletarian class consciousness that treatment might be. For example, *Sons and Lovers*, though it focuses on a protagonist, Paul Morel, whose dream is to be an artist and thus to escape work in the coal pits, does not denigrate working-class experience in the manner of so much mainstream British fiction. Indeed, Paul (though he sometimes views his coal miner father, Walter, as an uncivilized brute, seemingly preferring the attitudes of Gertrude, his more middle-class mother) retains a certain sense of loyalty to his working-class background and remains convinced that members of the working class have a certain vitality that is lacking in their more thoughtful, but more effete, middle-class counterparts. As he, himself, puts it, "I don't want to belong to the well-to-do middle class. I like my common people best" (298).

Paul's education and interest in art alienate him from the working class nevertheless, though Lawrence clearly depicts this alienation as a loss rather than a gain. At the same time, Lawrence carefully constructs *Sons and Lovers* in such a way that the relationship between Paul and his mother is decidedly problematic (and unhealthy), while Walter Morel, despite the antagonism that all of his children seem to feel toward him, remains the true heart of the family and the center of its most intimate and life-affirming moments. Indeed, it is only after the death of Mrs. Morel (induced by Paul and his sister, Annie, who give her an overdose of morphia to end her suffering from cancer) that Paul is able truly to begin a life of his own. Meanwhile, it is not Paul but Paul's older brother, William, who truly strives to escape his origins and to be a "gentleman." William's early death from pneumonia (after becoming engaged to a beautiful but pretentious and mindless "lady" who views working-class people as "clownish") thus symbolizes the lack of vitality in the world to which William aspires.

Sons and Lovers is a bildungsroman that describes the growth and maturation of Paul Morel from childhood to young adulthood. Sexuality is very much at the center of the story, and a great deal of Paul's development has to do with his highly oedipal relationship with his parents and with his exploration of his sexuality through his relationship first with the young, bovarystic, and sexually repressed Miriam Leivers and then with the earthier and more mature Clara Dawes, a married woman estranged from her working-class husband. Clara is also a crusader for women's rights, and through her Lawrence is able to introduce the important debates about redefinition of gender roles that were crucial to the political climate of British society at the beginning of the twentieth century. The frank treatment of Paul's sexual experiences with both Miriam and Clara was highly unusual for its time, but no more so than the book's intense focus on Paul's working-class background. Lawrence provides a detailed, essentially naturalistic account of the working-class culture in the Nottinghamshire mining village of Bestwood, centering on the Morel family but also encompassing the community as a whole. The book also pays considerable attention to Walter Morel's working experience. Thus, as Mary Eagleton and David Pierce point out, Walter is at his best and most human when he is working with his hands (103). Paul's working experience is important in the book as well, even if his job as a clerk (and later as an overseer) in a surgical appliances factory does not involve the kind of physical activity that is so life-affirming in the work of his father.

Clerking, in fact, is not an occupation that Walter views as a properly masculine one, suggesting the way in which most activities in *Sons and Lovers* tend to have a gendered character. The differences between Paul's parents illustrates the way in which Lawrence sometimes seems to confuse gender and class, equating working-class experience with masculinity and middle-class experience with femininity. For example, the relationship between Clara Dawes and her husband to some extent mirrors that of the Morel parents, with Baxter Dawes clearly serving as a sort of reinscription of Walter Morel. Thus, if Lawrence's treatment of class is somewhat hampered by his stereotypical tendency to think of middle-class individuals as people who think and of working-class individuals as people who feel, the same might be said for his vision of gender, in which men are driven by a strong phallic energy, while women, whose sexual energies are more repressed, tend to be thoughtful and ethereal. Of course, the opposition between the sensitive and introspective Paul and the physically passionate Clara seems to complicate Lawrence's treatment of gender and to reinforce what Dorothy Van Ghent has seen as the book's central idea: "an organic disturbance in the relationships of men and women" (247). But there is a class disruption involved here as well: it is, after all, also true that Paul becomes irreversibly estranged from the working class while Clara is drawn back into it and into her marriage with Baxter, who ultimately exercises a stronger sexual pull than Paul, whose intellect powerfully interferes with his ability to experience sexual passion.

Sons and Lovers is often regarded as the first genuinely working-class British novel. It is also widely regarded as a major milestone in the history of British literature, both for its working-class focus and for its innovative combination of naturalistic detail with a sometimes extravagant style and a strong modernist sense of crisis. However, one should not be too quick to dismiss, as many have since Lawrence's canonization, Christopher Caudwell's biting condemnation of Lawrence's vision as leading ultimately to fascism (56–57). There are, after all, significant flaws in Lawrence's vision, and these flaws, as in the frequent evocation of "the blood" as the central force in human life, can have potentially ominous consequences. On the other hand, Lawrence's treatment of class, however stereotypical, is in many ways quite complex. If nothing else, Lawrence recognizes—and attempts to reveal in his work—the invidiousness of class society, while treating the working class in a far less condescending manner than had most of his predecessors in British fiction. **Selected bibliography:** Black; Caudwell; Eagleton and Pierce; Fernihough; Holderness (*D. H. Lawrence*); Leavis; Martin; Van Ghent.

JOHN LEHMANN: *EVIL WAS ABROAD* **(1938).** John Lehmann, though of a middle-class background, was a leading figure in British leftist culture in the 1930s. An active editor, he founded (in 1937) and then edited the journal *New Writing*, which published works by a number of working-class, socialist, and antifascist writers, many of them previously unknown. Lehmann also wrote numerous works of his own, including the antfascist novel *Evil Was Abroad*. Though set primarily in Vienna, this novel resembles the works of Christopher Isherwood in that it focuses on the experiences of an English writer living in Europe during the tense years of the early 1930s as the Nazis rise to power in Germany, already with ominous hints that the rest of Europe is in danger as well. But *Evil Was Abroad* is also specifically a call to antifascist political action, and one of its main themes is the necessity for intellectuals to recognize fascism as a serious threat that they need move outside their ivory-tower worlds to oppose.

Lehmann's protagonist is Peter Rains, a middle-class English literary scholar who has come to Vienna to work on a biography of a well-known (though unidentified in the book) poet from the past. Though immersed in his research, Rains gradually becomes aware of the tense political climate around him. Vienna, however grand its past, is a city in decline.

Steeped in decadence and afflicted by a great deal of poverty and unemployment, the city is ripe for precisely the kinds of extreme political activity that are occurring in Berlin at the same time. Indeed, gangs of Nazi are already beginning to wander the streets of Vienna, menacing any of its inhabitants, especially socialists or communists, who might dare oppose them.

Rains, who has led a sheltered life of economic security surrounded by a world of books, begins to get in touch with the political reality of Vienna when he meets Rudi Slovanek, a young man who is a highly skilled cobbler but who has been unemployed for an extended period, and is now living a life of hardship and poverty. Rains befriends the young man and tries to help him as best he can, though it is clear that this help is offered with a certain amount of condescension and without any real understanding of Slovanek's world. Midway through the book, Rains goes to Prague to do some research there and to visit his newly married friends, Dick and Juliet. While Rains is in Prague, Dick, a journalist, goes to Berlin to cover the political developments there. He is there when the Reichstag fire occurs, and the Nazis ascend to power. Dick returns to Prague with alarming stories of Nazi atrocities and ominous warnings that a European war is inevitable.

Rains returns to Vienna with a vague plan to try to protect Rudi from the upcoming crisis, but finds that his friend has disappeared, possibly having committed suicide after contracting a venereal disease. As a result of this revelation and of his search for Rudi in Vienna's seedily decadent underworld, Rains begins to gain a better understanding of the true depth of Rudi's despair. Rains also begins to understand his own former separation from the material facts of the lives of most people. He comes to realize that fascism threatens privileged individuals like himself as much as downtrodden individuals like Rudi. He therefore resolves to try to get in touch with the masses, to "learn to feel as they felt" in order to be able to join with them in the upcoming struggle against fascism (255). As the book ends, he joins a crowd of people running through the streets in the aftermath of an antifascist political demonstration that has been broken up by the police, thus enacting a sort of allegory of the Popular Front alliance against fascism.

Evil Was Abroad is, first and foremost, a call for the middle class (especially middle-class intellectuals) to join together with the working class to mount a united opposition to fascism. In that, it is very much typical of its time. Though it is sometimes powerful in its evocation of the atmosphere of Vienna in 1932 and 1933, it is not an entirely successful novel. For example, though the book was praised by reviewers, such as Stephen Spender, for the "almost photographic" accuracy of its depiction of Vienna, Lehmann's attempts to reinforce his depiction of the nightmarish atmosphere of Europe in the 1930s by adding touches such as surrealistic scenes from Rains's dreams seem a bit artificial. Nevertheless, in its focus on both Czechoslovakia and Austria as prime targets for Nazi aggression, the book turns out to have been prophetic — though the accuracy of its prophecy also suggests the extent to which the West was long aware of the inevitable consequences of Nazi power and yet did little or nothing to stop it. *Selected bibliography:* Croft (*Red Letter Days*); Cunningham.

DORIS LESSING: *CHILDREN OF VIOLENCE* **(1952–69).** *Children of Violence* is the collective title for a five-volume sequence of novels that includes *Martha Quest* (1952), *A Proper Marriage* (1954), *A Ripple from the Storm* (1958), *Landlocked* (1965), and *The Four-Gated City* (1969). Together these five volumes trace the development of the protagonist, Martha Quest, from her adolescence in African "Zambesia" (based on colonial Rhodesia) in the late 1930s to her old age in London in 2000. The sequence also tracks important concurrent aspects of twentieth-century history, though by the fifth volume this "history" is projected into the future. The first three volumes are written in a relatively straightforward realistic mode, but the last two (written after the publication of Lessing's innovative *The Golden Notebook* in 1962) are more formally innovative. The sequence thus also traces the evolution of Lessing's writing practice over a period of the nearly twenty years. It also tracks certain developments in leftist literature as a whole, and Lessing's turn away from realism at the beginning of the 1960s is clearly symptomatic of the crisis in confidence that beset the British Left during and after the difficult decade of the 1950s. The content of the *Children of Violence* sequence mirrors this phenomenon as well. The early volumes begin as a leftist critique of capitalism, focusing on racism and colonialism as negative aspects of the capitalist system. The later volumes, however, focus less on politics and more on psychology and spirituality, suggesting Lessing's growing lack of faith in conventional political solutions to the problems that plague modern society. At the same time, the sequence remains critical of the capitalist system even in the mystical last volume, which ends in the aftermath of a nuclear holocaust which has been at least partly caused by capitalist greed and competition. To an extent, then, Lessing's sequence suggests the wide variety of formal strategies and political stances that are available to writers who would seek to use the novel form to provide a critique of capitalism.

Children of Violence also traces Lessing's development in the sense that Martha has a great deal in common with Lessing, who grew up in colonial Rhodesia and later moved to London. The first volume begins when Martha is fifteen and living with her parents on the colonial farm to which they had come years earlier with dreams of wealth, but on which they have barely been able to scratch out a living. Like most teenagers, Martha finds her parents insufferably conventional and narrow-minded. She is particularly appalled by their racism (a motif strongly reinforced by the colonial setting) and by her father's vision of warfare as a glorious activity (a motif with special resonances as war looms over Europe). Seeking broader horizons than are available in the rural society of her parents, Martha, at age eighteen, moves to the nearby town, where she takes an office job in a law firm headed by Jasper and Max Cohen, the uncles of Joss and Solly Cohen, two Jewish boys Martha has known for many years. Martha gradually adjusts to work in the office, improving her secretarial skills by taking courses at the local Polytechnic. In the meantime, she also expands her social horizons through participation in the local Sports Club, though the idealistic Martha (whose ideas about the world have been largely shaped by a bovarystic reading of literature) is constantly appalled by the hypocrisy and bigotry of most of the club's members.

Many of the events of *Martha Quest* involve Martha's gradual exploration of her sexuality, but Martha's encounters with racism and antisemitism are crucial to this volume as well, as is the ominous background of the looming threat of fascism and war in Europe. The book ends with her marriage to the priggish Douglas Knowell, a colonial official who is considered quite a catch by the society of the town, thus providing a conventional ending to the female bildungsroman plot of the novel. This romance ending is undercut, however, by hints of imminent war in Europe. Though this closure should conventionally be essentially the end of Martha's development as an individual, it is in fact merely another stage in her development. There are, after all, still four more volumes to come. In *A Proper Marriage*, Martha bears a child, but her relationship with Douglas deteriorates as she finds it increasingly difficult to maintain her sense of personal dignity within the marriage. In the course of the book she has an extramarital affair and begins to become more and more aware of politics, though her own vision of an ideal life remains located less in concrete political action than in a vaguely utopian vision of a "noble city" — which resurfaces in the "four-gated" city of the last volume.

A Ripple from the Storm turns to a more extensive exploration of potential political avenues toward the realization of this vision. At last free of her oppressive marriage, Martha joins a Marxist group that is dedicated to the liberation of the working classes of colonial Zambesia. Lessing treats this group as well meaning but fundamentally ineffectual, and the considerable skepticism in her portrayal of it foreshadows her later move away from leftist politics. Not only are their various political discussions presented with considerable irony, but the group, which is dedicated to black liberation, is composed entirely of whites — except for one black man who turns out to be a spy for the government. The group is eventually disbanded, and Martha, who has married the group's leader, finds herself once again trapped in an unfulfilling marriage, her foray into leftist political action having turned out to be as much a dead end as her earlier flirtation with the fashionable society of the Sports Club.

In *Landlocked*, Martha once again seeks solace in an extramarital affair, this time with a gardener, Thomas Stern, who, like her first lover in *Martha Quest*, is a Polish Jew. However, the relationship marks new territory in Martha's development as an individual and in Lessing's development as a writer. Moving away from the realism of the earlier volumes, Lessing has Martha and Stern communicate telepathically as a symbol of their intimacy, the first satisfying intimacy that Martha has ever experienced. This moment of happiness is cut short, however, and Stern soon dies, having become insane. His insanity is not, however, presented as a disease or deterioration, but simply as a movement into a different psychic state, thereby suggesting that the normal state we identify as sanity is unable to encompass the potential richness of the full range of human experience. This turn away from rationality is then completed in *The Four-Gated City*, which takes Martha into old age and into an increasing awareness of her paranormal psychic powers. In this volume, Martha comes to find a fulfillment in an inward turn to her own psychic resources that she had earlier failed to find in her private relations with others or her public participation in politics. Correspondingly, the novel itself moves still further away from realism, employing a complex concentric plot form rather than a linear narrative in its attempt to describe alternative realms of experience. As the book closes, modern civilization has been destroyed by a nuclear holocaust, but the survivors, Martha included, seem determined to rebuild the world based on mysticism and access to paranormal psychic experience, thus escaping the mistakes of the materialistic society that came before them.

One can certainly interpret the turn toward mysticism in the later volumes of *The Children of Violence* as an escapist move that ultimately deprives Lessing's work of any real political force. It is particularly telling, for example, that the final vision of the possibility of building a new and better world centrally depends upon the emergence of a new race of children born with fully developed paranormal psychic powers. On the other hand, Lessing's critique of modern society remains powerful, even if her alternatives become less viable and convincing. In the meantime, the sweeping coverage of the five books as a whole provides one of the most comprehensive accounts of modern experience available in all of literature. Moreover, the ultimate failure of the sequence in a political sense is, itself, instructive, suggesting that, once leftist political action has been abandoned, the only alternative available to late capitalist society is a turn toward individual subjective experience and an escape from material reality. *Selected bibliography:* Hite; Rubenstein; Sage.

DORIS LESSING: *THE GOLDEN NOTEBOOK* **(1962).** *The Golden Notebook* is a sophisticated work of postmodernist fiction that engages in extensive critical dialogues with both the history and politics of the 1950s and the tradition of realistic fiction, both bourgeois and socialist. The book is structurally complex, consisting of a number of interrelated layers. The ostensibly central layer consists of five separate segments that, together, constitute a seemingly conventional realistic novel entitled *Free Women*, the protagonist of which is Anna Wulf, a woman novelist. Interwoven with the *Free Women* segments are entries from Anna's four journals, or notebooks, which she keeps in an attempt to make sense of the different aspects of her life. These notebook segments then culminate near the end of the book when Anna abandons her multiple notebooks for a single, golden, notebook. The interrelationship among the different notebooks and between the notebooks and the *Free Women* segments is ironic and unstable, making any final interpretation of the text impossible. Nevertheless, the various segments address a number of significant issues and, together, constitute both a retrospective look at the failures of British leftist politics in the 1950s and an anticipation of the rise of feminism in the 1960s.

Free Women is described by Lessing in her 1972 introduction to the book as the "skeleton, or frame" of *The Golden Notebook*. It narrates Anna's experiences in 1957, which primarily involve her personal relationships with her daughter, Janet; her friend, Molly Jacobs; Molly's ex-husband, Richard Portmain; Richard's current wife, Marion; and Molly and Richard's twenty-year-old son, Tommy. The actual events of this narrative center on Tommy's failed suicide attempt (which leaves him permanently blind) and his subsequent, rather pathological, friendship with Marion, who is desperate for some sort of human contact because Richard, a wealthy cocoon, has abandoned her emotionally. Observing these events, Anna, herself, feels increasingly unstable and unable to cope with life. By the end of the narrative, however, she survives a particularly unsettling affair and decides to settle down, giving up writing and taking a job as a social worker and joining the respectable Labour Party. Molly similarly opts for stability and respectability and decides to marry a well-to-do businessman.

The black notebook consists of two different types of entries. In one, Anna details her experiences (in her early twenties) with a group of fellow European communists in central Africa during World War II. These experiences, which already suggest the futility of the communist project, prefigure Anna's experiences in Britain in the 1950s. They also provide the background for Anna's only published novel, *Frontiers of*

War, which was a minor bestseller in the early 1950s and the proceeds from which still support her in 1957, the present time of *The Golden Notebook*. The other entries in the black notebook concern the aftermath of Anna's novel, including critical reactions to it (especially from leftist critics, who find it frivolous and self-indulgent in its emphasis on private emotional experience) and the financial ramifications resulting from it (including negotiations with Western television and movie producers who hope to make impoverishing adaptations of it). In this way, Lessing announces her distaste for both the Marxist tradition of emphasis on realism and on the social and historical (rather than the individual and emotional), but she simultaneously critiques the tendency of Western popular culture to efface the social and historical and thereby to produce trivialized and romanticized representations of private experience.

The red notebook deals with Anna's political activities, and, in particular, with her involvement with the British Communist Party in the 1950s. The first segment of this notebook begins with Anna's decision officially to join the party in 1950. Subsequent segments deal with the increasing travails of the party, culminating in Anna's decision to leave the Party after the woeful year of 1956, in which Nikita Khrushchev's denunciation of Joseph Stalin and the Soviet intervention in Hungary led many members (including prominent scholars such as E. P. Thompson and Christopher Hill) to resign in protest against the party's inability or unwillingness to change its stance in response to these new developments. In these notebooks, many British communists are shown as hopelessly naive and idealistic in their belief in socialism and, especially, in their faith that the Soviet Union could lead the way to the establishment of socialist ideals worldwide. However, Anna (partly because of her previous experiences in Africa) is not one of these. The notebook suggests that, by 1952, she had already lost faith in the ability of the Party to achieve the goals of social and economic justice that she had initially associated with it. Indeed, there are suggestions that Anna never really believes in the Party's program but simply joins out of desire to be part of a genuine community of the kind otherwise unavailable in the alienating environment of capitalist England.

The yellow notebook consists primarily of fragments of a second novel, entitled *The Shadow of the Third*, that Anna has been composing for some time but which, by 1957, she has abandoned due to writer's block. This novel is rather transparently autobiographical, and its protagonist, Ella, seems to be an almost direct projection of Anna herself. The novel deals primarily with Ella's years-long love affair with a married psychiatrist, Dr. Paul Tanner, and with her attempts to come to grips with the end of this affair, which leaves her feeling empty and emotionally lost. These events clearly echo Anna's own five-year affair with Michael, a former Middle-European communist whom she still appears to love even years after he has ended their relationship. The entries in the yellow notebook eventually break down into fragmentary notes for potential short stories or novels, signaling Anna's increasing sense of psychic dissolution and her corresponding increasing inability to construct a coherent narrative based on her personal experience.

The final entries in the black and red notebooks are similarly fragmentary; they consist largely of newspaper clippings that Anna has pasted into the notebooks in an attempt to document events in a world of which Anna is less and less able to make sense. The blue notebook, meanwhile, records Anna's experiences through the 1950s in diary format and, thus, reiterates much of the material from the other notebooks (and from the *Free Women* narrative) from a slightly different perspective. The final entry in the blue notebook maintains a narrative coherence that the other notebooks by that time lack. On the other hand, this narrative largely involves Anna's growing sense of the dissolution of her identity and suggests that this breakdown is being furthered her difficult relationship with the American communist writer Saul Green (based on Lessing's lover, the American leftist writer Clancy Sigal), who is also experiencing radical psychic fragmentation.

The last notebook entry is the golden notebook, an expensive volume that Anna buys and begins in an apparent attempt to pull together the disparate elements of her life. This attempt fails, however, and the golden notebook actually narrates Anna's breakdown. This breakdown, however, is neither a simple matter of psychosis nor an entirely negative experience for Anna. It is, in fact, a symbolic representation of the fragmentation of individual experience in the modern world. Moreover, it is an experience that Anna and Saul share and that helps bring them both back to health. By the end, in fact, both are ready to resume writing. Saul will successfully complete a novel the first sentence of which is supplied to him by Anna, while Anna begins a new novel the first sentence of which is supplied by Saul.

This sentence, meanwhile, is also the first sentence of *The Golden Notebook*, which at first glance identifies the entire novel as Anna's subsequent production. However, such an interpretation results in a confusion of ontological levels that is impossible to untangle in any straightforward way. Indeed, as with much postmodernist fiction, the self-referential aspects of *The Golden Notebook* make any single, unambiguous interpretation of the book impossible. Moreover, a close comparison among the different segments of Lessing's novels reveals a number of inconsistencies. For example, *Free Women*, as the frame narrative, and the blue notebook, as Anna's personal diary, would seem to be the most authoritative of all the levels. Yet the endings of these two segments are entirely different. Other details vary as well. In the last segment of the blue notebook, for example, Tommy is married, apparently sighted, and traveling around England lecturing about the lives of coal miners. In *Free Women*, however, he is blind and withdrawn from the world except for his malicious attempts to involve Marion in leftist political activities of which she has no real understanding.

Among other things, the resistance to final interpretation that Lessing builds into *The Golden Notebook* has a mimetic function, suggesting the confusion and complexity that face individuals in their encounters with the modern world. Indeed, the book serves as a sort of fictional catalog of the symptoms of postmodernity ("schizophrenia," difficulty with "cognitive mapping") that observers such as Fredric Jameson would later associate with the phenomenon of postmodernism in their theoretical work. On the other hand, the complex textuality of *The Golden Notebook* also clearly serves as a response to the insistence of Marxist critics that fiction should have a clear and unambiguous political message. For example, Molly Hite notes the way in which Lessing's writing practice in the book challenges the orthodox Marxist aesthetics of her friend Jack Lindsay, who (in a mode resembling the work of Georg Lukács) called for a realistic engagement with the historical process and a unity of vision based on the class perspective of the proletariat (57).

The Golden Notebook suggests that, where Western literature has failed by focusing on the private at the expense of the public, socialist literature has failed in precisely the opposite direction. Lessing, on the other hand, seeks in the book to connect the public and the private, and the greatest strength of her novel is her insistence that Anna's political life and private life are intimately interrelated. As Lessing argues in her introduction, "the essence of the book, the organisation of it, everything in it, says implicitly and explicitly, that we must not divide things off, must not compartmentalise" (x). But Lessing's dismissive treatment of Marxist realist aesthetics may be unfair. After all, such connections between the private and the public are precisely what Marxists such as Lukács and Lindsay had been urging all along. Thus, Lorna Sage concludes that Marxist aesthetic statements, such as Raymond Williams's call in *The Long Revolution* for novels that represent life in its totality, might serve almost as "a synopsis for *The Golden Notebook*" (45).

Lessing's own aesthetics in *The Golden Notebook* are aligned almost directly with those of Western modernism and postmodernism, which may account for the fact that the book has been very popular in the West and has been incorporated into the syllabi of numerous college courses on the contemporary novel. The Modern Language Association of America has even published a guidebook for teaching the book in such courses (see Kaplan and Rose). Moreover, because of its vivid presentation of feminine experience, *The Golden Notebook* has gained something of a following as a feminist text, though feminists critics have been somewhat ambivalent toward the book, and Lessing, in her introduction, discounts the notion that the book is a "trumpet for Women's Liberation" (viii). Whatever attitude one takes toward the book, *The Golden Notebook* is certainly a valuable document of its time and one that raises a number of important political and aesthetic issues. In addition, to the extent that the book seeks to provide a sweeping historical document of its time and to the extent that it pays serious attention (however critical and skeptical) to leftist political activity, *The Golden Notebook* makes an important contribution to the British literature of the Left. ***Selected bibliography:*** Hite; Fredric Jameson (*Postmodernism*); Kaplan and Rose; McCrindle; Rubenstein; Sage; Williams (*The Long Revolution*).

JACK LINDSAY: *BETRAYED SPRING* (1953). *Betrayed Spring* is the first of what is essentially a trilogy of novels, which also includes *Rising Tide* (1953) and *The Moment of Choice* (1955). Together, these novels narrate the high hopes and ultimate disappointments that were associated with the election of the Attlee Labour government in Britain in 1945. *Rising Tide* centers on the dock strike of 1949 and, among other things, demonstrates that the political climate of the Cold War made it impossible for the Attlee government to move toward genuine socialism in Britain. *The Moment of Choice* is set in 1951, the year Attlee and the Labour Party were removed from power after calling an early election. Set at the beginning of the Korean War, it also pays a great deal of attention to the role of the Cold War in British domestic politics of the early 1950s. *Betrayed Spring*, however, is probably the best of these novels and the one that makes its points most clearly. Set in the six-month period from September 1946, to March 1947, this novel closely tracks the experiences of a number of individual characters while carefully and effectively setting those experiences against the background of the early years of the Attlee government and of events such as the nationalization of the coal industry. As the title indicates, Lindsay views the policies of the Attlee government as a betrayal of the working class, but he does so in an even-handed and considered manner.

Betrayed Spring consists of four separate, but interrelated, plot strands, labeled according to their settings in London, Lancashire, Yorkshire, and Tyneside. The London segments center on the working-class Tremaine family as it struggles to get by in the face of the father's unemployment. The most important character in these segments is daughter Phyl Tremaine, who struggles to help her family by working as a café waitress, while at the same time gradually becoming aware of politics and of the role of class in British society. The Lancashire segments focus primarily on Dick Baxter, a coal miner who has just returned from military service in the war. Dick, like Phyl, is in the early stages of political awareness. He returns to the pits after his demobilization, only to find that this decision contributes to the breakup of his engagement to typist

Patricia Hemans. During the remainder of the book he develops a growing sense of solidarity with the other miners as they attempt to cope with the failure of nationalization to give them any real say in the running of the mines.

Kit Swinton, the son of a wealthy mill owner, is the central character of the Yorkshire segments. Kit, who had served in the war with Dick Baxter, is something of a socialist, who at the start of the book is determined to side with the working class against their exploitation by capitalists such as his father. He begins work in his father's mill, still eager to help the workers there, but he gradually slides into a position of solidarity with his father against the workers, partly because his own romantic relationship with the communist Jill Wethers, a weaver in the mill, has gone sour. Finally, the Tyneside segments feature William Emery, a trade union official, who has worked hard his whole life to gain a position of some importance, but who then finds that he must begin to compromise his principles to keep that position. This compromise leads to his growing unhappiness and to the breakup of his marriage, leaving him lonely and miserable, seeking solace in an affair with this secretary, Barbara Pickering.

A fifth important character in *Betrayed Spring* is Harry Manson, a communist law student who had served in the war with Kit Swinton and Dick Baxter. Gavin MacKenzie, the brother of William Emery's wife, had served with them as well, but was killed in the war. Harry participates in various political meetings and activities at which Phyl Tremaine is present, so that he provides a central thread that links all four of the segments of the book together. In this way, Lindsay helps to create a sense of British society as an interrelated totality, much in the manner praised by Georg Lukács in relation to the great historical novels of nienteenth-century authors such as Walter Scott and Honoré de Balzac. The most theoretically sophisticated of the characters, Manson also provides some of the book's most important political statements. *Betrayed Spring* is thus structurally balanced: if the segments focusing on Swinton and Emery dramatize the betrayal of the working class by the Labour government, Lindsay also suggests that there is still hope for a better future in his positive portrayal of Manson and his suggestion that individuals such as Dick Baxter and Phyl Tremaine are growing in political awareness. In the meantime, the book provides a great deal of background detail to bring alive this crucial winter in British history when, among other things, the coldest weather in memory contributed to an economic crisis with which the Labour government found itself unable to cope without betraying its own principles and forming an alliance with big business. This emphasis on the extreme cold of the winter provides a useful reminder of the role played by such prosaic events as weather in the course of history. At the same time, this focus on the harsh winter symbolically reinforces the book's treatment of the Cold War, against the background of which the domestic events described in the book are carefully set. Many of the characters, for example, are alarmed at a world situation increasingly dominated by the Americans as Britain rapidly recedes from its former position of global imperial power. The book includes a number of ominous warnings that the postwar reaction against communism in various parts of the world (the repression of the opposition in Greece is singled out for detailed treatment) is becoming so severe that the victors in World War II are almost indistinguishable in their policies from the fascists they had supposed just defeated. All in all, *Betrayed Spring* is an effective historical novel that outlines the broken hopes of a crucial turning point in the history of the British Left, without becoming bitter or sentimental and without losing hope for a better future. Lindsay does not simply rail against the failures of the past: he insists that it might have been otherwise—and that it might still be. The remainder of the trilogy continues in much the same way, and Alick West is right to describe Lindsay's project in the three books (and in the rest of his work) as an attempt "to penetrate behind the mechanical abstraction into which political analysis is apt to degenerate when it becomes dogmatic, and to reveal the human energy which such analysis unthinkingly takes for granted" (208). **Selected bibliography:** Lukács (Historical Novel); David Smith (*Socialist Propaganda*); West (*Mountain*).

JACK LINDSAY: *MEN OF FORTY-EIGHT* **(1948).** *Men of Forty-Eight* is a historical novel that deals with the revolutionary uprisings that swept across Europe in 1848, though it focuses especially on English Chartism, an English working-class movement that had been agitating for greater political and economic equality in England since 1838, when the London Working Men's Association published the People's Charter, the document that gave the movement its subsequent name. The charter, which called for universal male suffrage and numerous other parliamentary reforms, was summarily rejected by parliament in both 1839 and 1842. The Chartist movement seemed to have lost much of its momentum by 1847, but it subsequently gained new energies, both from a new economic crisis in England and from the rebellions that began in Europe in early 1848, beginning with the February Revolution in Paris. At times seemed the Chartist movement seemed on the verge of becoming a revolution but the failure of new agitation for adoption of the Charter in 1848 left the movement essentially destroyed, especially in London, though some Chartist groups continued to be active in other parts of the country for several more years. Meanwhile, the revolutions on the continent, which often featured strong working-class participation, were repressed as well, usually through the combined efforts of the ruling aristocracies and the emergent bourgeoisie. Indeed, the year 1848 typically figures in Marxist accounts of modern history as a crucial turning point, not only because it saw the publication of *The Communist Manifesto*, but also because it marked the turn of the European bourgeoisie, long a radical and revolutionary historical force, to conservatism and reaction in an attempt to consolidate and solidify the gains they had made in the previous two centuries of dramatic social and political change.

Men of Forty-Eight is carefully based on real events, leading David Smith to complain that the book reads "like a left-wing history textbook, with large chunks of unassimilated material" (110). The coverage of the book is indeed large, as Lindsay seeks to situate the Chartist movement within the context of the revolutionary movements that were sweeping across the European continent at the same time. This undertaking is a difficult one, and it probably succeeds best with readers who are reasonably familiar with the events on which the book is based. However, the novel does gain a considerable amount of focus by concentrating on the involvement of Richard Boon, the son of a wealthy English landowner, in the revolutionary events of 1848. In Paris at the outbreak of the February revolution there, Boon becomes involved with the rebels, manning barricades in the streets and becoming much impressed with the idealism and commitment of the French revolutionaries. Called home to England by news that his mother is seriously ill, Boon takes a packet steamer across the channel. On the trip, he meets Thomas Scamler, who is actively involved in the Chartist movement in England and who introduces Boon to Chartism.

Most of the remainder of the text concerns the narration of historical events and of Boon's personal involvement in and reaction to these events. Many of the characters of the book are historical figures such as the Chartist leaders Feargus O'Connor (treated rather negatively in the book) and Ernest Jones (treated very positively). These historical figures interact directly with fictional characters, such as Boon, contributing to Lindsay's attempt to establish a connection between public historical events and the private experiences of individuals. This attempt is largely successful. For example, Boon's involvement with working-class revolutionaries in both France and England radically changes his view of his own personal life, leading him to realize the injustice and exploitation that are the sources of his family's wealth. The historical events of 1848 also greatly impact Boon's personal relationships, complicating his attitude toward his engagement to Mary Scawton, the daughter of a wealthy friend of his father. Believing that sexual repression is central to the political repression that he observes around him, Boon begins to seek sexual liberation, possibly through a relationship with Selina Neals, an earthy peasant girl who is presumably more natural in her sexuality than the bourgeois Mary. Unfortunately, Boon's insights into the repressive nature of Victorian sexuality have a rather modern ring to them, while his notion of the greater physicality of the working classes is rather stereotypical.

Partly because of his class, Boon is something of an outsider to the Chartist movement and to the other revolutionary events described in the book, thus remaining a sort of objective observer. However, he becomes more and more dedicated to revolution, especially after reading an early copy of *The Communist Manifesto*, which crystallizes many of his own formerly unarticulated insights. Late in the text, Boon and Mary are finally married, though there are still difficulties in their relationship. Meanwhile, with the revolutions all over Europe in a state of collapse, a fresh rebellion breaks out in Vienna. Boon decides that he must go there to try to contribute to this last chance for revolutionary success, leaving Mary, who turns out to be pregnant, back in London. In Vienna, Boon helps the revolutionaries who have taken control of the city defend it from counterrevolutionary attacks by Imperial Troops. But the troops eventually retake the city and Boon, along with numerous other revolutionaries, is captured and shot. The book then closes with an epilogue in which capitalism is again beginning to boom, while Mary is preparing to face the future without Boon and with their child.

Though written in 1939, *Men of Forty-Eight* was published in 1948, thus marking the anniversary of the events with which it deals. On the other hand, the book is in many ways very clearly a product of the late 1930s. In particular, Boon's relationship to the rebellions in continental Europe (and especially his decision to go to Vienna and his subsequent death there) reads very much like the relationship to the Spanish Civil War of numerous protagonists of British leftist fiction in the 1930s. In this and other ways, Lindsay's presentation of the 1848 revolutions quite often reads almost like an allegory of the situation in Spain in the late 1930s. Moreover, Lindsay carefully links the events of 1848 to subsequent events in Europe, treating 1848 as a pivotal turning point that turned Europe aside from the road to emancipation and enlightenment and put it on a dark course leading directly to the cataclysmic events of the twentieth century. At one point, for example, Scamler muses that, as a result of the failure of the 1848 rebellions, "the world is henceforth in for an accumulating series of wars, each war covering a larger area in a more destructive way; and the whole system of murder and greed will only end when the world-expansion splits and smashes on world-war" (388). Of course, Scamler here has access to a hindsight retrospectively supplied by Lindsay, who begins the book with an author's note that explicitly asks the reader to consider parallels between the world situation in 1848 and recent events surrounding the rise of fascism in the 1930s. Lindsay's characters seem to profit from hindsight at other times as well, as when Scamler predicts the centrality of colonialism to subsequent British history. Still, while Lindsay occasionally makes the mistake of modernizing his account of 1848, he establishes a sense of connection between historical events that is valuable and that is typical of the best historical novels. By establishing the rebellions of 1848 as a direct precedent to contemporary struggles for liberation, Lindsay contributes to the development of a potentially positive history of the British Left, especially given that most of the specific demands of the Chartist movement would eventually be met, despite the initial defeat of the movement. *Selected bibliography:* Charlton; Postgate (*Story of a Year*); Robertson; David Smith (*Socialist Propaganda*); Dorothy Thompson.

JACK LINDSAY: *1649: A NOVEL OF A YEAR* **(1938).** *1649* is a sweeping historical novel that attempts both to capture the feel of English life in the tumultuous year of 1649 and to suggest parallels between this time of dramatic social and political change and the late-1930s context in which Lindsay was writing the book. In particular, *1649* focuses on the attempts of the radical Levellers to establish an egalitarian society in the wake of the English Civil War, clearly identifying the Levellers as the predecessors of modern-day communists. While the book ends before the oppositions it sets in place are fully resolved, it also makes clear that the Leveller project is historically premature and cannot succeed. Instead, Lindsay suggests the historical inevitability of the rise to power of Oliver Cromwell, an event that is closely associated, in *1649*, with the rise of a capitalist economy and with the global expansion of trade as a source of English power and wealth. Indeed, this global expansion is a major motif in the text, which pays particular attention to Cromwell's invasion of Ireland as part of a general depiction of imperialism as a central element in English capitalism from the very beginning.

1649 tells the interrelated stories of a number of characters, most of whom are either members or acquaintances of the Lydcots, an affluent family of emerging bourgeoisie. No one character, however, can really be identified as the book's protagonist, thus reinforcing the book's collective vision. The most prominent fictional character is Ralph Lydcot, who, despite his family connections, begins the book devoted to the cause of the Levellers. In the course of the book, Ralph participates in the work of the Levellers,though in a rather marginal way; in the meantime, he becomes involved in the business activities of his uncle, Lionel Lydcot, thereby experiencing "the excitement of the hunt" and coming to appreciate the energies associated with the dynamic expansion of commerce in the mid-seventeenth century. He also comes to accept his uncle's view that the primary historical consequence of the recent Civil War was the opening of free markets, though he continues to believe that this opening is but a step toward eventual social justice: "He began to believe that his uncle was right. The free market was what was needed; then things would begin to move in the right direction; the wealth of the nation would be increased. And if the struggle between landlord, tributer, and spalliar was thereby increased at the same time, why sweep it over? Get on with the struggle" (314).

By the end of the book, Ralph has married and settled into a relatively bourgeois existence, still sympathizing with the Levellers in principle but no longer feeling that he is one of them. In this sense, Ralph's experience is essentially the mirror image of that of his friend Roger Cotton, who begins the book as a relatively respectable bookseller's apprentice but then becomes politicized, spending some time in the radically egalitarian Digger community on St. George's Hill and ending the book devoted to the Leveller cause, which is by that time in disarray. The majority of Roger's experiences in the novel have to do with his romantic relationship with Nell, a former prostitute. Among other things, this troubled relationship, in which the couple is never really able to establish effective intersubjective contact, becomes a sort of parable of the alienation of social relations under capitalism. Indeed, Roger's turn to political activism is clearly an attempt to overcome his radical sense of alienation not only from Nell but from the entire world around him. Thus, thinking of the gap between himself and Nell, he concludes late in the book that "the crack I saw was of all the world, and ran through the hearts of all men and women living, and no one of us will be whole till that crack is filled in" (434). The capitalism that is emerging in England in 1649 will not, of course, heal this rift but will make it worse. Lindsay is thus careful to indicate the negative consequences of the new system, which makes successful merchants astonishingly rich while most of the English population is languishing in poverty. At the same time, he makes it clear that the Diggers and Levellers do not yet hold the key to England's economic and social problems, which can only be solved after capitalism has run its course on the historical road to socialism. Indeed, the careful parallels drawn by Lindsay between the hard times of 1649 and those of the Depression of the 1930s suggest the two periods as the opposed ends of a continuous historical arc, one period of turmoil ushering in capitalism and the other ushering it out.

In this sense, it is important that Lindsay does not romanticize Roger Cotton as a predecessor of modern-day socialist activists. Instead, Roger is a humorless ascetic, a religious fanatic whose horror of the flesh torments Nell even as he is presumably trying to save her. And his political activism is more a turning away from the world than a participation in it. On the other hand, Ralph is treated rather positively, his seduction by the dynamic energies of a burgeoning system of capitalist commerce reflecting not his personal weakness but the simple fact that, in 1649, the tide of history is with capitalism. Lindsay's depiction of certain Leveller victories, such as the successful evasion of charges of treason by the Leveller leader, John Lilburne, indicate the possibility of collective resistance to oppression. But the main strength of *1649* is its ability to depict the triumph of capitalism in the seventeenth century as a historical inevitability that represented a necessary step toward the eventual establishment of socialism. As the Leveller Walwyn tells the Digger leader, Gerard Winstanley, "I can see no other way to your true commonwealth ... than by the way of Cromwell, which aims at raising the national wealth without concern for the fact that many will be trampled to death and degradation in the process" (537).

David Smith, while noting that the book is sometimes "overwritten," agrees that *1649* is an effective historical novel that gets its message across "without protruding too obviously the sharp elbow of ideology." In particular, Smith is impressed by Lindsay's ability to reflect the economic forces associated with the beginnings of capitalism in the seventeenth century: "Lindsay's world is an economic world. To a quite startling degree he convinces us of its reality: the small weavers in the north; the small smelting works; fishing in Yarmouth; the rudimentary ideas of trade unionism; the breaking down of the old craft system; the thrusting bourgeois impulse; the enclosures forcing the yeoman off the land into the newly burgeoning industries" (108). Of course, the subtlety with which Lindsay gets across his political message is not necessarily a virtue, and if *1649* has a major weakness as a political novel it is that many readers may now fail to miss the point, though that point would have undoubtedly been more clear in the late 1930s than it is today.

Indeed, *1649* is very much a work of the 1930s. Not only does its depiction of seventeenth-century England sometimes sound suspiciously similar to conditions in Depression England, but Lindsay's formal technique in the book is very much a product of its time. For example, as Valentine Cunningham notes, *1649* resembles a number of other works of the literature of the 1930s in making extensive use of the techniques of documentary realism (304). In particular, Lindsay reinforces the historical realism of his text by making real historical events, such as the execution of Charles I or the treason trial of Lilburne, central to his plot and by inserting a number of actual seventeenth-century documents, authored by Lilburne, Cromwell, and others, into his fictional text. Such techniques help Lindsay to do an excellent job of creating a picture of seventeenth-century English society as an interrelated totality. The book's numerous characters wander widely about the English landscape, coming into contact with almost every aspect of English society. At times the personal attitudes and relationships of the characters seem rather modern, but by and large they are effectively drawn as products of the historical forces of their time. They also frequently cross paths, not only with one another, but with historical figures such as Lilburne and Winstanley. Meanwhile, the important looming world-historical figure of

Cromwell, while literally appearing onstage only in a brief cameo role, is a specter constantly haunting the text from the margins. All in all, then, *1649* is a successful historical novel in the sense described by Georg Lukács in *The Historical Novel*. Its characters are vivid and distinct individuals who nevertheless clearly derive their individual identities from their participation in the larger historical forces that surround them. And these historical forces have a definite direction, sweeping the totality of seventeenth-century English society forward into capitalism in a way that clearly anticipates a further shift to socialism in the twentieth century, when the historical time is ripe at last. *Selected bibliography:* Croft ("Historical Novels of Jack Lindsay"); Cunningham; Lukács (*Historical Novel*); Montefiore; David Smith (*Socialist Propaganda*); West (*Mountain*).

JACK LINDSAY: *TIME TO LIVE* **(1946).** *Time to Live*, written and published shortly after the end of World War II, reflects the sense of a return to normalcy that was central to British life during that period. Not surprisingly, the book is relatively light in tone. It is, in fact, reminiscent of the British comedy-of-manners tradition, somewhat in the mode of the social satires of H. G. Wells. In keeping with this light tone, the book hardly mentions politics; instead it focuses on a street party organized by the inhabitants of London's Holly Street to celebrate the victorious end of the war and to provide their children with some hearty fun after the grim wartime years. On the other hand, *Time to Live* has its serious side as well, and the attempts, staunchly opposed by some of the grumpier denizens of Holly Street, to organize the party become, in the course of the book, a sort of allegory of the need to try to continue the popular solidarity of the war years into the postwar era. Moreover, the book is informed by a sort of running leftist joke in which the street party, a focal point for popular, communal energies that is frequently referred to simply as "the Party," becomes something of a stand-in for the Communist Party. *Time to Live* is unusual among British leftist fictions in its essentially comic tone, suggesting the heightened optimism that informed British society after the end of the war and the subsequent sweeping victory of the Labour Party in the 1945 elections.

Time to Live begins as insurance agent Robert Wylie conceives the idea for the street party and then proceeds as both support for and opposition to the idea spread rapidly through Holly Street. The supporters of the party are largely rallied together through the efforts of energetic young Polly Stipes, the daughter of Wylie's friend and neighbor. The oppponents, meanwhile, are led by another neighbor, Mrs. Luckins, and by Wylie's friend, the humorless shopowner Horace Tulse. Numerous side plots feature various inhabitants of the street as they go about their lives against the background of the upcoming party. The central character of the book, however, is Philip Smith, a young would-be intellectual who has only just moved to the street. Smith is employed as a reporter for Reuters, but his real ambition is to be a novelist, and much of the book concerns his efforts to immerse himself in the life of the street and therefore to derive creative inspiration from the communal energies of the people there.

As such, Smith is something of an autobiographical figure who reflects Lindsay's own career as a leftist novelist. Yet, the preposterously self-serious Smith is treated in a highly satirical way, and much of the humor of the book is at his expense—somewhat in the mode of James Joyce's satirical treatment of the young Stephen Dedalus. Thus, though Smith's notion that writers should derive their creative energies from popular life is basically sound, his bovarystic method of going about this process suggests his fundamental separation from popular life and his immersion not in the world of Holly Street but in the world of books. Smith is a thoroughly bourgeois figure who understands socialism in only the most romantic and literary of ways. Moreover, his writing is thoroughly derivative, while his principal technique for getting in touch with the lives of the people seems to be an attempt to seduce, one after another, the various teenage daughters of the street's families. After an initial fascination with Polly as she goes about the street organizing the party, Smith meets young Evangeline Blackie, a war orphan who has been adopted by the Rev. Winwood Blackie, the local clergyman. Evangeline seems highly impressed that Smith is an author, and he immediately begins to envision her as the source of a new era in his creative life. However, she quickly breaks off their relationship, apparently on the orders of the Blackies, and ends up running off with Peter Davenport, the disreputable brother of Delia Cunnington, a dissatisfied Holly Street housewife, who, herself, ends up running away from her overbearing husband. That leaves Smith with Maria Tulse, the rebellious daughter of the party's major opponent, and by the end of the book (after the party has successfully come off) Smith and Maria have declared their love for one another, causing him to become so inspired that he undertakes a brand-new novel, which begins precisely as does *Time to Live*. The book thus reflexively, and playfully, turns back on itself with the suggestion that Smith is the author of the entire work.

Among other things, *Time to Live* reflects the fact that numerous celebrations of the kind with which it deals were, in fact, being organized all over Britain at that time. But it reflects even more the kind of community participation that had been crucial to British society during the war, with the clear suggestion that, if this participation could only continue beyond the war, it might form the basis for an eventual movement toward genuine socialism. As Lindsay points out in *After the Thirties*, the "widening participation of the people in both enjoyment and creation" that had occurred during the war years was already, by the end of 1945, beginning to fade (76). The disappointing efforts of the Attlee Labour Government (which Lindsay bitterly refers to in *After the Thirties* — written, we should recall, ten frustrating years after *Time to Live* — as "right wing") served to erode these communal energies still further. In *Time to Live*, Lindsay seeks to stop this erosion and to remind the British people that, while their joint efforts have helped to defeat fascism, the fight for socialism is yet to be won. **Selected bibliography:** Andrew Davies; Lindsay (*After the Thirties*); David Smith (*Socialist Propaganda*).

JACK LINDSAY: *WE SHALL RETURN* (1942). *We Shall Return* was written during the early years of World War II, when the initial confidence of the British had been staggered, in the wake of their catastrophic retreat at Dunkirk, by the successes of a German military machine that seemed increasingly invincible. As such, the novel is clearly intended as an attempt to contribute to the war effort, exhorting the British people of all classes to stand together in the fight against fascism and assuring them that a united Britain will eventually emerge triumphant in this fight. In its treatment of fascism as a menace to civilization and its emphasis on the need for unity in opposition to this menace, *We Shall Return* is a clear continuation of the discourse of the Popular Front in the 1930s. On the other hand, the book is also a good illustration of the difficult position in which British leftist writers found themselves during the war, when the leftist Popular Front had been dissolved into the general British war effort. Most leftist writers, not wishing to criticize the British government in the midst of its fight against fascism, fell silent during the war. Lindsay was one of the few who continued to produce works such as *We Shall Return* that still espoused a leftist message. Indeed, David Smith points out that *We Shall Return* joins Lindsay's *Beyond Terror* (1943) as the only English war novels written from a communist perspective (134). But the political stance of these novels is a muted one, and Lindsay is careful to focus all of his negative commentary on the Germans, treating British society as a bastion of civilized decency in the face of a savage adversary.

We Shall Return is set in the very first months after the British and French, in response to the German invasion of Poland, had declared war on the Germans, hoping to bring a quick end to Nazi aggression. But initial events in the war strongly favored the Germans, who were far better organized and better prepared for war. On May 10, 1939, the German advance extended to Belgium and Holland, as airborne troops landed there, seizing airfields and bridges and even the great Belgian fortress Eben-Emael. The Dutch army surrendered four days later, after Germans bombers destroyed much of downtown Rotterdam. The Germans then immediately turned their main attack against the British and French forces that had rushed to the Belgian front. The German army, featuring highly mobile but heavily armored tanks and extensive air support, quickly drove the British and French armies back to the beach at Dunkirk, from which most of the main force was evacuated to Britain by means of a makeshift flotilla on May 26. Belgian King Leopold III officially surrendered the next day, and the rout appeared to be on. By June 17, the Germans had struck deep into France. Marshal Henri Philippe Pétain, a World War I hero who had become premier the day before, asked for an armistice, which was signed on June 25 on terms that gave Germany control of northern France and the Atlantic coast. Pétain then set up a new French government, essentially a puppet of the German Nazis, at Vichy in the unoccupied southeast of France.

Through a combination of straightforward narration, falshbacks, and stream-of-consciousness, *We Shall Return* follows its protagonist, Hugh Evans, through these events as he joins the British army, undergoes military training in Britain, then goes with his company to France. After an initial period of relative calm (when the men spend much of their time fraternizing with French women in the local town), Hugh and his company are rushed to the Belgian front, where they participate in the British defeats there. The book then ends as they participate in the Dunkirk evacuation. Lindsay includes a great deal of vivid narration of battle scenes, but his real focus is on the subjective experience of his protagonist. For one thing, he pays extensive attention to Evans's private life, suggesting that this life is not separate from the war effort but part of it. Evans is a highly introspective Hamletesque middle-class intellectual with leftist sympathies who begins the war powerfully alienated from his fellow soldiers but who gradually develops a sense of solidarity with them in the wake of their intense shared experience. This increasing sense of solidarity (whether it be during moments of shared recreation in French towns or in the heat of battle against the imposing German army) is, in fact, the central motif of the book. The importance of solidarity is overtly emphasized at several points in the book, culminating in a sort of epiphany as Hugh fights a rearguard action to facilitate the evacuation of the British forces from the beaches of Dunkirk, realizing that this early defeat will only make the British stronger and more able to band together in a genuine people's war against their fascist enemies: "It didn't matter, the defeat, it didn't matter if out of the broken structure of a dead world the new world was painfully coming to birth; if this meant the people of Britain. . . . The people have their own time, and that is history, and the first necessary humility is to know that and to live in the daily struggle, the daily liberation, and not to lose the sense of ultimates, of human freedom as a whole" (313).

The leftist orientation of this rhetoric is clear, as are numerous other aspects of the text, such as its positive treatment of the role of the Soviet Union as an ally against fascism at a time when much British popular opinion (in the wake of the controversial Nazi-Soviet pact of August 1939, and the Soviet invasion of Finland at the end of November of that year) had been strongly anti-Soviet for some time. But the principal perspective of the book is not so much leftist as antifascist—and pro-British. Despite the narration of Britain's early defeats, the tone of the book is strongly optimistic, as its title indicates. Thus, the book ends as Evans sails toward Britain, confident that "we shall return, this struggle can end only with the end of Fascism, and deepest of all he felt a powerful calm, a completion" (320). Lindsay's optimism is intended, of course, to raise the morale of the British people in support of the war effort. But it is not entirely manufactured, given that, by the end of 1941, there were signs that the tide of the war was beginning to turn. In August and September of 1940, the Germans launched a massive air assault on Britain, presumably in preparation for an invasion of the island. However, in what has become known as the Battle of Britain, the Royal Air Force inflicted heavy losses on the Germans, who were forced to postpone their invasion plans indefinitely. In the coming months, the German forces gradually became overextended, partially because so much of the German army was bogged down in Yugoslavia, where Tito and his communist partisans waged a courageous and highly effective guerrilla campaign against the German forces that had occupied the country. By the end of 1941, meanwhile, the vast majority of the German military machine was engaged on the Eastern Front, where Stalin's Red Army, buoyed by a decade of rapid industrialization in the Soviet Union and manned by millions of dedicated Soviet patriots, proved a far more formidable opponent than Hitler had anticipated. Thus, especially after the Americans entered the war at the end of 1941, the British had every reason to be optimistic. *We Shall Return* reflects this optimism, with the additional suggestion that victory in the war may pave the way to socialism in Britain. However, though the sweeping Labour victory in the first postwar elections in 1945 may have seemed to point in this direction, other events, which detailed in subsequent Lindsay novels such as *Betrayed Spring*, would prove Lindsay's optimism misplaced in this sense. **Selected bibliography:** Andrew Davies; David Smith (*Socialist Propaganda*).

RICHARD LLEWELLYN: *HOW GREEN WAS MY VALLEY* **(1940).** *How Green Was My Valley* is narrated by Huw Morgan, now in his sixties, who has lived his entire life in a Welsh mining valley but is about to move away because the massive slag heap that has gradually been built up as a result of the area's mining operations has become unstable and will soon bury the house in which he lives—and in which he grew up. The book consists of Huw's memories of his time in the valley, memories that are, as the title indicates, highly nostalgic evocations of bygone pastoral days.

As Huw puts it, "Beautiful were the days that are gone, and O, for them to be back. The mountain was green, and proud with a good covering of oak and ash, and washing his feet in a streaming river clear as the eyes of God" (164). The valley itself is, in fact, as much the central character of the book as his Huw, and the narrative relates both the story of Huw's early life and the history of the valley, covering the period roughly from the 1880s to 1910.

However, *How Green Was My Valley* is rather weak as a historical novel. Most of the book is devoted to evocations of the natural beauties of the valley and to accounts of the private affairs of the Morgan family, focusing on love, courtship, and marriage. Although the narrative does indicate certain pressures of modernity, symbolized by the creeping slag heap, that gradually undermine the traditional life of the valley, the book pays relatively little attention to political analysis of historical events, focusing on Huw's nostalgic memories of what he perceives, from his perspective in the 1930s, as having been better days. It is significant that all of the events narrated in the book occur well before the 1930s, keeping the narrative safely insulated from that highly politicized decade. Moreover, while the process that leads to the destruction of the traditional culture of the valley is presented as a sort of public tragedy, it is one from which Huw's memories retreat into visions of private contentment: "Even with the trouble coming flying to meet us, we grew, and we were happy" (324).

There are vaguely political intonations in Huw's suggestion of the gradual encroachment of the "English law" in the valley, but this encroachment is presented as strictly ethnic and cultural and is never related to capitalism or class conflict. Indeed, if there is a central political opposition in the book, it is not the class struggle between miners and mine owners but the ethnic one between the Welsh and the English. Huw's family are coal miners, and the book does indicate some of the difficulties and dangers associated with their work. It also suggests some of the ways in which the miners were exploited and unfairly treated by the mine owners. However, most of the men in the family gradually find work in other fields, while Huw's father during most of the book is not a miner per se but a mine superintendent. Labor activism hovers in the margins of the text, especially as Huw's brother, Davy, becomes an important leader in the drive to organize an effective union for the local miners. However, such matters are generally secondary and peripheral in the book. And when they become central they do so in problematic ways, as when Huw's father is killed at the end of the book in a cave-in while inspecting the mine for damage during a strike. Here, the strike (probably part of the 1910–11 Cambrian Combine Dispute detailed so vividly in Lewis Jones's *Cwmardy*, though not identified as such) is treated more as a chaotic interruption in the life of the valley than as an instance of heroic resistance to oppression. And it is more the strike than the exploitative labor practices that led to the strike that seems to be identified as the culprit causing Huw's father's death.

For such reasons, it is probably not surprising that *How Green Was My Valley* has been highly successful in a commercial sense and has remained continually in print since its first publication. John Ford's film adaptation, which is even more stereotypically sentimental than the book, won the 1941 Academy Award for Best Film over such competition as *Citizen Kane*. It is also not surprising that critics such as Dai Smith, upset by Llewellyn's romanticized and inaccurate depiction of life in Wales, have strongly criticized the book for its "glamorized nostalgia" and its falsification of Welsh history. Derrick Price summarizes such criticisms well, noting that critics, especially Welsh ones, have "attacked it for its lack of verisimilitude to working class life; for its obfuscation and reactionary analysis of significant historical struggles; for its individualist account of political action; and for its racism and sentimentality" (73). Moreover, Price concludes that these criticisms are largely justified, noting that the text gives us "an account of life in the valleys in which history, memory and political action are stripped of collectivity and presented as the qualities of heroic individuals" (75). Price also notes that *How Green Was My Valley* participates in a long tradition of literary accounts of Wales as a place of nature and romance — a fact that helps to account for Llewellyn's stance in the book but that also makes it all the more important to challenge the "social constructions" of the Welsh past that it helps to promulgate (93).

Although Llewellyn does not properly contextualize the process of historical transformation he is describing, and although his highly romanticized treatment of the lives of Welsh coal miners leaves out much of the real texture of those lives, he nevertheless treats the miners sympathetically and makes a contribution to the notion that miners and other workers are at least worthy subjects for literature. Given the baleful shortage of positive representations of working-class characters in canonical British literature, this contribution is significant, but the romanticized (and largely inaccurate) accounts of mining life presented by Llewellyn should be taken with a grain of salt, especially given the way they extend stereotypes about Wales that may stand in the way of any genuine solution to Welsh social problems. ***Selected bibliography:*** Price; Dai Smith.

PATRICK MacGILL: *CHILDREN OF THE DEAD END* (1914). *Children of the Dead End*, subtitled *The Autobiography of a Navvy*, is a colorful account of early twentieth-century working-class life based on the experiences of its author, who came as a youth from his native Ireland to Scotland, where he scratched out a living working at a variety of menial jobs, including significant stints as a potato digger and as a "navvy," or construction laborer. Because of his experience, MacGill is able to describe the hardships suffered by such workers convincingly and in great detail. But he is also able to avoid condescension, showing such workers as genuine human beings who sometimes take a great deal of pleasure in life despite their poverty and the grueling labor they must perform just to survive. In this sense, *Children of the Dead End* has a great deal in common with Robert Tressell's nearly contemporaneous *The Ragged Trousered Philanthropists*, with which it is often compared. MacGill's account of working-class life, like Tressell's, is explicitly political, clearly attributing the suffering of workers to their exploitation by a capitalist system and paying special attention to the strategies and institutions, especially religion, that this system uses to perpetuate its power.

Children of the Dead End is narrated by protagonist Dermod Flynn, a young Irishman who is rather transparently based on MacGill himself. Like MacGill, Dermod grows up in rural Donegal, and the book begins with a vivid description of the conditions of his childhood in Ireland. Dermod's family, like most of the families of Donegal, is abysmally poor, struggling to survive beneath the brutal domination of the local landlord and priest, both of whom continually demand sizable payments from the family. The greed of the Church is, in fact, a central theme of the book, which consistently depicts religion as a negative force in the lives of the poor, who are forced to pay a large portion of their meager incomes to support an institution that devotes itself to the support of the rich. As Dermod puts it later in the text, when he has gained more insight into the workings of organized religion, "The Church allows a criminal commercial system to continue, and wastes its time trying to save the souls of the victims of that system. Christianity preaches contentment to the wage-slaves, and hob-nobs with the slave drivers" (256–57).

At the age of twelve, Dermod goes to the hiring fair at Strabane, hoping to find work to help support his family. He does manage to get hired, working for six months for an abusive Protestant farmer who continually mocks Dermod for his Catholicism and pays the young boy a mere five pounds, ten shillings for six months of backbreaking labor. Dermod sends most of his pay home to his family, who, in turn, must pass it on to the landlord and priest. Returning to the hiring fair, Dermod contracts to work on a second farm, which he soon flees after learning that the farmer is being boycotted by most of his neighbors. He then manages to find a relatively pleasant job with a kindly farmer, with whom he stays for nineteen months. At this point, he learns that Jim Scanlon, a former neighbor, is organizing a crew of workers to go to Scotland to harvest potatoes. Dermod joins the group and goes to Scotland, where he finds that Norah Ryan, a girl he has known and admired since early childhood, is working in the same crew. The group moves from one farm to another, digging potatoes and living in generally squalid conditions. Dermod, greatly disappointed when Norah is seduced by a middle-class reformer during their stay in Scotland, decides to stay behind when Scanlon and the others return to Ireland. Penniless after losing his meager savings in a card game, Dermod goes on the tramp in Scotland, occasionally working at odd jobs and meeting a variety of colorful characters, including the irrepressible Moleskin Joe, with whom he establishes a lasting friendship. In the meantime, Dermod develops an interest in literature, reading Victor Hugo, Thomas Carlyle, and others. He also gradually becomes aware of politics after encountering socialists and anarchists on his journeys, eventually adding Marx and Henry George to his reading.

Dermod makes his way to urban Glasgow, where he joins the Socialist Party and helps to organize a strike of railway workers, but then leaves in disgust after the strike fails to materialize due to lack of support from the other workers. He then goes with Moleskin Joe to Kinlochleven in northern Scotland, where they work for an extended period as navvies on a construction project which they later learn to be a huge aluminum plant. Most of their work involves the dangerous job of rock-blasting, and several workers are, in fact, killed on the job while they are there. In the meantime, Dermod matures as a strong young man, gaining a reputation as a fighter after he knocks out Hell-fire Gahey, famous among the navvies as a fighter. It is in Kinlochleven that Dermod begins writing and even manages to get a story about the accidental death of a fellow worker published by a London newspaper. He also becomes increasingly devoted to drinking and gambling, taking what pleasure he can in the face of the dismal conditions under which the navvies live and work. Eventually, the excavation for the plant is completed, and the navvies are dismissed, tramping back southward like a ragged army. Dermod returns to Glasgow, where he encounters Norah on the street working as a prostitute after having been impregnated and abandoned by her middle-class lover. Dermod is infuriated at a social system that could drive such a pure and decent girl to such a fate. However, always squeamish about sexuality and the physicality of women, he is enough put off by her current condition that he quickly parts from her and does not try to reestablish their relationship.

Later, Dermod regrets this choice and attempts to find Norah again, but cannot. Eventually, he moves to London and takes a job as a reporter for the newspaper that published his first story. He does not find journalism to his taste, however, and he soon leaves the job after he is assigned to cover a coal miners' strike in Wales, realizing that he is not expected to portray the strikers in a positive light. He travels back to Glasgow, where he again meets Moleskin Joe, who helps him in his continued search for Norah. They eventually find her on her deathbed, suffering from injuries incurred when some hooligans attacked her on the street. In a somewhat sentimental ending, Norah dies with Dermod at her bedside while Gourock Ellen, an old bawd who had taken her in after her injuries and whom Dermod had earlier despised as a gross and revolting example of feminine impurity, weeps nearby.

This ending helps Dermod to understand that he had been overly hasty in his earlier rejection of Gourock Ellen, his reaction to whom had been part of a problematic attitude toward women that MacGill never effectively challenges. However, any real solidarity Dermod gains with the common people by virtue of his new understanding of Gourock Ellen is seriously limited. Perhaps because the Irish Dermod (and, presumably, MacGill in his earlier years) feels somewhat of an outsider in Scotland and, especially, England, he is unable to develop any strong sense of common cause with the workers there, particularly in the urban settings, where he in fact is often contemptuous of the workers he meets. Dermod's movement from rural Ireland to urban Glasgow and, eventually, to London in a sense recapitulates the historical growth of capitalism, leading Ruth Sherry to describe his story as "a novel about the *creation* of the working class" (113). But, in point of fact, Dermod develops little in the way of class solidarity and has little sense of participation in a common struggle to improve the conditions of workers. This lack is a serious political limitation in the novel, which, as Jack Mitchell notes, "entirely lacks a practical revolutionary perspective" despite its identification of the mistreatment of workers as a systematic characteristic of capitalism (79). Nevertheless, the book was greatly popular with working-class readers, who were heartened to see their perspective represented at last in British literature. Indeed, MacGill self-consciously seeks in the book to contribute to the development of a genuinely working-class literature, having Dermod conclude toward the end that "true art, the only true art, is that which appeals to the simple people" (271). *Selected bibliography:* Mitchell ("Early Harvest"); Ruth Sherry.

WILLIAM McILVANNEY: *DOCHERTY* **(1975).** *Docherty,* which follows the trials and tribulations of a single Scottish working-class family, the Dochertys, from the early years of the twentieth century to the hard times of the 1920s, remains perhaps McIlvanney's most important contribution to the tradition of British working-class fiction. The book centers very much on the father of the family, Tam Docherty, a coal miner and union activist who is presented in the text as a carrier of working-class values such as common decency and caring for others. A small man (only five feet, four inches tall), Tam is nevertheless renowned for his physical prowess, both as a miner and as a fistfighter, though he is a peaceful man who never looks for a fight. He is also a strong believer in working-class solidarity and in the possibility of achieving a better life if only the workers can stick together to resist their exploitation by their rich bosses. Greatly devoted to his family, he asserts that the family should be the central repository of the working-class virtues of sharing and togetherness to which he is so devoted.

Although Tam Docherty is very much the center of the text, McIlvanney reinforces Docherty's own emphasis on the importance of family by paying considerable attention to the other members of the Docherty clan as well. Meanwhile, Docherty's larger sense of working-class community is reinforced by a detailed treatment of the various inhabitants of the High Street neighborhood, in Graithnock, where the Docherty's live in a meager flat. This neighborhood is peopled by a variety of colorful characters, none of them with wealth or influence in the world, none of them particularly educated, but all of them genuinely human and thus worthy of compassion. Docherty is a central figure in the community, in which he is much loved as a neighbor and much respected as a fellow worker and leader in the fight for fair treatment for workers. But he is particularly crucial to his own family, which at the beginning of the book includes his wife, Jenny; his sons, Mick and Angus; and his daughter, Kathleen. In the book's prologue, set in 1903, a third son, Conn, is born, and much of the subsequent action is narrated from Conn's perspective as he grows from infancy to young adulthood.

The Dochertys are a close-knit and loving family, though there are signs of dissension. For one thing, Tam, viewing religion as a tool used by the ruling classes to perpetuate their domination of the workers, rejects the Catholicism to which his Irish father (also named Conn—perhaps for Connemara, where he was born and reared) is so devoted. For another, the pressures of the modern world gradually come to bear on the Dochertys and their neighborhood, leading to a general decline in the traditional values embodied by Tam. Meanwhile, Tam's hopes of building a better world for workers gradually decay as the mine owners win one battle after another with the workers. When World War I arrives, Mick enthusiastically joins the army, though Tam declares the war to be a battle of capitalists in which workers have nothing to gain. In the war, Mick is seriously wounded, losing one arm and the sight in one eye. He spends the rest of the book living at home with his parents, unable to work because of his disabilities.

Angus grows into a powerful young man who soon joins his father in the mines and seems a likely candidate to carry on the values espoused by his father. But Angus, despite his physical prowess and his willingness to work hard, does not share these values. He and Tam frequently argue, and the son shows little respect for the father. He leaves the pit where he works with Tam to work in a neighboring pit, where he will contract to deliver coal at a set price and pay wages to his own crew, becoming, in essence, one of the capitalists despised by his father. Angus also lacks his father's respect for family, refusing to marry a neighborhood girl whom he gets pregnant, then marrying another girl instead. Kathleen also has family problems, marrying a weak and abusive man who beats her to take out his own frustrations. It is, in fact, only the young Conn who seems to have any chance to carry on the legacy of his father, whom he greatly admires and loves.

When Tam is killed in a mining accident (while heroically saving the life of a fellow miner), Jenny reacts with nobility and strength, struggling to hold the family together in spite of the loss of her husband. She also supports Mick and young Conn in their controversial insistence that Tam be given a secular funeral, free of the priests against whom he had battled all his life. Though some are bothered by the exclusion of the priests, most of Tam's neighbors and coworkers come together in grief over his death, sharing their fond memories of his strength and goodness. After the funeral, Conn, coming more and more to realize the extent to which his father struggled and sacrificed for his family, challenges the imposing Angus to a fight in order to seek retribution for his disrespect of Tam. The two fight to a draw despite Angus's greater strength, signaling Conn's arrival at full manhood. Mick, meanwhile, has become a communist (and a reader of such works as Tressell's *The Ragged Trousered Philanthropists*) and vows to do all that he can to ensure that the workers' fight for justice goes on after Tam's death. Indeed, Tressell's book is an important predecessor of McIlvanney's, which clearly attempts to situate itself in the tradition of British working-class culture to which Tressell's book is central. Cairns Craig refers to *Docherty* as Scottish fiction's "major contribution to working-class fiction of the 1970s" (101). And McIlvanney, who is also the authors of such works as *Laidlaw* (1977), *The Papers of Tony Veitch* (1983), *The Big Man* (1985, film adaptation 1991), and *The Kiln* (1996) is certainly one of the most important contributors to Scottish, indeed British, working-class fiction in the past two decades. **Selected bibliography:** Cairns Craig; Dickson; Dixon; Murray and Tait.

JAMES LESLIE MITCHELL: *SPARTACUS* **(1933).** Mitchell, writing under the name Lewis Grassic Gibbon, produced in the trilogy *A Scots Quair* one of the most successful and enduring works of the British leftist culture of the 1930s. But he also wrote numerous books, including science fiction novels, collections of short stories, and even popular studies of archaeology, under his given name of Mitchell. Of these latter works, perhaps the best known is *Spartacus*, a historical novel about the famous slave rebellion led by the gladiator Spartacus against the Romans in 73–71 b.c. In the West, this rebellion became widely known largely due to the success of the 1960 film directed by Stanley Kubrick, though the film was based not on Mitchell's account but on the 1951 novel by the

American leftist novelist Howard Fast. The figure of Spartacus has long loomed large in leftist thought as a symbol of revolt against oppression, as is indicated by Marx's identification of him as "the most splendid fellow in the whole of ancient history" and as a "real representative of the ancient proletariat" (Marx and Engels 126). Mitchell's novel follows very much in this tradition, and occasionally his Spartacus envisions an egalitarian utopia that seems to have a vaguely socialist orientation. But Mitchell's novel is less informed by Marxism or socialism than by his own interest in "diffusionism," a current in the history and anthropology of the time informed essentially by a belief that all of human civilization represents a "hideous trade-off for the loss of original freedom" (Campbell x).

Mitchell's account of the rebellion is based on extensive research, but clearly relies on Plutarch's *Life of Crassus* as its principal source. The description in *Spartacus* of the rebel army of slaves and gladiators that moved about Italy alternately eluding and defeating the Roman legions is based fairly directly on his historical sources, though Mitchell also builds into his text a clear interpretation of these events based on his diffusionism. In particular, *Spartacus* pictures the Romans as the carriers of civilization (and thus, by definition, of oppression), while at the same time demonstrating that the behavior of the Romans (which culminates in the crucifixion of more than 6,000 rebels along the Appian Way) reaches levels of savagery and barbarity far beyond those attained by the "uncivilized" rebels. Yet Mitchell's rebels are extremely savage themselves, and most of the text is devoted to descriptions of abject violence perpetrated by both sides in the conflict (flavored with constant hints of sexuality), giving the book much the same feel as Gustave Flaubert's *Salammbo*, identified by Georg Lukács in *The Historical Novel* as a quintessential example of the decadence of the bourgeois historical novel in the second half of the nineteenth century. Largely because of the constant focus on violence and brutality, *Spartacus* was strongly criticized upon its publication by Jack Lindsay, probably the leading author of historical novels among British leftist writers of the 1930s (Croft 213). Lindsay also complained that Mitchell failed clearly to delineate the grounds of the struggle between Spartacus and the Romans, and, indeed, Mitchell says very little about the Romans at all, concentrating instead on accounts of the rebels. Oddly enough, he also says little about Spartacus, who remains a distant and mysterious figure in the text, which concentrates instead on his lieutenants, paying special attention to the roles played by the proud Jewish aristocrat Gershom ben Sanballat and the castrated Greek scribe Kleon.

Kleon is a particular devotee of Plato, and especially of *The Republic*, which he carries with him everywhere and which functions as one of several sources of utopian images in *Spartacus*. However, Spartacus himself rejects the ideal republic envisioned by Plato because it still allows slaves. Instead, he declares that "we come to free all slaves whatsoever, that in the new state we'll make even the Masters will not be enslaved" (136). Indeed, the political vision of Spartacus is radically egalitarian and at times clearly anticipates the Marxist vision of a classless society. At the same time, Spartacus does not reach this vision from careful and sophisticated analysis of the kind performed by Marx. Instead, he is presented as a sort of innocent who knows "nothing of the histories or plans of men" (165). This very naivete, in fact, is presented as a key to the greatness of Spartacus, who thereby remains uncontaminated by the corruption and intrigue of human society.

Spartacus is thus a text with several important limitations as a leftist novel. The book's seeming fascination with violence and sexuality (and the combination of the two) often comes dangerously close to prurience, while its privileging of innocence runs directly counter to the project of most leftist discourse, which is generally designed to contribute to a more sophisticated understanding of the workings of human social systems. These limitations become especially clear in comparison to Fast's novel, which does much more both to evoke the texture of the everyday life of the period and to explore the workings of the Roman society against which Spartacus and his followers rebel. Nevertheless, Mitchell's attempt to resurrect the story of Spartacus for his contemporary audience is certainly well meant and should be regarded, like the work of such writers as Fast and Lindsay, as a contribution to the development of a positive history for the modern Left that was emerging with new power in the 1930s. Indeed, while Mitchell at times portrays the specific rebellion of Spartacus as being doomed from the beginning, he also takes pains to treat that rebellion as the forerunner of future, potentially more successful rebellions. ***Selected bibliography:*** Campbell; Croft (*Red Letter Days*); Marx and Engels (*Correspondence*).

NAOMI MITCHISON: *THE CORN KING AND THE SPRING QUEEN* (1931). *The Corn King and the Spring Queen* is a long, ambitious historical novel covering the period 228 to 187 b.c. and focusing on the Scythian kingdom of Marob on the Black Sea. The book's central characters are Erif Der, a young Scythian witch, the Spring Queen of the title, and her husband, Tarrik, the chieftain of the local community and the Corn King on whose health and potency the fertility of the land depends. Marob is a sort of timeless, mythic land, and Mitchison's book often reads more like myth than history, often showing the clear influence of works such as *The Golden Bough*. History, however, does come to Marob when Tarrik, as its leader, recognizes that eventual change in the kingdom is inevitable. He therefore travels to Sparta, of which he has learned from a stoic philosopher shipwrecked on the coast of Marob, seeking knowledge that will help him lead his kingdom on the proper road to the future. There he observes an austere lifestyle that contrasts strongly with the sumptuousness of life in Marob. Tarrik is much impressed with the plans of the young Spartan leader Kleomenes, who plans to revolutionize Spartan society and to establish a communitarian state in Sparta. Tarrik joins Kleomenes in a battle against the hostile Achaean League. Tarrik is captured and imprisoned in Argos. Erif, however, rescues him, and they return to Marob where Tarrik reclaims his throne after a plot (led by Erif's father, Harn Der, and originally involving Erif as well) had sought to depose him. Erif kills her father, partially as retribution for his role in the death of her eldest child, but she must then leave Marob in order to be cleansed of the crime of patricide. Tarrik remains in Marob, while Erif travels first to Sparta, then escapes from there to Alexandria with Kleomenes and some of his loyal Spartans who are forced to flee from the advancing enemies of the revolution. In Alexandria, Kleomenes and the other Spartans are betrayed by enemies and die as a result. Erif, however, finds something of value in the decadent and corrupt Alexandrian court there when she is introduced to the cult of Isis, helping her to gain power that allows her to carry on Kleomenes's revolutionary ideas and eventually to be restored to the community of Marob.

The Corn King and the Spring Queen is an entertaining novel peopled with colorful characters and filled with compelling action. It is also quite effective at bringing to life the ancient world in which this action occurs. At the same time, the book is also a political novel of ideas that is clearly informed by a socialist-feminist message. Among other things, the novel includes important meditations on the relationship between the individual and society and, in particular, on the role of women in society. Indeed, as Janet Montefiore points out, there is a strong utopian component to Mitchison's depiction of the ancient world, particularly in her treatment of sexuality and of the role of women in the ancient societies she envisions. And there is a strong feminist orientation to this treatment. For example, as Jill Benton notes, the story of the Spring Queen is essentially that of "a woman's search for self in community" (66). Meanwhile, Mitchison's very positive depiction of Kleomenes clearly makes him and his communitarian followers the predecessors of modern-day communists, especially the Russian Bolsheviks, though, as Montefiore points out, the book is weak as a socialist novel, largely because of its focus on kings and queens to the almost total exclusion of any real description of the lives of common people (168). *Selected bibliography:* Benton; Montefiore.

WILLIAM MORRIS: *NEWS FROM NOWHERE* (1890). *News from Nowhere*, in its elaboration of a utopia based on relatively well thought out socialist principles, is one of the founding texts of the modern socialist novel in Britain. On the other hand, although Morris's utopia is set in the far future, it sometimes displays a nostalgia for a simpler past of a kind that informs a number of nineteenth-century utopian works. For example, the factory-based economy of the Industrial Revolution has been replaced in Morris's ideal future by an economy based on agriculture and individual craftsmanship following models provided by the Middle Ages. Morris's vision, although somewhat romantic, is fundamentally based on socialist principles and is, thus, an example of the kind of scientific utopianism praised by Friedrich Engels. Meanwhile, *News from Nowhere* represents a radical rejection of the Victorian ideology of progress and of the industrial and technological growth that fueled that ideology. The book's subtitle, *An Epoch of Rest*, indicates its emphasis on peace and harmony and its opposition to the dynamism of the nineteenth century. Morris's pastoral utopia is thus a direct challenge to the machine-oriented futures envisioned by a number of other nineteenth-century writers of utopian fictions. In particular, it responds to Edward Bellamy's *Looking Backward*, whose vision of a regimented future society based on principles of industrial efficiency was particularly appalling to Morris.

The form of Morris's book is in fact a direct parody of Bellamy's. Morris simply has his protagonist/narrator (suggestively named "William Guest") dream that he awakes in the far future in a time when an ideal society based on equality, simplicity, and harmony with nature has been established. This narrator then awakes at the end of the book back in the nineteenth century—unlike the future envisioned by Bellamy, whose sleeper really does awake in the future, Morris's future is merely a dream. Indeed, it is questionable whether Morris's romanticized view of the future should be read as a practical goal toward which society should strive or whether it simply represents a critique of Morris's contemporary society through the defamiliarization provided by an ideal opposite. Much of Morris's book is devoted to descriptions of the abuses of nineteenth-century capitalism, which the enlightened denizens of the future regard as a bizarre and nightmarish period in which society was founded on organized robbery and in which society seemed specifically designed to thwart the attempts of individuals to realize their human potential.

Morris, partly inspired by events surrounding the Great Dock Strike of 1889, presents a detailed description of the events leading to the establishment of his ideal society. This scenario includes considerable violence and death, and Morris's recognition that the forces that ruled nineteenth-century society would not cede their power without a fight seems far more realistic than Bellamy's suggestion of a smooth and peaceful transition. On the other hand, Morris's vision represents a far more radical transformation of society than does Bellamy's, and the violence he depicts can be taken as a symbol of the violence with which he rejects the mechanization of civilization that he associates with late-nineteenth-century capitalist society.

However, Morris provides little in the way of convincing argument that the ideal society he describes could work in practice. His deindustrialized society is quite prosperous, and all citizens live in considerable material comfort. The efficiency of their medieval economy comes about because of the elimination of the abuses of capitalism and because all citizens enjoy their work and take pride in it, encouraging them to work hard and well. In particular, goods in this socialistic society are esteemed for their value as genuinely useful objects rather than merely for their exchange value as commodities in a capitalist economy. The central change from the nineteenth century that underlies this future society is the pleasure that all citizens take in their work, either from anticipation of the recognition and rewards to be gained or from sheer enjoyment of the work itself. All occupations, no matter how menial, are honored and respected, and all workers have the status of artists. Each worker does the work that he does best and enjoys most, and each takes considerable pride in the quality of his or her work.

There are, however, no controls in this society to assure that "artists" will be available to perform all of the work that the continuing prosperity of the society might require. Morris's book shows a distaste for organization and bureaucracy of any kind, replacing the regimented efficiency of Bellamy's future with a radical volunteerism that somehow seems to work efficiently nevertheless. The educational system (or lack thereof) described by Morris is representative of this vision. Morris's future society has no organized schools, but simply depends on the natural curiosity of children, who presumably follow their own inclinations and thereby eventually gain, through independent study, the knowledge and skills they will need to pursue their eventual chosen occupations. In general, Morris seems to regard extensive formal education as an impediment to the harmony with nature and pleasure in productive work that are so central to his future society, and his students spend far more time in learning trades and crafts than in reading and studying books. As one of Guest's guides explains, "children are mostly given to imitating their elders, and when they see most people about them engaged in genuinely amusing work, like house-building and street-paving, and gardening, and the like, that is what they want to be doing; so I don't think we need fear having too many book-learned men" (25).

A similar lack of institutional structure informs all aspects of life in Morris's anarchistic society, which seeks in every way possible to remove societal restraints on individual liberty. The minimal workings of government proceed mostly by a kind of universal consent, and there are virtually no laws, because violent crime has become a thing of the past with the elimination of the social ills that led to such crime. The removal of these ills leads not only to an ideal society, but to ideal human beings who are superior to their nineteenth-century predecessors not only morally and intellectually, but even physically. Morris, in fact, repeatedly emphasizes the universal health and physical beauty of his future humans. Freed of the miserable working conditions prevailing in nineteenth-century factories, living in an environment free of the ugliness and pollution produced by the Industrial Revolution, and able to pursue individual talents and inclinations without the stifling restrictions associated with the family, religious, and other social institutions of Morris's Victorian England, the inhabitants of Morris's future live long, happy lives free of disease and of the ravages of early aging.

Morris does little to explain exactly how his future low-technology world (without modern medicine or surgery) would be able to maintain its high level of health and hygiene, just as he provides few details that make the economy of his future world seem viable in a practical sense. But then practicality is clearly not Morris's central concern in *News from Nowhere*. For one thing, the book is a highly self-conscious work of fiction. It is, thus, rightfully considered by many critics as one of the most successful utopian fictions in terms of its literary quality. Kumar, for example, identifies Morris's book, along with More's *Utopia* as utopian works that are genuinely great works of literature (25). In addition, many aspects of the future depicted by Morris are clearly symbolic, as when he suggests that in his future even the weather is ideal. Such idyllic images are obviously intended more as a challenge to the unquestioning faith in technology and industrial capitalism shown by many of Morris's contemporaries than as a literal prediction of what the world would be like without that faith. In this sense, Morris's book—while in some ways exemplifying the nostalgic and escapist aspects of utopian thought—well illustrates the powerful literary and satirical potential of the utopian genre. Moreover, what the book lacks in realism is more than made up for by the polemical power of its utopian emphasis, following Marx, on the ability of human beings to make their own history. **Selected bibliography:** Boos and Boos; Coleman; Holzman; Khouri; Kumar; Parrinder ("News"); Suvin.

ARTHUR MORRISON: *A CHILD OF THE JAGO* (1896). *A Child of the Jago* is a sort of bildungsroman detailing the grim and pathetic life of young Dicky Perrott, a denizen of the "Jago," based on the Old Nichol, a notorious slum in London's East End. However, it is not Dicky as an individual, but the Jago and the subculture it engenders in the debased poor who live there that are clearly the true protagonists of the novel. Dicky's story itself is highly predictable. Forced to commit various petty crimes in order to survive, Dicky is constantly in and out of trouble, moving from robbery to robbery and from street brawl to street brawl, despite a seeming basic goodness in his character. His brutish father, Josh Perrott, also survives by crime and is eventually hanged for the murder of the Fagin-like fence Aaron Weech (whose depiction is part of an unfortunate strain of antisemitism that runs through the novel) during a burglary of Weech's shop. Dicky himself is eventually killed in a street brawl at the age of seventeen, thus bringing the story to its logical end. In the meantime, Morrison produces a number of naturalistic descriptions of urban poverty that, at the time, were unusual in their vividness and candor. Peter Keating thus describes the book as a curious combination of the "English social-moralizing tradition and French naturalist objectivity" (179).

As a novel of urban squalor, *A Child of the Jago* addresses a widespread concern of its time, and is it is not surprising that numerous other late-nineteenth-century novels addressed similar issues. One might compare, in their different ways, George Gissing's *The Nether World* (1889) or Israel Zangwill's *Children of the Ghetto* (1892), the former a clear influence on Morrison and the latter an instructive variant that is much more sympathetic to the poor whose lives it describes. Keating has argued that *A Child of the Jago* is one of the most important of this genre and that it sets the tone for the slum fiction of the 1890s. On the other hand, while it is possible to an extent to read the debased and violent culture of the Jago as a result of class inequality under capitalism (and even as a sort of dark parody of the individualism and materialism of respectable bourgeois society), Morrison's book is a novel of the Left only in the loosest sense. From a leftist perspective the book is probably less valuable in its own right than for comparison to more genuinely political descriptions of urban squalor and poverty, such as the American Mike Gold's *Jews without Money* (1930), a book with which it has a number of superficial similarities. But, while Morrison writes as a presumably bourgeois observer for whom the Jagos are alien Others, Gold writes from the sympathetic perspective of one who has, himself, grown up in the slums of Manhattan's Lower East Side—and is proud of it. As Pamela Fox puts it, Morrison's book can serve as "an instructive 'double' for twentieth-century working-class writing" (110).

One problem with *A Child of the Jago* is that Morrison does not particularly identify with the Jagos, who are described via a series of demeaning images of irrationality and brutality—often involving comparison with animals such as rats—of the kind that Gill Davies has identified as typical of bourgeois descriptions of the working class at the end of the nineteenth century. Of course, the inhabitants of the Jago are members not of the proletariat, but of the lumpenproletariat. In any case, it is clear that Morrison's concern over the dehumanizing poverty experienced by the London underclasses has less to do with proletarian sympathies than with a fear that these conditions will eventually destabilize the bourgeois social order. Indeed, while Morrison himself was born to working-class parents in the East End, he was careful to disguise his class origins and actually went to the length of inventing a fictional middle-class biography for himself.

As John Kijinksi points out, Morrison's book is, among other things, a response to the growing fear among the British bourgeoisie in the 1890s that poor living conditions were causing England's lower classes to degenerate to the point that the English population would no longer have the talent or vitality to continue to rule Britain's vast global empire. Indeed, this fear of degeneration was, as R. B. Kershner describes, one of most common preoccupations of the popular imagination of the West at the end of the nineteenth century. In particular, Fox notes that Morrison's view of the Jagos is a version of the late-nineteenth-century theory of "hooliganism," and Morrison himself subscribed to the racist theory that London's working classes actually consisted of two different races, one respectable, and one degenerate. According to Fox, he even supported the building of Penal Settlements "to quarantine (and eventually exterminate)" this degenerate portion of the working class (112).

Kijinksi also asserts that the racialist overtones of *A Child of the Jago* directly parallel the kinds of ethnographic discourses that were at that time being used to describe the "exotic" populations of the British colonies. The urban poor of the Jago are treated very much as such a population, and Morrison applies to them many of the same stereotypes that were being used to describe the colonized peoples of Africa, Asia, and Ireland. The links thus established between the urban poor of London and the supposedly "primitive" peoples of Britain's colonies suggest that fears of degeneration of the urban poor were part of the same discourse as that which attempted to portray Africans, Asians, and the Irish as degenerate. Morrison's project is one of reform, and he obviously hopes that his book will lead to an improvement in living conditions in the London slums. Further, he went on to write two more novels of urban poverty—*To London Town* (1899) and *The Hole in the Wall* (1902)—t hat are somewhat more positive in their treatment of the lower classes of London. Nevertheless, while Richard Benvenuto may be correct that Morrison ultimately stresses the "responsibility of the larger community for the condition of its utter outcasts," even Benvenuto (who rather admires Morrison's book) admits that the Jago is treated in the book as "self-contained and enclosed, a world by itself" (154). And the inhabitants of the Jago are treated as a separate, exotic species, vastly and fundamentally different from London's more respectable inhabitants. The echoes of the "white man's burden" in Morrison's project of urban reform are all too disturbingly clear. **Selected bibliography:** Benvenuto; Davies; Pamela Fox; Keating (*Working Classes*); Kershner; Kijinski.

WILLIAM OAKHURST: *THE UNIVERSAL STRIKE* (1891). Narrated by a middle-class observer who purports to be writing in 1909 and, thus, looking back on events that occurred ten years in the past, *The Universal Strike* tells the story of the impact on London of a surprise international general strike that paralyzes the economies of the world's advanced industrial nations. As Eric Hobsbawm usefully summarizes in *The Age of Empire*, a global economic depression struck capitalist economies in the last quarter of the nineteenth century, leading among other things to agitation (including the founding of the Second International in 1889) on the part of workers for relief from hardships resulting partially from this depression. Like many other strike novels of the 1890s, Oakhurst's work responds to this historical situation. Gustav Klaus notes that it also clearly reflects specific recent phenomena from British history, including the Trafalgar Square Riot of February 1886 and the successful London Dock Workers' Strike of 1889. To some extent, Oakhurst's narrative also anticipates the British General Strike of 1926, though the fictional strike is far more successful and is global in scale.

Though the narrator consistently maintains his middle-class position and sympathies throughout the narrative, *The Universal Strike* is at least partially sympathetic to the cause of the workers involved in the strike. For example, Richard King, General Secretary of the British Section of the International Working Men's Society (the organization that plans and conducts the universal strike) is presented in a positive light as a selfless and indefatigable worker in the cause of social justice. Indeed, he works himself to death in support of his fellow workers. Moreover, the strike is largely successful in winning its demands, and the narrator concludes, at the end of the book, that life is generally better and society more humane as a result of the reforms triggered by the strike. Oakhurst thus anticipates the eventual success of the various efforts at democratization and institution of social programs that would, as Hobsbawm also describes, help to end the depression, avert revolution, and save capitalism from all-out collapse.

At the same time, Oakhurst and his narrator demonstrate many of the fears of working-class action that were prevalent among the British bourgeoisie at the end of the nineteenth century. For example, in the early days of the strike, with even the police and military refusing to work, London is taken over by roaming mobs, who destroy everything in their path in an outburst of senseless and animal-like violence. Such scenes, of course, are common in nineteenth-century British literature, in which attempts at working-class collective action often lead to senseless mob violence, as in Charles Dickens's *Barnaby Rudge*. In addition, the scenes of mob violence in *The Universal Strike* participate in a general fear of "degeneration" (see Kershner) that was rampant in Britain and elsewhere in the West in the late nineteenth century. However, unlike

Robert Louis Stevenson's *Dr. Jekyll and Mr. Hyde* and Joseph Conrad's *Heart of Darkness* (perhaps the two best-known degeneration narratives), *The Universal Strike* makes clear the extent to which these fears of degeneration were often specifically related to a growing fear of working-class power. As Oakhurst's narrator put it, this outbreak of mob rule demonstrated that "just beneath the outward veneer of decorum lie all the passions partially subdued by the wholesome dread of what the world will say if we let them loose; once relax this restraint, and they all start up, servants no longer, but lords" (35). Such class-oriented emphases, by the way, were not uncommon in British writing of the 1890s. Arthur Morrison's *A Child of the Jago* (1896) is another novel that concerns such themes. Indeed, as Gareth Stedman Jones notes, the impoverished East End of London came to be viewed as "an almost unalloyed centre of degeneration" (308).

Order is restored only when the middle-class organizes groups of vigilantes to patrol the streets. Meanwhile, the strike causes even more misery for the poor than for the rich, and all are relieved when it is called off after only a week, three days earlier than originally planned. The early end of the strike turns out to be highly fortuitous, for it occurs just in time to avert an invasion of Britain by a Russian force hoping to take advantage of Britain's helplessness during the strike and eventually to establish world domination. This fear of Russian expansionism runs throughout the rhetoric of British foreign policy in the nineteenth century; in this case, it participates in a general fear of internationalism in that one of the most important negative aspects of the strike is the fact that the International Working Men's Society is genuinely international and, thus, an apparent threat to British sovereignty. Further, the ruling board of the group is situated in Paris, the site of revolutionary energies that had been the object of fear and loathing in Britain since 1789 and that had undergone a fairly recent reinforcement during the Paris Commune of 1871. **Selected bibliography:** Hobsbawm (*Age of Empire*); Kershner; Klaus ("Strike Novel"); Stedman Jones (*Languages*).

GEORGE ORWELL: *BURMESE DAYS* **(1934).** *Burmese Days* provides an important description of British practices of power in colonial Burma and relates these practices directly to the economic underpinnings of imperialism. Burma, where Orwell spent five years as a member of the imperial police in the 1920s, had been gradually placed under British control via a series of colonial wars in the nineteenth century. Burmese resistance to British rule gradually grew from that time forward. Orwell's book, though ostensibly set in the mid-1920s, seems informed by the growing political tensions of the early 1930s as well; it was completed at a time when Burmese political discontent was reaching a high point, and the resulting air of crisis pervades the book. Many of the crucial events driving the plot of *Burmese Days* center on a growing sense of crisis in British colonial authority in Burma. The book features a number of small riots and demonstrations that contribute to an apocalyptic air that is well captured in the rumors of a native magician who has mysteriously appeared as if from nowhere, prophesying the end of British rule and supposedly distributing magic bulletproof jackets that will allow the Burmese successfully to resist the superior military technology of the British colonial army (111–12). Such rumors and the accompanying disturbances culminate late in the book in the outbreak of an all-out rebellion in Kyauktada, the Burmese town in which the book's action occurs. And, even though this rebellion is quelled relatively easily, there is a strong sense that it is the precursor of more cataclysmic events.

The British characters in *Burmese Days* are intensely aware of the air of crisis that pervades their situation. And Orwell's English colonials are nostalgic for bygone days when the "insolent" Burmese would not have dared to challenge British power. Ellis, the local manager of a British company and the nastiest of the colonials in Burma, is bitterly apocalyptic in his assessment of the situation, insisting that the empire has been ruined and that Burma, in particular, is "rotten with sedition," because the British have been "too soft" on the natives. His solution, of course, is to employ whatever means necessary to reassert English superiority over the Burmese. Similarly, speaking to the other denizens of the Kyauktada European Club, the last bastion of the all-English club in Burma, Orwell's Mrs. Lackersteen (who, with her husband, functions as a key marker of bourgeois vulgarity) complains that the political situation is making it more and more difficult to control her Burmese servants: "We seem to have no *authority* over the natives nowadays, with all these dreadful Reforms, and the insolence they learn from the newspapers. In some ways they are getting almost as bad as the lower classes at home" (29, Orwell's emphasis). Mrs. Lackersteen thus states the theme of crisis in British colonial authority that is central to the book, while at the same time introducing the more subtle, but extremely important, suggestion of parallels between the blatantly hierarchical structure of colonial power and the structure of bourgeois class society in England.

It is the timber merchant Flory, the principal protagonist of the book, who serves as Orwell's most vocal critic of British imperialism. Importantly, Flory's often bitter critique of British imperialism focuses on the economic, with theft as his central metaphor for the operations of empire. The decay of the British Empire, as depicted in the book, thus appears to suggest the decay of capitalism as well. Flory, knowing well the brutality of Ellis and the other English colonials in Burma, dismisses the "slimy white man's burden humbug" and insists that the British are in places like India and Burma purely in order to exploit the resources of the colonies for economic gain. Further, he suggests that the British have intentionally crippled the Indian and Burmese economic infrastructures in order to make them dependent on British administration. He notes that the British schools in India are designed to produce nothing but "cheap clerks," who are fit to do nothing more than work in the service of the British. Moreover, he argues that the British have systematically destroyed Indian industries, especially textiles, in order to assure that they cannot compete with their British counterparts (39–41).

Michael Shelden points out that Orwell would later recall that he had been pressured by his publishers to change some of the characters in *Burmese Days* from government officials to businessmen in order to make the book "less directly an attack on British imperialism" (183). But the focus on businessmen in the book actually enhances Orwell's most trenchant criticisms of imperialism by providing more emphasis on its economic basis. Flory's identification of economic exploitation as the principal motivation for British imperialism is reinforced by the fact that prominent British characters like Ellis, Lackersteen, and Flory, himself, are businessmen rather than government officials. Moreover, in his analysis of the British destruction of the Indian economy, Flory directly echoes the earlier comments of Karl Marx recorded in an 1853 article published in the *New York Daily Tribune*: "England has broken down the entire framework of Indian society, without any symptoms of reconstitution yet appearing" (Marx and Engels 655).

The potential Marxist intonation of Flory's critique of British economic imperialism participates in a larger fabric of imagery in Orwell's text that lends itself to Marxist interpretations. In an ironic anticipation of Orwell's own later appropriation as an anticommunist icon during the Cold War, one reason why Orwell's British colonials feel such a sense of crisis is that they are haunted by the specter of communism, which they often associate with Flory and his "Bolshie" nonconformist tendencies. The quintessential bourgeois Lackersteen, for example, equates Flory's suggestion that the Indian Dr. Veraswami be admitted to the Kyauktada Club with "downright Bolshevism" (235). When Flory attempts to court Lackersteen's niece Elizabeth, she is put off by the discovery that Flory has for some time kept a Burmese mistress. But she is even more violently disturbed by his "highbrow" tendencies, which for her associate him with the ultimate demon, Vladimir Lenin (200).

Elizabeth, meanwhile, is central to the text's treatment of the theme of commodification. Flory courts her purely because she is the only available Englishwoman in the vicinity; in fact, the Lackersteens have brought her to Burma on the assumption that they will be able to pass her along to a husband in short order. Women, both Burmese and English, are consistently treated as commodities by Orwell's characters, though it is also true that Ms. Lackersteen treats men as commodities as well, suggesting that, in Elizabeth's place, she would marry any young man who came along, one being just as good as another. Ellis, perhaps predictably, expresses the commodification of women in the book's most vulgarly overt terms. For Ellis, there can be only one reason why a young English girl would come to Burma: "to lay her claws into a husband." Warning the bachelor Flory of the "dangers" that Elizabeth represents, Ellis suggests, using an economic metaphor that makes the process of commodification quite explicit, that English girls come to the colonies only when they are desperate for a mate, having failed to find one at home: "The Indian marriage-market, they call it. Meat market it ought to be. Shiploads of 'em coming out every year like carcasses of frozen mutton, to be pawed over by nasty bachelors like you" (110). The Englishwoman Elizabeth is thus treated as a sexual commodity by the other English characters in the book, but the commodification of the Burmese woman Ma Hla May is even more extreme. Before Elizabeth's arrival, Flory, in the absence of any English women who might serve as outlets for his sexual desires, literally purchases Ma Hla May from her parents, and it is quite clear that he regards her not as a human being but as a kind of combination pet and sexual device. To Flory, she is "like a doll," with the "teeth of a kitten"; he strokes her "like a cat," and he has trained her to perform as obediently as a dog.

A few years after writing *Burmese Days*, Orwell expressed a reluctance to support what he saw as the "capitalist-imperialist" position of the British in the early days of World War II (Shelden 298). Orwell's most bitter denunciations of capitalism and imperialism, in fact, reside in his description in a letter to Geoffrey Gorer (September 15, 1937) of fascism as "only a development of capitalism." And he relates this suggestion directly to the British colonial presence in Asia: "We like to think of England as a democratic country, but our rule in India, for instance, is just as bad as German Fascism" (*Collected Essays I* 284). *Burmese Days* anticipates Orwell's socialist period, especially in its tendency to equate imperialism and capitalism. But Flory, the spokesman for such criticisms in the novel, is not a self-conscious Marxist, and his criticism of the British presence in Burma arises not from ideology but from his bitter sense of loneliness and isolation in the colonial environment. Indeed, critics like David Seed and Brian Matthews have argued that *Burmese Days* focuses so much on Flory's personal psychological problems that it fails to mount an effective critique of British imperialism. On the other hand, it might be argued that Flory's personal situation contributes in important ways to the book's potential Marxist critique of imperialism. In particular, Flory exemplifies the alienation typical of the characters in British colonial fiction, his intense self-consciousness of the "hideous birthmark" on his face serving as a symbol of his sense of separation from those around him. Flory himself attributes much of his sense of alienation to the strangeness of the Burmese environment, whose foreign flora, foreign landscape, and foreign alienation are as "alien as a different planet" (180).

Further, Flory's estrangement from Burma is exacerbated by his alienation from the other English colonials around him, and he believes that the tropical lushness of Burma could function as a sort of paradise on earth if only he had someone with whom to share it. Flory thus functions as a particularly vivid example of the alienation of individuals in modern capitalist society as a whole. The numerous indications in *Burmese Days* of parallels between the colonial situation in Burma and the domestic situation in England suggest the colonial environment as a locus in which the workings of bourgeois society in England reveal themselves in particularly obvious form. Orwell's representation of Burma thus becomes a tool for the demystification of English capitalism. ***Selected bibliography:*** Booker; Marx and Engels (*Reader*); Matthews; Orwell (*Collected Essays*); Seed; Shelden.

RAYMOND POSTGATE: *VERDICT OF TWELVE* (1940). *Verdict of Twelve* is a detective novel the author of which was a leading leftist historian and thinker of the 1930s. Postgate wrote such overtly Marxist works as *The New Bolshevik Theory* (1920) and *How to Make a Revolution* (1934). He was also the author of such leftist histories as *The Story of a Year: 1848* and the coauthor (with his brother-in-law, G.D.H. Cole, the husband of Postgate's sister, the leftist historian Margaret Cole) of *The Common People, 1746–1946* (1949, revised from the original version published in 1939). Meanwhile, Postgate went on to author such works as *The Plain Man's Guide to Win* (1953) and *The Good Food Guide* (several versions in the 1960s). His career thus stands as an excellent example of the variety of British leftist cultural production in the middle part of the twentieth century, just as *Verdict of Twelve* is evidence of the important role played by detective novels in that production.

Verdict of Twelve makes its principal message clear from the very beginning. It opens with two epigraphs, the first of which is a quotation from the British juror's oath in which prospective jurors swear to weigh the evidence objectively and to attempt to render "a true verdict . . . according to the evidence." The second epigraph then comes from the famous passage in *The German Ideology* in which Marx argues that "it is not the consciousness of men that determines their existence, but on the contrary their social existence determines their consciousness." The second epigraph, of course, undermines the first by suggesting that jurors cannot reach a fully objective judgment because their judgments will inevitably be affected by their own particular backgrounds and experiences. The remainder of the text is, essentially, an elaboration of this premise. Among other things, *Verdict of Twelve* differs from most detective fiction in that it pays a substantial amount of attention to the jurors in its central trial rather than focusing on the victims, criminals, and investigators who are involved in the case. Indeed, the entire first part of the book consists of a series of sketches of the diverse backgrounds of the various jurors, thereby establishing the possibility that these jurors might react very differently to the evidence that is about to be presented.

The second part of *Verdict of Twelve*, which narrates the crime itself, is the most conventional section. On the other hand, it still pays a substantial amount of attention to the important role played by each individual's social experience in determining his or her attitudes and behavior. In particular, it begins with a detailed explanation of the background of Mrs. Rosalie van Beer, the defendant in the case. Rosalie is a woman of working-class background who marries the wealthy Robert Arkwright shortly before he is killed in World War I. She then marries the "unpresentable" band leader, Henry van Beer, who is killed soon afterward in an automobile accident (85). Though looked down upon by the Arkwrights because of her class and her marriage to van Beer, Rosalie becomes the guardian of her young nephew, Philip Arkwright, when the boy's parents are killed in a plane crash, leaving her as his only living relative. Rosalie sees to it that most of the boy's basic needs are met, but she often treats him unkindly and is frequently abusive. This culminates in her brutal killing of Philip's beloved pet rabbit on the contrived grounds that the animal might pose a threat to the boy's precarious health. Soon afterward, Philip dies of poisoning, and a subsequent police investigation eventually leads to Rosalie's arrest for murder.

Part III of the book details the actual trial, in which the lawyers for both sides present their evidence, all of which is circumstantial. The prosecution notes Rosalie's cruel treatment of the boy, including the killing of the rabbit. They also note that there is evidence she may have been conducting research into the properties of the poison used in the killing and that she, and only she, seems to have had ample opportunity to commit the crime. They also make the point that she had an excellent motif to commit the crime, given that she stands to inherit the Arkwright family fortune upon the boy's death. The defense, meanwhile, bases its case on the theory that Philip inadvertently poisoned himself in an attempt to murder Rosalie in retribution for the death of his rabbit. There is circumstantial evidence to support this theory as well, including the fact that the rabbit seems to have derived its name from a pet in a short story by H. H. Munro ("Saki") in which a young boy plots the killing of his cruel aunt. Much of Part III, however, deals with the deliberations of the jurors, who predictably react to this evidence in different ways depending upon their backgrounds. Nevertheless, they reach a unanimous verdict (not guilty) rather quickly, suggesting that such verdicts do not always indicate that all twelve jurors legitimately agree about the case.

The text then ends with a twist, as Rosalie reveals to her lawyers that both the defense and the prosecution theories of the case were essentially correct. It turns out that Philip was trying to poison her, but that she found out about his plan and turned the tables, arranging matters so that he would be sure to poison himself instead. This final revelation is entirely appropriate to the remainder of the text in that it indicates the complexity of the situations about which jurors are asked to make unequivocal judgments. The clever and ironic tone of this ending is also consistent with the rest of the text, which is written in a lively and often quite amusing style throughout. Postgate thus manages to level a number of important criticisms against the British legal system, which turns out to be based on universalist assumptions that are consistent with the bourgeois ideology of the Enlightenment but inconsistent with the lived experience of human beings. At the same time, he demonstrates that such criticisms can be contained within a highly entertaining work of popular fiction. *Selected bibliography:* Cole and Postgate; Postgate (*How to Make a Revolution*); Postgate (*New Bolshevik Theory*); Postgate (*Story of a Year*).

J. B. PRIESTLEY: *BRIGHT DAY* **(1946).** A prolific writer who produced a vast amount of output in a variety of genres and media over the course of a career spanning more than five decades, Priestly is widely regarded as one of the central figures of modern British culture. His work varies greatly in attitude as well as form, but much of it has at least vaguely leftist inclinations. The son of a schoolmaster, he clearly regarded himself as a sort of spokesman for the common man, and in a volume of memoirs, *Margin Released*, he describes his political stance as "pink" if not outright red (227). Priestley is often mentioned in the 1930s as one of the bright new "proletarian" writers who came to the forefront of British culture during that decade. His 1930s novel, *Angel Pavement*, is a grimly realistic account of urban life in London that is very much in the vein of much proletarian fiction of that decade, while *Let the People Sing* (1939) is very much in the tradition of Popular Front opposition to fascism that came to the forefront of British leftist fiction in the late 1930s. However, some of Priestley's most interesting work with clearly leftist inclinations appears during and after World War II, at a time when leftist fiction in general was at a low point. In particular, the sequence *Daylight on Saturday* (1943), *Three Men in Suits* (1945), and *Bright Day* (1946) in many ways helps to set the tone for British leftist fiction in the next two decades.

Bright Day, which is probably Priestley's most respected novel, is a partly autobiographical work that centers on screenwriter Gregory Dawson, now fifty, as he works to complete a film script in the wake of World War II while at the same time coming to grips with his memories of the years just before World War I, when he (like Priestley) worked as a clerk in a wool trading company. Dawson's attempts to unravel certain mysteries that still remain from his earlier life provides much of the plot interest of the book, which often reads like a sort of detective story. But much of the dual temporal perspective of the book simply serves to explain Dawson's sense that something has been lost in British culture in the course of the twentieth century. In particular, Dawson believes that a growing focus on monetary gain has gradually eroded many of the traditional values that had formerly been central to British culture. Dawson, as a screenwriter who has spent several years in Hollywood and has had considerable success there, is particularly well situated to observe this phenomenon, the dominance of Hollywood films in the contemporary popular culture of the 1940s serving as one of the principal symptoms of the Americanization of British culture, which for Dawson (and Priestley) is a central consequence of the creeping commodification of the twentieth century.

Tired of his own participation in the Hollywood Culture Industry, Dawson has decided to remain in Britain and work on British films, even though such films have difficulty competing with Hollywood products in the international marketplace. But British commercial films are becoming more like Hollywood films all the time; by the end of the text, his memories of his earlier life having reminded him of more innocent days, Dawson decides to give up screenwriting altogether. At this point, however, he comes into contact with a group of young people who hope to begin producing, with trade union support, alternative films that avoid the formulaic commercial glitz of Hollywood. Impressed by the group's desire to make films that "show how real people behaved in a real world," Dawson agrees to begin writing scripts for the group and thereby discovers a new sense of meaning in his chosen profession (352). As the text ends, Dawson, realizing that there are still idealistic young people who value more than money, feels a new optimism about his own future and the future of Western culture. *Selected bibliography:* Braine; Susan Cooper; DeVitis and Kalson; Priestley (*Margin Released*); David Smith (*Socialist Propaganda*).

J. B. PRIESTLEY: *DAYLIGHT ON SATURDAY* **(1943).** Written and published in the midst of World War II, *Daylight on* Saturday is clearly intended as a contribution to the British war effort. The book is very much in the tradition of British working-class fiction in that it concentrates on the workers in a factory, in this case a plant run by the Elmdown Aircraft Co., Ltd., to produce military aircraft. The title of the book refers to the fact that these workers put in such long hours inside the plant that they only see natural daylight on weekends. On the other hand, many of the major characters are in management, including James Cheviot, the general manager of the factory. And, while the book suggests that some in management need to learn to understand that their workers are human beings and not merely pieces of production equipment, most of the management personnel, particularly Cheviot, are treated quite positively. The overall message of the book is that workers and managers need to work together because they are on the same side in the battle against fascism. The book is thus most directly in the tradition of the Popular Front of the late 1930s.

To a large extent, *Daylight on Saturday* is a series of character sketches, presenting various employees of the factory and their diverse backgrounds, interests, and desires. These employees include Joyce Deerhurst, an attractive young woman from London who has just begun work in the factory; Gwen Ockley, one of the few women employees who is a longtime factory hand from well before the war; Maurice Angleby, a young working-class man who has managed, with the help of his sacrificing parents, to become a professional engineer; Alfred Cleeton, an "old-fashioned radical"; Mr. Ogmore, a devoted communist; Mr. Stonier, a withdrawn religious fanatic; and Freda Pinnell, a woman from a genteel (but impoverished) family who is still adjusting to life in the working world. The plot itself is rather minimal, and centers largely on the antagonism between Cheviot's two chief lieutenants, Elrick, the works superintendent, and Blandford, the assistant manager. Elrick comes from a working-class background and has worked his way up through the ranks, devoting his entire adult life to the Elmdown. Blandford, on the other hand, comes from a rich and powerful family that has members in both houses of parliament. Believing that technology is the way of the future, Blandford has to some extent deviated from family tradition by studying engineering at Cambridge, then beginning work as a professional engineer, but he maintains many of the attitudes and mannerisms of his class. In particular, he has a difficult time relating to the workers in the factory as human beings. Elrick, on the other hand, understands the humanity of the workers, though his gruff manner does not make him particularly popular with many of them, especially the new hands who have come on as part of the war effort.

Elrick and Blandford constantly clash over various matters of factory policy, while at the same time competing for the role of successor to Cheviot. Blandford is eventually chosen to succeed Cheviot after the latter is promoted to take over a new series of plants that are being converted to defense work. This development leaves Elrick bitter and on the verge of resignation, declaring that he will not work under Blandford. In the meantime, Elrick becomes involved in an embarrassing incident when he makes an unwelcome pass at Joyce Deerhurst, leading to his dismissal from the plant, though Cheviot still plans to put him in charge of one of the new plants. Elrick, however, is killed in a fight with Stonier after the latter finally goes off the deep end and tries to make one of the young women working in the factory into a human sacrifice. Gwen Ockley, who has long secretly been in love with Elrick, is crushed by his death. But life goes on in the plant, and the book proceeds to a sort of romance ending. Angleby succeeds Elrick and in the meantime becomes engaged to marry Freda Pinnell, despite their class differences. Cheviot prepares to leave for his new job, urging Blandford to learn to view the workers as human beings and then proudly standing outside the plant, watching the workers as they depart at the end of the shift. Meanwhile, there are hints that a recent production lag is over and that production on the plant will soon be on the upswing — partially because of improved worker morale resulting from recent Allied victories in the war.

Daylight on Saturday is obviously very rooted in its World War II context, though the book clearly seeks to present images of cooperation between classes that might extend beyond the end of the war. Priestley, in *Margin Released*, expresses a hope that *Daylight on Saturday* can continue to function for future generations as a document that shows "how people lived and worked in World War Two" (193). In this sense, *Daylight on Saturday* is quite effective. However, the book's very muted can't-we-all-just-get-along political message, understandable within the context in which the book was written, would also extend beyond the war, anticipating the relatively moderate (and sometimes incoherent) political orientation of much British working-class fiction of the 1950s and 1960s. **Selected bibliography:** Braine; Susan Cooper; DeVitis and Kalson; Priestley (*Margin Released*); David Smith (*Socialist Propaganda*).

BERNARD SHAW: *AN UNSOCIAL SOCIALIST* (1883). George Bernard Shaw is unquestionably one of the major literary figures of the twentieth century, primarily because of his work as a dramatist. However, he began his career as a novelist, writing and publishing five novels from 1879 to 1883. The last of these, *An Unsocial Socialist*, was written just after Shaw's conversion to socialism, at a time when he was highly enthusiastic about the work of Marx and convinced that capitalism was entering its death throes. In an introduction written in 1930 for later editions of the novel, Shaw looks back and explains that the book began as part of a project to depict "capitalist society in dissolution, with its downfall as the final grand catastrophe" (v). Moreover, he argues in this introduction that his literary vision has become a reality in the Soviet Union: "My unsocial socialist has come to life as a Bolshevist; and my catastrophe has actually occurred in Communist Russia. The opinions of the fictitious Trefusis anticipated those of the real Lenin" (v). Indeed, Shaw was an enthusiastic supporter of the Soviet Union in the 1930s, returning from a trip there a self-declared Stalinist. Granted, Shaw's political opinions were by this time a bit quirky and unreliable (he also expressed admiration for Hitler at times in the 1930s), but it is nevertheless the case that, as a founding figure of the Fabian Society (and thus, indirectly, of the Labour Party) and longtime professor of socialist beliefs, he is an important figure in the history of British socialism.

An Unsocial Socialist, which begins in Alton College, an exclusive British girls' school, focuses primarily on upper-class characters. And, although one might argue that this focus simply demonstrates the universal relevance of Marxist ideas, it is also the case that Shaw falls far short of depicting a genuine working-class perspective or calling for proletarian revolution. The plot of the book combines Shaw's socialist message with traditional elements derived from British literature, and the book is really more of a social comedy than the apocalyptic announcement of the downfall of capitalism that Shaw would describe in his later introduction. The early parts of the book deal with the attempts of Sidney Trefusis, the socialist protagonist, to escape from his recent marriage to Henrietta Jansenius on the premise that his passion for her distracts him from his political work. He runs away to the pastoral setting of Alton College, where he dons a working-class disguise, calling himself Jeff Smilash and beginning work as a freelance handyman. He also begins a flirtation with young Agatha Wylie, a student at Alton College. Henrietta discovers him there, but conveniently dies soon afterward, leaving Trefusis to continue his work of organizing the local laborers (none of whom are vividly represented in the text) to fight against their oppression by the capitalist system, thus presumably laying the groundwork for the coming revolution. Several romantic complications and entanglements later, Trefusis marries Agatha, whom he believes can help, rather than hinder, him in his work. The book then ends with a letter, purportedly from Trefusis, complaining to Shaw that he has represented him unfairly and suggesting that Shaw should perhaps put his talents to better use than writing novels.

Of course, Shaw's Fabian socialism, relying on evolutionary political change rather than class-based revolution, is specifically non-Marxist (and non-Leninist) in nature, and the gestures toward revolution in *An Unsocial Socialist* are halfhearted at best. Trefusis actually has little in common with Lenin, despite Shaw's later claim. Further, Shaw's novel, with its cast of primarily upper-class characters (the wealthy Trefusis seems motivated to political action largely because of a guilty conscience over the fact that his father has made a fortune within the exploitative capitalist system), has little in common with the British tradition of working-class culture. Nevertheless, *An Unsocial Socialist* is an important early marker of the beginnings of socialist fiction in Britain, even if it also fails to overcome (and thus demonstrates the extent of) the exclusion of the working class from most of the mainstream British literature of the nineteenth century. ***Selected bibliography:*** Dietrich; Julian Kaye; Sypher.

ALAN SILLITOE: *THE LONELINESS OF THE LONG-DISTANCE RUNNER* **(1959).** Like the earlier *Saturday Night and Sunday Morning*, the short novel *The Loneliness of the Long-Distance Runner* was adapted for the screen by its author, produced in a film version (directed by Tony Richardson) in 1962. Together, these two novels and their film adaptations helped to establish Sillitoe's reputation as one of the leading working-class writers in post–World War II Britain. The latter book (published as the title story in a collection that included several other shorter stories of working-class life) deals with the experience of Smith, a working-class youth in Nottingham who runs afoul of the law and is sent to a Borstal for rehabilitation. The story, narrated by Smith in first person, is striking not only for its vivid evocation of his life on the fringes of British society but for Smith's attitude of unmitigated hostility to the rulers of mainstream Britain and their bourgeois values. Unlike the contemporaneous protagonists of writers such as John Braine, Stan Barstow, and Keith Waterhouse, Smith has no desire to rise into the middle class, for which he has nothing but contempt. Instead, he seeks to maintain his independence from the mainstream of British life and to use his "cunning" to score whatever victories he can in a sort of guerrilla campaign against respectable society..

The title of the book refers to the fact that, as the book opens, Smith is training as a long-distance runner in the Essex Borstal where he has been sent as a result of his involvement in a burglary at a Nottingham bakery. The book includes some extremely effective descriptions of the sense of isolation (and exhilaration) Smith feels while training alone on the roads surrounding the Borstal in the early morning hours. This isolation, of course, mirrors the radical alienation that he experiences in his life as a whole, and indeed that alienation is the major topic of the book. Moreover, given this alienation and given Smith's sense that social life in Britain consists primarily of a Manichean struggle between "us" (the outcasts like Smith) and "them" (the forces of authority in respectable society), it comes as no surprise that, train as he might, Smith has no intention of bringing home the Prize Cup that the governor of his Borstal dreams of winning in the upcoming All-England Borstal Long Distance Cross Country Running competition.

The first section of the story develops Smith's attitude toward his running and his view of life as a war between In-laws, like the authorities in his Borstal, and Out-laws, like himself. The second section of the story then details Smith's life in Nottingham before his arrest and incarceration, including a description of the robbery in which he and his friend Mike climbed over a wall and broke into a bakery, stealing a cashbox containing more than one-hundred-fifty pounds. This section also includes a description of the police investigation that eventually leads to Smith's arrest when a rainstorm causes the money to wash out of a drainpipe in which it had been hidden while a detective stands in the rain interrogating Smith nearby. Most of the third section of the story is devoted to a description of the Prize Cup race itself, though much of this description involves a narration of Smith's thoughts as he runs, including his memory of having discovered his father in a pool of blood, dead from cancer. Smith gains the lead in the race and briefly muses on the possibility of winning, but then comes to a near stop as he approaches the finish, allowing the runner from Gunthorpe, a rival Borstal, to win the race. As punishment, Smith is assigned only the most undesirable jobs for the remaining six months of his stay in the Essex Borstal, but he accepts this treatment with good humor, feeling that his "victory" in losing the race was worth it. Soon after his release, he contracts pleurisy (partially as a result of his training), but this, too, turns out to be a victory over the forces of authority because it keeps him out of the army. He resumes his life of crime and uses his leisure time to write the story that we have just read.

Smith joins Arthur Seaton, the protagonist of *Saturday Night and Sunday Morning*, as a cultural icon of an entire generation of angry young men in Britain. Smith, however, is a far more rebellious figure than Seaton, who reliably goes to work every day despite his sexual transgressions in his off hours. Smith is a particularly striking figure of the working-class rebel who feels radically disenfranchised by and excluded from the system around him. At the same time, he feels that he is more alive than those who reside within this spiritually deadening system, with its emphasis on the following of rules and the preservation of order. Moreover, while Smith's particular rebellion is partially a youthful rejection of the authority of his elders, *The Loneliness of the Long-Distance Runner* makes it clear that the opposition sensed by Smith is primarily one of class against class, even if Smith himself does not have a sophisticated understanding of this fact.

While Smith's rebellion is entirely personal, the book also makes it clear that this individualist rebellion can never hope to bring about fundamental change in the conditions that have driven him to rebellion in the first place. Only collective rebellion can do that, and, in the final analysis, Sillitoe's story may therefore be less about rebellion than about the difficulty of effective collective rebellion within the radically alienating social conditions of capitalism. Indeed, though Smith believes that he rejects all of the central values of his society, he has thoroughly accepted the individualism that is perhaps the most important of these values and the one most crucial to maintaining the current social order. Thus, while *The Loneliness of the Long-Distance Runner* to some extent suggests the possibility of rebellion by detailing the failed interpellation of Smith by bourgeois ideology, it also demonstrates the success of that ideology in channeling rebellion into the relatively innocuous realm of individual transgression. **Selected bibliography:** Atherton; David Craig ("The Roots"); Hitchcock (*Working-Class Fiction*); Penner; Rollins; Vaverka.

ALAN SILLITOE: *SATURDAY NIGHT AND SUNDAY MORNING* **(1958).** *Saturday Night and Sunday Morning* was the first novel by Sillitoe, who would come to be known as one of the most successful chroniclers of working-class experience in post-World War II British fiction. The book, which became a major bestseller, received immediate acclaim as a demonstration of the possibilities of a genuine working-class novel (despite Sillitoe's own rejection of that term) and is one of the highlights of a sudden explosion of working-class novels produced at about the same time, including John Braine's *Room at the Top* (1957), Keith Waterhouse's *Billy Liar* (1959), and Stan Barstow's *A Kind of Loving* (1960). Like many of these other texts, *Saturday Night and Sunday Morning* was made into a film, and the 1960 film adaptation, written by Sillitoe and directed by Karel Reisz, was so successful that it is widely regarded as one of the landmarks of modern British cinema. Sillitoe's novel resembles most of the other working-class texts produced at the time in that it focuses more on depictions of working-class experience under capitalism than on the presentation of specific political alternatives to the capitalist system. *Saturday Night and Sunday Morning* does, however, gesture toward leftist political solutions in ways that most of the working-class texts of its time do not. It also differs from most of those texts in that its protagonist, the young factory machinist Arthur Seaton, is an ordinary worker who has no intellectual pretensions or aspirations to join the middle class. Seaton is also important because he has come to be regarded as a fictional exemplar of the "angry young man" and thus as an important icon of British culture in the late 1950s.

Saturday Night and Sunday Morning is written in a vigorous and energetic, yet straightforward and highly accessible style. It opens at a furious pace as the twenty-one-year-old Arthur, who has just triumphed in a drinking contest in a local Nottingham pub, falls down a flight of stairs due to his drunkenness. He staggers to his feet, vomits on some of the other customers, then leaves and makes his way to the home of his girlfriend, Brenda, wife of his mild-mannered coworker, Jack, who is away at the races for the night. Arthur spends the night with Brenda, slipping out just as Jack arrives the next morning. The frenetic action of these first few pages well characterizes Arthur's life on weekends, when he seeks, through booze and sex, to escape from the tedium of his humdrum Monday-through-Friday life as a lathe operator in the local bicycle factory. Not surprisingly, this solution is less than entirely effective and, in fact, leads him into more and more trouble. Arthur spends an increasing amount of his time either drunk or recovering from the effects of drinking. Brenda eventually becomes pregnant, apparently by Arthur, who in the meantime also begins (without Brenda's knowledge) an affair with Brenda's sister, Winnie, whose husband, Bill, is away in the military. Arthur also begins a more conventional courtship with nineteen-year-old Doreen Greatton. Arthur's attempts to juggle these three women are interrupted when Bill returns and, along with a fellow soldier, corners Arthur in an alley and gives him a severe beating, though Arthur defends himself furiously. Thus ends Arthur's pursuit of Winnie and Brenda, but Doreen sticks by him, even after he confesses his other affairs to her. Their courtship proceeds, and they soon become engaged, even though Arthur has proclaimed throughout the book his determination never to be married. As the book ends, Arthur is about to marry Doreen and to move in with her and her mother, thus making his home life nearly as routine as his life on the job. In a final scene he goes fishing and catches a fish, but throws it back, sympathizing with its predicament that so resembles his own.

One of the strengths of *Saturday Night and Sunday Morning* is its very effective description of Arthur actually working at his lathe, perhaps because Sillitoe himself spent time working in a bicycle factory in his teen years. David Craig thus concludes that one such description early in the book "is the first passage I know of in our literature (nearly two centuries after the first power-loom was patented!) which evokes a factory-worker's experiences from the inside with the finesse that writers have given to all others in the human range" (103). The book also nicely captures Arthur's complex attitude toward his work and his relationship with the factory's management and his fellow workers. A skilled machinist, Arthur takes pride in a job well done and often loses himself in his work. It is not the work itself that makes him angry, but the factory system in which that work must be performed. He remains radically alienated from the products of his labor and knows that most of the benefits of his work go to his bosses, not to him. He thus views his highly regimented workplace as a sort of prison despite the pleasure he takes in his craftsmanship, consistently describing the factory in carceral terms and viewing the years ahead of him in his job as a "life sentence" (206). Arthur's alienation also extends to his personal life, causing him to treat women merely as sexual objects toward whom he feels as much animosity as attraction and leading him to prefer married women to single ones because the former already have husbands and will not be tempted to try to ensnare him in marriage. Yet Arthur, whose only experience with genuine human contact comes from fleeting moments of family community (especially with his Aunt Ada and her numerous progeny), is also lonely and longs to have a home and wife of his own; thus, his eventual engagement to Doreen, despite the fact that he is highly ambivalent about her.

Among other things, Arthur's engagement demonstrates the true power of the interpellating forces around him. Viewing himself as a rebel who radically rejects the received values of his society, especially as they are purveyed through mass culture, Arthur nevertheless confines his rebellion to harmless and apolitical realms, while ultimately tending to behave in precisely the manner prescribed by the society for which he supposedly has so much contempt. *Saturday Night and Sunday Morning* does an excellent job of capturing Arthur's frustration and bitterness at the society around him, while making clear the lack of political consciousness that makes him unable fully to articulate the source of his anomie. He has a clear sense of himself as a worker and a concomitant sense that bosses are his enemy, but he does not really formulate that opposition in terms of class struggle, focusing his animosity on the "government" as the vague embodiment of all of the forces that limit and control his existence (220–22). Indeed, Arthur rebels as much against the traditional ethos of the British working-class as against capitalism. To the radically alienated Arthur, virtually everyone around him, whatever his or her class, is a potential enemy, making his life one of constant combat. He sums up this view at the end of the book: "And trouble for me it'll be, fighting every day until I die. Why do they make soldiers out of us when we're fighting up to the hilt as it is? Fighting with mothers and wives, landlords and gaffers, coppers, army, government. If it's not one thing it's another, part from the work we have to do and the way we spend our wages. There's bound to be trouble for me every day of my life, because trouble it's always been and always will be" (238–39).

Given this insight, Arthur actually approaches his life with relative good humor, despite his underlying bitterness and anger. He does not appear to realize that the antagonistic basis of social relationships in the society around him is the direct result of the capitalist system. His political insights are thus scattered and largely incoherent, though socialism and communism do circulate in the margins of the text as potential alternatives, so much so that Nigel Gray complains that Sillitoe's own political sympathies and insights (perhaps gained from his father, a Communist Party member) sometimes color Arthur's thoughts in unlikely ways (131–32). For example, Arthur admits early in the text that he voted (illegally since he was underage) for the communists in the last election, not because he supported their program but simply because he likes to root for the underdog and because they were at least different from the Tories whom he so despises. Similarly, Arthur has little sympathy for the barrage of anti-Soviet propaganda with which he is constantly bombarded in these Cold War years, finding the Soviet Union vaguely intriguing and musing to himself that if he is ever asked to fight in a war against the Russians he might be tempted to turn his gun against the powers that be in Britain instead (31–32).

Gray admits, however, that Sillitoe's presentation of Arthur's experience in the bicycle factory is impressive. Moreover, the brief hints toward political material that punctuate the text can just as easily be seen as an important enhancement of this presentation rather than a diversion from it, leading critics such as Ronald Dee Vaverka to see a commitment to leftist politics as the major strength of Sillitoe's writing. Indeed, Sillitoe's socialist sympathies become even more clear in some of his later work, leading David Craig to remark that "Communism" functions in his work "like an incantation," though Craig argues that Sillitoe fails to follow through on this incantation to present clear images of class struggle (109). While Gray finds Sillitoe in this book inferior as a literary craftsman to such writers as David Storey and Barry Hines, others have found *Saturday Night and Sunday Morning* technically impressive. For example, Peter Hitchcock views the book as an effective and complex mixture of a variety of discourses and as "an articulation of the strengths and dilemmas of the very possibility of a working-class fiction" (57). In any case, Sillitoe's first novel stands as one of the most important—and sophisticated—fictional explorations of working-class experience in postwar British culture. *Selected bibliography:* Atherton; David Craig ("Roots"); Nigel Gray; Hauge; Hitchcock (*Working-Class Fiction*); Paul (*Fire*); Penner; Vaverka.

ALAN SILLITOE: *A TREE ON FIRE* **(1967).** *A Tree on Fire* is the middle volume in a trilogy of novels that also includes *The Death of William Posters* (1965) and *The Flame of Life* (1974). The first volume begins in the Nottingham setting of Sillitoe's own working-class background and features a protagonist, Frank Dawley, who, at least initially, has a great deal in common with earlier Sillitoe protagonists such as Arthur Seaton of *Saturday Night and Sunday Morning*. However, Dawley gradually develops a greater political consciousness than any earlier Sillitoe protagonist, eventually leaving Nottingham (also leaving his job, wife, and children) to seek ways of becoming involved in the political questions that increasingly trouble him. Dawley goes to London, where he becomes romantically involved with Myra Bassingfield, the estranged wife of an English writer who is afterward killed in an attempt to run down both Myra and Frank in his car. Dawley and Myra go abroad together, eventually winding up in North Africa, where Frank decides to go with Shelley Jones, an American he meets on the trip, to deliver a load of arms to the National Liberation Front (FLN) guerrillas fighting against French colonial rule in Algeria. Myra, now pregnant, reminds behind in Tangier, hoping for Frank's quick return.

As *A Tree on Fire* begins, Dawley has decided to stay in Algeria to fight for the FLN. Myra, who has given birth to a boy, returns to England, realizing that Frank may not return soon, if ever. Back in England,

Myra meets Albert Handley, a successful artist who had been a close friend of Dawley. The remainder of the novel fluctuates between descriptions of events in England (centering on Handley and his large and colorful family) and a narration of Dawley's experiences in Algeria. The latter are vivid and convincing and are quite successful at capturing the physical hardships endured by Dawley and the other FLN guerrillas as they struggle against the inhospitable climate of the Algerian desert and the vastly superior military technology of the French colonial army against which they are battling for their independence. The Algerian sections are rich in thematic content as well, containing not only a detailed exploration of the continuing evolution of Dawley's political thought, but extending the range of Sillitoe's earlier fiction to encompass colonialism, while making clear the continuing vitality of the Left in the so-called Third World. Sillitoe's depiction of the struggles of the Algerian guerrillas against all odds gains a special energy from the knowledge that, by 1967 when *A Tree on Fire* was published, the French have in fact been driven from Algeria, which is now under the rule of the leftist Houari Boumedienne, the former head of the military wing of the FLN. Events in Algeria of the 1990s give this outcome a further, darker twist; nevertheless, the resultant implication that struggles for justice can, in fact, be won in the modern world is reinforced by the title of the book, which refers to Dawley's observation of a tree in the desert that survives being set afire by French napalm and begins to sprout new growth.

There is also a strong, if subtle, utopian dimension to the English portions of the book. For one thing, Handley is a figure of almost Rabelaisian vitality whose sympathies are fiercely anticapitalist, even if he remains skeptical of traditional oppositional political institutions such as the Communist Party. He therefore pursues his own form of subversion, such as investing the considerable income from his painting in corporate stocks, then donating the income from those investments to various groups who work in opposition to the capitalist system. Handley himself espouses the view that "revolution is the only remaining road of spiritual advance. . . . I don't mean the revolution of those middle-class English marxists who live in Hampstead or the juiciest of the Home Counties, because at the first sniff of civil strife they'd join the government militia or run to hide in the nearest police station. . . . What I'm talking about is the common quest for spiritual energy that you get from the idea of revolution" (313–34).

Handley's belief in revolution is not merely "spiritual," but leads to specific action. When his rambling home burns to the ground, he and his large family move, at Myra's invitation, to her large estate in Buckinghamshire. There, they are joined by Frank, who returns to England to work there for the FLN cause after injuries suffered in combat render him ineffective as a guerrilla fighter. The estate becomes an armed compound within which the Handleys, Frank, and Myra found a sort of utopian community, living according to their own principles while waging their own form of guerrilla warfare against various reactionary elements in the surrounding area. Of course, these subversive actions seem feeble compared to those of the FLN in Algeria, and one might even read this portion of the book as a parodic mockery of the ineffectuality of the British Left in comparison to the more vital leftist movements in the Third World. However, given Sillitoe's generally positive treatment of the Handley clan, it is probably best to read this motif as a suggestion that one can, in fact, seek to build a better world and to fight for justice even in the relatively sedate and conservative environment of postwar England.

The concluding volume of the trilogy, *The Flame of Life*, follows the efforts of Dawley, Handley, and Handley's sons to build a successful life in this utopian community. Much of this volume is rather abstract and theoretical as Sillitoe explores the various possibilities open to such a community. As a result, *The Flame of Life* is more overtly political than the earlier two volumes in the series, though all three are quite consistent in their political stance and in their thoughtful and sophisticated exploration of the opportunities for radical political action in Britain during the 1950s and 1960s, when sweeping revolutionary change no longer seems an immediate possibility. All three volumes are also remarkably successful at combining their public political content with vivid depictions of the thoughts, feelings, and experiences of specific individuals. Together, the volumes of the trilogy reaffirm Sillitoe's status as one of the leading literary spokesman of the British working class in the decades since World War II, while also representing a substantial increase in his scope as a novelist. Further, they maintain an anticapitalist stance, at least through 1974, despite Sillitoe's growing skepticism toward the possibilities of leftist political action through the 1970s. *Selected bibliography:* Atherton; David Craig ("Roots"); Penner.

JOHN SOMMERFIELD: *MAY DAY* (1936). *May Day* is an essentially utopian work that narrates events in London during the three days leading up to and including May 1, the International Workers' Day, in a "typical" year, presumably soon after the one in which the book was presented. The events of the book center on a series of strikes surrounding the holiday, including a busmen's strike that begins on the holiday itself. As such, the book is dominated by an increasingly powerful workers' movement, led by a Communist Party that is rapidly gaining in strength and influence at the expense of the more traditional and conservative trades unions. This hopeful projection, rather unusual even in the 1930s, helps to make *May Day* one of the most intriguing productions of British leftist culture in that crucial decade. The book combines extensive naturalistic detail (reminiscent of the documentary realism that became prominent in the 1930s) with experimental, essentially modernist, narrative techniques. It also presents a strong socialist message, in terms of both its subject matter and its attempt to go beyond the conventions of bourgeois fiction in a number of ways. Probably the most striking of these is the largely successful attempt to avoid the individualistic emphasis of the bourgeois novel by refusing to concentrate on a few individual characters and, instead, paralleling the experiences of dozens of characters in London during the three days covered by the book's actions. This technique makes the people of London, especially those who belong to the working class, a sort of collective protagonist.

May Day is probably more notable for its technique than its content, which is a relatively straightforward imaginative projection of a near-future London in which working-class collective action, coordinated by Communist Party leadership, becomes a formidable political force at last. The action covers numerous characters and settings but focuses to some extent on the workers and bosses in a single factory, Langfier's Carbon Works. Among other things, Sommerfield contrasts the impoverished and difficult lives of the mostly virtuous workers with the luxurious lives of their decadent bosses. Importantly, however, he treats the British capitalist system not as a fixed fact but as part of a dynamic historical process. Long owned by the Langfier family and still nominally owned and run by Sir Edwin Langfier, the Longfier Works, along with many other operations both in London and worldwide, are increasingly coming under the domination of Amalgamated Industrial Enterprises (AIE), a giant, predatory conglomeration that embodies the worst aspects of a British capitalism that is gradually drifting toward fascism. Langfier's works are now for all intents and purposes managed by William Dartry, a representation of AIE. Dartry has instituted a number of changes that greatly exacerbate the existing injustices of the factory system, forcing the workers to work more and more rapidly and under increasingly unsafe conditions. These changes lead to a series of accidents, culminating in a gruesome May Day incident in which a woman worker is scalped when her hair is caught in a machine. The workers refuse to continue under the current unsafe conditions and go out on strike, joining the striking busmen and the other marchers who are already demonstrating against capitalist exploitation in the streets of London. These events lead to violent clashes with the police in which one character, James Seton, is killed. But the marchers win the field, and the police are forced to withdraw. The marchers continue to the Marble Arch, bearing the body of the martyred Seton in a scene that clearly suggests their growing power, even as certain sinister elements conclude that these events will lead to the establishment of a fascist police state.

The central narrative technique of the book involves a sort of synchronization in which Sommerfield presents brief narrative segments centered on a single character or group of characters, then immediately shifts, using a variety of ingenious transitional devices, to another segment that shows the parallel activities of a different character or characters at the same moment. As such, the entire book is in many ways reminiscent of the "Wandering Rocks" chapter of James Joyce's *Ulysses*, which employs a similar technique of synchronization. Meanwhile, as Gustav Klaus notes, many aspects of the book's style and structure also recall the work of modernists such as John Dos Passos and (especially) Virginia Woolf (116–20). Klaus also notes that the fragmented style of the book might render it vulnerable to the criticisms leveled against modernist literature by Marxist critics such as Georg Lukács. Although Klaus concludes that Lukács's remarks are not relevant to Sommerfield's book because that book is not written in the tradition of bourgeois realism, this point does not address Lukács's real argument, which is that leftist literature should, in fact, draw upon the realist tradition. More to the point is the fact that the structure of Sommerfield's book, though seemingly fragmented, is actually designed to battle against fragmentation by indicating subtle connections between the activities of seemingly unrelated individuals in various parts of the city, which is itself presented as a complexly integrated totality. As Stuart Laing puts it, "Sommerfield is not interested in making the readers share any sense of isolation or disconnection that the characters may feel; this novel's task is to *reveal* the connections and relations" (149). This project is a difficult one, but Sommerfield achieves a certain amount of success, especially given that this attempt at connection is strongly reinforced by the content of the book, which continually emphasizes the need for and potential of collective working-class action. Laing is thus probably correct to conclude that "*May Day* is a novel which, in the context of its political perspective, deserves credit and attention for its answers to this problem" (158). **Selected bibliography:** Klaus (*Literature of Labour*); Laing ("Presenting"); David Smith (*Socialist Propaganda*).

CHRISTOPHER ST. JOHN SPRIGG: *THE CORPSE WITH THE SUNBURNED FACE* (1935). Writing under the name Christopher Caudwell (perhaps to negate the upper-class resonances of his given name) Christopher St. John Sprigg became one of the leading Marxist thinkers in Britain in the 1930s. In particular, with essays eventually collected in such as volumes as *Illusion and Reality* (1937), *Studies in a Dying Culture* (1938), and *Further Studies in a Dying Culture* (1949), Caudwell became one of the founding figures in the development of a genuine Marxist literary criticism in Britain. Though his career was cut short when he was killed in 1937 while fighting in the British Battalion of the International Brigade in the Spanish Civil War, Sprigg/Caudwell was a prolific writer who published several nonfiction books about science and aeronautics. He also published *This My Hand* (1936, a sort of anti-detective novel) under his adopted name and a number of successful detective novels under his given name. The latter include *Crime in Kensington* (1933, published in America as *Pass the Body*), *Fatality in Fleet Street* (1933), *The Perfect Alibi* (1934), *Death of an Airman* (1934), *Death of a Queen* (1935), *The Corpse with the Sunburned Face* (1935), and *The Six Queer Things* (1937). All are clever, ingenious, and entertaining, though they also address, in subtle ways, issues of importance to the British Left. Indeed, Urszula Tempska has argued that Sprigg's novels and Caudwell's criticism should not be viewed separately but as part of the same project—despite some of Caudwell's dismissive remarks about his own novels and detective novels in general. Tempska considers Sprigg's novels to be "proto-avant-garde experiments with an institutionalized, conservative genre" and describes them as "novels of considerable intellectual adroitness, formal insubordination, and a radical political program seemingly out of place in the staid genre of detective fiction" (126-27).

The Corpse with the Sunburned Face is an excellent example of Sprigg's detective fiction, though it does not involve Charles Venable, the detective who figures in the majority of Sprigg's novels. The basic plot is complex, but reasonably conventional. In fact, it resembles in many ways the plot of Wilkie Collins's *The Moonstone* (1868), which is often identified as the first detective novel. On the other hand, Sprigg's plot has just enough of an ironic twist to make it read almost like a parody of the traditional plots of formulaic detective fiction. The first part of the book is set in the conventional English village of Little Whippering, where a mysterious stranger, who gives his name as O'Leary, has moved to town two years earlier, taking up residence in a rented cottage and living there in total seclusion. As events proceed, a former associate of O'Leary's from their days in Africa comes to town to meet with him but is soon found dead in his hotel room, ostensibly by suicide. However, certain details of the case arouse the suspicions of Gregson, the local police investigator, especially when he questions O'Leary and finds him to be deeply tanned despite apparently never emerging from his house for the past two years. Gregson calls in Inspector Archibald Campbell of Scotland Yard for help in unraveling the clues. Campbell subsequently discovers some African treasures hidden on the premises of O'Leary's cottage, but when O'Leary himself is then found killed, the treasure has vanished.

Campbell, knowing that O'Leary and a man named Crumbles had been involved years earlier in the theft of some sacred treasures in the African kingdom of Balooma, puts two and two together when he realizes that Neptune Jones, an African studying law in London but recently living in Little Whippering, is, in fact, the Nga-ma-Nwama (a prince and sea god) of Balooma. He concludes that O'Leary murdered Crumbles and that Jones then murdered O'Leary in order to recover the treasure and take it back to Balooma. However, Campbell cannot prove his theory, and some questions remain unanswered. So he makes a trip to Balooma, where much of his theory is substantiated, except that the bodies have been misidentified. Crumbles, it turns out, was actually murdered in Africa by Tuffy Samson, a third figure involved in the earlier robbery. The body in the hotel was actually O'Leary's, while the body thought to be O'Leary's was actually Samson's. Campbell insists on bringing charges against Jones for the killing of Samson, even though he is warned by the colonial Chief Commissioner that such charges might provoke serious unrest in the colony. However, subsequent experiences give Campbell new appreciation for the importance of the stolen treasures to the culture of Balooma, and he eventually agrees to conceal Jones's involvement in the case, though this decision also causes him to feel that he must subsequently resign from Scotland Yard. The book ends as Campbell is offered the post of chief of police in the colony (an offer he neither accepts not rejects), while Campbell himself offers his hand in marriage to Virginia Ridge, an American anthropologist doing field work in Balooma. This offer is also neither rejected nor accepted in the text, thus leaving at least two loose ends of a kind that seem designed to poke fun at the neat closure typical of the traditional detective novel. This conventional closure is undermined even more radically by the fact that the "murderer" in this case is not brought to "justice"—and under circumstances that call into question the validity of conventional notions of the very concepts of murder and justice.

However, the real value of *The Corpse with the Sunburned Face* lies not in its play with the detective-story plot but in its treatment of a number of important issues, especially those relating to colonialism and colonial politics. Though the text itself occasionally seems to slip into Africanist stereotypes (understandable given the prevalence of such stereotypes in the 1930s), by and large the book functions as an extended challenge to the kind of stereotypes through which the British and other Europeans consistently portrayed Africans in negative and demeaning ways clearly designed to justify European colonial rule in Africa. *The Corpse with the Sunburned Face* thus differs dramatically from predecessors texts such as *The Moonstone*, which draws upon and reinforces Orientalist stereotypes about India and Indians. In addition to the respect that Campbell gains for African culture in the course of the book, Sprigg uses a number of motifs to deconstruct (often quite humorously) typical notions of the differences between Africa and England. In what functions among other things as a critique of conventional European anthropology as the study of primitive societies, the inhabitants of Little Whippering are shocked when the anthropologist Ridge comes to their town to study the local customs, much in the way she had earlier studied Africa. Meanwhile, Mr. Wykeham, the vicar in Little Whippering, is stunned when he travels to Balooma and finds the local people and customs there surprisingly similar to those he had encountered at home. In addition, the British Chief Commissioner for Balooma Territory, Colonel Max Wittington-Hopeful-Smythe, shows a sophisticated and enlightened attitude that allows him to argue, among other things, that the British society itself relies upon a number of superstitions and fetishes and thus does not differ from the society of Balooma as much as the British would like to think. All in all, *The Corpse with the Sunburned Face* is a text very much ahead of its time in terms of its critique of the ideology of colonialism, thus demonstrating the important way in which Sprigg's detective fiction subtly reinforced Caudwell's political project. **Selected bibliography:** Cunningham; Tempska; E. P. Thompson ("Christopher Caudwell").

OLAF STAPLEDON: *LAST AND FIRST MEN* **(1930).** The British philosopher Olaf Stapledon is widely regarded as one of the most important pioneers in the development of the genre of science fiction, and several of his imaginative works from the 1930s and 1940s are among the early classics of that genre. These classics include *Last and First Men* (1930), *Odd John* (1935), *Star Maker* (1937), and *Sirius* (1944). All are marked by a serious attempt to explore important ethical and philosophical issues through an imaginative projection of alternatives to the social and political context of Stapledon's contemporary world. On the other hand, they also remain firmly rooted in that world, addressing highly topical issues, such as the rise of fascism, in ways that show a profound concern with and understanding of those issues. And, while one might describe Stapledon's approach as being more philosophical than political, his work is informed by a consistent antipathy toward fascism, a belief that capitalism is on the wane, and a tendency toward socialist attitudes in the British tradition of H. G. Wells.

Last and First Men is a future history that begins with the world situation at the end of the 1920s, then follows it two billion years into the future until the human race is extinguished at last after proceeding on a grand journey through eighteen different species of humanity (with widely varying characteristics) and the development of numerous different civilizations on three different planets. The narrative is presumably projected backward by one of the last species of men in an attempt to communicate with the past and thus make a positive contribution to the evolution of humankind. It includes a complex combination of utopian and dystopian ideas. On the one hand, in Stapledon's future history there is an overall tendency toward gradual improvement in the race, and, in particular, toward the evolution of new forms of consciousness that are less individualistic and more group oriented. These developments lead to great achievements in culture and society. At the same time, human civilizations cyclically decline and perish, largely due to the inability of the race to adapt rapidly enough to changing conditions, but also due to the continuing recurrence of baser tendencies, such as nationalism and racism, already present in the late 1920s.

The first sections of the book, which trace the gradual decline of contemporary civilization after the rise to global dominance of a relatively valueless ultracapitalist America, seem almost prescient from the point of view of American global dominance at the end of the twentieth century. On the other hand, Stapledon makes clear in his preface to the book that he is not trying literally to predict the future, but simply to explore various ideas and possibilities through the motif of future history. These ideas, always informed by Stapledon's basic model of cyclical history, often focus on individualism vs. collectivism, with individualism (a major force behind the American hegemony projected early in the book) generally being treated as a cause of social decline and collectivism treated as the consequence of advances in society and in the human race. At the same time, Stapledon shows humanity repeatedly unable to sustain its peaks of collectivism, which tend to lead to stagnation and decline. Only the Last Men, now living on Neptune because of changing solar conditions, seem to have attained a level of civilization in which a genuine collective life is sustainable. But their civilization is cut short by a natural disaster in which the sun is finally destroyed, ending mankind's great journey.

This seemingly pessimistic ending is tempered, however, by the insistence of the last born of the Last Men that the career of humanity has been a beautiful one that must be judged, like a work of music, in its entirety and not just by its ending. There is even hope that the race might be reborn in that the Last Men have projected into the cosmos biological seeds from which the race might potentially evolve once again. More importantly, however, the cosmic view of *Last and First Men* is a grand one in which humanity is only one small, if significant, phenomenon in the overall scheme of things, a notion examined more extensively in the later *Star Maker*, which explores a number of other civilizations throughout the universe. **Selected bibliography:** Crossley; Fiedler; Goodheart; McCarthy; McCarthy, Elkins, and Greenberg; Curtis Smith.

OLAF STAPLEDON: *STAR MAKER* **(1937).** *Star Maker* is in many ways a sequel to Stapledon's earlier *Last and First Men* in that it extends the earlier book's exploration of the future history of the human race to an imaginative vision of the course of intelligent life throughout the cosmos. *Star Maker* is also a sequel in that it clearly shows the influence of the seven years that came between the two books, particularly in its awareness of the ominous rise of fascism in the 1930s. Like Stapledon's other imaginative works, *Star Maker* is a work of science fiction only in the broadest sense. That is, the book shows little interest in science or in the details of technological developments but instead concentrates on philosophical issues. The book thus begins as the narrator, an Englishman in the 1930s, suddenly ascends mentally into the heavens and discovers that he has inexplicably developed the capability of disembodied interstellar flight through both space and time. Stapledon provides no scientific explanation for this ability, which is nothing more than a device to allow the kind of mobility necessary to explore the ideas with which the book is concerned.

The narrator first travels to an earthlike planet where he spends an extended period observing and eventually making telepathic contact with the "Other Men," a race that resembles humans in many ways, including the fact that their society eventually decays into a form of fascism. The narrator makes especially close contact with Bvalltu, one of the Other Men who then accompanies him on his travels around the cosmos seeking out other civilizations. This premise allows Stapledon to explore a number of possibilities, as the narrator and his companion visit a wide variety of civilizations developed by a diverse array of intelligent species. Despite this diversity, however, the overall course of intelligent life generally follows the same basic cyclical pattern of rise and fall postulated by Stapledon with respect to human societies in *Last and First Men*. Stapledon provides an explanation for the consistency of this basic pattern by introducing the Star Maker, a sort of superintelligent being who is the elemental creative force that is behind all activity in the cosmos. Although this vision may appear religious, it is also the case that the Star Maker is neither loving nor benign relative to his creatures but merely curious, using their experiences to feed his own gradually increasing understanding.

As with *Last and First Men*, this vision of the universe appears to be fundamentally pessimistic, or at least to downplay the significance of humanity in the cosmos. However, as with the earlier book, *Star Maker* also has its utopian aspects. One of these involves a dream in which the narrator envisions the Star Maker's creation of the Ultimate Cosmos as the culmination of all of his learning through the eons. In the end, the book returns to its contemporary setting in England, as the narrator awakes to find that he is once again back on earth. There, he concludes that the insights gained from his recent travels suggest not that human activity is pointless and insignificant but that the fight for justice in the contemporary world is all the more important. In what is clearly a sort of Popular Front call for action against fascism, the narrator concludes that, in the light of all he has learned, "the human crisis does not lose but gains significance. Strange, but it seems more, not less, urgent to play some part in this struggle" (434). *Selected bibliography:* Crossley; Fiedler; McCarthy (Special Stapledon Issue); McCarthy (*"Star Maker"*); McCarthy, Elkins, and Greenberg.

DAVID STOREY: *PASMORE* **(1972).** The author of such works as *This Sporting Life* (1960), *Flight into Camden* (1960), *Radcliffe* (1963), *Pasmore* (1972), *Saville* (1976), and *Present Times* (1984), David Storey, son of a Yorkshire coal miner, is one of the leading British working-class novelists of the past few decades. He has been equally successful as a dramatist, authoring such plays as *The Restoration of Arnold Middleton* (1967), *In Celebration* (1969), *The Contractor* (1970), *The Changing Room* (1972), and *The March on Russia* (1989). Storey's work, although not in general openly political, nevertheless maintains a fairly consistent focus on the working class. Many of his characters are upwardly mobile individuals who move, or seek to move, beyond the working class. Such upward mobility, however, is not an unmixed blessing, and one of Storey's major themes is the psychic dislocation that occurs in characters whose mobility leaves them without a firm footing in any class and therefore without any stable sense of participation in a community.

Pasmore is one of the most straightforward examples of Storey's treatment of this motif of *déclassement*. It tells the story of a young man, Colin Pasmore, who is the son of a coal miner but who has managed to acquire enough education to become a college lecturer in history. As the book begins, Pasmore, nearly thirty, seems relatively settled in his job, in his home in suburban London, and in his family, which consists of his wife, Kay, and three young children. However, Pasmore has been feeling increasingly alienated from those around him and, though he is unable fully to articulate the source of his unhappiness, he experiences a growing sense of despair. It is clear to the reader, though not to Pasmore, that much of his difficulty comes from the fact that his upward mobility has alienated him from his working-class roots without allowing him truly to feel that he belongs to any other class. His problem is exacerbated by the fact that his family has placed so many of their hopes and dreams on his shoulders, leaving him with a sense that more is expected of him than he can possibly deliver. Seeking solace, he begins an affair with a slightly older woman whom he meets after she attends some of his evening lectures. The affair is oddly dispassionate and seems motivated, at least from Pasmore's point of view, as much by the fact that the woman is wealthy (and thus offers to him a new world of class experience) as by any sexual attraction that he feels for her. After feeling momentarily invigorated by the affair, Pasmore sinks back into despondency and decides to leave his wife, moving full-time into the flat he had rented for the assignations with Helen, his lover.

The affair with Helen ends soon after her wealthy husband learns of it and begins to make threatening gestures, including hiring a thug to beat Pasmore up on the street. Soon afterward, Pasmore visits his parents to inform them that he has left his wife. They react strongly, feeling that his irresponsible departure from his home violates the values that they have lived for all their lives. His mother, hurt, tries to be understanding, but his father is furious and castigates Pasmore for wasting all of the sacrifices that the family has made on his behalf. Pasmore returns to London and sinks into almost total inactivity, spending most of his time sitting alone on the bed in his flat, which becomes more and more squalid. When Kay overcomes the initial pain of his departure and begins an affair of her own, Pasmore is near hysteria. Finally, realizing that the separation from his family has made his alienation even worse, Pasmore asks Kay if he can come home. She agrees, and the family is reunited, though the root cause of Pasmore's unhappiness has not really been addressed. Indeed, the experience has separated him even more from the world of his parents, while still leaving him with no new world (or class) to which he feels he truly belongs.

Pasmore is a powerful exploration of the way the experience of *déclassement* can lead to psychic fragmentation in the individual. However, Pasmore's individual predicament is related to larger phenomena as well, his personal psychic dissolution paralleling his own sense that his entire society is experiencing an "era of disintegration" (20). The book thus recalls the descriptions of the postmodern experience as described by Marxist cultural critics such as Fredric Jameson. Indeed, Pasmore's experiences in the book recall Jameson's analyses of postmodernism in a number of ways in addition to the obvious way his psychic fragmentation corresponds to Jameson's identification of "schizophrenia" as the quintessential postmodern experience. For example, his lack of passion recalls Jameson's description of the "waning of affect" in the postmodern era, while his radical alienation recalls Jameson's comments on the difficulty of "cognitive mapping" in the postmodern world. Thus, while *Pasmore* is a relatively brief and straightforward exploration of the phenomenon of *déclassement* in modern British society, it still manages to address a number of important and complex issues. And, while the book does very little to suggest collective working-class action as a remedy for the ills of modern capitalist society, it does indicate that capitalism as a system does not lead to happiness, even for those who are successful. **Selected bibliography:** David Craig ("Storey's Vision"); Eagleton and Pierce; Fredric Jameson (*Postmodernism*).

DAVID STOREY: *SAVILLE* (1976). David Storey was awarded the 1976 Booker Prize for *Saville*, thus becoming the first working-class writer to win that prestigious honor. *Saville* is essentially a bildungsroman that deals with the growth and maturation of Colin Saville, a bright young working-class man who uses his intelligence and education to escape the pits in which his miner father works. As David Craig describes it, the book is "something like the complete history of the working-class child who changes class via schooling, told with the detailed lifelike fullness of classic naturalism" (134). As such, it participates in a long tradition of British working-class fiction that goes back at least to D. H. Lawrence's *Sons and Lovers*. However, Storey shows more respect for working-class life than does Lawrence, and it is clear that for him Saville's escape from the working-class is far from an unequivocal blessing. Indeed, Saville experiences a radical alienation that can be attributed largely to his estrangement from his family and their working-class culture, leaving him a man without a class. Or, as another character in the book puts it, he is "alienated from his class, and with nowhere to go" (439).

Saville actually begins well before the birth of its protagonist, detailing the arrival of his parents, Harry and Ellen Saville, with their first son, Andrew, in the mining village of Saxton in the late 1930s. Andrew dies suddenly from an illness at the age of three, with Ellen already pregnant with another child. That child, Colin, is born shortly before the outbreak of World War II, which provides the context for most of his early childhood. A good student, Colin is encouraged in his studies by his father, who is determined that his son will never work in the mines. Colin passes the examinations that allow him to go on to the grammar school in the nearby city, which he does, clad in his new uniform and filled with fear and anticipation. He works hard and becomes a successful student, despite suffering from class prejudice at the hands of some of the teachers. The war eventually ends, and the coal mines are nationalized, but Harry finds that the new system hardly makes life easier for the miners. Colin, who has had dreams of becoming a poet, is encouraged by one of this teachers to try to go on to the university, but he decides to opt for a briefer college education that will allow him to become a teacher and thus begin to earn a living as soon as possible.

By the time he finishes college, Colin has grown estranged from the boys he had known during his childhood in the village. He has also undertaken a series of unsuccessful courtships, including one that nearly led to marriage until his would-be financée, Margaret, dropped him in favor of Stafford, one of Colin's closest friends in grammar school. Class is very much at the center of this development. Margaret is the daughter of a medical doctor, and her middle-class view of Colin's background makes him much more intensely aware of the poverty of his home and his village. Stafford, meanwhile, is the son of a wealthy mill owner, and it is clear that his superior class position is a key factor in Margaret's attraction to him. Colin's two younger brothers show few signs of following in his footsteps, and, though Colin attempts to help them with their studies, it is clear that neither will make it to grammar school. Colin, in fact, feels that his parents are putting little pressure on his brothers to succeed and bitterly resents the fact that they had always put such pressure on him. At this point, however, Colin's father, worn out and diminished from years of work in the mines, simply lacks the energy to push his younger sons in the way he had pushed Colin. Indeed, the whole village seems to be wearing out and declining. The remainder of Colin's personal life continues to go badly as well, as he puts much of his energy into an ill-fated affair with Elizabeth Bennett, an older married woman. Nor is his professional life very fulfilling. Colin, still living at home, gets a job teaching English at a village school that caters to working-class students. However, he soon comes to realize that he is expected to teach his students to submit to their roles as members of a subaltern class rather than encourage them to aspire to something more. And his attempts to employ innovative teaching strategies win the disapproval of the headmaster, leading to a confrontation that ends in Colin's dismissal. The affair with Elizabeth eventually comes to an end as Colin decides to go to London to try to make a new start, both personally and professionally.

As Colin prepares to go, Elizabeth warns him that he is not likely to escape his troubles by moving to London, but that he will take the real source of his unhappiness with him. That source, as Elizabeth has pointed out earlier, is the *déclassement* that results from his alienation from his working-class roots, a problem that he is not likely easily to solve. Indeed, as Richard Hoggart has shown, this problem has haunted any number of British scholarship boys, whose educations have opened new professional vistas but have left them without a sense of genuine connection to any community or class. *Saville* is an important fictional exploration of this phenomenon that is relatively free of overt political statement; however, like Storey's *Pasmore*, it carefully places the alienation of its protagonist within the context of the kind of class-based society that is inevitably furthered by capitalism. **Selected bibliography:** David Craig ("Storey's Vision"); Hoggart; Pittock.

GWYN THOMAS: *ALL THINGS BETRAY THEE* (1949). Though published in 1949 and set in the 1830s, *All Things Betray Thee* grows directly out of the political climate of the 1930s. As Dai Smith outlines, the 1930s had a great formative influence on Thomas, despite the fact that he addresses the politics of the 1930s directly only in his first novel, *Sorrow for Thy Sons*, which was written in the 1930s but not published until 1986 (140–43). *Sorrow for Thy Sons* is a furious and impassioned indictment of the social system that brought about the intense suffering that characterized life in the Welsh mining and industrial regions in that decade. *All Things Betray Thee* is less furious, yet still firm in its suggestion of the evils of a capitalist system that makes bosses and owners rich while plunging workers into dire poverty, dehumanizing the latter and reducing them to the status of production machinery to be used and discarded at the convenience of those who own the means of production of which the workers are merely a part.

All Things Betray Thee is narrated in the first person by Alan Hugh Leigh, an itinerant harpist who comes to the newly industrialized town of Moonlea seeking his friend and old traveling companion, John Simon Adams, whom he hopes to convince to accompany him on his subsequent travels. Adams, however, is in no mood to leave, having established a love relationship with the Katherine Brier, despite the fact that she is married (to a childlike simpleton). More important, Adams has become involved as a leader of the workers of the town, who are struggling to adjust to a new way of life, having mostly moved to Moonlea in the past few years after earlier lives in the countryside. Not only is town life confining and restricting, but the workers, most of whom are employed at the local ironworks, find that they are ruthlessly exploited for the economic gain of their bosses. Soon after Leigh's arrival the growing tensions in the area explode in a region-wide rebellion of the workers against their treatment under this new system.

Richard Penbury, owner of the Moonlea ironworks, is a sensitive and rather sickly sort who takes to his bed as the rebellion erupts, leaving the dirty work of putting down the uprising to his henchman, Radcliffe, and Lord Plimmon, the local aristocrat. The loosely organized workers are no match for Plimmon and his well-armed yeomanry, and the rag-tag rebel armies are quickly defeated. In the meantime, both Leigh and Adams are arrested for the killing of one Bledgely, a hired thug who had earlier murdered one of the rebel leaders. Leigh is pardoned through the ministrations of Penbury, but Adams, as one of the rebel leaders, is condemned to hang. Leigh then leads a rebel force to Tudbury Castle to try to rescue his friends, but they arrive too late to prevent the hanging. Leigh is then given some money and a passage to America by Penbury's daughter, Helen, with whom Leigh has had a flirtation throughout his stay in Moonlea, but who is scheduled to wed Plimmon, thus sealing the alliance of the aristocracy and the bourgeoisie against the Moonlea workers. As the book closes, Moonlea is in ruins, much of it having been burned in the uprising. Leigh departs, looking back upon a Penbury mansion that is brightly lit in celebration of the victory over the workers. Nevertheless, there is a hint of optimism in the ending as the musician Leigh feels in his fingers "the promise of a new enormous music" that can be taken as the accompaniment to the birth of proletarian class consciousness in Britain (318).

All Things Betray Thee nicely illustrates Smith's point that Thomas's literary descriptions of Welsh working-class life, while striking for their presentation of the details of material deprivation among workers and their families, are powerful not because of the vividness of their depiction of everyday material life but because of the way they capture the intellectual life of the miners. Thomas, a poor child of the Welsh Rhondda who nevertheless received an elite education at Oxford and the University of Madrid, may have been particularly well suited for this task, which is an important one. Based on the real Merthyr Rising of that period, the book presents the social and political climate of the 1830s in convincing detail and in a language and style that convincingly captures the rhythms of Welsh life. It also resonates in its depiction of a growing class consciousness among workers with such accounts of working class history as E. P. Thompson's *The Making of the English Working Class*.

All Things Betray Thee not only captures the quality of working-class life in a time of dramatic historical transformation but also indicates the oppressive nature of these changes for many workers and the complicity between the British bourgeoisie and aristocracy against the workers amid these changes, a complicity that, as Tom Nairn has pointed out, was unique in nineteenth-century Europe. Indeed, the historical location of *All Things Betray Thee* makes it a work of particular interest, placing it at an early moment in the growth of capitalism, when vestiges of a former way of life are still within memory of the current generation. The book's suggestion of the sense of loss felt by this generation thus serves as a powerful reminder of the true nature of the history of capitalism, while its unusual ability to combine private experience with the sweeping events of history could serve as an important object lesson in leftist historical fiction. Thus, Raymond Williams finds it a powerfully "authentic" work not only in its presentation of the 1830s, but in its reminder of the continuing relevance of that historical moment to our own (ix-x). **Selected bibliography:** Nairn; Dai Smith (*Wales! Wales?*); E. P. Thompson (*Making*); Williams (Introduction).

GWYN THOMAS: *SORROW FOR THY SONS* (1986). *Sorrow for Thy Sons* is a powerful evocation of the impact of unemployment on a Welsh coal-mining community in the 1930s—so powerful, in fact, that it was unable to find a publisher when first completed in 1937. A reader for the Gollancz publishing house thus explained to Thomas that "some of the physical descriptions were so realistic as to produce actual nausea in the reader, but it is worth while to remember that, as your audience will be 99 per cent more or less tender-stomached, you will frighten them all away if you write in this fashion" (qtd. in Dai Smith, Introduction 8). The manuscript was then tucked away for decades, only to be rediscovered in 1983, two years after Thomas's death. It was finally published in 1986 and now stands as an important contribution to the literature of the Depression. Smith calls it "a central coping stone now restored to the canon of twentieth century Welsh literature and a 'genuinely proletarian novel'" (Introduction 9). Elsewhere, Smith argues that if this novel had been published and if Thomas had continued to write in this vein, "he would now be considered one of the major socialist writers in Britain this century" (*Wales* 143).

Sorrow for Thy Sons focuses on three brothers, Herbert, Alf, and Hugh Evans, all of whom live together in a small house left to them by their deceased parents. As the book begins in 1931, the closing of an important local coal pit has just led to Hugh's unemployment. The youngest, Alf, a promising student, is still in school, while Herbert remains employed as the manager of a local grocer's shop. Alf, accustomed to long hours of work, finds idleness oppressive and is especially resentful when Herbert suggests that he assume the role of housekeeper. He grudgingly takes on those duties nevertheless, while feeling more and more humiliated and dehumanized by the experience of unemployment and of relying on the public dole as his only source of income. Meanwhile, poverty prevents Alf from going through with a planned marriage with Gwyneth, his longtime love, though they are finally married late in the book as Gwyneth, stricken with a tuberculosis that is exacerbated by her long hours of work in a millinery shop, nears death. Alf's frustrations eventually lead him to assault the supervisor of the local Labor Exchange, and the book ends with him awaiting arrest for that action, having considered fleeing the valley but simply being too firmly rooted there to do so. In his last appearance in the text, he describes the impact of unemployment on the valley in a way that well summarizes the flavor of the text: "All around me I see chaps who wake up in the morning and find a little bit less in their lives than there was the day before. They're going grey and rotten. They are being sucked down into the earth before they've even found out the things they could do if they had the chance" (272).

Herbert is a figure of the petty bourgeois who has had just enough economic success to turn his back on his working-class origins. He admires his middle-class customers, who always pay promptly, and has nothing but contempt for the poor and unemployed who come into his shop and are unlikely to be able to pay their bills. Not surprisingly, tensions arise between Herbert and the other brothers, and by the end of the text he has asked them to move out so he can have the house for himself and the woman he plans to wed. Herbert, however, is not a villain so much as a victim of *déclassement*, or estrangement from his class, and the events that drive a wedge between himself and his brothers also separate him from any genuine sense of community within which to root his personal identity.

Déclassement is also an important motif in the experience of Hugh. In particular, Hugh's experiences at school dramatize the way in which the education system is designed to interpellate students safely within the confines of the liberal-humanist ideology of bourgeois England, as when they assemble to hear a guest speaker who warns the students against "troublemakers" who might agitate for strikes or other forms of opposition to the status quo. In short, they are taught to be loyal to the British system and not to the working class in which many of them have their roots. An important figure in this respect is Hugh's schoolmaster, a man who has himself turned his back on his working-class origins. As Hugh tells one of his fellow students, "'I've heard he comes from a family as poor as any of ours. You'd think that would make him kind of friendly to us, wouldn't you? Instead of that, he tries to fool himself into thinking that his family was the richest and the strongest in the land'" (117).

The schoolmaster is particularly harsh in his treatment of Hugh and Hugh's friend, Lloyd, both promising students who do not seem ideologically to be falling in line. Indeed, both Hugh and Lloyd go on to win scholarships that allow them to go to college, but both remain loyal to the working class—as did the Oxford-educated Thomas. Initially excited about the economic opportunities presumably opened to him by his education, Hugh soon finds that there are no such opportunities. Educated or not, he joins Alf in the ranks of the unemployed. His education does, however, help him to understand the unfolding events in a more sophisticated way. At the end of the book, Hugh leaves the valley by train in search of work elsewhere, but his loyalty to the valley's workers remains strong. In a letter of farewell to a woman with whom he has recently been having an affair, he describes the dehumanizing effects of unemployment and advises her, "Don't consider me a human being, capable of running luxury buses between the two distinct depots of good and bad. Mark me down as a historical force, a flesh and blood symbol of everything that unemployment is" (269).

Lloyd also becomes an important figure late in the text, where he acts as a sort of mentor to Hugh, who is beginning to be estranged from his class. In particular, Lloyd counsels his former classmate to stop worrying about the benefits he might reap from his education and start worrying about putting his education to work in the pursuit of social and economic justice (253). Lloyd also plays a central role in the massive demonstrations (based on the early 1935 marches against newly passed unemployment legislation that lowered unemployment benefits and instituted the means test) that mark the last part of the book. These demonstrations are broken up by police and seem to achieve little in the way of immediate effects, but the impressive solidarity shown by the demonstrators clearly provides a utopian suggestion of possibilities for the future. If Hugh declares himself an allegorical representative of the unemployed, Lloyd becomes an almost allegorical embodiment of the protest movement itself. Seriously injured when police attack the demonstrators, he is brought up on charges of rioting. As the book closes, he awaits trial, yet he sees Hugh off at the train station with a final statement of utopian optimism, assuring his departing friend that "'something great and glorious will rise from this shambles. Poverty, unemployment, Means Test, hovels, filth . . . those things are just manure for the harvests to come'" (274).

The focus on the three brothers (in addition to Lloyd) rather than a single character helps *Sorrow for Thy Sons* to escape the individualist orientation of the typical bourgeois novel. Indeed, the real "protagonist" of the book is not these four characters but unemployment itself and its tragic dehumanizing consequences for individuals whose identities have been shaped by the experience of work. Partly as a result of this collective focus, and partially because it does suggest the positive potential of collective action, the book is far more effective at describing the impact of unemployment from a genuine working-class perspective than are better-known novels on the same subject, such as Walter Greenwood's *Love on the Dole* or Walter Brierley's *Means-Test Man*. Smith's encapsulation of the novel in his introduction describes its overall impact well: "What it does . . . is to explore self-awareness, discuss choice, explain the necessary displacement from roots and certitude and community that "coal capitalism" entailed and then, moving beyond that . . . the novel declared [sic] its allegiance, in a unity of mind and heart, to the significance of a class experience and to the consciousness that comes, albeit like lightning flashes, with that class history" (9). ***Selected bibliography:*** Dai Smith (Introduction); Dai Smith (*Wales! Wales?*).

FRANK TILSLEY: *I'D DO IT AGAIN* **(1936).** Narrated in a lively, brisk, and entertaining style that is in many ways more reminiscent of American authors such as Dashiell Hammett and Ernest Hemingway than of most British fiction, *I'd Do It Again* tells the story of one year in the life of its narrator, a young British clerk. And it is an exciting year, indeed. Tired of dragging out a meager existence on his paltry wage of three pounds per week and feeling, because of his low income, increasingly inadequate as a husband to his dazzlingly beautiful wife, Helen, the narrator decides that he must do something to improve his life. When his request for an increase in his wage is categorically denied, he undertakes a series of minor embezzlements from his firm that allow him to increase his effective income to five pounds per week—just enough to buy Helen a few of the luxuries he thinks she deserves and, more importantly, to purchase a suburban home so that the couple can escape the noise and squalor of the lodgings in which they have been living.

This increase in their standard of living results in a dramatic improvement in their personal relations as well, as Helen gains a new respect and admiration for her husband now that he can provide such things for her. Indeed, Helen's avariciousness and her stated desire to be dominated by a strong and capable man combine with her treatment as a sexual object to represent an obvious weakness of Tilsley's book, though it is also the case that the problematic characterization of Helen is quite consistent with the narrator's Hemingway-Hammet hard-boiled style and potentially suggests a subtle critique of the individualist ideology that lies behind that style. The text is certainly dominated by its nameless narrator, whose perspective is the only one we see and whose activities, both personal and professional, form the entire substance of the plot.

The plot is compelling, as the narrator moves from one embezzlement strategy to the next, narrowly negotiating a series of near-misses that keep him on the verge of being discovered and, thus, of disaster. Meanwhile, the stuff of the plot allows Tilsley to address an important central theme: that the narrator's petty crimes are perfectly at place in a capitalist system that is little more than an organized method of theft. The narrator justifies his thefts on the basis of the fact that his firm employs shady and unscrupulous business practices to bilk its mail-order customers of their hard-earned cash—and that he, himself, is essentially being robbed by the firm because his labor is of much greater value than the low wages he receives. Much of the narrator's activity becomes a sort of personal contest between himself and Mr. Gaskell, the firm's managing director. This contest comments directly on the British class system. In particular, the narrator continually muses on the fact that he is just as talented and intelligent as his boss but has simply had fewer opportunities in life due to their different class origins.

In the final analysis, the narrator triumphs. At last he finds another job at a higher wage and gives notice to Gaskell that he is leaving the firm. Soon afterward, however, Gaskell offers him a raise and a promotion. In the end, the narrator stays with his original firm, with great prospects for future advancement. Meanwhile, his relationship with the now-pregnant Helen is better than ever. The narrator concludes at the end that the past year of crime has been the best year of his life and that he would gladly do it all again. In the British society of the 1930s, crime apparently does pay. Indeed, it would seem that only criminals have a chance to prosper under the conditions that obtain under modern capitalism. Tilsley makes this point well, though one could argue that his touch is a bit too light and his roguish narrator a bit too charming. All in all, however, *I'd Do It Again* is an excellent demonstration of the variety of modes and strategies that have been employed by British leftist novelists, especially during the 1930s, when the leftist novel flourished as never before. The novel, Tilsley's second, was in fact quite successful and spurred him to a highly productive writing career that included such works as the antifascist novel *Little Tin God* (1939). Tilsley remained a popular novelist through the 1950s, though his later work tends to be less oriented toward politics and more toward pure entertainment. *Selected bibliography:* Croft (*Red Letter Days*).

WILLIAM EDWARDS TIREBUCK: *MISS GRACE OF ALL SOULS* **(1895).** *Miss Grace of All Souls* details the everyday lives of the coal miners who live and work in the Yorkshire coal mining community of Brockerton-beyond-Brow. Gustav Klaus calls the book "the first closely observed and sympathetic view of a mining community in English fiction" (89–90). Similarly, Peter Keating calls it "the most important industrial novel to be published in England since *Hard Times*" and goes one to describe the book as "the most successful portrayal of industrial working-class life since *Mary Barton* (235). Tirebuck focuses on a single family, the Ockleshaws, but he clearly presents their experiences as typical of working-class families in this community, while this community is described as representative of mining communities all over England and Wales. He vividly describes the extreme hardships wrought on this family by poverty and clearly identifies class inequality as a major source of these hardships. In particular, Tirebuck parallels his depiction of the lives of the Ockleshaws with a description of the wealth and luxury in which the Brookster family, owners of most of the local mines, live. Indeed, much of the action of the novel revolves around a strike that is triggered when the family patriarch, Peter Brookster, cuts wages so low that the miners can no longer live off of their pay. Work in the mines therefore ceases, which suits Brookster perfectly because he has large existing stocks of coal that he can now sell off at higher prices. The miners persist valiantly in the strike (which is really more of a lock-out), even as they near starvation and even in the face of official persecution, as when soldiers are sent to the area to keep them in check.

To this extent, *Miss Grace of All Souls* closely resembles Émile Zola's *Germinal*, a book from which Tirebuck obviously drew considerable inspiration, as Ingrid von Rosenberg demonstrates. However, it is also important to recognize that Tirebuck's book is largely based on real historical events surrounding the great lock-out of 1893. Moreover, the book differs from Zola's in important ways. For example, Tirebuck provides very little in the way of details concerning the actual work of mining, nor does he engage in Zola's frank treatment of sexuality. More importantly, Tirebuck is considerably more optimistic than Zola in his treatment of his materials. Tirebuck's strikers are more successful and manage to get their wages restored to the former level—though only, of course, after Brookster has depleted his reserve of coal. For another, the Ockleshaws and the other members of their community are depicted with a considerable warmth and affection, and the vitality and solidarity with which they and the other families in Brockerton-beyond-Brow deal with adversity is impressive. *Miss Grace of All Souls* also includes a number of utopian gestures that indicate hope for the future. For example, the generations of the Ockleshaw men progressively move from old Dan, who passively accepts conditions as they are, to his son Ned, who rages against the system but without any theoretical understanding of it, to Ned's son Dan, a sort of organic intellectual whose reading helps him to gain an understanding of the forces aligned against the workers and of the strategies needed to oppose those forces and to begin to build a better (socialist) world.

The central utopian imagery of *Miss Grace of All Souls* (and the most obvious difference between Tirebuck's book and *Germinal*) involves the presence of Tirebuck's title character, Miss Grace Waide, daughter of the Reverend Egerton Waide, vicar of All Souls Church. Tirebuck shows Waide and the official Church as being entirely in complicity with the rich, causing Grace, whose sympathies lie entirely with the workers, to reject her father and his organized religion. In the course of the book, Grace, who has earlier rejected a marriage proposal from Harry Brookster, not only provides what support she can to the striking workers but falls in love with Sam Ockleshaw, leading to what Kiernan Ryan calls "a truly heroic marriage, which cuts across class divisions and convincingly prefigures the real human possibilities beyond them" (16). On the other hand, the depiction of the saintly Grace is rather idealized and participates in a constellation of images that tend to suggest that Tirebuck's vision of socialism is derived more from Christianity than from Marx. Indeed, von Rosenberg concludes that the final union between Grace and Sam "impairs the final political message of the novel by substituting a Christian dream of brotherhood of man for the socialist perspective" (168). It is certainly the case that the most positive character in *Miss Grace of All Souls* is not, herself, a member of the working classes. And, as Pamela Fox notes, the suggestion of Grace's innate superiority to working-class women is particularly problematic (121-22). Nevertheless, the book's sympathetic presentation of the lives of workers and their families is effective—and, for its time, unusual. **Selected bibliography:** Pamela Fox; Keating, (*Working Classes*); Klaus ("Strike Novel"); Ryan ("Citizens"); von Rosenberg ("French Naturalism").

RUTHVEN TODD: *OVER THE MOUNTAIN* (1939). Like many other works of British literature in the 1930s, *Over the Mountain* is primarily intended as a critique of fascism. The book is an absurdist dystopian fantasy that is somewhat reminiscent of the novels of Franz Kafka, though its closest literary relative is probably Rex Warner's *Wild Goose Chase*. Unfortunately, Todd's "Kafkaesque" satire lacks Kafka's subtlety and profundity and tends to spill over into caricature. Todd's book is unusually comic in its tone, presenting fascism as a ludicrous movement of degenerates made possible only by the inattention and inaction of ordinary people. This approach to criticizing fascism may be based on an insight expressed by one of Todd's characters, who notes that what the fascist regime in the book fears most is "being laughed at" (173). On the other hand, Todd does not treat fascism lightly, and his comedy has a definite dark side. While he mocks fascism throughout the book, by the end it is clear that the dystopian fascist dictatorship being described in the book symbolically exists not in some alien locale (i.e., Germany) but in the narrator's own country (i.e., England). Thus, while *Over the Mountain* depicts fascism as absurd and preposterous, it is also suggests that certain elements already present in British society make fascism a genuine threat there.

The protagonist and narrator, known through most of the book simply as Michael, is a young man who grows up in the village at the foot of a high mountain range that has never been successfully crossed. Even as a child he is fascinated by the unknown regions on the other side of the mountains, and he resolves to scale the peaks to discover those regions. When he becomes a young man he decides to make the attempt. After a difficult and arduous journey, he awakes on what he presumes to be the other side, in the home of a local clergyman who is helping to tend him. Unfortunately, Michael has almost entirely lost his memory of his own land, so he is unable to compare this new society to his own. He is greeted as an intrepid explorer and asked by the clergyman, Father Podmore, to make a speech in his church urging the congregation to obey authority and accept the status quo. Michael agrees to do so, but quickly realizes that Podmore is merely using religion as a tool to further the dystopian conditions that obtain in this strange land. So Michael instead begins to deliver a subversive speech urging the people to take action against oppression. This speech is soon interrupted by the secret police, but Michael manages to escape, largely because the police are entirely incompetent. He then spends much of the rest of the book in hiding from the authorities with the help of the local Reds. In the process, he learns a great deal about the fascist regime that rules in this land via an extensive system of police agents who are mostly mental defectives. He also encounters numerous inhabitants of the land whose apathy and selfishness have made the current condition of the country a possibility.

As Michael explores this strange land, there are numerous hints that it is, in fact, his own homeland. For example, he comes upon several books that he has read before and hears music with which he is familiar. In the end, he again attempts to scale the peak to return to his home, only again to wind up at Father Podmore's. This time, Michael realizes that Podmore is his own father and that he has never left his own land. By this time, however, the revelation is not especially surprising, thus decreasing the effect. In fact, as David Smith notes, the impact of the book is consistently diminished by the crudeness and simplicity of the satire—

and by the fact that the underground resistance movement in the book seems almost as absurd as the fascist regime they are resisting (101). In addition, a great deal of the text is devoted to the description of various scenes, hallucinations, and adventures that really have very little to do with Todd's satirical point. The book cannot be judged a success, though its project is certainly an important one. *Selected bibliography:* Croft (*Red Letter* Days); David Smith (*Socialist Propaganda*).

JEFF TORRINGTON: *THE DEVIL'S CAROUSEL* (1996). *The Devil's Carousel*, Torrington's second novel, followed the earlier *Swing Hammer Swing!* to help place him in the leading ranks of the numerous innovative working-class writers in contemporary Scotland. Torrington's work, like that of James Kelman, derives a great deal of linguistic energy from the working-class speech of Glasgow. However, Torrington's work relies more on verbal effects than does Kelman's. Torrington has, in fact, sometimes been compared to James Joyce in his effective use of experimental language. At the same time, Torrington's work remains strongly rooted in Glaswegian working-class experience. *The Devil's Carousel*, which is set in a fictional Glasgow automobile plant, nicely illustrates this combination of innovative style with everyday working-class content.

The Devil's Carousel has only a minimal plot, which involves growing rumors that the American-owned Centaur Company may be in financial trouble and culminates in the shut-down of the company's Glasgow plant so that the work can be transferred to a plant in Spain, where the workers lack the effective union organization of the workers at the Scottish plant. Meanwhile, most of the book consists of a series of vignettes that are essentially character sketches, presented in a highly comic, informal style, of the various colorful people who work in the plant. One of the most striking of these figures is Curly Brogan, a powerfully odiferous, but highly effective, shop steward who is eventually fired for faking his own death in order to get time off from work to attend his son's wedding. Another is Alf Sheridan, a foreman and religious fanatic, who eventually commits suicide after his daughter becomes a pornographic model whose pictures are among those that adorn the inspection booth manned by Jack Boag, a connoisseur of such photographs. Other colorful figures include "Laurel and Hardy," a pair of door-handle fitters who are among the plant's leading practical jokers; Midge Stacey, a four-foot-high forklift operator with a legendary giant penis; Twitcher Haskins, a retiring security chief much given to birdwatching; Ratzo Runciman, the plant exterminator who stocks the premises with live cockroaches and rats to increase his job security; and "The Human Sardine," the most gung-ho of the plant's senior shop stewards.

Each of the sketches that, together, make up the main text is followed by an intercalary insertion that consists of an issue from the plant's badly typed, but highly irreverent, underground newspaper, KIKBAK, published by a group known as the "Laffing Anarkists." These brief issues consist of poems and short vignettes that are written in an extremely sarcastic style that provides the book's most striking examples of the use of Glasgow demotic as a source of innovative literary language. In general, these insertions are related to the main text in only the most oblique of ways, though occasionally the connection is more direct, as when issue 105 announces Curly Brogan's return from death. All in all, the main segments and the KIKBAK segments reinforce each other in more subtle ways, combining to produce an effective overall picture of life in the plant from a variety of perspectives, ranging from that of the lowliest of assembly-line workers to that of the plant's top-ranking managers, or "Martians."

The Devil's Carousel is an impressive demonstration that an automobile plant can, in fact, provide an effective setting for literary fiction and that the workers in an automobile plant can provide the basis for interesting and entertaining literary characters. The book also demonstrates the effectiveness of working-class speech as a source of linguistic innovation of the kind normally associated with the generally more elitist texts of literary modernism. Meanwhile, the book suggests that the attempts of the Centaur Car Company to increase its profits through the unfair exploitation of workers are part of a larger systemic phenomenon, as when new employee Steve Laker concludes that "to give credence to the preposterous notion that there was such a thing as a humane car plant was only a step away from accepting the tyrant's claim that his regime was a benign one because at executions his firing squads always fixed silencers to their weapons" (17). On the other hand, Torrington does not approach the relations between management and workers in the plant within anything like a coherent political framework. Indeed, the book's own political perspective seems to be somewhat aligned with the "laffing anarkism" of KIKBAK, a position that the narrator acknowledges to have been judged irresponsible by the plant's "Marxists, Trots, and Maoists, not to mention a scattering of lesser lefties" (212). The problematic political position of the book can probably best be seen in its suggestion that the plant's effective unionization, while leading to certain benefits for the workers, also leads to unemployment for all of the plant's workers. In short, workers without effective union representation are exploited by their employers; workers with such representation are replaced by workers without it. Granted, this motif is not inconsistent with the traditional Marxist argument that labor organization needs to be international in order to be effective or with recent analysis by Marxist thinkers, such as Ernest Mandel and Fredric Jameson, of the global nature of "late capitalism." But Torrington does not really make this point, stopping instead at the mere suggestion, without real comment, that capitalism is growing increasingly global at the end of the twentieth century, thus making relations between labor and management all the more complicated. *The Devil's Carousel* is an effective and innnovative fictional representation of working-class experience, but it does little to suggest potential remedies to any of the problems it describes. **Selected bibliography:** Fredric Jameson (*Postmodernism*); Mandel.

JEFF TORRINGTON: *SWING HAMMER SWING!* **(1992).** *Swing Hammer Swing!*, reportedly the product of almost thirty years of work, was Torrington's first novel. It immediately established him as a major figure on the Glasgow literary scene, winning considerable critical praise as well as the 1992 Whitbread Book of the Year award in Britain. The book is a lively and highly comic account of several days in the life of narrator Tom Clay, a lovably irresponsible antihero. Clay, a striking creation whose characterization one might suspect to derive a great deal from Torrington himself, is an unemployed denizen of the slums of 1960s Glasgow with aspirations to be a novelist. The distinctive working-class rhythms of his voice dominate the book, as do his irreverent attitudes toward all forms of official authority in modern British society. There is, however, a dark side to the book, which is set in the Gorbals section of Glasgow, where Clay has lived all his life but which is now being demolished in the interest of urban renewal. Clay and his wife are among the last inhabitants of the tenement in which they live and are being pressured by the authorities to remove to "Castlemilk," a new high-rise housing complex. Indeed, the contrast between the somehow lively squalor of the dark and decaying Gorbals and the shiny, but sterile and inhuman newness of Castlemilk is a major symbol of the book, as the fiercely independent Clay battles not only against this particular move but against the regimentation and routinization that modern society seeks to impose on his life as a whole. The destruction of the Gorbals, while treated in some ways as an inevitable consequence of modernization, is also treated as an example of the destruction of working-class neighborhoods by a society that essentially has nothing but contempt for working-class culture.

Swing Hammer Swing! is a sort of modern picaresque tale that has very little in the way of plot, though it is chock full of events, most of them darkly absurd, as when Matt Lucas, the chief projectionist at the Planet Cinema, is struck down by a car while wandering about Glasgow in a mummy costume to promote a current feature at the fading theater. Clay himself, in a discussion of his own writing practice, explains that "plots are for graveyards," preferring instead to base his work on ideas (162). And Clay, well read despite having little formal education, has plenty of ideas. A would-be novelist, he has read widely in the classics of world literature, and his narration is liberally sprinkled with allusions to an eclectic collection of authors that includes Walt Whitman, Leo Tolstoy, Miguel de Unamuno, Samuel Beckett, George Orwell, and Norman Mailer. Clay is also an amateur devotee of philosophy, meditating throughout the book on the meaning of human existence while contemplating the ideas of such thinkers as Plato, Berkeley, Pascal, Nietzsche, Bergson, and Sartre. On the other hand, Clay's down-to-earth perspective deflates the pretentiousness of conventional philosophy. His own attitude is a sort of comic proletarian existentialism, as when he explains the meaning of life: "A helluva thing is existence: a wee splutter of light, that's all there is to it. You learn to eat; where to shit; what your given name is. You're made to take a job and to live by the rigours of its working conditions; then, one day, usually when you don't expect it—they drop a coalmine on your head. Finito" (298).

Clay's irreverent attitude toward both literature and philosophy is centrally informed by his strong sense of himself as a member of the working class. Both the style and the content of his narration are avowedly working class and therefore antiauthoritarian, given his own firm belief that the discourses of authority in modern Britain, and especially Scotland, are oriented toward the exploitation of the working class in the interest of its bourgeois masters. This consistent sense of class perspective is, in fact, the strongest aspect of the book. On the other hand, Clay's class consciousness is seriously compromised by his radical individualism. Thus, though he has some sense of common cause with the various other colorful working-class characters described in the book, he is essentially a loner. He has numerous acquaintances, but no real friends. Throughout the book, his wife, Rhona, is in a maternity hosptial due to complications in her first pregnancy, leaving Clay to inhabit their seedy flat alone. His periodic visits to Rhona, whose family looks down on him as a deadbeat and loser, show little in the way of intimacy between them. Indeed, Clay's only "intimate" relationship in the book consists of an overnight sexual marathon with the passionate Becky McQuade—to whom he identifies himself as Matt Lucas in order to avoid too much involvement and to evade her jealous and violent truck driver husband. In the end, it is not surprising that Clay conceives the idea of emigrating to Australia to escape the conditions around him. One suspects, of course, that this plan would never actually be carried out. And, even if it were, Clay would discover that the modernization and routinization he seeks to escape in Scotland have come to Australia as well.

As an exploration of the postmodern predicament, which is defined here as a seemingly paradoxical combination of regimentation and disorientation, from a distinctively working-class perspective, *Swing Hammer Swing!* is a highly effective work. Torrington nicely illustrates the literary possibilities of the working-class dialect of Glasgow while also presenting, through Clay, a convincing argument that working-class individuals are perfectly capable of the kinds of sophisticated thought typically associated in British literature with bourgeois characters. Meanwhile, Clay is also capable (as most bourgeois characters are not) of seeing through the pretensions of bourgeois discourse. He is not, however, capable of conceiving of collective working-class action to improve the sordid conditions that he finds around him, which he seems to accept as an inevitable consequence of ongoing modernization. His only solution is to escape, but, within the context of global late capitalism, there is nowhere left to go. *Selected bibliography:* Fredric Jameson (*Postmodernism*).

ROBERT TRESSELL: *THE RAGGED TROUSERED PHILANTHROPISTS* **(1914).** *The Ragged Trousered Philanthropists* is one of the founding texts of modern British working-class fiction and is still considered one of the most important examples of the genre. The book is particularly striking for its vivid depiction of British working-class life, made all the more effective by the fact that Tressell himself, an Irish-born house painter whose real name was Robert Noonan, had experienced such life first hand. Indeed, Brian Mayne calls the book "the first realistic novel of working-class life by a member of the working classes" (73). And Tressell's own working-class perspective comes through not only at the level of content (though he clearly knows more about the actual experiences of workers than do most novelists), but also in the form and style of his book. As Raymond Williams argues, "there is no finer representation, anywhere in English writing, of a certain rough-edged, mocking, give-and-take conversation between workmen and mates" (254). Moreover, as Wim Neetens points out, *The Ragged Trousered Philanthropists* engages in an extended subversive dialogue with the tradition of bourgeois fiction, succeeding in negating "the dictates of the literary market place by being intelligent without being trivial, oppositional without being marginal, instructive without being patronising or dull" (88). According to Neetens, the book is thus an excellent "example of how through constructing for itself unorthodox cultural conditions a text may become a vital part of a popular political consciousness on the side of the opposition" (81).

Or, as Raymond Williams puts it, in *The Ragged Trousered Philanthropists*, Tressell sought to break "with precisely the inherited assumptions of what it was to write a novel, and to write a good, competent novel" (242). Tressell's most important violation of the accepted decorum of the bourgeois novel, of course, is to make his work an avowedly political tract. David Smith stresses the fact that *The Ragged Trousered Philanthropists* is "fundamentally a work of propaganda" (28). He notes that Tressell draws upon a wide variety of socialist thinkers in the development of his own political vision and argues that "part of his appeal lies in his very unsectarian willingness to borrow from various strands of Socialist ideology" (28). But Smith also insists that the book is "both a masterpiece of polemic and also an extremely good novel" (30). And Smith is right to conclude that the real power of the book lies in its vivid (and sympathetic, though not idealized) evocation of the lives of British workers. These workers, Smith notes, come alive in both their "comic and tragic aspects," and their experience is related with a dignity and to an extent unrivaled in works such as those of Charles Kingsley, Benjamin Disraeli, and Charles Dickens, who occasionally show the horrors of sweatshops and factories, but who represent workers themselves in little or no detail and who establish no organic connection between workers and their work (33).

Given the strong prejudice against political statement in literature that has long informed the tradition of bourgeois aesthetics, it is perhaps a wonder that Tressell's book has survived at all. Indeed, the continued survival and even popularity of Tressell's text, despite the fact that it has seldom received serious critical attention from scholars in the official academy, is a remarkable story in itself. The informal dissemination of information about Tressell's book—and of the book itself—is itself one of the most interesting phenomena in the modern history of British working-class culture. The textual history of the book is interesting as well. First published in a greatly condensed version three years after Tressell's death, the book was reissued in an even shorter "abridged" edition in 1918. It was not published in a full edition (based on Tressell's handwritten manuscript, newly rediscovered in 1946) until 1955 by Lawrence and Wishart, largely through the efforts of their editor, F. C. Ball, whose own book, *One of the Damned*, provides a number of details concerning the publication history of *The Ragged Trousered Philanthropists* and the life of the rather mysterious Tressell. Since that time, the reputation and popularity of the book have constantly grown, even during the dark years of the Cold War, when conditions were hardly advantageous.

Tressell's own preface to the book begins by stating that his intention in writing it was "to present, in the form of an interesting story, a faithful picture of working-class life—more especially of those engaged in the Building trades—in a small town in the south of England" (11). *The Ragged Trousered Philanthropists* succeeds admirably in this task. It relates in great detail the lives of building-trades workers, especially house painters, in the fictional town of Mugsborough, including their experiences on the job, in their private homes with their families, and in various public activities in their community. But the book goes beyond mere representation of everyday life among workers to develop a detailed and systematic theoretical explanation for why their lives are the way they are. As Tressell goes on to state in his preface, "I wished to describe the relations existing between the workmen and their employers, the attitude and feelings of these two classes towards each other" (11). The book succeeds in this task as well, in the process presenting both a sweeping indictment of the capitalist system and a sort of beginning course on socialism as a potential alternative. In doing so, the book addresses a number of important social and political issues that have remained fundamental to British working-class fiction ever since.

As a book written about workers by a worker who comes home from his job every day to do his writing, *The Ragged Trousered Philanthropists* presents the process of work as a craft and as a social interaction with an immediacy that is unsurpassed in any literary representation of the working class. However, Williams points out that the book gains its unique power from the fact that Tressell is writing from a perspective that is very much within the working class and simultaneously outside a typical working-class position, given Tressell's wide reading and experience. Tressell is thus able to undergird his representation of working-class life with a sophisticated theoretical framework. For example, his workers are skilled craftsmen who take pride in doing a good job, but they are constantly pressured to do slipshod work so that their endlessly greedy bosses can make higher profits. The book thus suggests the tendency of capitalism to devalue genuine craftsmanship and to reduce the real quality of life in the interest of purely economic advancement. In addition, the insatiable thirst for profit that drives the capitalist system reduces the workers themselves to profit-making tools, treated not as human beings, but as commodities, ruthlessly exploited on the job and often unemployed (with little in the way of social services) when business is slow.

The protagonist, Frank Owen, is a highly intelligent, self-educated sign painter who provides the central point of view from which Tressell observes the complex workings of the capitalist system. Owen observes abundance of production all around him, while he and his fellow workers live in abysmal poverty: "he saw that the people who enjoyed abundance of the things that are made by work, were the people who did Nothing: and that the others, who lived in want or died of hunger, were the people who worked" (16). Such observations run throughout the book and are reinforced with detailed introductory explications of socialist theory, centered in the two great teaching chapters, "The Oblong" and "The Great Oration," which, together, serve as a sort of introduction to socialism, helping to make the book, as Peter Miles puts it, "a self-contained kit for the dissemination of ideas" (10).

Much of *The Ragged Trousered Philanthropists*, meanwhile, is devoted to a depiction of the cultural practices by which the capitalist system maintains its hegemony by blinding the workers to their own exploitation. Religion, for example, comes in for particular criticism as an opiate of the masses in a way that recalls Marx's famous observation, but that also resembles the diagnoses of religion as a mind-numbing force that appear in the works of Tressell contemporaries such as James Joyce and Arnold Bennett. Where Tressell differs from these writers in his clear understanding of the participation of religion in a class-oriented economic system. One working-class character, for example, observes, "As for all this religious business, it's just a money-making dodge. It's the parson's trade, just the same as painting is ours, only there's no work attached to it and the pay's a bloody sight better than ours is" (153). Similarly, in a way that anticipates later Marxist thinkers such as Max Horkheimer and Theodor Adorno, Tressell identifies popular culture, in the form of devices such as the *Daily Obscurer* newspaper, as a major factor in the workers' lack of understanding of the true nature of the capitalist system and of their antagonism toward socialism as an alien force supposedly contrary to their interests.

Tressell's book attempts to engage these cultural forces head-on and to provide an alternative cultural voice, both as a cultural artifact in its own right and in the ways Owen and his fellow socialist, Barrington, attempt to counter the hegemony of bourgeois ideology by winning their fellow workers over to their ideas through extended rational argumentation. The difficulty of these efforts is indicated in the title itself, which refers to the way that most of the workers in the book, despite their own conditions of poverty and deprivation, are willing to work so diligently in order to support their rich bosses, who do little or no real work at all. Indeed, Tressell's depiction of the ignorance and stubbornness with which most of his workers continue to support the existing system comes very close to the depiction of workers as "irredeemably incapable of improving their conditions" that is often found in reactionary literature (Williams 249).

But Tressell successfully negotiates this pitfall by building into his book a profound respect for workers and their work. He also lightens his criticism of them with a liberal dose of humor. Thus, Smith, placing the book in a number of literary traditions, notes that it particularly recalls the English humorous tradition of Fielding, Swift, Shaw, Wells, and especially Dickens (36). Ronald Paul, meanwhile, notes how the book participates in an early-twentieth-century surge in leftist fiction from around the world, but that it stands apart from the works of contemporaries such as Gorky, Nexö, and Jack London in its effective use of humor (247). Tressell's humor, sometimes bitingly sarcastic, sometimes warmly affectionate, is in fact one of characteristics of *The Ragged Trousered Philanthropists* that has made the text so popular for so long.

Despite its sometimes pessimistic-sounding presentation of the difficulty of convincing workers of the value of socialism, *The Ragged Trousered Philanthropists* maintains a consistent underlying tone of optimism. As the book ends, Owen, sick with tuberculosis and in desperate need of money, is suddenly saved when Barrington (who turns out to be a rich man who has been working just to observe working-class conditions) supplies him with the needed cash. Sudden changes for the better, this motif seems to say, are possible. And the book then ends on a note of utopian optimism, anticipating the coming triumph of socialism as "the light that will shine upon the world wide Fatherland and illumine the gilded domes and glittering pinnacles of the beautiful cities of the future, where men shall dwell together in true brotherhood and goodwill and joy. The Golden Light that will be diffused throughout all the happy world from the rays of the risen sun of Socialism" (630). *Selected bibliography:* Ball; Pamela Fox; Mayne; Miles; Mitchell (*Robert Tressell*); Neetens; Paul ("Tressell"); David Smith (*Socialist Propaganda*); Williams (*Writing*).

EDWARD UPWARD: *JOURNEY TO THE BORDER* (1938). *Journey to the Border* is a brief, allegorical tale that relates the alienation of a young intellectual, "the tutor," from his upper-class employers and his eventual conversion to socialism as the only way to improve the conditions by which he is so appalled. Most of the book concerns the tutor's trip to the races with his employer, Parkin, a pretentious snob with nothing but contempt for the working classes. Here, surrounded by a bourgeois extravaganza that suggests not only the ultimate of inauthenticity of bourgeois life but the complicity of this life with forces such as colonialism and fascism, the tutor undergoes a number of surreal hallucinations as he attempts to come to grips with his growing alienation from the injustice and hypocrisy of the world around him. On the verge of suicide or insanity, he is saved when a voice advises him to join the Internationalist Movement for Working-Class Power. This suggestion gives his life a direction and a purpose and therefore stabilizes his mind. At the end of the novel, the tutor refuses to return home with Parkin and instead sets out on foot for a nearby town where he hopes to get in touch with the Internationalist Movement.

While John Lehmann has called this ending "extraordinarily lame," it should be remembered that the point is allegorical and should not be taken in a literal sense (57). Though its surreal technique might prove confusing to some readers, the major point of *Journey to the Border*—that socialism is the only solution to the insanity of capitalism—is quite clear. As Peter Widdowson puts it, the book narrates "a journey to the border of insanity, beyond which lies the sanity of commitment to Marxism" (145). Indeed, the book is an avowedly didactic work that is in many ways a companion piece to Upward's essay "Sketch for a Marxist Interpretation of Literature" in C. Day Lewis's collection *The Mind in Chains* (1937). In this essay, Upward vigorously argues that intellectuals must reject the lure of the bourgeois life and work to bring about fundamental change through support of the proletarian class struggle. Unfortunately, *Journey to the Border* seems to need this essay as a supplement. It merely posits socialism as a solution and does not present a convincing explanation of why this is the case. Indeed, the book leaves open the possibility that some readers might read the ending call to socialism as simply another in the tutor's sequence of hallucinations. Nevertheless, while lacking convincing arguments for the efficacy of socialism (and failing to represent working-class struggle in any direct way), Upward's book is an interesting and effective exploration of the dilemma of the intellectual trapped within a bourgeois society in which he does not believe. *Selected bibliography:* Lehmann; C. Day Lewis; David Smith (*Socialist Propaganda*); Widdowson.

EDWARD UPWARD: *THE SPIRAL ASCENT* (1962-77). *The Spiral Ascent* is the collective title for a trilogy of works consisting of *In the Thirties* (1962), *The Rotten Elements* (1969), and *No Home but the Struggle* (1977). Written by one of the major figures of British leftist culture from the 1930s, the trilogy is a retrospective fictional treatment of Upward's own attempts to reconcile his political commitment with his literary ambitions within the context of the rise of British leftist culture in the 1930s and its decline in prominence from World War II onward. The protagonist of the trilogy is Alan Sebrill, who resembles Upward both in his middle-class origins and in his commitment to leftist political action. Sebrill is a poet and teacher who begins as an enthusiastic young Marxist in the first volume, grows into middle age (and growing disillusion) in the second, and reaches a sort of resolution in his old age in the third, realizing at last that his political commitment and poetic creation need not be at odds but should be part of the same project. Together, these volumes provide a firsthand account of a number of important (and vexing) issues in the history of leftist culture in modern Britain.

In the first volume, Sebrill concludes that his desire to live a "poetic life" cannot be fulfilled under capitalism and that to achieve this life he must join the political struggle to build socialism and, thus, a society more amenable to poetry. He joins the Communist Party (as did Upward) and works for its goals, meanwhile pursuing his ambition to be a poet and working as a teacher at Condell's Secondary School, just as Upward spent many years working at Alleyn's School. Through Upward's description of Sebrill's activities and observations, *In the Thirties* provides an important document of the troubled, but often optimistic, political life of the 1930s. *The Rotten Elements* then moves to the postwar period, drawing upon Upward's own sense of political isolation after his resignation from the Party on the grounds that it had abandoned its commitment to revolutionary Marxist-Leninist ideas in favor of a more politically expedient reformism. Sebrill, much like Upward, is so torn by his conflicts with the Party that he becomes unable to write and literally falls ill. At the end of the book, however, he resolves to resume the writing of poetry with a renewed energy and a restored commitment to making a contribution to the kinds of revolutionary change for which he believes the Party should be working. *No Home but the Struggle* begins with Sebrill living in a quiet home on the Isle of Wight, having retired from teaching. He remains politically active, though outside the Party. For example, it now being the 1960s, he spends a considerable amount of effort protesting against the war in Vietnam. But most of his time and energy is now devoted to his poetry, in particular to the writing of a long autobiographical poem that in many ways parallels the trilogy itself. He struggles mightily with the composition of this poem, but finally completes it as the volume draws to a close, having reached the recognition that his true home has always been within the struggle for justice itself, and not necessarily within the Communist Party. Meanwhile, he remains dedicated to his poetry as well but realizes that the "poetic life" need not conflict with his political activism and that the struggle must remain at the heart of his poetry: "I shall make my main contribution to the struggle in the way I am best fitted to make it, through poetic creation.... I now know that the only way I can bring poetic vitality into the poetry I want to write in future is by writing it to serve the political struggle" (293).

Sebrill thus presumably achieves a dialectical synthesis that overcomes the opposition between poetry and politics that has long troubled him, and the suggestion that the political and the poetic need not be at odds is a valuable one. On the other hand, it is not at all clear that Sebrill (or Upward) really overcomes the aestheticist tendencies that mark his own attitude toward art as being fundamentally bourgeois. For example, the intense focus on Sebrill as the protagonist of the trilogy (the third volume even shifts to first-person narration) suggests a tendency toward individualism and subjectivism. In addition, it is not at all clear how "the struggle" can possibly succeed without the leadership and direction of a well-organized group such as the Party. Nevertheless, *The Spiral Ascent* is a unique document of British leftist culture that provides an intelligent discussion of important aesthetic issues as well as valuable details about the history of the British Left from the 1930s to the 1960s. ***Selected bibliography:*** Arblaster; Munton and Young.

REX WARNER: *THE WILD GOOSE CHASE* **(1937).** *The Wild Goose Chase* is a long allegorical fantasy involving a search for a utopian future in a surreal world threatened with total domination by sinister and oppressive political forces. As such, it comments in a fairly obvious way upon the political climate of the 1930s, in which economic depression created tremendous hardships in the bourgeois societies of the West, while the looming threat of fascism created a growing sense of political crisis. Malcolm Bradbury describes the book as a "'fable' of ethical and existential quest, filled with strong scenes, flavoured with the spirit of Marx and Freud, influenced by Kafka" (234). However, the book's political (and specifically Marxist) inclinations are surely more dominant than Bradbury here indicates, as Peter Widdowson suggests in his description of the book as a "vigorous and self-confident fable of revolution" (146).

The Wild Goose Chase begins as three brothers set out by bicycle on a journey to a distant "frontier" where they hope to find the "wild goose," the book's central symbol of utopian hopes for a better future. These brothers include Rudolph (an adventurous athlete), David (an intellectual), and George (an ordinary man). In the course of the book, Rudolph has numerous colorful adventures, none of which really further the quest for the wild goose, thus suggesting the inefficacy of the kind of swashbuckling individualism that he represents. David, on the other hand, reaches the ominous dystopian city that lies across the frontier, but is there appropriated by the powers that be and goes to work in the "Convent," a sort of official think tank in which artists and intellectuals can pursue their work in complete isolation from social reality, thus assuring that they will do nothing to challenge the power of the fascistic regime that rules both the city and the surrounding countryside.

George, on the other hand, remains true to the quest, despite the numerous obstacles he encounters along the way. Refusing the lure of the Convent and ignoring the advice of the musician Bob (an embodiment of bourgeois popular culture) George becomes intimately involved with a revolutionary movement that is centered in a village under the essentially colonial domination of the evil city. George and the revolutionaries eventually storm the walls of the city, the defenses of which turn out to be far weaker than they appear. This assault this quickly turns into a successful workers' revolution that topples the city's government (represented by a series of absurd "kings") and establishes a government of the masses. George describes the new order in a triumphant speech near the end of the book, as a symbolic flock of wild geese fly overhead: "What our old leaders most respected we chiefly despise — the frantic assertion of an ego, do-nothings, the over-cleanly, deliberate love making, literary critics, moral philosophers, ball-room dancing, pictures of sunsets, money, the police; and to what they used to despise we attach great value — to comradeship, and to profane love, to hard work, honesty, the sight of the sun, reverence for those who have helped us, animals, flesh and blood" (440).

In short, the new order represents a complete rejection of bourgeois values, of which fascism was merely an extreme case, and an endorsement of the principles of socialism. Moreover, in keeping with the dynamic nature of socialism, this new utopia is open ended. George still faces more adventures as the book closes, while the new regime still faces important challenges, as symbolized by the fact that the generals of the old regime look at George "with an odd expression in their eyes and their mouths smiling" in the last sentence of the book (442).

Though the emphasis on collective action in *The Wild Goose Chase* is clear, Widdowson is probably correct to argue that the book foreshadows Warner's later turn to a more liberal-humanist perspective in novels such as *The Professor* (1938) and *The Aerodrome* (1941). Noting the central role played in the text by the heroic George, Widdowson concludes that "despite the materialist conception of history which the fable proposes, the book inclines to a form of romantic individualism" (147). Meanwhile, David Smith notes that *The Wild Goose Chase* is unnecessarily repetitive and that there is much about the book that is "facile and hastily worked out." Nevertheless, he also agrees that "its overall construction, especially the concept of the Wild Goose itself, still remains striking and distinctive. Various of its episodes ... also remain absorbing and effective to a degree" (95). For all its strengths, however, Smith concludes that "it emerges as a book of potential rather than realisation, of scattered fragments rather than one successful, integrated whole" (96). This sense of fragmentation may be an inevitable result of the book's surrealist method, and one could argue that the abstract and allegorical nature of the book is itself inimical to the effective representation of the material forces of history. Nevertheless, the book is in many ways powerful, especially in its depiction of the disengaged intellectuals of the Convent, whiling away their time in decadent and self-indulgent pursuits while the society around them crumbles into chaos. The main value of the book, in fact, is as a call to bourgeois intellectuals to drop such pursuits and give their support to revolutionary working-class action. **Selected bibliography:** Bradbury; David Smith (*Socialist Propaganda*); Widdowson.

SYLVIA TOWNSEND WARNER: *AFTER THE DEATH OF DON JUAN* **(1938).** Sylvia Townsend Warner, a committed communist who remained loyal to the Party well into the 1950s, was one of the leading leftist women writers in Britain in the 1920s and 1930s. Of her numerous novels, *After the Death of Don Juan* is one of the most clearly communist in its political stance. The book, though set in an eighteenth-century Spanish village, is a fable of class conflict that is clearly meant to refer to the Civil War raging in Spain at the time the book was written. In an often quoted statement, Warner herself described the book in a letter to Nancy Cunard as "a parable if you like the word, or an allegory ... of the political chemistry of Spain, with the Don Juan—more of Molière than of Mozart—developing as the Fascist of the Piece" (*Selected Letters* 51).

After the Death of Don Juan is loosely based on the well-known Don Juan legend and begins with a prologue that briefly details that legend. The book itself then features such familiar characters from the legend as the roguish libertine, Don Juan; his servant and sidekick, Leporello; and Doña Ana, the latest object of Don Juan's lustful manipulations. The book opens after Don Juan has presumably been killed by the father of Doña Ana, the virtuous virgin whom Don Juan has attempted to seduce (or rape). Doña Ana, meanwhile, has just married the army officer Ottavio but insists on honeymooning in Tenorio Viejo, the distant native village of Don Juan, to whom she is still devoted. There, she brings the news of Don Juan's death to his father, Don Saturno, who is less than crushed by the loss of his rather troublesome son, partly because he is not convinced that Juan is actually dead.

Much of the novel centers on Don Saturno's relationship with the local peasants, for whom he has some feeling and whom he hopes to help via his interest in modern (especially scientific) ideas. Of course, Don Saturno also exploits the peasants, living in great wealth off the fruits of their labor, while they live in great poverty. His various well-meaning schemes for reform generally tend to make the lives of the peasants worse, rather than better. One project that does seem promising is his plan to irrigate the local lands, a plan that has a genuine chance to succeed, especially given the increased resources available with the extravagant spendthrift Don Juan out of the picture. Unfortunately, this project is so promising that Juan, who is not dead but merely in hiding, reappears to try to take advantage of the increased opportunities for profit offered by the possibility of irrigation. The peasants rebel, surrounding and besieging the castle in which Don Juan resides. He nevertheless manages to get a message to a nearby army detachment, which sends soldiers to put down the revolt. The poorly armed rebel army of peasants fights bravely but is no match for the well-equipped soldiers, who massacre them.

This confrontation obviously foreshadows the Spanish Civil War of the 1930s. Indeed, as Janet Montefiore points out, the imagery of the last scenes directly reflects W. H. Auden's poem *Spain 1937* (158). On the other hand, despite the allegorical nature of *After the Death of Don Juan* and despite the fact that the plot is largely based on legend rather than historical fact, the book is a genuine historical novel that is filled with period details that richly evoke the eighteenth-century setting. The presentation of such details was, in fact, one of Warner's major strengths as a writer throughout her career. Moreover, the connections between the events described in the book and those occurring in Spain in the 1930s are established more through general thematic parallels than through specific one-to-one correspondences, so that the eighteenth-century narrative stands on its own, even without allegorical interpretation. The book's characters are vividly drawn as individuals, but never dominate the text as in bourgeois individualist narratives.

As Wendy Mulford notes, Warner resembled other Marxist writers of the period in her attempt to make society as a whole, rather than individuals, her protagonist (x). The characters, especially the peasants, are more important as members of a group rather than as individuals. Moreover, most of them bear clear (though often double) allegorical meanings. Thus, Don Juan represents the traditional political and economic oppression of the Spanish peasantry, first by the aristocracy, then later by fascism. The sacristan Don Gil, probably the book's most evil character, represents the traditional ideological oppression of the peasantry by the Catholic Church, long in league with the aristocracy and then, in the 1930s, with fascism. Don Saturno, meanwhile, represents a gesture toward modernity in his opposition to such forces of oppression, though through the ineffectual means of liberal reform. More radical (and potentially more successful) change in the pursuit of justice and modernization is represented in the person of the peasant leader Ramon, a sort of proto-Marxist organic intellectual. Thus, the book's characters are both richly realized as individuals and representative of larger social forces, much in the manner of the typical characters described by Georg Lukács.

Warner also does a good job of working her political message into the narrative in an effective and organic way. Thus, as Montefiore notes, "the political perceptions are not tacked on to the narrative by means of authorial commentary or 'abstract' anachronistic dialogues, but grow, as Lukács required, out of the peasants' own life and work" (160). Meanwhile, Warner presents her narrative in an engaging fashion, detailing her dark allegory of the roots of Spanish fascism in a mode that is often informed by wry irony, even farce. The book is also sometimes self-consciously literary, pointing with good humor to its own obvious fictionality. Montefiore argues, however, that this fictionality enhances, rather than weakens the political message of the book (162). In any case, despite the frequent use of humor and self-consiously literary devices, *After the Death of Don Juan* is always serious in its passionate concern for the Spanish peasants it so vividly evokes and in its rage at the failure of Western democracies to take action to end the fascist takeover of Spain. **Selected bibliography:** Montefiore; Mulford; Warner (*Selected Letters*).

SYLVIA TOWNSEND WARNER: *SUMMER WILL SHOW* (1936). *Summer Will Show* centers on the revolution of 1848 in Paris, which provides the background for the gradual awakening of revolutionary consciousness in its heroine, a wealthy British women who begins the book with no interest in politics and nothing but a snobbish disdain for the working classes. However, Sophia Willoughby is, from the beginning, a rather unconventional woman of her time and her class. By 1847 she has already decided to live apart from her husband and to bring up her two children on her family estate without his help. And this sense of independence from masculine support stays with her throughout the novel, which centers at least as much on issues related to gender as ones related to class. On the other hand, the Marxist inclination of the book is clear, and Sophia's conversion to revolutionary politics becomes complete only at the end of the book as she discovers an underground copy of the recently published *Communist Manifesto* and begins to read it with fascinated absorption.

As Andy Croft puts it, *Summer Will Show* "opens like a historical novel, turns into a radical appropriation of romantic conventions and ends with all the breathlessness of a thriller. It is probably Sylvia Townsend Warner's strongest work, a lesbian re-working of the revolutionary tradition and a personal statement about political faith" (215). The book begins as both of Sophia's children die of smallpox, after which she resolves to have another child with her husband, Frederick, despite their estrangement. She then travels to Paris, where Frederick has been living with his mistress, Minna Lemuel, a Jewish actress. There, Sophia hopes to convince Frederick to impregnate her, though she by this time has nothing but contempt for him and his mistress. The relationship between Frederick and Minna soon dissolves, however, and Sophia soon finds herself befriending her husband's former mistress. Sophia and Minna end up growing close and living together in poverty after Frederick, jealous of Sophia's new involvement with Minna, manages to gain control of all of her assets and to cut her off without a penny. Meanwhile, momentous events are afoot in Paris as the revolution, part of the revolutionary wave that would sweep across Europe in that year, drives King Louis-Philippe from the throne and leaves several provisional governments vying for power. These revolutionary events do a great deal to open Sophia's eyes to the injustices that have long been suffered by the poorer members of society, as does the experience of living in poverty herself. But it is her friendship with the leftist Minna, who has long lived in poverty and whose parents were murdered by Christian zealots in her childhood, that does the most to transform Sophia's consciousness. This transformation is as much sexual as political, and the book pays a great deal of attention to Sophia's feelings of sexual liberation after she breaks off her involvement with Frederick once and for all and begins instead a relationship with Minna. And, while this relationship is never explicitly described as sexual, its lesbian undertones (emphasized in a recent study by Terry Castle) are unmistakable.

Sophia becomes directly involved in revolutionary activity when she agrees to collect scrap metal for a group of communists who need it to make ammunition for the upcoming battles in the streets. She also agrees to deliver several packets of subversive pamphlets for Josquin Ingelbrecht, a leftist intellectual she has met through Minna. In the end, Minna is killed while helping to defend a barricade in the streets from reactionary troops attempting to restore "order." Sophia is arrested in that same battle, then imprisoned among a group of revolutionaries who are earmarked for execution. Most of the prisoners are executed, but Sophia is freed because she is a woman and from an upper-class background. Afterward, the revolution suppressed, she returns to the room she had shared with Minna and opens the last remaining packet from Ingelbrecht, finding that it contains *The Communist Manifesto*.

Upon its publication, *Summer Will Show* was praised by Jack Lindsay as a good example of the almost unlimited potential of the historical novel as a mode of expression of leftist ideas. Janet Montefiore agrees, treating the book as one of the leading examples of leftist historical novels in the 1930s. In particular, Montefiore, though noting the important lesbian resonances of the novel, points out the crucial importance of Marxism to the text, arguing that *The Communist Manifesto* is not simply tacked on at the end but is an integral part of the book's many intertextual dialogues. Further, she insists that to read the book only as a parable of feminine desire is mistakenly to ignore its Marxist politics and its powerful engagement with history (176–77). She also notes the timeliness of the book in the 1930s, arguing that, despite its setting in 1848, it serves as a statement against fascism that joins many other more overtly antifascist texts of the period. **Selected bibliography:** Brothers; Castle; Croft (*Red Letter Days*); Foster; Maslen; Montefiore; David Smith (*Socialist Propaganda*).

KEITH WATERHOUSE: *BILLY LIAR* (1959). *Billy Liar*, which was adapted by Waterhouse, in collaboration with Willis Hall, into the screenplay for a successful 1963 film of the same title, is probably one of the best-known works of post–World War II British fiction dealing with working-class experience. However, like much of this fiction, *Billy Liar* is more concerned with attempts to rise from the working class into the middle class than with working-class experience under capitalism or on the presentation of specific political and economic alternatives to capitalism. Thus, the protagonist, Billy Fisher, is concerned not with the improvement of working-class life through collective political action, but simply with improving his own life through escaping from the working class altogether. And Billy apparently has a good chance of succeeding, given that his own father has already risen from working-class origins to the ownership of his own haulage firm. Billy, however, is uninterested in joining the family business, especially as he finds his family a key source of the very oppression that he seeks to escape through fantasy. Indeed, the oppositions perceived by Billy as central to his society are generally based more on age than class, and he feels oppressed not by members of the bourgeoisie but by his parents and other elders, who simply cannot understand his youthful dreams. Nevertheless, the book contains a number of implied criticisms of British class society. Billy's fantasies, while directly stimulated by the culture in which he lives, are largely unrealizable in that culture, which is therefore presented as dishonest. Meanwhile, this dishonesty has a specific political function, serving to divert the energies of talented and imaginative members of the working class from political action to personal fantasy.

Waterhouse explores Billy's predicament largely through a comic exploration of the disjunction between Billy's inner dreams and his outer reality, much in the mode of James Thurber's classic story "The Secret Life of Walter Mitty." The book begins as Billy lies in his bed in the dismal Yorkshire town of Stradhoughton contemplating a future that will take him away from his dingy surroundings and his boring job as a clerk for a local undertaker, the comical Mr. Shadrack. In particular, Billy has high hopes of wealth and fame under the bright lights of London, perhaps as a scriptwriter for comedian Danny Boon. Meanwhile, Billy also dreams of sexual adventure and romance that will take him beyond his current engagement to the unalluring Barbara, and much of the action of the book deals with Billy's comic attempts to seduce other women, including Rita, a sexy waitress, and Liz, a woman whose frumpy appearance disguises a passionate nature and a secret life of sexual intrigue. Unfortunately, Billy's attempts at seduction, considerably hampered by his own tendency to drift off into fantasy, lead only to comic misadventures, though with dark undertones that suggest the fundamental alienation of Billy from his surroundings and from other people.

Billy's hope of a new job in London (or, preferably, of becoming the much-adored ruler of the mythical realm of Ambrosia) also comes to naught. As the book ends, Billy waits at the station for a train to London, then retreats when the train arrives and returns to his life of tedium in Stradhoughton, realizing that his dreams of success in London are unlikely to come about. Ambrosia may be a utopia, but it is not a utopia that can be reached from Stradhoughton via the train or any other means that Billy finds at his disposal. He retreats from a potential marriage to Liz as well, and, by the end of the book, Billy is in very much the same predicament as at the beginning. His dreams of blowing away all of his enemies with an "Ambrosian repeater gun" are replaced with an acceptance of the fact that there is little he can do to eliminate the restrictions and limitations that govern his life. The suggestion that he is trapped in this life, however active his imagination, thus makes a powerful statement about the myth of opportunity and upward mobility with which bourgeois society has long justified its class structure with the argument that those who deserve to rise will do so, while those who remain in the lower classes do so because of their fundamental inferiority. Meanwhile, Billy's treatment of the women in his life as fantasy objects rather than human beings makes a comment about the general reification of social relations under capitalism and about the way in which dreams of upward mobility encourage individual ambition but discourage the treatment of other individuals as human beings with the same feelings and needs as oneself. *Selected bibliography:* Paul (*Fire*).

H. G. WELLS: *TONO-BUNGAY* **(1909).** Though now best remembered (especially in the popular imagination) for science-fiction works such as *The Time Machine* and *The Island of Dr. Moreau*, H. G. Wells also wrote many other works, including a number of novels that directly addressed social conditions and problems in the England of his day. Of these latter novels, *Tono-Bungay* is probably the most important. *Tono-Bungay* is, in a sense, the culmination of all of Wells's early works, and it includes elements of all of the other genres in which he worked. As John Hammond puts it, *Tono-Bungay* combines all the different aspects of Wells's career, and in it "the humorist, the sociologist, the scientific romancer, the prophet, the novelist—fuse together in a narrative of compelling richness and power" (41). On the other hand, the book has been criticized by some as lacking unity because of its generic multiplicity and its diverse array of materials. In this sense, Arnold Kettle's characterization of the book as an example of Wells's "incurably slapdash, slip-shod method of composition," is a typical critical response (91). All in all, however, most contemporary critics seem to agree with David Lodge that *Tono-Bungay* is an important "condition of England" novel that shows Wells at the height of his powers as a novelist. While noting that Wells's novel violates most of the conventions of the well-made novel as put forth by Henry James, Lodge suggests that these violations are largely intentional and at least partially motivated by a mimetic desire to reflect the confusion and complexity of life in Edwardian England: "I suggest that if we read *Tono-Bungay* with an open mind, with attention to its language, to the passages where that language becomes most charged with imaginative energy, we shall find that it is an impressive, and certainly coherent, work of art" (111).

Tono-Bungay is structured as a bildungsroman that tells the story of the life of George Ponderevo, its narrator. It begins with his early childhood as the son of a housekeeper at genteel Bladesover House, which George views (at the time) as a sort of microcosm of Victorian society. At age fourteen, however, George is banished from the estate after he gets into a fight with another boy, Archie Garvell, the cousin of the estate's owner, Lady Drew. Expelled from the ostensibly Edenic Bladesover, George then begins to learn that there is far more to the world than he had realized. He eventually goes to live with his uncle Teddy Ponderevo, who is in many ways the major character of the remainder of the novel. Teddy at the time is running a small apothecary shop in the rural village of Wimblehurst, hoping to strike it rich via various schemes for the marketing of patent medicines. George is thus introduced to the world of commerce, about which he learns more and more as he follows Teddy from an initial failure that leads to bankruptcy and the loss of his shop on through the eventual development of a burgeoning empire built upon the success of "Tono-Bungay," a worthless, but highly marketable patent medicine. The empire grows rapidly, and Teddy becomes an increasingly important and powerful man of business until his business suddenly collapses and he loses everything, sinks into bankruptcy, and dies in miserable surroundings after fleeing with George to Spain to escape arrest.

We also follow George's personal affairs, particularly his highly unsatisfactory love life, which George himself identifies as emblematic of life in the modern world: "Love, like everything else in this immense process of social disorganization in which we live, is a thing adrift, a fruitless thing broken away from its connexions" (338). Indeed, it is this kind of careful connection between the private lives of George and Teddy and the public events that surround them that makes *Tono-Bungay* an important political novel. As Lodge puts it, "The organizing principle of *Tono-Bungay* is to be found in the web of description and commentary by which all the proliferating events and characters of the story are placed in a comprehensive political, social, and historical perspective" (115).

Decline and decay are the central metaphors of *Tono-Bungay*, and those phenomena lie at the heart of George's description of Edwardian society. In one of his numerous commentaries on his own text, George, late in the book, sums up his diagnosis of England as "a feudal scheme overtaken by fatty degeneration and stupendous accidents of hypertrophy" (350). Thus, George concludes that the refined and genteel order he had observed at Bladesover in his youth was merely a veneer hiding the realities of ruthless competition for wealth under modern capitalism. While modern England may continue to attempt to cloak itself in the robes and finery of aristocratic tradition, for George the "realities are greedy trade, base profit-seeking, bold advertisement—and kingship and chivalry, spite of this wearing of treasured robes, are ... dead " (348). Bladesover itself, in fact, becomes an image of this transition when George visits there again late in his life only to find it much diminished in relation to his memory, now owned by a family of rich Jewish entrepreneurs who lack even the pretence of traditional aristocratic dignity. The change, for George (possibly reflecting a certain amount of antisemitism, but mostly reflecting skepticism toward the commodification of everything under capitalism), is not an improvement: "There was no effect of a beneficial replacement of passive unintelligent people by active intelligent ones. One felt that a smaller but more enterprising and intensely undignified variety of stupidity had replaced the large dullness of the old gentry, and that was all" (55).

From a leftist perspective, it is the critique of capitalism as a historical phenomenon that is the most important aspect of *Tono-Bungay*. The Tono-Bungay patent medicine is itself the quintessential capitalist commodity. Endowed with a tremendous amount of exchange value, it has no use value whatsoever. George describes the workings of the Tono-Bungay empire in terms that obviously refer to capitalism in general: "We sold our stuff and got the money, and spent the money honestly in lies and clamour to sell more stuff" (134). Thus, the rise of Teddy Ponderevo, based largely on deceit and illusion, becomes an image of capitalism itself. As George puts it, "all this present commercial civilization is no more than my poor uncle's career writ large" (198). Meanwhile, Teddy, echoing the description of capitalism in *The Communist Manifesto*, cannot be content with past successes, but continues to strive for more until he finally overextends his operations and causes the collapse of his entire empire. And Teddy's fall from the heights suggests both the fundamental instability of capitalism and the ultimate lack of security for all individuals under the capitalist system, again recalling the famous diagnosis in *The Communist Manifesto* of capitalism as an insubstantial system under which "all that is solid melts into air" (Marx and Engels 476).

Tono-Bungay also echoes *The Communist Manifesto* in its clear suggestion of the centrality of colonialism and global expansion to the operations of capitalism. As is often the case in British fiction, the colonies continually lurk in the margins of the text as a potential source of wealth. Yet, they also remain a locus of fantasy and romance, despite their very real economic importance. Thus, George notes in relation to the colonial world that "the places of origin of half the raw material of the goods we sold had seemed to us as remote as fairyland or the forest of Arden" (202). Meanwhile, Teddy demonstrates a typical British (and capitalist) sense that the ingenuity and enterprise of the British make them the rightful rulers of their empire: "There's the millions over seas, hundreds of millions, Chinee, M'rocco, Africa generally, 'Merica. . . . Well, here we are with power, with leisure, picked out—because we've been energetic, because we've seized opportunities, because we've made things hum when other people have waited for them to hum" (235). He thus envisions London generally, and his business particularly, as the center of a vast interrelated network that stretches around the world (235). Given this insight, it is not surprising that one of George's major capitalist undertakings involves a trip to Mordet Island, off the coast of Africa, to salvage a huge deposit of the radioactive substance "quap" and thus to save Uncle Teddy's failing business.

On the other hand, although the indictment of capitalism in *Tono-Bungay* is both bitter and insightful, Wells ultimately fails to suggest a viable alternative. While socialism is a constant presence in the margins of the text (many characters, including George, express an occasional sympathy with socialist ideas), the socialism suggested by *Tono-Bungay* is more the Fabian than the Marxist variety. Moreover, capitalism is analyzed in the text not as a system of exploitation of one class by another, but merely as a symptom of universal social decay. The book presents an entirely top-down view of capitalism, and if Uncle Teddy's ultimate failure nicely illustrates the vicissitudes of capitalism, it is also true that Teddy, though described as "modern species of brigand" is presented in a relatively sympathetic light. He is as much a victim of large historical forces as a victimizer of his own numerous customers and employees. Indeed, the latter, though the source of Teddy's wealth, have virtually no presence in the book at all. Thus, Arnold Kettle complains that the rather snobbish George, though the son of a servant, seems "incapable of looking at the poor . . . except with contempt as a species almost sub-human" (95). The only genuinely utopian potential in the book lies not in proletarian revolution, but in a rather elitist vision of science and technology, as when George concludes that scientific truth is "the one reality I have found in this strange disorder of existence" (249). *Tono-Bungay* thus illustrates Christopher Caudwell's conclusion that all of Wells's writing is ultimately hampered by the author's inability to transcend his own petty-bourgeois class perspective, but the book nevertheless stands as an important analysis of turn-of-the-century capitalism and of the early rise of capitalist consumer culture. ***Selected bibliography:*** Caudwell; Hammond; Herbert; Kettle; Lodge; Marx and Engels (*Reader*); Sommers.

JAMES WELSH: *THE UNDERWORLD* (1920). *The Underworld* was the first of three novels by Welsh, a former Scottish coal miner and candidate for Parliament (on the ticket of the Independent Labour Party), who had earlier published a volume of poetry, *Songs of a Miner* (1917). Welsh thus became one of the leading working-class writers of the 1920s, making him, as David Smith puts it, something of a "link between Tressell and the proletarian novelists of the 1930s" (42). On the other hand, as Gustav Klaus points out, Welsh's three novels tend to drift gradually to the right in their political stance (94). *The Underworld* is clearly socialist in its perspective; *The Morlocks* (1924) still leans toward the left but expresses a strong opposition to the use of violence to effect political change; *Norman Dale, M. P.* (1928) abandons the leftist perspective altogether, treating its only truly socialist character as a villain and espousing a watered-down politics that amounts to little more than acceptance of the status quo.

The Underworld draws directly on Welsh's experience as a miner. It is essentially a bildungsroman that relates the growth and maturation of Robert Sinclair, who begins work in the mines at an early age and, on his first day at work, sees his father killed beside him in an accident. As Sinclair reaches adulthood, he also grows in political awareness and gradually becomes a fierce fighter for the socialist cause, especially after he is inspired by a visit of Keir Hardie to his small mining town. Sinclair becomes an increasingly important figure in the movement, but he dies young when he is killed while heroically trying to save some men who have been trapped in another mine accident. The book suggests, however, that the movement will go on even without Sinclair, thus avoiding the individualist emphasis of the conventional bourgeois bildungsroman. Welsh avoids this emphasis in other ways as well, paying considerable attention to other characters throughout. There is, for example, a subplot involving the competition between Sinclair and Peter Rundell, son of a mine owner, for the hand of Mysie Maitland, a young working-class woman. This competition is won by Rundell, but Mysie's subsequent attempt to escape from her community and her class through her relationship with him leads to disaster and her death. Her disloyalty to class and community is meanwhile contrasted with Sinclair's staunch loyalty to both.

The entire mining community in which Sinclair lives is presented by Welsh with admiration and affection, and it is this community that is the true protagonist of *The Underworld*. And the real narrative of the book is the history of this community over the twenty-five year period from the 1880s to the extensive labor unrest of 1910 and 1911. One of the strengths of the book is its emphasis on community and its confidence that collective working-class action can bring about better working and living conditions for workers. On the other hand, the kind of action portrayed by Welsh in the book is not revolutionary but essentially conventional trade union activity, foreshadowing the more unequivocal denunciation of revolutionary action that would inform Welsh's later novels. **Selected bibliography:** Klaus ("Silhouettes"); David Smith (*Socialist Propaganda*).

ELLEN WILKINSON: *CLASH* (1929). *Clash* is probably the single best-known work by an author who was one of the most important women activists in British labor politics from the 1920s to the 1940s. Wilkinson came from a working-class background and maintained a strong sympathy with the workers' perspective throughout a career that saw her participate in a central way in such important events as the 1926 General Strike and the Jarrow Crusade of 1936. In addition to *Clash*, she was the author of the 1931 novel *The Division Bell Mystery*. She also wrote such nonfiction social documents as *The Town That Was Murdered* (1939) and *A*

Workers' History of the General Strike (1927, coauthored with J. F. Horrabin and Raymond Postgate) as well as regular columns for a number of newspapers. Consistently working for the cause of labor, Wilkinson became a member of Parliament and eventually, in the Attlee Labour government of 1945, the first woman minister of education in Britain. Her writing and her political work both show a strong consciousness of gender, as well as class issues, and she is regarded as an important pioneer in British feminism.

Clash centers on the General Strike and relates the story of protagonist Joan Craig, a young woman employed as a trades union activist in the North of England. Joan obviously has a great deal in common with Wilkinson, and much of the book can be taken as at least partly autobiographical. As such, it provides a number of inside looks at the workings of the General Strike and its aftermath. But the real focus of the book is Joan, herself; the real clash of the title is not so much the battle between labor and government-backed management as the various internal conflicts that Joan encounters in the course of the book. Many of these are class oriented as Joan finds that her work takes her into middle-class circles in ways that threaten to alienate her from her own working-class origins. The most important conflicts of the book, however, are gender related. Not only does Joan encounter certain specific professional obstacles because of her gender, but she also finds that, within the expected gender roles of modern British society, her devotion to her work powerfully clashes with her desire for a fulfilling sexual life.

Clash is essentially a variation on the romance plot, and its principal suspense derives not from the General Strike (which, as most readers would already know, failed quickly) but from Joan's attempts to mediate between her career and her love for writer Tony Dacre, a somewhat older middle-class married man. In the beginning, Tony's wife refuses to grant him a divorce, and Joan is afraid that an extramarital liaison with him would compromise her effectiveness as a political worker. Then, even after Tony's wife agrees to a divorce, Joan finds that he, despite the feminist orientation of his writing, believes that Joan would have to give up most of her political work if she married him. The situation is further complicated by the fact that Gerry Blain, a man from a wealthy background who has recently converted to socialism, is also in love with Joan. Joan likes and respects Gerry, but finds him far less sexually exciting than the dashing Tony. In the end, however, Joan decides to marry Gerry despite her passion for Tony, and she and Gerry plan a life together based not on sex but on mutual devotion to the cause of justice for British workers.

As Betty Vernon notes in her introduction to the 1989 re-publication of the book, *Clash* manages to deal with a number of important issues within the framework of what is essentially a romance plot: "*Clash*, racy and witty, with a vivid turn of phrase, though superficially slight, can be read at various levels. It reflects the collision of capital and labour; exposes conflicts inherent in class loyalty; and lays bare the contradictory demands which pull a woman, eager for a career, away from the obligations of love and marriage." The book is especially strong on its treatment of the latter gender issues, though its political position is somewhat questionable. For one thing, as Pamela Fox points out, the book does not really challenge Tony Dacre's position that Joan's private and public lives are two entirely different phenomena, thus endorsing precisely the sort of perceived split between private and personal experience that is one of the keys to bourgeois ideology as a whole (174). For another, Joan Craig is explicitly antirevolutionary and anticommunist. She also seems to have no consciousness of issues related to race or colonialism. In fact, she is given to making as racist remarks, such as referring to a hidden cause as a "nigger in the woodpile." Most importantly, the book is not entirely successful in resolving the various clashes it notes between the politics of class and the politics of gender. Nevertheless, *Clash* is firm in its support for workers in their battle with capitalists and clear in its understanding of that battle as a question of the overall economic system rather than individual personalities. ***Selected bibliography:*** Pamela Fox; Vernon.

RAYMOND WILLIAMS: *BORDER COUNTRY* (1960). Raymond Williams, though best known as one of the most important leftist theorists and cultural critics of postwar Britain, also wrote a significant amount of fiction, most of which draws upon Williams's Welsh background and emphasizes the importance of that background to his thought. *Border Country* is the first of three novels that are often considered to constitute Williams's "Welsh trilogy," the others being *Second Generation* (1964) and *The Fight for Manod* (1979). He also wrote *The Volunteers* (1978), a political thriller, and *Loyalties* (1985), a far-ranging historical novel that traces a variety of developments in the British Left from the 1930s and the Spanish Civil War to the 1980s and the 1984 Miners' Strike. In addition, Williams conceived and began an even vaster historical novel tracing the history of Wales from 23,000 b.c. to the present. This latter project, entitled *People of the Black Mountains*, was planned as a trilogy but was cut short after two volumes (published, respectively, in 1989 and 1990 as *The Beginning* and *The Eggs of the Eagle*) by Williams's death in 1988. All of these novels bear relations to the realist tradition, but they do so in innovative ways that show strong influences of modernism and other movements. Indeed, Tony Pinkney argues, in the most extensive critical discussion of Williams's novels to date, that Williams's fiction is best regarded as postmodern.

Border Country introduces Matthew Price, a young man whose education has taken him from his upbringing in a Welsh village to a career as a university lecturer in economic history in London. The book is centrally concerned with Price's attempt to come to grips with his growing alienation from the legacy of his working-class past. *Second Generation* features a new protagonist, Peter Owen, the son of Welsh working-class parents who have migrated to an English university city in search of economic opportunity. But the book deals with many of the same issues as its predecessor, following Owen as he pursues an academic career and becomes the focal point of Williams's examination of the impact of radical cultural change on individuals. In *The Fight for Manod*, both Price and Owen return as two academic experts appointed to evaluate a government proposal to build a new model city in rural Wales. In the process, both men continue the process of dealing with their separation from the traditions of their past begun in the earlier two novels. Owen, meanwhile, uncovers a complex conspiracy of corruption associated with the model project, and the remainder of the plot involves the reactions of the two men to this revelation.

Border Country provides an excellent introduction to the themes and concerns of the entire trilogy. As the book begins, Price is called back to his childhood village of Glynmawr when his father, Harry, suffers a near-fatal heart attack. Matthew loves and respects his father, a railway signalman, but has grown apart from the life of his village and the communitarian working-class culture of his childhood. This alienation is symbolized in the book by the fact that Price is known in London as Matthew (his actual given name), but has always been called Will in Glynmawr. He is, thus, a man with two separate identities, much like Williams himself, who was called Raymond at Cambridge, but grew up being called Jim in his home village. Price, in fact, has a number of things in common with his author, and much of his story can be taken as at least partly autobiographical. As Dai Smith puts it, "Williams wrote the final version of *Border Country* as a settling of accounts with his father, with himself and with the kind of Wales that had sent him away" (47).

On his return to Glynmawr, Price finds that much of the formerly familiar life of the village now seems quite foreign to him. Accustomed to the alienated individualism of modern London, he has become totally estranged from the communal culture of the village. For example, he finds the well-meaning attentions of the neighbors to his recovering father rude and intrusive rather than helpful and supportive. Realizing his alienation from his roots and worried that his father, who is his most important link with the past, may not survive, Price struggles to establish a sense of connection between his rural Welsh past and his urban English present. The book formally pursues this dialogue between past and present by alternating chapters set in the present and in earlier years. The chapters set in the past begin with the arrival of Price's newlywed parents in Glynmawr and trace their life together through Matthew/Will's birth and childhood, ending with his departure by train to attend the university at Cambridge. In the meantime, the private history of the Price family is related to the public history of Wales through an engagement with a number of historical events, the most important of which is the 1926 General Strike, Harry's participation in which helps to place events in Glynmawr within a broader context.

The contrast between London and Glynmawr (or between Matthew and Will) is, in many ways, the central device of the book, the principal motif of which thus becomes an opposition between tradition and modernity of a kind reminiscent of the work of Thomas Hardy (especially in *Jude the Obscure*), an author Williams greatly admired. But Williams goes to great pains to demonstrate that a dichotomy between urban modernity and rural tradition is far too simplistic to encompass the cultural situation in which Matthew Price finds himself, just as Williams demonstrated the complexity of the urban-rural opposition in works of criticism such as *The Country and the City*. It is, in fact, characteristic of all of Williams's work to reject such easy dichotomies. In *Border Country* there are many other oppositions at stake in addition to that between tradition and modernity, centrally including that between Wales and England. This opposition, however, is quite complex and is among other things intertwined with the class-based oppositions of capitalism. A central motif of the book is Price's anxiety over his work, not only because it is done in England but because it seems a violation of the working-class ethic of productive physical labor that his father values.

By the end of the text, Harry Price has died, and his son has returned to London to his wife and his own two sons. Matthew's experience in Glynmawr has, however, given him a new perspective that among other things teaches him to understand the value and complexity of "lived experience"—a key notion in all of Williams's critical work. Matthew comes to see his difference from his father not as the result of a personal betrayal of his class origins but of larger historical processes that make all sorts of changes inevitable. And Matthew comes to realize that his different life does not necessarily mean that he cannot remain a member of the community represented by the people of Glynmawr. Among other things, this realization will apparently reenergize his stalled research on the history of population movements in Wales, because by the time of *The Fight for Manod* that research has been successfully completed and published. But it also provides a subtle commentary on the nature and meaning of historical change as a process experienced and lived through by actual human beings. ***Selected bibliography:*** Di Michele; Eldridge and Eldridge; Gorak; Pinkney; Ryan ("Socialist Fiction"); Dai Smith ("Relating to Wales"); Ward; Williams (*Country*).

RAYMOND WILLIAMS: *THE VOLUNTEERS* (1978). *The Volunteers* is typically described as a political thriller, and that description is certainly appropriate. However, Williams draws upon a number of popular literary traditions in the book to produce what is actually a complex multigeneric work. The political thriller clearly provides the central model for the book, though it is narrated in a tone and constructed in a manner reminiscent of hard-boiled detective fiction. The book is set in 1988, though it was published in 1978. This near-future setting allows Williams to project a rather authoritarian Britain in a mode that has much in common with the tradition of dystopian fiction. In addition, Williams's protagonist in the book is an employee of a global satellite television news service, and the book builds upon a number of projected developments in communications technology in a mode reminiscent of science fiction. Finally, Williams draws upon the tradition of the British novel of the Left by combining these popular forms with complex meditations on a variety of issues, including specific questions such as the relationship between England and Wales as well as more general questions such as the nature and consequences of political commitment and the possibility of achieving radical change through oppositional political action. Perhaps the central subject of the book, however, is the media and its role in the evolution of what Guy Debord has called the "society of the spectacle."

The Volunteers is narrated in the first person by its protagonist, Lewis Redfern, an ex-radical activist who is now employed by the Insatel television news service to do investigative reporting and analysis of oppositional political activity. As the book begins, he is assigned to go to Wales to cover the recent attempted assassination there of Edmund Buxton, the right-wing British secretary of state for Wales. This assassination is thought to be directly connected to the earlier killing of a striking Welsh coal miner in Pontyrhiw by soldiers who were ordered to occupy the Pontyrhiw railway depot as part of a plan to ensure the continued distribution of coal (and generation of electricity) in the midst of a miners' strike. In the course of his investigation, Redfern verifies this connection, though the actual circumstances of the attack on Buxton turn out to be far more complex than was originally thought. Redfern also manages to obtain copies of secret government documents confirming that Buxton had indeed ordered the attack at Pontyrhiw, demonstrating the callous attitude of the British government toward both Wales and the working class.

The title of the book refers to the fact that Redfern's investigation also uncovers the existence of a secret organization known as the "Volunteers," which includes a number of radical opponents of the existing system who have for years been involved in a careful and extensive penetration of several important organizations in business and government, establishing themselves in positions of power and authority and working toward the day when they can use those positions to disrupt and hopefully overturn the existing order. Central to this organization is the prominent Welsh politician Mark Evans, who has long operated on the borderline between conventional politics and radical opposition to the conventional political system. Realizing that the existence of the Volunteers is about to be revealed in the press, Evans decides to salvage what he can, destroying all of his papers relating to the operation and supplying to Redfern the documents that implicate Buxton in the Pontyrhiw killing.

Redfern experiences a number of ethical dilemmas in the course of his investigation. Though he is not entirely in agreement with either the clandestine methodology of the Volunteers or the more overt methods of the terrorist group (including Evans's son, David) responsible for the shooting of Buxton, his radical instincts are still strong enough to allow him to sympathize with the goals of both groups. In the meantime, the reaction of Insatel to the unfolding events brings home to Redfern the extent to which his employers (and, by implication, the media as a whole) are working in complicity with official power and in opposition to any group that might pose a legitimate threat to that power. In the end, Redfern resigns from Insatel and produces the Pontyrhiw documents as part of a public inquiry into the matter. He does not, however, reveal what he has learned about Evans's involvement with the Volunteers; nor does he reveal that he has learned the identity of Buxton's attackers, an identity that, in contrast to the conventions of detective fiction, has by this time become largely irrelevant, anyway.

The Volunteers is an entertaining work of fiction that manages to engage readers both in the epistemological questions that drive its plot and in the political and philosophical questions that provide its real substance. The book is particularly memorable for its presentation of a number of striking central images, such as the description of the Welsh Folk Museum at St. Fagans, near Cardiff. Among other things, this description comments upon the commodification of the Welsh past in ways that clearly recall recent Marxist discussions of postmodernism and that tend to substantiate Tony Pinkney's argument that Williams is rightly regarded as a postmodern novelist. In fact, images are crucial to the entire fabric of the book, which treats events such as political demonstrations and the attack on Buxton as staged spectacles for consumption by the media. This motif combines with Williams's suggestion of the complicity between the media and official power to make *The Volunteers* an important exploration of the role of the communications media in late capitalist society. As such, it provides a useful supplement to Williams's late cultural criticism, which, in works such as *Television: Technology and Cultural Form*, often focused on the impact of television and other new communications technologies on contemporary world culture. **Selected bibliography:** De Bord; Eldridge and Eldridge; Gorak; Pinkney; Ryan ("Socialist Fiction"); Dai Smith ("Relating to Wales"); Ward; Williams (*Television*).

AMABEL WILLIAMS-ELLIS: *TO TELL THE TRUTH . . .* **(1933).** Amabel Williams-Ellis was a member of the Communist Party and a leading figure on the British Left in the 1930s. The sister of John Strachey and the wife of prominent leftist architect Clough Williams-Ellis she participated extensively in Party activities and represented Britain at a number of international leftist conferences. A founding editor of *Left Review*, she was particularly important as a journalist, editor, and fiction writer. She was the author of several novels, including *The Wall of Glass* (1927), *Volcano* (1931), *The Big Firm* (1938), and *Learn to Love First* (1939). Her writings also include an autobiography, *All Stracheys Are Cousins* (1983), which extensively documents her life on the British Left. Of all of her works, the 1933 novel *To Tell the Truth . . .* is one of the most imaginative.

A satiric reversal of the anti-Soviet travelogue, the book details the visit of a young Soviet, Pavel Pedersson to Britain, where he hopes to learn about the workings of capitalism. Meanwhile, set in the early 1940s, the book also participates in the genre of dystopian fiction. Though written in a comic mode, it details a Britain in which the worst tendencies of the early 1930s have continued to develop, producing a grim, authoritarian, and impoverished society.

As the book begins, Pedersson is a member of a Soviet delegation meeting with Western representatives at a conference in Skaal, Denmark, hoping to break a long trade embargo that has economically isolated the Soviet Union from the Western world. Skaal is a model city, clean, neat, and efficient, and Pedersson is much impressed with it as an example of the results of capitalism. He thus begins to doubt the negative vision of capitalism he has received throughout his education in the Soviet Union and decides to slip away from the Soviet delegation to try to find out for himself the truth about capitalism. Immediately, he finds some evidence that the inhabitants of Skaal are not quite as free and prosperous as they appear on the surface, but he soon realizes, on the advice of American journalist William Hake, that Skaal is not in any case a typical capitalist city and that, to see the real face of capitalism, he will have to go to Britain or America.

Hake then arranges to fly Pedersson to Britain for a tour. They arrive in the industrial town of Bradstoke, where the atmosphere is dark, grimy, and depressing. Pedersson witnesses several signs of social and political injustice, as when a family is being evicted from their home even though they have paid the rent or when a man is being unfairly arrested for the murder of his wife, who actually committed suicide to escape the horrors of continued poverty. In the course of his trip, Pedersson also visits London and an unnamed university town. Highly impressed with the technological advancement of much of England (and especially with the traffic and bustle of London), the young Russian is nevertheless appalled at the conditions under which the majority of British workers are forced to live, even while the society as a whole shows signs of plenty. He is particularly horrified when he realizes that, for the poor, the birth of a child is often a cause for grief rather than joy, because of the difficulty in providing sustenance for the new infant. What especially concerns him is the low level of morale of most of the working-class people he encounters in England, most of whom see little hope for a better future. Indeed, though Pedersson encounters a few communists and other politically aware workers, by and large he finds that the cultural apparatus in Britain has been almost entirely successful in suppressing any sense that concerted working-class action might bring about a change in the grim conditions he has observed.

In the end, Pedersson decides to return to the Soviet Union, where the technology may be relatively undeveloped and overall material conditions relatively grim, but where all children are guaranteed the basic needs of life and where workers are treated with a dignity and respect that helps them to maintain an optimistic faith that their own joint efforts were helping to bring about a coming better future: "His Russia might be poor still, and clumsy and rough as a colt.... But neither hope, nor skill, nor life, was being wasted. Slowly all these wants were being fulfilled, because they all had their faces turned the same way and they were awake. The clothes were on people's backs and the food in their bellies, and not stored behind plate glass in the shops" (201). *Selected bibliography:* Croft (*Red Letter Days*); Williams-Ellis (*All Stracheys*).

4

SELECTED POSTCOLONIAL NOVELS OF THE LEFT

PETER ABRAHAMS: *MINE BOY* **(1946).** Peter Abrahams was one of the important founding figures of black South African literature in English. He became politically aware in the 1930s and then went into exile in 1939 better to pursue his ambition to be a writer. After two years at sea, Abrahams settled in London, where he married an English woman and became an editor of the Communist Party organ *Daily Worker*. His first two novels, *Song of the City* (1945) and *Mine Boy* (1946), show the influence of his political commitment with their overtly Marxist themes of opposition to class-based oppression under industrial capitalism (which, in South Africa as in the United States, is inseparable from racial oppression). Abrahams's third novel, *The Path of Thunder* (1948), is optimistic in its treatment of the possibility of love across racial barriers; taken together, his first three novels are informed by a powerful hope that conditions in South Africa can be greatly improved if only white South Africans can be taught to see beyond their traditional habit of racial hatred. With the publication of *Wild Conquest* (1950), Abrahams turned his attention to more historical themes in an attempt to locate the roots of apartheid in the early history of encounters of Afrikaner settlers with the indigenous Matabele people during their "Great Trek" into the interior of South Africa in the 1830s and 1840s. One of Abrahams's most important works is his 1954 autobiography, *Tell Freedom*, the first published autobiography by a black South African. The novel *A Wreath for Udomo* (1956) is also especially important in the way its indictment of colonialism and its understanding of the dangers of neocolonialism anticipate the works of later writers such as Chinua Achebe, Ayi Kwei Armah, and Ngugi wa Thiong'o. Abrahams extends this theme in *This Island Now* (1966), a critique of neocolonialism in an island nation modeled on Haiti and Jamaica. Other important works by Abrahams include *A Night of Their Own* (1965) and *The View from Coyaba* (1985), which employ South African and Jamaican settings, respectively, to explore the role of the writer in the liberation of the black race.

Despite his long and productive career, the early *Mine Boy* remains one of Abrahams's most important and representative works. The plot of the book is simple and minimal, as Abrahams depends upon the description of characters to achieve most of his effects. The central character is Xuma, a young man who comes to Johannesburg to work in the nearby gold mines and thereby to seek an escape from the poverty of his rural village. These mines are a central image of the book, calling attention to the contrast between the abysmal poverty of most South African blacks and the vast material wealth of South Africa as a whole. Xuma has trouble adjusting to the city, where the fast pace and alienated social relations differ dramatically from the more communal conditions to which he is accustomed. Fortunately, he is befriended by a group of inhabitants of the Malay Camp, a black area on the outskirts of the city. Centering around the woman Leah, who makes her living selling illegal beer to the local blacks, this group includes the mine worker Johannes Williamson, the old couple Daddy and Ma Plank, and two beautiful young women, the educated and ambitious Eliza and the more traditional Maisy. Together, the members of this group allow Abrahams to make numerous points about the difficulty of life for blacks in a South Africa that, in 1946, was fast moving toward the official implementation of the policy of apartheid. For example, Leah is a good woman forced to live a life of crime in order to get by — and, at that, her beer-selling business would be perfectly legal were she only white. Daddy, meanwhile, is a once proud and powerful man who has been defeated by life and eventually dies a broken-down drunk.

Johannes helps Xuma to get a job in the mine working as a gang leader for Paddy O'Shea, one of the white foremen. The hardworking and muscular Xuma quickly becomes one of the mine's most valuable workers. But his personal life is more troublesome. He falls in love with Eliza almost immediately, but she rejects his advances, having promised herself that she would marry an educated man who might be able to help her fulfill her dream of escaping poverty and living in the way white people live. Dazzled by the lure of the commodity culture that signifies the gap between whites and blacks in South Africa, Eliza can see no other road to success than to try to be as much like white people as possible. She does not seem to realize that the whites of South Africa will never allow her to live like them. Maisy, meanwhile, falls in love with Xuma, and they have a brief affair, but he is unable to get his mind off of Eliza. Xuma and Eliza eventually become romantically involved as well, but this relationship breaks off when she suddenly leaves town by train in order to escape an entanglement with the poor and uneducated Xuma. Leah, meanwhile, does her best to survive by bribing the police and manipulating the corrupt system as best she can, though she is eventually arrested and sentenced to nine months in jail for selling beer.

One of the most important characters in the book is Paddy O'Shea, who treats Xuma kindly and who genuinely believes in justice for people of all colors. When a mine accident leads to the deaths of Johannes and his white boss, Paddy joins Xuma in a protest of the unsafe working conditions that led to the accident. Their crew refuses to return to work until these conditions are corrected, leading the mine management to call in the police to deal with the "strikers." When the police arrive, they attack the men. Paddy is beaten and arrested, though Xuma manages to escape. He returns to the Malay Camp where he and Maisy have a final encounter in which he concludes that Maisy is the one he truly loves after all. But, given the situation in preapartheid South Africa, there is no room for the couple to have a peaceful and happy life together. Despite having found his true love, Xuma leaves Maisy at the end of the book to go to the police station to try to help Paddy and to speak out for racial justice.

Abrahams's focus on the romantic adventures of Xuma may at times divert attention from his political message, though this aspect of the book is useful for its important reminders of the way in which black South Africans struggle to live as human beings amid radically dehumanizing conditions. A more serious problem may be the use of the developing relationship between Xuma and Paddy as a utopian image of racial harmony in *Mine Boy*, a motif that seems to suggest that such harmony can be achieved by individual action rather than sweeping systemic change. In fact, racial relations in South Africa would get far worse before they would get better; in light of subsequent events, Abrahams's 1946 vision of racial equality based on individual decency and transethnic friendship seems a bit idealized. Nevertheless, his book, published more than a decade before Chinua Achebe's *Things Fall Apart*, which is often considered the first black African novel in English, is valuable as an early effort to use literature to call attention to the racial injustice of South African society. It is also important for its implied understanding of the economic roots of this injustice, even if none of the characters of the book are themselves politically sophisticated enough to understand this phenomena in a genuinely historical way. *Selected bibliography:* Ensor; Harris; Ogungbesan; Wade.

MULK RAJ ANAND: *COOLIE* (1936). Along with R. K. Narayan and Raja Rao, Mulk Raj Anand is usually identified as one of the three leading Indian novelists writing in English prior to the 1980s, when Salman Rushdie spearheaded a veritable explosion in production of English-language novels by Indian writers. Anand is also typically identified as India's most politically committed writer. For example, Saros Cowasjee, who believes that *Coolie* is probably Anand's best novel, argues that "no Indian writer of fiction in English comes anywhere near Mulk Raj Anand in providing a social and political portrait of India from the time of the Delhi Durbar of 1911 to the demise of the Indian princes following Indian Independence in 1947" (96). In this vein, R. K. Dhawan, in a discussion of Anand's novel *Coolie*, notes that Anand has often been characterized by detractors as more a propagandist than a novelist. But Dhawan concludes that Anand has effectively integrated his political message into his fictional framework to produce "an intensely realised and credible narrative that is both political thesis and absorbing fiction" (18). Dhawan also notes the abiding popularity of Anand's novels worldwide, attributing much of this popularity to the passion and sincerity with which the novels express Anand's political convictions (2). Thus, *Coolie*, a book that grows very much out of Anand's extensive involvement with the Left in England in the 1930s, continues to be popular in England, India, and elsewhere at the end of the twentieth century.

Dhawan usefully details Anand's engagement with Western literature and Western, especially English, politics as background to *Coolie*. In particular, he notes that Anand, who lived in London from 1924 to 1945, was powerfully influenced by events such as the 1926 British General Strike, an event that fundamentally changed Anand's attitude toward British society and propelled him in a leftist direction that would inform all of his writing for decades to come. Anand, in fact, became prominently involved in leftist literary circles in England in the 1930s, as can be seen by the fact that he wrote the preface to a 1944 edition of Ralph Fox's important Marxist literary study, *The Novel and the People*. Along with numerous others in his circle in England, Anand joined the International Brigades and participated in the Civil War in Spain on the Republican side. Novels such as *Untouchable* (1935) and *Coolie*, while strongly informed by Anand's Indian background, thus also stand as important works of *British* leftist culture in the 1930s.

Coolie, focusing on the experiences of the lowly worker Munoo, has a great deal in common with the proletarian novels published in Britain and the United States in the 1930s. Munoo, the child of impoverished parents in a rural village, is orphaned early on and forced to go, at age fourteen, to the town of Shampur to work as a much-abused household servant in order to support himself. As the book proceeds, he moves on to the small city of Daulatpur, where he works in a pickle factory and then as a coolie seeking odd jobs in the city's market. Eventually he comes to Bombay, where he works in a large British-owned textile mill, in the end moving from there to Simla to become the servant of Mrs. Mainwaring, a somewhat disreputable, though socially ambitious, Anglo-Indian woman. Munoo's movements thus present the reader with a broad cross-section of Indian society in the interwar period. They also make *Coolie* a sort of historical novel that traces Munoo from his childhood in a remote rural area through a variety of experiences that bring him into increasingly modern and urban environments, thus, to an extent, tracing the arc of world history in the last several centuries. In so doing, the book also suggests the element of exploitation and inequity that has been central to the historical process of modernization, presenting Munoo as an emblem of the poor and oppressed whose labor has fueled the growth of global modernization but who have themselves been largely excluded from the benefits of that process.

Munoo's life is difficult from the very beginning, but his sense of suffering grows steadily through the book, partly because of the increasingly oppressive situations in which he finds himself and partly because his increasing maturity makes him more and more aware of the unfairness of the ways in which he is being treated. He also becomes more and more frustrated and disappointed as each move, intended to open new vistas and bring new opportunities, sinks him deeper into exploitation and misery. Much of Munoo's experience is specifically Indian, and Anand, despite his numerous Western contacts and influences, does an excellent job of embedding his book in the cultural and historical context of India. At the same time, especially in the Bombay sections when Munoo works in a modern factory, many of the experiences depicted parallel those of Western workers quite closely. Granted, much of what is at stake in this section of the book has to do with British colonial exploitation of Indian workers, but Anand carefully constructs this segment in such a way as to suggest that Western workers are also exploited and that the racial element of Munoo's mistreatment at the factory is an intensified form of the class differences that lead to such abuse in all capitalist societies. Class, for Anand, is the principal social category and the primary source of Munoo's misfortunes.

Anand presents vivid depictions of the squalid conditions under which the poor of India, including the Bombay workers, must work and live. He also offers socialism as a key to the improvement of these conditions. In Bombay, Munoo takes up with a poor family and lives with them on the street. The father of the family, Hari, then takes Munoo with him and his family to find work in the cotton mill, which they manage to do only by paying a bribe to the corrupt English foreman, Jimmie Thomas, who also rents them a straw hut in which to live. Conditions in the mill are not only hellish, but highly dangerous, and Hari's son is soon seriously injured in an accident. After their hut is destroyed in a storm, the family is taken in by a fellow worker, Ratan, called "the wrestler" because of his powerful physique. Ratan defends Hari and Munoo from the abuse of Thomas and also urges them to join the union to fight for better treatment. In general, however, the union's leaders pursue such a moderate course that they pose no real threat to the existing system at the factory. Only the local communists work for real change, eventually organizing an alternative union that poses such a threat that the factory's owners, in order to undermine solidarity among the workers, spread rumors intended to lead to dissention between Hindus and Muslims. This strategy is so successful that Muslim–Hindu riots break out. Munoo is injured in the ensuing confusion when he is struck by Mrs. Mainwaring's automobile. She then takes him with her to Simla as a personal servant, harboring sexual thoughts about him as well. Munoo's objectification and humiliation are thus complete, though Mrs. Mainwaring actually treats him kindly and the natural beauty of Simla revives some of his fonder memories of his rural childhood. However, he soon contracts tuberculosis and dies at the age of sixteen, at last putting an end to his miseries. Despite this outcome, however, Anand makes clear his belief that the efforts of the communists in Bombay to organize collective opposition to oppression carry a great potential for eventual success.

Anand presents the program of the communist union in Bombay primarily through the speeches of the leader, Sauda, as when he urges the workers to demand to be treated like "human beings and not soulless machines" (261). His other demands (including decent housing, better education, more job security, shorter hours, and higher pay) are very much those made by leftist labor leaders the world over. Indeed, R. K. Dhawan suggests that the program of the communist union "reads like manifesto of the Progressive Writers' Association of the thirties" (15). In any case, *Coolie* combines a bitter denunciation of existing oppression with a clear suggestion of a utopian alternative, which may account for the fact that many critics, as Asha Kaushik notes, have seen the book as Anand's "most satisfying political novel" (134). **Selected bibliography:** Cowasjee (*Studies*); Dhawan; Kaushik; Rajan; Tagore.

MULK RAJ ANAND: *UNTOUCHABLE* (1935). *Untouchable* is perhaps the best-known novel by Anand, an Indian writer who had numerous connections with the literary Left in England during the 1930s. The book tells the story of one day in the life of Bakha, a young Indian "Untouchable." Fated by his low birth to work as a latrine sweeper — and thus to be regarded as an unclean outcaste by Hindus born into higher castes, Bakha suffers a number of undeserved abuses and humiliations in the course of the day. In its depiction of these humiliations and of Bakha's painful emotional reaction to them, the book presents a powerful critique of the Indian caste system. At the same time, the book's treatment of the caste system can also be read as a more general critique of the inequities of class society, including that which prevails in the presumably more modern and democratic Britain. Finally, Anand supplements his critique of Hindu tradition with suggestions of the ways in which the British colonial domination of India, while bringing a certain amount of modernization, has actually exacerbated, rather than ameliorated, the suffering of outcastes such as Bakha.

Bakha lives with his father, brother, and sister in abject poverty. Moreover, Bakha's father, Lakha, constantly abuses him though the boy generally works hard and tries his best to please the aging man. To make matters worse, much of Bakha's childhood has been spent as a latrine cleaner in the nearby British barracks, which has led him to develop a great admiration of all things British and to dream of being like the impressive-looking soldiers he sees in the barracks. Brutally mistreated by his own society, Bakha accepts virtually without question the superiority of the only alternative society he knows, failing to ask whether that society contains its own forms of injustice. Bakha does feel vaguely uncomfortable about his admiration for the British "Tommies," but he admires them greatly nevertheless. In any case, however, such splendors are not for the likes of the lowly Bakha, who is lucky to be able to scrounge enough food to keep himself alive. On the day covered by the book, his life is made particularly difficult when, distracted by the sights of the busy town where he goes to clean latrines and sweep streets, he accidentally brushes against a higher-caste Hindu. This incident precipitates a major crisis, as the Hindu, feeling that he has been defiled, screams in outrage, causing a crowd to gather. The crowd abuses Bakha, who runs away in shame.

Next, Bakha goes to the temple to sweep the courtyard. Once there, however, he is overcome by curiosity and creeps up the steps of the temple to peer inside, even though it is forbidden for an Untouchable to come so near to the sacred building. A priest sees Bakha on the steps and cries that the temple has been defiled, leading to another crisis and another round of abuse for Bakha. In the ensuing confusion, another priest appears, crying that he has been defiled by the touch of Sohini, Bakha's beautiful sister. Fortunately, no one pays attention due to the uproar over the contamination of the temple, so Sohini manages to escape. Later, however, an enraged Bakha learns that the priest had actually tried to seduce Sohini and had accused her of defiling him in retribution for her rejection of his advances. Bakha then returns home for his midday meal. There, he and his father experience a rare moment of contact when Bakha tells Lakha of the abuse he has suffered, and Lakha responds with the story of a similar humiliation from his own youth.

As they begin to eat, however, Bakha finds himself sickened by the uncleanliness of his own family. He then seeks solace in a visit with his friends Chota and Ram Charan, who are of higher caste but who have always treated him as an equal. Bakha has a few pleasant moments during the afternoon, especially when he is given an almost new hockey stick at the British barracks by the locally renowned hockey star Charat

Singh. However, when Bakha and his friends get involved in a hockey match, a fight breaks out between the two teams, resulting in the injury of a small boy who is looking on. Bakha picks up the boy and carries him home, where the boy's mother abuses him for touching her son and accuses him of causing the injury. Bakha returns to his own home, once again humiliated, only to suffer more humiliation at the hands of his father. Fed up, Bakha runs away, seeking to escape the constant shame that is his lot in life.

Having effectively and graphically described the sorts of humiliations to which Bakha is subjected as an Untouchable in India, Anand spends the remainder of the text describing Bakha's attempts to find a solution to his difficulties. First, he meets Colonel Hutchinson, a Salvation Army preacher who assures him that Christ knows no caste and that all men are viewed as the same by the Christian God. Impressed by this egalitarian rhetoric, Bakha returns with Hutchinson to the latter's home to learn more about this new religion. When they arrive, however, Mrs. Hutchinson excoriates her husband for wasting his time on "blackies," and Bakha again runs away, realizing that, while Christians might view him as the equal of other Indians, they do not in general view him as the equal of white Europeans (132). Next, Bakha joins a crowd that gathers to hear Gandhi speak against the doctrine of untouchability, urging all Hindus to reject the doctrine. The speech, based upon an actual address delivered by Gandhi in 1921, is a bit disjointed and suggests that Anand, who would later identify Gandhi as a powerful inspiration in his work, was at this stage somewhat suspicious of Gandhi, as were many on the Indian Left (Cowasjee 99–104). Bakha, however, is thrilled to hear himself referred to by Gandhi not as a *bhangi*, the usual derogatory term for an Untouchable, but as a *harijan*, or man of God (141). After the speech, Bakha is somewhat troubled to hear an Anglicized Indian Muslim, the barrister R. N. Bashir, complain that Gandhi is hopelessly old-fashioned and that his programs cannot possibly work in the modern world. Bakha then listens as Bashir's companion, the poet Iqbal Nath Sarshar, responds that Gandhi's ideas are basically sound, though they need some updating. In particular, Sarshar grants that the key to liberation for India lies not in Eastern spirituality, but in Western technology, like it or not. In particular, he insists that the best way to end the doctrine of untouchability would be to install flush toilets all over India so that no one would be required manually to remove human waste and thus be considered unclean.

As the book closes, a confused Bakha mulls over all that he has heard. He is not quite sure what to make of all the arguments, but the idea of a flush system that would liberate his people strikes him as an exciting possibility. The possibility clearly excites Anand as well, and there can be no doubt that Anand endorses the modernization of India via Western technology, even as he realizes that certain positive aspects of traditional Indian life may be lost in the process. The book does suggest, however, especially in the speech of a babu waiting in the crowd to hear Gandhi speak, that the strength of traditional Indian spirituality may be such that India can incorporate modern innovations without necessarily succumbing to the rampant materialism and commodification that has swept across capitalist Europe (139). On the other hand, Anand does not simply endorse Orientalist notions of Eastern mysticism and spirituality. Indeed, as Saros Cowasjee points out, one of the major strategies of the book is to destroy such stereotypes of the East as "contentment," "mystical silence," and "spiritual attainments" ("Mulk Raj Anand's *Untouchable*" 33). Thus, through the voice of the poet Sarshar, Anand insists that the real strength of traditional Indian culture is its fundamental realism and its basic ability to deal with the realities of the world as they come. As Sarshar succinctly puts it, subtly reversing certain Orientalist stereotypes, "We can see through the idiocy of these Europeans who deified money. They were barbarians and lost their heads in the worship of gold" (153).

One could, of course, argue that Anand here wants to have it both ways, and P. J. Rajan does, in fact, suggest that the text is torn by an inherent contradiction arising from Anand's ambivalent attempt both to hang on to the traditional strengths of Hindu society and to modernize that society through technological innovation (37). Moreover, Rajan notes that this tension between East and West resides not just in the theme of the book but in its very form and structure. He points out, for example, that *Untouchable* is a brief and simple novel that, despite its essentially realist (Western) mode of narration, can be appropriately be seen as a moral fable that draws directly upon Indian narrative traditions (32). It might be best, however, to view this ambivalence not as a flaw but as an expression of the extreme difficulty and complexity of the issues with which this seemingly simple book deals. In its attempt to come to grips with the issues raised by the colonial confrontation between Indian tradition and British modernity, *Untouchable* carefully avoids the simple privileging of either side and suggests that a new kind of society might emerge dialectically out of this confrontation, a new society that avoids the evils and injustices of both East and West. *Selected bibliography:* Cowasjee ("Mulk Raj Anand's *Untouchable*"); Cowasjee (*Studies*); Kaushik; Rajan.

AYI KWEI ARMAH: *THE BEAUTYFUL ONES ARE NOT YET BORN* (1968). *The Beautyful Ones Are Not Yet Born* focuses on the failure of postcolonial Ghanaian society, under the leadership of Kwame Nkrumah, to live up to the utopian hopes generated by the Nkrumah-led independence movement in the 1950s. In particular, the book focuses on the phenomenon of neocolonialism and on the way independence has led not to the liberation of utopia, but to the enslavement of a new form of colonial domination. In this sense, *The Beautyful Ones* has much in common with the Western genre of dystopian fiction. Thus, S. A. Gakwandi has compared the tone and atmosphere pervading Armah's text to those of George Orwell's *Nineteen Eighty-Four* (102-3). However, Armah's particular focus on the postcolonial situation, underwritten by the theoretical work of Frantz Fanon, sets it apart from Western works such as Orwell's.

Armah creates his dystopian atmosphere through the use of a number of striking images and motifs. On the one hand, the real texture of everyday life in postcolonial Ghana is characterized through patterns of imagery involving corruption, decay, garbage, and excrement. On the other hand, the false promises presented both by the rhetoric of Nkrumahism and by the lure of Western commodity culture are represented by images of brightness and cleanliness that turn out to obscure an even more thorough corruption underneath. The central image of this corrupt brightness is the "gleam," a metaphor for the almost hypnotic lure of Western commodities that enthralls the Ghanaian populace with fantasies of wealth they can never hope to achieve except through dishonesty. To some extent, the gleam is a literal, physical phenomenon. Material symbols of Western wealth, such as the Atlantic-Caprice tourist hotel, tend in the book to be painted in dazzling white and bathed in bright light. But this brightness merely obscures the exploitation and injustice that allow such wealth to exist amid the general poverty of Ghana. Among other things, Armah's presentation of the gleam serves to invert the traditional Western image structure in which whiteness and light tend to be associated with good, darkness and black with evil. In addition, the use of the gleam in both a literal and a figurative sense exemplifies a technique that Armah uses throughout the book in which the two senses are conflated. Thus moral corruption and physical rot become inextricably intertwined in the book. According to Neil Lazarus, by focusing the attention of the impoverished masses on the possibility (however remote) of future wealth, the gleam diverts their attention from their current suffering and helps to ensure that they will take no effective action to change the system: "Armah suggests that they continue in bondage because the gleam now prevents them from seeing their manacled condition for what it is" (62).

The plot of *The Beautyful Ones* largely involves the efforts of the protagonist, simply called "the man," to resist the lure of the gleam in the face of pressure from his family and friends to succumb. The pressure to succumb is made all the greater by the man's realization that the gleam has conquered virtually everyone else in Ghana, including his own family. He is thus made to feel an alien in his home, "the land of the loved ones," where "it was only the heroes of the gleam who did not feel that they were strangers" (35). By the end of the book, however, the man's wife, Oyo, seems to have come to appreciate his integrity in the face of the gleam, especially after she has witnessed the ignominious fall and flight of the corrupt government minister Koomson, the book's central image of an individual whose life is entirely consumed with the pursuit of the gleam.

This focus on the man's family life illustrates the way in which *The Beautyful Ones*, while concentrating on public political and social issues in postcolonial Ghana, presents the issues primarily through their impact on the lives of individual characters. Central among these is the protagonist, whose namelessness may suggest his almost total lack of a genuine identity in the context of this corrupt society. Another nameless central character in the book is the man's friend, Teacher, a frustrated former Nkrumahist intellectual who has now retreated into seclusion to escape the corrupt society that he finds around him. Labeled by profession rather than by name, Teacher can be taken as a representative character whose alienation and despair are typical of many postcolonial intellectuals. Indeed, it is tempting to see the Teacher as a sort of spokesman for Armah himself, and some critics have done so. Moreover, this view of Teacher at first seems to be reinforced by the fact that the long sixth chapter, dominated by Teacher, diagnoses the ills of postcolonial Ghana in a vein very much reminiscent of Frantz Fanon, one of the major influences on all of Armah's work.

Lazarus suggests that *The Beautyful Ones* is Armah's "most Fanonian novel" (41), and it is certainly the case that Fanon's work, especially *The Wretched of the Earth*, provides a crucial background to Armah's novel. Teacher, however, is not merely a spokesman for the positions espoused by Fanon. In his cynicism and despair, he is also an embodiment of the postcolonial decadence that Fanon warns against. In particular, his withdrawal from the world is precisely the opposite of the intense engagement with the everyday life of the people that Fanon sees as crucial to the function of intellectuals in postcolonial societies. For Fanon, the "native intellectual" must "return to the people" and through his contact with popular life learn to provide intellectual leadership in the ongoing struggle against cultural imperialism in the postcolonial era (47). In short, as Lazarus points out, a careful reading shows that *The Beautyful Ones* ultimately rejects Teacher's escapist reaction to the troubles of postcolonial Ghana, seeing it as a form of "living death" (72).

Critics such as Leonard Kibera have accused *The Beautyful Ones* of being entirely negative and devoid of hope and of presenting its political message in a dogmatic and overly simplistic fashion. The first of these charges, however, can be countered by the fact that numerous aspects of the book can, in fact, be taken to suggest possible sources of hope. For one thing, as Robert Fraser argues, the book subtly extends its historical scope beyond the 1960s by setting this period against "a backdrop of centuries of oppression, a recurring cycle of despair" (26). But, lest this suggestion of the long legacy of corruption and oppression in Ghana be taken as a sign that things can never improve, Fraser also notes that characters like Teacher and the man are still able to "discern the original wholesomeness that lies somewhere beneath the festering refuse" (27). If this wholesomeness can still be discerned in this fashion, it can perhaps be recovered—a motif that would become the central idea of Armah's later *Two Thousand Seasons*. If nothing else, the book's title certainly suggests a coming future in which the "beautyful ones" will be born at last, especially given that this title is taken from a legend the man sees at the end of the book on the back of a bus that surrounds a picture of a flower, a traditional symbol of rebirth (183). This image, meanwhile, links up with Teacher's earlier reminder that "out of the decay and the dung there is always a new flowering" (85). Lazarus, meanwhile, argues that *The Beautyful Ones* supplements its basically dystopian tone with a strong utopian element. For him, the book does not convey a sense of hopelessness. Instead, Lazarus concludes that Armah seeks in the book "to describe the preconditions of and prevailing constraints to change. The novel is formulated upon the premise that it is only by knowing one's world, by seeing it for what it is, that one can ever genuinely aspire to bring about its revolutionary transformation" (48).

The charge that Armah's political message is simplistic has also been leveled by Derek Wright, who argues that only the inventiveness of Armah's language saves *The Beautyful Ones* from "the cartoonlike banality of its political themes" (30). In a somewhat similar vein, Gakwandi complains of the "shoddiness of Armah's political sentiments" (108). Among other things, such critics are responding to a long tradition of critical prejudice against political statements of any kind in literature. According to this tradition, which is exemplified by American New Criticism, all political sentiments are shoddy, and all political themes are banal. But, within the context of postcolonial Ghana (or postcolonial Africa in general), politics is a very real and palpable part of the texture of everyday life. Any literary representation of postcolonial life that ignores politics would be irresponsible and unrealistic at best. In terms of the specifics of Armah's very clear political stance against neocolonial corruption and oppression in Ghana, one might first seek to remember this context. In addition, it is useful from a Western perspective to recall that *The Beautyful Ones* is a work of satire and that satire as a genre works through methods of simplification and emphasis that call attention to specific ills that might otherwise be obscured by the complexities of everyday life. From this point of view, the political statement made by Armah's book is not simplistic, but focused. Ultimately, Armah's book is powerful and aesthetically successful not despite his political engagement, but because of it. *Selected bibliography:* Fraser; Fanon; Gakwandi; Kibera; Lazarus; Wright.

BRENDAN BEHAN: *BORSTAL BOY* **(1959).** *Borstal Boy,* strictly speaking, is not a novel but a partial autobiography. It relates, in first person, the experiences of the young Behan in the period 1939-42, during which he, at age sixteen, was arrested in Liverpool as an Irish Republican Army (IRA) terrorist, then imprisoned and eventually sent to a juvenile detention institution, or "Borstal." However, the book reads very much like a novel and one can probably assume that many of the events in the book are fictionalized to an extent. Moreover, *Borstal Boy* is worth reading within the context of the novel of the Left because it addresses so many of the issues that are central to such novels. Given the context of the book, it is not surprising that Behan's narrative provides important commentary on colonialism and the postcolonial condition, the continuing British presence in Northern Ireland serving as a particularly overt example of the neocolonial condition in which European rulers maintain influence and power in their former colonies well after the moment of ostensible independence. But the treatment of these issues in *Borstal Boy* is distinctive for its focus on class rather than nationality and for its clear suggestion that the working classes of England and Ireland have a great deal in common and that both are the exploited victims of the British ruling classes.

The book begins as British agents arrive at Behan's rooming house to arrest him, discovering a suitcase full of bomb materials in his room. The prisoner receives rather rough and insulting treatment from his captors, especially after he refuses their offer of leniency in return for information about the activities of the IRA. After having been notified that he will be denied a public trial for security reasons, Behan is then shipped off to Walton Jail to be held for a week, which actually turns into months after several delays, while he awaits trial. Conditions in the jail are grim, especially for the Irishman Behan, though he manages to gain a certain amount of respect from his fellow prisoners by showing his willingness (and ability) to defend himself with his fists. He also begins a friendship with Charlie Millwall, an English boy sent to Walton at the same time. In the meantime, Behan bears the persecution he receives from the guards and some of the other prisoners as part of his due as an IRA man. What he finds particularly offensive, however, is the attempt of the prison priest to convince him to turn against the IRA. In response, Behan delivers a long diatribe against the historical complicity between the Catholic Church and the British Empire in the domination of Ireland (65-67). This stance leads not only to a sound beating at the hands of the guards but to

Behan's excommunication from the Church, which remains a strong object of critique throughout the book.

In the meantime, Behan's litany of betrayals of the Irish people by the Church is only one part of a carefully constructed narrative of the Irish past that is woven into his narrative. For example, he spends much of his time in Walton remembering the experiences of other IRA men at the hands of the British authorities and constructing, in fact, a history of Irish anticolonial resistance to British rule. Reminiscences of famous figures such as Wolfe Tone, Robert Emmet, Michael Collins, Tom Clarke, Eamon de Valera, and Terence McSwiney punctuate Behan's thoughts as he awaits trial, as does his awareness that two other IRA men are currently awaiting execution for a bombing for which they were apparently wrongly convicted. Indeed, memories of indignities and injustices suffered by Irish prisoners at the hands of the British authorities are central to Behan's thoughts, helping to steel his resolve, even as they lead him to expect the worst in his own case. Due to his age, however, he receives rather lenient treatment and is sentenced to three years in the relatively comfortable Hollesley Bay Borstal Institution, despite delivering a rousing denunciation of the British colonial domination of Ireland at his trial.

Behan finds life at Hollesley Bay surprisingly easy to bear, especially as Charlie Millwall is sent there as well. In fact, Behan forms a number of friendships with the other prisoners, who develop a sense of solidarity based on their common working-class origins that goes well beyond the differences in religion or national origin. Indeed, as Ronald Paul puts it, the central theme of the book is Behan's movement "from a rather isolated and sectarian position of ideological abstraction to a broader and more basically class identification and fusion with the mutual working-class experiences of backstreets, factories, and work of his fellow English prisoners" (112). The primacy of class is particularly demonstrated in the text in the story of Ken Jones, a middle-class English prisoner who feels far more alienated from the other prisoners than does the Irishman Behan, to the point that Jones is driven to try to escape. Behan, as an outsider himself, is the only prisoner who seems to sympathize with Ken's plight: "In a way, as the middle class and upper class in England spend so much money and energy in maintaining the difference between themselves and the working class, Ken was only getting what his people paid for but, still and all, I couldn't help being sorry for him, for he was more of a foreigner than I" (227).

Most of Behan's experiences at Hollesley Bay are rather positive, especially as he soon manages to get himself assigned to work in the institution's painting party, work for which he had prepared as an apprentice painter before his incarceration. Indeed, Behan places great emphasis on the rewards of work and of the central role played by work in the constitution of working-class identity. While working with the painters, he meets another important friend, Tom Meadows, also a former apprentice painter. Tom is an avowed socialist whose diatribes against British capitalism and the class society that supports it provide some of the strongest political statements in the book, though Tom himself feels alienated from most of the other prisoners, whom he regards as members of the lumpenproletariat rather than as genuine workers. As fellow workers in the same trade, Tom and Brendan become friends instantaneously, especially as they share many leftist political sentiments. They also have some common cultural background, given that each, growing up among leftist painters, has been raised with Robert Tressell's *The Ragged Trousered Philanthropists* as a central part of his cultural heritage (286).

Behan, of course, is proud to note that Tressell was an Irishman, though what is clearly most significant to both boys is that Tressell was a painter like themselves. The importance of Tressell's book to both Tom and Brendan (and to the other painters with whom they have worked druing their apprenticeships) suggests the crucial role that literature can play in the development of working-class consciousness, just as cultural practices such as the numerous songs and poems shared by the prisoners contribute to their sense of solidarity. Books, in fact, are important throughout *Borstal Boy*, and Behan spends as much of his time as possible in reading virtually anything he can get his hands on. He is a great admirer of Irish writers such as James Joyce and Sean O'Casey, and he tends to seek Irish books whenever he can. Among the books that influence him most while incarcerated are Frank Harris's life of Oscar Wilde and a book by Robert Collis (*the Silver Fleece*) about Irish rugby players. Not surprisingly, however, most of the books to which Behan is exposed while incarcerated are by canonical British writers such as Charles Dickens, Elizabeth Gaskell, Thomas Hardy, and John Galsworthy. Behan, a great lover of these (and most other) books, reads them with relish and without animosity, though there is a subtle suggestion running through his very love of British literature that this literature contributes in important ways to the British cultural domination of Ireland.

All in all, *Borstal Boy* is an optimistic, even comic, book that emphasizes, especially after Behan reaches Hollesley Bay, the utopian dimension that adheres in the strong sense of solidarity that links the imprisoned boys, whatever their backgrounds. Nevertheless, they do remain prisoners whose regimented lives are punctuated by the constant threat of violence. Meanwhile, the carceral settings of the book emphasize the oppressive nature of the societies from which the boys come, whether British or postcolonial Irish. Sometimes, in fact, this connection is quite overt, as when Behan points out the carceral nature of Catholicism by suggesting that his excommunication from the Church was "like being pushed outside a prison and told not to come back" (322). Hollesley Bay at times seems almost a haven from civil society, where various divide-and-conquer strategies, such as animosities between the English and the Irish, effectively impede the growth of the kind of class consciousness that obtains inside the Borstal. Meanwhile, if violence is a fact of life for the prisoners, it is also the case that World War II looms in the outside world as a subtle background to the book. Charlie, for example, will be killed in the war soon after his release from incarceration. Behan maintains his Irish neutrality toward the war, and one of his most powerful indictments of the British consists of his argument that there is little to distinguish British tyranny from the tyranny of Nazi Germany. Thus, despite the almost pastoral presentation of Hollesley Bay, *Borstal Boy* has considerable power as a political statement. As a simultaneous commentary on class as the most important social category and on the continuing British neocolonial domination of Ireland, the book is an important example of both working-class and postcolonial literature. *Selected bibliography:* Nigel Gray; Kearney; Paul (*Fire*).

RALPH DE BOISSIÈRE: *CROWN JEWEL* **(1952).** Born in Trinidad in 1907, Ralph de Boissière developed an interest in writing in the 1920s under the encouragement of C.L.R. James and Alfred Mendes. In 1937, he observed the major social upheavals that engulfed Trinidad at the time in the wake of a bitterly fought strike by the island's oilfield workers. As a result, he became involved in radical trade union activism, a commitment that would greatly inform his subsequent writing. In 1947, after a brief stay in the United States, he immigrated to Australia, where he worked in a General Motors plant in Melbourne, thus enriching his understanding of and sympathy for the urban proletariat. Among other things, this experience led him substantially to revise his first novel, already in manuscript when he came to Australia. De Boissière's interactions with militant Australian workers influenced him to move more and more to the Left. He studied Marxism extensively and then joined the Communist Party in 1951; his three novels were all initially published by a left-wing publishing house in Australia. One novel, *No Saddles for Kangaroos* (1964), is based directly on his Australian experience, though the two earlier novels, *Crown Jewel* and its sequel *Rum and Coca-Cola* (1956), are firmly rooted in the history of the Caribbean. These remain his best-known works, especially as they were reissued, in well-received and substantially revised versions, by the British publishing house Allison and Busby in the 1980s.

Written in a mode of critical realism, *Crown Jewel* and *Rum and Coca-Cola* are sweeping historical novels that indicate, in the manner praised by Georg Lukács in relation to the great European historical novels of the early nineteenth century, the interconnectedness of all aspects of Trinidad's society during the period 1935-45. Moreover, as de Boissière points out in a brief introduction to *Crown Jewel*, the events of these years are viewed as the culmination of more than four hundred years of colonial history in the Caribbean. Also recalling the work of Lukács, de Boissière carefully connects the large public events of his narrative with the private experience of specific individuals by interweaving the life histories of individual characters from a variety of backgrounds with one another and with the history of Trinidad. For example, *Crown Jewel*, which focuses on the two years leading up to the tumultuous labor disputes of 1937, features André de Coudray, roughly based on the author, a member of the mixed-race middle class who begins to feel guilty about his relatively privileged position as the near-white son of a solicitor; André gradually develops his political consciousness and ends up an active participant in the movement for working-class liberation. He is paralleled by the character Cassie, who evolves from a timid servant into a confident, self-assertive, and effective member of the working-class movement. Both Cassie and André are counterpointed by Joe Elias, who becomes involved in working-class politics as an opportunistic way of achieving fame, then moves in the other direction, away from a commitment to the working class.

Labor activism forms a crucial part of the novel, which revolves around events such as the 1937 oilfield strikes in its presentation of recent Trinidadian history as centrally informed by the growing power of the working class as a collective agent. De Boissière's sympathies with the workers are clear, and one of the book's most admirable figures is the oilfield labor leader Ben Le Maître, who is loosely based on a combination of the historical Trinidadian working-class leaders Jim Barrette, leader of the Negro Welfare Association, and Uriah Butler, leader of the British Empire Workers and Citizens Home Rule Party. Le Maître serves as something of a mentor for both André and Cassie. Le Maître eventually marries Cassie, and his treatment of her as an intellectual equal and her role in the book as a whole, which is even more pronounced in the 1981 edition, help to make her a symbol of equality of the genders, so that gender joins race as a principal focus of the book's critique of social inequalities; at the same time, de Boissière maintains a consistent emphasis on class as the most important social category of all.

As Reinhard Sander notes, "*Crown Jewel* does not merely reconstruct Trinidad history during the late 1930s: It interprets this history from a militant, working-class perspective" (131). This historical vision combines with the book's critical presentation of social injustice and positive focus on the potential of working-class action to end injustice to make *Crown Jewel* a highly effective novel of the Left. Indeed, Trinidadian critic Clifford Sealy has described the book as Trinidad's "most important political novel" and as "the fundamental work of fiction in our society" (1-3). *Selected bibliography:* Lukács (*Historical Novel*); Rennie; Sander; Sealy.

NADINE GORDIMER: *BURGER'S DAUGHTER* (1979). *Burger's Daughter*, like all of Gordimer's fiction, is closely related to her historical context in South Africa, and, as a group, her works track the history of South Africa from the early years of apartheid to the early aftermath of apartheid's demise. Stephen Clingman is surely right when he argues that the most important characteristic of Gordimer's fiction is its intense engagement with its historical context, marked by Gordimer's ability to "maintain an extraordinarily close observation of the world in which she lives" (7). *Burger's Daughter*, one of Gordimer's better-known and most respected novels, is also one of the most representative in this sense. Events such as the Sharpeville and Soweto massacres inform the narrative of the book in crucial ways, while the individual life of Gordimer's protagonist, Rosa Burger, is inextricably intertwined with the history of South Africa, especially the history of resistance to apartheid. Indeed, *Burger's Daughter* can be seen as a complex, dialogic combination of two of the most important European novelistic genres: in telling the story of the growth and maturation of Rosa Burger, the book clearly participates in the tradition of the bildungsroman; in connecting the experience of its characters to a narrative of the national history of South Africa, the book recalls the great European historical novels of the nineteenth century.

This combination of genres parallels the book's consistent attempt to connect public and private realms of experience, a connection that begins in the very first scene of the *Burger's Daughter*, in which we are introduced to fourteen-year-old Rosa as she waits outside a South African prison with a group of people who have come to deliver clothing and other items to some of the prisoners within. We soon learn, however, that this schoolgirl's participation in this public political event has a strong personal dimension; she has come to bring a quilt and hot-water bottle to her mother, Cathy Burger, who is being held in the prison for her antiapartheid political activities. The major issues that will be central to the remainder of the text are already put into place in this relatively brief introductory scene. Most obviously, Rosa and her parents are identified and placed within the historical context of resistance to apartheid. We learn that Rosa's father, the communist leader Lionel Burger, is a particularly prominent opponent of apartheid, that Cathy is an important dissident as well, and that Rosa has had to assume unusual responsibility in her young life because of her parents' frequent arrests and imprisonment for their political activities.

Burger's Daughter consists of three major sections. The first deals primarily with the historical and political situation in South Africa and with the attempts of the Burgers and their circle to change that situation.

Among other things, it narrates the history of leftist politics in South Africa, focusing in particular on Lionel's final trial, which leads to a life sentence and to his death in prison only a few years later. This section thus might be seen as public in its orientation, though Gordimer maintains a focus on the effects on Rosa of the oppressive South African political system and of the Burgers' opposition to that system. In the second section, Rosa, unable any longer to deal with the abject political realities of apartheid South Africa, flees to the south of France, where she seeks personal happiness in the carefree lifestyle pursued there by Lionel's first wife, Katya, and her circle. The orientation of this section is thus primarily private. In the third section, Rosa realizes that her flight was irresponsible and returns to South Africa to do what she can to help the situation there. One might, then, view this third section as a sort of resolution of the conflict between public and private orientations that informs the contrast between the first two sections. Indeed, critics have argued that the plot structure of the novel is dialectical. That is, they believe the plot moves from the thesis of public responsibility in the first section, to the antithesis of the search for personal happiness in the second section, to a synthesis of these emphases in the third section. However, the public and private spheres are actually interwoven throughout the text. Thus, in the first and most "public" of the sections, Rosa's first-person speeches are addressed to her lover, the apolitical Conrad, whose relationship to her is personal and who is, himself, an almost allegorical representative of the private sphere. The second, most "private" section revolves around Katya, but Katya herself is a former communist, and hints of politics creep in even in the sun-and-fun world of the French Riviera. Meanwhile, the dialogic generic combination of bildungsroman and historical novel infuses the entire text.

In its attempt to link public and private realms of experience, *Burger's Daughter* can be seen as an attempt to recover some of the energies of the early nineteenth-century novels praised by Georg Lukács, a suggestion that gains support from the fact that Gordimer has frequently commented upon Lukács and has identified him as one of the major influences on her work. Clingman thus suggests that Gordimer found in Lukács a theorist whose work reflected the historical consciousness she was seeking to convey in her fiction (8–10). Moreover, while Clingman sees the major parallel between Gordimer and Lukács as a general insistence on thinking historically, Dominic Head is more precise in concluding that the major parallel with Lukács in Gordimer's work is her emphasis on "a dialectical interaction between public and private realms" (13–4). Clingman notes that such typification is common in Gordimer's writing, especially in *Burger's Daughter*, where Rosa, herself, is perhaps the clearest example of Gordimer's creation of characters who are typical in the Lukácsian sense (Clingman 173). In fact, many of the book's characters have typical aspects, so that the interaction among them dramatizes the interaction among large historical forces. Rosa's name identifies her as a point of confluence of the private and the public. Christened "Rosemarie," but called "Rosa," she is named both for her grandmother Marie Burger (a private connection) and for the important communist thinker and revolutionary activist Rosa Luxemburg (a public connection). Meanwhile, the Burger name itself has the same root as "bourgeois," introducing further ironies into the family's position as opponents of bourgeois ideology even as they enjoy upper-class economic privileges—and, in South Africa, the privileges associated with being white.

In addition, Lionel Burger is clearly representative of the general leftist opposition to apartheid, though he is also a complex and carefully drawn individual. Gordimer is careful to make Burger a figure of genuine compassion and humanity who has a successful professional career and a rich personal life enriched by numerous important personal relationships, despite his devotion to his political cause. Far from adopting a rigid and doctrinaire "party line," the Burgers and their associates are willing to adapt their beliefs to historical circumstances and, in particular, to the special situation in apartheid South Africa. Rosa, herself, makes it clear that the communism of her parents was carefully tailored to "local conditions" rather than simply following Soviet or Chinese models., and she insists on the particularly personal, human nature of the Burgers' communism. Lionel Burger's individual humanity is further reinforced by the fact that he is not merely a generalized figure of abstract political ideas, but seems to have been based largely on Bram Fischer, an important South African communist whose antiapartheid activities, extensive enough to cause some to compare him to Nelson Mandela, led to his own imprisonment for life in 1966. Meanwhile, Gordimer's own admiration for Fischer's political commitment and genuinely warm humanity make it highly unlikely that she intends Burger, based on Fischer in a very direct way, to be seen as anything other than admirable.

In short, Burger is a genuinely typical figure in that he embodies both public and private forces, while Conrad, who represents private concerns divorced from the public world, is a far flatter figure who might be described as more allegorical than typical. Of course, Gordimer's characterization of Conrad in this way is entirely appropriate in the sense that it suggests the divorce between the private and public that is central to the decadent bourgeois ideology that Conrad represents. The relative richness of Burger's characterization, meanwhile, suggests the relative richness of his communist social vision, which inherently seeks to establish links between the public and private worlds. That the affluent white Afrikaner Burger is the text's central figure of opposition to both capitalism and apartheid is also indicative of the complexities of politics in South Africa. As a Marxist, Burger understands that history is driven primarily by economic conflict between classes; as a South African, he knows that race, not class, is the most obvious source of division and conflict in his society. In South Africa, as in America, race and class are closely interrelated. Clingman's suggestion that under apartheid "lines of class and race coincide" is probably a slight exaggeration, but it is certainly the case that in South Africa whites are likely to occupy professional and management positions, while blacks can hope at best for positions as workers (15). Burger understands this situation quite well and further understands that racism arises primarily as an attempt to justify and maintain the class structure of South African society. In this sense, he again resembles Fischer, who, according to Gordimer, "sees the colour problem in South Africa as basically an economic one: the white man's fear of losing his job to the overwhelming numbers of Africans" (*Essential* 73).

In *Burger's Daughter*, Gordimer openly endorses the contributions of the South African Communist Party to the antiapartheid movement, even as she acknowledges the complexity of South African politics, including in her text criticisms of the Communist Party by other antiapartheid, groups such as the Black Consciousness movement. In this sense, it is important that her main historical source seems to have been the essay "South Africa—No Middle Road," by the important South African communist Joe Slovo (Clingman 186-87). In fact, Gordimer often employs unattributed quotations from Slovo and other Marxist writers, including Marx and Engels, making *Burger's Daughter* a sort of collage of leftist writing. Given that Gordimer quotes primarily from Marxist thinkers, one could see her use of unattributed quotation as an expression of solidarity with these thinkers and as an acknowledgment of their belief in collective action and rejection of individualism and bougeois property relations. In any case, *Burger's Daughter* is an impressive evocation of recent South African history and a convincing demonstration that the history of the South African Communist Party is, as Clingman puts it, "a proud one" (173). **Selected bibliography:** Clingman; Ettin; Gordimer (*Essential*); Head; Peck (*One Foot*); Wagner.

NADINE GORDIMER: *A SPORT OF NATURE* **(1987).** *A Sport of Nature* is, ostensibly, a bildungsroman that relates the story of its protagonist, Hillela Capran. As the title indicates, Hillela is a highly unusual figure. As a white Jewish female in Africa, she is triply marginal to the society around her. Moreover, she is reared by two aunts and eventually expelled from both households, thus emphasizing her status as an outsider. She also violates many of the expectations of modern bourgeois society, both because her specific conduct (sexual and otherwise) often breaks accepted rules of feminine behavior and because, as a strong, independent, and capable woman, she generally fails to conform to her society's stereotypes of feminine subjectivity. At the same time, however, Hillela is centrally involved in a number of important historical events that shape the world in which she lives. *A Sport of Nature* is, in fact, an ambitious historical novel as well as a bildungsroman. In this sense, it resembles the earlier *Burger's Daughter*, except that *A Sport of Nature* has an even broader scope and suggests more strongly the possibility of historical change. In particular, the book is centrally informed by historical energies deriving from earlier African anticolonial independence movements, projecting those energies forward in what would turn out to be a prophetic vision of the fall of the system of apartheid in South Africa.

A Sport of Nature begins with Hillela attending a boarding school in Salisbury, in what was then colonial Rhodesia. She is then expelled from her school for fraternizing with a boy of mixed race. She stays for a while in Salisbury with her father and his English second wife, then returns to Johannesburg to live with the family of her aunt Olga, the sister of Hillela's mother (who is living in Mozambique, having moved there to follow her Portuguese lover). After a disagreement with Olga, Hillela moves in with her other aunt, Pauline, who, with her husband Joe, is active in South African liberal politics. Joe, in fact, is part of the legal defense team for Lionel Burger, and Rosa Burger, the title character of *Burger's Daughter*, at one point visits the family. Hillela thus grows up in a political atmosphere, but controversies over her unconventional behavior (she secretly works as a go-go dancer in a shop window and engages in sex play with her cousin, Sasha) eventually leads her to leave the family and strike out on her own.

The tumultuous nature of Hillela's life is thus established early on, as is the tumultuous nature of South African politics, details of which are carefully filled in amid the narration of Hillela's personal experiences. Once on her own, Hillela gets a job as a psychiatrist's receptionist but soon leaves to avoid the sexual advances of her employer. She then becomes involved with Andrew Rey, a journalist who is also active in the underground resistance movement. Eventually, the two flee to Tanganyika, where Rey (who may be a double agent working for the South African government) suddenly disappears, leaving Hillela on her own in the foreign environment. She lives in a colony of exiles on Tamarisk Beach, suffering poverty and the threat of deportation until she joins the household of a foreign ambassador, working for the ambassador's wife in a variety of domestic roles but eventually becoming the mistress of the ambassador as well.

When the ambassador is reposted to Ghana, Hillela moves there with the family. In Accra, she marries Whaila Kgomani, a black revolutionary whom she had met earlier in Dar es Salaam. Pregnant, she studies revolutionary theory and joins the discussions of Kgomani's group of leftist dissidents. Their child, a girl, looks black and is named Nomzamo, after Mrs. Mandela. The family moves to London for a time, then on to Lusaka, where Kgomani is involved in the planning of a major guerrilla action against South Africa. There, Hillela, again pregnant, meets Oliver Tambo. The planned campaign goes awry, and, as the guerrillas attempt to regather their forces, Kgomani is assassinated by agents of the South African government, who may have actually been seeking Tambo. Amid the trauma of her husband's death, Hillela loses her baby.

At the age of twenty-five, Hillela travels to Eastern Europe to rally support for the movement. She works there for two years, then moves on the America in the hope of gaining more financial support for the cause. In America, Hillela is a hit on the lecture circuit and advances to a position of prominence. She becomes sexually involved with Bradley Burns, the son of a longtime leftist white family, and nearly marries him. However, on a trip to Africa she meets the black African guerrilla leader Reuel and becomes involved with him instead. Reuel, referred to in the text primarily as "The General," is a former general in the anticolonial resistance movement and has briefly been president of his country (unspecified in the text) before being deposed in a coup supported by his country's former colonial rulers. When Hillela meets him he is working to regain power and to restore the legitimate government of his country. Hillela works closely with him in the effort, sending Nomzamo to England to boarding school. The General retakes his capital and Hillela (now bearing the official name of Chiemeka, Igbo for "god has done very well") ascends to power at his side, though he also has two black wives.

The new nation thrives under the General's rule, and Hillela/Chiemeka remains active in affairs of state. The situation remains grim in South Africa, however, and Hillela's cousin, Sasha, now a trade union activist, receives a lengthy prison sentence for his opposition to the apartheid regime. He serves his sentence and is eventually released. Meanwhile, President Reuel becomes a prominent pan-African leader, and the system of apartheid finally collapses. The book ends as the President and Hillela attend a huge ceremony in South Africa celebrating the birth of the new postapartheid nation. The ending is thus strongly utopian, so much so that critics such as Richard Peck attacked it as simplistic and unrealistic when the book was first published (*What's a Poor White* 83). In retrospect, of course, Gordimer's projection of the South African future was quite accurate, adding force to the historical movement that informs her entire narrative.

A Sport of Nature is a complex and ambitious work, though not without its flaws. For example, while the book is consistently sympathetic to leftist political positions, neither the book nor its protagonist shows a coherent, well-developed political philosophy. In particular, the book's political position is based primarily on opposition to apartheid, without making a particularly strong case for the complicity between apartheid and capitalism. Further, Hillela's political position is largely based on a problematic project for interracial equality that is symbolized by her sexual relationships with black men. Thus, as Brenda Cooper has argued, *A Sport of Nature* tends to focus on issues of race at the expense of an inadequate treatment of class and gender. In addition, while Hillela is certainly the central figure of the book, her most important asset seems to be her sexuality and her most important accomplishments are achieved through her sexual liaisons with powerful men. There has, in fact, been a significant amount of critical disagreement over the characterization of Hillela. Dominic Head, for example, believes that Hillela's sexuality is treated positively as something that allows her to "break restrictive taboos, and inspire in herself and in others productive committed action" (142–43). Peck believes that the book is informed by an ironic gap between the narrator and the protagonist that suggests a potential disapproval of Hillela's actions. He also concludes that this gap results in an ultimate ambivalence that undermines the book's political message. Barbara Temple-Thurston, on the other hand, argues that any confusion over the interpretation of Hillela is intentional and serves as part of a consistent ambiguity that can be seen as an attempt to explore a new aesthetics that rejects the simplistic oppositions of apartheid. Such ambiguities are also central to Head's vision of *A Sport of Nature* as a metafictional postmodernist text. Ultimately, however, these ambiguities may weaken the book's political message. Nevertheless, the book has important assets as a political novel, including its strong sense of a historical drive toward a utopian future and the strong sense of connection between the private experiences of Hillela and public events from African and world history. This powerful engagement with political reality marks the book as an excellent example of the often intense political engagement of the postcolonial African novel. **Selected bibliography:** Cooper; Head; Peck (*What's a Poor White*); Temple-Thurston.

FESTUS IYAYI: *HEROES* (1986). In the late 1960s, the dissatisfaction of the Igbo people with their position in Nigeria led to the secession of the eastern region, led by Lt. Col. Chukwuemeka O. Ojukwu, from the nation. Ojukwu proclaimed the region the Republic of Biafra on May 30, 1967. A bloody civil war ensued, leading eventually to Biafra's surrender on January 15, 1970, and to the restoration of the original boundaries of Nigeria. In addition to massive casualties from the actual fighting, it is estimated that more than a million Igbos starved to death as a result of the war. This civil war is one of the major defining events of the postcolonial history of Nigeria and has been, understandably an important focus of Nigerian fiction in the last quarter of a century. Of the numerous novels to deal with the war (one might cite Buchi Emecheta's 1982 *Destination Biafra* and Isidore Okpewho's 1976 *The Last Duty* as prominent examples), Festus Iyayi's powerful *Heroes* (which won the Commonwealth Book Prize in 1986) is the one that treats the war most trenchantly from a leftist perspective. The central point made by Iyayi in the book is a simple one: the intertribal warfare that informed the civil war was instigated by a few powerful leaders on both sides who stood to gain both power and wealth from the war. Meanwhile, the common soldiers who fought on both sides were being manipulated by these leaders into slaughtering one another when in fact their real enemies were not the soldiers on the other side but the generals and politicians instigating the war from both sides. Among other things, *Heroes* deconstructs myths of heroism in war, so that its title is largely ironic. But the book is far from a sentimental cry for peace and universal brotherhood. In fact, the book, which at one point quotes Mao Zedong's dictum that political power grows out of the barrel of a gun, is a direct call for class warfare in which all of the common people of Nigeria would unite to destroy the ruling class that has oppressed them since the beginning of independence in 1960.

Although the direct focus of *Heroes* is on the civil war, the book identifies this war as a symptom of the general corruption of postcolonial Nigerian society and not as a unique aberration in Nigerian history. Using graphic images of filth and decay, *Heroes* describes the corrupt ambience of postcolonial Nigeria in a mode that is highly reminiscent of Ayi Kwei Armah's *The Beautyful Ones Are Not Yet Born*. Iyayi's book also resembles Armah's in its understanding of this postcolonial corruption from a theoretical perspective that obviously owes a great deal to Frantz Fanon's *The Wretched of the Earth*. In fact, *Heroes* might be described as a graphic dramatization of Fanon's point that independence from colonial rule was only a first step toward liberation for the common people of Africa, who could achieve genuine freedom only through a class revolution that would remove the postcolonial bourgeoisie from power and institute direct rule by the masses. This perspective is made clear early on when Iyayi's protagonist visits a country club that had formerly served as the mansion of a British colonial official. Repelled by the luxury in which the official had lived, this protagonist concludes that economic inequalities in Nigeria are now even worse: "*The black master took over all the white colonial man's vices and when he added his own, society became blacker than darkness, selfish, greedy, dirty*" (40, Iyayi's italics).

The protagonist of *Heroes* is Osime Iyere, a journalist who works as a political correspondent for the Benin City *Daily News*. As the book begins, Benin City is under occupation by the Biafran rebels, but federal troops, whom Iyere welcomes as liberators, are on the outskirts of the city, advancing toward it. As the troops occupy the city, their senseless slaughter of the remaining Biafrans leads Iyere to begin to reconsider his position. Later, Iyere is himself kicked and beaten by soldiers for no apparent reason. Finally, Iyere's Igbo landlord, Mr. Ohiali (the father of Iyere's fiancée, Ndudi) is summarily executed by federal soldiers, even though he has had no involvement with the Biafran cause. These events lead Iyere to realize that the opposition between the Nigerians and the Biafrans is not one of good versus evil (or even legality versus illegality) and that the entire war is senseless. Iyere comes to realize the extent to which powerful leaders on both sides of the conflict are profiting from this senseless slaughter of the people of Nigeria.

Iyere agrees to help Ndudi and her mother return Ohiali's body to his home village of Oganza. They make their way there with great difficulty, passing through numerous military checkpoints on the way. Iyere then leaves them there and resolves to return to Benin City to work against the war in his capacity as a journalist. However, he makes it only to the large federal army camp at nearby Asaba, where he gets to know some of the federal soldiers and realizes that most of them are not monsters but decent human beings who have been driven to commit atrocities at the prompting of their corrupt leaders and by the pressures of the insane civil war. This camp is commanded by Brigadier Otunshi, the husband of Iyere's former lover, the ravishingly beautiful Salome. Iyere resists Salome's offers to renew their relationship and in the meantime decides to accompany the federal troops in their assault on the Biafran stronghold at Onitsha, which Otunshi hopes to capture as a wedding present for Yakubu Gowon, the Nigerian head of state whose oppressive military government had created conditions leading to the Biafran succession. In the heat of the ensuing battle, the Nigerian officers desert their men, who are routed, suffering heavy casualties. Humiliated and frustrated, the soldiers return to Asaba and massacre the nearly two hundred Biafran prisoners who are being held there. Despite the fiasco, Otunshi (who has become wealthy during the war, largely by selling arms to the Biafrans) is promoted to the rank of general. As a way of keeping up morale, the army then advances on Oganza, which is now in the hands of the Biafrans. The federal troops take the village easily, but Ndudi is raped by Biafran soldiers as they prepare to flee, then again by federal soldiers as they occupy the village. Iyere remains with her, comforting her, as the soldiers move out to attack the next village.

The message implied by these events is simple and clear, and Iyayi's compelling narration drives this message home with a visceral power. Much of the book consists of italicized passages in which Iyere, in a mode of internal monologue, meditates on the events of the book and reaches clearly stated conclusions that indicate the message of the book in direct fashion. For example, he concludes that "*the war is only another market with opportunities for profit*" and that someone needs to tell the soldiers on both sides that "*this is not their war, that they are shooting at the wrong enemies. The real enemies are the politicians who robbed the country blind, who looted the country and prompted the generals to intervene*" (90). And Iyere's ruminations are supplemented by graphic scenes that dramatize the shocking horrors of the civil war and the corruption of postcolonial Nigeria. At the same time, the book—despite its focus on the horrific atrocities being committed by both sides in the war—is not entirely negative. In fact, it contains an important utopian component and shows a strong faith in the possibility of a better future for Nigeria and for common people everywhere. For one thing, Iyayi shows the basic human decency of the common people of Nigeria, despite the horrors to which they have been exposed and in which many of them have participated. For another, he is convinced that, even if the class warfare for which he calls cannot succeed at the present time, the working class (the true "heroes" of the book and its title) will almost inevitably triumph in the long run. Iyere thus concludes that, while corrupt rulers may establish local kingdoms, "*the kingdom of the working class is the earth itself*" (133). Further, as the book ends, Iyere, holding the sobbing Ndudi in his arms, reflects on the fact that generals always seem to get the glory from war, while common soldiers do most of the work and suffer most of the casualties. He remains convinced, however, that the class inequalities implied by this situation cannot survive indefinitely, that "*it will not always be like that because a movement is bound to emerge from this war and if not from this war, then after this war. A movement which will write the history of this war and give each man and woman his or her proper due*" (247). **Selected bibliography:** Fanon; Ni Creachain; Wendt.

FESTUS IYAYI: *VIOLENCE* (1979). Festus Iyayi is a committed socialist whose novels have much in common with the Soviet movement of socialist realism and the proletarian fiction that was produced during the Depression years of the 1930s in Britain and the United States. His first novel, *Violence* (1979), relates the travails of a young Nigerian couple, Idemudia and Adisa, as they attempt to make a life for themselves in a modern Lagos dominated by the corrupt manipulations of politicians and business people. In particular, this working-class couple is structurally opposed to Obufun and Queen, a rich couple whose activities dramatize the exploitation of the Nigerian people by a corrupt postcolonial comprador bourgeoisie. Narrated in a straightforward, down-to-earth style that should make its message accessible to large numbers of Nigerian readers, *Violence* addresses a number of crucial issues, including the exploitation of workers by dishonest bosses and the ill functioning of public services, such as hospitals, because of corruption and incompetence among administrators and managers. The book also includes, in its description of the relationship between Idemudia and

Adisa, a sensitive exploration of relations between the genders in modern Nigeria. In its vivid contrast between the dire poverty of the honest, hard-working couple, Idemudia and Adisa, and the decadent luxury of the rich couple, Obufun and Queen, *Violence* presents a striking indictment of the inequities in postcolonial Nigerian society. In particular, the book demonstrates, as its title indicates, the violence (both physical and psychological) that is perpetrated by the rich against the poor. On the other hand, in the final solidarity between Idemudia and Adisa and in certain hints of the potential for successful collective action among workers against their unscrupulous bosses, the book includes a strong utopian dimension that suggests the possibility of a better future.

As the book opens, Idemudia is unemployed and he and Adisa are living in dire poverty. Upset by Adisa's impatience with his inability to find a job, Idemudia beats her, and she threatens to leave him for another man. He then goes out into a pouring rain to try to borrow money to buy food. When Idemudia and some others help to push Queen's Mercedes out of a gutter where it has gotten stuck, she hires them to unload a newly arrived shipment of cement. Queen, who has no scruples about using the allure of her voluptuous body to aid in her corrupt business dealings, pays them for their grueling labor only meagerly and reluctantly. Idemudia goes home and collapses in a fever from overwork in the heavy rain. Adisa returns home to dsicover him in a delirium and struggles to find medical help for him, eventually getting him into the Ogbe Hospital, which is so overcrowded that he has to lie on the floor because there are no available beds.

Adisa, walking in the rain to the market to buy medicine for Idemudia, accepts a lift from Obufun, who finds her attractive and offers her a job. Though lacking the money for food or for adequate medical care for Idemudia, the virtuous Adisa resists Obufun's proposal, which involves engaging her to sell bootleg whisky, which he will supply in return for sexual favors. Frustrated by her continual resistance, Obufun eventually rapes her, then supplies the whisky (plus a small amount of money) out of remorse. Idemudia, meanwhile, is held in the hospital, which refuses to release him until he pays his bill. There, he hears stories of the brutal oppression and exploitation suffered by some of the other patients. He also watches a play that is put on in the hospital as part of a festival honoring Florence Nightingale (174–89). This play, an agitprop production entitled "Violence," is a biting political satire that calls for revolution as the only cure for the ills it exposes. As the title indicates, the play is in many ways the heart of Iyayi's novel and of his revolutionary political message.

The play consists of a courtroom scene in which a laborer on trial for "robbery with violence" explains his actions in terms of the need to feed his children when an exploitative economic system refuses to allow him sufficient wages on which to live, regardless of how hard he labors. The man is ordered chained and removed from the courtroom by the outraged judge, a staunch defender of the status quo. Then, the trial of a second defendant, a school teacher also accused of theft, begins. His counsel also pleads hardship and points out that numerous figures of authority in Nigeria have committed far worse crimes in their rise to wealth and power. Indeed, the counsel suggests that the majority of the people of Nigeria have more than adequate reason to turn to crime, given the overall corruption of the society. This defendant, too, is ordered out before his defense can be completed, at which time a third accused robber is brought into the courtroom. This third defendant, finally, has been mostly jobless for years, driven to robbery in order to survive. The counsel again defends him on the basis of need and points out that the man's violence against property is nothing compared to the violence against human dignity perpetrated by the capitalist system of postcolonial Nigeria: "We often do not realize that it is the society, the type of economic and political system which we are operating in our country today that brutalises the individual, rapes his manhood. We often do not realise that when such men of poor and limited opportunities react, they are only in a certain measure, answering violence with violence. What I would like to see, however, is not just for a handful of men to take up arms to rob one individual. I feel and think it is necessary that all the oppressed sections of our community ought to take up arms to overthrow the present oppressive system" (185). This tactic causes the judge to panic and to sentence all of the accused robbers to death, but word then comes that the verdict is void because the judge has already been dismissed from his position for refusing to share his revenues from bribes with his superiors. The play thus ends, causing a powerful reaction from a newly enlightened Idemudia and the other members of the audience.

Finally released from the hospital, Idemudia gets a job working for Queen in the construction of a government housing project. He finds that the workers on the project are cruelly exploited and, though afraid of losing his job, he soon becomes involved in efforts to organize the men for a potential strike. In so doing, he continues to gain new insights into his life that explain the significance of the book's title: "His unfinished education, his joblessness, his hunger, his poverty, all these he found out were different forms of violence. It consisted not of physical, brutal assault but of a slow and gradual debasement of himself, his pride as a man" (243).

The site engineer warns Queen of the possibility of a strike and identifies Idemudia as the ringleader. She then tries to bribe Idemudia to avert the strike, but he refuses her offer of money. She then makes him foreman in an effort to estrange him from the workers, who begin to distrust him in his new position. Queen then lures Idemudia to her room at the Freedom Motel and offers him sex in return for his cooperation. When he again refuses, the embittered Queen tells him that Adisa has slept with Obufun. Enraged, Idemudia returns home determined to kill Adisa, but then realizes that she must have done it for him, just as he had earlier been willing to sell his blood to get money for her. In the end, they are reconciled, determined to face the tribulations of life in postcolonial Nigeria together. Clearly, however, the final relationship between Idemudia and Adisa is not romanticized and idealized but stands as an emblem of the necessity of solidarity among members of the oppressed classes of Africa.

Violence has been characterized by Udenta Udenta as a successful example of "revolutionary aesthetics" that is informed by "an ideology of dialectical changes, of great transitions from quantity into quality; and of leaps from a particular situation to another that is radically different" (71). The book combines a vivid presentation of both the hardships of Africa's poor and the contribution made to these hardships by the selfishness and corruption of Africa's decadent postcolonial ruling class. And it does so in a way that clearly elaborates the material and economic bases of the situation it describes. Furthermore, as Chidi Amuta emphasizes, the proletarian characters of *Violence* "do not simply accept, fatalistically, their plight. They act in concert with a view to challenging the system and changing it" (157). In that sense, the book is one of the most successful leftist novels from Africa or anywhere else. Critical of the capitalist present and clear about the steps necessary to attain a possible socialist future, *Violence* is formally sophisticated, yet straightforward and imminently accessible. The book thus stands as an exemplary effort to enlighten the working class of the true causes of their impoverished lives and to stir them to action to eliminate those causes. **Selected bibliography:** Amuta; Udenta.

C.L.R. JAMES: *MINTY ALLEY* **(1936).** Important as an editor, activist, historian, cultural critic, political theorist, and novelist, C.L.R. James is one of the central figures in the intellectual history of the modern Caribbean. Indeed, James was one of the world's leading intellectuals of the twentieth century. Born in Trinidad, James spent a great deal of time in both Britain and the United States and was highly influential in both countries as well as throughout the Third World. In 1937, James published *World Revolution*, a study of the Communist International that established him as a major voice in modern Marxism. The book was opposed to many of the bureaucratic tendencies of Stalinism and importantly influenced by Leon Trotsky; at the same time, it provided an analysis of world Marxism from a Third World perspective distinct from the main trends in Marxist thought in Europe. *The Black Jacobins* (1938), a history of the slave rebellion that began in the French colony of Saint-Domingue in 1791 and eventually led to the birth of Haiti as the first black-ruled postcolonial state in 1804, may be his most important single work. A founding work of Third World anticolonial historiography, *The Black Jacobins* provided inspiration for such later historians as Eric Williams and Walter Rodney. It was reissued in a revised 1962 edition that included an appendix by James linking the revolution in Haiti to the recent revolution in Cuba as part of a historical quest for an independent Caribbean national identity. James is also the author of *Beyond a Boundary* (1963), a complex and highly original work of cultural history that was to be one of the founding texts in the burgeoning field of cultural studies. Among James's numerous other works was *American Civilization*, a sweeping posthumously published Marxist study of American society and culture emphasizing the crucial role played by mass production in their development.

As a central figure in the political and literary group that formed around such Trinidadian journals as *The Beacon* in the 1930s, James made crucial contributions to the birth of the Caribbean novel as an important phenomenon in cultural history of the Caribbean and in the literature of the world in the twentieth century. With the publication of his own novel, *Minty Alley*, James, himself, made a major contribution to the growth of the Caribbean novel as a cultural and political force. *Minty Alley* focuses on the poor dwellers of No. 2 Minty Alley, which features a front house inhabited by the landlady, Mrs. Rouse, and a backyard containing a number of outbuildings that she rents out to poorer tenants. James makes clear the harsh conditions under which these tenants — and even Mrs. Rouse herself — must exist, but he concentrates less on naturalistic descriptions of their impoverished living conditions than on the sense of communal cooperation that marks the lives of the alley's inhabitants. In this sense, the book anticipates the positive emphasis of most of James's later work as a historian and cultural critic.

Conditions in the alley are described largely from the point of view of the protagonist Haynes, who is based to some extent on James. Haynes leaves his middle-class home after the death of his mother and, as a sort of declaration of his coming of age, goes to live in the less commodious surroundings of Minty Alley. Initially, his middle-class background and perspective set him apart from the yard's other inhabitants, but, as the book proceeds, he becomes more and more involved in the life of the yard. Merle Hodge, in a review of the 1971 re-publication of the book has argued, in fact, that the book's central project is a demonstration that cooperation between the Caribbean working class and the educated middle class is of value to both classes (11). On the other hand, as Reinhard Sander points out, Haynes remains somewhat alienated from the other inhabitants of No. 2 Minty Alley during his stay there, even in midst of the sexual relationship he establishes with one of them, Maisie (Sander 101). Indeed, even Maisie continues to address him as "Mr. Haynes," and she is aware from the beginning of their relationship that their class difference will preclude anything more serious between them than a brief fling. The naïve Haynes learns a great deal about sex from Maisie, who also teaches him important lessons about friendship and life in general. At the end of the book, however, Haynes leaves Maisie and the yard. Though he occasionally visits Mrs. Rouse after moving away, he gradually begins to forget his former neighbors, again emphasizing the alienation between his middle-class perspective and the working-class perspectives of the other characters.

Though James leaves this important problem of alienation between the classes in Trinidadian society unsolved in *Minty Alley*, the book at least begins to address it. Further, as Sander notes, the "pioneering achievement of James's novel lies in its presentation of lower-class life itself" (102). *Minty Alley* makes clear the difficulties faced by its working-class characters without sensationalizing or romanticizing their plights. In its sympathetic understanding that its working-class characters, of both genders, are not merely victims of economic oppression but genuine human beings with rich interior lives and considerable personal resources, *Minty Alley* broke new ground in the literary representation of Britain's colonial subjects and of Britain's working class in general. Though James would concentrate, after *Minty Alley*, on the writing of history and political commentary, his one book-length work of fiction is a successful and important contribution to both Caribbean literature and international working-class literature. ***Selected bibliography:*** Buhle (*Artist as Revolutionary*); Buhle (*Life and Work*); Cudjoe and Cain; Grimshaw; Hodge; Nielsen; Worcester.

ALEX LA GUMA: *IN THE FOG OF THE SEASONS' END* **(1972).** The political commitment central to all of La Guma's work is not unusual in African literature, but *In the Fog of the Seasons' End*, in its elaboration of the possibilities for armed resistance to apartheid, represents a step toward the advocacy of violent revolution that is distinctive in African literature and a significant turning point in La Guma's career. The book focuses on the activities of a secret underground organization dedicated to the destruction of apartheid in South Africa. Its two principal protagonists are the "colored" operative Beukes, who gives up a happy personal life to devote himself to revolutionary activity, and the black organizer Elias Tekwane, who is captured by the South African police, then tortured and beaten to death. La Guma refuses to romanticize revolutionary activity, showing in stark fashion the sacrifices that must be made in the interest of a cause the ultimate success of which is by no means certain. Tekwane's fate is gruesome, while Beukes's work is more tedious than glamorous, and he is forced to endure extreme physical and mental hardship in the course of his day-to-day political activities. At the same time, *In the Fog of the Seasons' End* does contain a strong utopian dimension. During his torture, Tekwane refuses to reveal any information the police can use against the movement. Meanwhile, partly because of Tekwane's heroic silence, Beukes escapes from the police and succeeds in his mission of smuggling three other revolutionaries out of South Africa for military training in preparation for a possible all-out war against apartheid.

Most of the events in the narrative of *In the Fog of the Seasons' End* involve the efforts of Beukes to distribute antiapartheid pamphlets and otherwise work against the system while at the same time avoiding the South African secret police. In the course of these activities, Beukes frequently recalls earlier happy times spent with his wife, Frances, though Beukes has not seen Frances or their young child for some time, since being forced underground. Beukes sometimes longs simply to lead a normal, peaceful life with his family apart from the dangerous world of revolutionary politics, but he also knows that, as a "colored" South African, he can never do so. He is willing to sacrifice his personal life for the movement because he knows that the destruction of apartheid is crucial to any hope he and his family might have of living a life free of oppression and humiliation.

If it is through Beukes that La Guma gives us a glimpse of the daily lives of those who work in the underground resistance to apartheid, it is through the story of Tekwane that La Guma presents the brutal realities that make such resistance necessary. Not only does Tekwane's torture at the hands of the South African authorities dramatize the cruelties of apartheid, but La Guma's presentation of the humiliations suffered by Tekwane throughout his life simply because of his skin color serves as a vivid reminder that apartheid's evils were not limited to prisons and police stations but were an integral part of everyday life for the citizens of South Africa. La Guma makes it clear that Tekwane's case is not unique and that his experience, however horrifying, is that of many nonwhites in South Africa.

For La Guma, apartheid reduces nonwhites to dehumanized, interchangeable objects and is thus a particularly brutal and overt example of the ways in which individuals are inevitably reduced to the status of commodities under capitalism. Tekwane, the most theoretically sophisticated of the major characters in *In the Fog of the Seasons' End*, is perfectly well aware that there is more than racism at stake in apartheid. There is also a strong economic motivation behind the system. Tekwane thus realizes as he watches a crowd of blacks standing outside a government labor bureau hoping to be assigned menial jobs, that these men, like himself, are oppressed at least as much because of their class positions as their skin color. "We are not only humbled as Blacks," he thinks to himself, "but also as workers; our blackness is only a pretext" (131).

Tekwane, like La Guma, believes that, in order to end their oppression, South African workers must band together to oppose their exploitation by their rich bosses. Indeed, La Guma is careful to make the revolutionary movement in *In the Fog of the Seasons' End* multiracial, emphasizing the fact that its members belong to a common class rather than a common race and that their ultimate struggle is against the class structure of capitalism, of which apartheid is but a particularly perverse and brutal form. La Guma thus stresses the need for the development of a strong proletarian class consciousness, that is, of a sense of solidarity and common interest among workers of whatever race. In this sense, La Guma's work recalls that of Frantz Fanon, who insists that any genuine liberation from the brutal racial inequities of colonialism (of which apartheid is an extension) requires a complete transformation not simply of racial power structures, but of class structure. As Abdul JanMohamed puts it, the "major imperative" of La Guma's fiction is a search for viable, nonexploitative communities that will allow their members to escape the oppression they have experienced under apartheid; JanMohamed identifies the "mutual care, concern, and respect" of the members of the underground movement in *In the Fog of the Seasons' End* as an important example of such a community (255). The movement, in short, represents an important step toward the development of a viable proletarian class consciousness that can lead to a class-based revolution.

While La Guma's focus in *In the Fog of the Season's End* is on the physical brutality of apartheid and the concomitant need for violent resistance to the apartheid regime, La Guma also acknowledges the ideological and cultural practices that were long used to shore up the system of apartheid. In particular, he clearly indicates that the popular culture of global capitalism, largely American in origin, helps to create a mindset in South Africa that works in the interest of the perpetuation of apartheid. Beukes, himself, sometimes feels that his cloak-and-dagger existence is like something from a film (25). At the same time, he realizes that the filmlike nature of his existence is an aberration brought about by the unnatural system of apartheid. But other South Africans are not so adept at seeing beyond the complex entanglement of fiction and reality that characterizes their society.

This motif is most obvious in the portrayal of Beukes's friend, Tommy, a decent young man who nevertheless has little interest in political activism, largely because his mind is too immersed in the escapist world of popular culture. Tommy responds to almost every event in his life through reference to the images and ideas conveyed by (mostly American) film and popular music. Tommy, in short, retreats into the escapist world of popular culture in order to avoid dealing with the cruel world of reality in South Africa. As the narrator puts it (from a perspective filtered through the consciousness of Beukes), reality for Tommy "could be shut out by the blare of dance-bands and the voices of crooners. From this cocoon he emerged only to find the means of subsistence, food and drink. Politics meant nothing to him" (53).

What in the West passes for "high" art (that is, art that is intended for consumption by the ruling classes rather than the working classes) also comes in for criticism in *In the Fog of the Seasons' End*. Realizing that Tommy, despite his fascination with Western culture, knows nothing about classical music, Beukes remarks that "There's things poor people just don't get to hear" (57). Meanwhile, at one point the South African authorities attempt to demonstrate their enlightened attitude by proposing (in the manner of Marie Antoinette's famous "let them eat cake") to allow nonwhites occasional access to a new opera house, though they will be unlikely to be able to afford to go there. Beukes thus dismisses the plan as a ruse, and Elias rejects it as well. Access to an opera house is of very little use to a population that is starving to death: "What a peculiar way of thinking they have," he tells Beukes, "Opera house and no bread" (131).

Indeed, for South Africa's oppressed majority, access to this opera house may not only be of little use, but may contribute to the problem by creating a diversion from the real problems of South African society. This suggestion that the niceties of Western bourgeois aesthetics are irrelevant or even harmful in the crisis context of apartheid South Africa can be read as a sort of allegorization of La Guma's own literary project, which dispenses with common Western expectations that art will present pleasant and beautiful images disengaged from the world of politics. This is not, however to say that aesthetic and formal concerns are irrelevant to La Guma's project in *In the Fog of the Seasons' End*. For example, JanMohamed notes that the fragmented formal structured of the book helps to convey the chaotic nature of life for guerrillas involved in revolutionary activity (257). It is important, however, to recognize that La Guma's use of formal techniques is intended not to set his work apart from the world of politics and history, but to effect a more intense engagement with that world. In short, La Guma's work, like all literature, depends on a certain aesthetic dimension for its effects, but the aesthetics of the book differ significantly from those of Western bourgeois literature. The particular urgency of the political message of *In the Fog of the Seasons' End* marks it as an African—and especially as a South African—text. Indeed, African revolutionary writers such as Ngugi wa Thiong'o and Ousmane Sembène are clearly La Guma's closest literary comrades. But La Guma has important predecessors among European writers, as well. Many of these are Russians, whose marginality to European history may have appealed to La Guma, though La Guma's most important Russian influence,

Maxim Gorky, is regarded worldwide as one of the great figures of socially engaged literature, and leftist writers all over the world have identified Gorky as an important model. This mutual interest in Gorky suggests that readers who would wish to find Western analogues to La Guma's fiction should search for them not in the canonical "Great Tradition" of Western bourgeois literature, but in the works of American proletarian writers such as Mike Gold and Jack Conroy or British socialist writers such as Robert Tressell and Lewis Grassic Gibbon. **Selected bibliography:** Asein; Balutansky; Chandramohan; JanMohamed; Ngara; Rabkin; Scanlon.

GEORGE LAMMING: *IN THE CASTLE OF MY SKIN* **(1953).** George Lamming is one of the leading figures in Caribbean literature. His first novel, *In the Castle of My Skin*, won immediate recognition and provided an important boost to the Caribbean novel, then still in its infancy. Lamming went on to write several more important novels, including *The Emigrants* (1954), *Of Age and Innocence* (1958), *Season of Adventure* (1960), *Water with Berries* (1971), and *Natives of My Person* (1971). He also gained a substantial reputation as an intellectual and theorist of the postcolonial condition, as represented in such nonfiction collections as *The Pleasures of Exile* (1960) and *Conversations: Essays, Addresses, and Interviews, 1953–1990* (1992). Though continuing to regard his native Barbados as his permanent home, Lamming has traveled widely and has taught at important universities in the Caribbean and on almost every continent.

In the Castle of My Skin is a largely autobiographical work based on Lamming's childhood and adolescence in Barbados. However, like all of his work, it moves beyond the personal dimension to establish an important dialogue with the history of Barbados and of the Caribbean. Although the book is essentially a bildungsroman, relating the growth and maturation of its protagonist, designated simply as G., *In the Castle of My Skin*, as Lamming notes in his introduction, focuses on the "collective human substance" of the village in which G. lives, so that "community, not person, is the central character" (xxxvi). Thus, as Sandra Pouchet Paquet points out in her foreword, "G.'s individual predicament is always dissolving into the collective predicament of other village boys, and into the adult world of social and political relations of which the child has only partial awareness" (xvi). Lamming, however, is highly aware of these relations. He addresses in a sophisticated way a number of issues that would later become central to the field of postcolonial studies, focusing on the difficulty of establishing viable and stable individual or communal identities amid the fundamentally alienating context of colonialism. He does so through both content and form, detailing G.'s experience with and growing awareness of the impact of colonialism on the society around him in a mode that departs in many ways from the conventions of the Western bourgeois novel. The book derives important energies from Caribbean oral folk culture, representing the rhythms of popular life in Barbados, while eschewing the focus on plot and individual characterization typical of the Western novel. In particular, Lamming seeks, through a variety of strategies, such as alternating between first-person and third-person narrative voices, to establish a connection between public and private experience of precisely the kind that has been obliterated in the bourgeois novel (and bourgeois society) since the middle of the nineteenth century.

In the Castle of My Skin begins with G.'s ninth birthday, as a damaging flood sweeps through his village and forces the cancellation of his much-anticipated birthday party. This disappointment is only one of many he will suffer amid the poverty of his upbringing living with his mother in a village that is completely dominated by the white landlord, Mr. Creighton. G. does derive important sustenance from the communal cultural traditions of the poor villagers, but, as he grows older, he becomes more and more estranged from the life of the village. In particular, as he attends school, he comes to believe that education, which in this school means mastering the language and knowledge of the British colonial rulers of Barbados, is the key to a better and more prosperous life. Much of the book, in fact, focuses on the school and on the way its curriculum distorts the history and culture of the Caribbean in an attempt to convey the ideology of empire to its students. Thus, G. is faced early on with a central dilemma of the colonial subject: to succeed and to receive recognition of this success from official authority, he must learn to master discourses that are designed to demonstrate his own fundamental inferiority.

History frequently intrudes into the relatively insulated worlds of the school and the village, as when one day classes are suddenly dismissed when a strike in the nearby city leads to violent clashes between workers and police. Labor relations in Barbados are, in fact, central to the novel, which makes clear the role of the colony as a cheap source of labor for international capital. The police and other officials consistently support the employers in their battles against labor, while the workers are hampered in their efforts to organize by the betrayal of their own would-be advocates, such as the unscrupulous former teacher, Mr. Slime. Near the end of the book, major changes come to Barbados as a result of the seemingly distant outbreak of World War II. A course of military training is instituted in G.'s high school, and the reality of the war is brought home to Barbados when a large merchant ship, anchored off the island, is torpedoed. But modernity marches on, and the disruption of life in G.'s village due to economic changes, already under way before the war, continues. In particular, Creighton is selling off his properties piecemeal (to private investors that include, among others, Mr. Slime), leading to significant disruptions in the village when the new owners begin to evict tenants who have occupied the same houses and shops for decades.

Although most of the book's treatment of the foreign domination of Barbados is, understandably, focused on Great Britain, the United States also plays a major role. Late in the book, G.'s longtime friend, Trumper, returns to the island for a visit after an extended stay working in the States. Among other things, Trumper's experiences with African Americans have given him a new racial consciousness and a better understanding of what it means to be black in a world dominated by white capitalists. He also makes trenchant observations about the nature of life in America, particularly of the way in which the fast pace and constant innovation that inform American capitalism lead to a fundamental sense of unreality (284). G. listens carefully to Trumper's stories of America, but does not yet have the experience fully to comprehend them. As the book closes, however, G. is about to broaden his experience considerably, as he prepares to depart for Trinidad to take a teaching job.

Lamming, a longtime supporter of Castro's Cuba, has made his leftist politics clear in a number of ways. *In the Castle of My Skin* is centrally informed by this leftist orientation. Not only does the book's critique of colonialism imply a critique of international capitalism, but Lamming is careful to couch his observations of colonial Barbados in terms that are fundamentally economic and that are based first and foremost on class as a category of social inequities. In a mode highly reminiscent of the work of Frantz Fanon, Lamming notes, in his introduction, that the "overwhelming torment of race has made it difficult for Afro-Americans to perceive how central is the conflict of class in the ultimate liberation of black countries" (xliii). And Lamming seeks, throughout *In the Castle of My Skin*, to call attention to class and to avoid falling into the trap of obscuring the reality of class through a focus on race, although race is an obvious locus of colonial oppression. In his treatment of America, meanwhile, he warns that nominal independence from colonial rule does not necessarily mean liberation for the Third World, but may, in fact, merely lead to the replacement of British political domination by American cultural and economic domination. For example, Lamming makes clear his understanding of the threat posed to the Caribbean by the spread of an American capitalist system that seems determined to devour everything in its path: "Sometimes the twilight darkens and threatens to obliterate all memory in the tidal wave of capitalist consumerism. America spreads itself like a plague everywhere, capturing the simplest appetite with the fastest foods and nameless fripperies the advertising industry instructs us are essential needs" (xlv–xlvi). In its understanding of such issues and in its general treatment of the economic, cultural, linguistic, and historical foundations of colonialism and its successor, global capitalism, *In the Castle of My Skin* is a major contribution to the world literature of the Left. *Selected bibliography:* Fanon; Gikandi; Lamming (Introduction); Nair; Pouchet Paquet (Foreword); Pouchet Paquet (*Novels*).

PATRICK McCABE: *THE BUTCHER BOY* (1992). *The Butcher Boy* relates the story of Francie Brady, a young boy growing up in a small Irish town in the early 1960s. As such, it features many of the expected boyhood scenes, as Francie and his friend, Joe Purcell, pass their time reading comics, building hideouts, and pretending to be explorers, American Indians, or superheroes, somewhat in the mode of an updated Huckleberry Finn and Tom Sawyer. However, as the narrative proceeds, it soon becomes clear that McCabe's book is anything but a charming and heartwarming story of the innocent joys of childhood. Francie is, as Rosemary Mahoney put it in a review, "part Huck Finn, part Holden Caulfield, part Hannibal Lecter." Francie's life is, it turns out, a nightmare version of the postmodern predicament, and the various deprivations and humiliations he experiences gradually drive him into madness, culminating in his permanent incarceration in a mental hospital after his grisly murder of a local woman. In the meantime, McCabe avoids a descent into lurid sensationalism by carefully detailing the context of Francie's deterioration in ways that make the book a powerful political statement about life in modern Ireland—and under the global system of late capitalism.

For one thing, Francie's shame is very much a matter of class. The son of an abusive, alcoholic father and a mother so disappointed by life that she has long been drifting toward insanity, Francie grows up in a household that radically fails to live up to the visions of the perfect domestic situation that he has derived from the portrayals of families in Western, largely American, popular culture. The boy is dimly aware that his family, abysmally poor and emotionally dysfunctional, is an object of pity in the community at large. And this vague humiliation is crystallized when Francie and Joe pilfer the prize comic collection of Philip Nugent, the prissy son of a middle-class family that has just moved to town from England. Mrs. Nugent comes to the Brady home demanding that Francie be punished and angrily refers to the entire Brady family as slovenly pigs whose son is not fit to be in the company of her own. The young Francie is terribly wounded by this characterization, particularly because it comes painfully close to his own assessment of his family, so unlike the ones he sees on television. Soon afterward, Francie experiences another blow when Uncle Alo, his father's brother, visits from England. The family prepares a grand celebration in honor of Alo, who presumably has an important job in London and is thus the one successful member of the family. When Alo is revealed to be a failure and a fake, Francie is unable to deal with this further disappointment, so he runs away from home and walks to nearby Dublin, where he hopes to strike it rich.

In Dublin, Francie robs the till of a chip shop and starts to live it up on the take, fantasizing a rise in class by pretending to be Algernon Carruthers, a rich Englishman featured in one of the comic books he has read. Then he attends a science-fiction film about an attempted alien takeover of the earth, recalling the sorts of films that were so popular in the West at the time and that served as transparent allegories of the perceived menace of communism during the Cold War. Indeed, McCabe reinforces this interpretation of the film by having Francie overhear a woman talking about communists just before he goes into the film (40). The film makes Francie begin to get sentimental about his home, so he buys a gift for his mother and heads back to his town, only to discover when he arrives that his mother, apparently in reaction to his disappearance, has committed suicide. Francie subsequently begins to lose touch with reality, drifting in and out of a fantasy world constructed as an amalgam of clichés from popular culture and romanticized visions of the courtship and honeymoon of his parents. Meanwhile, he focuses more and more on the Nugent family as a locus of his own frustrations and humiliations. He is finally arrested and sent to a Catholic reform school after he breaks into the Nugent home, a spotless rendition of a middle-class home of precisely the kind Francie has long seen on television and in films, pretends that it is his own, then defecates on the floor.

After a poor start, Francie resolves to be on his best behavior in the reform school so that he can be released and return home. The priests are much impressed when he pretends to religiosity and even claims to have communicated directly with the Virgin Mary, though his principal experience with priests occurs when he becomes an object of sexual fascination for the pederast Father Sullivan. Eventually, Francie is driven to a violent assault on Sullivan, but he is soon released nevertheless, returning to his town only to find that Joe has now become best pals with Philip Nugent. Francie begins to reacquaint himself with the town, but finds himself shunned by Joe and hounded by Buttsy, Mrs. Nugent's brother. Meanwhile, the text takes an increasingly Gothic turn as Francie comes home one day to find his father dead, but he pretends that he is merely ill and resolves to become a good son and care for his father. Francie then helps support himself and his deccomposing father by taking a job in Leddy's Slaughterhouse, where the work well accords with Francie's increasingly morbid turn of mind.

Francie finally descends into complete madness, but within a context that emphasizes the fundamental insanity of the society around him. Popular culture remains central to McCabe's depiction of modern Irish society, which is increasingly dominated by images from America, especially during the presidency of John F. Kennedy, whose picture hangs on the walls of most of the homes in Francie's town, occupying a position of reverence rivaled only by that of the Pope. Indeed, much of the crucial action of the text occurs during the Cuban Missile Crisis of October 1962, as the inhabitants of the town grow more and more excited about the confrontation, in which they look forward to an American (and thus Irish, given Kennedy's background) triumph over Nikita Khrushchev and the Russians. Francie, however, sees little in the town that is worth defending, concluding that "Khrushchev hasn't much work to do about this place its done already" (185). The 1963 assassination of Kennedy serves as a retrospective reminder of the violence that lies at the heart of the American culture that is gaining so much influence in Ireland, a motif reinforced by the fact that Francie's favorite figure from American culture is John Wayne, hero of numerous violent films. As if the apocalyptic expectations associated with the missile crisis were not enough, the town becomes caught up in an additional apocalyptic frenzy when a local girl (appropriately enough, the daughter of the town TV repairman) announces that she has been visited by the Virgin Mary, who has announced to her that the world will soon end but that this town will be spared. Soon after, the text comes to its inevitable conclusion as Francie murders Mrs. Nugent with a bolt pistol used to slaughter pigs at Leddy's, then dumps her body in the offal heap at the slaughterhouse. He is arrested, abused by the police, and finally incarcerated in a mental hospital, apparently permanently.

Narrated by Francie in his own voice and idiom, *The Butcher Boy* impressively captures his descent into madness, while at the same time establishing a musical style that sharply contrasts with the banality of the language used by the other inhabitants of Francie's town and leads readers into sympathy with Francie's plight, despite his crimes. Thus, Denis Donoghue, identifying *The Butcher Boy* as a "proletarian novel," argues that McCabe "implies that Francie had the right instincts but should have kept them under better control" (48). But of course matters are beyond Francie's control from the very beginning. It is clear from the beginning that he is faced not just with small-town bigotry, but with a global capitalist system that has focused its awesome cultural resources on anti-Russian propaganda, thereby diverting attention from the kinds of injustices suffered by unfortunates such as Francie and assuring that no action will be taken to alleviate these injustices. In the meantime, the culture of Western capitalism has constructed a strictly defined image of appropriate and proper behavior, leaving Francie, with his background, little choice but to become an outcast and an outlaw, denied any real sense of belonging or community. **Selected bibliography:** Donoghue; Mahoney.

NGUGI WA THIONG'O: *DEVIL ON THE CROSS* (1982). *Devil on the Cross* is the author's own English translation of *Caitaani Mutharaba-ini*, a novel written by Ngugi in the Gikuyu language while detained in Kenya's Kamiti Maximum Security Prison for "subversive" activities. The book is an angry and biting satire of neocolonial oppression and corruption in Kenya. It draws upon the long heritage of courageous Kenyan resistance to colonial domination, as when positive references to the Mau Mau guerrillas of the 1950s provide examples of the kind of collective action that is again needed in opposition to oppression in Kenya (37–40). Moreover, the text draws in central ways upon indigenous Gikuyu cultural traditions. The narrator initially introduces himself as the "Prophet of Justice" and as the "Gicaandi Player," thus announcing both that the text will deal with questions of justice and that it will be narrated in the mode of the traditional Gikuyu oral storyteller. This narrator to a certain extent recedes into the background as the novel proceeds, but the initial narrative framework remains in place.

The impact of orality in *Devil on the Cross* goes well beyond mere references to oral tradition. Orality is, in fact, a fundamental aspect of the texture of the book, which Ngugi specifically designed for oral performance in order to make it more accessible to an audience of Kenyan peasants and workers, many of whom are illiterate. This profound use of Gikuyu oral traditions makes *Devil on the Cross* a crucial turning point in Ngugi's career. The book is also an important departure in that it is the first novel written by Ngugi in his native Gikuyu after he had already established a major reputation as an English language novelist. Indeed, *Devil on the Cross* marks the point at which the choice of language becomes central to Ngugi's writing, making him one of the most important figures in the ongoing debate over this issue, on which he has commented extensively in works such as *Decolonising the Mind*. By writing in Gikuyu, Ngugi signals, among other things, his focus on an audience of Kenyan peasants and workers who are, by and large, not literate in English. Thus, an overt declaration of the intended audience of *Devil on the Cross* is built into the very fabric of the book's language. The book draws extensively upon Gikuyu oral culture, and its narrative is liberally punctuated with proverbs, songs, and other elements normally associated with oral performances rather than printed novels, establishing a further line of communication with Ngugi's anticipated audience. Critics like Sam Adewoye, Bayo Ogunjimi, and Edward Sackey have thus emphasized this link to the oral tradition as one of the most important characteristics of *Devil on the Cross*.

Ngugi's book engages in a number of rich dialogues with the Western literary tradition as well. For example, the basic plot of the book parallels that of the nineteenth-century bildungsroman. *Devil on the Cross* centrally concerns the education and development of the young woman

Wariinga. As the book begins, Wariinga is a passive victim of the kind of sexual expoitation that Ngugi suggests is typical of that experienced by Kenyan women. Wariinga's consciousness is then raised when she meets the woman Wangari, who had formerly worked with the Mau Mau guerrillas, and the worker Muturi, a former Mau Mau who is now a dedicated socialist working for revolution in Kenya. She also meets the composer Gatuiria, who is trying to help build an indigenous Kenyan cultural tradition free of Western domination. He thus helps her to become aware of the importance of building a new Kenya free of foreign cultural domination. Wariinga goes with her new acquaintances to an allegorical "Thieves's Competition" in the village of Ilmorog. There she observes various "thieves and robbers," who proudly boast of their wickedness and corruption as businessmen working in league with foreign companies to exploit the Kenyan people, especially women.

Wariinga therefore abandons her earlier passive attitude, in which she hoped to find happiness through finding a man to love her and take care of her, and goes back to school to finish her engineering degree. By the end of the book she has become a competent mechanical engineer and has gained the respect and admiration of her male coworkers. She is engaged to marry Gatuiria, but it is clear that she does not rely on him for her sense of self-worth. The new, independent Wariinga thus serves as a potentially powerful positive role model for Kenya as a whole, and especially for Kenyan women.

Ngugi makes clear, however, that even Wariinga's newfound education and professional competence are not sufficient to ensure that she will be treated with dignity and respect in her society. As the book comes to a close, Wariinga discovers, to her great horror, that Gatuiria's father is none other than the Rich Old Man who seduced and abandoned her in her youth, the father of her child, Wambui. When the Rich Old Man recognizes Wariinga, he insists that she not marry his son and offers instead to resume their former relationship and again to make her his mistress. Wariinga suddenly realizes that no Kenyan woman—even one with her education and professional skills—can be free of sexual oppression as long as the country remains in the hands of Rich Old Men like this one. She takes out a gun and shoots the old man dead, thus declaring her intention to embark on a program of violent revolution against the prevailing order. As the book ends, Wariinga's fate is left undetermined, but it is clear that she can never again seek comfort merely in personal achievement. She has now committed herself to the revolutionary transformation of Kenyan society as a whole, and she has done so without the help or support of any man: Gatuiria stays behind with his slain father, unsure which side he should take. By the end of the book, therefore, Wariinga has grown from a frightened, passive, exploited woman, to a proud, defiant woman warrior.

Devil on the Cross is a didactic work designed to educate Kenyan peasants and workers in the true nature of capitalism, much in the way that proletarian novels of the 1930s sought to educate British and American workers. As G. D. Killam points out, *Devil on the Cross* can be seen as a literary enactment of the political and artistic program described in Ngugi's essays and prison diary. Killam thus notes that the book is aesthetically innovative, but suggests that this artistic innovation is employed in the service of political statement: in the book "Ngugi is not ... concerned with finding new ways to be new; he is concerned with finding new ways to be effective" (142). In this sense, the best analogue for Ngugi's project in the tradition of Western leftist literature may be the epic theater of Bertolt Brecht, which also employs aesthetic innovation in the interest of Marxist political statement. Indeed, Ngugi greatly admires Brecht as an artist, quoting Brecht's work frequently in his own nonfiction writings. *Devil on the Cross* makes particularly prominent use of some of Brecht's favorite metaphors for the workings of capitalism. Indeed, the central metaphor of *Devil on the Cross* is the very Brechtian notion that capitalism is little more than an organized system of thievery and corruption. The various competitors in the Thieves' Competition that is the centerpiece of the book are not criminals in the normal sense (the one "ordinary" thief who shows up for the competition is quickly expelled as unworthy because of the meager level of his crimes) but businessmen who make their wealth by exploiting the workers of Kenya. Ngugi also gets a great deal of symbolic mileage in *Devil on the Cross* from the central Brechtian motifs of prostitution and cannibalism. Prostitutes feature prominently in Brecht's work, where they are used as especially obvious examples of the overt commodification of human beings. Meanwhile, prostitution itself serves in Brecht's work as an image of the way even the most "personal" of relationships under capitalism are converted into mere economic transactions. *Devil on the Cross* makes frequent reference to the fact that women, the most oppressed sector of the postcolonial Kenyan populace, are frequently forced to resort to prostitution (either directly or in more subtle forms) in order to survive. Thus *Devil on the Cross* includes the story of an aged American tourist who comes to Kenya because his wealth can buy the sexual favors of young girls, whom he regards as just another example of the exotic indigenous species, such as lions and elephants, that make Kenya so attractive to foreign tourists (70–71).

Just as Brecht frequently uses cannibalism as a metaphor for the commodification of human beings under capitalism, Ngugi uses this metaphor throughout *Devil on the Cross* as a symbol of the way foreign business interests and their Kenyan collaborators are literally feeding off of the people of Kenya, though in an African novel the motif has the additional effect of reversing and thus undermining conventional European stereotypes of Africans as savage cannibals. Ngugi also links the motifs of prostitution and cannibalism directly together. He notes that, Wariinga, in her teenage years, was offered by the corrupt uncle with whom she lived to a rich acquaintance in return for his help in securing a bank loan and buying some land. The element of prostitution in this transaction is clear, but Ngugi describes it in terms that smack of cannibalism as well by suggesting that the uncle regards Wariinga as a young chick whose tender flesh will provide "soft food for a toothless old man" (142). Ngugi also extends his use of cannibalism to reinforce his suggestion throughout *Devil on the Cross* of a close complicity between Christianity and the colonial and neocolonial oppression of Kenya, which (as Odun Balogun notes) is a major element of the book.

Devil on the Cross thus effects a rich combination of Western and African generic traditions. In his use of a relatively simple and straightforward plot and of forms of Gikuyu oral narration, Ngugi has created a text that is highly accessible to Kenyan readers with relatively little experience in reading novels. Moreover, the book is easily understood when read aloud in a literal oral performance. At the same time, the book continues to present multiple layers of literary complexity for Western readers who are accustomed to the work of Joseph Conrad, William Faulkner, and other modern Western novelists. Western readers unacquainted with Gikuyu oral culture will miss important dimensions of *Devil on the Cross*; likewise, African readers or listeners unacquainted with the European novel will be unable to appreciate the profundity of Ngugi's dialogue with various forms of the Western literary tradition. The ideal reader of the book, then, is one who is highly familiar with both African and European cultural traditions. The real accomplishment of *Devil on the Cross* is that readers unacquainted with one or the other (and maybe even both) of these traditions can still find the book enjoyable and appreciate its important political message. **Selected bibliography:** Adewoye; Balogun ("Ngugi's *Devil*"); Cook and Okenimkpe; Killam; Ngugi (*Decolonising*); Ngugi (*Detained*); Ogunjimi; Sackey; Sicherman.

NGUGI WA THIONG'O: *MATIGARI* (1987). *Matigari*, translated into English by Wangui wa Goro, was the second of Ngugi's novels written in the Gikuyu language. The book draws heavily upon traditions of Gikuyu oral narrative to tell the story of its title character, a seasoned Mau Mau warrior, who emerges from the forests of Mount Kenya several decades after Kenyan Independence only to discover that very few of the goals of the Mau Mau anticolonial struggle have actually been accomplished. Enraged, Matigari vows to renew the fight for freedom in Kenya. Matigari is probably modeled upon a real-life Mau Mau hero, the famous general Stanley Mathenge, who disappeared with two hundred fighters at the end of the Mau Mau rebellion. Indeed, many Kenyans to this day believe that Mathenge and his warriors will emerge from the forests and continue to fight for the people suffering under neocolonialist regimes. (For a discussion of Mathenge see Paul Maina.) On the other hand, Matigari is clearly an allegorical figure who stands as a general representation of the Kenyan people and their spirit of resistance, reemerging after a period of neocolonial slumber. In particular, he serves as a dramatization of Frantz Fanon's warnings, in *The Wretched of the Earth*, that independence alone could not lead to liberation but must be followed by a class-based revolution of the masses.

As the book begins, Matigari emerges from the Kenyan forest, having at long last won his long war against Settler Williams and John Boy (i.e., the British and their Kenyan collaborators). Triumphant, Matigari comes to reclaim his house (i.e., Kenya), only to discover that it has been usurped by Settler Williams's sons and his black servant John Boy (i.e., Western capital, the Kenyan comprador bourgeoisie, and the postcolonial Kenyan regime of Jomo Kenyatta and Daniel arap Moi). The novel depicts Matigari's attempts to reclaim his house via a picaresque search for truth and justice throughout Kenya. Matigari finds, however, that most of the Kenyans he encounters are afraid to answer his questions about justice, truth, and freedom, thus emphasizing the stark absence of these elements in postcolonial Kenyan society. The novel thus dramatizes the need for change in present-day Kenya, namely for the elimination of the heirs of colonialism.

Matigari reflects Ngugi's revolutionary standpoint in many ways. For example, the issue of messianism, which was present in earlier Ngugi novels such as *The River Between* and *A Grain of Wheat*, is again prominent in *Matigari*. However, while Ngugi focuses in the earlier novels on the negative aspects of messianism, which actually paralyze the characters into inaction and alienate them from the community, in *Matigari* the treatment of messianism is more complex. Here Ngugi continues his warnings against the passive reliance on the coming of a savior; at the same time, he taps into the positive energies that this Gikuyu tradition of messianism potentially contains. Thus, Matigari is often associated with the messianic hopes that the legendary prophet Mugo wa Kibiro once instilled in the Gikuyus and that formed a central part of Mau Mau cultural identity. Moreover, Ngugi frequently associates Matigari with Christ, as when Ngugi has Matigari spend a night in prison where he shares his dinner with twelve other inmates (of whom one is a police informer). And when Matigari's fame spreads around the country, rumors begin to spread that Matigari is the Second Coming of Christ.

But *Matigari* is hardly a Christian text, and Ngugi's "Christ" is not the son of the Christian God, but rather a symbol of resistance to illegitimate authority. When two boys ask Matigari if he is the one whose

Second Coming is prophesied, he replies, "The God who is prophesied is in you, in me and in the other humans" (156). Thus Ngugi avoids the quietist mentality often associated with Christian salvationism, urging the Kenyan people to look to themselves for "salvation" rather than awaiting the coming of a savior. Indeed, Ngugi suggests throughout the novel that the salvation mentality amounts not just to passive obedience to authority, but to effective complicity with oppression. This complicity dates back to colonial times, when John Boy helped Settler Williams in his fight against Matigari and continues today in various forms, as in the black bourgeoisie's complicity in exploitation, the neocolonial scholars' justification of the regime, and the willingness of the military and police to serve such masters.

But the kind of complicity with which Ngugi is most concerned is the complicity of ordinary, oppressed people with the regime. In *Matigari* a whole group of spectators silently watches and does nothing to help a woman being abused by the police. And when Matigari, who arrives at the scene late, chides them for such passivity, they simply disperse in fear, leaving it to Matigari to save the woman. Ngugi thus suggests that the Kenyan people have been intimidated to such a degree that they are unable to resist oppression, hoping instead that a messiah will come to liberate them. But Matigari is not such a savior. As the embodiment of the Mau Mau tradition, he provides symbolic inspiration for the Kenyan people to throw off their own shackles. In the novel, he does not magically solve the problems of Kenyans by striking down their neocolonial oppressors. Instead, he provides a model through which Kenyans can begin to mount their own resistance. Thus, at the end of the novel Matigari disappears, leaving his weapons in the hands of the boy Muriuki, who prepares to carry on the fight against the heirs of John Boy and Settler Williams.

The theme of messianism in *Matigari* serves as part of Ngugi's overall critique of the postcolonial regime of Jomo Kenyatta. During the 1940s and 1950s, Kenyatta was widely believed by the Gikuyus to be the messiah whose appearance Mugo wa Kibiro had prophesied. But Ngugi suggests that Kenyatta failed to live up to the trust that his people invested in him. During the 1950s, a large part of Kenyatta's popularity was based upon his anticolonial struggle both in Great Britain (where he lived during the 1930s and 1940s) and in Kenya upon his return in 1947. During the Emergency he was imprisoned by the colonial government as the leader of the Mau Mau from 1952 to 1961, despite his denials of any involvement with the Land and Freedom Army and his vehement denouncement of their armed struggle. Kenyatta's imprisonment only increased his authority among the Gikuyus, and, upon his release, he resumed his political leadership, eventually to become the first president of the newly independent Kenya in 1963. But for Kenyatta and his supporters independence came to mean capitalism in Kenya, not a just redistribution of land and resources among all Kenyans. His government never acknowledged the Land and Freedom Army and its role in the struggle for independence. Instead, Kenyatta argued specifically that the freedom fighters deserve no special place in the new society.

Ngugi, in fact, notes that Kenyatta actively sought to "remove Mau Mau and other patriotic elements from the central stage of Kenyan politics," going so far as to send his army, "inherited from colonial times" to hunt down the Mau Mau guerrillas who remained in the Kenyan forest, wary (justifiably as it turned out) of the new regime (Ngugi, *Detained* 88–89). In so doing, and in failing to pursue the equitable land reforms that were of such crucial importance to the Kenyan people, Kenyatta and his supporters merely stepped into the role of the exploiters of the national wealth once occupied by the British colonial government. By accepting the premise of the political, cultural, and economic superiority of the European bourgeois system, the new regime preserved the colonial division of labor and wealth, meanwhile perpetuating the suppression of the indigenous cultures (except in museums) and social and political institutions. This development, coming on the heels of the long, heroic, and painful struggle for Uhuru, explains the bitterness of Ngugi's critique of the new regime.

On the other hand, Ngugi is careful to supplement his blistering critique of the society of postcolonial Kenya with the elaboration of positive utopian elements that might potentially contribute to the building of a better society. The most important of these utopian elements is the long tradition of anticolonial resistance. Taken together, Ngugi's novels present the history of this resistance, from its beginnings in the vague dissatisfactions of the 1920s through the development of direct armed conflict in the Mau Mau period. But Ngugi also seeks, especially in his later work, to depict nascent forces of resistance that remain alive in the present and that might eventually emerge to challenge the neocolonial domination of Kenya. In *Matigari* these forces are closely related to class. One of the book's central events is a major labor strike, and the book, as a whole, depicts the working class as a slowly and painfully emerging political force. For Ngugi the Marxist, the transformation of Kenyan society is directly connected to the development of the class consciousness of the society's oppressed and underprivileged majority. For Ngugi the postcolonial writer, this class consciousness is essentially synonymous with a viable Kenyan cultural identity. ***Selected bibliography:*** Balogun ("Ngugi's *Matigari*"); Fanon; Gikandi ("Epistemology"); Gurnah ("*Matigari*"); Maina; Ngugi (*Detained*); Sicherman.

NGUGI WA THIONG'O: *PETALS OF BLOOD* (1977). *Petals of Blood* is the first of Ngugi's novels to focus on Kenyan postcolonial society. It is also the first to be informed by his new dedication to an essentially Marxist vision of society and history, inspired by his reading of Frantz Fanon, Lenin, Marx, and others. In its depiction of postcolonial life in the fictional Kenyan town of Ilmorog, the novel focuses on the discrepancy between the reality of postcolonial Kenyan and the ideals for which so many, especially those in the Mau Mau movement, fought and died in the struggle for independence. *Petals of Blood* is also Ngugi's most formally complex novel, mixing modernist techniques with a detective-story plot and a basic mode of social realism to condemn the evils of neocolonialism in Kenya. In his later novels, Ngugi turned to simpler forms and to writing in the Gikuyu language, realizing that the complex technique of *Petals of Blood* could only be appreciated by "a reader acquainted with the convention of reading novels, and particularly the modern novel in European languages" (*Decolonising* 77).

Petals of Blood is a crucial part of Ngugi's attempt to counter colonialist versions of Kenyan history and to produce a new narrative of Kenyan history centering on the long tradition of Kenyan anticolonial resistance. The book centers on the transformation of the fictional Kenyan town of Ilmorog from a backwater into a boomtown where tourism, alcohol, prostitution, and rapid industrial development have brought misery and poverty to most of the inhabitants. The plot revolves around the murder of three prominent Kenyan capitalists, who are burned to death in an Ilmorog brothel. In the course of narrating the events leading up to this murder, the book introduces a number of characters, most of whom have come to Ilmorog in an attempt to escape from the destructive neocolonial society of Kenya. These include the prostitute Wanja (who flees a world of bars and prostitution to Ilmorog where she hopes to start over), Godfrey Munira (a teacher and religious zealot), Abdulla (owner of a small pub in Ilmorog who has profited little from his former heroic participation, as a Mau Mau rebel, in liberation of Kenya), the worker Karega (who has been hired by Munira as a teacher's aide in the school at Ilmorog), and a first-person plural narrator who represents the villagers of Ilmorog.

Each of these characters represents a segment of society that has not fared well in neocolonial Kenya. Ngugi paints a bleak picture of postcolonial Kenya as he shows how the new society has been constructed for the benefit of the few, and how the attempts of the majority of ordinary Kenyans to create decent living conditions are thwarted. In particular, in a mode clearly influenced by the work of Fanon, he attributes the woeful conditions in postcolonial Kenya to the effects of Western capital and of the comprador bourgeoisie who serve as its agents in Kenya. These effects involve, among other things, a violent rupture in the history of Kenya, a theme Ngugi dramatizes in *Petals of Blood* in the story of Mwathi, the one-time "guardian spirit" of the people of Ilmorog. Before the coming of modernization, Mwathi was "guarding the secrets of iron works and native medicine" and was for the villagers the highest authority on virtually all subjects (281). From a Western perspective, Mwathi is a fictional entity—his various prophecies and pronouncements are clearly produced by a village elder who plays the role of Mwathi. From the point of view of the villagers of Ilmorog, however, the Mwathi tradition, passed down from generation to generation, had long provided a vital link with their cultural past. Mwathi's prophecies actively guided and defined the everyday lives of the people of Ilmorog. But when a major trans-African highway is build through Ilmorog, Mwathi's compound is "discovered" by the builders and turned into a fenced archaeological site. The Mwathi tradition dies, and his former abode becomes "only a site for the curious about the past," which does not participate in the present (266). The living connection that the people of Ilmorog had with their past and their culture has thus been effectively ruptured.

Many of the characters of *Petals of Blood* have had significant or traumatic breaks with their past. This is especially the case with Munira, who comes from a distinguished, wealthy family from Limuru. Regarded by his family as a failure because of his lack of financial success, Munira has come to Ilmorog specifically to escape his unpleasant past: "It was the tyranny of the past that he had always tried to escape" (249). Given Munira's escapist attitude toward the physical, temporal world it is not surprising that he eventually becomes a Christian religious fanatic in his attempt to overcome his oppressive sense of inadequacy. Consistent with his attempt to disengage himself from the past, Munira shows little or no awareness of the role played by Christianity in the former colonial domination of Kenya. However, Ngugi is quite aware of the destructive role of Christianity which "set in motion a process of social change, involving rapid disintegration of the tribal set-up and the framework of social norms and values by which people had formerly ordered their lives and their relationship to others" (*Homecoming* 31). Therefore, he continually reminds his readers, in *Petals of Blood*, that the church has preserved its alignment with the rich comprador bourgeoisie in their exploitation of the masses in neocolonial Kenya. For example, Munira's father, Ezekieli, uses Christian ideology as a righteous justification of his ruthless exploitation of the landless peasants who till his land. Any peasants who protest this treatment are thus declared "devilish" and summarily dismissed (14). Christianity also drives Munira to commit murder. Consistent with his Christian ethics, he sees the woman Wanja as the major culprit for his and Karega's woes. He sees her as the source of all evil and as a vile temptress who will ruin Karega with her seductions, thus dramatizing the role of Christinaity in the special oppression and exploitation suffered by women in postcolonial Kenya. In an attempt to save Karega from sin, Munira decides to burn the brothel owned by Wanja. In the process he inadvertently kills the three prominent local businessmen, leading to the investigation that forms a central part of the plot of the novel.

One of Ngugi's major criticisms of Munira is that his rejection of the historical world in favor of a heavenly paradise leads to a political quietism that makes it impossible successfully to improve conditions in the real world. Late in *Petals of Blood*, for example, Ngugi's narrator tells the story of a labor union led by Karega at an important Ilmorog factory that was weakened when many of the workers were seduced by a new charismatic religion for which "the only meaningful struggle was a spiritual battle with Satan" (305). Karega, in fact, functions in the book very much as a positive counter to Munira, and his activities (focused both on a positive connection with the anticolonial past and an active participation in the class struggles of the present) point in the direction of a better Kenyan future. During Karega's many searches for the causes of his own hardships, he wants to learn more about the history of his country because "it had seemed to him that history should provide the key to the present, that a study of history should help us to answer certain questions: where are we now? How did we come to be where we are?" (198). But Karega soon realizes that official versions of history tend merely to endorse colonialism as the bringing of civilization to a savage Africa. Disappointed with the scholarship of official historians, Karega eventually realizes that "Africa, after all, did not have one but several pasts which were in perpetual struggle" and that he must choose whether to accept the history of the colonial collaborators or the history of the resistance to colonialism (214).

Karega can be usefully read as a representative of the young, pauperized generation of postcolonial Kenyans who have been estranged from a history relevant to their present lives by the discourse of neocolonial history. Ngugi suggests that, in order to overcome present hardships, the young generation must restore the ties with the past that have been ruptured by the colonial and neocolonial experience. *Petals of Blood* traces Karega's development from a helpless victim into an active fighter in the ongoing workers' struggle against capitalism. Part of Karega's maturation into a conscious labor activist arises from his newly acquired knowledge about neocolonialism and about the necessity of active resistance to it. But, his maturity is also a result of his new awareness of the importance of history, in particular the history of resistance, which becomes his main inspiration.

Because Karega is successful in establishing a meaningful relation to the history of his people, he can creatively apply the lessons from that history in his own present-day struggles. He finally learns that the past is usable only if it is relevant to the present struggles of the people: "We must not preserve our past as a museum: rather, we must study it critically, without illusions, and see what lessons we can draw from it in today's battlefield of the future and the present" (323). Meanwhile, Ngugi suggests that the regime in present-day Kenya is perfectly willing to pay lip service to the past, but that this supposed respect tends to reduce the past to the status of a museum artifact, divorced from everyday life in the present. *Selected bibliography:* Cook and Okenimkpe; Fanon; Killam; McLaren; Ngara; Ngugi (*Decolonising*); Ngugi (*Homecoming*); Sicherman; Craig Smith.

PEADAR O'DONNELL: *ON THE EDGE OF THE STREAM* **(1934).** Although some of the best-known writers normally associated with the British novel of the Left have actually been from Ireland (Robert Tressell and James Hanley are good examples), the novel of the Left has not been an especially prominent phenomenon in modern Irish literature. However, the novels of Peadar O'Donnell, although not well known outside of Ireland, represent a notable exception. O'Donnell was not only a productive leftist writer but a socialist activist whose fight for justice can, as Patrick Delaney notes, be placed directly in the tradition of Irish anticolonial resistance (104). Amid the repressive climate of the Irish Free State of the 1920s and 1930s, O'Donnell was a prominent crusader for the rights of the common people of Ireland and for Irish independence from domination by international capitalism and the Catholic Church. This struggle is vividly portrayed in O'Donnell's novels of this period, which derive strength from age-old Irish traditions of community, while avoiding sentimentality and nostalgia through an insistence on modern socialism as the road to freedom and justice in Ireland. This task, of course, is not easy, and one can trace its development through O'Donnell's five novels, which tend to become increasingly successful, from *Storm* (1925), through *Islanders* (1928), to *Adrigoole* (1929), which is sometimes considered his finest work. These first three novels are striking for the vividness of their evocation of certain specific aspects of Irish life, but their focus on the experience of the "Gael" is so intense that they are unable adequately to reflect larger concerns. In *The Knife* (1930), O'Donnell attempts to broaden the scope of his work by presenting the Irish quest for freedom as a nonsectarian class-based struggle. It is in *The Edge of the Stream* (1934), however, that he fully develops his portrayal of the Irish struggle for nationalist liberation as an integral part of a worldwide working-class struggle. After 1934, O'Donnell concentrated his energies on political activism and on encouraging younger writers, such as Brendan Behan, though he did eventually publish two additional novels, *The Big Window* (1955) and *Proud Island* (1975).

The Edge of the Stream, despite its socialist orientation, is still a very Irish book, in both its subject matter and its style, which is informed by a distinctive use of Irish slang and syntax. The rhythms of O'Donnell's English sentences are also very Irish and suggest a heavy influence of Irish oral speech patterns on the prose style. Nevertheless, the book is quite accessible to non-Irish readers, though such readers may at times have to work out the meanings of certain expressions from their context. The book focuses on the inhabitants of the Donegal "Townland" of Derrymore, a small rural community on the outskirts of "The Town," as the residents of Derrymore invariably refer to the nearby town of Carrick. The people of Derrymore are proud and independent, but they live under the economic domination of The Town, and especially of the Garvey family, which controls most of the commerce in the area. The Garvey store provides both the only viable market for the agricultural goods produced in Derrymore and the only available source of most consumer goods in the region. As a result, the unscrupulous Garveys are able to pay low prices for produce and to charge high prices for their own goods. This combination has forced most of the inhabitants of the area into considerable debt to the Garveys, giving the family even more leverage.

As *On the Edge of the Stream* opens, Phil Timony, a Derrymore man who will become the book's central figure, has for several years been living in Scotland, after Nelly McFadden, his longtime sweetheart, has been married off by her mother to Ned Joyce, the principal teacher of Derrymore School and a man with a considerable political and economic future. Timony, who has become a socialist activist while in Scotland, returns to Derrymore after hearing that his old mother is ill. He then immediately sets about putting the lessons he has learned in Scotland to good use by organizing opposition to the power of the Garveys. In particular, he tells the locals about the cooperative stores that have been set up in Glasgow to break the tyranny of exploitative merchants like the Garveys. He then begins to organize such a store on an informal basis in his own barn, gaining considerable support from most of the people of Derrymore (and from some of the Garveys' enemies in Carrick as well), but also drawing the attention of the Garveys, who immediately begin to mobilize to crush Timony and his cooperative store. The schoolmaster, Joyce, and the priest, Father Cassell, are among the leaders of this effort, and through them O'Donnell is able to suggest the complicity of the Irish intelligentsia and the Catholic Church in the oppression of the common people of Ireland.

The Church is especially prominent in the opposition to Timony, and O'Donnell makes clear the way in which not only Cassell, but the Church as a whole functions as a tool of rich merchants like the Garveys. A religious procession featuring a number of nuns descends upon Derrymore with the intention of encircling Timony's barn and declaring his effort sinful; but the procession is scattered when Donal Breslin releases his prize bull, which charges the procession and scatters it in a rout. However, the tide turns against Timony and his supporters when the bull subsequently falls ill and dies, causing the more superstitious among the inhabitants of Derrymore to conclude that the animal has been cursed by God. Timony continues his efforts nevertheless, opening a formal shop in Carrick itself, but his support dwindles still more when a mission of Holy Fathers comes to town to preach against his efforts and in support of the Garveys. This mission stirs the people to a frenzy, and they rush into the street to sack the cooperative store. Dan Boyle and Red Charlie, Timony's strongest supporters, are captured and locked in a cellar, leaving Timony to defend the store alone. However, Nelly Joyce, who still loves Timony and sympathizes with his cause, alerts Michael Boyle, Dan's brother, to this fact, and Michael releases the two prisoners from the cellar. Meanwhile, Nelly has learned that Breslin's bull was actually poisoned by the supporters of the Garveys. She finally manages to get the attention of the crowd and to reveal this fact, causing the crowd to turn on the Garveys' store, which they sack under the leadership of Dan Boyle and Red Charlie. At the end of the book, Timony speaks to the gathered crowd, which is finally ready to listen to his socialist message.

On the Edge of the Stream calls attention to certain special aspects of Irish society, as when it focuses on rural life rather than the life of an urban proletariat. The book is also particularly Irish in its concentration on the role played by the Catholic Church in the continuing political and economic domination of the Irish people by the postcolonial bourgeois elite that is exemplified by the Garveys. In this sense, the book can be especially well illuminated by the warnings of Frantz Fanon that nominal independence from colonial rule cannot bring true emancipation unless accompanied by a subsequent class-based revolution to overturn the rule of the postcolonial bourgeoisie, who continue essentially as a less competent and energetic extension of the former colonial rulers. At the same time, O'Donnell's suggestion that the lessons learned by Timony in Scotland can also be useful in Ireland makes the point that Ireland, despite the special nature of its history, is not a unique society but part of the larger system of global capitalism. ***Selected bibliography:*** Delaney; Doyle; Fanon; Freyer; O'Leary.

V. S. REID: *NEW DAY* **(1949).** Victor Stafford Reid was born in Jamaica in 1913. In 1938, he took a job as a clerk for a sugar estate and subsequently gained an intense awareness of the issues that had recently led to riots by sugar workers. His work grows directly out of the tumultuous political climate of Jamaica in the late 1930s, when widespread labor unrest combined with anticolonial agitation to produce social upheavals. These upheavals eventually led, in 1944, to the establishment of a new constitution, which mandated universal adult suffrage and the end of direct colonial rule of Jamaica by Great Britain, though complete independence would not be gained until 1962. *New Day* is a sweeping historical novel that begins with the anticolonial violence of the Morant Bay uprising in1865 and culminates on Constitution Day in November, 1944.

Reid continued his interest in the history of anticolonial resistance with the publication of *The Leopard* (1958), a historical novel set in colonial Kenya, focusing on the Mau Mau rebellion of the early 1950s. Anticipating the later work of Kenyan novelist Ngugi wa Thiong'o, Reid presents the Mau Mau movement as a legitimate and heroic response to colonial oppression, rather than an outbreak of native African savagery, as it was often portrayed in the Western press at the time. Reid returns to Jamaican history in *The Jamaicans* (1976) and *Nanny-Town* (1983), both of which seek to provide a positive usable past for a postcolonial Jamaica undergoing considerable economic hardship and social turmoil. Reid is also the author of a number of children's novels that focus on Jamaican history and of *The Horses of Morning* (1985), a biography of Jamaican independence leader Norman Manley.

New Day is narrated by John Campbell, nearly ninety years old, as he sits alone on the eve of Constitution Day and ponders the historical changes he has observed in Jamaica during his long life. The story begins with the Morant Bay uprising of 1865 and is closely based on historical accounts of that event. John, eight years old in 1865, has only a vague understanding of the issues at stake in the rebellion as it occurs, but he supplements this understanding with knowledge gained through the years, describing the rebellion in a way that authentically represents his eight-year-old perspective while at the same time making clear the political and economic foundations of the uprising. John's brother, Davie, is among the rebels, who are led by Deacon Paul Bogle and supported by prominent planter and assemblyman George Gordon. Governor Edward John Eyre brutally suppresses the uprising. Many of the rebels are killed in clashes with government troops, and both Bogle and Gordon are hanged. Davie is forced to flee Jamaica and to take refuge, along with John and a young woman, Lucille Dubois, on an uninhabited cay off the coast of the main island.

In the aftermath of the uprising, Eyre is recalled as governor, and Jamaica's semiautonomous representative government is deposed by Great Britain in favor of direct colonial rule. Davie receives a pardon for his involvement in the uprising after testifying in the Crown's investigations of the event. He remains on the cay, founding a utopian community there based initially on essentially socialist principles. As time goes by, however, the responsibility of heading the community, called Zion, begins to wear on Davie. He becomes more and more somber and humorless, gradually descending into religious fanaticism. Nevertheless, the community prospers until a hurricane destroys much of the island, killing Davie and leaving Lucille shipwrecked in Cuba, where she is forced into prostitution. In 1882, the survivors on the cay, now led by a twenty-five-year-old John, petition Great Britain to take possession of their small island in order to protect them from the increasing danger of domination by American companies that are beginning more and more to seek economic control of the Caribbean.

John moves to the main island and begins, with the help of James Creary Campbell, the son of Davie and Lucille, to build a prosperous family business, producing bananas, sugar, and rum. In 1920, both James Creary and his English wife die of smallpox, and John assumes the care of seven-year-old Garth Campbell, who will become the real protagonist of the second half of the book. Garth, loosely based on Norman Manley, has inherited both Davie's fervent desire for justice and John's cautious wisdom. A promising student, he is educated in England and becomes a successful solicitor and advocate for the poor and downtrodden of Jamaica. Though the violence of 1938 represents a substantial setback, Garth eventually leads the way to the new constitution, with the aid of his cousin, the trade union leader Carlos Fernandez, who is loosely based on Jamaican labor leader Alexander Bustamante (in reality a distant cousin of Manley). Indeed, *New Day* emphasizes the importance of trade union activity, in which Garth has also been involved, as a key element in Jamaica's quest for a more democratic society. As the book closes, Garth is expected to become the head of the new Jamaican government, as Manley would, in fact, become.

Campbell's narration is presented in an adapted form of Jamaican dialect that captures much of the character and rhythm of Jamaican speech while remaining easily accessible to non-Jamaican readers. It was the first Caribbean novel to be narrated in dialect, and in this and other ways was an important founding work of Caribbean literature, which would become a major phenomenon in world literature beginning in the 1950s. In particular, Reid's engagement with history from an anticolonial perspective and his strong sense of his fiction as a potential weapon in the fight for social and economic justice would strongly inform the works of Jamaican novelists such as John Hearne, Roger Mais, and Michael Thelwell. Reid's combination of a critique of economic inequality with a utopian vision of a possible better future makes his book an effective novel of the Left, especially given its consistent endorsement of trade unionism and sympathy with the perspective of the working class. *Selected bibliography:* Bakan; Baugh; Richard Hart; Holt; Louis James.

MICHAEL THELWELL: *THE HARDER THEY COME* (1980). Although Michael Thelwell is the author of only one novel, he enjoys a prominent place in contemporary Caribbean and African American culture. His novel, *The Harder They Come*, is one of the most important works of Caribbean literature. Thelwell has also made important contributions as a teacher (at the University of Massachusetts in Amherst) and as a civil rights activist. He has written a number of short stories (many focusing on the American Civil Rights movement) and essays. The most important of the essays is probably "Modernist Fallacies and the Responsibility of the Black Writer," which is included, along with several other essays and stories, in the volume *Duties, Pleasures, and Conflicts* (1987). In this essay, Thelwell lambastes modernist literature for its fascination with technique and consequent disengagement from historical reality. He urges black writers to adhere to a realist aesthetic in their representation of black experience. Thelwell very effectively follows his own advice in his short stories and in his only novel, which powerfully evoke the realities of black experience in the United States and in his native Jamaica.

The Harder They Come is based on the 1972 Perry Henzell film of the same title and was written by Thelwell at the request of the publisher, Grove Press. Thelwell details the process of adapting the film, which was the first genuinely Jamaican film, to novel form in his essay "*The Harder They Come:* From Film to Novel." In the novel, he adheres fairly closely to the plot of the film, which was in turn based, though somewhat loosely, on the real story of notorious Jamaican gunman Ivanhoe "Rhygin" Martin, who became something of a popular hero in Jamaica in the late 1940s. As one might expect, the novel includes a bit more background information on Martin and his historical context, beginning in Book I with an account of Martin's childhood in the care of his grandmother in rural Jamaica that is not included in the film. This first book is entitled "The Hills Were Joyful," in an obvious allusion to the novel *The Hills Were Joyful Together* (1953) by Roger Mais, one of Thelwell's most important predecessors in the realistic depiction of the plight of the poor and downtrodden of Jamaica.

Book II of the novel begins approximately at the beginning of the film, as Martin, in the wake of his grandmother's death, travels to Kingston, where his mother has been living for some time. In Kingston, the naïve Martin has a number of new experiences, including seeing Rastafarians for the first time. The book is powerful in its presentation of the squalor and poverty of Kingston, while at the same time making clear that the plight of the poor is not due to historical necessity but to the manipulations of a rich upper class of Jamaicans and foreigners, especially Americans, who exploit the poor and make huge profits from them. Martin struggles to make a living by honest means. In his spare time, he becomes more and more enthralled by Western films, the heroes of which begin to become his role models. However, he runs afoul of the law after knifing a man who cheats him; as punishment, he is whipped so severely that he barely survives.

Martin becomes involved in the urban gangs of Kingston, which are the only sources of communal activity in the city. Meanwhile, he pursues his ambition to be a star in the rising Jamaican music industry — a motif added to the story apparently to take advantage of the availability of reggae star Jimmy Cliff to star in the film as Martin, but one that also effectively reinforces some of the suggestions in both the film and book that popular culture can, in complex ways, serve as a means of both exploitation and resistance. Eventually, Martin makes a record but is paid only fifty dollars by the unscrupulous record producer, Hilton, who orders his minions not to promote the record. Martin becomes increasingly involved in Jamaica's thriving "ganja" (marijuana) industry as a means of supporting himself. Thelwell does an excellent job of showing how the major profits from this industry go not to Jamaicans but to Americans, while also indicating the complex relationship between the ganja trade and forces of official authority, including the army and the police, especially the sinister, U.S.-trained Detective Superintendent Ray Jones.

After Martin realizes that most of the profits of the ganja trade are going to foreigners, he complains and demands a bigger cut for himself and his friends. As a result, he is set up for a police ambush. He escapes after killing several policemen in a gun battle. News reports of this battle and the subsequent manhunt stir the popular imagination and make Martin, now called "Rhygin,' or "Raging," a hero to the masses. His record suddenly gets extensive play on the radio and becomes a hit, allowing Hilton to cash in on Martin's new fame. But, fearing his sudden popularity as a figure of insurrection, most of the wealthy in Jamaica want Martin dead. The manhunt intensifies, and the badly wounded Martin is finally trapped on a beach as he prepares to attempt to escape to Cuba by boat. His memory remains alive, though, and the book ends with a group of boys playing games of Rhygin versus police in the streets of Kingston.

The Harder They Come is powerfully effective in its description of life in neocolonial Jamaica and in its careful delineation of the role of international capitalism in the continuing poverty of the Jamaican masses. Various forces, including official corruption, popular culture, and traditional Christian religion (most of which are heavily influenced by foreign, especially American, pressures), are specifically identified as crucial to the oppression of the Jamaican poor. On the other hand, the poor do have some resources, and they are able to convert many of these forces into sources of resistance, as exemplified by the development of reggae music and the Rastafarian religion. Thelwell develops all of this material in a consistently realistic mode, though the book also makes sophisticated use of linguistic effects, such as authentic Jamaican dialects, and literary techniques, such as multiple points of view and the use of reggae rhythms as a structural device, in presenting its points. *Selected bibliography:* Thelwell (*Duties*); Thelwell ("*The Harder They Come:* From Film to Novel").

APPENDIX
Novels of the Left Listed by Subject

ART AND POLITICS

Berger, *A Painter of Our Time*
Calder-Marshall, *Pie in the Sky*
Jameson, *The Mirror in Darkness*
Lessing, *The Golden Notebook*
Ngugi, *Devil on the Cross*
Sillitoe, *A Tree on Fire*
Torrington, *Swing Hammer Swing!*

CLASS INEQUALITY

Anand, *Untouchable*
Barstow, *A Kind of Loving*
Braine, *Room at the Top*
Calder-Marshall, *Pie in the Sky*
Fox, *This Was Their Youth*
Harkness, *A City Girl*
Harkness, *Out of Work*
Iyayi, *Heroes*
Iyayi, *Violence*
James, *Minty Alley*
Lawrence, *Sons and Lovers*
Lehmann, *Evil Was Abroad*
Storey, *Saville*
Thelwell, *The Harder They Come*
Tilsley, *I'd Do It Again*
Upward, *Journey to the Border*
Waterhouse, *Billy Liar*

THE COLD WAR

Berger, *A Painter of Our Time*
Heinemann, *The Adventurers*
Lessing, *The Golden Notebook*
McCabe, *The Butcher Boy*
Sillitoe, *Saturday Night and Sunday Morning*

COLONIALISM

Anand, *Coolie*
Anand, *Untouchable*
Armah, *The Beautyful Ones Are Not Yet Born*
Behan, *Borstal Boy*
Brunner, *Stand on Zanzibar*
Caute, *The Decline of the West*
De Boissière, *Crown Jewel*
Eagleton, *Saints and Scholars*
Gordimer, *Burger's Daughter*
Gordimer, *A Sport of Nature*
Iyayi, *Heroes*
Iyayi, *Violence*
James, *Minty Alley*
Lamming, *In the Castle of My Skin*
Lessing, *Children of Violence*
Ngugi, *Devil on the Cross*
Ngugi, *Matigari*
Ngugi, *Petals of Blood*

O'Donnell, *On the Edge of the Stream*
Reid, *New Day*
Sillitoe, *A Tree on Fire*
Thelwell, *The Harder They Come*

DÉCLASSEMENT

Braine, *Room at the Top*
Brierley, *Sandwichman*
Chaplin, *The Thin Seam*
Common, *The Ampersand*
Greene, *It's a Battlefield*
Heinemann, *The Adventurers*
Kelman, *A Disaffection*
Storey, *Pasmore*
Storey, *Saville*
Williams, *Border Country*

DETECTIVE / CRIME NOVELS

Blake, *A Question of Proof*
Cole and Cole, *Corpse in Canonicals*
Postgate, *Verdict of Twelve*
Sprigg, *The Corpse with the Sunburned Face*
Tilsley, *I'd Do It Again*
Williams, *The Volunteers*

DYSTOPIAS

Brunner, *Stand on Zanzibar*
Burdekin, *Swastika Night*
Jameson, *In the Second Year*
Stapledon, *Last and First Men*
Stapledon, *Star Maker*
Todd, *Over the Mountain*
Warner, Rex, *The Wild Goose Chase*
Williams-Ellis, *To Tell the Truth* ...

FASCISM

Briffault, *Europa*
Burdekin, *Swastika Night*

Heslop, *Last Cage Down*
Isherwood, *Goodbye to Berlin*
Isherwood, *Mr. Norris Changes Trains*
Jameson, *In the Second Year*
Jameson, *The Mirror in Darkness*
Lehmann, *Evil Was Abroad*
Todd, *Over the Mountain*
Upward, *Journey to the Border*
Warner, Rex, *The Wild Goose Chase*

GENDER AND SEXUALITY

Barker, *The Century's Daughter*
Barker, *Union Street*
Blumenfeld, *Jew Boy*
Braine, *Room at the Top*
Burdekin, *Swastika Night*
Calder-Marshall, *Pie in the Sky*
Carnie Holdsworth, *This Slavery*
Doherty, *A Miner's Sons*
Hanley, *Boy*
Harkness, *A City Girl*
Hines, *Unfinished Business*
Jameson, *The Mirror in Darkness*
Lawrence, *Sons and Lovers*
Lessing, *Children of Violence*
Lessing, *The Golden Notebook*
Mitchison, *The Corn King and the Spring Queen*
Ngugi, *Devil on the Cross*
Ngugi, *Petals of Blood*
Warner, Sylvia Townsend, *After the Death of Don Juan*
Warner, Sylvia Townsend, *Summer Will Show*
Wilkinson, *Clash*

HISTORICAL NOVELS

Barke, *The Land of the Leal*
Barker, *The Century's Daughter*
Bates, *Lean Men*
Bates, *The Olive Field*
Berger, *Into Their Labours*

Appendix

Briffault, *Europa*
Caute, *Comrade Jacob*
Cronin, *The Stars Look Down*
De Boissière, *Crown Jewel*
Fox, *Storming Heaven*
Fox, *This Was Their Youth*
Gibbon, *A Scots Quair*
Isherwood, *Goodbye to Berlin*
Isherwood, *Mr. Norris Changes Trains*
Jameson, *The Mirror in Darkness*
Jones, Mervyn, *Today the Struggle*
Lindsay, *Betrayed Spring*
Lindsay, *Men of Forty-Eight*
Lindsay, *1649*
Lindsay, *Time to Live*
Lindsay, *We Shall Return*
Mitchell, *Spartacus*
Mitchison, *The Corn King and the Spring Queen*
Reid, *New Day*
Thomas, Gwyn, *All Things Betray Thee*
Warner, Sylvia Townsend, *After the Death of Don Juan*
Warner, Sylvia Townsend, *Summer Will Show*
Williams, *Border Country*

INTELLECTUALS

Day Lewis, *Starting Point*
Doherty, *A Miner's Sons*
Heinemann, *The Adventurers*
Kelman, *A Disaffection*
Lehmann, *Evil Was Abroad*
Lessing, *The Golden Notebook*
Upward, *Journey to the Border*
Upward, *The Spiral Ascent*
R. Warner, *The Wild Goose Chase*
Williams, *Border Country*

MEDIA AND POPULAR CULURE

Brunner, *Stand on Zanzibar*

Chaplin, *The Day of the Sardine*
Hines, *Kes*
McCabe, *The Butcher Boy*
Priestley, *Bright Day*
Thelwell, *The Harder They Come*
Williams, *The Volunteers*

RACE AND ETHNICITY

Abrahams, *Mine Boy*
Behan, *Borstal Boy*
Blumenfeld, *Jew Boy*
Fox, *Storming Heaven*
Gordimer, *Burger's Daughter*
Gordimer, *A Sport of Nature*
La Guma, *In the Fog of the Seasons' End*
Lamming, *In the Castle of My Skin*
Lessing, *Children of Violence*

RELIGION

Barke, *The Land of the Leal*
Behan, *Borstal Boy*
Clarke, *The Red Flag*
Harkness, *Out of Work*
O'Donnell, *On the Edge of the Stream*
Tirebuck, *Miss Grace of All Souls*

REVOLUTION

Bates, *The Fields of Paradise*
Bates, *Lean Men*
Bates, *The Olive Field*
Caute, *Comrade Jacob*
Fox, *Storming Heaven*
Gordimer, *A Sport of Nature*
La Guma, *In the Fog of the Seasons' End*
Lindsay, *Men of Forty-Eight*
Lindsay, *1649*
Ngugi, *Devil on the Cross*
Ngugi, *Matigari*

Warner, Sylvia Townsend, *Summer Will Show*

SATIRES OF CAPITALISM

Brown, *Breakfast in Bed*
Brown, *Daughters of Albion*
Brunner, *Stand on Zanzibar*
Greene, *It's a Battlefield*
Wells, *Tono-Bungay*

SOCIALISM

Blatchford, *The Sorcery Shop*
Clarke, *The Red Flag*
Jones, Lewis, *Cwmardy*
Jones, Lewis, *We Live*
Shaw, *An Unsocial Socialist*
Tressell, *The Ragged Trousered Philanthropists*

SPANISH CIVIL WAR

Barke, *Land of the Leal*
Bates, *Lean Men*
Bates, *The Olive Field*
Brown, *Breakfast in Bed*
Day Lewis, *Starting Point*
Jones, Mervyn, *Today the Struggle*
Warner, Sylvia Townsend, *After the Death of Don Juan*

STRIKES AND LABOR ACTIVISM

Anand, *Coolie*
De Boissière, *Crown Jewel*
Doherty, *A Miner's Sons*
Gibbon, *A Scots Quair*
Heinemann, *The Adventurers*
Heslop, *The Gate of a Strange Field*
Heslop, *Goaf*
Heslop, *Last Cage Down*
Iyayi, *Violence*
Jones, Gwyn, *Times Like These*
Jones, Lewis, *Cwmardy*
Jones, Lewis, *We Live*
Oakhurst, *The Universal Strike*
Reid, *New Day*
Sommerfield, *May Day*
Thomas, *All Things Betray Thee*
Tirebuck, *Miss Grace of All Souls*
Welsh, *The Underworld*
Wilkinson, *Clash*

UNEMPLOYMENT

Barke, *Land of the Leal*
Barker, *Union Street*
Blumenfeld, *Jew Boy*
Brierley, *Means-Test Man*
Brierley, *Sandwichman*
Calder-Marshall, *Pie in the Sky*
Carnie Holdsworth, *This Slavery*
Clarke, *The Red Flag*
Greenwood, *Love on the Dole*
Jones, Gwyn, *Times Like These*
Thomas, *Sorrow for Thy Sons*
Torrington, *Swing Hammer Swing!*

UTOPIAS

Blatchford, *The Sorcery Shop*
Mitchison, *The Corn King and the Spring Queen*
Morris, *News from Nowhere*
Sommerfield, *May Day*
Stapledon, *Last and First Men*
Stapledon, *Star Maker*

WORKING-CLASS LIFE

Barker, *Union Street*
Brierley, *Means-Test Man*
Chaplin, *The Day of the Sardine*

Chaplin, *The Thin Seam*
Common, *The Ampersand*
Common, *Kiddar's Luck*
Doherty, *A Miner's Sons*
Gissing, *The Nether World*
Grant, *The Back-to-Backs*
Green, *Living*
Greenwood, *Love on the Dole*
Hines, *Kes*
Hines, *Unfinished Business*
James, *Minty Alley*
Jones, Gwyn, *Times Like These*
Jones, Lewis, *Cwmardy*
Jones, Lewis, *We Live*
Kelman, *The Busconductor Hines*
Kelman, *How Late It Was, How Late*
Lamming, *In the Castle of My Skin*
Lawrence, *Sons and Lovers*
Llewellyn, *How Green Was My Valley*
MacGill, *Children of the Dead End*
McIlvanney, *Docherty*
Morrison, *A Child of the Jago*
Sillitoe, *The Loneliness of the Long-Distance Runner*
Sillitoe, *Saturday Night and Sunday Morning*
Storey, *Saville*
Tirebuck, *Miss Grace of All Souls*
Torrington, *The Devil's Carousel*
Torrington, *Swing Hammer Swing!*
Tressell, *The Ragged Trousered Philanthropists*
Waterhouse, *Billy Liar*

WORKS CITED

NOVELS OF THE LEFT

Abrahams, Peter. *Mine Boy*. 1946. Oxford: Heinemann, 1989.
Anand, Mulk Raj. *Coolie*. 1936. New York: Liberty P, 1952.
Anand, Mulk Raj. *Untouchable*. 1935. London: Penguin, 1986.
Armah, Ayi Kwei. *The Beautyful Ones Are Not Yet Born*. London: Heinemann, 1969.
Barke, James. *The Land of the Leal*. 1939. Edinburgh: Canongate, 1987.
Barker, Pat. *The Century's Daughter*. 1986. New York: Ballantine, 1987.
Barker, Pat. *Union Street*. 1982. New York: G. P. Putnam's Sons, 1983.
Barstow, Stan. *A Kind of Loving*. London: Michael Joseph, 1960.
Bates, Ralph. *The Fields of Paradise*. New York: Dutton, 1940.
Bates, Ralph. *Lean Men*. 1934. 2 vols. Harmondsworth: Penguin, 1938.
Bates, Ralph. *The Olive Field*. 1936. Rev. ed. London: Hogarth, 1986.
Behan, Brendan. *Borstal Boy*. 1959. Boston: Godine, 1982.
Berger, John. *G*. New York: Viking, 1972.
Berger, John. *Into Their Labours*. Includes *Pig Earth*, 1979; *Once in Europa*, 1987; and *Lilac and Flag* (1990). New York: Pantheon, 1992.
Berger, John. *A Painter of Our Time*. 1958. New York: Simon and Schuster, 1959.
Blake, Nicholas. *A Question of Proof*. London: Crime Club, 1935.
Blatchford, Robert. *The Sorcery Shop: An Impossible Romance*. London: Clarion P, 1909.
Blumenfeld, Simon. *Jew Boy*. 1935. London: Lawrence and Wishart, 1986.
Braine, John. *Room at the Top*. Boston: Houghton Mifflin, 1957.
Brierley, Walter. *Means-Test Man*. 1935. Nottingham: Spokesman, 1983.
Brierley, Walter. *Sandwichman*. 1937. London: Merlin, 1990.
Briffault, Robert. *Europa*. 1935. New York: MacFadden-Scribner's, 1963.
Briffault, Robert. *Europa in Limbo*. 1937. New York: MacFadden-Scribner's, 1963.
Brown, Alec. *Breakfast in Bed*. London: Boriswood, 1937.
Brown, Alec. *Daughters of Albion*. 1935. New York: Doubleday, Doran, 1936.
Brunner, John. *Stand on Zanzibar*. 1968. New York: Ballantine, 1969.

Burdekin, Katharine (a.k.a. Murray Constantine). *Swastika Night*. 1937. Old Westbury, NY: Feminist P, 1985.
Calder-Marshall, Arthur. *Pie in the Sky*. New York: Scribner's, 1937.
Carnie Holdsworth, Ethel. *This Slavery*. London: Labour Publishing Company, 1925.
Caute, David. *Comrade Jacob*. 1961. New York: Pantheon, 1962.
Caute, David. *The Decline of the West*. New York: Macmillan, 1966.
Chaplin, Sid. *The Day of the Sardine*. London: Eyre and Spottiswoode, 1961.
Chaplin, Sid. *The Thin Seam*. London: Phoenix House, 1950.
Clarke, Allen. *The Red Flag: A Tale of the People's Woe*. London: Twentieth Century P, 1908.
Cole, G.D.H., and Margaret Cole. *Corpse in Canonicals*. London: Collins, 1930.
Common, Jack. *The Ampersand*. London: Turnstile P, 1954.
Common, Jack. *Kiddar's Luck*. 1951. Newcastle upon Tyne: Bloodaxe Books, 1990.
Cronin, A. J. *The Stars Look Down*. Boston: Little, Brown, 1935.
Day Lewis, C. *Starting Point*. London: Jonathan Cape, 1937.
De Boissière, Ralph. *Crown Jewel*. 1952. London: Allison and Busby, 1981.
Doherty, Len. *A Miner's Sons*. London: Lawrence and Wishart, 1955.
Eagleton, Terry. *Saints and Scholars*. 1987. London: Futura, 1990.
Farrell, J. G. *The Singapore Grip*. 1978. New York: Carroll and Graf, 1986.
Fox, Ralph. *Storming Heaven*. London: Constable, 1928.
Fox, Ralph. *This Was Their Youth*. London: Secker and Warburg, 1937.
Gibbon, Lewis Grassic. *A Scots Quair*. 1932–34. Includes *Sunset Song*, *Cloud Howe*, and *Grey Granite*. New York: Schocken, 1977.
Gissing, George. *The Nether World*. 1889. New York: Oxford UP, 1992.
Gordimer, Nadine. *Burger's Daughter*. 1979. New York: Penguin, 1980.
Gordimer, Nadine. *A Sport of Nature*. 1987. New York: Penguin, 1988.
Grant, J. C. *The Back-to-Backs*. London: Chatto and Windus, 1930.
Green, Henry. *Living*. 1929. In *Living, Loving, Party Going*. London: Penguin, 1978. 205–382.
Greene, Graham. *It's a Battlefield*. 1934. London: Penguin, 1977.
Greenwood, Walter. *Love on the Dole*. 1933. London: Penguin, 1969.
Hamilton, Patrick. *Hangover Square, or The Man with Two Minds*. 1941. New York: Random House, 1942.
Hanley, James. *Boy*. 1931. London: Penguin, 1990.
Harkness, Margaret. (John Law). *A City Girl*. 1887. New York: Garland, 1984.
Harkness, Margaret. (John Law). *Out of Work*. 1888. London: Merlin, 1990.
Heinemann, Margot. *The Adventurers*. New York: Marzani and Munsell, 1961.
Heslop, Harold. *The Gate of a Strange Field*. New York: Appleton, 1929.
Heslop, Harold. *Goaf*. London: Fortune, 1934.
Heslop, Harold. *Last Cage Down*. 1935. London: Lawrence and Wishart, 1984.
Hines, Barry. *Kes*. London: Michael Joseph, 1974. Rpt. of *A Kestrel for a Knave*. 1968.
Hines, Barry. *Unfinished Business*. London: Michael Joseph, 1983.
Isherwood, Christopher. *Goodbye to Berlin*. 1939. London: Chatto and WIndus, 1952.

Isherwood, Christopher. *Mr. Norris Changes Trains.* 1935. London: Hogarth, 1952.
Iyayi, Festus. *Heroes.* Harlow: Longman, 1986.
Iyayi, Festus. *Violence.* 1979. Harlow: Longman, 1987.
James, C.L.R. *Minty Alley.* 1936. Jackson: UP of Mississippi, 1997.
Jameson, Storm. *Company Parade.* 1934. London: Virago-Penguin, 1985.
Jameson, Storm. *In the Second Year.* New York: Macmillan, 1936.
Jameson, Storm. *Love in Winter.* 1935. London: Virago, 1984.
Jameson, Storm. *None Turn Back.* 1936. London: Virago, 1984.
Jones, Gwyn. *Times Like These.* 1936. London: Gollancz, 1979.
Jones, Lewis. *Cwmardy: The Story of a Welsh Mining Valley.* 1937. London: Lawrence and Wishart, 1978.
Jones, Lewis. *We Live: The Story of a Welsh Mining Valley.* 1939. London: Lawrence and Wishart, 1978.
Jones, Mervyn. *Today the Struggle.* London: Quartet, 1978.
Kelman, James. *The Busconductor Hines.* Edinburgh: Polygon, 1984.
Kelman, James. *A Disaffection.* 1989. London: Picador, 1990.
Kelman, James. *How Late It Was, How Late.* 1994. New York: Norton, 1995.
Kennedy, Bart. *Slavery.* London: Treherne, 1905.
La Guma, Alex. *In the Fog of the Seasons' End.* London: Heinemann, 1972.
Lamming, George. *In the Castle of My Skin.* 1953. Ann Arbor: U of Michigan P, 1991.
Lawrence, D. H. *Sons and Lovers.* 1913. London: Penguin, 1994.
Lehmann, John. *Evil Was Abroad.* London: Cresset, 1938.
Lessing, Doris. *The Four-Gated City.* 1969. New York: HarperCollins, 1995.
Lessing, Doris. *The Golden Notebook.* 1962. New York: Simon and Schuster, 1972.
Lessing, Doris. *Landlocked.* 1965. New York: HarperCollins, 1995.
Lessing, Doris. *Martha Quest.* 1952. New York: HarperCollins, 1995.
Lessing, Doris. *A Proper Marriage.* 1954. New York: HarperCollins, 1995.
Lessing, Doris. *A Ripple from the Storm.* 1958. New York: HarperCollins, 1995.
Lindsay, Jack. *Betrayed Spring: A Novel of the British Way.* London: Bodley Head, 1953.
Lindsay, Jack. *Men of Forty-Eight.* London: Methuen, 1948.
Lindsay, Jack. *1649: A Novel of a Year.* London: Methuen, 1938.
Lindsay, Jack. *Time to Live.* London: Andrew Dakers, 1946.
Lindsay, Jack. *We Shall Return: A Novel of Dunkirk and the French Campaign.* London: Andrew Dakers, 1942.
Llewellyn, Richard. *How Green Was My Valley.* 1940. New York: Collier-Macmillan, 1992.
MacGill, Patrick. *Children of the Dead End: The Autobiography of a Navvy.* 1914. London: Caliban, 1985.
McCabe, Patrick. *The Butcher Boy.* 1992. New York: Delta-Dell, 1994.
McIlvanney, William. *Docherty.* London: Allen and Unwin, 1975.
Mitchell, James Leslie. *Spartacus.* 1933. Edinburgh: Scottish Academic P, 1990.
Mitchison, Naomi. *The Corn King and the Spring Queen.* London: Jonathan Cape, 1931.

Morris, William. *News from Nowhere, or an Epoch of Rest*. 1890. London: Routledge and Kegan Paul, 1970.
Morrison, Arthur. *A Child of the Jago*. 1896. Chicago: Academy Publishers, 1995.
Ngugi wa Thiong'o. *Devil on the Cross*. Trans. from the Gikuyu by the author. 1982. London: Heinemann, 1988.
Ngugi wa Thiong'o. *Matigari*. Trans. Wangui wa Goro. 1987. London: Heinemann, 1989.
Ngugi wa Thiong'o. *Petals of Blood*. London: Heinemann, 1977.
Oakhurst, William. *The Universal Strike*. London: Odhams, 1891.
O'Donnell, Peadar. *On the Edge of the Stream*. London: Jonathan Cape, 1934.
Orwell, George. *Burmese Days*. 1934. San Diego: Harcourt Brace Jovanovich, 1962.
Postgate, Raymond. *Verdict of Twelve*. 1940. Chicago: Academy Publishers, 1986.
Priestley, J. B. *Bright Day*. 1946. Chicago: U of Chicago P, 1983.
Priestley, J. B. *Daylight on Saturday*. New York: Harper, 1943.
Reid, V. S. *New Day*. New York: Knopf, 1949.
Shaw, George Bernard. *An Unsocial Socialist*. 1883. St. Clair Shores, MI: Scholarly P, 1970.
Sillitoe, Alan. *The Loneliness of the Long-Distance Runner*. 1959. London: Plume-Penguin, 1992.
Sillitoe, Alan. *Saturday Night and Sunday Morning*. 1958. London: Plume-Penguin, 1992.
Sillitoe, Alan. *A Tree on Fire*. 1967. Garden City, NY: Doubleday, 1968.
Sommerfield, John. *May Day*. 1936. London: Lawrence and Wishart, 1984.
Sprigg, Christopher St. John. *The Corpse with the Sunburned Face*. New York: Doubleday, Doran, 1935.
Stapledon, Olaf. *Two Science-Fiction Novels:* Last and First Men [1930] *and* Star Maker [1937]. New York: Dover, 1968.
Storey, David. *Pasmore*. New York: Dutton, 1972.
Storey, David. *Saville*. New York: Harper and Row, 1976.
Thelwell, Michael. *The Harder They Come*. New York: Grove, 1980.
Thomas, Gwyn. *All Things Betray Thee*. 1949. London: Lawrence and Wishart, 1986.
Thomas, Gwyn. *Sorrow for Thy Sons*. London: Lawrence and Wishart, 1986.
Tilsley, Frank. *I'd Do It Again*. New York: Dodd, Mead, 1936.
Tirebuck, William Edwards. *Miss Grace of All Souls*. New York: Dodd, Mead, 1895.
Todd, Ruthven. *Over the Mountain*. New York: Knopf, 1939.
Torrington, Jeff. *The Devil's Carousel*. New York: Harcourt, Brace, and Company, 1996.
Torrington, Jeff. *Swing Hammer Swing!* 1992. San Diego: Harcourt Brace, 1994.
Tressell, Robert. *The Ragged Trousered Philanthropists*. London: Lawrence and Wishart, 1955.
Upward, Edward. *In the Thirties*. 1962. London: Quartet, 1978.
Upward, Edward. *Journey to the Border*. 1938. Rev. ed. London: Enitharmon Press, 1994.

Upward, Edward. *No Home But the Struggle*. 1977. London: Quartet, 1979.
Upward, Edward. *The Rotten Elements*. 1969. London: Quartet, 1979.
Warner, Rex. *The Wild Goose Chase*. London: John Lane the Bodley Head, 1937.
Warner, Sylvia Townsend. *After the Death of Don Juan*. 1938. London: Virago, 1989.
Warner, Syliva Townsend. *Summer Will Show*. New York: Viking, 1936.
Waterhouse, Keith. *Billy Liar*. London: Michael Joseph, 1959.
Wells, H. G. *Tono-Bungay*. 1909. London: Everyman-Dent, 1994.
Welsh, James. *The Underworld: The Story of Robert Sinclair, Miner*. London: H. Jenkins, 1920.
Wilkinson, Ellen. *Clash*. 1929. London: Virago, 1989.
Williams, Raymond. *Border Country*. 1960. London: Hogarth P, 1988.
Williams, Raymond. *The Volunteers*. 1978. London: Hogarth P, 1985.
Williams-Ellis, Amabel. *To Tell the Truth* . . . London: Jonathan Cape, 1933.

CRITICAL AND HISTORICAL WORKS

Adewoye, Sam A. "The Strength of the Rhetoric of Oral Tradition in Ngugi wa Thiong'o's *Devil on the Cross*." *Commonwealth Novel in English* 5.1 (1992): 11-19.
Allott, Kenneth, and Miriam Farris. *The Art of Graham Greene*. New York: Russell and Russell, 1963.
Althusser, Louis. *Lenin and Philosophy and Other Essays*. Trans. Ben Brewster. London: Monthly Review P, 1971. 170-83.
Amuta, Chidi. *Towards a Sociology of African Literature*. Oguta, Nigeria: Zim Pan, 1986.
Anderson, Perry. *Considerations on Western Marxism*. 1976. London: Verso, 1979.
Arblaster, Anthony. "Edward Upward and the Novel of Politics." *Practices of Literature and Politics*. Proceedings of the Essex Conference on the Sociology of Literature, July 1978. Vol. 2. Ed. Francis Barker et al. Colchester: U of Essex, 1979. 179-96.
Asein, Samuel Omo. "The Revolutionary Vision in Alex La Guma's Novels." *Phylon* 39 (1978): 74-86.
Ashraf, Phyllis Mary. *Introduction to Working-Class Literature in Great Britain. Part II: Prose*. Berlin: VEB Kongres und Werbedruck Oberlungwitz, 1979.
Atherton, Stanley S. *Alan Sillitoe: A Critical Assessment*. London: W. H. Allen, 1979.
Auerbach, Eric. *Mimesis: The Representation of Reality in Western Literature*. Trans. Willard R. Trask. Princeton, NJ: Princeton UP, 1968.
Bakan, Abigail B. *Ideology and Class Conflict in Jamaica: The Politics of Rebellion*. Montreal: McGill-Queen's UP, 1990.
Bakhtin, Mikhail M. *The Dialogic Imagination*. Ed. Michael Holquist. Trans. Caryl Emerson and Michael Holquist. Austin: U of Texas P, 1981.
Ball, F. C. *One of the Damned: The Life and Times of Robert Tressell, Author of* The Ragged Trousered Philanthropists. London: Lawrence and Wishart, 1979.

Balogun, F. Odun. "Ngugi's *Devil on the Cross*: The Novel as Hagiography of a Marxist." *Ufahamu* 16.2 (1988): 76-87.

Balogun, F. Odun. "Ngugi's *Matigari* and the Refiguration of the Novel as Genre." *The World of Ngugi wa Thiong'o*. Ed. Charles Cantalupo. Trenton, NJ: Africa World P, 1995. 185-96.

Balutansky, Kathleen. *The Novels of Alex La Guma: The Representation of a Political Conflict*. Washington, DC: Three Continents P, 1990.

Bargainnier, Earl F., ed. *Twelve Englishmen of Mystery*. Bowling Green, OH: Bowling Green UP, 1984.

Baugh, Edward, ed. Special V. S. Reid Issue. *Journal of West Indian Literature* 2.1 (1987).

Behrend, Hanna. "Second Thoughts on an Unfinished Business." *Literarische Diskurse und historischer Prozess: Beitrage zur englischen und amerikanischen Literatur und Geschichte*. Ed. Brunhild de la Motte. Potsdam: Pedagogische Hochschule "Karl Liebknecht," 1988. 151-58.

Bell, David. *Ardent Propaganda: Miners' Novels and Class Conflict, 1929-1939*. Umeå, Sweden: U of Umeå, 1995.

Benjamin, Walter. *Illuminations*. Ed. Hannah Arendt. Trans. Harry Zohn. New York: Harcourt, Brace and World, 1955.

Benton, Jill. *Naomi Mitchison: A Biography*. London: Pandora, 1990.

Benvenuto, Richard. "The Criminal and the Community: Defining Tragic Structure in *A Child of the Jago*." *English Literature in Transition, 1880-1920* 31.2 (1988): 153-61.

Berger, John. *Permanent Red*. London: Methuen, 1960.

Bergonzi, Bernard. "Fictions of History." *The Contemporary English Novel*. Ed. Malcolm Bradbury and David Palmer. New York: Holmes and Meier, 1980. 43-65.

Binns, Ronald. *J. G. Farrell*. London: Methuen, 1986.

Black, Michael H. *D. H. Lawrence:* Sons and Lovers. Cambridge: Cambridge UP, 1992.

Blatchford, Robert. *Britain for the British*. London: Clarion P, 1902.

Blatchford, Robert. *Merrie England*. London: Clarion P, 1894.

Booker, M. Keith. *Colonial Power, Colonial Texts: India in the Modern British Novel*. Ann Arbor: U of Michigan P, 1997.

Boos, Florence S., and William Boos. "*News from Nowhere* and Victorian Socialist-Feminism." *Nineteenth-Century Contexts* 14.1 (1990): 3-32.

Bradbury, Malcolm. *The Modern British Novel*. London: Penguin, 1994.

Braine, John. *J. B. Priestley*. New York: Barnes and Noble, 1979.

Branson, Noreen, and Margot Heinemann. *Britain in the 1930s*. New York: Praeger, 1971.

Brenner, Robert. *Merchants and Revolution: Commercial Change, Political Conflict, and London's Overseas Traders, 1150-1653*. Princeton, NJ: Princeton UP, 1993.

Briffault, Robert. *Breakdown: The Collapse of Traditional Civilization*. New York: Brentano, 1932.

Brothers, Barbara. "*Summer Will Show:* The Historical Novel as Social Criticism." *Women in History, Literature and the Arts*. Ed. Lorrayne Y. Baird-Lange and

Thomas A. Copeland. Youngstown, OH: Youngs-town State UP, 1989. 262–74.

Brown, Alec. *The Fate of the Middle Classes*. London: Gollancz, 1936.

Brunner, John. "The Genesis of *Stand on Zanzibar* and Digressions." *Extrapolation* 11.2 (1969): 34–43.

Buhle, Paul. *C.L.R. James: The Artist as Revolutionary*. London: Verso, 1988.

Buhle, Paul, ed. *C.L.R. James: His Life and His Work*. London: Allison and Busby, 1986.

Burns, John. Introduction. *The Land of the Leal*. By James Barke. Edinburgh: Canongate, 1987. xi–xvi.

Burton, Deirdre. "A Feminist Reading of Lewis Grassic Gibbon's *A Scots Quair*." *The British Working-Class Novel in the Twentieth Century*. Ed. Jeremy Hawthorn. London: Edward Arnold, 1984. 35–46.

Campbell, Ian. Introduction. *Spartacus*. By James Leslie Mitchell. Edinburgh: Scottish Academic P, 1990. vii–xxix.

Cannadine, David. "The Context, Performance, and Meaning of Ritual: The British Monarchy and the 'Invention of Tradition', c. 1820–1977." *The Invention of Tradition*. Ed. Eric Hobsbawm and Terence Ranger. Cambridge: Cambridge UP, 1983. 101–64.

Castle, Terry. *The Apparitional Lesbian: Female Homosexuality and Modern Culture*. New York: Columbia UP, 1993.

Caudwell, Christopher. *Studies in a Dying Culture*. London: John Lane, 1938.

Caute, David. *The Demonstration: A Play*. London: Deutsch, 1970.

Caute, David. *Frantz Fanon*. New York: Viking, 1970.

Caute, David. *The Illusion: An Essay on Politics, Theatre, and the Novel*. New York: Harper and Row, 1972.

Caute, David. *The Occupation*. London: Panther-Granada, 1972.

Chandramohan, Balasubramanyam. *A Study in Trans-Ethnicity in Modern South Africa: The Writings of Alex La Guma, 1925–1985*. Lewiston, ME: Mellen Research UP, 1992.

Charlton, John. *The Chartists: The First National Workers Movement*. London: Pluto, 1997.

Clark, Jon, Margot Heinemann, David Margolies, and Carole Snee, eds. *Culture and Crisis in Britain in the Thirties*. London: Lawrence and Wishart, 1979.

Clingman, Stephen. *The Novels of Nadine Gordimer: History from the Inside*. Johannesburg: Ravan, 1986

Cole, G.D.H. *A Short History of the British Working-Class Movement, 1789–1947*. London: Allen and Unwin, 1948.

Cole, G.D.H., and Margaret Cole. *The Condition of Britain*. London: Gollancz, 1937.

Cole, G.D.H., and Raymond Postgate. *The Common People, 1746–1946*. 1949. London: Routledge, 1992.

Cole, Margaret. *Growing up into Revolution*. London: Longmans, Green, 1949.

Coleman, Roger. "Design and Technology in *Nowhere*." *Journal of the William Morris Society* 9.2 (1991): 28–39.

Constantine, Stephen. "*Love on the Dole* and Its Reception in the 1930s." *Literature and History* 8.2 (1982): 232–47.

Cook, David, and Michael Okenimkpe. *Ngugi wa Thiong'o: An Exploration of His Writings*. London: Heinemann, 1983.
Cooper, Brenda. "New Criteria for an 'Abnormal Mutation'? An Evaluation of Gordimer's *A Sport of Nature*." *Rendering Things Visible: Essays on Recent South African Writing*. Ed. Martin Trump. Athens: Ohio UP, 1990. 68-93.
Cooper, Susan. *J. B. Priestley: Portrait of an Author*. New York: Harper and Row, 1971.
Couto, Maria. *Graham Greene: On the Frontier: Politics and Religion in the Novels*. New York: St. Martin's, 1988.
Cowasjee, Saros. "Mulk Raj Anand's *Untouchable*: An Appraisal." *Perspectives on Mulk Raj Anand*. Ed. K. K. Sharma. Atlantic Highlands, NJ: Humanities P, 1982. 27-38.
Cowasjee, Saros. *Studies in Indian and Anglo-Indian Fiction*. New Delhi: Harper-Collins, 1993.
Craig, Cairns. "Resisting Arrest: James Kelman." *The Scottish Novel Since the Seventies: New Visions, Old Dreams*. Ed. Gavin Wallace and Randall Stevenson. Edinburgh: Edinburgh UP, 1993. 99-114.
Craig, David. "David Storey's Vision of the Working Class." *The Uses of Fiction: Essays on the Modern Novel in Honour of Arnold Kettle*. Ed. Douglas Jefferson and Graham Martin. Milton Keynes, England: Open UP, 1982. 125-38.
Craig, David. "The Roots of Sillitoe's Fiction." *The British Working-Class Novel in the Twentieth Century*. Ed. Jeremy Hawthorn. London: Edward Arnold, 1984. 95-110.
Croft, Andy. "'Extremely Crude Propaganda?': The Historical Novels of Jack Lindsay." *Jack Lindsay: The Thirties and the Forties*. Ed. Robert Mackie. London: U of London, 1984. 32-45.
Croft, Andy. Introduction. *Last Cage Down*. By Harold Heslop. London: Lawrence and Wishart, 1984. vii-xiii.
Croft, Andy. Introduction. *Means-Test Man*. By Walter Brierley. Nottingham: Spokesman, 1983. vii-xvi.
Croft, Andy. *Red Letter Days: British Fiction in the 1930s*. London: Lawrence and Wishart, 1990.
Cronin, James E. *Labour and Society in Britain, 1918-1979*. London: Batsford, 1984.
Cross, Colin. *The Fall of the British Empire*. New York: Coward-McCann, 1969.
Crossley, Robert, ed. *Olaf Stapledon: Speaking for the Future*. Syracuse, NY: Syracuse UP, 1994.
Cudjoe, Selwyn R., and William E. Cain, eds. *C.L.R. James: His Intellectual Legacies*. Amherst: U of Massachusetts P, 1995.
Cunningham, Valentine. *British Writers of the Thirties*. New York: Oxford UP, 1988.
Davies, Andrew. "Lindsay and the Radical Culture of the 1940's." *Jack Lindsay: The Thirties and the Forties*. Ed. Robert Mackie. London: U of London, 1984. 74-80.
Davies, Gill. "Foreign Bodies: Images of the London Working Class at the End of the 19th Century." *Literature and History* 14.1 (1988): 65-79.

Day Lewis, C., ed. *The Mind in Chains: Socialism and the Cultural Revolution.* London: F. Muller, 1937.
Day Lewis, Sean. *C. Day Lewis: An English Literary Life.* London: Unwin, 1980.
De Beauvoir, Simone. *The Second Sex.* 1949. Ed. and trans. H. M. Parshley. New York: Bantam, 1961.
Debord, Guy. *Society of the Spectacle.* Trans. anon. Detroit: Black and Red, 1977.
Delaney, Patrick. "Politics and Art: The Novels of Peadar O'Donnell." *Working-Class and Feminist Literature in Britain and Ireland in the Twentieth Century.* Part II. Ed. Hanna Behrend and Isolde Neubert. Berlin: Humboldt U, 1990. 104-109.
DeVitis, A. A., and Albert E. Kalson. *J. B. Priestley.* Boston: Twayne, 1980.
Dhawan, R. K. "Mulk Raj Anand: *Coolie.*" *Major Indian Novels: An Evaluation.* Ed. N. S. Pradhan. New Delhi: Arnold-Heinemann, 1985. 1-21.
Dickson, Beth. "Class and Being in the Novels of William McIlvanney." *The Scottish Novel Since the Seventies: New Visions, Old Dreams.* Ed. Gavin Wallace and Randall Stevenson. Edinburgh: Edinburgh UP, 1993. 54-70.
Dietrich, Richard Farr. *Bernard Shaw's Novels: Portraits of the Artist as Man and Superman.* Gainesville: UP of Florida, 1996.
Di Michele, Laura. "Autobiography and the 'Structure of Feeling' in *Border Country.* *Views beyond the Border Country: Raymond Williams and Cultural Politics.* Ed. Dennis L. Dworkin and Leslie G. Roman. New York: Routledge, 1993. 21-37.
Dixon, Keith. "Writing on the Borderline: The Works of William McIlvanney." *Studies in Scottish Literature* 24 (1989): 142-57.
Dodd, Kathryn, and Philip Dodd. "From the East End to *EastEnders*: Representations of the Working Class, 1890-1980. *Come on Down?: Popular Media and Culture in Post-War Britain.* Ed. Dominic Strinati and Stephen Wagg. London: Routledge, 1992. 116-32.
Donoghue, Denis. "Kicking the Air." *New York Review of Books* 42.10 (June 8, 1995): 45-48.
Doyle, Paul A. "Peadar O'Donnell: A Checklist." *Bulletin of Bibliography* 28 (1971): 3-4.
Dyer, Geoff. *Ways of Telling: The Work of John Berger.* London: Pluto, 1986.
Eagleton, Mary, and David Pierce. *Attitudes to Class in the English Novel from Walter Scott to David Storey.* London: Thames and Hudson, 1979.
Eagleton, Terry. *Criticism and Ideology: A Study in Marxist Literary Theory.* London: New Left Books, 1976.
Eagleton, Terry. *The Ideology of the Aesthetic.* Oxford: Basil Blackwell, 1990.
Eagleton, Terry. *Literary Theory: An Introduction.* Minneapolis: U of Minnesota P, 1983.
Eagleton, Terry. *Marxism and Literary Criticism.* Berkeley: U of California P, 1976.
Eldridge, John, and Lizzie Eldridge. *Raymond Williams: Making Connections.* London: Routledge, 1994.
Elistratova, Anna. "The Works of Harold Heslop." *International Literature* 1 (1932): 99-102.

Empson, William. *Some Versions of Pastoral*. 1935. Rev. ed. New York: New Directions, 1974.
Ensor, Robert. *The Novels of Peter Abrahams and the Rise of Nationalism in Africa*. Essen: Verlag Die Blaue Eule, 1992.
Ettin, Andrew V. *Betrayals of the Body Politic: The Literary Commitments of Nadine Gordimer*. Charlottesville: UP of Virginia, 1993.
Fanon, Frantz. *The Wretched of the Earth*. Trans. Constance Farrington. New York: Grove P, 1968.
Fernihough, Anne. *D. H. Lawrence: Aesthetics and Ideology*. Oxford: Oxford UP, 1993.
Fiedler, Leslie A. *Olaf Stapledon: A Man Divided*. New York: Oxford UP, 1983.
Foley, Barbara. *Radical Representations: Politics and Form in U. S. Proletarian Fiction, 1929-1941*. Durham, NC: Duke UP, 1993.
Foster, Thomas. "'Dream Made Flesh': Sexual Difference and Narratives of Revolution in Sylvia Townsend Warner's *Summer Will Show*." *Modern Fiction Studies* 41.3-4 (1995): 531-62.
Fox, Pamela. *Class Fictions: Shame and Resistance in the British Working-Class Novel, 1890-1945*. Durham, NC: Duke UP, 1994.
Fox, Ralph. *The Novel and the People*. 1937. London: Lawrence and Wishart, 1979.
Fox, Ralph. *People of the Steppes*. London: Constable and Company, 1925.
Fraser, Robert. *The Novels of Ayi Kwei Armah: A Study in Polemical Fiction*. London: Heinemann, 1980.
Freyer, Grattan. "An Irish Revolutionary: Regionalism and Realism in the Writings of Peadar O'Donnell." *Kwartalnik Neofilologiczny* 24 (1977): 511-26.
Gakwandi, S. A. "Freedom as Nightmare: Armah's *The Beautyful Ones Are Not Yet Born*." *Critical Perspectives on Ayi Kwei Armah*. Ed. Derek Wright. Washington, DC: Three Continents P, 1992. 102-15.
Gikandi, Simon. "The Epistemology of Translation: Ngugi, *Matigari*, and the Politics of Language." *Research in African Literatures* 22.4 (1991): 161-68.
Gikandi, Simon. *Writing in Limbo: Modernism and Caribbean Literature*. Ithaca, NY: Cornell UP, 1992.
Gindin, James. *British Fiction in the 1930s: The Dispiriting Decade*. New York: St. Martin's, 1992.
Gloversmith, Frank, ed. *Class, Culture, and Social Change: A New View of the 1930s*. Sussex: Harvester, 1980.
Goode, John. *George Gissing: Ideology and Fiction*. New York: Barnes and Noble, 1979.
Goode, John. "Margaret Harkness and the Socialist Novel." *The Socialist Novel in Britain: Towards the Recovery of a Tradition*. Ed. H. Gustav Klaus. New York: St. Martin's, 1982. 45-66.
Goodheart, Eugene. "Olaf Stapledon's *Last and First Men*." *No Place Else: Explorations in Utopian and Dystopian Fiction*. Ed. Martin H. Greenberg and Joseph D. Olander. Carbondale: Southern Illinois UP, 1983. 78-93.
Gorak, Jan. *The Alien Mind of Raymond Williams*. Columbia: U of Missouri P, 1988.

Gordimer, Nadine. *The Essential Gesture: Writing, Politics, Places.* 1988. New York: Penguin, 1989.
Gorski, Philip. Introduction. *Sandwichman.* By Walter Brierley. London: Merlin, 1990. vii–xx.
Gråboek, Mette. "John Braine and *Room at the Top.*" *The Angry Young Men.* Ed. Michael Skovmand and Steffen Skovmand. Copenhagen: Akademisk Forlag, 1975. 104–32.
Gramsci, Antonio. *Selections from the Prison Notebooks.* Ed. Quintin Hoare and Geoffrey Nowell Smith. New York: International Publishers, 1971.
Grant, Elliott M. *Émile Zola.* New York: Twayne, 1966.
Gray, John. *Enlightenment's Wake: Politics and Culture at the Close of the Modern Age.* London: Routledge, 1995.
Gray, Nigel. *The Silent Majority: A Study of the Working Class in Post-War British Fiction.* New York: Barnes and Noble, 1973.
Green, Henry. *Pack My Bag: A Self-Portrait.* London: Hogarth P, 1940.
Greene, Graham. *Ways of Escape.* London: Bodley Head, 1980.
Grimshaw, Anna, ed. *The C.L.R. James Reader.* Oxford: Blackwell, 1992.
Grylls, David. *The Paradox of Gissing.* London: Allen and Unwin, 1986.
Gurnah, Abdulrazak. "*Matigari*: A Tract of Resistance." *Research in African Literatures* 22.4 (1991): 169–72.
Hammond, John R. *H. G. Wells and Rebecca West.* New York: St. Martin's, 1991.
Hanley, James. *Broken Water: An Autobiographical Excursion.* London: Chatto and Windus, 1937.
Harris, Michael T. *Outsiders and Insiders: Perspectives of Third World Culture in British and Post-colonial Fiction.* New York: Peter Lang, 1992.
Hart, Francis Russell. *The Scottish Novel from Smollett to Spark.* Cambridge, MA: Harvard UP, 1978.
Hart, Richard. *Rise and Organize: The Birth of the Workers and National Movements in Jamaica, 1936–1939.* London: Karia, 1989.
Harvie, Christopher. "Gnawing the Mammoth: History, Class and Politics in the Modern Scottish and Welsh Novel." *The Scottish Novel since the Seventies: New Visions, Old Dreams.* Ed. Gavin Wallace and Randall Stevenson. Edinburgh: Edinburgh UP, 1993. 187–205.
Hauge, Hans. "Alan Sillitoe and *Saturday Night and Sunday Morning.*" *The Angry Young Men.* Ed. Michael Skovmand and Steffen Skovmand. Copenhagen: Akademisk Forlag, 1975. 133–56.
Hawthorn, Jeremy, ed. *The British Working-Class Novel in the Twentieth Century.* London: Edward Arnold, 1984.
Head, Dominic. *Nadine Gordimer.* Cambridge: Cambridge UP, 1995.
Heilbrunn, Carolyn, ed. Special Christopher Isherwood Number of *Twentieth Century Literature* 22.3 (1976).
Heinemann, Margot. *Britain's Coal: A Study of the Mining Crisis.* London: Gollancz, 1944.
Heinemann, Margot. *Coal Must Come First.* London: F. Muller, 1948.
Herbert, Lucille. "*Tono-Bungay*: Tradition and Experiment." *H. G. Wells: A Collection of Critical Essays.* Ed. Bernard Bergonzi. Englewood Cliffs, NJ: Prentice-Hall, 1976. 140–56.

Heslop, Harold. *Out of the Old Earth*. Newcastle upon Tyne: Bloodaxe, 1994.

Hicks, Granville. *Figures of Transition: A Study of British Literature at the End of the Nineteenth Century*. New York: Macmillan, 1939.

Hill, Christopher. *The World Turned Upside Down: Radical Ideas during the English Revolution*. 1972. Harmondsworth: Penguin, 1975.

Hitchcock, Peter. *Dialogics of the Oppressed*. Minneapolis: U of Minnesota P, 1993.

Hitchcock, Peter. *Working-Class Fiction in Theory and Practice: A Reading of Alan Sillitoe*. Ann Arbor, MI: UMI Research P, 1989.

Hite, Molly. *The Other Side of the Story: Structures and Strategies of Contemporary Feminist Narrative*. Ithaca, NY: Cornell UP, 1989.

Hobsbawm, Eric. *The Age of Capital, 1848-1875*. New York: Scribner, 1975.

Hobsbawm, Eric. *The Age of Empire, 1875-1914*. New York: Pantheon, 1987.

Hobsbawm, Eric. *The Age of Extremes: A History of the World, 1914-1991*. New York: Pantheon, 1994.

Hobsbawm, Eric. *The Age of Revolution, 1789-1848*. London: Weidenfeld and Nicolson, 1962.

Hodge, Merle. "Peeping Tom in Nigger Yard." *Tapia* 25 (April 2, 1972): 11-12.

Hoggart, Richard. *The Uses of Literacy*. London: Chatto, 1957.

Holderness, Graham. *D. H. Lawrence: History, Ideology and Fiction*. Dublin: Gill and Macmillan, 1982.

Holderness, Graham. "Miners and the Novel: From Bourgeois to Proletarian Fiction." *The British Working-Class Novel in the Twentieth Century*. Ed. Jeremy Hawthorn. London: Edward Arnold, 1984. 19-32.

Holmesland, Oddvar. *A Critical Introduction to Henry Green's Novels: The Living Vision*. New York: St. Martin's, 1986.

Holt, Thomas C. *The Problem of Freedom: Race, Labor, and Politics in Jamaica and Britain, 1832-1938*. Baltimore: Johns Hopkins UP, 1992.

Holzman, Michael. "Anarchism and Utopia: William Morris's *News from Nowhere*." *ELH* 51.3 (1984): 589-603.

Horkheimer, Max, and Theodor W. Adorno. *Dialectic of Enlightenment*. Trans. John Cumming. New York: Seabury P, 1972.

Hoskins, Katharine Bail. *Today the Struggle: Literature and Politics in England during the Spanish Civil War*. Austin: U of Texas P, 1969.

Hutcheon, Linda. *A Poetics of Postmodernism: History, Theory, Fiction*. London: Routledge, 1988.

James, Louis. *The Islands in Between: Essays on West Indian Literature*. London: Oxford UP, 1968.

Jameson, Fredric. *Marxism and Form: Twentieth-Century Dialectical Theories of Literature*. Princeton, NJ: Princeton UP, 1971.

Jameson, Fredric. *The Political Unconscious: Narrative as a Socially Symbolic Act*. Ithaca, NY: Cornell UP, 1981.

Jameson, Fredric. *Postmodernism, or, The Cultural Logic of Late Capitalism*. Durham, NC: Duke UP, 1991.

Jameson, Fredric. *Signatures of the Visible*. New York: Routledge, 1992.

Jameson, Storm. *Journey from the North*. New York: Harper and Row, 1970.

Jameson, Storm. "Writing in Revolt: Documents." *Fact* 4 (July 1937): 9-18.

JanMohamed, Abdul R. *Manichean Aesthetics: The Politics of Literature in Colonial Africa*. Amherst: U of Massachusetts P, 1983.
Johnson, Roy. "The Proletarian Novel." *Literature and History* 2.2 (1975): 84–95.
Johnson, Roy. "Walter Brierley: Proletarian Writer." *Red Letters* 2 (Summer 1976): 5–8.
Jones, Glyn. Foreword. *Times Like These*. By Gwyn Jones. London: Gollancz, 1979. 5–7.
Kaplan, Carey, and Ellen Cronan Rose. *Approaches to Teaching Lessing's* The Golden Notebook. New York: Modern Language Association of America, 1989.
Kaushik, Asha. *Politics, Aesthetics, and Culture: A Study of Indo-Anglian Political Novel*. New Delhi: Manohar, 1988.
Kaye, Harvey J. "Historical Consciousness and Storytelling: John Berger's Fiction." *Mosaic* 16.4 (1983): 43–57.
Kaye, Julian B. *Bernard Shaw and the Nineteenth-Century Tradition*. Norman: U of Oklahoma P, 1958.
Kearney, Colbert. *The Writings of Brendan Behan*. New York: St. Martin's, 1977.
Keating, Peter. *The Haunted Study: A Social History of the English Novel, 1875–1914*. London: Secker and Warburg. 1989.
Keating, Peter J. *The Working Classes in Victorian Fiction*. New York: Barnes and Noble, 1971.
Keating, Peter, ed. *Into Unknown England, 1866–1913: Selections from the Social Explorers*. Manchester: Manchester UP, 1976.
Kershner, R. B., Jr. "Degeneration: The Explanatory Nightmare." *Georgia Review* 40 (1986): 416–44.
Kettle, Arnold. *An Introduction to the English Novel. Vol. II: Henry James to the Present Day*. London: Hutchinson's, 1953.
Khouri, Nadia. "The Clockwork and Eros: Models of Utopia in Edward Bellamy and William Morris." *College Language Association Journal* 24.3 (1981): 376–99.
Kibera, Leonard. "Pessimism and the African Novelist: Ayi Kwei Armah's *The Beautyful Ones Are Not Yet Born*." *Critical Perspectives on Ayi Kwei Armah*. Ed. Derek Wright. Washington, D.C.: Three Continents P, 1992. 92–101.
Kijinski, John L. "Ethnography in the East End: Native Customs and Colonial Solutions in *A Child of the Jago*." *English Literature in Transition, 1880–1920* 37.4 (1994): 490–501.
Killam, G. D. *An Introduction to the Writings of Ngugi*. London: Heinemann, 1980.
Kirwan, Bernadette. Introduction. *Out of Work* by Margaret Harkness. London: Merlin, 1990. vii–xix.
Klaus, H. Gustav. *The Literature of Labour: Two Hundred Years of Working-Class Writing*. Sussex: Harvester, 1985.
Klaus, H. Gustav. "New Bearings in Scottish Writing: Alasdair Gray, Tom Leonard, James Kelman." *Proceedings Anglistentag 1992 Stuttgart*. Ed. Hans Ulrich Seeber and Walter Göbel. Tübingen: Max Niemeyer Verlag, 1993. 186–95.

Klaus, H. Gustav. "Silhouettes of Revolution: Some Neglected Novels of the Early 1920s." *The Socialist Novel in Britain: Towards the Recovery of a Tradition.* Ed. H. Gustav Klaus. New York: St. Martin's, 1982. 89-109.

Klaus, H. Gustav. "The Strike Novel in the 1890s." *The Rise of Socialist Fiction, 1880-1914.* Ed. H. Gustav Klaus. Sussex: Harvester, 1987. 73-98.

Klaus, H. Gustav, ed. *The Rise of Socialist Fiction, 1880-1914.* Sussex: Harvester, 1987.

Klaus, H. Gustav, ed. *The Socialist Novel in Britain: Towards the Recovery of a Tradition.* New York: St. Martin's, 1982.

Kumar, Krishan. *Utopia and Anti-Utopia in Modern Times.* Oxford: Basil Blackwell, 1987.

Laing, Stuart. "Presenting 'Things as They Are': John Sommerfield's *May Day* and Mass Observation." *Class, Culture, and Social Change: A New View of the 1930s.* Ed. Frank Gloversmith. Sussex: Harvester, 1980.

Laing, Stuart. "*Room at the Top*: The Morality of Affluence." *Popular Fiction and Social Change.* Ed. Christopher Pawling. New York: St. Martin's, 1984. 157-84.

Lamming, George. Introduction. *In the Castle of My Skin* by George Lamming. Ann Arbor: U of Michigan P, 1991. xxxv-xlvi.

Lazarus, Neil. *Resistance in Postcolonial African Fiction.* New Haven, CT: Yale UP, 1990.

Leavis, F. R. *D. H. Lawrence, Novelist.* 1955. Harmondsworth: Penguin, 1994.

Lee, James W. *John Braine.* New York: Twayne, 1968.

Lehmann, John. *Christopher Isherwood: A Personal Memoir.* New York: Holt, 1988.

Lehmann, John. *New Writing in Europe.* Harmondsworth: Penguin, 1940.

Lehmann, John. *The Whispering Gallery.* New York: Harcourt Brace, 1955.

Lehmann, John, T. A. Jackson, and C. Day Lewis. *Ralph Fox: A Writer in Arms.* New York: International Publishers, 1937.

Lewis, Peter. "Region and Class: An Introduction to Sid Chaplin (1916-86)." *Durham University Journal* 85.54 (1993): 105-109.

Lieske, Stephan. "Robert Briffault's Portrait of History in *Europa*." *Working-Class and Feminist Literature in Britain and Ireland in the Twentieth Century.* Part I. Ed. Hanna Behrend and Isolde Neubert. Berlin: Humboldt U, 1990. 79-84.

Lindsay, Jack. *After the Thirties: The Novel in Britain, and Its Future.* London: Lawrence and Wishart, 1956.

Lodge, David. "*Tono-Bungay* and the Condition of England." *H. G. Wells: A Collection of Critical Essays.* Ed. Bernard Bergonzi. Englewood Cliffs, NJ: Prentice-Hall, 1976. 110-39.

López Ortega, Ramón. "The Language of the Working-Class Novel of the 1930s." *The Socialist Novel in Britain: Towards the Recovery of a Tradition.* Ed. H. Gustav Klaus. New York: St. Martin's, 1982. 122-44.

Lukács, Georg. *The Historical Novel.* 1937. Trans. Hannah Mitchell and Stanley Mitchell. Lincoln: U of Nebraska P, 1983.

Lukács, Georg. *History and Class Consciousness: Studies in Marxist Dialectics.* 1923. Trans. Rodney Livingstone. Cambridge, MA: MIT P, 1971.

Lukács, Georg. *The Meaning of Contemporary Realism.* Trans. John Mander and Necke Mander. London: Merlin, 1963.

Lukács, Georg. *Studies in European Realism*. New York: Grosset and Dunlap, 1964.

Lukács, Georg. *The Theory of the Novel: A Historico-Philosophical Essay on the Forms of Great Epic Literature*. 1916. Trans. Anna Bostock. Cambridge, MA: MIT P, 1971.

Mahoney, Rosemary. "Part Huck Finn, Part Hannibal Lecter." *New York Times Book Review*, May 30, 1993.

Maina, Paul. *Six Maumau Generals*. Nairobi: Gazelle Books, 1977.

Mandel, Ernest. *Late Capitalism*. Trans. Joris De Bres. London: New Left Books, 1975.

Martin, Graham. "D. H. Lawrence and Class." *The Uses of Fiction: Essays on the Modern Novel in Honour of Arnold Kettle*. Ed. Douglas Jefferson and Graham Martin. Milton Keynes, UK: Open UP, 1982. 83–97.

Marwick, Arthur. "*Room at the Top*: The Novel and the Film." *The Arts, Literature, and Society*. Ed. Arthur Marwick. London: Routledge, 1990. 249–79.

Marx, Karl, and Friedrich Engels. *Correspondence 1846–95*. Ed. Dona Torr. New York: International Publishers, 1934.

Marx, Karl, and Friedrich Engels. *Literature and Art*. New York: International Publishers, 1947.

Marx, Karl, and Friedrich Engels. *The Marx-Engels Reader*. Ed. Robert C. Tucker. New York: Norton, 1978.

Maslen, Elizabeth. "Sizing Up: Women, Politics, and Parties." *Image and Power: Women in Fiction in the Twentieth Century*. Ed. Sarah Sceats and Gail Cunningham. London: Longman, 1996. 195–204.

Matthews, Brian. "'Living with the Stream': George Orwell's *Burmese Days*." *Only Connect: Literary Perspectives East and West*. Ed. Guy Amirthanayagam and S. C. Harrex. Adelaide, Australia: Centre for Research in the New Literatures in English, 1981. 93–106.

Mayne, Brian. "*The Ragged Trousered Philanthropists:* An Appraisal of an Edwardian Novel of Social Protest." *Twentieth Century Literature* 13.2 (1967): 73–83.

McCallum, Pamela. "Postmodernist Aesthetics and the Historical Novel: John Berger's *G*." *Minnesota Review* 28 (Spring 1987): 68–77.

McCarthy, Patrick. "*Star Maker*: Olaf Stapledon's Divine Tragedy." *Science-Fiction Studies* 8.3 (1981): 266–79.

McCarthy, Patrick, ed. Special Olaf Stapledon Issue. *Science-Fiction Studies* 9.3 (1982).

McCarthy, Patrick, Charles Elkins, and Martin Harry Greenberg, eds. *The Legacy of Olaf Stapledon: Critical Essays and an Unpublished Manuscript*. Westport, CT: Greenwood, 1989.

McCrindle, Jean. "Reading *The Golden Notebook* in 1962." *Notebooks / memoirs / archives: Reading and Rereading Doris Lessing*. Ed. Jenny Taylor. London: Routledge, 1982. 43–56.

McKay, George. "Metapropaganda: Self-Reading Dystopian Fiction: Burdekin's *Swastika Night* and Orwell's *Nineteen Eighty-Four*." *Science-Fiction Studies* 21.3 (1994): 301–314.

McLaren, Joseph. "Ideology and Form: The Critical Reception of *Petals of Blood.*" *The World of Ngugi wa Thiong'o*. Ed. Charles Cantalupo. Trenton, NJ: Africa World P, 1995. 73–92.

McMahon, Joseph H. "Marxist Fictions: The Novels of John Berger." *Contemporary Literature* 23.2 (1982): 202–24.

Mengham, Rod. *The Idiom of the Time: The Writings of Henry Green*. Cambridge: Cambridge UP, 1982.

Messmer, Michael W. "Apostle to the Techno/Peasants: Word and Image in the Work of John Berger." *Image and Ideology in Modern/Postmodern Discourse*. Ed. David B. Downing and Susan Bazargan. Buffalo: State U of New York P, 1991. 199–227.

Miles, Peter. "The Painter's Bible and the British Workman: Robert Tressell's Literary Activism." *The British Working-Class Novel in the Twentieth Century*. Ed. Jeremy Hawthorn. London: Edward Arnold, 1984. 1–17.

Milne, Drew. "James Kelman: Dialectics of Urbanity." *Swansea Review* (1994): 393–407.

Mitchell, Jack. "Early Harvest: Three Anti-Capitalist Novels Published in 1914." *The Socialist Novel in Britain: Towards the Recovery of a Tradition*. Ed. H. Gustav Klaus. New York: St. Martin's, 1982. 67–88.

Mitchell, Jack. *Robert Tressell and the Ragged Trousered Philanthropists*. London: Lawrence and Wishart, 1969.

Mitchell, Jack. "Tendencies in Narrative Fiction in the London-Based Socialist Press of the 1880s and 1890s." *The Rise of Socialist Fiction, 1880–1914*. Ed. H. Gustav Klaus. Sussex: Harvester, 1987. 49–72.

Montefiore, Janet. *Men and Women Writers of the 1930s: The Dangerous Flood of History*. London: Routledge, 1996.

Moretti, Franco. *The Way of the World: The Bildungsroman in European Culture*. London: Verso, 1987.

Morgan, Edwin. "Tradition and Experiment in the Glasgow Novel." *The Scottish Novel since the Seventies: New Visions, Old Dreams*. Ed. Gavin Wallace and Randall Stevenson. Edinburgh: Edinburgh UP, 1993. 85–98.

Mulford, Wendy. Introduction. *After the Death of Don Juan* by Sylvia Townsend Warner. London: Virago, 1989. v–xvii.

Munton, Alan, and Alan Young. *Seven Writers of the English Left: A Bibliography of Literature and Politics, 1916–1980*. New York: Garland, 1981.

Murphy, Patrick. "Dialogics and Didacticism: John Brunner's Narrative Blending." *Science-Fiction Studies* 14.1 (1987): 21–33.

Murray, Isobel and Bob Tait. *Ten Modern Scottish Novels*. Aberdeen: Aberdeen UP, 1984.

Nair, Supriya. *Caliban's Curse: George Lamming and the Revisioning of History*. Ann Arbor: U of Michigan P, 1996.

Nairn, Tom. *The Break-up of Britain: Crisis and Neo-Nationalism*. London: New Left Books, 1981.

Neetens, Wim. "Politics, Poetics, and the Popular Text: *The Ragged Trousered Philanthropists*." *Literature and History* 14.1 (1988): 81–90.

Neubert, Isolde. "Walter Brierley's *Means-Test Man*—The Literary Value of the Novel." *Working-Class Literature in Britain and Ireland in the Nineteenth and*

Twentieth Century. Part I. Ed. Hanna Behrend, et al. Berlin: Humboldt U, 1985. 40-46.

Ngara, Emmanuel. *Art and Ideology in the African Novel: A Study of the Influence of Marxism on African Writing*. London: Heinemann, 1985.

Ngugi wa Thiong'o. *Decolonising the Mind: The Politics of Language in African Literature*. London: James Currey, 1992.

Ngugi wa Thiong'o. *Detained: A Writer's Prison Diary*. London: Heinemann, 1981.

Ngugi wa Thiong'o. *Homecoming: Essays on African and Caribbean Literature, Culture and Politics*. New York: Lawrence Hill, 1972.

Ni Chreachain, Firinne. "Festus Iyayi's *Heroes*: Two Novels in One?" *Research in African Literatures* 22.1 (1991): 43-53.

Nielsen, Aldon Lynn. *C.L.R. James: A Critical Introduction*. Jackson: UP of Mississippi, 1997.

North, Michael. *Henry Green and the Writing of His Generation*. Charlottesville: UP of Virginia, 1984.

Ogungbesan, Kolawole. *The Writing of Peter Abrahams*. London: Hodder and Stoughton, 1979.

Ogunjimi, Bayo. "Language, Oral Tradition and Social Vision in Ngugi's *Devil on the Cross*." *Ufahamu* 14.1 (1984): 56-70.

O'Flaherty, Liam. Introduction. *The Back-to-Backs*. By J. C. Grant. London: Chatto and Windus, 1930.

O'Leary, Philip. "The Donegal of Seamus O Grianna and Peadar O'Donnell." *Éire-Ireland* 23.2 (1988): 135-49.

Orwell, George. *The Collected Essays, Journalism, and Letters of George Orwell*. Ed. Sonia Orwell and Ian Angus. 4 vols. New York: Harcourt, Brace, and World, 1968.

Orwell, George. *Homage to Catalonia*. San Diego: Harcourt, Brace, and World, 1952.

Orwell, George. *The Road to Wigan Pier*. 1937. San Diego: Harcourt Brace and Company, 1958.

Parrinder, Patrick. "News from the Land of No News." *Foundation* 51 (Spring 1991): 29-37.

Patai, Daphne. "Imagining Reality: The Utopian Fiction of Katharine Burdekin." *Rediscovering Forgotten Radicals: British Women Writers, 1889-1939*. Ed. Angela Ingram and Daphne Patai. Chapel Hill: U of North Carolina P, 1993. 226-43.

Patai, Daphne. Introduction. *Swastika Night* by Katharine Burdekin. Old Westbury, NY: Feminist P, 1985. iii-xv.

Patai, Daphne. *The Orwell Mystique: A Study in Male Ideology*. Amherst: U of Massachusetts P, 1984.

Paul, Ronald. *"Fire in Our Hearts": A Study of the Portrayal of Youth in a Selection of Post-War British Working-Class Fiction*. Göteborg: Acta Universitatis Gothoburgensis, 1982.

Paul, Ronald. "Tressell in International Perpsective." *The Rise of Socialist Fiction*. Ed. H. Gustav Klaus. Sussex: Harvester, 1987. 231-50.

Peck, Richard. "One Foot before the Other into an Unknown Future: The Dialectic in Nadine Gordimer's *Burger's Daughter*." *World Literature Written in English* 29.1 (1989): 26–43.

Peck, Richard. "What's a Poor White to Do? White South African Options in *A Sport of Nature*." *Ariel* 19.4 (1988): 75–93.

Penner, Allen Richard. *Alan Sillitoe*. New York: Twayne, 1972.

Petrey, Sandy. *Realism and Revolution: Balzac, Stendhal, Zola, and the Performances of History*. Ithaca, NY: Cornell UP, 1988.

Pfeil, Fred. "Between Salvage and Silvershades: John Berger and What's Left." *TriQuarterly* 88 (Fall 1993): 230–45.

Pickering, Michael, and Kevin Robins. "The Making of a Working-Class Writer: An Interview with Sid Chaplin." *The British Working-Class Novel in the Twentieth Century*. Ed. Jeremy Hawthorn. London: Edward Arnold, 1984. 139–50.

Pickering, Michael, and Kevin Robins. "'A Revolutionary Materialist with a Leg Free': The Autobiographical Novels of Jack Common." *The British Working-Class Novel in the Twentieth Century*. Ed. Jeremy Hawthorn. London: Edward Arnold, 1984. 77–92.

Pierce, John J. *Foundations of Science Fiction: A Study in Imagination and Evolution*. Westport, CT: Greenwood P, 1987.

Pinkney, Tony. *Raymond Williams*. Bridgend, UK: Seren, 1991.

Pittock, Malcolm. "David Storey and *Saville*: A Revaluation." *Forum for Modern Language Studies* 32.3 (1996): 208–27.

Poole, Adrian. *Gissing in Context*. Totowa, NJ: Rowman and Littlefield, 1975.

Postgate, Raymond. *How to Make a Revolution*. New York: Vanguard, 1934.

Postgate, Raymond. *The New Bolshevik Theory*. London: G. Richards, 1920.

Postgate, Raymond. *The Story of a Year: 1848*. London: Cassell, 1955.

Pouchet Paquet, Sandra. Foreword. *In the Castle of My Skin* by George Lamming. Ann Arbor: U of Michigan P, 1991. ix–xxxiii.

Pouchet Paquet, Sandra. *The Novels of George Lamming*. London: Heinemann, 1982.

Price, Derrick. "*How Green Was My Valley*: A Romance of Wales." *The Progress of Romance: The Politics of Popular Fiction*. Ed. Jean Radford. London: Routledge and Kegan Paul, 1986. 73–94.

Priestley, J. B. *Margin Released: A Writer's Reminiscences and Reflections*. London: Heinemann, 1962.

Pykett, Lyn. "The Century's Daughters: Recent Women's Fiction and History." *Critical Quarterly* 29.3 (1987): 71–77.

Quillian, Bill. "*Pig Earth*: Writing Inside the Wall." *Minnesota Review* 28 (Spring 1987): 85–97.

Rabkin, David. "La Guma and Reality in South Africa." *Journal of Commonwealth Literature* 8.1 (1973): 54–61.

Rajan, P. K. *Mulk Raj Anand: A Revaluation*. New Delhi: Arnold, 1994.

Rao, A. V. Krishna. "History and the Art of Fiction: J. G. Farrell's Example: *The Siege of Krishnapur*." *The Literary Criterion* 23.3 (1988): 38–48.

Rennie, Bukka. *The History of the Working Class in the 20th Century (1919–1956): The Trinidad and Tobago Experience.* Toronto: New Beginning Movement, 1973.

Rignall, J. M. "Walter Scott, J. G. Farrell, and Fictions of Empire." *Essays in Criticism* 41.1 (1991): 11–27.

Robbins, Bruce. "Feeling Global: Experience and John Berger." *Boundary 2* 11.1–2 (Fall/Winter 1982/83): 291–308.

Robbins, Bruce. "John Berger's Disappearing Peasants." *Minnesota Review* 28 (Spring 1987): 63–67.

Robbins, Bruce. *The Servant's Hand: English Fiction from Below.* New York: Columbia UP, 1986.

Robertson, Priscilla. *Revolutions of 1848: A Social History.* Princeton, NJ: Princeton UP, 1952.

Rollins, Janet Buck. "Novel into Film: *The Loneliness of the Long-Distance Runner.*" *Literature/Film Quarterly* 9.3 (1981): 172–88.

Rosenthal, Michael. "Isherwood, Huxley, and the Thirties." *The Columbia History of the British Novel.* Ed. John Richetti. New York: Columbia UP, 1994. 740–64.

Roskies, D. M. "Lewis Grassic Gibbon and *A Scots Quair*: Ideology, Literary Form, and Social History." *Southern Review* 15.2 (1982): 178–202.

Rubenstein, Roberta. *The Novelistic Vision of Doris Lessing.* Urbana: U of Illinois P, 1979.

Ryan, Kiernan. "Citizens of Centuries to Come: The Ruling-Class Rebel in Socialist Fiction." *The Rise of Socialist Fiction, 1880–1914.* Ed. H. Gustav Klaus. Sussex: Harvester, 1987. 6–27.

Ryan, Kiernan. "Socialist Fiction and the Education of Desire: Mervyn Jones, Raymond Williams and John Berger." *The Socialist Novel in Britain: Towards the Recovery of a Tradition.* Ed. H. Gustav Klaus. New York: St. Martin's, 1982. 166–85.

Sackey, Edward. "Oral Tradition and the African Novel." *Modern Fiction Studies* 37.3 (1991): 389–407.

Sage, Lorna. *Doris Lessing.* London: Methuen, 1983.

Said, Edward. *Orientalism.* New York: Vintage-Random House, 1979.

Salveson, Paul. "Allen Clarke and the Lancashire School of Working-Class Novelists." *The Rise of Socialist Fiction, 1880–1914.* Ed. H. Gustav Klaus. Sussex: Harvester, 1987. 172–202.

Salwak, Dale. *A. J. Cronin.* Boston: Twayne, 1985.

Salwak, Dale. *A. J. Cronin: A Reference Guide.* Boston: G. K. Hall, 1982.

Sander, Reinhard W. *The Trinidad Awakening: West Indian Literature of the Nineteen-Thirties.* Westport, CT: Greenwood, 1988.

Scanlon, Paul A. "Alex La Guma's Novels of Protest: The Growth of the Revolutionary." *Okike* 16 (1979): 39–47.

Scholes, Robert, and Eric S. Rabkin. *Science Fiction: History, Science, Vision.* New York: Oxford UP, 1977.

Schwerdt, Lisa M. *Isherwood's Fiction: The Self and Technique.* New York: St. Martin's, 1989.

Sealy, Clifford. "*Crown Jewel:* A Note on Ralph De Boissière." *Voices* 2,3 (March 1973): 1-3.

Seed, David. "Disorientation and Commitment in the Fiction of Empire: Kipling and Orwell." *Dutch Quarterly Review of Anglo-American Letters* 14.4 (1984): 269-80.

Shelden, Michael. *Orwell: The Authorized Biography*. New York: HarperCollins, 1991.

Sherry, Norman. *The Life of Graham Greene, Volume I: 1904-1939*. New York: Viking-Penguin, 1989.

Sherry, Ruth. "The Irish Working Class in Fiction." *The British Working-Class Novel in the Twentieth Century*. Ed. Jeremy Hawthorn. London: Edward Arnold, 1984. 111-23.

Sicherman, Carol M. *Ngugi wa Thiong'o: The Making of a Rebel: A Source Book in Kenyan Literature and Resistance*. London: Hans Zell, 1990.

Sinfield, Alan. *Literature, Politics, and Culture in Postwar Britain*. Berkeley: U of California P, 1989.

Singh, Frances B. "Progress and History in J. G. Farrell's *The Siege of Krishnapur*." *Chandrabhaga* 2 (1979): 23-39.

Smith, Craig. "'Rainbow Memories of Gain and Loss': *Petals of Blood* and the New Resistance." *The World of Ngugi wa Thiong'o*. Ed. Charles Cantalupo. Trenton, NJ: Africa World P, 1995. 93-108.

Smith, Curtis C. "Olaf Stapledon: Saint and Revolutionary." *Extrapolation* 13.1 (1971): 5-15.

Smith, Dai. Introduction. *Sorrow for Thy Sons* by Gwyn Thomas. London: Lawrence and Wishart, 1986. 5-10.

Smith, Dai. "Relating to Wales." *Raymond Williams: Critical Perspectives*. Ed. Terry Eagleton. Boston: Northeastern UP, 1989. 34-53.

Smith, Dai. *Wales! Wales?* London: Allen and Unwin, 1984.

Smith, David. Introduction. *Cwmardy* by Lewis Jones. London: Lawrence and Wishart, 1978. n.p.

Smith, David. Introduction. *We Live* by Lewis Jones. London: Lawrence and Wishart, 1978. n.p.

Smith, David. *Socialist Propaganda in the Twentieth-Century British Novel*. Totowa, NJ: Rowman and Littlefield, 1979.

Smith, Grahame. *The Achievement of Graham Greene*. Sussex: Harvester, 1986.

Snee, Carole. "Working-Class Literature or Proletarian Writing?" *Culture and Crisis in Britain in the Thirties*. Ed. Jon Clark, Margot Heinemann, David Margolies, and Carole Snee. London: Lawrence and Wishart, 1979. 165-91.

Sommers, Jeffrey. "Wells's *Tono-Bungay*: The Novel Within the Novel." *Studies in the Novel* 17.1 (1985): 69-79.

Stedman Jones, Gareth. *Languages of Class: Studies in Working-Class History, 1832-1982*. Cambridge: Cambridge UP, 1983.

Stedman Jones, Gareth. *Outcast London: A Study in the Relationship between Classes in Victorian Society*. Harmondsworth: Penguin, 1976.

Stokes, Edward. *The Novels of Henry Green*. London, Hogarth P, 1959.

Stokes, Edward. *The Novels of James Hanley*. Melbourne: Cheshire, 1964.

Suvin, Darko. "Anticipating the Sunburst—Dream and Vision: The Exemplary Case of Bellamy and Morris." *America as Utopia*. Ed. Kenneth M. Roemer. New York: Burt Franklin, 1981. 57–77.

Sypher, Eileen. "Fabian Anti-Novel: Shaw's *An Unsocial Socialist*." *Literature and History* 11.2 (1985): 241–53.

Tagore, Leo. "Social Justice in Anand's *Coolie* and Achebe's *Things Fall Apart*." *The Novels of Mulk Raj Anand*. Ed. R. K. Dhawan. New Delhi: Prestige, 1992. 84–97.

Taylor, A. J. P. *English History 1914–1945*. Oxford: Oxford UP, 1992.

Temple-Thurston, Barbara. "Nadine Gordimer: The Artist as *A Sport of Nature*." *Studies in Twentieth Century Literature* 15.1 (1991): 175–84.

Tempska, Urszula. "'Beauty That Must End': English Avant-Garde Aesthetics in the 1930s." Diss. U of Texas, 1993.

Thelwell, Michael. "*The Harder They Come:* From Film to Novel." *Grand Street* 37 (1991): 135–65.

Thelwell, Michael. *Duties, Pleasures, and Conflicts: Essays in Struggle*. Amherst: U of Massachusetts P, 1987.

Thompson, Dorothy. *Outsiders: Class, Gender, and Nation*. London: Verso, 1993.

Thompson, E. P. "Christopher Caudwell." *Making History: Writings on History and Culture*. New York: New P, 1995. 78–140.

Thompson, E. P. *The Making of the English Working Class*. New York: Vintage-Random House, 1966.

Udenta, Udenta O. *Revolutionary Aesthetics and the African Literary Process*. Enugu, Nigeria: Fourth Dimension, 1993.

Updike, John. Introduction. *Loving, Living, Party Going* by Henry Green. London: Penguin, 1993. 7–15.

Van Ghent, Dorothy. *The English Novel: Form and Function*. 1953. New York: Harper and Row, 1961.

Vaverka, Ronald Dee. *Commitment as Art: A Marxist Critique of a Selection of Alan Sillitoe's Political Fiction*. Stockholm: Almqvist and Wiksell, 1978.

Vernon, Betty. Introduction. *Clash* by Ellen Wilkinson. London: Virago, 1989.

Vicinus, Martha. *The Industrial Muse: A Study of Nineteenth-Century British Working-Class Literature*. London: Croom Helm, 1974.

Von Rosenberg, Ingrid. "French Naturalism and the English Socialist Novel: Margaret Harkness and William Edwards Tirebuck." *The Rise of Socialist Fiction, 1880–1914*. Ed. H. Gustav Klaus. Sussex: Harvester, 1987. 151–71.

Von Rosenberg, Ingrid. "Militancy, Anger and Resignation: Alternative Moods in the Working-Class Novel of the 1950s and Early 1960s." *The Socialist Novel in Britain: Towards the Recovery of a Tradition*. Ed. H. Gustav Klaus. New York: St. Martin's, 1982. 145–65.

Wade, Jean-Philippe. "*Song of the City* and *Mine Boy*: The 'Marxist' Novels of Peter Abrahams." *Research in African Literatures* 21.3 (1990): 89–101.

Wade, Stephen. *Christopher Isherwood*. Basingstoke, UK: Macmillan, 1991.

Wagner, Kathrin M. *Rereading Nadine Gordimer*. Bloomington: Indiana UP, 1994.

Ward, John Powell. *Raymond Williams*. Cardiff: U of Wales P, 1981.

Warner, Sylvia Townsend. *Selected Letters*. Ed. William Maxwell. London: Chatto and Windus, 1982.

Watt, Ian. *The Rise of the Novel: Studies in Defoe, Richardson, and Fielding*. Berkeley: U of California P, 1957.

Webster, Roger, "*Love on the Dole* and the Aesthetic of Contradiction." *The British Working-Class Novel in the Twentieth Century*. Ed. Jeremy Hawthorn. London: Edward Arnold, 1984. 49–61.

Weibel, Paul. *Reconstructing the Past:* G. *and* The White Hotel, *Two Contemporary "Historical" Novels*. New York: Peter Lang, 1989.

Wendt, Albert. "An Interview with Festus Iyayi." *Landfall* 44.4 (1990): 412–22.

West, Alick. *Crisis and Criticism*. London: Lawrence and Wishart, 1937.

West, Alick. *The Mountain in the Sunlight: Studies in Conflict and Unity*. 1958. Westport, CT: Greenwood P, 1980.

Widdowson, Peter. "Between the Acts?: English Fiction in the Thirties." *Culture and Crisis in Britain in the Thirties*. Ed. Jon Clark, Margot Heinemann, David Margolies, and Carole Snee. London: Lawrence and Wishart, 1979. 133–64.

Wilde, Alan. *Christopher Isherwood*. New York: Twayne, 1971.

Williams, Raymond. *The Country and the City*. New York: Oxford UP, 1973.

Williams, Raymond. *Culture and Society, 1780–1950*. New York: Columbia UP, 1958.

Williams, Raymond. Introduction. *All Things Betray Thee* by Gwyn Thomas. London: Lawrence and Wishart, 1986. iii–x.

Williams, Raymond. *The Long Revolution*. 1961. London: Hogarth P, 1992.

Williams, Raymond. *Television: Technology and Cultural Form*. New York: Schocken, 1975.

Williams, Raymond. "Working-Class, Proletarian, Socialist: Problems in Some Welsh Novels." *The Socialist Novel in Britain: Towards the Recovery of a Tradition*. Ed. H. Gustav Klaus. New York: St. Martin's, 1982. 110–21.

Williams, Raymond. *Writing in Society*. London: Verso, 1983.

Williams-Ellis, Amabel. *All Stracheys Are Cousins*. London: Weidenfeld, 1983.

Wilson, Angus. *Émile Zola, an Introductory Study*. New York: Morrow, 1952.

Wolmark, Jenny. "Problems of Tone in *A Scots Quair*." *Red Letters* 11 (1981): 15–23.

Worcester, Kent. *C.L.R. James: A Political Biography*. Albany: State U of New York P, 1996. U of Michigan P, 1991. ix–xxxiii.

Worpole, Ken. Introduction. *Jew Boy* by Simon Blumenfeld. London: Lawrence and Wishart, 1986. 3–7.

Wright, Derek. "'Dystropia' in the African Novel: A Critique of Armah's Language in *The Beautyful Ones Are Not Yet Born*." *Commonwealth Novel in English* 5.2 (1992): 26–38.

INDEX

Abrahams, Peter, 317-19
Adewoye, Sam A., 358, 361
Adorno, Theodor W., 9, 11, 21, 24, 292
Africa: anticolonial struggle in, 262, 371; apartheid in, 317-19, 334-41, 348-51; colonialism in, 135-36, 210, 213-14, 244, 267-69, 305; neocolonialism, 90-92, 194, 341, 346, 358-68; postcolonial, 101-104, 328
Alienation, 5, 6, 30, 37, 122, 170, 302, 331; artists and, 64, 65, 206; capitalism and, 103, 104, 124, 192, 214, 223, 258-61; class and, 42, 45, 73, 77, 113-15, 148, 160, 171, 272-75, 308, 310, 347, 348; colonialism and, 249, 250, 318, 330; individualism and, 76, 124, 166, 197, 201-203, 257, 310; intellectuals and, 148, 198-201, 228, 272, 293, 327
Allott, Kenneth, 149
Althusser, Louis, 12, 13, 25
Amuta, Chidi, 346
Anand, Mulk Raj, 18, 319-25; *Coolie*, 319-22; *Untouchable*, 320, 322-25
Anderson, Perry, vii, 19, 21, 32
Arblaster, Anthony, 295
Armah, Ayi Kwei, 317, 325-29, 341
Ashraf, Phyllis Mary, 99
Atherton, Stanley S., 259, 262, 264
Attlee, Clement, 160, 217, 227, 308

Bakan, Abigail B., 372
Bakhtin, Mikhail, 3, 4, 6, 15, 90, 125, 126
Ball, F. C., 21, 290, 293
Balogun, F. Odun, 361, 364
Balutansky, Kathleen, 352
Bargainnier, Earl F., 67
Barke, James, 18, 41-44
Barker, Pat, 19, 44-50; *The Century's Daughter*, 44-47; *Union Street*, 47-50
Barstow, Stan, 19, 50, 51, 171, 257, 259
Bates, Ralph, 18, 51, 52, 53, 54, 55, 56, 57; *The Fields of Paradise*, 51-53; *Lean Men*, 51, 53-56; *The Olive Field*, 51, 55-57
Baugh, Edward, 372
Behan, Brendan, 34, 127, 329, 330, 331, 368
Behrend, Hanna, 173
Bell, David, 22, 48, 49, 153, 161, 163, 165, 168, 189, 192, 307
Benjamin, Walter, 8, 9, 11, 16, 24, 25, 69, 147, 290
Benton, Jill, 239
Benvenuto, Richard, 244
Berger, John, 19, 32, 57-65; *G.*, 19, 57-59, 80, 110, 112, 127, 161, 164, 193, 225, 250, 269, 303; *Into Their Labours*, 59-62; *A Painter of Our Time*, 62-65; *Permanent Red*, 62, 65

Bergonzi, Bernard, 101-104
Bildungsroman, 57, 79, 137, 138, 186, 190, 207, 211, 242, 273, 303, 307; postcolonial, 334, 335, 337, 352, 358
Binns, Ronald, 127, 131
Black, Michael H., 208
Blake, Nicholas, 18, 26, 65-67, 119. *See also* Day Lewis, C.
Blatchford, Robert, 17, 67, 68
Blumenfeld, Simon, 18, 69, 70, 71
Booker Prize, 19, 46, 57, 201, 202, 273
Booker, M. Keith, 64, 65, 131, 250
Boos, Florence S., 242
Boos, William, 242
Bradbury, Malcolm, 296, 297
Braine, John, 19, 50, 73, 74, 171, 253, 255, 257, 259
Branson, Noreen, 161
Brenner, Robert, 101
Brierley, Walter, 18, 23, 74-79, 189, 206, 280; *Means-Test Man*, 18, 74-79; *Sandwichman*, 77-79
Briffault, Robert, 79-81
British Empire, 66, 94, 127, 130, 157, 247, 329, 333. *See also* Colonialism; Imperialism
Brothers, Barbara, 301
Brown, Alec, 81-89, 136; *Breakfast in Bed*, 81-84; *Daughters of Albion*, 81-82, 84-89; *The Fate of the Middle Classes*, 81
Brunner, John, 89-91
Buhle, Paul, 348
Burdekin, Katharine (Murray Constantine), 92-94
Burns, John, 43, 44
Burton, Deirdre, 138, 140, 141

Cain, William E., 348
Calder-Marshall, Arthur, 94-96
Campbell, Ian, 237, 238
Cannadine, David, 158, 159
Capitalism, late, 10, 61, 92, 134, 197, 201, 286, 289, 355
Carnie Holdsworth, Ethel, 17, 32, 97-99

Castle, Terry, 300, 301
Caudwell, Christopher, vii, 18, 22, 208, 266, 269, 306; *Studies in a Dying Culture*, 22, 266. *See also* Sprigg, Christopher St. John
Caute, David, 19, 99-104; *Comrade Jacob*, 99-101; *The Decline of the West*, 101-104
Chandramohan, Balasubramanyam, 352
Chaplin, Sid, 105, 106, 107; *The Day of the Sardine*, 104-106; *The Thin Seam*, 106-108
Charlton, John, 222
Chartist Movement, 15, 16, 31-34, 38, 219, 220, 221, 222
Churchill, Winston, 160, 186
Clarke, Allen, 17
Clarke, Allen, 17, 97, 108-10
Clingman, Stephen, 334, 335, 337
Coal mining, 34, 38, 42, 160, 217, 274, 312; novels about, 77-79, 106-108, 123-25, 143-45, 161-71, 183-92, 229-36, 277-80, 282, 283
Cold War, 1, 2, 9, 11, 14, 15, 18, 26, 29, 35, 37, 63, 64, 101, 123, 125, 160, 217, 219, 248, 261, 290, 356
Cole, G.D.H., 18, 110-12, 164, 250, 252
Cole, Margaret, 18, 110-12, 250
Coleman, Roger, 242
Colonialism, 19, 135, 195, 309, 317, 329; capitalism and, 127-31, 210, 246-50, 293, 305; Caribbean, 332-34, 346-48, 352-55, 371-75; French, 101-103, 262-64; racism and, 64, 91, 133, 136, 158, 210, 268, 269, 350; violence and, 63, 101-103. *See also* Africa; British Empire; Imperialism; India; Ireland
Commodification, 5, 6, 10, 72, 128, 248, 253, 304, 305, 313, 318, 325, 326, 360
Common, Jack, 18, 27, 34, 112-16; *The Ampersand*, 18, 112-14; *Kiddar's Luck*, 114-16
Communist Party, 2, 14, 25, 27, 34, 46,

Index

65, 71, 95, 119, 121–25, 140, 147, 189, 194, 214, 225, 314, 317, 332; Cold War and, 125; German, 177; South African, 337; Soviet Union and, 53; Spanish Civil War and, 54, 83
Conrad, Joseph, 30, 31, 102, 148, 246, 361
Constantine, Murray. *See* Burdekin, Katharine
Constantine, Stephen, 92, 151, 152
Cook, David, 361, 368
Cooper, Brenda, 340
Cooper, Susan, 253, 255
Couto, Maria, 149
Cowasjee, Saros, 319, 322, 324, 325
Craig, Cairns, 197, 198, 201, 205, 236
Craig, David, 171, 259, 260, 262, 264, 273–75
Croft, Andy, 74–76, 94, 165, 167, 168, 225, 315; *Red Letter Days*, 19, 71, 94, 96, 123, 144, 145, 154, 175–78, 180, 210, 237, 238, 282, 285, 301, 315
Cronin, A. J., 116-19
Cronin, James E., 23
Cross, Colin, 130, 131
Crossley, Robert, 270, 272
Cudjoe, Selwyn R., 348
Cunningham, Valentine, 23, 27, 65, 67, 154, 155, 174, 176, 178, 210, 224, 269

Davies, Andrew, 227, 229
Davies, Gill, 243, 244
Day Lewis, C., 18, 65, 95, 96, 119-23, 135, 293; *Starting Point*, 119-23. *See also* Blake, Nicholas
Day Lewis, Sean, 67
De Beauvoir, Simone, 76
De Boissière, Ralph, 332-34
Debord, Guy, 312
Déclassement, 30, 73, 108, 114, 185, 198, 200, 272, 273, 275, 278
Delaney, Patrick, 368, 370
Detective fiction, 18, 22, 65-67, 110, 111, 119, 153, 177, 250, 253, 258, 266-69, 312, 313
DeVitis, A. A., 253, 255
Dhawan, R. K., 320, 322
Di Michele, Laura, 311
Dickens, Charles, 15, 16, 31, 39, 200, 245, 290, 292, 331
Dickson, Beth, 236
Dietrich, Richard Farr, 256
Disraeli, Benjamin, 16, 147, 290
Dixon, Keith, 236
Dodd, Kathryn, 50
Dodd, Philip, 50
Doherty, Len, 123-25, 206
Dole, the, 74, 150, 151, 278
Donoghue, Denis, 205, 357
Doyle, Sir Arthur Conan, 66
Doyle, Paul A., 370
Dyer, Geoff, 59, 63, 65
Dystopian imagery, 14, 89, 92, 93, 94, 179, 269, 283, 284, 296, 312, 314, 326, 328

Eagleton, Mary, 50, 51, 207, 208, 273
Eagleton, Terry, vii, 3, 12, 14, 19, 24, 25, 125-27; *Saints and Scholars*, 125-27
Eldridge, John, 311, 314
Eldridge, Lizzie, 311, 314
Elistratova, Anna, 163
Elkins, Charles, 270, 272
Empson, William, 2, 25
Engels, Friedrich, 5, 16, 25, 26, 33, 61, 84, 86, 89, 155, 157, 184, 186, 237, 238, 240, 248, 250, 305, 306, 337
English Civil War, 99, 108, 222
Enlightenment, 9, 29, 61, 252
Ensor, Robert, 319
Ettin, Andrew V., 337

Factory work, 2, 48, 69, 70, 104, 105, 109, 135, 253–55, 259, 260–62, 265, 320-22
Fanon, Frantz, 102, 104, 326, 327, 329, 341, 343, 350, 354, 362, 364, 365, 368, 370
Farrell, J. G., 127-31
Farris, Miriam, 149

fascism, 22, 33, 81, 208, 227, 249, 269, 283–85, 296, 301; British, 17, 71, 83, 92–94, 136, 139, 153, 167, 179–83, 265; European, 57, 83, 136, 189, 209, 211, 228, 271; German, 94, 174, 176, 178–80; Italian, 12; Spanish, 34, 42, 43, 51, 52, 57, 82, 83, 122, 190, 299
Fernihough, Anne, 208
Fiedler, Leslie A., 270, 272
Films, 8, 24, 28, 50, 67, 71, 95, 113, 116, 151, 152, 168-70, 173, 174, 192, 231, 236, 252, 253, 257, 259, 301, 350, 356, 357, 373, 374
Foley, Barbara, 14, 141
Foster, Thomas, 301
Fox, Pamela, 25, 75, 76, 99, 138, 140, 141, 243, 244, 283, 293, 309
Fox, Ralph, vii, 18, 25, 26, 53, 55, 131-37, 320; *The Novel and the People*, 25, 26, 320; *Storming Heaven*, 26, 131-35, 137; *This Was Their Youth*, 26, 135-37
Fraser, Robert, 328, 329
Freyer, Grattan, 370

Gakwandi, S. A., 326, 328
Gaskell, Elizabeth, 15, 16, 147, 281, 331
Gender, 96, 171, 183, 207, 300, 308, 344; class and, 47, 99, 140, 173, 309; inequality, 42, 47, 92, 94, 153, 192, 333; sexual objectification and, 70, 89; stereotyping, 91, 133, 134, 172
General Strike (1926), 43, 120, 162, 163, 181-84, 189, 245, 307, 308, 311, 320
Germany, 8, 70, 80, 92, 94, 103, 135, 153, 168, 173, 176, 178, 179, 180, 182, 190, 193, 208, 228, 284, 332
Ghana, 325-29, 338
Gibbon, Lewis Grassic, 18, 26, 27, 32, 35, 39, 43, 137-41, 236, 352. *See also* Mitchell, James Leslie
Gikandi, Simon, 355, 364
Gindin, James, 67, 154

Gissing, George, 16, 27, 30, 31, 78, 141-43, 243
Gloversmith, Frank, 27
Goode, John, 141, 143, 157, 159
Goodheart, Eugene, 270
Gorak, Jan, 312, 314
Gordimer, Nadine: *Burger's Daughter*, 334-37; *A Sport of Nature*, 337-40
Gorski, Philip, 78, 79
Gråboek, Mette, 74
Gramsci, Antonio, 12, 21, 190, 192
Grant, J. C., 143-45
Gray, John, 62
Gray, Nigel, 261, 262, 332
Green, Henry, 17, 26, 145, 146
Greenberg, Martin Harry, 270, 272
Greene, Graham, 22, 102, 146-49, 176
Greenwood, Walter, 18, 23, 27, 74, 149-52, 189, 280
Grimshaw, Anna, 348
Grylls, David, 141, 143
Gurnah, Abdulrazak, 364

Hamilton, Patrick, 26, 152-54
Hammond, John R., 303, 306
Hanley, James, 18, 154, 155, 368
Hardie, Keir, 160, 161, 307
Harkness, Margaret (John Law), 17, 31, 32, 97, 155-59; *A City Girl*, 155-57, 159; *Out of Work*, 157-59
Harris, Michael T., 319, 331
Hart, Francis Russell, 43, 44
Hart, Richard, 372
Harvie, Christopher, 201
Hauge, Hans, 262
Hawthorn, Jeremy, 19
Head, Dominic, 335, 337, 340
Heilbrunn, Carolyn, 176, 178
Heinemann, Margot, 159-61
Herbert, Lucille, 306
Heslop, Harold, 18, 22, 32, 38, 123, 125, 161-68, 206; *The Gate of a Strange Field*, 38, 161-63, 165; *Goaf*, 161, 163-65; *Last Cage Down*, 18, 161, 163, 165-68
Hicks, Granville, 27
Hill, Christopher, 101, 214

Index

Hill, Joe, 95
Hines, Barry, 19, 34, 168-73, 206, 262; *Kes*, 168-71; *Unfinished Business*, 171-73
Hitchcock, Alfred, 152
Hitchcock, Peter, 28, 46, 49, 259, 262
Hite, Molly, 213, 216, 217
Hitler, Adolph, 93, 174, 175, 179, 229, 255
Hobsbawm, Eric, vii, 19, 28, 29, 127, 168, 245, 246
Hodge, Merle, 347, 348
Hoggart, Richard, 30, 148, 149, 275
Holderness, Graham, 76, 171, 189, 191, 192, 208
Holmesland, Oddvar, 146
Holt, Thomas C., 372
Holzman, Michael, 242
Horkheimer, Max, 9, 292
Hoskins, Katharine Bail, 53
Hutcheon, Linda, 57, 59

Imperialism, 27, 28, 128, 129, 130, 131, 137, 222, 246, 247, 248, 249, 327. *See also* British Empire; Colonialism
Independent Labour Party, 67, 108, 162, 306
India, 42, 129, 131, 157, 247, 249, 268, 319-25
Ireland, 27, 63, 125-27, 138, 193, 222, 231-35, 244, 329-32, 355-57, 368-370
Isherwood, Christopher, 23, 173-78, 208; *Goodbye to Berlin*, 173-76; *Mr. Norris Changes Trains*, 173, 175-78
Iyayi, Festus, 340-46; *Heroes*, 340-43; *Violence*, 343-46

Jackson, T. A., 135, 137
Jamaica, 317, 370-75
James, C.L.R., 332, 346-48, 368, 372; *Minty Alley*, 346-48
James, Louis, 372
Jameson, Fredric, 9-11, 197, 216; *The Political Unconscious*, 10, 11, 65, 141-43; *Postmodernism*, 9, 10, 59, 92, 135, 198, 217, 273, 286, 287, 289
Jameson, Storm: *In the Second Year*, 179-80; *The Mirror in Darkness*, 180-83
JanMohamed, Abdul R., 350, 351
Johnson, Roy, 75, 76, 78, 152, 170, 171
Jones, Ernest, 16, 38, 220
Jones, Glyn, 185, 186
Jones, Gwyn, 183-86
Jones, Lewis, 18, 22, 23, 32, 123, 125, 186-92, 206, 230; *Cwmardy*, 18, 186-90, 230; *We Live*, 18, 189, 190-92
Jones, Mervyn, 192-95
Joyce, James, 7, 31, 38, 89, 126, 127, 163, 200, 201, 226, 266, 285, 292, 331

Kafka, Franz, 7, 200, 202, 203, 283, 296
Kalson, Albert E., 253, 255
Kaplan, Carey, 216
Kaushik, Asha, 322, 325
Kaye, Harvey J., 62, 65, 256
Kearney, Colbert, 332
Keating, Peter, 30, 31, 143, 157, 243, 244, 282, 283
Kelman, James, 19, 195-205, 285; *The Busconductor Hines*, 195-98; *A Disaffection*, 198-201; *How Late It Was, How Late*, 201-205
Kennedy, Bart, 97, 195
Kenya, 358-68, 371
Kershner, R. B., Jr., 244-46
Kettle, Arnold, 31, 303, 306
Khouri, Nadia, 242
Kibera, Leonard, 327, 329
Kijinski, John L., 158, 159, 244
Killam, G. D., 360, 361, 368
Kirwan, Bernadette, 159
Klaus, H. Gustav, 19, 32, 57, 97, 99, 108, 110, 168, 174, 198, 200, 201, 245, 246, 266, 282, 283, 306, 307
Kumar, Krishan, 242

La Guma, Alex, 348-52
Labour Party, 1, 46, 118, 122, 160-64,

179, 180, 184, 213, 217, 218, 225, 227, 229, 256, 266, 308
Laing, Stuart, 27, 74, 266
Lamming, George, 352-55
Law, John. *See* Harkness, Margaret
Lawrence, D. H., 21, 27, 31, 39, 78, 146, 205-208, 274, 290
Lazarus, Neil, 326-29
Leavis, F. R., 208
Lee, James W., 74
Lehmann, John, 26, 135, 137, 176, 178, 208, 209, 293
Lenin, Vladimir, 12, 26, 80, 248, 255, 256, 365
Lessing, Doris, 19, 210-17; *Children of Violence*, 210-13; *The Golden Notebook*, 19, 210, 213-17
Lewis, Peter, 108
Lieske, Stephan, 80, 81
Lindsay, Jack, 18, 101, 216-29, 237, 238, 301; *Betrayed Spring*, 217-19, 229; *Men of Forty-Eight*, 219-22; *1649*, 101, 222-25; *Time to Live*, 225-27; *We Shall Return*, 227-29
Llewellyn, Richard, 229-31
Lodge, David, 164, 303, 304, 306
London Dock Workers Strike (1889), 16, 240, 245
López Ortega, Ramón, 32, 88, 89, 140, 146, 150, 152, 184, 185
Lukács, Georg, 4-11, 21, 25, 26, 32, 33, 44, 60, 80, 90, 102-104, 128, 136, 188, 191, 192, 195, 216, 218, 225, 237, 266, 299, 332, 334, 335

MacDonald, Ramsay, 118
MacGill, Patrick, 232, 234
Mahoney, Rosemary, 355, 357
Mandel, Ernest, 92, 134, 286
Marriage, 82-88, 142, 208, 211, 251
Martin, Graham, 208
Marwick, Arthur, 74
Marx, Karl, 16, 61, 84, 97, 129, 132, 164, 184, 200, 233, 237, 248, 250
Marxism, vii, 2, 87, 88, 101, 140, 153, 211, 286, 293, 317, 346; history and, 59, 81, 127, 168, 220, 242, 337, 365
Marxist literary theory, 3-14, 18, 19, 21, 22, 24-29, 31, 32, 38, 39, 131, 155, 214, 216, 266
Maslen, Elizabeth, 301
Matthews, Brian, 249, 250
Mayne, Brian, 289, 293
McCabe, Patrick, 355-57
McCallum, Pamela, 59
McCarthy, Patrick, 270, 272
McCrindle, Jean, 217
McIlvanney, William, 234-36
McKay, George, 69, 94
McLaren, Joseph, 368
McMahon, Joseph H., 59, 65
Means test, 18, 74-76, 78, 79, 150, 152, 279, 280
Mengham, Rod, 146
Messmer, Michael W., 62
Miles, Peter, 291, 293
Milne, Drew, 198, 201, 205
Mitchell, Jack, 109, 110, 234, 293
Mitchell, James Leslie, 236-38. *See also* Gibbon, Lewis Grassic
Mitchison, Naomi, 18, 33, 238, 239
Modernism, 2, 7-10, 25, 30, 33, 59, 70, 89, 201, 286, 373; in the novel of the Left, 18, 94, 119, 140, 147, 183, 208, 216, 265, 266, 309, 365
Montefiore, Janet, 33, 180, 183, 225, 239, 298, 299, 301
Moretti, Franco, 4
Morgan, Edwin, 201
Morris, William, 17, 27, 67, 97, 239-42
Morrison, Arthur, 16, 31, 242-44, 246
Mosley, Oswald, 182
Mulford, Wendy, 299
Munton, Alan, 53, 55, 57, 295
Murphy, Patrick, 90, 92
Murray, Isobel, 236

Nair, Supriya, 355
Nairn, Tom, 277
Narayan, R. K., 319
Neubert, Isolde, 76
Ngara, Emmanuel, 352, 368
Ngugi wa Thiong'o, 317, 351, 358-68,

Index 411

371; *Devil on the Cross*, 358-61; *Matigari*, 361-64; *Petals of Blood*, 364-68
Nigeria, 340-46
Nkrumah, Kwame, 325
North, Michael, 146

Oakhurst, William, 245, 246
Ogungbesan, Kolawole, 319
Ogunjimi, Bayo, 358, 361
Okenimkpe, Michael, 361, 368
Orwell, George, 3, 22, 27, 34, 39, 92, 107, 246-50, 288, 326; *Burmese Days*, 246-50; *Homage to Catalonia* 34; *Nineteen Eighty-Four*, 92, 326; *The Road to Wigan Pier*, 34, 107

Parrinder, Patrick, 242
Patai, Daphne, 94
Paul, Ronald, 32, 34, 51, 105, 106, 113, 114, 116, 173, 262, 292, 293, 303, 330, 332
Peck, Richard, 337, 339, 340
Penner, Allen Richard, 259, 262, 264
Pfeil, Fred, 57, 59, 61, 62
Pickering, Michael, 106-108, 113, 114, 116
Pierce, David, 50, 51, 207, 208, 273
Pierce, John J., 92
Pinkney, Tony, 309, 312, 313
Pittock, Malcolm, 275
Poole, Adrian, 143
Popular culture, 9, 13, 29, 90, 105, 106, 113, 115, 169, 170, 199, 214, 253, 292, 296, 350, 355, 356, 374
Postgate, Raymond, 110, 112, 222, 250, 252, 308
Postmodernism, 24, 125, 216, 273, 313, 340; capitalism and, 10, 197; in the novel of the Left, 19, 57, 59, 128, 197, 200, 213, 215, 216, 309, 340
Price, Derrick, 193, 231, 310, 311
Priestley, J. B., 26, 181, 252-55; *Bright Day*, 252, 253; *Daylight on Saturday*, 252-55
Pykett, Lyn, 44, 46

Quillian, Bill, 62

Rabkin, David, 352
Rabkin, Eric S., 92
Racism, 48, 89, 210, 211, 231, 244, 270, 309, 317, 319, 321, 337, 349, 350, 354
Rajan, P. K., 322, 325
Rao, A. V. Krishna, 128, 131
Rao, Raja, 319
Reid, V. S., 370-72
Reification, 5, 6, 7, 9, 45, 65, 72, 84, 86, 104, 136, 303
Religion: capitalism and, 67, 97, 106, 187, 232, 235; class and, 37, 42, 292; as false consciousness, 55, 142, 291, 292, 367; as mode of oppression, 43, 93, 284, 374; as mode of resistance, 374
Rignall, J. M., 131
Robbins, Bruce, 35, 60, 62
Robertson, Priscilla, 222
Robins, Kevin, 106-108, 113, 114, 116
Rollins, Janet Buck, 259
Rose, Ellen Cronan, 216, 217
Rosenthal, Michael, 176, 178
Roskies, D. M., 137, 141
Rubenstein, Roberta, 213, 217
Russia, 26, 63, 71, 80, 125, 246, 315, 351. *See also* Soviet Union
Russian Revolution, 17, 29, 58, 79, 131-35, 187, 195, 239
Ryan, Kiernan, 57-59, 195, 283, 312, 314

Sackey, Edward, 358, 361
Sage, Lorna, 213, 216, 217
Said, Edward, 132, 135-37
Salveson, Paul, 108, 109, 110
Salwak, Dale, 119
Sander, Reinhard W., 333, 347, 348
Scanlon, Paul A., 352
Scholes, Robert, 92
Schwerdt, Lisa M., 176, 178
Science fiction, 18, 89, 90, 92, 236, 269, 271, 303, 312, 356
Science, 9, 11, 13, 24, 79, 90, 92, 122,

236, 240, 267, 298, 303, 306, 312
Scotland, 41–44, 137–41, 162, 195-205, 231-36, 285–89, 369, 370
Sealy, Clifford, 333
Second International, 16, 110, 245
Seed, David, 249, 250
Shakespeare, William, 39, 200
Shaw, George Bernard, 17, 22, 38, 80, 111, 255, 256, 292
Shelden, Michael, 248, 249, 250
Sherry, Norman, 147, 149
Sherry, Ruth, 234
Sicherman, Carol M., 361, 364, 368
Sigal, Clancy, 215
Sillitoe, Alan, 19, 27, 28, 34, 50, 257-64; *The Loneliness of the Long-Distance Runner*, 50, 257-59; *Saturday Night and Sunday Morning*, 28, 50, 257-62; *A Tree on Fire*, 262-64
Sinfield, Alan, 35
Singh, Frances B., 127, 131, 324
Smith, Craig, 368
Smith, Curtis C., 270
Smith, Dai, 231, 275, 277, 280, 310, 312, 314
Smith, David, 186, 191, 192; *Socialist Propaganda in the Twentieth-Century British Novel*, 35, 36, 43, 44, 54–57, 69, 80, 81, 84, 88, 89, 120, 166, 219, 220, 222, 224, 225, 227, 229, 253, 255, 266, 284, 285, 289, 290, 293, 294, 297, 301, 306, 307
Smith, Grahame, 147
Snee, Carole, 23, 74, 76, 78, 152, 188, 189, 191, 192
Socialist realism, 343
Sommerfield, John, 18, 27, 265, 266
Sommers, Jeffrey, 306
South Africa, Republic of, 317-19, 334-40, 348-52
Soviet Union, 17, 25, 26, 63, 71, 131-35, 163, 165, 167, 168, 176, 228, 229, 255, 314, 315. *See also* Russia; Russian Revolution
Spanish Civil War, 30, 34, 43, 122, 147, 194, 221, 297-99, 309; background, 53–57; British writers and, 22, 161, 190, 267, 268, 320; International Brigades, 22, 26, 82-84, 189, 190, 267, 268, 320
Sprigg, Christopher St. John, 18, 22 266-69. *See also* Caudwell, Christopher
Stalin, Josef, 160, 167, 168, 194, 214, 229
Stapledon, Olaf, 18, 269, 270, 271, 272
Stedman Jones, Gareth, 19, 36, 246
Stokes, Edward, 145, 146, 155
Storey, David, 19, 262, 272-75; *Pasmore*, 272, 273, 275; *Saville*, 272-75
Strikes, 98, 99, 108, 196, 217, 233, 245, 246, 264, 265, 332, 333, 345, 353, 364; London Dock Workers' of 1889, 16, 240; miners', 47, 160, 165, 186, 187, 230, 282, 309, 312. *See also* General Strike
Suvin, Darko, 242
Sypher, Eileen, 256

Tagore, Leo, 322
Tait, Bob, 236
Taylor, A.J.P., 151, 152
Temple-Thurston, Barbara, 340
Tempska, Urszula, 133, 135, 267, 269
Thatcher, Margaret, 35, 45, 50
Thelwell, Michael, 372-75
Thomas, Gwyn: *All Things Betray Thee*, 275-77; *Sorrow for Thy Sons*, 275, 277-80
Thompson, Dorothy, 222
Thompson, E. P., 15, 19, 36-38, 127, 192, 214, 269, 277; *The Making of the English Working Class*, 15, 36-38, 127, 192, 277
Tilsley, Frank, 280-82
Tirebuck, William Edwards, 17, 30-32, 282, 283
Todd, Ruthven, 283-85
Torrington, Jeff: *Swing Hammer Swing!*, 285, 287-89; *The Devil's Carousel*, 285-87
Tressell, Robert, 17, 21, 27, 30-32, 35,

Index

39, 109, 140, 150, 151, 232, 236, 289-93, 306, 331, 352, 368; *The Ragged Trousered Philanthropists*, 17, 21, 35, 151, 232, 236, 289-93, 331
Trinidad, 332-34, 346-48, 354
Trotsky, Leon, 346

Udenta, Udenta O., 346
Unemployment, 23, 34, 42, 48, 69, 70, 74-77, 96, 97, 109, 118, 141, 153, 158, 166, 183, 184, 191, 198, 200-202, 209, 217, 277-80, 286, 287, 291, 344
United States, 1, 2, 5, 10, 14, 24, 28, 60, 67, 69, 70, 89, 91, 102, 105, 132, 134, 142, 152, 173, 176, 178, 195, 216, 267, 270, 276, 314, 317, 320, 332, 337, 339, 343, 346, 354, 356, 373
Updike, John, 146
Upward, Edward, 18, 22, 24, 293-95; *Journey to the Border*, 18, 293, 294; *The Spiral Ascent*, 294, 295
Utopian imagery, 9, 11, 14, 17, 18, 32, 35, 43, 49, 52, 53, 57, 61, 68-70, 79, 92, 95, 98, 99, 104, 106, 110, 142, 163, 167, 185, 195, 200, 204, 211, 237, 239, 242, 263, 264, 269, 271, 279, 283, 293, 295-97, 302, 306, 319, 322, 325, 328, 331, 339, 340, 343, 344, 349, 364, 371, 372

Van Ghent, Dorothy, 207, 208
Vaverka, Ronald Dee, 259, 262
Vernon, Betty, 308
Vicinus, Martha, 38

Wade, Jean-Philippe, 319
Wade, Stephen, 176, 178
Wagner, Kathrin M., 337
Wales, 17, 32, 72, 111, 138, 154, 160, 183, 184, 186-89, 229-31, 233, 275, 276, 277, 280, 282, 309-13
Ward, John Powell, 312, 314
Warner, Rex, 18, 22, 24, 120, 283, 295-97

Warner, Sylvia Townsend, 18, 33; *After the Death of Don Juan*, 297-99; *Summer Will Show*, 299-301
Waterhouse, Keith, 19, 50, 171, 257, 259, 301, 302
Webster, Roger, 152
Weibel, Paul, 59
Wells, H. G., 17, 22, 30, 123, 124, 161, 225, 269, 292, 303-306
Welsh, James, 17, 306, 307
Wendt, Albert, 343
West, Alick, 325, 351, 356
West, Rebecca, 33
West, Alick, vii, 18, 28, 38, 163, 219
Widdowson, Peter, 22, 293, 296, 297
Wilde, Alan, 176-78
Wilde, Oscar, 27, 331
Wilkinson, Ellen, 17, 307-309
Williams, Raymond, 13, 15, 19, 32, 38, 39, 138, 139, 141, 188, 189, 216, 217, 277, 289, 291-93, 309-14; *Border Country*, 309-12; *The Country and the City*, 13, 15, 38, 39, 138, 139, 141; *Culture and Society*, 39; *The Volunteers*, 309, 312-14; *Writing and Society*, 39, 289, 291-93
Williams-Ellis, Amabel, 314, 315
Wolmark, Jenny, 140, 141
Worcester, Kent, 348
World War I, 8, 17, 18, 21, 23, 29, 42, 43, 46, 58, 79-81, 83, 95, 97, 114, 117, 118, 135, 138, 186, 228, 235, 251, 252
World War II, 18, 29, 31, 34, 35, 46, 57, 72, 104, 108, 127, 128, 147, 153, 160, 176, 181, 213, 219, 225, 227, 249, 252, 253, 255, 274, 332, 353
Worpole, Ken, 69, 71
Wright, Derek, 328
Wright, Ralph, 176

Young, Alan, 53, 55, 57, 295
Yugoslavia, 58, 86, 229

Zola, Émile, 117, 125, 156, 190, 282

About the Author

M. KEITH BOOKER is Professor of English at the University of Arkansas. He is the author of numerous articles and books on modern literature and literary theory, including *Dystopian Literature: A Theory and Research Guide* (Greenwood, 1994), *The Dystopian Impulse in Modern Literature: Fiction as Social Criticism* (Greenwood, 1994), *Bakhtin, Stalin, and Modern Russian Fiction: Carnival, Dialogism, and History* (Greenwood, 1995), *Joyce, Bakhtin, and the Literary Tradition* (1996), *A Practical Introduction to Literary Theory and Criticism* (1996), and *Colonial Power, Colonial Texts: India in the Modern British Novel* (1997).

ISBN 0-313-30343-6

HARDCOVER BAR CODE